SAN FRANCISCO •

A

LOS ANGELES •

— 30° N

N

B

HONOLULU
HAWAII

PEARL HARBOR

— 15° N

C

CHRISTMAS

— EQ

MARQUESAS
ISLANDS

D

— 15° S

BORA BORA

TUAMOTU ISLANDS

TAHITI

FRENCH
POLYNESIA

COOK
ISLANDS

E

— 30° S

PACIFIC OCEAN

F

Place	Grid
American Samoa	D5
Angaur	C1
Australia	E, F1, 2
Beru	D4
Bikini	C3
Borneo	C1
Bora Bora	E6
Bougainville	D3
Butaritari/Makin	C4
Cape Gloucester	D2
Christmas	C6
Chúuk/Truk	C3
Cook Islands	E6
Corregidor	C1
Efate	E4
Espiritu Santo	E4
Federated States of Micronesia	C2, 3
Fiji	E4
Funafuti	D4
Guadalcanal	D3
Guam	C2
Hawaii	B6
Hiroshima	A1
Honolulu	B6
Iwo Jima	B2
Japan	A1, 2
Kanton/Canton	D5
Kiribati/Gilbert Islands	C4
Kwajalein	C3
Leyte	C1
Luzon	B1
Manila	C1
Marquesas Islands	D7
Midway	B5
Mindanao	C1
Munda	D3
Nadi	E4
Nagasaki	A1
Nauru	D4
New Britain	D2
New Caledonia	E4
New Zealand	F4
Northern Mariana Islands	B2
Okinawa	B1
Pago Pago	D5
Palau	C1
Papua	D2
Papua New Guinea	D2
Pearl Harbor	B6
Peleliu	C1
Philippines	C1
Pohnpei/Ponape	C3
Port Moresby	D2
Rabaul	D3
Saipan	B2
Samoa	D5
Sarmi	D2
Solomon Islands	D3
Tahiti	E7
Taiwan	B1
Tanna	E4
Tarawa	C4
Tinian	B2
Tokyo	A2
Tonga	E5
Tuamotu Is.	E7
Tulagi	D3
Tuvalu/Ellice Island	D4
Vanuatu/New Hebrides	D, E4
Wake	B3
Yap	C2

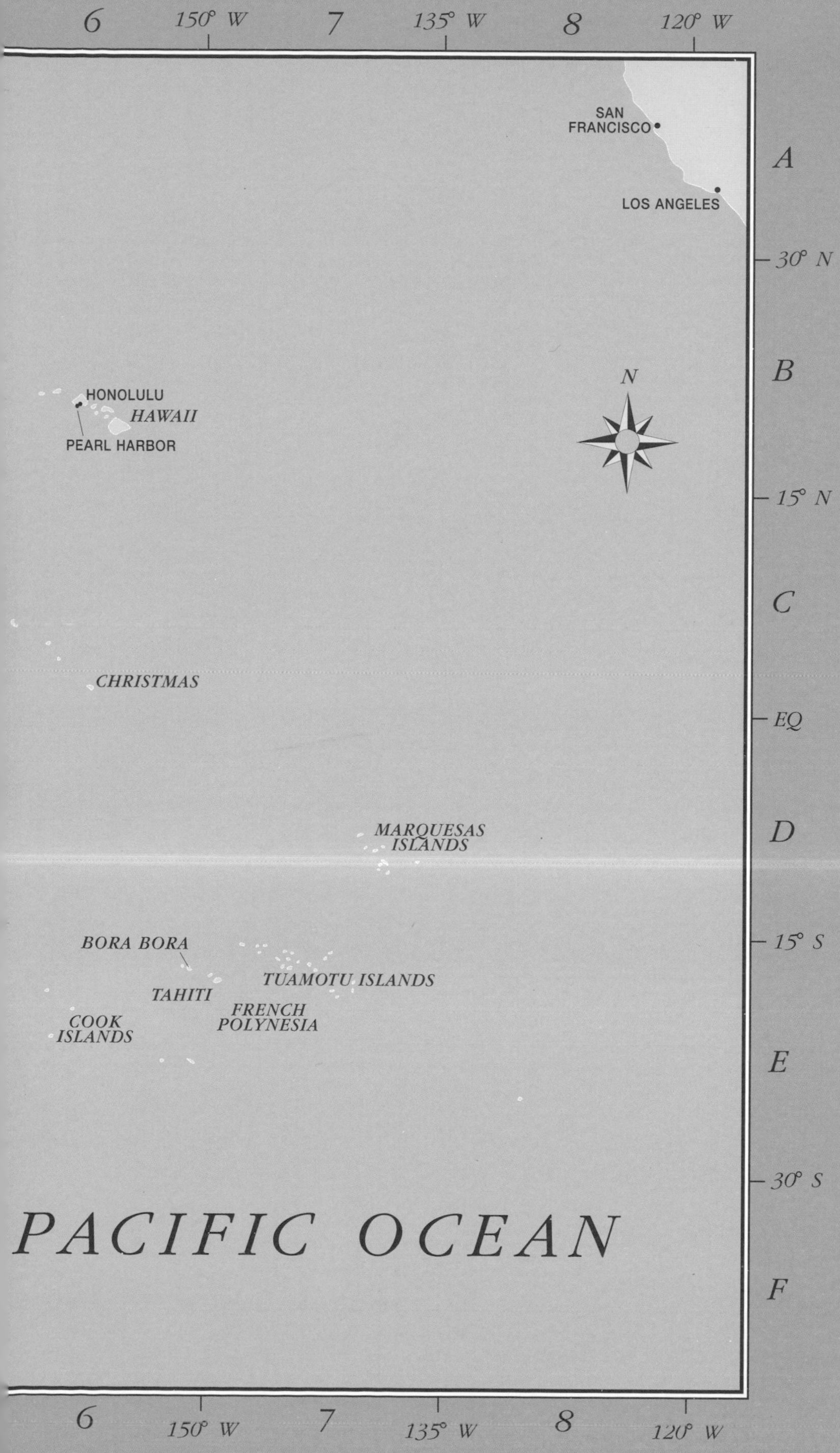

PACIFIC
LEGACY

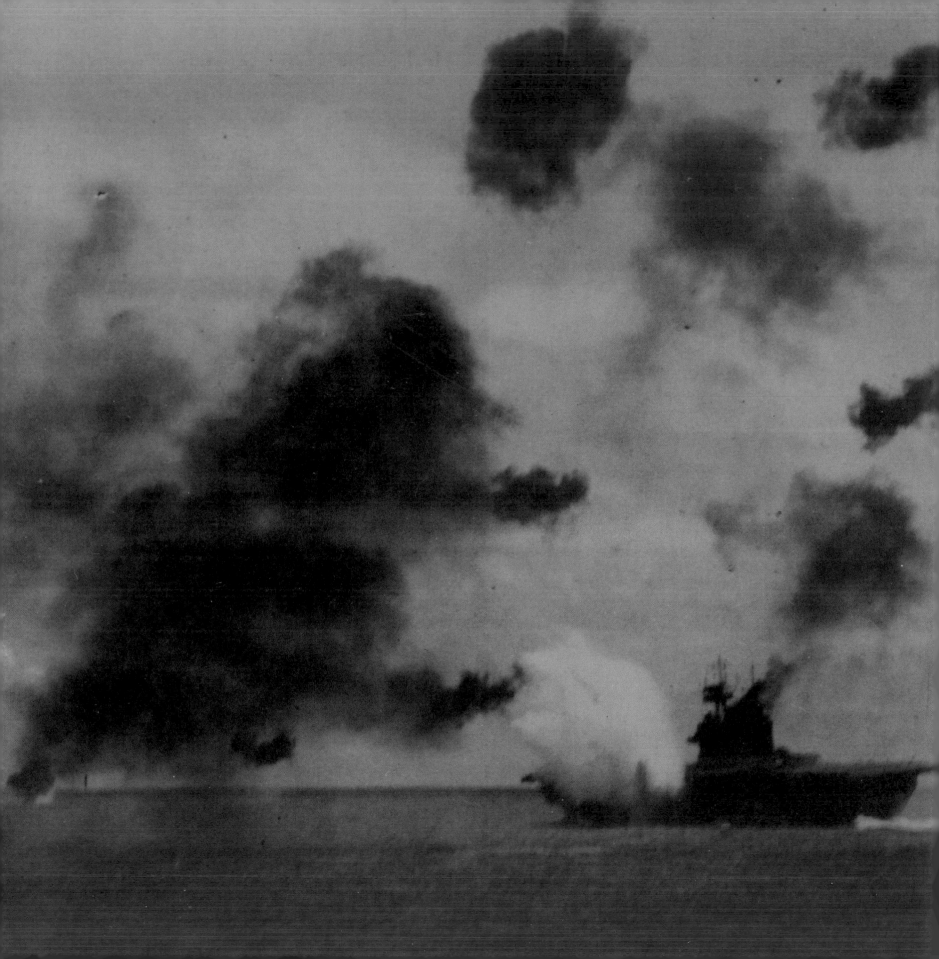

PACIFIC
LEGACY

IMAGE AND **MEMORY** FROM
WORLD WAR II IN THE **PACIFIC**

Rex Alan Smith & Gerald A. Meehl

ABBEVILLE PRESS

NEW YORK · LONDON

Project Manager: **SUSAN COSTELLO**
Editor: **WALTON RAWLS**
Copyeditor: **MARIAN K. GORDIN**
Designer: **JIM WAGEMAN**
Production Manager: **LOUISE KURTZ**

Printed in China

Second Edition
10 9 8 7 6 5 4 3 2 1

ISBN 978-0-7892-1333-4

A previous edition of this book was cataloged as follows.

LIBRARY OF CONGRESS CATALOGING-IN-PUBLICATION DATA

Smith, Rex Alan.
    Pacific Legacy / image and memory from World War II in the Pacific / Rex Alan Smith & Gerald A. Meehl.
        p.   cm.
    Includes index.
        1. World War, 1939–1945—Campaigns—Pacific Area. 2. Pacific Area—History, Military—20th century. 3. World War, 1939–1945—United States.
    I. Meehl, Gerald A. II. Title.

D767 .S584 2002
940.54'26—dc21   2002025417

For bulk and premium sales and for text adoption procedures, write to Customer Service Manager, Abbeville Press, 655 Third Avenue, New York, NY 10017, or call 1-800-ARTBOOK.

Visit Abbeville Press online at www.abbeville.com.

FRONT COVER: This U.S. tank still sits in the shallow water offshore where it was put out of action during the 1944 invasion of Saipan.

BACK COVER (CLOCKWISE FROM TOP LEFT): Japanese defenders inflicted heavy casualties on Marines as they waded in to these beaches on Tarawa; Japanese Zero in the second attack wave takes off from the *Akagi* on December 7, 1941; U.S. flag raising on Iwo Jima in 1945; simple, graceful memorial straddles the sunken remains of the USS *Arizona* at Pearl Harbor; representatives of the government of Japan sign surrender documents on the deck of the USS *Missouri* in Tokyo Bay; PT 59 maneuvers off the coast of Guadalcanal early in the war.

ENDPAPER MAP: Michael Shibao.

HALF TITLE: A Grumman F4F Wildcat returns to Henderson Field on Guadalcanal after raiding Japanese positions in December 1942.

TITLE SPREAD: USS *Yorktown* under attack during the battle of Midway, June 4, 1942.

CONTENTS: Japanese troops on the march in early 1942 near Subic Bay, Philippines.

PAGE 4: Pfc. Paul Isen sprints through Japanese machine gunfire across one of Okinawa's battlefields.

THIS BOOK IS DEDICATED to those veterans of the 1941–1945 War in the Pacific—both living and dead, who swallowed their fear and rose to the need—fighting from ships, planes, foxholes, slit trenches, and bullet-lashed landing beaches until the job was done, and who, in doing it, all too often paid the ultimate price.

IT IS DEDICATED ALSO to Rex's wife, Wanda, for her patience during his endless hours of preoccupation with this project; to editor and old friend Walton Rawls; to our many veteran friends for their inspiration and contributions of personal accounts; to Jerry's father, B-17 crew chief Paul Meehl; to his uncles who fought the Japanese in the Pacific—Al Hahn, Harlan Wall, and Louis Meehl; and especially to his wife, Marla, who has seen more far-flung Pacific island battlefields than she had ever thought imaginable.

Contents

PACIFIC WAR CHRONOLOGY

1941

December 7: Japanese attack Pearl Harbor, Hawaii, and also bomb the Philippines, Wake Island, Guam, Malaya, Thailand, Shanghai, and Midway.

December 10: Guam overrun by invading Japanese

December 12: First Japanese invasion of Wake Island turned back by U.S. defenders

December 12, 19, 22: Japanese troops land on Mindanao and Luzon, Philippines

December 23: Second Japanese landing on Wake Island is successful; U.S. Marines, Naval personnel, and civilian construction workers taken prisoner

December 24 (Manila time): In the face of advancing Japanese forces, MacArthur and staff evacuate Manila and move headquarters to island of Corregidor in Manila Bay

1942

February 15: Singapore falls

February 19: Japanese bomb Darwin, Australia

February 27: Battle of Java Sea; of fleet of 18 Allied ships, only American cruiser *Houston* and Australian light cruiser *Perth* survive, and these both are sunk a few days later

March 11: After being ordered to return to Australia to take command of Allied Forces, MacArthur leaves Corregidor on PT boat and arrives in Australia seven days later

April 9: American and Philippine forces surrender on Bataan, Philippines; Japanese attention turns to last American stronghold, Corregidor Island

April 10: Bataan Death March begins

April 18: Doolittle's planes bomb targets in Tokyo and other cities, taking off from the aircraft carrier *Hornet*

May 6: Corregidor falls, and all U.S. forces in Philippines surrender

May 7–8: Battle of Coral Sea; Japanese carrier *Shoho* and U.S. carrier *Lexington* sunk

June 4–6: Battle of Midway; four Japanese carriers and the U.S. carrier *Yorktown* sunk

August 7: U.S. forces land on Guadalcanal and Tulagi in the Solomon Islands, the first U.S. amphibious landings in the Pacific war; Guadalcanal campaign will last until February 1943

August 16: Marines raid Makin Island (Butaritari)

August 21: Marines defeat Japanese at Ilu River (Tenaru), Guadalcanal

September 5: Australian and New Zealand forces stop Japanese army 32 miles from Port Moresby on the Kokoda Track in Papua New Guinea

September 13–14: Battle of Bloody Ridge, Guadalcanal; Marines stop the Japanese advance on Henderson Field

October 26: Naval battle of Santa Cruz Islands; USS *Hornet*, the carrier that launched the planes of the Doolittle Raid, is sunk

November 12–14: Naval battles of Guadalcanal

1943

June 21: New Georgia landings begin in Solomon Islands in drive to take Munda

August 12: PT 109, skippered by John F. Kennedy, is rammed and sunk by a Japanese destroyer in the Solomon Islands near Kolombangara Island

August 28: Japanese evacuate Munda and New Georgia area to consolidate their forces on New Britain and Bougainville

September: Allies work their way up the north coast of Papua New Guinea in a series of landings

November 1: Marines land on Bougainville

November 20–23: Marines take Tarawa; U.S. Army forces invade and secure Makin (Butaritari)

December 26: Marines invade Cape Gloucester on New Britain Island

1944

January 31: Landings begin in Marshall Islands

February 7: U.S. forces invade Kwajalein in the Marshalls

February 17–18: U.S. carrier-based aircraft sink numerous Japanese ships and destroy facilities at large Japanese base on Truk (now Chuuk)

May 17, 27: U.S. Army lands on Wakde and Biak, respectively, in Papua New Guinea

June 6: D-Day invasion of France

June 15: Marines land on Saipan; Army troops land the next day; organized Japanese resistance ends on July 9

July 21: Marines and Army units land on Guam; organized resistance ends on August 10

July 24: Marines land on Tinian; organized resistance ends on August 1

September 15: Marines land on Peleliu; battle finally ends on November 27

September 17: U.S. Army invades Angaur near Peleliu

October 20: U.S. Army forces land on Leyte, Philippines, and MacArthur returns; Leyte declared secure December 26

November 24: First Saipan-based B-29s bomb Tokyo

December 15: U.S. Army forces land on Mindoro, Philippines

1945

January 9: U.S. Army forces land at Lingayen on Luzon, Philippines

February 16: U.S. Army paratroopers land on Corregidor

February 19: Marines land on Iwo Jima

February 23: Marines raise U.S. flags on Mt. Suribachi, Iwo Jima

March 26: Last Japanese defenders on Iwo Jima launch banzai attack

April 1: U.S. forces land on Okinawa

April–May: Hundreds of Japanese planes attack U.S. ships off Okinawa in concentrated kamikaze attacks

April 12: President Franklin Roosevelt dies; Harry Truman becomes president

May 8: Germany surrenders, V-E day

June 21: Okinawa campaign ends with U.S. victory

June 26: Philippine campaign declared ended, but fighting continues

July 16: World's first atomic bomb detonated at Trinity site, New Mexico

July 26: USS *Indianapolis* delivers atomic bomb components to Tinian

August 6: Atomic bomb dropped on Hiroshima from B-29 *Enola Gay*

August 8: Soviet Union declares war on Japan

August 9: Atomic bomb dropped on Nagasaki from B-29 *Bock's Car*

August 14: Japan accepts Allied unconditional surrender terms; Truman announces cease fire

September 2: Japanese representatives sign surrender documents on deck of USS *Missouri* in Tokyo Bay ending the Pacific war, V-J day

FOREWORD

Joe Foss MEDAL OF HONOR WINNER

WITH MARINE FIGHTER SQUADRON VMF 121, I LANDED MY F4F WILDCAT on the island of Guadalcanal on October 9, 1942. From the air it looked like a tropical paradise, but, for a guy from the plains of South Dakota, terra firma came as something of a rude shock. We landed right after a Japanese bombing raid, and Guadalcanal turned out to be what the Australians had called it: "a bloody, stinking hole." There were leeches, poisonous spiders, scorpions, and malarial mosquitoes, and the island had only two seasons: wet, hot, and steamy, and wetter, hotter, and steamier. It was a climate in which nothing ever dried out, including us, and fungus infections flourished.

We were there because, after conquering everything else in the western Pacific, Japan now wanted Australia. Well aware that Australia, with most of her fighting men in Europe or North Africa with the British, could only survive through steady supplies and support from the United States, the Japanese were building on Guadalcanal a bomber base that if completed would enable them to sever the vital America-to-Australia supply line. The consequences of that happening would be so serious that in August 1942 the U.S. First Marine Division was sent to Guadalcanal to see that it did not come about.

It was a drastic decision, for America was far from ready for such an operation. Because of widespread pacifist sentiment in the 1930s and lack of preparation for war, America's armed forces in 1942 were still seriously under-equipped and under-trained. Moreover, to secure Guadalcanal, the Marines would have to be landed from the sea in small boats, facing a well-entrenched enemy—a hazardous type of operation with a bad history of failure and high casualties.

Still, on August 7, 1942, the Marines arrived at Guadalcanal, began landing, and received more bad news. Having promised the invasion force seventy-two hours of Naval protection, the commander of the battle fleet, fearing loss of his aircraft carriers from a Japanese counterattack, decided to withdraw his support at the end of the second day. Left unprotected, the transports and supply ships also withdrew, carrying with them some of the invasion force and about half of the operation's supplies.

All of this should have meant certain disaster for the Americans when Admiral Isoroku Yamamoto dispatched an experienced Japanese battle force charged with pushing the invaders into the sea. Most of the Marines meeting this force had never seen combat. Many were in their teens. A year or so earlier, most had not even been Marines. And yet, on the night of August 21, 1942, those untested, under-equipped, and seemingly unqualified young men didn't just beat back the attacking force, they wiped it out, handing the Japanese Army its first defeat in a thousand years.

And that was only the beginning. By the time I got there those young, civilian-soldier Marines had withstood every attack the Japanese could throw at them and were still at it—enduring the stress of almost nightly bombings and shellings from Japanese ships. On one night that I remember well, the shelling lasted from one to three in the morning, and over that time nine hundred shells exploded on the island in the vicinity of the airfield. For minutes at a time the roar of explosions was so loud and the pain in my ears so intense that I could do nothing but hold my hands over my ears and cringe. Those two hours were indescribable. Unless you've been through it, you just can't imagine what it's like.

But the Marines hung in there and took America's first step on the road to victory, creating a turning point in the war by being first to recapture territory that Japan had seized. Ordinary men, swallowing their fear, rising to the need, and, against heavy odds, got the job done. But it was just a sample of what would take place later on other beaches and other islands in the Pacific.

There was another side to the war. My old friend Jack Conger attempted to rescue a Japanese pilot who had parachuted into the sea. When Jack reached down to grab the enemy airman's life vest to pull him into the boat, the pilot smiled and extended an arm up to his rescuer. As the two clasped hands, the Japanese pilot whipped his other arm around and rammed the barrel of a cocked 8mm Nambu pistol between Conger's eyes and pulled the trigger. The gun misfired, but Conger threw himself so violently backward against the other side of the boat that back problems plagued him the rest of his life. Oddly enough, in April 1990, Jack met this same Japanese pilot, Shiro Ishikawa, and the two veterans shook hands and talked for the first time since their encounter forty-eight years earlier. And there was Saburo Sakai, Japan's top fighter ace to survive the war. I ended up sharing the platform with him at university symposiums after the war, and one time he told me that I was his best friend in America.

Significant moments like these may be locked in history, but time heals, and God gives us a forgiving heart. The fact that after the bitterness of war such friendships could grow is for me a significant legacy of the Pacific war.

PREFACE TO THE SECOND EDITION

It has been sixteen years since my coauthor Rex Alan Smith and I put together the first edition of *Pacific Legacy*. Our intention was to tell the story of World War II in the Pacific with then-and-now images of its principal battlegrounds. The challenge, however, was to place these images in a coherent historical narrative without becoming overwhelmed by the many facets and infinite details of the war in the Pacific—a monumental action that encompassed forty million square miles, with only scattered bits of islands to focus the battles. And it was not just the battles that made the Pacific war unique. Due to the incredible distances involved, the defense and supply chains stretched thousands of miles through hundreds of islands. Only a very small fraction of those who served in the Pacific ever saw action, with many thousands more stationed on remote, isolated, exotic, and, under other circumstances, romantic island outposts across the watery expanse of the Pacific. We decided that the best way to recount this complicated and compelling story, and to convey the significance of the photographs, was through the voices of the veterans themselves. As we wrote in our 2002 preface, "The vivid images and memories in the minds of the veterans are the key elements . . . to recapture impressions of the war and its times, the sight, sound and feel—thereby enabling readers who lived through those times to remember and relive them, and to allow those many more who were never there to get a sense of how it really was."

To that end, Rex and I interviewed many surviving Pacific war veterans in the late 1990s. At that time, most were in their late seventies and retained memories so vivid that little editing was required. We only had to choose the quotes most appropriate to bring the images and history alive. The oral histories were so evocative that we subsequently compiled and published complete stories from about seventy Pacific war veterans, a group that included Americans, Japanese, and Pacific islanders, in a separate volume entitled *Pacific War Stories* (2004).

Since *Pacific Legacy*'s original publication, most of the veterans we interviewed have passed away, along with most others who had any firsthand memories of the war years. Any of that generation who have survived to date, the remaining eyewitnesses to history, are now in their nineties. *Pacific Legacy* has turned into a history rescue project. With the rapid passing of the World War II generation, there are few eyewitnesses left to tell the story. We must now rely on images,

recordings, and written accounts of their experiences to bring that history back to life, and these are what *Pacific Legacy* provides.

Some of the eyewitnesses we have lost were directly involved in the preparation of this book. Joe Foss, who wrote the foreword, was a Medal of Honor winner for his heroics as a Marine fighter pilot in the skies above Guadalcanal in the desperate early days of the war. Joe passed away at age eighty-seven in 2003, a year after *Pacific Legacy* was published. My coauthor Rex Alan Smith, himself a Pacific war veteran, followed Joe in 2010. Two of my uncles who were veterans of the Pacific War have subsequently passed away—PT boat motor-mac Al Hahn and army artilleryman Harlan Wall. They both fought the Japanese in the Philippines.

One of the few veterans who remains to tell his story is ninety-five-year-old Everett Hyland. He was seriously injured when a Japanese bomb exploded next to him on the battleship USS *Pennsylvania* during the attack on Pearl Harbor on December 7, 1941. He awoke from a coma on Christmas Day, 1941, with shrapnel wounds and severe burns over much of his body. He recovered, spent the rest of the war on another ship in the Atlantic, and became a schoolteacher in Las Vegas. When he was in Hawaii for the fiftieth-anniversary commemoration of the Pearl Harbor attack in 1991, he met a lovely Japanese travel planner at his hotel in Waikiki. Miyoko and Everett ended up getting married, and they retired to Honolulu. The irony is not lost on Everett that some of the members of the Japanese military machine that almost killed him on December 7 became his in-laws. As of 2018, Everett is the only veteran who was on a ship in Pearl Harbor on December 7 still residing in Honolulu today. Every Sunday he makes his way to what is now the World War II Valor in the Pacific National Monument (formerly the USS *Arizona* Memorial), to sign copies of *Pacific War Stories* and *Pacific Legacy* in front of the bookstore at the visitors' center. His very presence enthralls long lines of tourists who marvel at seeing an actual surviving eyewitness to the December 7 attack. Visitors crowd around to ask if they can take their photo with him or if they can shake his hand to thank him for his service. Others stand silently by, gawking in wonder at what they rightly view as an historical treasure. Though arthritis now makes it difficult for him to sign his name, Everett patiently affixes his stamped signature to anything people put in front of him.

There are a few others on the dwindling list of Pearl Harbor survivors. Of the few hundred sailors and Marines who made it off the USS *Arizona* alive, in 2018 only five are still left to tell the tale. One, Don Stratton, who by all rights should have died on December 7 but narrowly escaped with his life from the burning ship, is the unofficial spokesman for the USS *Arizona* veterans. He traveled to Hawaii for the annual December 7 commemorations for years, although none of the five remaining survivors was able to attend the 2018 ceremony. Stratton has told his harrowing story countless times to honor the service of his 1177 USS *Arizona* shipmates who died that fateful morning. A few years ago, the sailor responsible for saving the lives of five USS *Arizona* crewmen, including Stratton, was finally identified as Joe George. The lifeline he threw across to the *Arizona* from his post on the repair vessel USS *Vestal* allowed the five crewman to escape the burning ship. Though George passed away in 1996, he was posthumously awarded the Bronze Star on December 7, 2017. Two of the men he saved, ninty-five-year-old Stratton and ninety-seven-year-old Lauren Bruner, were there to witness George's daughter receive her father's Bronze Star on the USS *Arizona* Memorial, literally yards away from where the dramatic rescue took place seventy-six years before.

To date, the remains of forty-three USS *Arizona* survivors have been interred inside the ship, fulfilling their desire to join their shipmates who still remain at the posts where they died on December 7 Only the crewmen who were assigned to the USS *Arizona* on December 7 are allowed this privilege. Other Pearl Harbor survivors can have their ashes scattered over those famous waters, and many have left instructions with family members to return them to the location of an event that irrevocably changed their lives.

A little over four months after the Pearl Harbor attack, the Doolittle Raiders performed an unprecedented launch of sixteen Army Air Corps twin-engine B-25 bombers off the pitching deck of the aircraft carrier USS *Hornet* as it steamed through the western Pacific toward Japan. They then flew to the home islands and totally surprised and demoralized the Japanese by dropping bombs on Tokyo and surrounding cities. Most of the Raiders then continued on to China, where the crews bailed out of the planes at night. After a harrowing evacuation from China, many of the Doolittle Raiders continued in active service in the Asian and European theaters. A number lost their lives in subsequent missions, despite having survived their daring attack on Japan. One of those who survived World War II was my neighbor in Boulder, Bill Bower, who piloted the twelfth B-25 off the deck of the *Hornet*. Until he passed away in 2011, Bill patiently and humbly entertained visitors with his recollections of the most important event of his life.

Meanwhile, Jimmy Doolittle, the famous air-race pilot who led the mission, initiated a "last man" ceremony. Every year, the remaining Raiders gathered and toasted their comrades who had died in the past year. A set of eighty silver goblets, each inscribed with the name of one of the original Raiders, was used for the toast; the goblets of those who had passed away were inverted. A bottle of cognac, vintage 1896 (the year of Doolittle's birth), was kept with the goblets. Doolittle's instructions stipulated that when there were only two Raiders left alive, they would open the bottle and toast all who had gone before them. In 2013, the four surviving Raiders decided not to wait any longer. In an emotional ceremony at the National Museum of the U.S. Air Force in Dayton, Ohio, the three Raiders who could still travel opened the bottle of cognac and made the toast. As of this writing, there is only one goblet not yet turned over. It has Dick Cole's name inscribed on it. He was Doolittle's copilot, and he is now 103.

One would think that with the passage of time, and the passing of the World War II generation, interest in the Pacific war would fade. If anything, it has intensified. The sprawling National World War II Museum in New Orleans, one of the biggest tourist attractions there, opened a new Pacific war pavilion in 2015. The National Museum of the Pacific War in Fredericksburg, Texas, completed a major expansion of its facility in 2009. Both museums are repositories of the physical artifacts of the war as well as many recorded oral histories that give visitors a chance to hear about the Pacific war from those who experienced it.

Other organizations are returning to the Pacific to find the men and ships that were lost there more than seventy years ago. The government-funded Defense POW/MIA Accounting Agency (DPAA), as well as several volunteer groups, scour brilliantly colored tropical lagoons and jungle-enshrouded islands looking for the long-lost remains of the Pacific war's MIAs. One such group, Bent Prop, has focused on plane crash sites in and around the islands of Palau in the western Pacific. Over the course of numerous expeditions, they have been able to locate the wrecks of crashed World War II aircraft as well as the remains of the fliers who died in them. When human remains are located in crumpled aluminum wreckage in the aquamarine lagoons of the Rock Islands of Palau, or scattered among fragments of crashed aircraft deep in the islands' rain forests or mangrove swamps, the DPAA is called in to make an official identification. Once there is a positive ID, the remains are returned to the family for burial. These ceremonies are powerfully emotional, even though more than seven decades have passed since the young men disappeared "somewhere in the South Pacific."

Most of the people doing the searching now are two generations removed from the Pacific war. Clay Bonnyman Evans grew up hearing about the exploits of his grandfather, Alexander Bonnyman. Known by his nickname "Sandy," Alexander Bonnyman won the Medal of Honor in spectacular fashion by leading a group of Marines in a charge to the top of a huge sand-covered concrete bunker in the latter stages of the battle for the tiny island of Betio in Tarawa Atoll in late 1943. The charge was successful, and one of the last points of Japanese resistance was eliminated, but Sandy was killed at the top of the bunker. He was soon buried nearby in an impromptu cemetery with a group of other dead Marines. Such scattered burials needed to happen quickly, as bodies decomposed rapidly in the oppressive tropical heat. As the Marine survivors left the island after the seventy-six-hour-long battle, Navy Seabee construction crews were already frantically at work to expand the coral runway and taxiways on the tiny island to make a suitable base from which to carry the war farther west to the Japanese. Although all burials were marked and recorded at the time, the location of Sandy's shallow grave was promptly lost to history. Of the thousand or so Marine dead, only about six hundred bodies were recovered after the war. The missing dead of Tarawa remained unaccounted for and missing for the next seventy years.

Enter another volunteer group searching for World War II remains, History Flight, led by Mark Noah. After extensive historical research and high-tech procedures on the ground amidst the many structures on the small but heavily populated island, they thought they had a good lead on where Sandy's remains might be found. Meanwhile, Clay had become interested in finding out more about his grandfather, and he was present when History Flight volunteers unearthed Sandy's remains. The only one of the four Tarawa Medal of Honor winners whose body had never been recovered emerged, ghostlike, from the embrace of the sand that had held him since that day in 1943 when he was buried in a shallow trench with about twenty of his fellow Marines. He was lying facedown in a relaxed position. His boots, including the rubber composition soles, were still on his feet, a reminder that he was buried exactly as he was killed, in combat gear. A cigarette lighter, engraved with a hand-scratched B, was found underneath his remains where his left-front pants pocket would have been. Though it was obvious from his unique gold dental work that the remains were Sandy's, his body had to be officially identified by the DPAA. He then was returned to the Bonnyman family in Knoxville, Tennessee, for a military burial. This was final closure to the legend of Sandy Bonnyman, and Clay described the experience in his 2018 book *Bones of My Grandfather*.

But, in recent years, perhaps nothing has drawn more attention to the legacy of the Pacific war than the high-profile finds of sunken ships by the Paul Allen–funded research and exploration vessel RV *Petrel*. Using the latest in scanning equipment and submersibles, the *Petrel* has located and photographed a number of historically notable American and Japanese ships that were sent to the bottom during the Pacific war. One was the heavy cruiser USS *Indianapolis*, found in 2017. Illuminated in the lights of a submersible, its bow, with the clearly legible hull number "35," loomed from the darkness about 18,000 feet below the surface, nearly seventy-two years after the ship was last seen by its crew as it sunk minutes after being torpedoed by a Japanese submarine on July 30, 1945. Just days before, the *Indianapolis* had delivered the components of the first atomic bomb to Tinian. Of the crew of 1196, 880 died, many taken by sharks during four interminable days in the water, in what was perhaps the largest mass shark attack in history. Inexplicably, the Navy had lost track of the ship and did not know it was missing until a passing aircraft spotted groups of agonized survivors in the water.

In another significant find, in March 2018 the *Petrel* discovered the remains of the USS *Lexington*, the aircraft carrier that was lost during the Battle of Coral Sea in May 1942. Scattered across the ocean floor near the sunken ship were a number of combat aircraft that had been on the decks of the "Lady Lex." One, an incredibly preserved F4F-3 fighter, still had all its original paint and markings intact. Below the cockpit were four Japanese flags, indicating that the pilot had downed four Japanese aircraft. A black fragmentation bomb was painted next to one of the flags. Also clearly visible ahead of the flags was the Felix the Cat fighter-squadron emblem. With this evidence, it was determined that the aircraft had been flown in combat by Lieutenant Noel Gayler. The plane had made its final landing on the *Lexington* during the battle and was on the flight deck when the ship was attacked. Gayler survived the sinking of the *Lexington* and went on to become a Navy admiral.

Other recent finds by the *Petrel* include the cruiser USS *Juneau*. It was lost in late 1942 during the Naval Battle of Guadalcanal, in an action that took 687 men, including the five Sullivan brothers, to their widely publicized deaths. Only ten of the crew survived. Another find was the destroyer USS *Ward*, the first US ship to fire a shot in anger in World War II, when it sank a Japanese mini-submarine outside the entrance to Pearl Harbor shortly before the attack began. The *Ward* was taken down in 1944 by a kamikaze off Leyte in the Philippines, and was next seen by the *Petrel*'s submersibles in 2017.

A shocking recent development involved perhaps the most iconic image to emerge from World War II, Joe Rosenthal's photo of the flag-raising on Mount Suribachi during the battle for Iwo Jima. In June 2016, research on several fronts, officially confirmed by the Marine Corps, determined that the original identification of the flag-raisers in the photo was wrong. John Bradley, the Navy corpsman who was one of three flag-raisers to survive the battle and was the subject of his son's moving 2000 book *Flags of Our Fathers* (as well as

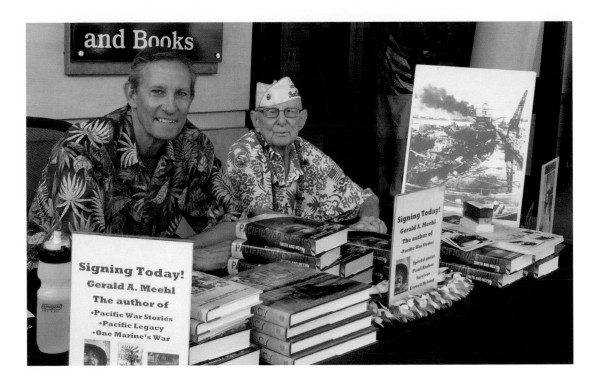

Author Gerald A. Meehl and Pearl Harbor survivor Everett Hyland sign copies of *Pacific Legacy* and *Pacific War Stories* at the World War II Valor in the Pacific National Monument (also known as the USS *Arizona* Memorial), Pearl Harbor, Hawaii, March 2015. Everett barely lived through December 7, 1941, as a Japanese bomb exploded next to him on the USS *Pennsylvania* in Pearl Harbor (the ship in the photo at right). He awoke from a coma on Christmas Day, 1941, with extensive burns and shrapnel wounds. He recovered and spent the rest of the war on a Navy ship in the Atlantic.

the Clint Eastwood–directed 2006 movie of the same name), turned out not to have been in the photo. Though he participated in the first flag-raising that morning on Mount Suribachi, Bradley, who died in 1994, took to his grave the secret of why he passed himself off as one of the men in the famous photo of the second flag-raising. After further scrutiny of the photographs taken on Mount Suribachi that day in 1945, it was determined that the previously unknown Private First Class Harold Schultz was present in the famous photo. And it didn't end there. The photographic analysis revealed that the man previously identified as Bradley was Franklin Sousley, and Schultz was the man thought to have been Sousley in the photo. Schultz died in 1995, and never mentioned his role in the flag-raising.

Another indication of the growing interest in the Pacific war is its ever more frequent depiction in books, on television, and in Hollywood and international movies. The sequel to *Flags of Our Fathers*, entitled *Letters from Iwo Jima* (2006) and also directed by Clint Eastwood, told the story of the battle from the Japanese viewpoint. *Unbroken*, the moving 2010 book by Laura Hillenbrand, adapted into a 2014 film directed by Angelina Jolie, tells the amazing wartime story of Louis Zamperini, a runner who had competed in the 1936 Olympics. A bombardier whose B-24 crashed in the ocean, Zamperini survived for forty-seven days in an open raft before washing up on a Japanese-held island. Although he was tortured and abused as a POW, he came to terms with and forgave his captors after the war.

We ended the first edition of *Pacific Legacy* with a quote from James Michener's *Tales of the South Pacific*. Michener, a Pacific war veteran, described what he thought would happen when he and his fellow eyewitnesses passed from the scene: "They, like their victories, will be remembered as long as our generation lives. After that, like the men of the Confederacy, they will become strangers. Longer and longer shadows will obscure them, until their Guadalcanal sounds distant on the ear like Shiloh and Valley Forge." It turns out that Michener's prediction has not come to pass. If he were alive today, he would be surprised, and probably pleased, to see that the Pacific war actually is and will be remembered long after his time. There are intensifying efforts to recover the remains of MIAs from the Pacific; to locate ships sunk during the conflict; and, in an ongoing stream of books and movies, to tap the seemingly endless supply of incredible stories of service and sacrifice by those who served in the Pacific. The difference, sixteen years later, is that these stories are now largely told second- and thirdhand. But *Pacific Legacy* is a treasure trove of stories told by the eyewitnesses themselves, interwoven with photographic evidence of what their islands were like then and what has happened to them since. What we said in our original preface is more true now than ever: *Pacific Legacy* truthfully recounts the experiences of the veterans of the Pacific war, and relates "the central events of lifetimes played out on islands all across the vast Pacific, and . . . how essential it is now to pass on those experiences."

Gerald A. Meehl, Boulder, Colorado, October 2018

PREFACE TO THE FIRST EDITION

This generation has a rendezvous with destiny.
—Franklin D. Roosevelt

FOR THOSE TOO YOUNG TO HAVE EXPERIENCED IT, IT MAY BE almost impossible to understand, or feel vicariously, the shock, the shiver that ran down America's spine on December 7, 1941, or the mixture of feelings engendered in both the United States and Japan. Or that during the following forty-four months these two countries would play out their conflict on the bloody beaches of a hundred Pacific islands, nearly all of which, when the war began, were terra incognita to most of the combatants on both sides.

It was a war such as the world had never seen before, and almost certainly will never see again. Fought over an area five thousand miles wide and eight thousand miles deep—encompassing at least forty million square miles—there was hardly more than 1 percent of it dry land. It was a war in which battleships, once thought invincible, turned out to be vulnerable indeed, ending up their wartime service as mainly artillery platforms for bombarding enemy island invasion sites. There were sea battles in which ships of the opposing sides never once came in sight of each other, in which the true, deadly offensive weapons were airplanes borne to battle by aircraft carriers, and there was probably the last naval battle the world will ever know where fleets did engage each other and slug it out in a duel of heavy guns. It was a war of blazing battles for tiny coral spits where, in one case, five thousand men would die defending an island half the size of New York's Central Park. Rank after rank of soldier-laden landing craft, looking from the air like rows of white-tailed water bugs, dashed through splashes of artillery to land their troops on bullet-swept shores. In a mere few hours they had deposited the population of a medium-sized town on beaches usually far too small to accommodate the numbers, a population that had to be immediately and constantly kept supplied with the necessities of life, as well as the necessities of warfare.

This, then, in words and pictures, is the story of the Pacific War —as it looked and felt to those who fought there, and how it looks now to visitors who seek out those Pacific battlefields. The vivid images and memories in the minds of the veterans are the key elements. And it is a history worth remembering—of looking back, of trying to recapture impressions of the war and its times, the sight, sound, and feel—thereby enabling readers who lived through those times to remember and relive them, and to allow those many more who were never there to get a sense of how it really was.

It is almost certain that no one who did not experience what the veterans endured can understand what they lived through on the beaches of Betio, the jungles of Guadalcanal, the ridges of Peleliu and Okinawa, the corrosive, sulfur-reeking sands of Iwo Jima, or within the flaming hell of a kamikaze-stricken destroyer. There were also those many more who were on islands thousands of miles from the fighting, or on ships endlessly at sea, or on island bases where B-29s roared off into the early morning skies to rain destruction on the cities of Japan. In fact, given the benevolent workings of human memory, which over time tends to soften past horrors while enhancing the images of what was good, it may be that many of those Pacific war veterans really no longer understand what they went through either, the sheer immensity of it. But they certainly remember the experiences that forever changed their young lives, the central events of lifetimes played out on islands all across the vast Pacific, and agree how essential it is now to pass on those experiences. This book is an attempt to tell that story—area by area, island by island—to tell how it was for those who fought by truthfully relating their actions and experiences, and to describe as well the lives of "those who also served" by standing and waiting.

We could not cover every campaign in detail, nor was it our purpose to present a comprehensive history of the Pacific war. Rather, we tried to create for the reader, while the veterans themselves can recall it, what that war was like—how it looked and felt and smelled—and to examine the legacy today of a war so fiercely fought on faraway Pacific islands.

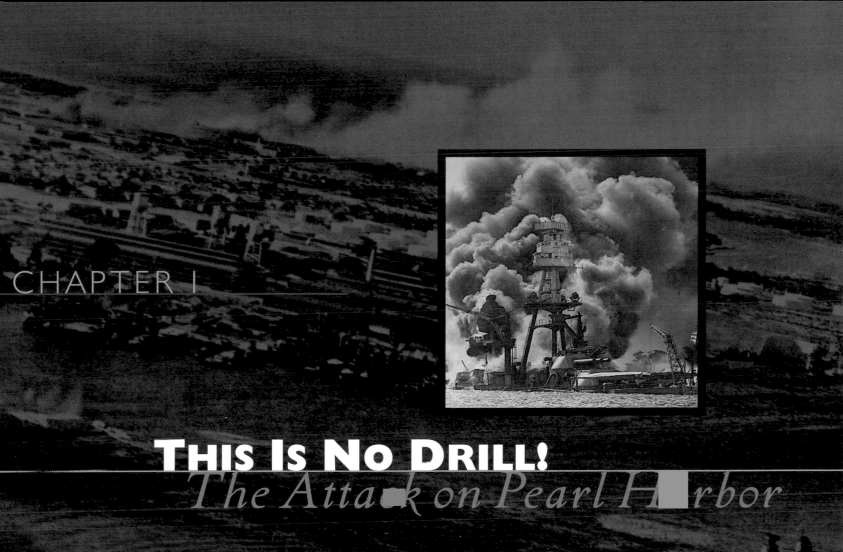

CHAPTER I

THIS IS NO DRILL!
The Attack on Pearl Harbor

FEW AMERICANS more than ten years old that December Sunday have ever forgotten precisely where they were or what they were doing when they heard the news. At one moment their homeland was at peace, and in the next it was not; the world turned, and never again would things be the same.

In Honolulu and on the ships in Pearl Harbor the day began as placidly as any other Hawaiian Sunday. On the night before, however, things had not been so placid. The Pacific Fleet was in—eight battleships along with eighty-four other vessels—and the ships' crews were enjoying a Saturday night on liberty. Men from Oahu's Army installations—Schofield Barracks, Fort Shafter, Hickam Field, Wheeler Field, and others—were also in for a night on the town. More civilians than usual were in the streets, too, for on this evening Honolulu was to turn on its celebrated Christmas lights and thereby open the 1941 holiday season. "Those decorations were really beautiful," recalled civil engineer Bob Noble. "A lot of energy had gone into building them, and there were millions of lights. Elmer Taft and I took cameras downtown to shoot pictures. But it was too crowded. The ships were in. The soldiers were in town. All those kids were Christmas shopping, and we couldn't find any place to stop to take pictures or even to stop, period. We just kept being swept along the sidewalk by thousands and thousands of uniforms. Finally, we just said, 'Ah, the hell with it. Tomorrow night they'll be back on duty and we can get our pictures then.'"

Now it is early on that Sunday morning, and the island of Oahu drowses under cotton-puff clouds drifting in a soft, tropical sky. The air is fragrant with the perfume of tropical flowers, and out on the west or "Ewa" side of Honolulu early risers are awakening to a delightful aroma of baking bread drifting from Love's Bakery to mingle with the fruity, sweet smell of the Dole Pineapple cannery.

It is five minutes before eight, according to the big clock on Aloha Tower. A few early churchgoers and sightseers are in the streets, some eager swimmers are already splashing about in the surf at Waikiki, and motor whale-boats put-put across Pearl Harbor's still, gray waters carrying parties of white-clad sailors bound for sightseeing or church services ashore. Private Wayne H. "Jim" Johnson and a couple of his buddies, lounging on their cots in the big Consolidated Barracks at Hickam Field, are waiting for the bus to John Rogers Airport where they plan to do some private flying. Engineers Bob Noble and Elmer Taft, planning a Sunday of sightseeing and picture-taking, are at breakfast in their boardinghouse up on the side of the Punchbowl, and Harvey and Jean Fraser are asleep on a pair of army cots, the only furniture still remaining in their house at Schofield Army Barracks twenty miles north of Honolulu.

"I'd just been relieved of command of Company A, Third Engineer Combat Battalion, and reassigned to Camp Beauregard, Louisiana," said Harvey, a first lieutenant who ultimately will become a brigadier general. "We were due to sail on the eighth, and all our furniture and belongings had been packed up and were down at the docks. There'd been a going-away party the night before, and we were sleeping late."

Delmar Aldrich, an electrician's mate aboard the DMS (Destroyer-Minesweeper) *Ramsay* in Pearl Harbor, has been spending the morning "mess cookin'—workin' out of the galley on the main deck." And at this particular moment he is walking aft on the main deck, "carryin' a load of food back to the quarters where the black-gang ate, and yellin', 'Come and get or I'll throw it out!.'"

The blue "prep" ("Prepare for Morning Colors") flag has just been hoisted above Pearl Harbor's tall water tank and answered in kind by all ships in the harbor. It signals the approach of that solemn eight o'clock moment when Naval vessels raise the Stars and Stripes—smaller craft observing the occasion with boatswains' pipes, larger ones with buglers or recordings of the National Anthem, and the largest, often, with a performance by the ship's band, as was happening on the battleship *Nevada*. Bandleader Oden McMillen has his musicians poised to strike up The Star-Spangled Banner, and the war is now only one minute away.

There have been warnings this morning—ominous indications of a coming storm. Unfortunately, however, they have been seen by only a tiny handful of military leaders—none of whom has taken them seriously—and by no civilians at all. At half-past-six the ancient destroyer *Ward,* patrolling offshore, spotted and sank an odd-looking little submarine trying to sneak into Pearl Harbor in the wake of a supply ship. Immediately afterward *Ward'*s captain, Lieutenant William Outerbridge, tried to inform the Fourteenth Naval District Communications Office of the incident, but with no luck. The ensign manning the office had fallen asleep. Fifteen minutes later Outerbridge tried again: "Attacked, fired upon, depth bombed, and sank submarine operating in defensive sea area."

This time the ensign was awake, recorded the message, and passed it on. But even then its passage through the various command levels was unhurried. There was debate about whether or not it was just another case of a trigger-happy destroyer crew depth-bombing a whale. Also, there was confusion about who should be notified and how to locate them after that had been decided. When the report finally did make its way up to Chief of Staff Captain John Earle he, too, was skeptical. "We get too many of these false sightings," he said. "We can't afford to go off half-cocked. Get it verified." By the time it is verified, however, it will no longer matter.

Privates George Elliott and Joseph Lockard at the Opana Radar Station on a mountaintop on the north end of the island have picked up an even more ominous warning. Radar is a new thing in December 1941, semi-experimental and not entirely to be trusted. Accordingly, Opana is the only one of Oahu's three radar stations operating this morning, and that, said George Elliott, was only because he and Lockard had decided to run a training problem. But the problem they dealt with was far different from what they had planned.

"At 7:02," remembered Elliott, "We picked up a very large blip, such as we had never seen before." Calculating it to represent a group of at least fifty airplanes 137 miles north and approaching at 180 MPH, they try to report it to the appropriate information center. And they have no more success than Outerbridge with his submarine report.

"The switchboard operator told me there was no one in the center," Elliott said, "and asked if I'd like a call back when someone did show up."

Eighteen minutes later someone does call—an Air Corps first lieutenant named Kermit Tyler. Elliott describes their mysterious blip, now within ninety miles of Oahu and still approaching.

Tyler replies that they are no doubt seeing planes from Hickam Field, or from the carrier *Enterprise* (known to be in the area), or maybe a flight of twelve B-17s expected momentarily from the West Coast. Whatever it is, he says, "Don't worry about it."

Well, Elliott and Lockard may be just privates but they are no dummies. They know twelve aircraft do not appear on a radarscope as more than fifty, and they continue their watch.

At 7:39 the incoming planes, now only twenty-two miles out and coming fast, "seemed to disperse to the right and to the left," pass behind a screen of mountains, and disappear from the scope.

With nothing left to see, Elliott and Lockard shut Opana down, and at five minutes before eight they are in a pickup truck bouncing down the mountain on their way to breakfast.

For the United States and its Western Allies, that was when the Pacific War began: December 7, 1941, at 7:55 A.M. in Hawaii, 10:25 A.M. in San Francisco, and 1:25 P.M. in Washington, D.C. For Japan, however, it had begun years before, back in the 1930s.

Japan was controlled in those days by a clique of militarists dreaming of empire and steeped in the code of their country's ancient warriors, the Samurai. They dreamed of "gathering the eight corners of the world under one roof"—a Japanese roof. And their warrior code, which they were trying with considerable success to impose upon the population as a whole, was jingoistic, militaristic, and brutal.

Children, as newsman Ian Mutsu later put it, "were taught to believe their Emperor was invincible, their people were a chosen race, and their country was divine." Women were told their main purpose in life was to produce warrior sons for the Emperor. Those sons, in turn, were told that fighting for their Emperor God was the noblest possible pursuit and that to be killed while so fighting was to die the noblest possible death, to fall as the cherry blossom falls—at the moment of perfection. In fighting to the death there was immortal honor. In surrendering or submitting to capture there was eternal disgrace—disgrace so foul that to avoid it one must commit suicide. As for any captives so craven as to have chosen surrender over suicide—well, they were beneath contempt and were to be treated accordingly.

The Japanese warlords began their empire building in 1931 with a bloody invasion and takeover of Manchuria, China's richest province. They continued in 1937 by launching an all-out war for the rest of China, a war waged as their Samurai ancestors would have waged it—as a rampage of pillage and slaughter and torture and rape that shocked the world. The United States, long-time friend and trading partner of China, condemned the attack and especially its viciousness. In reply, the Japanese sent twenty-four planes to bomb and strafe the U.S. gunboat *Panay* as it lay at anchor in China's Yangtze River, killing three men and wounding sixteen. Then they said they were sorry, that the bombing had been just an unfortunate mistake. The United States accepted the Japanese apology and did it "so eagerly," according to historian William Manchester, that "Japan's leaders knew now the United States was a paper tiger."

But as the Japanese assault on China continued and grew ever more savage, the "Paper Tiger" began to growl. When it did, Japan's militarists decided they had to get the United States out of their way once and for all—by negotiation and/or intimidation if possible, by war if not. In 1940, in an appearance before the Senate Naval Affairs Committee, Admiral Joseph Taussig, one of too-few Americans willing to recognize what Japan was up to, tried to warn Congress—and was roundly damned for his pains.

"The most provocative, inflammatory and dangerous testimony of any Naval man in our time," roared New York's Hamilton Fish, Jr. "No matter how many ships Navy men have it is not enough!" thundered Missouri's Bennett Champ Clark, who went on to state that the admiral should be court-martialed for saying what he did.

Another who saw the storm gathering in the Pacific was newspaper columnist Raymond Clapper, who wrote on June 22, 1939: "Japan is determined to dominate the Orient and adjacent raw materials supplies [i.e., the minerals, oil, and timber of Australia, the Netherlands East Indies, and the Philippines]." When pacifist politicians continued to insist on allowing Japan a free hand in the Orient, Clapper, on June 13, 1940, condemned their demands as a "craven betrayal" that "would leave Australia, New Zealand, The Philippines, and Dutch East Indians to the tender mercies of the Japanese army . . . scuttle every international ideal [and] gain us nothing but another Munich."

"Read your newspapers," Clapper continued two weeks later. "The Japanese Minister of War [has announced] that 'Japan's hour has come [and she] will no longer allow any foreign power to interfere in East Asia, including French Indo-China and the Netherlands Indies.'"

But Americans weren't listening. They remembered the horrors of the World War, with its louse-infested trenches and mustard gas and body-littered no-man's-lands. And whereas they may not have agreed with the strident preaching of North Dakota's Senator Gerald Nye, as he insisted that wars were nothing but commercial enterprises fomented by munitions makers and bankers— "Merchants of Death" he called them—they did agree that the United States should never get into another one. Accordingly, remembering the Great War, as it was called, and scarred by the hardships of the Great Depression, they saw no reason for spending money on national defense. After all, safely tucked away between two vast oceans, they were clearly immune to foreign attack. And it was this sort of unrealistic complacency that made it easy for Japan to slip a naval spy into Hawaii and easy for him to operate once there.

He came to Honolulu as Tadashi Moramura, an employee of the Japanese Embassy. Actually, however, he was Takeo Yoshikawa, an ensign in the Japanese Navy. He had been sent by Admiral Isoroku Yamamoto, commander-in-chief of the Japanese Combined Fleet, who believed that "[in a] war with America we have no hope of winning unless the U.S. Fleet in Hawaiian waters can be destroyed," and he wanted all the intelligence about that fleet that he could get.

Arriving in Hawaii on March 26, 1941, Yoshikawa immediately set out to learn all he could about its military installations, especially Pearl Harbor. And with the aid of the embassy's Captain Kanji Ogawa, Honolulu taxi-driver Johnny Mikama, and his own disarming charm, he found the learning easy. By tucking a lunch box under his arm, he was able to join a group of Navy Yard laborers entering Pearl Harbor and then to spend the day wandering unchallenged throughout the base.

By pretending to be meeting an officer friend he also got into Hickam Field and drove about, again unchallenged, counting airplanes, noting facilities, and diagramming runways. "Also," he recalled years later: "I often went Japanese tea house in Alewa Height. From there I saw the fleet in Pearl Harbor. Sometimes I go around Pearl Harbor by taxi or by bus. Sometime I walk along with this [sailor] or that one and drink a beer to get information. I did a lot of fishing [and thus] made out the depths of the sea [harbor]." With the exception of Johnny Mikama, however, he got no help at all from the local Japanese.

In January 1941 Japan demanded control of the oil fields of the Dutch East Indies. The Dutch refused. The United States backed them up by suspending all shipments to Japan of American scrap iron and steel. And now Raymond Clapper perceived really big trouble ahead. "We see the distant fire rolling toward us," he wrote on May 27, 1941. "It is not being put out. It is still some distance away but the evil wind blows it toward us."

As things turned out, Clapper was more of a prophet than even he could know. Exactly one month after he wrote those words the "evil wind" became a gale and the "distant fire" was no longer "rolling" but racing. For on that day, June 27, the Japanese Army took over South Indo-China, and the United States promptly responded by placing an embargo on all trade with Japan and declaring it would remain in place until the Japanese troops were withdrawn.

Now, Japan faced a major crisis. Having little iron of her own and no oil at all, she had been depending on supplies almost entirely from the United States, which had plenty of both. To keep her industries going and dreams of empire alive Japan had to have unlimited access to both —especially oil. Without it, said her admirals, her fuel-thirsty navy would soon be reduced from the most powerful fleet in the Pacific to a pitiful collection of immobilized hulks. But to get it by giving in to American demands: Impossible! Unthinkable! Not only would that halt Japan's empire building, it would actually reverse it. Even worse, it would cost the Japanese an unbearable loss of "face." But there was an alternative source: the petroleum-rich Dutch East Indies. The militarists already had secretly made plans for seizing these resources. Now they would simply speed up their timetable. To insure success, however, they must first do something about America's Pacific Fleet. And at this point a plan for attacking Pearl Harbor, called Operation Z, was put into high gear.

The physical problems pilots would encounter in attacking Pearl Harbor—a shallow bay surrounded by a city and smokestacks and mountains—also existed at Kagoshima Bay on the island of Kyushu. There, Commander Minoru Genda, a Japanese naval aviation genius, began endlessly drilling his pilots in dropping torpedoes under such conditions. At the same time he was also solving another problem. American admirals knew that in Pearl Harbor their ships were safe from torpedoes. Pearl was too shallow, they said, only fifty feet at the deepest, and everyone knew air-dropped torpedoes needed at least seventy-five feet of water, and a hundred was better. Genda, however, didn't "know" it. He knew instead of a British torpedo attack in November 1940 on the Italian fleet at Taranto. There, too, the water was presumed too shallow for torpedoes.

But with only twenty-one obsolete open-cockpit airplanes the British had managed to sink one battleship and to heavily damage two others. Their secret: wooden fins fitted to their torpedoes. Another problem: battleships in Pearl Harbor were usually moored side-by-side in pairs. Accordingly, the inner ship of each pair would be shielded by the outer one and therefore invulnerable to torpedoes. But Genda had a solution for that too: bombs made by putting fins on sixteen-inch, armor-piercing naval shells. These should be capable of penetrating a battleship's heavy decks to explode with devastating effect deep inside.

NOVEMBER 4, 1941: Genda sets his pilots to memorizing a seven-foot-square model of Pearl Harbor that, thanks to Takeo Yoshikawa's spying, shows the exact locations of ships to be hit.

NOVEMBER 7: Admiral Yamamoto sets the time for attack—early morning, Sunday, December 7, a day of the week when most of the American Pacific Fleet can be expected to be in the harbor, and an hour when most of its men are likely to be off-duty or off-guard. Not until long after Yamamoto's death will the world learn that he does not want to carry out this plan. He has studied at Harvard, lived in Washington, D.C., as a Japanese naval attaché, and traveled the country extensively—usually by bus. He likes America and its people and opposes the whole idea of war against Americans. He knows the vast resources and industrial might of the United States and has warned Japan's militarists of the disaster they may bring upon themselves if they attack. But Yamamoto's first loyalty is to his Emperor. When the decision is made to attack he accepts it and chooses Pearl Harbor as the place to strike. But at the same time he writes in his private diary: "It is terrible to think that this is God's will [but] I am determined to do my duty even though it is completely opposite to my personal convictions . . . for I am the sword of my Emperor. It is a heavy fate."

NOVEMBER 27: The *Kido Butai*, as the Japanese attack force is named, gathers at a secret rendezvous in the Kurile Islands north of Japan proper. The most formidable fleet ever assembled in the Pacific so far, it includes two battleships, three cruisers, eight destroyers, oil tankers, supply ships, and six aircraft carriers (including the world's two largest), carrying 360 aircraft. And it is ready to go. Japan's diplomatic emissaries are continuing to negotiate with the United States, but (though they do not know it) only as a smoke screen for a die already cast.

NOVEMBER 30: Tokyo radios its embassies in the U.S. and other Allied countries the message "East winds raining," meaning, "Destroy your files. Burn your papers."

DECEMBER 1: Tokyo radios the *Kido Butai*, now halfway to Pearl Harbor and still undetected, "Climb Mount Niitake," meaning, "Attack as planned."

DECEMBER 5: Takeo Yoshikawa flies over Oahu in a rented Piper Cub, and then radios Tokyo: "The following ships were in port on December 5: 8 battleships, 3 light cruisers, sixteen destroyers." The Americans, who have broken the Japanese diplomatic code, intercept his message. But this is Friday and so the intercept is put in a "hold" basket for action after the weekend.

DECEMBER 6: The Japanese fleet, maintaining radio silence, picks up an evening broadcast of dance music from radio station KGMB in Honolulu. Played on the ships' PA systems to entertain the crews, it is also used by their navigators as a beacon to maneuver the fleet into final attack position.

DECEMBER 7, 1941, 3:30 A.M.: Japanese aircrews are awakened, don their good luck belts-of-a-thousand-stitches, and assemble for a ceremonial breakfast of red snapper and red rice.

6:10 A.M. (twelve minutes before sunrise): Turning at flank speed into a raw, gusting wind and spray-blown seas the carriers begin launching airplanes. First up are forty-three Mitsubishi "Zero" fighters, one of which crashes on take-off. Next come forty-nine Nakajima "Kate" level-bombers, then fifty-one Aichi "Val" dive-bombers. Finally, burdened by heavy torpedoes slung beneath their bellies, forty "Kate" torpedo-bombers manage to struggle into the air.

6:25 A.M.: All 182 first-strike planes are in the air now, and led by Lieutenant Commander Mitsuo Fuchida they disappear in droning vee's over the southern horizon. Behind them, spread over a hundred square miles of sea only 190 miles from Pearl Harbor but still undetected, the *Kido Butai* lies waiting, listening, and preparing a second attack to be launched an hour after the first.

7:49 A.M.: Fleet Commander Vice Admiral Chuichi Nagumo hears Fuchida's first report—his voice, radio-distant and tinny, exclaiming, "To, To, To!" (Abbreviations of *totsugeki*, meaning, "Charge!")

7:53 A.M.: The Japanese strike force is now swarming southward down Oahu's central valley. And despite its buzzing and rumbling and clear visibility against the sky it seems, unbelievably, not to have alerted a single defender. Or, for that matter, anyone else.

Elated, Fuchida radios his second coded report. "Tora! Tora! Tora!" ("We have achieved complete surprise!") Simultaneously he fires a blue flare and airplanes bank and wheel into many smaller formations, each heading for a preplanned target.

Their first chore is to neutralize the American air defenses, and Fuchida's flare has hardly stopped falling when the island's airfields—Wheeler, Hickam, Ewa, Bellows, Kaneohe, and Pearl Harbor's Ford Island—are all swept by storms of bombs and bullets.

Asleep in their Schofield Barracks quarters only one block from the edge of Wheeler Field, Harvey and Jean Fraser are awakened by planes buzzing overhead like swarming bees. At first they think it is only a Wheeler exercise. Then, "there was a loud crash!" said Jean, "and we jumped out of bed to find all our windows blown out and a smoking crater in the yard across the street."

"Planes flew right up our alley," said Harvey: "Planes with the Rising Sun on 'em, machine guns wide open, flying so Goddam low you could see the white neckerchiefs on the pilots. I ran to get my pistol, then remembered I'd turned it in because I was leaving. So there I was with those damn planes and nothing to shoot back with!"

At Hickam Field, mechanics Jess Gaines and Ted Conway see an approaching vee of planes and notice a tiny something falling from one of them.

"He lost a wheel," says Gaines.

"Wheel, Hell!" yells Conway. "Those are Japs!"

A moment later the "wheel" explodes in a row of parked B-18 bombers and sets them afire.

In Hickam's Consolidated Barracks, Jim Johnson and his buddy, "takin' life easy and waitin' for the bus," hear a loud bang: "but we had a guy who'd shake things up now and then by rolling a big cherry-bomb firecracker down the hall, so we don't think much about it. But when there were more bangs I looked out the window and there was an airplane with a Rising Sun on its wing! We'd been told we were so invulnerable that nobody'd dare attack us, but there the damn buggers were, right over our roof!"

At Ford Island Naval Air Station, Patrol Wing Commander Logan Ramsey hears an airplane screaming down toward the seaplane ramp. Thinking it is one of his pilots engaged in forbidden low-level "flat-hatting," he rushes out to get the offender's number. But the plane not only isn't one of his, it isn't even American. Unlike any American fighter it has a fixed landing gear that gives it a predatory look—like a hawk diving with talons extended—and is, unbelievably, a Japanese Val. But before that fact can really register it is driven home by one bomb exploding on the ramp and another inside a hangar. Now, with more bombs falling and the air full of smoke and flame and flying debris, Ramsey radios Navy Headquarters: "Air raid Pearl Harbor. This is no drill."

At the other airfields the story is the same. Personnel caught by surprise and unprepared are left confused and disbelieving. And the worst of it is, fear of sabotage by disloyal Japanese locals had led American commanders to order all military aircraft removed from their protective bunkers and bunched neatly together on the aprons, so they would be easier to guard. And also, as it unfortunately turned out, to be easier targets for air attacks, so much so that most are already bullet-riddled and burning where they stand. At Wheeler Field Harvey Fraser sees planes "lined up in front of the hangars so close together that it took only two or three bombs to set 'em all on fire. They just burned and melted and fell down like dead people right there on the tarmac. Perfectly lined up little piles of cooling junk."

What it all adds up to is this: with the war less than five minutes old, the Americans' air-defense capability is already destroyed. A few fighter-planes will become airborne, but too few and too late even to annoy those Japanese now proceeding to the business for which they came—the destruction of the United States' Pacific Fleet.

7:56 A.M.: The cruiser *Honolulu* radios a report of planes attacking Hickam Field. The cruiser *New Orleans* announces an attack in progress on Ford Island. The cruiser *Phoenix* reports unidentified aircraft approaching Pearl Harbor. Then radios begin sputtering and crackling with similar announcements from all over the base. Now, everywhere, boatswain's pipes, buglers, and PA systems can be heard sounding "General Quarters!" and "This is No Drill!" And the harbor area becomes a shaken anthill of milling inhabitants scurrying to battle stations, or to shelter, or simply to where they can see what is going on.

7:59 A.M.: Flying only sixty feet above the water ("came over the *Ramsay* at masthead height," said Del Aldrich), a half-dozen Kate torpedo-bombers sweep in from the west to strike at ships moored on the west side of Ford Island. A torpedo misses the cruiser *Detroit* and explodes against the shore. Another strikes the cruiser *Raleigh*, blowing a hole in her forward engine room, and she begins to list, but her damage control crews will save her from sinking. Astern of *Raleigh* the old *Utah*, once a battleship but now spending her dotage as a target ship, is less fortunate. Two torpedoes blast great holes in her port side, and the sea pours in.

Continuing eastward, the Kates hop over Ford Island and the ships in East Loch. Passing *Nevada*, one fires its machine guns at the band assembled on deck for Morning Colors. Bandleader McMillen has never yet begun the National Anthem without finishing it. He is not about to let a little hostile gunfire stop him now, and the band plays on. *Nevada*'s newly raised flag is shredded, but no musicians are hit. The moment the Anthem is finished, however, they drop their instruments and race to battle stations.

A torpedo fired at the cruiser *Helena*, tied up at Ten-Ten Dock, passes under the old minelayer *Oglala* moored alongside and explodes against *Helena*'s port engine room. *Helena* takes in water and begins to list, though she will not sink. *Oglala*, however, will sink—her ancient seams sprung open by concussion.

Destructive as all this action has been it is only a mild preliminary—the wind before the storm. Some thirty or more Kate torpedo-bombers that have flown past Pearl Harbor now reverse course to drop their torpedoes in Southeast Loch—a finger of water pointing like a gun barrel at the ships neatly lined up in Battleship Row like ducks in a shooting gallery. They come, fighter pilot Yoshio Shiga will recall, "flying low and in a line, dropping torpedoes like dragonflies dropping their eggs."

Being moored outboard of *Maryland* and *Tennessee* and the most directly in line with Southeast Loch, *Oklahoma* and *West Virginia* are the first to be hit, and great columns of water erupt from their sides as torpedoes strike home. The first explodes in *Oklahoma* and puts out all her lights. Three more blast away much of her port hull. *West Virginia* is hit twice. *Nevada* is hit, as are *California* and *Arizona*—the latter by a torpedo passing under the repair ship *Vestal* tied up alongside. Then *California* is hit again, and *West Virginia* perhaps as many as four more times, though in all the uproar and confusion it is hard to keep an accurate accounting of exactly what is happening to whom.

Oil streams from explosion-rent bunkers to form a floating, stinking gummy mess in which dozens of men who have been blown overboard now struggle for their very lives. Seeing them there, Torpedo Squadron Leader Hirata Matsumura feels momentary pity. "They looked," he will recall, "as if they were swimming in glue."

On *West Virginia*'s bridge, Captain Mervyn Bennion says, "This is in keeping with Japan's history of surprise attacks," and then he is dead—struck by a sliver of flying shrapnel. Although both *California* and *West Virginia* are hard-hit, their damage control officers manage by counter-flooding to keep them from capsizing, and they settle down upright on the bottom of the shallow bay.

Oklahoma, however, is beyond saving. Water pours in through her ruined side and she lists and keeps on listing. Inside, all the lights are out, and as the list increases everything there starts breaking loose. In pitch-dark handling-rooms trapped men dodge thousand-pound shells rumbling across tilting decks, and men in other spaces scramble to avoid a hundred other kinds of rolling, tumbling hardware. In dozens of below-decks compartments they splash and fumble in a dark and topsy-turvy world where (in landlubber's terms) floors have become walls and walls have become floors, frantically seeking an escape that too many will not find. The trouble is, there is no time. Less than ten minutes after *Oklahoma* is first hit, Chief Petty Officer Albert Molter, watching from Ford Island, sees her rolling over, "slowly and stately . . . as if she were tired and wanted to rest."

Minutes later the old *Utah,* on the far side of Ford Island, also turns bottom up. At the same moment on the nearby *Ramsay,* Del Aldrich is running to his battle station and overhead a flight of Japanese Zeros is roaring in to strafe the harbor with machine-gun fire. "One of 'em sees me runnin' and starts shooting, but his bullets go into the water. I don't know what the hell is goin' on. I'm just a twenty-year-old kid from Salem, South Dakota, and all I know is, the old *Utah* is rollin' over and an airplane is firin' its guns and lookin' for Del Aldrich."

It is the same with almost everyone else in the harbor. They, too, don't know what the hell is going on but run to battle stations to do their frantic best against an unexpected onslaught by enemies who seem to be looking for them, personally. Too often, however, their response is confused by excitement and frustrated by conditions. Ammunition lockers on many ships have to be smashed open with fire axes. On ships hard-hit and listing or without electric power, heavy ammunition has to be passed hand-to-hand through slanting passageways and over slippery decks. Age-worn ammunition belts of heavy machine guns break, causing gunners to say things their mothers would never approve of. On shore, Army supply sergeants, following regulations, often refuse to issue guns or ammunition without first having proper requisitions and signatures. Overexcited antiaircraft gunners forget to fuse their shells for air bursts, and any that strike nothing in the air (as ninety-nine out of a hundred will not) explode upon striking the earth. Many fall in downtown Honolulu. There are casualties, and residents there believe they, too, are being bombed.

At breakfast in their Thurston Street boardinghouse, Bob Noble and Elmer Taft heard "one hell of an explosion. . . . We ran outside and there about six hundred feet up the street was what was left of a car that had had four guys in it. Had just started to go fishing when they got hit, and now they all were dead. Later turned out they'd been hit by one of our own antiaircraft shells."

Aboard the cruiser *New Orleans*—or so it will later be told—Chaplain Howell M. Forgy utters a phrase that is to become one of the most famous and enduring of the entire war. According to one survivor of that day Forgy had no battle station, but being concerned with crew morale "was marchin' up and down the gun deck saying, 'Praise the Lord and pass the ammunition.'" Historian Walter Lord will record the event in much the same way. But the February 2, 1942, issue of *Time* magazine will carry a suspiciously more colorful version: "The Chaplain dropped his bunting, ran to an antiaircraft gun and began preaching lead to the Japanese. A few minutes later he was heard to intone: 'Praise the Lord and pass the ammunition. I just got one of the sons of bitches!'" Forgy himself is to deny having said it at all in any form. But whatever the case, "Praise the Lord and Pass the Ammunition" is to become one of the war's inspirational slogans and the basis for one of its most popular songs.

Immediately behind the Kate torpedo planes come other Kates carrying Genda's specially designed armor-piercing bombs. They score two hits each on *Nevada* and *Maryland.* They hit *West Virginia* twice also, but fortunately both bombs turn out to be duds. A bomb explodes atop a *Tennessee* gun turret. Another penetrates a magazine of antiaircraft ammunition on *California* and sets off a massive below-decks explosion. Yet another plunges through *Vestal*'s hull and explodes beneath her.

It is *Arizona,* however, that seems to have drawn the lion's share of bombs. It has been hit by seven (according to one possibly exaggerated report), and these were in addition to one and perhaps two torpedoes. Surprisingly, all these seem to have done is support a boast that appeared only eight days earlier in the program of the Army-Navy football game. There, under a picture of

Arizona steaming tall, proud, and invincible-looking into flying spray, was the statement: "It is significant that despite the claims of air enthusiasts no battleship has yet been sunk by bombs."

But when an eighth bomb plunges down into *Arizona's* forward magazine, that image of battleship invincibility is destroyed forever. There are more than a million pounds of high explosives in that magazine—equal to more than twenty-thousand cases of dynamite—and it all explodes with a deep, earthshaking *Whuff!* (a titanic *"Swish!"* as some survivors will remember it) that shivers the air and the water and even the buildings on shore. A plume of black smoke spurts upward, instantly, hundreds of feet into the air. Then, just as instantly huge flashing sheets of gray smoke and white fire obscure it. The whole forward end of the great ship appears to leap up and then fall back, its massive foremast structure now wrenched and tattered and leaning at a crazy angle over the water. Pieces of ship as large as small houses sail like chips through the air. Debris of all kinds showers down—and not just debris. "When the *Arizona* blew up it just rained sailors," one Pearl Harbor veteran will grimly recall and then go on to observe that many of these were the lucky ones, saved by the very fact that they were blown away from the burning wreck. For there, now, death is more common than life, and in the cases of many blasted and scalded men, preferable to it.

Aviation Machinist's Mate D. A. Graham will never forget: "Yellowish smoke pouring out of the hatches.... Men coming out on the quarterdeck with every stitch of clothing and even their shoes blown off . . . all painfully burned."

And branded forever into the memory of Marine Corporal E. C. Nightingale is the picture of "Lieutenant Simonson lying with blood on his shirtfront . . . dead. Everything forward of the mainmast aflame . . . bodies of the dead thick everywhere. Badly burned men headed for the quarterdeck only to fall dead or badly wounded . . . charred bodies everywhere."

But amid the horror and chaos there is heroism, too, and performance far beyond what anyone could expect in such a holocaust. As Lieutenant Commander S. G. Fuqua

remembers, "I could hear guns firing on the ship long after the boat deck was a mass of flames. [Their crews] conducted themselves with the greatest heroism and bravery."

"There was no 'going to pieces' or panic," said Graham. "Courage and performance of all hands was of the highest order."

Radioman's Mate (third class) G. H. Lane will agree: "I saw no signs of fear.... Everyone was just surprised and pretty mad."

Not only was the explosion a disaster for *Arizona* but for nearby vessels as well. Captain C. E. Reardan aboard *Tennessee* will recall, "burning powder, oil, and debris falling on the quarterdeck," and *Nevada* and *West Virginia* are similarly showered. Debris—sharp-edged and flaming—also rains down on the near shore of Ford Island and on men struggling for survival in the oily water.

Burning oil flowing from *Arizona* ignites other oil already in the water, and the whole flaming mess drifts outward, setting other ships ablaze. A fire will burn in *Tennessee* for two-and-a-half hours, gutting her stern and warping and buckling her hull plates aft. There are fires on *Maryland,* too, but small and soon controlled. (In fact, *Maryland,* suffering relatively little damage, will be back in service before Christmas.)

On *West Virginia,* on the other hand, things are bad indeed. Hit by possibly six torpedoes, she sits on the bottom with her main deck awash and with a fire in her superstructure burning so fiercely that it will take thirty-six hours to put it out. But in spite of it all, her crew still defiantly flies the Stars and Stripes from her fantail.

8:30 A.M.: The first wave of attackers is gone, and for the moment, at least, there is no more danger from the sky.

8:40 A.M.: The battleship *Nevada* begins to move. One torpedo and two bombs have hit her and she is hurt. Some of her forward spaces are flooded and she is somewhat down by the head. Even so, she has managed to get up steam, and all over the harbor men wave and cheer to see her towering gray shape gliding majestically, colors flying, out of the smoke of the burning *Arizona* and toward the channel to the sea. Unfortunately, however, just as she passes Ten-Ten

Dock the Japanese second-strike arrives—170 planes bent on finishing what the first strike started.

Blocked up for repairs in Dry Dock No. One, the battleship *Pennsylvania* and destroyers *Cassin* and *Downes* were not hit at all during the first attack. Now, they are. A bomb explodes on *Pennsylvania*'s starboard boat deck. Then *Downes* is hit and begins burning so fiercely that the dry dock is flooded to extinguish the fire. But the flooding intended to help *Downes* causes *Cassin* to rise from her blocks and roll onto *Downes*. Then torpedo warheads on both destroyers begin exploding, and *Pennsylvania* is showered with flaming debris. When it all ends both destroyers will be a total loss, but *Pennsylvania*, though damaged, will sail under her own power to San Francisco for repairs.

But it is *Nevada* that gets the most attention this time, and for good reason. If the attackers can but sink her in the channel she will seal the harbor like a cork in a bottle—thirty thousand tons of inert steel keeping the ships inside from getting out and those outside from getting in—thus rendering the channel useless to the Americans for weeks or even months to come.

Nevada's gunners shoot down three planes (these in addition to two they got during the first attack), but there are just too many of them to be stopped. Six bombs strike home. *Nevada*'s bridge and fore-structure begin to burn. To prevent the possibility of her being sunk in the channel she is ordered to run herself aground before reaching it.

9:45 A.M.: Again the skies are clear of enemy planes, and this time there will be no more. But no one on the island knows that, and rumors are rife and wild, though none too wild to be believed by frightened people.

"Japs are landing at Diamond Head."

"Forty troop transports are lying off Barber's Point."

"Paratroopers have landed in the cane fields near Ewa."

"Sampans are landing troops at the Navy Ammunition Depot."

Nor do fearful civilians spawn all the rumors. Some have an official origin. For example, a Navy communication time-stamped 11:50 A.M.: "COM14 to CINCPAC. Parachutists landing at Barber's Point."

People rush to stock up on groceries. Many dig themselves foxholes and trenches. Those who have guns get them out, fully expecting to have to defend themselves and their families on the beaches, in the streets, or in their own front yards.

Civilians by the hundreds volunteer themselves and their cars for whatever service they can perform—transporting wounded, moving supplies, helping in hospitals—whatever they can do.

Military units rush to set up defensive measures, many of them sensible. But there are some that because of the confusion and rumors and fright range from ridiculous to downright dangerous. Harvey Fraser is ordered to resume command of his old company at Schofield:

And when I got over there it was just pandemonium. Things confused as all hell. The Colonel said to me, "Harvey, we gotta have a whole bunch of slit trenches in the residence areas." "Colonel," I said, "remember the time you ordered me to dig a trench in the housing area and it cut the phone cable to Honolulu and I nearly got court-martialled for it?" "Damn you!" he yelled, "Just start diggin'!" Well, we dug the damn things and did cut the phone cable to Honolulu again, and cut water and electric lines as well. We got a lot of slit trenches—many of 'em full of water—and also wound up out of communication with Honolulu and with water running a foot deep in the street.

Troops from Schofield and Shafter rush to defensive positions on the island's beaches, and sentries rush to wherever various commanders think sentries ought to be. But both troops and sentries are excited and jumpy and inclined to shoot first and investigate later.

Pearl Harbor itself has become a beehive of rescue activity. Hundreds of burned and wounded men need to be transported to where they can be cared for. Dozens and maybe hundreds of trapped men need to be rescued from the wreckage. It is a massive effort requiring the use of every available small craft that has a motor and will float, and launches, motor whaleboats, cabin cruisers, captain's gigs, and landing craft are scooting over the bay like water bugs over a pond.

The most frustrating job, and the most heartbreaking, is that of trying to save men trapped below the waterline in sunken ships, especially the capsized *Oklahoma* and *Utah*. Those still alive will be in spaces where there is captive air and often plenty of it. But how even to get to them, let alone get the men out—through the mazes of drowned ladders and water-filled passageways lying between them and freedom—this is a tragic problem that in too many cases will be impossible to solve.

Then there is the matter of rescuing men trapped in compartments next to the hulls of *Oklahoma* and *Utah*, and this involves the hardest decisions of all. Their tappings can be heard along the whole length of the exposed bottoms of both ships, and the first impulse, obviously, is just to cut holes and let them out. But those same holes are likely also to release trapped air holding back water in other compartments, thus drowning any survivors who may be in them. Engineers and naval architects are on both hulls, now, studying page after page of the ships' plans while making life-and-death decisions on just where and how to cut. And as passing time will prove, they are doing it well and saving many more lives than could be reasonably expected.

Night comes at last, and with the night comes danger that, because of misinformation and confusion and rumors, could be almost as terrifying as that in the morning. Two Schofield Army units assigned to beach defense mistake each other for invading Japanese and get into a small shooting war. A sentry at an Army pack-train corral challenges and then shoots an "invader," only to find that he's killed one of his own mules. All this panic-spawned recklessness is upsetting to Lieutenant Harvey Fraser, now out supervising preparation of beach defenses: "Jesus! Anything that moved got shot at. It was worth your life to go out, and if I'd been a pilot I'd never have gone up in an airplane there. Everybody shot at anything that flew."

He would have been even more upset if he had known that among those moving and therefore being shot at is his wife, Jean. She and some other officers' wives are being evacuated from Schofield Barracks to Honolulu by truck, and, she said, "It was a nightmare. Trigger-happy sentries, or somebody, kept taking shots at us, and we'd have to pile out and take cover in a ditch. Happened five times in twenty miles."

Six F4F Wildcat fighters coming in from the carrier *Enterprise* learn that people are indeed shooting at anything that flies, and learn it the hard way. Having received radio clearance to land on Ford Island, they are in the landing pattern when some nervous soul begins firing a machine gun at them—and triggers a panic. Searchlights instantly stab into the sky—brilliant fingers of light probing for and finding targets. Streams of tracer bullets follow, rising from both ships and shore, and within moments five of the six American planes are shot down and three of their pilots are dead.

A little later Jean Fraser's truck passes Pearl Harbor and she witnesses "the greatest fireworks display I've ever seen. Spectacular but horrible, too. Great fires burning, clouds of rolling smoke, and so many flares it was like daylight out there. Reason for the flares was, they were still trying to rescue people."

They will continue trying to rescue people, day after day, night after night, round the clock, until there is no hope of rescuing any more. They will save many but they cannot save all. When, for instance, *West Virginia* is raised some weeks later they will find in Storeroom A-III the bodies of three trapped men who counted the remaining days of their lives by making xs on the bulkhead. They made sixteen, the last one two days before Christmas.

Much time will pass before it is generally realized how little material harm was actually done to American naval power at Pearl Harbor. However, Admiral Yamamoto realizes it immediately and considers the raid a failure. The U.S. Pacific Fleet still has its fuel—4.5 million barrels of it in two tank farms beside the harbor. And it still has its Yard facilities—machine shops, cranes, docks, drydocks, and the power to operate them—all still intact. Had Admiral Nagumo ordered a third attack, as Genda and Fuchida had urged him to do, those exposed and vulnerable tank farms could have been set ablaze and destroyed. With American air-defenses wiped out, those Yard facilities could have been massively damaged. And these two things together would have put the American Pacific Fleet out of action for months to come. As it happened, however, most of the harm done was to old battleships, which without extensive modernization and refitting wouldn't have been much of a threat anyhow. For the fact was that battleships no longer ruled the seas. Aircraft carriers had taken their place. There were admirals of all nations who still refused to accept this, but it was true, and to Yamamoto's great disappointment there had been no carriers in Pearl Harbor when the attack took place.

The real damage—the terrible damage—is not material. It is human. When the final figures are tabulated they will show that at a cost of only twenty-nine planes and fifty-five men of their own on this bloody morning, the Japanese have killed more than 2,400 Americans—68 civilians, 109 Marines, 218 soldiers, 2,008 sailors. And of these, 1,178—49 percent of the total—are sailors who died when *Arizona* blew up.

These things, of course, will not be known until much later. All that is known now is that the Japanese have attacked Pearl Harbor. That they have done enormous damage and taken a great many American lives. And that they did it by sneaking in like assassins in the night to pounce upon and slay unsuspecting people who thought they were at peace. Accordingly, those few Americans who know anything about the Japanese calendar will find it grimly appropriate that in Japan the year 1941, the sixteenth year of Hirohito's reign, called *Showa* and meaning "Enlightened Peace," is also and more appropriately the Year of the Serpent.

Shortly after sunrise on December 7, 1941, crewmen cheer as an A6M2 "Reisen" (Zero) fighter, coded AI-101 and flown by Lieutenant Commander Shigeru Itaya, takes off from *Akagi* in the second attack wave. *Akagi* has turned into the Northeast Trade Winds to launch planes for the strike, and the low sun barely above the eastern horizon off the starboard bow casts long shadows across the flight deck. No photos of the launch of the first wave, which occurred in predawn darkness, are known to exist.

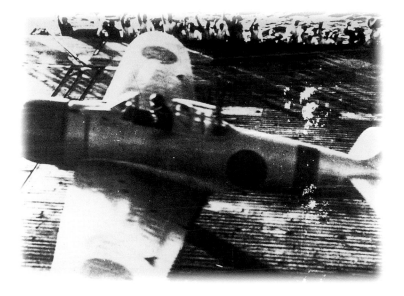

PEARL HARBOR

Sunday's horoscope is noteworthy because of its strange, sudden and wholly unpredictable and inexplicable occurrences, affecting all phases of life.

——"Your Horoscope," **L. A. Evening Herald Express**, SATURDAY, DECEMBER 6, 1941

IRONICALLY, the most immediately recognizable legacy from the war in the Pacific is a symbol of U.S. defeat: the battleship *Arizona,* still lying today on the muddy bottom of Pearl Harbor where it came to rest on Sunday morning, December 7, 1941. Salvagers sheared off its rusting superstructure during the war, and now a gleaming white memorial stands over the ship's sunken remains. Of all the war relics in the Pacific, this one has captured America's heart like no other. Each year thousands of Americans (and a large number of Japanese as well) visit the *Arizona* Memorial, one of the major tourist destinations in Hawaii. Nearly two million people go there annually. On a single busy day, more than five thousand visitors pay their respects to the remains of *Arizona,* and a large Visitor Center has been built to accommodate the crowds. Yet if you don't arrive there before about nine in the morning and get in line, you can expect to wait at least a couple of hours for one of the launches that will take visitors out to the memorial. Such crowds are literally unbelievable to anyone who has visited many war relics left to rust on other islands spread across the Pacific. Today the names of most of these once-famous islands are not at all recognizable to the majority of Americans. Oddly, it is the vanquished Japanese veterans and their descendants that are now the most frequent visitors to battlegrounds symbolic of American victory: Guadalcanal, Tarawa, Saipan. Yet the *Arizona* Memorial, if anything a symbol of Japanese triumph, is swamped with Americans, who often cannot all jam into a facility designed to hold three thousand. They spill out onto the landscaped grounds, clutching their tickets for the launch trip out to the memorial and often wait one, two, or even three hours or more.

The crush of tourists at the Visitor Center can tend to distract visitors from the true significance of the *Arizona* Memorial, which is not only the relic of a terrible war but an underwater tomb for hundreds of Americans. Except for the *Utah* and *Arizona,* all of the other battleships sunk or damaged in the December 7 attack were eventually salvaged and

removed. Most were refurbished, returned to combat, and for the rest of the war bombarded enemy-held islands across the Pacific in preparation for the numerous beach landings that characterized island combat in the Pacific.

In October 1944, the Battle of Surigao Strait (in the Philippines) featured the last line-of-battle naval surface engagement of the war, and probably the last ever. It was fought with four battleships, *Maryland, West Virginia, Tennessee,* and *California,* that had been sunk and one, *Pennsylvania,* that had been heavily damaged at Pearl Harbor. The old battleships, humiliated at Pearl Harbor, got their revenge by wiping out most of what remained of Japan's once-powerful navy.

The ultimate fate of the Pearl Harbor battleships:

Pennsylvania returned to duty in 1942, barely survived a torpedo attack at Okinawa in August 1945, became a target ship for the atomic bomb tests of Operation Crossroads, and was mercifully sunk at sea by U.S. aircraft on February 10, 1948.

Tennessee also returned to duty in 1942, and after several re-builds was decommissioned in 1947 and scrapped in 1959.

California was raised and rebuilt to return to duty in 1944, avoided being sunk in a kamikaze attack on January 6, 1945, was decommissioned in 1947 and scrapped in 1959.

Maryland returned to duty in 1942, survived a torpedo attack on June 22, 1944, and extensive damage from kamikaze attacks during November 1944 and April 1945, was decommissioned in 1947 and scrapped in 1959.

West Virginia was raised in 1942, rebuilt and returned to duty in 1944, survived a kamikaze attack in 1945, was decommissioned in 1947 and scrapped in 1961.

Nevada, the only battleship to get underway during the Pearl Harbor attack, was then beached to avoid being sunk in the channel. Rebuilt and returned to duty in 1943, it also survived a kamikaze attack in March 1945, only to be used as a target for the Operation Crossroads atomic bomb tests. It

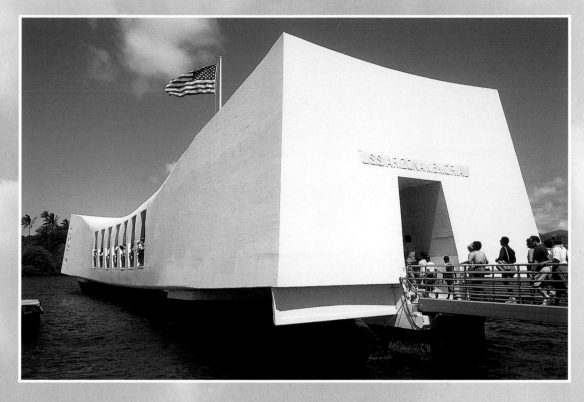

A stark, simple memorial now marks the resting place of the USS *Arizona,* which went down on December 7, 1941, with more of her crew than any other U.S. vessel in Naval history. A wall of white marble records the names of her casualties, and the Stars and Stripes has flown daily from the sunken hulk since 1950.

survived the atomic blasts and was decommissioned in 1946. *Nevada* remained at Pearl Harbor for two years as a target ship, and was finally sunk off Hawaii by torpedoes on July 31, 1948. *Oklahoma* was agonizingly raised from where it had capsized and sunk on December 7, only to be decommissioned in 1944. Some of its guns went to refurbish *Pennsylvania.* In 1947 en route to San Francisco to be scrapped, the hulk broke loose from its tow rope and sank in mid-Pacific on May 17, 1947.

Ironically, the two battleships sunk on December 7, 1941, and never salvaged, *Arizona* and *Utah,* are the ones that ultimately have survived and can still be seen today.

The Japanese ships that participated in the attack that precipitated the Pacific war were all gone by Pearl Harbor Day 1944. All six of the Japanese aircraft carriers involved in the attack already had been sunk. *Kaga, Akagi, Soryu,* and *Hiryu* went down at Midway in 1942. *Shokaku* was sunk in the first Battle of the Philippines Sea, June 19–20, 1944, and *Zuikaku* was sent to the bottom on October 25, 1944, in the second Battle of the Philippines Sea.

Arizona did not easily yield the 1,177 men who were entombed onboard. Efforts to retrieve the bodies by Navy salvage divers during the war were frustrating and gruesome. Inevitable deterioration of the remains made identification and recovery extremely difficult. Sporadic efforts continued into 1943 before it was decided to leave the wreck as a tomb and memorial to those who had died aboard ship on December 7. It is impossible to know exactly how many bodies are still aboard *Arizona.* Current estimates range anywhere from 900 to 1,000 seamen, forever frozen in time where they died on that morning in 1941.

Other than *Arizona,* the remaining original naval relic from December 7 at Pearl Harbor is *Utah.* Visitors on more extensive launch tours of Pearl Harbor go past her final resting place. A 1909-vintage battleship, she was already obsolete by 1941 and was being used as a target ship. Yet when she was torpedoed and capsized, she became a tomb for fifty-eight of her crew. *Utah* was never salvaged and rests today opposite a simple memorial built on the west side of Ford Island.

Of the more than 150 ships on duty December 7 in and around Pearl Harbor, only two are known to remain afloat in the early twenty-first century. The first, the

yard tug *Hoga* (YT146), was very active during the attack. She pulled *Vestal* away from the burning Arizona, assisted the stricken *Ogalala,* helped beach *Nevada,* and fought fires on *Arizona* and elsewhere around Pearl Harbor for three days without a break. After the war she operated for many years as a fireboat for the Port of Oakland, renamed *City of Oakland.* She has been decommissioned, and in 2001 awaits her fate at the Navy's Inactive Ship Maintenance Facility at Suisun Bay, north of San Francisco. Efforts to bring her back to Pearl are being mounted by a group called "Friends of Pearl Harbor Tug *Hoga."* The second ship, the Coast Guard Cutter *Taney,* was anchored at Pier Six in Honolulu Harbor as the attack began six miles away. The first attack wave was too distant for *Taney*'s antiaircraft guns to be very effective. But during the second wave, *Taney* opened fire on the high-level carrier bombers flying overhead. Even more significantly, *Taney*'s antiaircraft fire is credited with breaking up a five-plane glide-bombing formation headed for the Honolulu power plant. The USCGC *Taney* continued in service after the war, was subsequently retired, and is now a museum ship anchored in Baltimore's Inner Harbor.

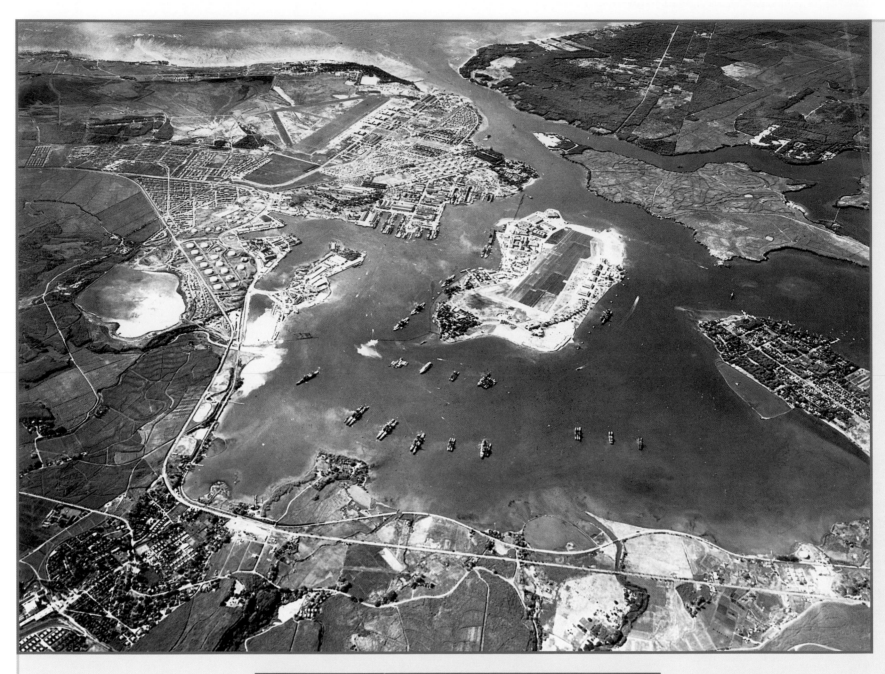

ABOVE: Aerial photograph of Pearl Harbor taken two months before the Japanese attack. Ford Island is at center, with the ship channel above it leading out to the Pacific at the top. Battleship Row, where the remains of *Arizona* still lie today, is just to the left of Ford Island. The runways of Hickam Field are at upper left. Honolulu International Airport, the major point of airline access to Hawaii, was later built on the vacant land above and to the left of Hickam Field.

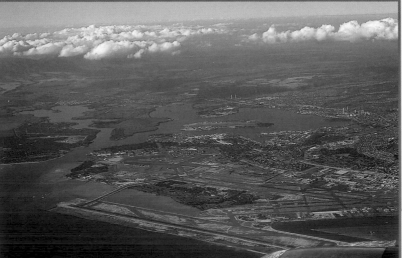

LEFT: Aerial view from the south of Pearl Harbor and Hickam Field in the early 1990s. Ford Island is at center, and the white dot near the north end of the island at right is the *Arizona* Memorial. Just below and to the left of Ford Island are the runways of Hickam Field. In the foreground is the reef runway for Honolulu International Airport. The basic configuration of the area around Ford Island shown in this photo remained for fifty-seven years nearly identical to how it appeared to attacking Japanese pilots on that long-ago fateful morning. Then in 1998 the Navy opened a $78 million bridge connecting the north end of Ford Island to the Pearl Harbor Naval Base immediately to the north of the *Arizona* Memorial Visitor Center. The bridge was built to facilitate development of Ford Island for Navy housing, forever altering the historic island that was at the center of the 1941 attack. In mid-1998 USS *Missouri* was towed into Pearl Harbor from Bremerton, Washington. It was docked at Ford Island just south of the remains of *Arizona,* near where *Oklahoma* was berthed the morning of the attack. On January 29, 1999, fifty-five years to the day after President Harry S. Truman's daughter, Margaret, christened it, *Missouri* was dedicated as a memorial to the end of World War II and opened to tourists. Thus the beginning of the war in the Pacific, as represented by the sunken *Arizona,* is juxtaposed with the end, where on the deck of *Missouri* the Japanese surrender was signed.

TOP: The flight deck of *Akagi,* flagship of the Japanese Pearl Harbor attack force. The photo was taken at Hittokappu Bay, Kurile Islands, shortly before the fleet departed on the long run to Hawaii on November 26, 1941. This is believed to be the only photo that shows all six attack carriers in one image. Directly behind *Akagi* is *Kaga.* To the right in the far distance are the dim shapes of *Shokaku* and *Zuikaku.* Somewhat closer and a little bit farther right is *Hiryu,* and at far right is the stern of *Soryu.*

BOTTOM: Captured Japanese photo taken during the early stages of the attack. Military personnel on Ford Island and sailors on board the ships in the harbor are just waking up to the start of World War II as a Japanese plane can be seen in this photo banking away to the south above Ford Island. A geyser from an exploding torpedo erupts from a direct hit on Battleship Row on the far side of Ford Island. *Utah* (second in the line of three ships on the near side of Ford Island) already has been hit and is listing to port.

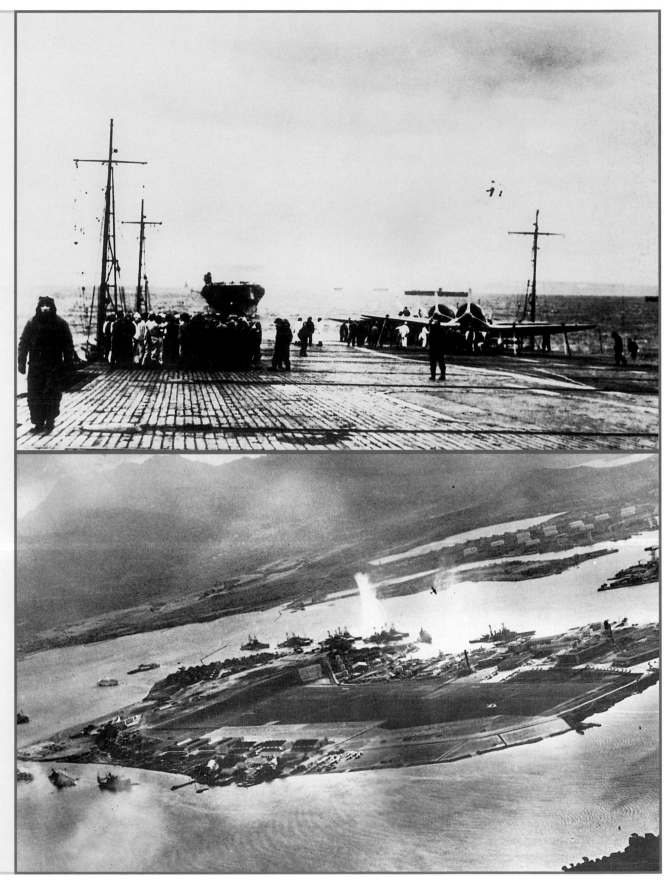

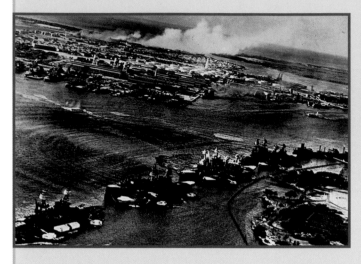

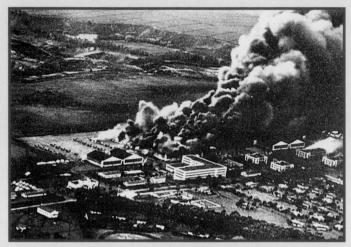

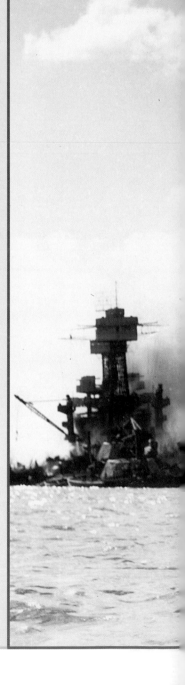

ABOVE: Another Japanese photo taken during the initial stages of the attack. The ships of Battleship Row, from lower left, are *Nevada, Arizona* with *Vestal* tied up to port, *Tennessee* with *West Virginia* tied up to port, *Maryland* with *Oklahoma* on her port side, and the tanker *Neosho.* Smoke rises in the distance from Hickam Field, while tracks of torpedoes dropped from Japanese planes (and possibly from a Japanese midget submarine) can be seen to the left of Battleship Row. Two of the tracks can be traced all the way to *West Virginia.* Ripples from the concussion of the first radiate away and oil has started to spread. An explosion from the second has just occurred as a spout of water rises from the port side. The white patch of foam on the surface of the water at right center is thought to be bubbles rising from the turning propellers of an errant Japanese aerial torpedo dropped by pilot Tomoe Yasue from *Akagi.* His torpedo went nose-down into the mud of the harbor bottom and was recovered intact in 1991 during routine dredging of the harbor. Unfortunately it could not be preserved due to the potentially unstable unexploded warhead, and

it was detonated at sea in May 1991. The rear part of the torpedo survived the explosion, and the remains are now on display in the *Arizona* Memorial Visitor Center.

BOTTOM LEFT: Japanese photo of a B5N2 (Kate) level-bomber, coded EII-307 from *Zuikaku* over Hickam Field during the attack on December 7, sometime between 8:10 and 9:30 A.M. *Arizona* and Battleship Row are marked by a column of black smoke just below and behind the plane. The runways of Hickam Field are directly below the plane in the foreground, and the hangars and Hale Makai barracks at Hickam are beneath the column of black smoke below the front of the plane.

TOP RIGHT: Planes parked close together to prevent sabotage at Wheeler Field burn with bonfire-like intensity after being set afire by Japanese attackers.

CENTER RIGHT: This Japanese Val dive-bomber, one of only twenty-nine aircraft lost by the Japanese, was salvaged from the waters of Pearl Harbor shortly after the attack. Curious American sailors inspect what remains of the front portion of the stricken plane suspended like a trophy fish from a crane. If even one of the wrecked Japanese planes had survived until today, it would be a valuable war relic. As it turns out, all were scrapped during or after the war. A few small pieces of a couple of the attacking planes are on display in several Honolulu museums. A joint National Park Service–U.S. Navy underwater survey in 1988 failed to turn up any trace of downed aircraft left in Pearl Harbor.

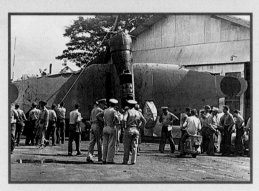

RIGHT: The forward section of the sunken *Arizona* burns fiercely in this photo of Battleship Row taken from astern of the ship. Visitors on the National Park Service launch approach the Memorial today from this same angle.

BELOW: A similar view from the *Arizona* Memorial Visitor Center. Japanese tourists prefer to have their photos taken in front of the symbol of their victory, *Arizona,* marked by the white memorial next to Ford Island in the distance, as opposed to the ship to the left of the *Arizona,* the USS *Missouri,* where Japan's surrender was signed.

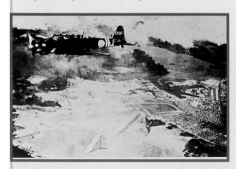

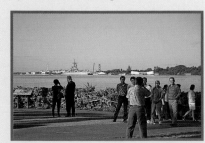

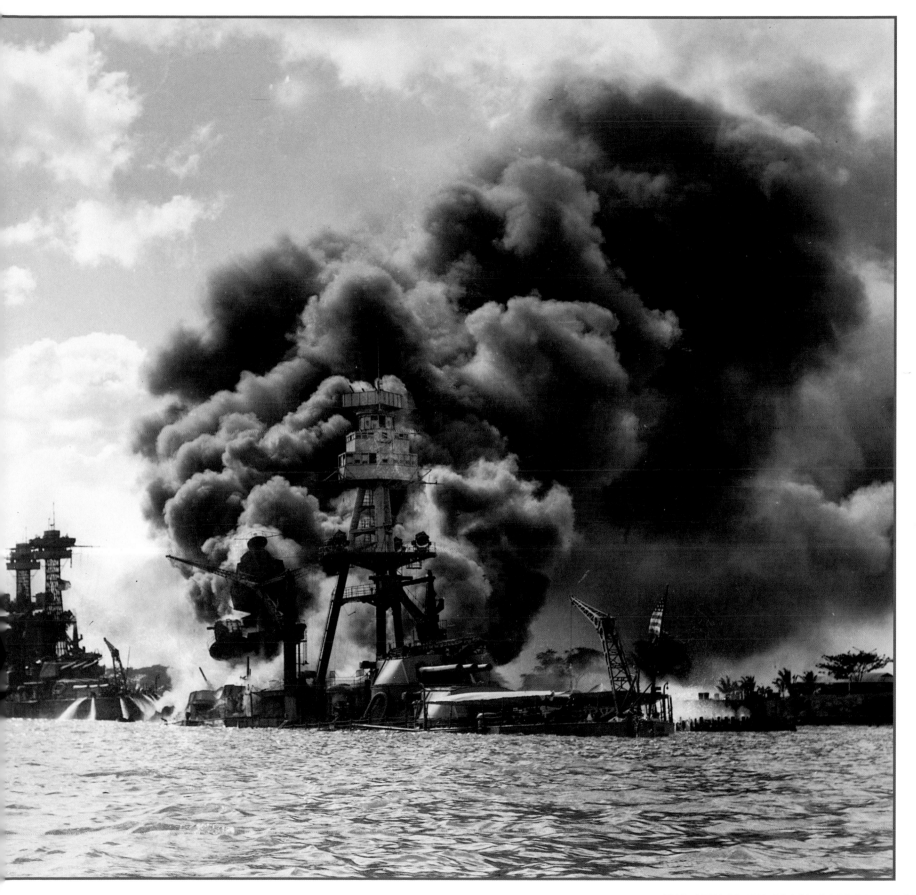

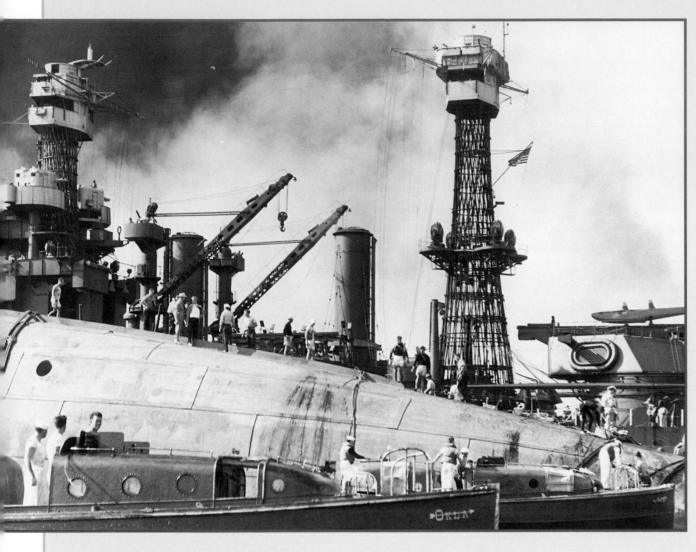

OPPOSITE TOP: The *Arizona* Memorial straddles the ship but does not rest directly on the hulk. The flagpole is affixed to the sawed-off stump of *Arizona*'s mainmast in the foreground, one of three legs that supported the rear fire-direction tower, or "fighting top." This is the only part of the ship that visitors can actually inspect from close range. Inside the old mainmast are electrical cables that ran up to the overhead tower. A steel ladder, long disused, can be seen inside the mast, leading down into the bowels of the wreck, now the tomb of more than nine hundred men.

OPPOSITE BOTTOM LEFT: A rendering shows the present-day remains of *Arizona,* the result of an underwater survey performed in the early 1980s by the U.S. National Park Service, caretakers of the *Arizona* Memorial. Note that the only remaining fourteen-inch guns on the ship are in the No. One turret, the rest having been salvaged during the war.

OPPOSITE BOTTOM RIGHT: After the superstructure of *Arizona* was sheared off at the waterline when salvage efforts were abandoned during the war, the largest visible part of the ship left above water was the No. Three gun turret mount, seen beyond the stump of the mainmast in this view from the Memorial looking toward the stern (marked by the small orange float at upper center). Some of the large concrete moorings of Battleship Row remain and can be seen at upper left. *Nevada* was anchored at these particular moorings on the morning of December 7.

The capsized hulk of *Oklahoma* (and one of her launches in the foreground) and *Maryland* (behind) following the attack. Men were still alive inside the ship when this photo was taken. Some were pulled out by rescue efforts that involved cutting through the upturned hull to free trapped sailors inside. Others could not be reached and died slow deaths, trapped in the dark iron tomb of their ship. Incredibly, *Oklahoma* was righted after a Herculean salvage effort in 1943, only to have her decommissioned in 1944 and lost at sea while being towed back to California. *Tennessee* and *West Virginia* were tied to moorings directly northeast on the morning of December 7. *Tennessee* was freed from her berth on December 16. After repairs she rejoined the fleet in February 1942, and ended up earning seven battle stars. *West Virginia* was outboard of *Tennessee.* Her port side was ripped open by torpedoes, and she settled to the bottom. When she was finally refloated in May 1942, after a major salvage effort, sixty-six bodies were removed from her flooded compartments. Three men had been able to survive for seventeen days in an air pocket deep inside the ship with access to a fresh water supply. A calendar near their bodies had the days marked off one by one, from December 7 to December 23. Their old ship was eventually repaired and rejoined the fleet in 1944. After seeing considerable action, she was present for the Japanese surrender in Tokyo Bay.

RIGHT: *Arizona* after the attack (photo taken off the port bow). The ship has settled to the bottom, but in the shallow waters of Pearl Harbor the main deck is only ten or so feet below the surface. After salvage efforts were abandoned, almost all of the ship visible above water was cut away, leaving only an underwater hulk to be viewed today by the nearly two million annual visitors.

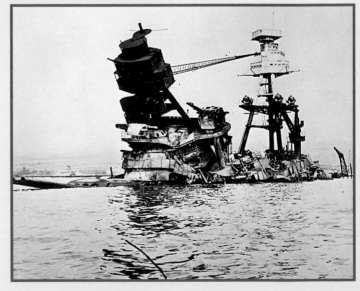

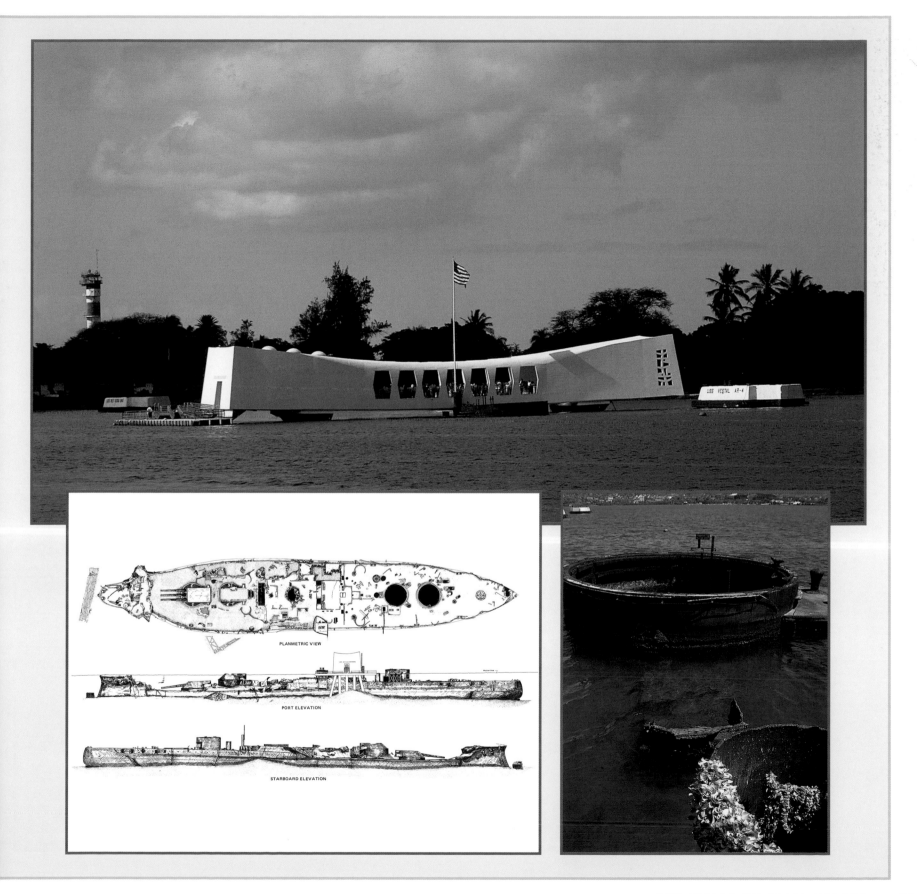

PLANMETRIC VIEW

PORT ELEVATION

STARBOARD ELEVATION

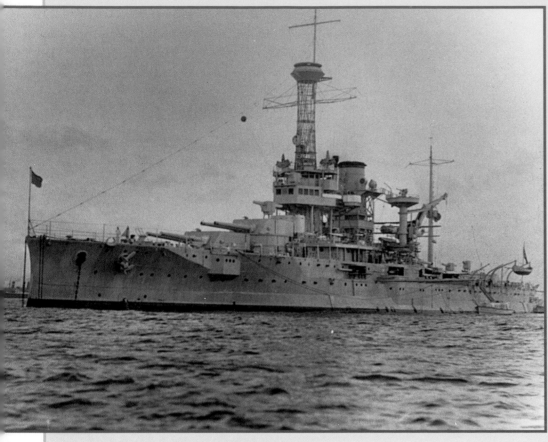

The other remaining ship relic from the Japanese attack on Pearl Harbor is the USS *Utah*. This 1909-vintage ship, shown here in a prewar photo, served in World War I and in 1918 became the flagship of Rear Admiral Thomas Rodgers. When the war ended, she was one of the ships, along with *Arizona,* in the honor escort accompanying Woodrow Wilson to the Versailles Peace Conference. In 1932 *Utah* was converted for testing sophisticated radio control equipment, and by 1935 she had been rigged as an antiaircraft training ship. After extensive refitting with new shipboard armament and protective deck planking, *Utah* sailed from the West Coast for Hawaii in September 1941.

BELOW LEFT: *Utah* was one of the first ships attacked on December 7. Shortly after at least two torpedoes slammed into her side, she capsized and sank, entombing fifty-eight of her crew. This photo was taken minutes after she was hit.

BELOW: Salvage attempts were eventually abandoned, leaving *Utah* resting on her left side. Just a small portion of the rusting ship is visible above the water in the background of this memorial dedicated in 1972. Only visitors passing by on launch tours can view *Utah,* the forgotten ship of the Pearl Harbor attack. The Ford Island Memorial is rarely read today because it is in an area off-limits to civilians.

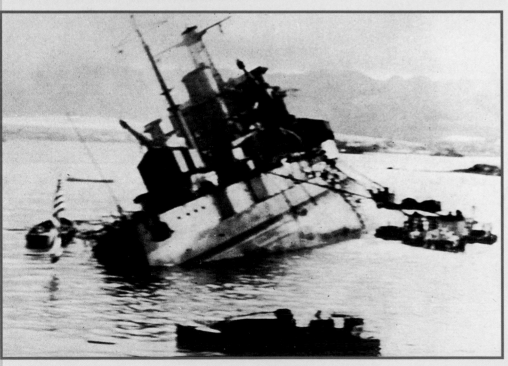

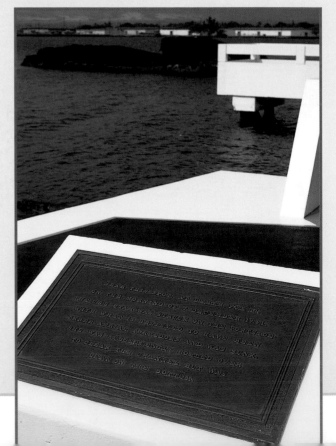

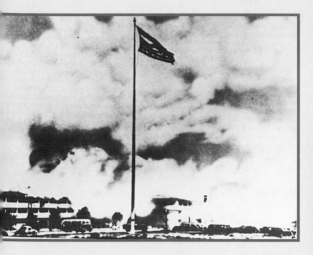

In a photo published in many newspapers following the attack, fires started by Japanese bombs in Hale Makai barracks send columns of smoke skyward, while a torn, smoke-stained American flag still flies in the foreground. That flag is on display in a glass case in the building's lobby.

RIGHT: Old Glory still flies from the same flag-pole in front of Hale Makai. The building was repaired after the attack, and today serves as headquarters for the U.S. Pacific Air Force.

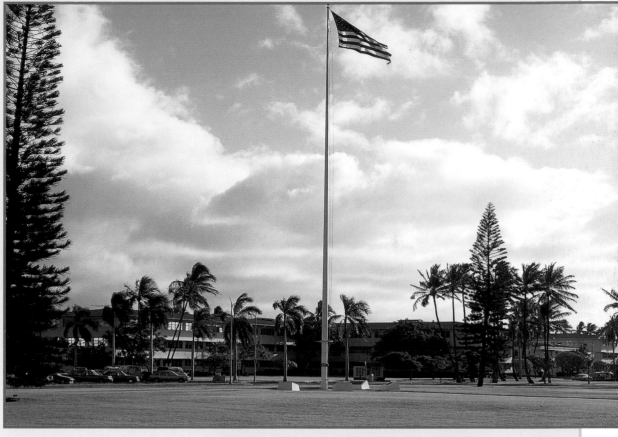

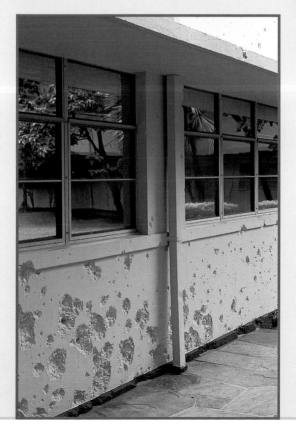

LEFT: The concrete exterior walls of Hale Makai still bear scars of the bombing and strafing inflicted by some of the first Japanese planes to attack the airfield. Men eating breakfast and others just waking up were greeted by a rain of bombs, and thirty-five Americans were killed outright. Many more were wounded and died shortly thereafter in and around this building. It is thought that the final death toll numbered around sixty men.

RIGHT: Visitors to the *Arizona* Memorial through the 1990s and into the twenty-first century have heard compelling eyewitness accounts by Pearl Harbor survivors. Joe Morgan describes how he spent the morning of December 7, 1941, sitting behind a machine gun mounted on a grounded airplane on Ford Island.

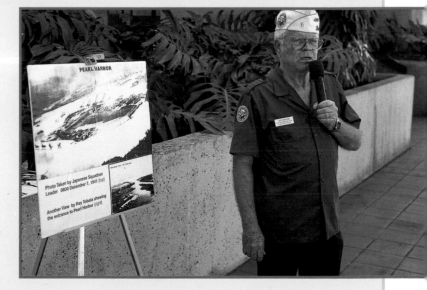

"**R**EMEMBER WAKE ISLAND!" screamed the headlines at Christmastime, 1941. The widely acclaimed "gallant defenders of Wake" had pulled off the impossible right up to the end. Not only had they held out against the seemingly invincible Japanese, but they actually turned back the initial invasion. And this with just a skeleton force of Marine pilots flying a few bullet-riddled F4F Wildcat fighters, several hundred Marines on the ground, and some civilian construction workers caught on the island on December 7.

Before that date, Wake had been known mainly as one of the island stepping-stones for Pan American's trans-Pacific flying boats. As the first bombs fell on Pearl Harbor, about twelve hundred civilian contract construction workers were fortifying Wake. On the morning of December 7 the Pan Am flying boat *Philippine Clipper* had already taken off for Guam, and it was called back when news of Pearl Harbor came through on the radio. Shortly afterward, at about noon, the first Japanese bombing raid devastated the tiny atoll, but miraculously the *Philippine Clipper* was not destroyed. After the raid was over, it was loaded up with as many Pan Am employees as it could carry. The big plane was barely able to lift off from the lagoon for its flight back to Midway and Pearl Harbor. Left behind was the stranded group of men destined to make one of the most notable "last stands" in all of World War II.

Major James Devereux was in command of the Marines on Wake, but the media was unaware that Navy Commander Winfield Scott Cunningham had arrived shortly before the siege to assume overall command of the island. Americans listening to their radios daily to find out how the little force on Wake was holding out heard the name Devereux over and over. It was only after the war when Cunningham was released from Japanese POW camps that authorities acknowledged his role during the siege. Cunningham later wrote that he had given the fateful order early on the morning of December 12 to hold fire until the first Japanese invasion force was within point-blank range. When American guns opened fire, they sank one ship and severely damaged seven others. Another ship limped away from the island after being hit by artillery fire and sank while under air attack from Wake's patched-up F4F fighters.

This was an incredible initial victory over the Japanese, one of the first bright spots in that otherwise dismal December. It was the ultimate underdog story, David and Goliath revisited, and the media made the most of it. But when a U.S. rescue flotilla sent from Pearl Harbor was recalled, the island was doomed. The Japanese returned with a more powerful invasion force and overwhelmed the defenders on December 23, 1941. A total of about sixteen hundred Americans surrendered, nearly twelve hundred of them civilian construction workers. Initially, some of the Japanese soldiers seemed almost reticent. Trying to cheer up a disconsolate American Marine, a Japanese soldier said, "Pretty soon war over. Then everybody shakes hands."

Shortly after the surrender, the Japanese posted information that clarified exactly for the captives their new situation:

PROCLAMATION

Here it is proclaimed that the entire Islands of Wake are now the state-property of the Great Empire of Japan.

PUBLIC NOTICE

The Great Empire of Japan who loves peace and respects justice has been obliged to take arms against the challenge of President Roosevelt. Therefore, in accordance with the peace-loving spirit of the Great Empire of Japan, Japanese Imperial Navy will not inflict any harms on those people—though they have been our enemy—who do not hold hostility against us in any respect. So they be in peace!

But whoever violates our spirit or whoever is not obedient shall be severely punished by our martial law. Issued by The Headquarters of Japanese Imperial Navy.

Such notices, though chilling, gave only a slight hint of what lay ahead for the captives. Those who were loaded onto ships for transport to POW camps in China and Japan got a better idea when they read a posting entitled "Regulations for Prisoners":

1. The prisoners disobeying the following orders will be punished by immediate death:
a) Those disobeying orders and instructions.
b) Those showing a motion of antagonism and raising a sign of opposition.
c) Those disordering the regulations by individualism, egoism, thinking only about yourself, rushing for your own goods.
d) Those talking without permission and raising loud voices.

OPPOSITE: Wake Island from the air around 1990. The modern runway was built on top of the World War II American and Japanese runway. The two Japanese invasion forces attacked the beaches in the foreground. The first attack was turned away by a ferocious and accurate artillery barrage and harassment from Wake's tiny air force that consisted of a few F4F fighter planes. The second invasion succeeded in landing a large force under heavy fire on those same beaches, ultimately overwhelming the American defenders.

e) Those walking and moving without order.

f) Those carrying unnecessary baggage in embarking.

g) Those resisting mutually.

h) Those touching the boat's materials, wires, electric lights, tools, switches, etc.

i) Those climbing ladder without order.

j) Those showing action of running away from the room or boat.

k) Those trying to take more meal than given to them.

l) Those using more than two blankets.

The Japanese retained only ninety-eight of the American civilian workers on the island. They were to operate the American construction equipment as part of the Japanese effort to heavily fortify the island for the invasion they were sure would come. But American military planners decided not to retake Wake, part of an overall strategy of island-hopping, of cutting off islands and letting them "die on the vine." However, Wake would not be forgotten. An almost incessant series of air raids and shellings from passing aircraft carriers and ships kept the Japanese close to their air-raid shelters.

After a couple of years, some of the Japanese officers apparently became convinced that the American construction workers were somehow directing the raids on the island with a secret radio transmitter. So the Japanese rounded up the ninety-eight Americans on the night of October 7, 1943, tied their hands behind them, lined them up on the beach, and machine-gunned them. All were killed. After the war island commander Rear Admiral Shigematsu Sakaibara, his adjutant, Lieutenant Commander Soichi Tachibana, and nine others were found guilty in a war crimes trial and executed. Five other Japanese received prison terms extending from ten years to life. Just before the verdict was delivered, Sakaibara addressed the court. Alluding to those who developed and dropped the atomic bombs on Hiroshima and Nagasaki, he stated that they "should be regarded in the same light as we."

Wake Island remained an important stop for trans-Pacific military and civilian aircraft after the war. During the Korean War, General Douglas MacArthur and President Harry Truman had a historic meeting on Wake. Also, it was an important stopover for troops heading to and from Southeast Asia during the Vietnam War. Wake was subsequently used as a staging point for Vietnamese refugees on their way to being resettled in the United States.

A visit to Wake by a civilian today is difficult at best, since the only transport to and from the island, which is administered by the U.S. Air Force, is by military aircraft. The island is run by a handful of Air Force personnel, and populated by about 100 to 150 maintenance and construction workers, mostly from Thailand. A small number of rough-and-tumble American contract workers, the same types who assisted in the defense of Wake nearly sixty years ago, return to the island on occasion to help with construction projects. When any excavation work is done on Wake today, archeologists are present to help extricate corpses that are unearthed, casualties from the initial battles or from the subsequent Japanese occupation period. It is thought that around thirteen hundred Japanese died from starvation after the Americans cut off supplies to the island, and perhaps another six hundred were killed in American air raids. During construction work in 1989 on the southeast tip of Wake, two corpses from the war were uncovered in a three-month period.

For the most part Wake has been left in much the same state that returning Americans found it after the Japanese surrendered in 1945. Evidence of the frenzied Japanese preparations for the anticipated U.S. invasion is everywhere. Huge concrete bunkers, tank trenches, and "hills" (mounds of coral heaped over bombproof bunkers) stand out incongruously on the little atoll. Only a few traces of the American efforts can be found. Notably, the coral-covered, concrete storage bunkers near the airfield remain. One housed the Marine command post manned by Major Devereux and his aides during the final phases of the defense; two others were used as hospitals.

In the one-room "museum" in the terminal building, traces of the battle remain: a twisted propeller from one of the F4F fighters, corroded cartridges, a rusted machine gun. Yet the lonely desolation of the place is what leaves the deepest impression. It is not hard to imagine what it must have felt like to be abandoned on the tiny island to face the might of Imperial Japan, literally thousands of miles from any help or relief; to stare out over the endless sweep of ocean from horizon to horizon, straining to listen for the drumming of Japanese airplane engines, the signal for yet another bombing; or to search for signs of a Japanese invasion force in the far distance. Wake has again reverted to the desolate speck of land it was before the war, mostly forgotten and rarely visited, another lost footnote to the Pacific War.

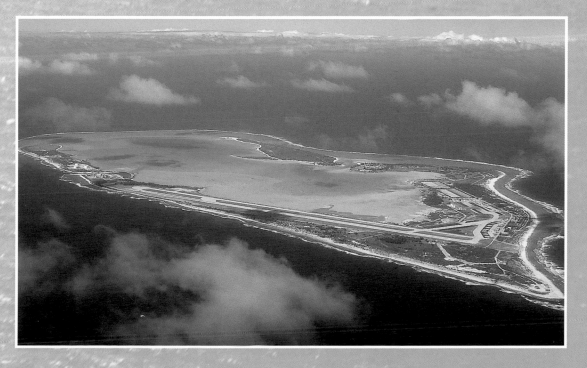

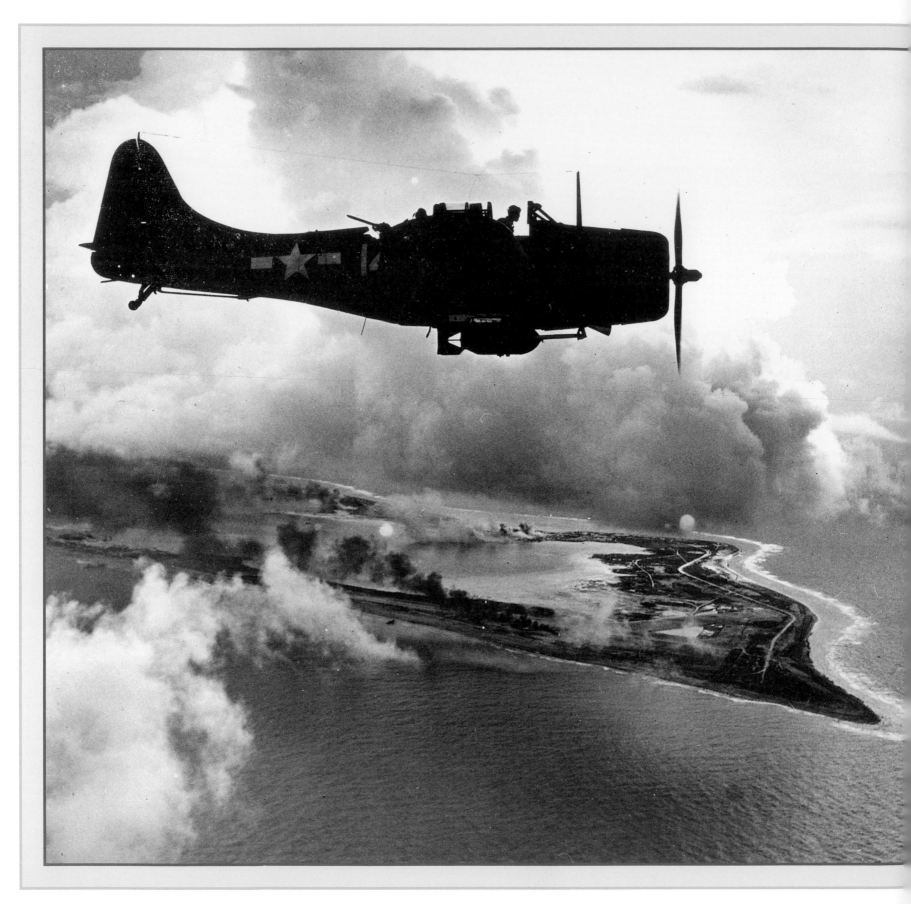

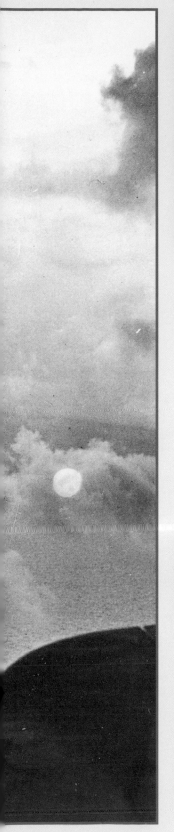

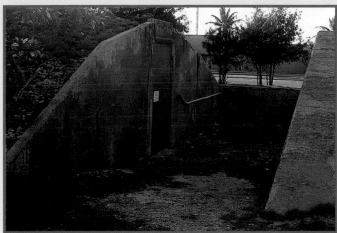

One of the few remaining traces of the battle for Wake is this coral-covered, concrete storage bunker on the east end of the island. Major Devereux and his staff took shelter here from incessant Japanese air raids in the final phases of the defense of the island.

Shortly after the capture of the island, the Japanese took this photo of one of the American F4F Wildcats in a covered shelter.

No photos taken by Americans during the siege of Wake are known to have survived. This photo was made during a bombing mission over the island in 1943 and shows the outline of Wake Island most familiar before the war to Pan Am flying-boat captains.

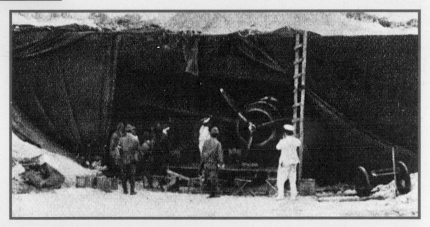

The "boneyard" of disabled American F4F fighters on Wake was photographed by the Japanese shortly after capturing the island.

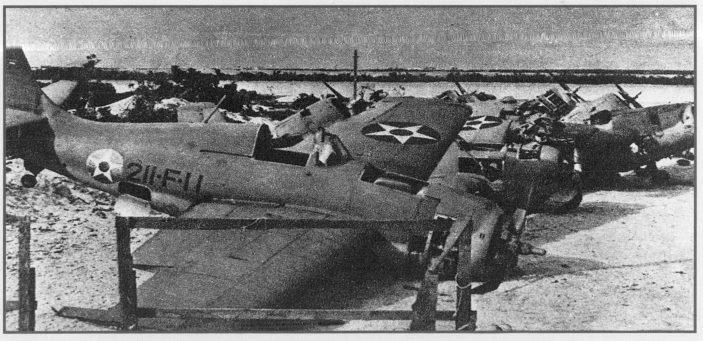

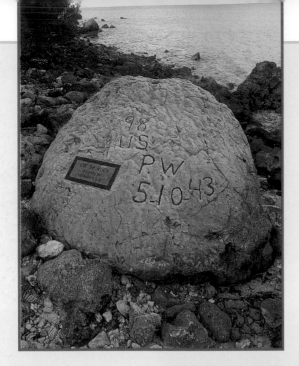

LEFT: This eerie message was carved by one of the ninety-eight American civilian construction workers used as slave labor on Wake by the Japanese. Now called "98 Rock," the message indicates that ninety-eight prisoners of war ("PW") were still alive on May 10, 1943. When this message was carved, they had only five months to live.

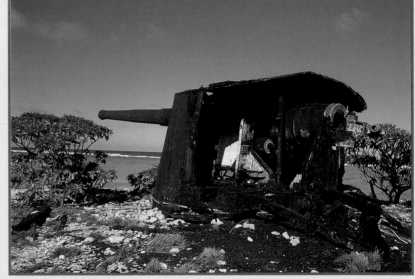

CENTER LEFT: When the Americans returned to Wake in September 1945, to accept the formal surrender of the Japanese, they found extensive fortifications and armaments on the island. In effect, the Japanese had spent four years building defensive positions for an American invasion that never came. Pictured is an eight-inch coastal defense gun on Peale Island, Wake.

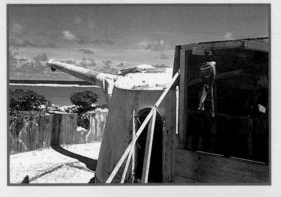

CENTER RIGHT: The same gun today. It is said to have been brought to Wake by the Japanese either from Hong Kong or Singapore.

BOTTOM LEFT: In addition to a heavily fortified island, the Americans returned to Wake to find a starving Japanese garrison. These malnourished Japanese soldiers line up for sick call on September 20, 1945.

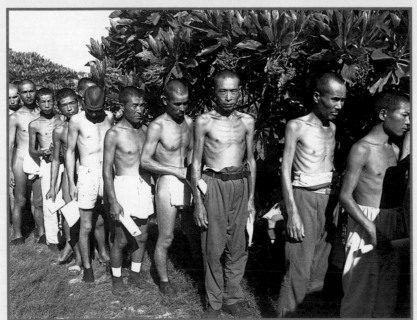

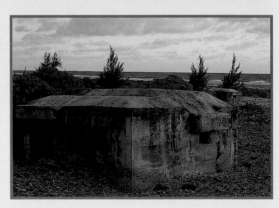

ABOVE: Today, abandoned Japanese concrete bunkers stare out over the invasion beaches on the southern shore.

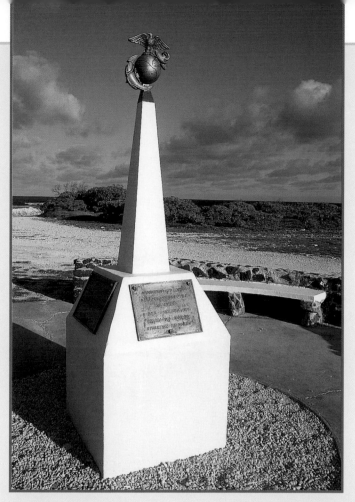

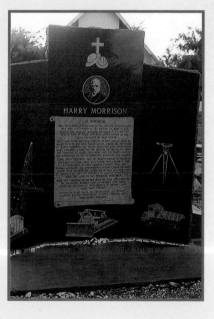

LEFT: The United States Marine Corps memorial on Wake Island.

BOTTOM LEFT: Japanese memorial on Wake.

RIGHT: Monument to the civilian construction workers on Wake. Of the estimated twelve hundred civilians on the island when it was invaded, several hundred actively assisted in the defense and thirty-seven were killed before the capitulation. The necessity for a military construction force ready to build or fight as the need arose became clear after Wake. This contributed to the formation of the Navy Seabees, designed for just such functions.

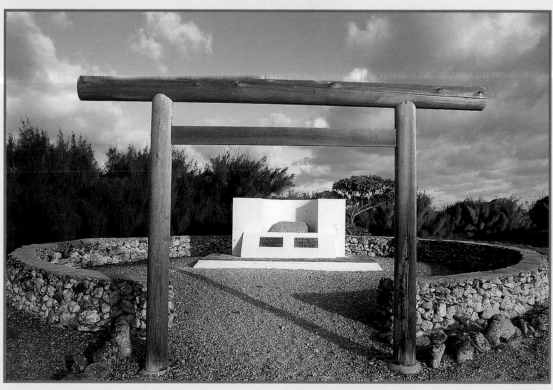

THE DOOLITTLE RAID ON TOKYO

THINGS COULDN'T have looked much worse for the U.S. and her allies in early 1942. The seemingly invincible Japanese Army was sweeping relentlessly toward Australia and New Zealand. And with the whole-sale surrender of Allied forces in the Philippines and Southeast Asia, there appeared little that could be done to slow up, much less stop, the Japanese onslaught.

However, something did need to be done, and President Roosevelt was obsessed with the idea of somehow bombing Japan. Realizing that a bombing raid on the Japanese home islands would have a tremen-

the mission were summed up in a question to aviation expert James Doolittle. "What airplane," asked General Henry H. "Hap" Arnold, "have we got that will get off in 500 feet with a 2,000-pound bomb load and then fly 2,000 miles?" Conventional carrier fighter planes couldn't do it, so land-based medium bombers, B-25s, were chosen for their longer range, which could be extended even farther by adding supplemental fuel tanks. The longer the planes could remain aloft, the farther away from Japan the task force could stay and still launch the planes. This would reduce the risk of

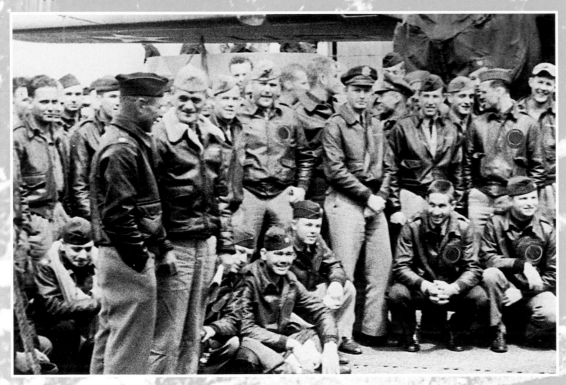

Hornet captain Admiral Marc Mitscher and Lieutenant Colonel Jimmy Doolittle pose for a photo with Doolittle's aircrews on board *Hornet* before the raid. For many of his men, most of whom were in their early twenties, Doolittle had been a childhood hero.

OPPOSITE: The aircraft carrier *Hornet* en route to Japan in early April 1942, with the B-25s lined up nose-to-tail.

dous morale effect on both Americans and the enemy, Roosevelt began dreaming. Fortunately, Captain Francis Low, operations officer for Navy Chief of Staff Admiral Ernest J. King, came up with an idea for flying medium bombers from the deck of a carrier. Roosevelt, King, and the Army Air Forces liked the idea. The plan was to ferry the bombers as close to Japan as possible, launch them at dawn, bomb targets in Japan at midmorning Tokyo time, fly to forward airstrips in friendly areas of China by sunset, refuel, and then fly farther south the next day to deliver the planes to the Nationalist Chinese. The seemingly impossible requirements of

being detected by the Japanese Navy and having to fight a superior force. It was a one-way trip, though. Once launched from the carrier, the planes had to fly far enough to reach friendly airstrips in China.

The twin-engine B-25 Mitchell bomber was a relatively new plane in early 1942 and not too many squadrons had them. It was known to have short takeoff capability, but no one had ever demonstrated whether a land-based plane like the B-25 could take off from an aircraft carrier. However, with an aircraft carrier steaming at full speed into a brisk wind, the B-25 had only to generate a speed of about thirty-five miles per hour relative to the deck in a space of about four hundred feet to take off. Jimmy Doolittle, legendary air racer of the 1930s and personal hero to many pilots at that time, was confident that it could be done. He was put in command and ended up arranging for himself to personally fly the lead plane.

Only the very best B-25 pilots were picked for the mission, and some had already survived close calls in the new planes. Bill Bower was destined to pilot the twelfth B-25 off the deck of *Hornet,* the carrier chosen for the mission, but before he earned that distinction he raised a few eyebrows at the assembly plant. "I had a little accident with about the fourth B-25 off the assembly line," he recalled. "I met an airliner on the same runway, ran off the pavement, and sheared off the wings."

The pilots and crews were not given any information on the mission, but still had to decide whether or not to volunteer. "They asked for volunteers," said Bower, "and all we knew was that the mission was something special, and of course we wanted to get out of Oregon [where they were based at the time]." It was only later that they learned to their amazement and delight that their idol, Jimmy Doolittle, was to lead the mission. Bower's feelings about Doolittle were typical of all the pilots and crews: "There wasn't a blind response to Doolittle that we would do what he said. He never took away your power of reason. He just set the example, and it wasn't difficult to follow that example. So we knew if he was going to go we were going to go, and we could make it. He conditioned us to the point that we knew we were capable of operating as well as he could, that we had that competence."

By March 1, 1942, aircrews were practicing short-field takeoffs at Eglin Field, Florida. Modifications were made to the planes besides the addition of extra fuel tanks. The troublesome belly turrets were removed after Doolittle noted, "A man could learn to play a violin in Carnegie Hall before he could learn to fire that thing." After much speculation, the first real confirmation that they had been training for a mission against Japan was when the sixteen crews flew their planes to Alameda Naval Base near San Francisco and boarded the aircraft carrier *Hornet.*

After a crane hoisted the planes up onto the deck one by one, *Hornet* sailed from San Francisco on April 2, 1942. The task force accompanying *Hornet* consisted of the aircraft carrier *Enterprise,* eight destroyers, two oilers,

and the cruisers *Northampton, Vincennes,* and *Nashville.*

"The sailors on the *Hornet* were very hospitable for the most part," said Bower.

They spread us Air Corps guys all over the ship, since we had to share bunk space with the Navy. I was put right up in the front near the anchor chain. The sailors let me have a bunk and they slept on the floor. They didn't have to do that. I always wondered what happened to those guys and if they went down with the *Hornet* [which was sunk seven months after the Doolittle raid]. I didn't get seasick like some of the guys, but I didn't really enjoy being on the ship either. It was boring, and there wasn't much to do but play cards—mostly poker and acey-deucey. The Navy pilots were not real pleased either. Our B-25s were up on the deck strung out nose-to-tail and the Navy pilots couldn't fly their planes. There was a guy that gave us lectures almost every day. He had been a naval attaché in Tokyo before the war. He discussed topography, what Japan looked like, what he'd seen, and tried to give us as much information about Japan as he could. One day we were told we could pick our targets from a list. I noticed that one was a plant in Yokohama that belonged to the Ford Motor Company. I picked that one. I thought that was a pretty good deal because I drove Fords! As we got closer to Japan the atmosphere on the ship got tenser. We heard that if we were discovered and couldn't take off, we'd have to dump the planes over the side and make a run for it.

The aircrews were permitted to pick from a list of targets located in Tokyo, Yokosuka, Yokohama, Nagoya, and Kobe. Orders were to bomb and set fire to the chosen military targets only, no schools or hospitals. Above all else the crews were warned to be sure to avoid bombing the Imperial Palace. If the task force was detected outside the B-25s' range, the planes would indeed have been dumped. But a more depressing possibility existed if the task force was detected within range of Japan, which was summed up by Doolittle: "We were agreed that if we were intercepted within range of Japan . . . we would go ahead and complete our bombing mission even though we had to land immediately afterward and fall into Japanese hands."

On the morning of April 18, 1942, the day before the mission was scheduled to begin and with the task force

still over six hundred miles from Japan (but well within the range of B-25s), a Japanese picket boat was sighted by an SBD Dauntless dive-bomber pilot. The message he dropped on the deck of *Enterprise* read:

"Enemy surface ship—latitude 36-04 long. 153-10e, bearing 276 true—42 miles. Believe seen by enemy."

The Japanese ship, *Nitto Maru,* was destroyed shortly thereafter by gunfire from *Nashville* (which required "938 rounds of six-inch ammunition to do it," because the small craft was bobbing in heavy seas), but not before it sent a radio message back to Japan:

"Three enemy aircraft carriers sighted near our position 650 miles east of Inubo Sake at 0630 [Tokyo time]."

The position of the ships of the task force, including two precious aircraft carriers (misinterpreted to be three by the Japanese picket boat), was no longer a secret. What to do? After some quick conferences, the decision was made to launch the B-25s. To Admiral Marc A. Mitscher on *Hornet,* Admiral Halsey signaled from *Enterprise* at 8:00 A.M.: "Launch planes. To Colonel Doolittle and his gallant command, good luck and God bless you."

"It was early in the morning and I was laying around in my bunk and didn't hear the call to quarters," said Bill Bower. "All of a sudden Jack Hilger came in and got us up. I think he did that because my plane was ahead of his on the deck, and he wanted to make sure I showed up! By the time Jack got to me they had all the hatches secured for battle stations, and we had to go back through all those hatches, one after another, about four hundred feet back from the bow before we could go up on deck. I didn't have time to put on my flight suit—I just ran out of there in what I had on. We got up on deck and there was no doubt or hesitation and no one thought it was a suicide mission. Doolittle had made the decision, and there was no question that we could do it. We were highly trained, we had a weather report from a submarine in Tokyo Bay, we knew the winds, we just loaded up and went."

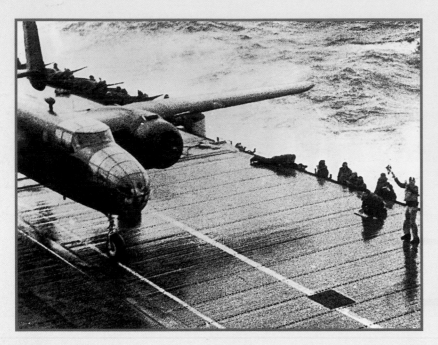

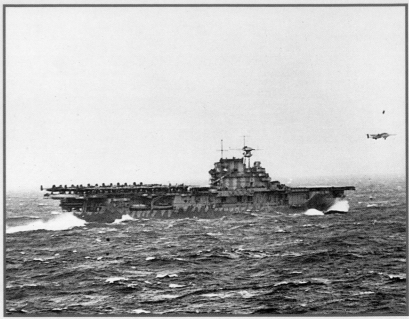

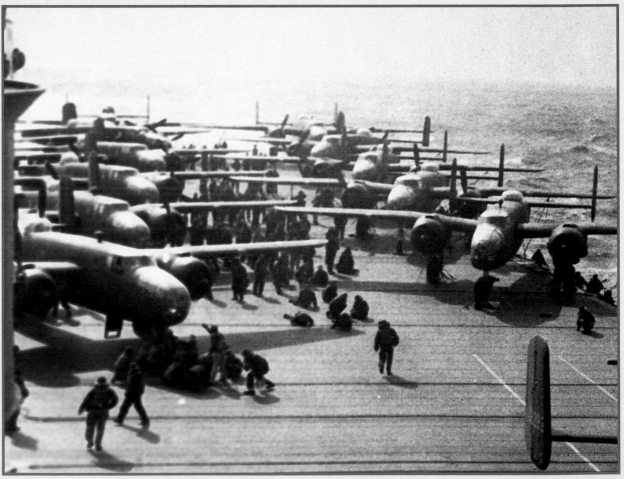

ABOVE LEFT: All hands hold their breath as the first of sixteen B-25s, with Doolittle at the controls, guns its engines with brakes locked, awaiting the signal to take off.

ABOVE RIGHT: Doolittle lifts off the deck of *Hornet* with relative ease and gains altitude rapidly in the stiff head wind. Seven months later the Japanese off the Santa Cruz Islands would sink the *Hornet.* For the fiftieth anniversary of the Doolittle Raid in 1992, two B-25s took off from the deck of a modern aircraft carrier along the California coast, the first B-25s to accomplish this feat since the sixteenth plane left the deck of *Hornet* in 1942. Two more took off from the deck of the moored museum carrier *Lexington* at Corpus Christi for the filming of the movie *Pearl Harbor* in 2000.

RIGHT: Each of the remaining planes lined up one by one and took off after Doolittle. Here the tail of the fifth B-25 can be seen at lower right as it is positioned for takeoff. Planes six and seven have started their engines and prepare to follow.

Even though everyone had supreme confidence in Doolittle, it still remained to be seen if a fully loaded B-25 could take off from the deck of a carrier. A couple of empty B-25s had earlier demonstrated that it was possible, but no one had done it with a B-25 weighted down with a full load of gasoline and bombs. *Hornet* turned into a brisk thirty-knot wind and ran up to full steam. Combined with the speed of the carrier, Doolittle's plane had fifty knots of airspeed before he even turned a wheel. There was a large swell running with whitecaps and spray being driven over the flight deck. Doolittle was piloting the number one plane. The left wheel of his aircraft was on a white stripe that had been painted down the left side of the flight deck, and the center wheel was on a second white stripe down the middle of the deck. The white stripes were important aids, since the flight deck was only seventy-five feet wide and the B-25 wingspan was sixty-seven feet. The plane had to be positioned so that the right wingtip would not hit the control island during the takeoff roll. Doolittle locked the brakes, revved the engines, and waited for the signal. When the carrier plunged into a trough between waves, the signal was given. The plane leapt forward, and within the first hundred feet had enough airspeed to lift the front wheel from the deck. Doolittle then backed off a bit to gain more sustained airspeed, and, as the flight deck rose to the top of the swell, he lifted off. A cheer went up from all those lucky enough to have watched the first-ever takeoff of a fully loaded bomber from the deck of a carrier. Doolittle later wrote, "Took off at 0820 ship time. Takeoff was easy. . . . Circled carrier to get exact heading and check compass. Wind was from around 300 degrees." Each succeeding plane rolled forward and lurched off the deck until by 9:20 A.M. all sixteen were on their way to Japan.

Bower's plane, nicknamed *Werewolf*, was twelfth off *Hornet*. He had no problem on takeoff and headed for Japan. "We were flying right down on the deck," he recalled, "just off the surface of the ocean, to avoid detection. We were in single file mostly, and our plane flew alone all the way to Japan. It was a beautiful sunny day when we got there. We ended up north of Yokohama, hit the coast and turned south. I was impressed with the countryside. It was a beautiful country, green, well manicured, and neat. All of a sudden we flew right over an airport at the same altitude as the planes in the traffic pattern. They didn't seem to notice us, and we went on. The target looked just like they said it would. We had climbed a bit by then so

we were at about 1,500 feet when we released the bombs. Then we had only one thought: get out of there!"

The Japanese people had been led to believe that an American air raid was not a threat. On April 16, 1942, two days before the Doolittle raid, Radio Tokyo reassured the people of Japan: ". . . it is absolutely impossible for enemy bombers to get within five hundred miles of Tokyo. Instead of worrying about such foolish things the Japanese people are enjoying the fine spring sunshine and the fragrance of cherry blossoms."

Ironically, the very morning of the raid the Japanese Government held Tokyo's first full-dress air-raid drill. Yet there was still considerable surprise when the American planes suddenly appeared at midday over Tokyo. Akira Kasahara was a student in Tokyo that day. "The American bombers came right overhead," he said. "It was scary. You could see bombs dropping out. We were all very surprised. The American planes I saw were flying low and they seemed quite large, bigger than the other planes we had seen flying over Tokyo. Afterwards, there was not much mentioned about the bombing in the newspapers. My friends and I knew you couldn't believe the media anyway because it was controlled by the government, but everyone was talking about the American planes and knew about the bombing right after it happened."

What did appear in the Japanese media was meant to enrage the Japanese populace. Each of the B-25s had been ordered specifically to bomb strategic, not civilian, targets. Unfortunately a hospital, a couple of schools, and some houses were accidentally hit with a few stray incendiary bombs. The media reports were intended to convince the Japanese people that civilians were the sole targets, such as this one from *Asahi Shimbun*: ". . . fleeing helter-skelter to avoid the curtain of shells which burst forth from our antiaircraft batteries, the enemy planes chose innocent people and city streets as their targets. . . . they carried out an inhuman, insatiable, indiscriminate bombing attack on the sly, and the fact they schemed to strafe civilians and non-combatants demonstrates their fiendish behavior."

In another press report, presumed attacks on civilian targets were specified: "The cowardly raiders purposefully avoided industrial centers and the important military establishments and blindly dumped their incendiaries in a few suburban districts, especially on schools and hospitals."

As the Japanese were left to contemplate the seemingly impossible appearance of American

bombers, the fliers themselves were facing long odds. "Before we took off we had discussed what was going to happen," said Bower. "We knew we wouldn't get to China until after dark, so all our plans for landing were out the window. After we released the bombs we turned south, started to climb slowly, and the weather socked in. We kept trying to climb to get above it but it was real deep. It was dark when we crossed the coast of China, but since we were flying in clouds we couldn't see a thing. We were just flying by dead reckoning to the area where the airstrip was that we were supposed to have landed on. We didn't really know how far we had come, but when the red lights came on indicating we were out of gas we just jumped."

Most of the planes ended up as Bower's did. Out of fuel, the crews bailed out into the chilly, cloudy night sky over China. Two planes attempted to crash-land on the shore. Another flew to Russia against strict orders. Bower chuckles today when he recalls that "the pilot who flew to Russia was the only West Pointer in our group." Amazingly, many of the planes ended up near their original destination in China despite the longer distance they had to fly on account of the early launch. It is probable that the weather system they flew through provided a tailwind that got the planes closer to their destinations. Crew after crew bailed out at about ten thousand feet into the dark, not knowing where they were. Most survived.

"I left the plane, the chute opened, I couldn't see a thing in the dark, and all of a sudden I was on the ground," said Bower. "I landed right by a tree and within fifty to seventy-five feet of a sharp cliff."

The next morning Doolittle went with crew chief Paul Leonard to see the pile of junk that just the day before had been the first plane off the deck of *Hornet*. Doolittle was extremely depressed. He had been ordered not only to bomb Japan, but also to deliver sixteen new B-25s to China for use against the Japanese. Since all sixteen planes must surely be piles of wreckage like his, he felt that he had failed.

Leonard asked what he thought would happen when he got home. "Well," said Doolittle, "I guess they'll send me to Leavenworth." "No," Leonard replied, "they're going to make you a general." Which is exactly what happened. Back home a few weeks later, Doolittle was given the Medal of Honor and jumped from lieutenant colonel to brigadier general. The raid had been a huge propaganda success and had finally given the Allies some good news. Harlan Wall, a high school student in Colorado at the time who would later fight the Japanese in the Philippines, recalled, "If we could fly right over there and bomb Tokyo, we thought that maybe they weren't so hot after all." The Japanese military government had also been put on notice. Their cities were not immune to air attack, and the citizens of Tokyo and the other cities that were bombed now knew it.

Dodging Japanese patrols and hiding the airmen in a succession of locations, friendly Chinese civilians smuggled most of the crews south to Chunking over the next few weeks. From there they were able to find rides on Allied planes that flew them back to the U.S. Out of eighty crewmen on sixteen B-25s, one man died on the parachute jump into China, four either drowned or died in landing accidents, and eight were captured in Japanese-occupied China. From the plane that bombed Nagoya, Sergeant Harold Spatz and Lieutenant Harold Farrow were executed on October 15, along with pilot Lieutenant Dean Hallmark. The other five were sentenced to "life imprisonment" for "war crimes." Of these, one died of malnutrition. The remaining four were released at the end of the war. Fifteen aircraft were lost, and one was interned in the Soviet Union. It was a year before that crew finally managed to escape into Iran. Meanwhile, the United States received a bill from the Russians every month for the internees' room and board.

"At the time the raid seemed exciting to us, but we didn't think it was a real big deal," recalled Bower. "Most of us ended up doing much more dangerous flying in Italy, and we didn't think too much about what they ended up calling the Doolittle Raid. It was only in later years that there was a lot of interest built up. We have been getting together for years now. It's influenced our whole lives. We are a pretty tight family."

Jimmy Doolittle, revered head of that family of fliers, went on to even greater achievements as head of the Eighth Air Force in Europe. Yet today he is most often associated with the daring Doolittle Raid, the first offensive strike at the Japanese homeland in World War II. He lived to be ninety-six, and died peacefully at his son's home in September 1993.

The Doolittle Raiders have had annual reunions over the years, highlighted by a ceremony honoring the members who have passed on since their last gathering. A set of mugs, one for each Raider, is kept in a case at the Air Force Academy and transported to the ceremony every year. The surviving Raiders' mugs are upright, and the mugs of those who have passed on are turned upside down. The last two surviving Raiders will tap a bottle of champagne, vintage 1896, the year of Doolittle's birth, and make a toast to all the Raiders.

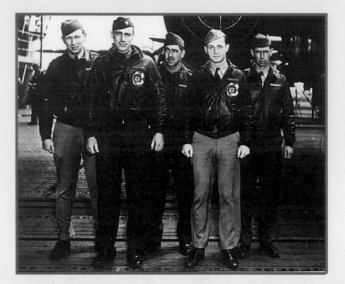

Bill Bower (second from left) and his crew on *Hornet* in mid-Pacific.

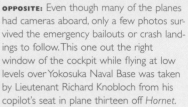

OPPOSITE: Even though many of the planes had cameras aboard, only a few photos survived the emergency bailouts or crash landings to follow. This one out the right window of the cockpit while flying at low levels over Yokosuka Naval Base was taken by Lieutenant Richard Knobloch from his copilot's seat in plane thirteen off *Hornet*.

BELOW: Rough outline for the nose art on Ross Greening's B-25 painted during the trip. The plane's name, *Hari Carrier*, and color rendering of the woman were added after the photo was taken.

Ross Greening bails out of his plane *Hari Carrier* over China. Greening painted this picture while in a German POW camp after being shot down over Italy later in the war.

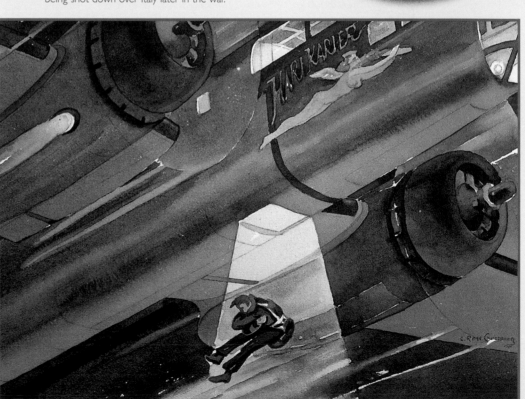

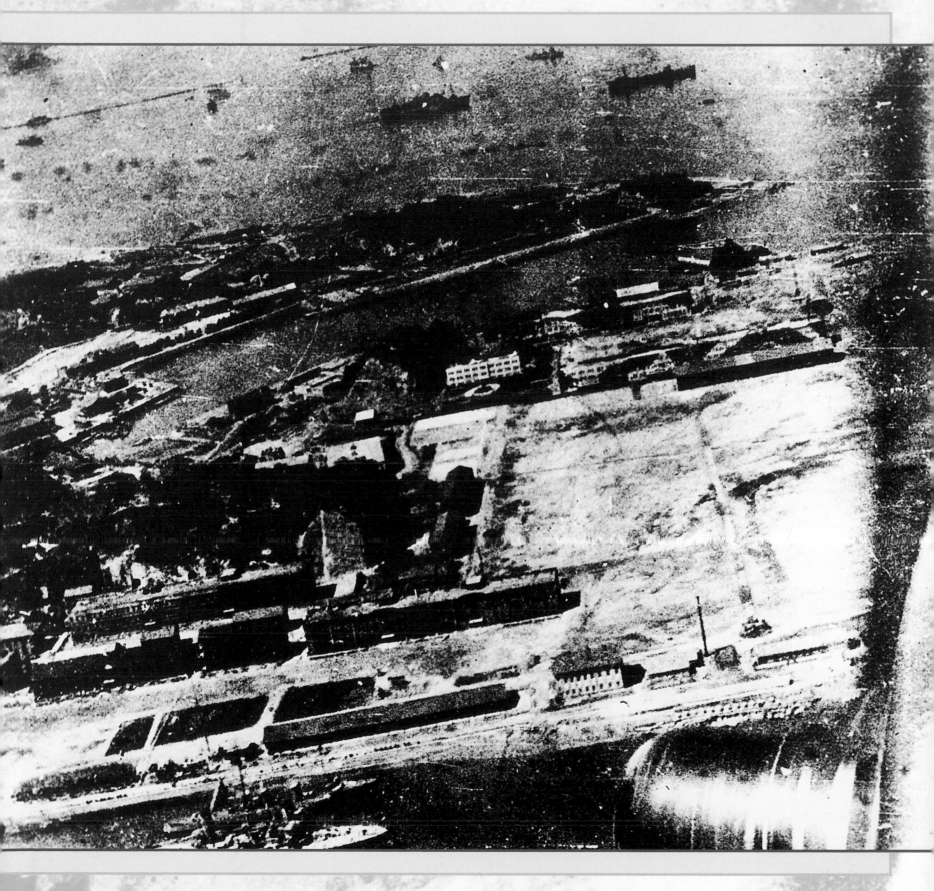

Jimmy Doolittle (fourth from right) and some of his men are pictured after ditching in China.

A group of Doolittle Raiders gathered together outside a cave (at right) where they were hidden for about a week after bailing out over China. Bill Bower is fifth from left in the second row from the front.

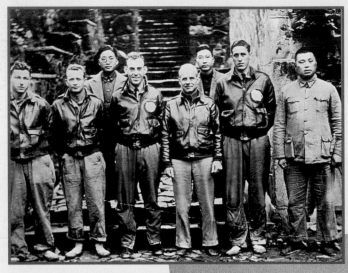

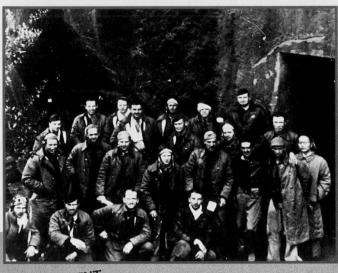

RIGHT: A letter from Jimmy Doolittle to a relative of Bill Bower, relating that he was alive. The censor deleted Bower's location.

BELOW: Doolittle Raiders receive decorations from General Hap Arnold and Jimmy Doolittle after returning to the U.S.

Bower in 1998 in Boulder, Colorado, with a copy of Ross Greening's collection of paintings (done while a POW in Europe) and reminiscences entitled *Not As Briefed.*

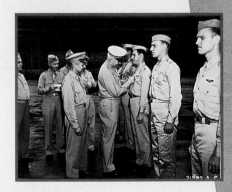

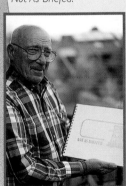

WAR DEPARTMENT
HEADQUARTERS OF THE ARMY AIR FORCES
WASHINGTON

May 22, 1942

Miss Edith L. Marsh
2905 Franklin Avenue
Cleveland, Ohio

Dear Miss Marsh:

Thanks for your sincere wishes.

I may tell you in the greatest of confidence that Bill is in ▆▆▆▆▆ I don't know where he will be sent but the first time I see him I will convey your wishes in person and if I am in communication with him I will send them by mail.

I want to thank you for your kind letter.

Sincerely yours,

J. H. DOOLITTLE

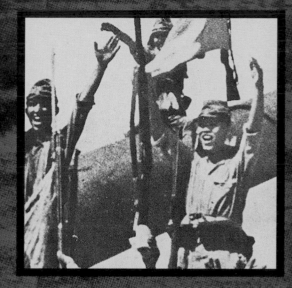

CHAPTER 2

THE TIME BUYERS
Losing the Philippines

AMERICAN SOLDIERS AND SAILORS assigned to the Philippines in the years immediately preceding World War II usually discovered, and often to their astonishment, that they'd been sent to one of the best duty stations anywhere. Many went there expecting a hinterland whose inhabitants would likely be found running about in the jungle wearing bones through their noses and little else, with the disturbing habit of having their neighbors for lunch—literally. Many Americans were arrogantly confident (as most were in those days) of the superiority of Americans over all other peoples, and Caucasian Americans over all other races. And to such as these the Philippines must have come as something of a shock. For what they actually found was a civilized, devoutly religious people (mostly Catholic), among whom even the lowest classes were generally well mannered and gracious and whose upper classes could be said to operate at a cultural and educational level at least equal to that of American counterparts.

Culturally inclined newcomers soon found, at least in Manila, an abundance of concerts, museums, art exhibits, performances at the Manila Opera House, and educational events of all kinds at the capital's seven universities. For the sports-minded there were baseball and football games at the huge Rizal Stadium, polo at the polo grounds, golf courses, swimming pools, tennis courts, and excellent lake and saltwater fishing. There were many outstanding restaurants, among which the cuisine of almost any nation would not be found missing. And for lovers of nightlife there was, of course, almost a surfeit of nightclubs, dance halls, and bars.

In sum, in the Manila area at least (where most American military personnel were based), most of the amenities and amusements to be found in any major stateside city were there, and all considerably cheaper than at home. At fine tailor-shops such as Duran's a man could get a made-to-measure white drill suit for four dollars, a woman a hand-tailored sharkskin suit for five, and in both cases delivery within twenty-four hours guaranteed. You could play golf all day for a dollar, swim all day for a dime, and tennis cost ten cents per game. You could rent a three-bedroom house with garage and servants' quarters in one of the best districts for fifty dollars a month, hire a skilled full-time cook for fifteen, a houseboy for seven-fifty, and a laundress for ten.

Add to this the Philippines' lush tropical setting and, yes—until December 8, 1941—it was a fine place to live for American servicemen and their families. But on that day their world fell apart, and for both Americans and Filipinos life became a nightmare.

At 3:30 on that morning, General Douglas MacArthur, commander of all American forces in the Philippines and also of the army of the Philippine Commonwealth, was awakened by a telephone call from Washington to tell him the Japanese had attacked Pearl Harbor. He was not alarmed, however—or so he wrote in his memoirs—because, given no details, he thought the attack had failed.

Four hours later he received another call, this one from Major General Lewis Hyde Brereton, his Air Corps commander, telephoning from the Philippines' principal military air base at Clark Field, asking for permission to send his B-17 bombers to attack Japanese airfields on Formosa, five hundred miles to the north.

"No," responded General MacArthur. "We must not make the first overt act."

At 9:25 Brereton asked again, this time pointing out that the bombing of Pearl Harbor most certainly could be considered overt. Once more MacArthur refused, saying they didn't have enough intelligence about Formosan fields for an effective attack.

At 12:35 the argument was finally settled, not by the generals but by fifty-four Japanese bombers and thirty-five fighters that attacked Clark Field. The raid lasted only forty-five minutes, but when it was over General Brereton no longer had very much with which to bomb anything, let alone enemy bases on Formosa. When the Japanese raid began, Generals MacArthur and Brereton had known of the attack on Pearl Harbor for a full eight hours, and it seems almost inconceivable that the attackers could have caught Clark Field by surprise. But they did.

An artilleryman of the New Mexico National Guard first saw the planes approaching and remembers shouting, "Here Comes the Navy!" Impressed by the precision and beauty of their formations, Sergeant Dwaine Davis snatched up his movie camera and began taking pictures. Then someone called out, "Why are they dropping tin foil?" and he was answered by smoke and flame when the "tin foil" began striking the ground.

A Signal Corps telephone operator hurried to report the raid to General MacArthur's headquarters in Manila, and even as he reported it, bombs already were blasting craters in the airfield's runways, exploding inside hangars and repair shops and barracks buildings, and in the oil dump, where great fires were beginning to burn and spread.

Next came Zero fighters, sweeping in and strafing everything in sight, but with particular attention paid to the field's parked airplanes. Just as in Hawaii, they were out of their bunkers and neatly lined up on the aprons. And minutes later these, too, were no longer airplanes but piles of flaming junk. What it came down to was this: the Japanese in one quick stroke had reduced the Philippines' air defense from major threat to minor nuisance.

Next, on December 10, the attackers turned their attention to the big United States Navy Yard, home of the American Asiatic Fleet, ten miles southwest of Manila at Cavite. From the destroyer *Ford* Gunner's Mate J. Daniel Mullin saw them coming: "Two-engined bombers leisurely circling" and "sizing up targets" then dropping bombs that killed eight men and left thirty-four wounded or missing on the destroyer *Peary*, heavily damaged the submarine *Sea-dragon* and minelayer *Bittern*, and left the submarine *Sea Lion* damaged beyond repair.

"For more than an hour," wrote naval historian Captain Robert Bulkley, "[they] swept over, out of anti-aircraft range, dropping their explosives at will. . . . [Soon] the entire yard and one third of the city of Cavite were ablaze. . . . So complete was the destruction, that all remaining facilities had to be set up in new locations."

"Dead and wounded were everywhere," recalled Gunner's Mate Mullin. The dead, according to General E. M. Flanagan, Jr., totaled "about 2,200 people," almost as many as died at Pearl Harbor.

While Japanese bombers were pounding Cavite, twelve Japanese transports were landing the first invasion forces,

part at Aparri on the extreme north of Luzon Island and the rest at Vigan on the northwest coast. These, however, represented only a preliminary move. The real invasion came twelve days later when, on the morning of December 22, seventy-six troop transports steamed into Lingayen Gulf 110 miles north of Manila and began unloading forty-three thousand men of General Masaharu Homma's Fourteenth Army.

General Brereton's four surviving B-17s made a bombing run on the unloading transports, dropping one-hundred-pound bombs with little but psychological effect. Then, as they had been ordered to do, they headed south to Australia.

Still believing he could depend on help from home and desperate now for air support, General MacArthur radioed Army Chief of Staff George C. Marshall to ask that aircraft carriers be sent to attack the Japanese transports.

"Can I expect anything along that line?" he asked, only to be promptly told he could not.

A Philippine Army battalion was first to challenge the invaders, and initially it put up a spirited resistance. Consisting, however, of new, half-trained recruits rather than the highly capable Philippine Scouts, it was no match for the invaders and finally broke and ran.

As word of the Luzon landings reached other Philippine islands, their residents became more and more nervous. Though unmolested themselves they knew they could not remain so. Still, there were many who simply could not comprehend the seriousness of their situation and how critical it was likely to become.

At the IXL gold mine on Masbate, the staff had built a bomb shelter, and then scheduled practices for its use. Louise Spencer, wife of the mine's engineer, wrote about this later: "The wife of the resident manager came over all in a flurry saying, 'My Dear, I simply haven't a thing to wear. I do hope the barrio tailor can alter a pair of jodhpurs for me' . . . and off she went busily, to prepare her outfit for the air raids!" And when the first air-raid practice was conducted, "The manager's wife wore her altered jodhpurs, a tailored white shirt, a riding hat and a pair of white silk gloves. 'You know, Louise, going down the ladder and all that—one really does need gloves.'"

Then came Christmas eve, approaching grimly this year, and marked not by joyous celebrations but with great clouds of smoke boiling up from Cavite where men of the withdrawing Asiatic Fleet were burning everything they could not take with them, including a million gallons of oil. And smoke was rising also from ruined buildings in Manila where bomb-blasted bodies littered the streets.

Even so, the traditional Christmas party was held at the palatial Manila Hotel that evening, an elegant affair with all the men in dress uniforms or tuxedos, the women in evening gowns, and with bowls of punch and dancing and the singing of Christmas carols. But because Japanese soldiers were relentlessly approaching and the partygoers knew the city was doomed to fall, the affair was not so much a party as a gesture: a set piece of fate-defying gallantry like that performed by those *Titanic* bandsmen who continued to play their music while the ship was sinking beneath them.

Although residents of the hotel, General MacArthur and his family were not at the party. There had been another enemy landing, this time of ten thousand men at Antimonan on Limon Bay. So now the Japanese had more than seventy thousand men on shore and more undoubtedly on the way—all of them well supplied and all well equipped, and most hardened from campaigns in China.

To resist this juggernaut MacArthur had only a few PT boats for a navy, no air force at all, and an army that was outnumbered, ill supplied, and comparatively inexperienced. Therefore, he abandoned any notion of trying to defend Luzon either on the beaches or in the city. Instead, he now set in motion an alternative plan, Operation Orange 3, by which he hoped to withdraw all his forces into the Bataan Peninsula, which flanked the entrance to Manila Bay, and onto the fortified island of Corregidor, just off the peninsula's tip. There he would hold out until the arrival of reinforcements and supplies from the States.

Accordingly, "On Christmas eve I evacuated Manila and moved my headquarters to Corregidor." Where, four days later, MacArthur was present for the first of the more than three hundred Japanese bombings this tiny two-and-a-half-square-mile island was to endure before surrendering. "They came," wrote the general, ". . . glittering in the brilliant blue sky like silver pieces thrown against the sun. [But] their currency was death. . . . The long white barracks, a concrete straight line, cracked and splintered like a glass box. . . . A 500 pound burst took the roof off my quarters. . . . The lawn became a smoking crater. Blue sky turned to dirty gray. Then came strafing, and again bombing. They kept it up for three hours. . . . Then they left as shaking earth yielded to this pulverizing attack."

Until the raid the general's headquarters had been located on "Topside," which was "the flattened summit of the highest hill of the island," but no more. He now moved his headquarters and all other remaining vital Topside operations down into the Malinta Tunnel, a huge complex consisting of a central tunnel from which branched twenty-three laterals and from them another twenty-three sub-lateral tunnels totaling nearly two miles of passages all together, deep within a mountain of solid rock.

From there he continued to direct Orange 3 through the dangerously complex wheeling and sidestepping maneuvers necessary for funneling all of Luzon's American and Filipino troops into Bataan, while at the same time keeping them from any disastrous involvements with the hordes of Japanese now flowing toward Manila from three directions. And, against all odds he succeeded. Shortly after New Year's Day his troops were busy sealing off the neck of the Bataan peninsula with a defensive complex they called the Abucay Line.

By this time the enemy had arrived at the outskirts of Manila, and local radio stations exhorted the citizens: "Keep calm. Stay at home. Pour all liquor down the drain." And on January 2, Manila, known as the Pearl of the Orient, fell to the Japanese, an event recorded this way by Louise Spencer: "The noonday broadcast from Manila came in clearly . . . 'your announcer is Osias. I have to tell you Manila has fallen to the Japs.' His voice broke. He could say no more. After a moment the Philippine National Anthem came in strong. We stood at attention, tears streaming down our cheeks. Writing of it I experience again the choked, impossible emotions of that moment. . . . Accept defeat? Never! The sun went on shining on Masbate. The mill went on grinding. We stood, in tears, as the radio went silent."

Back in the United States, meanwhile, people had not yet begun to get used to the idea of being at war, nor did most yet comprehend its full meaning. They knew the war was going badly in Europe. They knew that in the Pacific the Japanese seemed able to take whatever they wanted whenever they wanted it. Even so, for most Americans the war still had an air of unreality about it. Distant and invisible, it had seemed so far to exist mainly in radio broadcasts and newspaper pages and as yet hadn't touched more than one in a thousand with its tragic realities. On the contrary, at this point most people were benefiting from it. The massive unemployment of the Great Depression years was over, replaced by massive hiring for the defense industry. Anyone could get a job now, qualified or not. Wages were higher than ever, and on most jobs there was as much time-and-a-half overtime work available as anyone could desire or handle. Before long, however, there would be little for those wages to buy. Civilian supplies of meat, gasoline, sugar, shoes, and a hundred other items would be severely curtailed and strictly rationed. But that was still in the future, and in January 1942, a great many Americans were suddenly living better and with less financial worries than ever before.

True, thousands of young men were being drafted into the Armed Forces. And although this was soon to change, at present they, too, had not been touched by war's realities. Joining the Armed Forces was for many an exciting thing, lifting them from a usually humdrum and often unemployed existence into a new world of experiences and of travel to faraway places they had never dreamed of being able to see. It was, moreover, a highly applauded patriotic adventure in uniforms that invested previously ordinary young men with instant public prestige, which had a considerable aphrodisiac effect upon many a young woman.

On Bataan American and Filipino soldiers, too, were still trying to get used to the war, but to another side of it—the grim and ugly side. Their most immediate problem was food. Bataan's five hundred square miles of mostly jungle and precipitous mountainsides were totally incapable of producing food for eighty thousand soldiers plus the populations of the peninsula's nine villages. Accordingly, to conserve such subsistence as they did have, their daily ration was reduced to two thousand calories, half the normal allotment and barely enough to keep the men alive and able to fight.

Still, in the beginning things didn't seem all that bad, for in the beginning there was hope. All "knew" that their country would soon come to their aid, either with the supplies and reinforcements they needed to hold Bataan or with ships to take them home. Hospital Corpsman Eugene Rogers recalled it this way: "We lived with rumors. We lived with hope that help was on the way, yes, help was on the way. . . ."

Meanwhile they could at least be amused by the fractured English and scrambled thoughts in Japanese propaganda broadcasts and leaflets. Major John Coleman, Jr., would recall a leaflet, "showing the private parts of a beautiful, blonde woman and captioned, 'You, too, can enjoy if you surrender.'"

"Tokyo Rose poked fun at our predicament," recalled Captain Steve Mellnik (later to become a brigadier general): "You're out on the end of a six-thousand-mile limb," she said in dulcet tones. "The Japanese Imperial forces are sawing that limb in two. Get smart and give up. Why starve in the stinking jungle while folks back home make big profits?"

The name "Tokyo Rose," though never used in broadcasts, was attached by the Americans to any female voice speaking English on Japanese radio. Since there were probably at least a dozen women who spoke on Japanese-controlled radio at one time or another, it became difficult after the war to identify a "real," possibly treasonous Tokyo Rose. Yet the Americans ended up arresting one of these women and labeling her Tokyo Rose. She was an American of Japanese descent named Iva Toguri who grew up in southern California and graduated from UCLA with a B.A. in zoology. She started graduate school but fatefully decided to take a trip to visit relatives in Japan in the summer of 1941. Stranded there after Pearl Harbor, she took a clerical job at Radio Tokyo to make enough money to survive. Though she had no experience behind the microphone, an Australian POW named Norman Cousens recruited her to be an announcer on the *Zero Hour* program. He and several other POWs, who were put in charge of writing and staging the program, tried to make their production sound as ludicrous as possible to discredit the Japanese propaganda embedded in it. Cousens figured that Toguri's "rough," untrained voice would add to the effect. Her radio name became "Orphan Ann," and she typically greeted her Allied listeners at the beginning of a broadcast by saying, "Hello to all my little orphans wandering in the Pacific." From 1943 to 1945 she shared this role with several other women who would occasionally substitute for her on the show.

The *Zero Hour* program consisted mostly of big-band music interspersed with news and sprinkled with mostly laughable attempts at propaganda, made so by skillful scriptwriting by Cousens and other POWs. They convinced their Japanese supervisors that they were simply using American slang to make the program more palatable to their audience on Pacific islands. American servicemen usually took the broadcasts the way Cousens intended them to—as laughable entertainment. But somehow a legend grew up around a mythical Tokyo Rose, visualized as an Asian enchantress who had the uncanny ability to know what the Allies were doing. Japanese intelligence would pass along tidbits of Allied unit movements and naval actions to the female announcers to fuel this perception, yet Toguri herself never used such material.

Even though she tried to convince the Americans she was not the Tokyo Rose of South Pacific legend, she was arrested and tried for treason in San Francisco from July to September 1949. The U.S. government trumped up a bizarre case full of contradictions and coerced witnesses, and Toguri was convicted of treason, sentenced to ten years in prison, and fined $10,000. She served six years and two months of her sentence, and finally paid the last dollar of her fine in 1972. In the meantime, several groups trying to expose the government's case finally succeeded in convincing President Gerald Ford to pardon Toguri in January 1977. Virtually everyone involved with her trial agreed later that she never made a treasonable broadcast.

On January 10 General MacArthur received and rejected an enemy demand for surrender, and General Homma retaliated with a shower of leaflets that read: "The outcome of the present combat has already been decided and you are cornered to the doom . . . blinded General MacArthur has stupidly refused our proposal. . . . 'Dear Filipino soldiers! . . . surrender to the Japanese force before it is too late and we shall protect you. Surrender at once and build your new Philippines for and by Filipinos.'" The result, wrote MacArthur, "was that night every foxhole on Bataan rocked with ridicule."

Now that the American and Filipino troops had been backed up into Bataan, General Homma thought he had them at his mercy and on January 13 set out to prove it. He found he had been mistaken. Hitting the Abucay Line with what MacArthur later described as headlong attacks of unabated fury, Homma's troops did punch a two-mile hole in it, but were able to hold the ground only briefly before being driven back out.

During the next few days the Japanese attacked again and again, and yet again, but the line still held. Finally, on January 21, they did manage to pry loose the China Sea end of the line. Threatened with being outflanked, defenders fell back ten miles and established a new line running from Pilar on Manila Bay to Bagac on the South China Sea. Here Bataan's beleaguered resisters would hold the Japanese forces at bay for seventy days, and so effectively that at the beginning of February General Homma—complaining that his Bataan campaign had already cost him seventy-seven hundred men killed plus another ten thousand incapacitated by malaria, beriberi, and dysentery—felt forced to suspend operations until he could be reinforced.

Despite these American and Filipino successes, however, it was clear they couldn't continue for very long. The Japanese had access to food, weapons, ammunition, medicines, and replacements for their killed and wounded. Bataan's beleaguered defenders had none of these things. Their numbers were steadily reduced by death, wounds, sickness, and capture, and their effectiveness further diminished by dwindling essential supplies—food, medicines, weapons, munitions, clothing, tents, trucks, tools, and fuel—as they became used up, worn out, or lost to enemy fire.

Filipinos, during all this time, had been learning just what it meant to be liberated by the Japanese, and learning it the hard way. The Japanese had come, they said, to rescue their "brown brothers," to free them from the evil yoke of Western colonialism, brutality, and greed they had suffered for the past four hundred years, first under the Spanish, then the Americans. But now they were free. Free to become an independent nation and to become an equal partner with the Japanese and other "liberated brown brothers" in a new alliance called the Greater East Asia Co-Prosperity Sphere. Soon, however, the Filipinos had discovered that this new "freedom" was freedom only to do what the Japanese ordered them to do. And the "prosperity" in this new alliance was turning out to apply only to the Japanese. For all Japan's other "partners" a better name would have been the East Asia Co-Poverty Sphere.

To begin with, the Japanese had begun confiscating all "alien held" property in the Philippines, finding it convenient to describe as "alien" whatever property they happened to want. Next they began stripping all the islands of their stocks of rice, sugar, and coconut oil. And any owners rash enough to object could expect at best to be beaten and at worst to be executed. In fact, the Filipinos were being told that simply "annoying" a Japanese soldier would be considered grounds for execution.

A natural result of all this was that Filipino men by the hundreds were melting away into the jungle and forming the nucleus of what was ultimately to become a massive underground army of resistance. Unfortunately, however, there was no way for that army to become organized and effective in time to help the troops trapped on Bataan and Corregidor. There, the troops were still hanging on and making General Homma pay double and even triple for every gain. But, malnourished and disease-ridden, they were finding it ever harder to do this.

On February 22, on Corregidor, General MacArthur received from President Roosevelt a message ordering him to leave the Philippines and assume command of the Allied Forces in Australia. Before going, however, Mac-

Arthur made his first (and only) visit to the men on Bataan. "My heart ached," he wrote, "as I saw my men slowly wasting away. Their clothes hung on them like tattered rags. Their bare feet stuck out in silent protest. Their long, bedraggled hair framed gaunt bloodless faces. . . ."

Not privy to how the general felt, the men generally were not very impressed. Only this once during their three miserable months on Bataan had he left the tunnels of Corregidor to visit them. So, as armies have been doing since time immemorial, they made a song about it:

Dugout Doug's not timid; he's just cautious, not afraid.
He's protecting carefully the stars that Franklin made.
Four-star generals are rare as good food on Bataan,
And his troops go starving on.

At 7:15 on the evening of March 11 General MacArthur, along with his wife and son and certain members of his staff, left Corregidor on a motor-torpedo boat and headed south. Six days later they were met on the island of Mindanao by a B-17 bomber and flown to Australia.

It made sense for the general to go. There was nothing more he could accomplish where he was, and he was far too valuable a leader to be wasted by spending the rest of the war years in some Japanese prison. To the men left behind on Bataan, however, it reinforced the opinion they'd had of him. And so they added another verse to "Dugout Doug":

Dugout Doug is ready in his Chris-craft for the Flee,
Over bounding billows and the wildly raging sea.
For the Japanese are pounding on the gates of
*   old Bataan,*
And his troops go starving on.

Bataan's defenders were receiving some encouragement via radio and continued to get worldwide praise for their valiant stand. From President Roosevelt they heard, "Congratulations on the magnificent stand you are making. We are watching you with pride. . . ." From Secretary of War Henry Stimson, "Every one of us is inspired to greater efforts by [your] heroic, skillful fight. . . ." And from King George VI of England, "Your countrymen must indeed be proud of the United States and Philippine troops who are fighting with such dauntless heroism. . . ."

But these messages and the additional dozens like them filled no stomachs, treated no wounded, healed no sick. What Bataan's defenders really needed was help, and not only were they not getting it they were losing all hope of ever getting it. This inspired yet another verse to their growing repertoire:

We're the battling bastards of Bataan:
No momma, no poppa, no Uncle Sam,
No aunts, no uncles, no nephews, no nieces,
No rifles, no guns, or artillery pieces,
And nobody gives a damn.

By April 1 it had become obvious that the end was near. Of the seventy-eight thousand American and Filipino troops on Bataan only twenty-seven thousand could still be listed as combat effective, and that only by applying the term loosely. Their main enemy now, greater even than disease or the Japanese, was hunger. After their own supplies had run out they had eaten their horses and mules (three hundred according to one account), but now they were gone. And they had eaten Bataan's carabao—the water buffalo that was the Philippine farmer's beast of burden—but now they, too, were gone. The defenders were left with nothing but such things as pythons, iguanas, monkeys, and other wildlife they might manage to bag, but there was no way they could exist on that fare. "They are so exhausted," Major General Edward King wrote in his daily report, "that they cannot move a hundred yards out of their foxholes before collapsing."

To accelerate the now inevitable surrender of the Bataan defenders, the Japanese began bombing them even more intensely, with no particular regard for what their bombs might hit. On April 4 Army nurses Lieutenants Willa Hook and Juanita Redmond were busy in the wards of Hospital No. One when "Bombers came overhead . . . hitting the receiving wards, mess hall, doctors' & officers' quarters and . . . the nurses dormitory, setting fire to all buildings. . . ."

Two hours later, via Manila Radio, the Japanese apologized. So sorry about bombing the hospital, they said. It was a regrettable accident that wouldn't happen again. But three days later, on April 7, "Another wave of bombers came over. . . . An ammunition truck passing the hospital got a direct hit. . . . Patients, even amputation cases, were falling and even rolling out of the triple-decker beds. . . . [A bomb] hit directly in the middle of our hospital ward. . . . Beds were swaying and tumbling down. Desks were doing a jitterbug. Red flashes of heat burned our eyes. Through it all we could hear [Chaplain] Father Cummings' voice in prayer. His clear voice went through to the end. Then he turned and said, 'Put a tourniquet on my arm, would you?' And we saw that he had been badly hit by shrapnel."

By midnight on April 8–9, wrote General George Parker in his Second Corps Official Report, "All organized resistance had ceased. . . . The II Corps, which had taken the brunt of Japanese pressure since 6 January, ceased to exist as a fighting unit. Major General King ordered the destruction of artillery and ammunition, and all equipment except transportation, by 6 A.M., 9 April. At that time II Corps sent a flag of truce to the Japanese line. Corps headquarters surrendered at its command post. Troops surrendered wherever found by the enemy."

But even then, as Ray Thompson was to recall, "Many of the troops did not want to give up their arms. [We] would not give up our rifles, until we were given a direct order. [Then] we were told to strip the bolts from our rifles and throw them as far as we could into the jungle. . . . The Ordnance Companies then blew up the ammo dumps and that was some explosion. The ground shook, and you could hear the blast for many miles."

George Idlett wrote that he would "never forget that last night on Bataan before the surrender; [but] I am not sure that I can put it into words that will convey the memory. . . . We . . . set about destroying all of the equipment we could, and also gathering any food that we could find. . . . It was an unbelievable sight when the main Ammo Dump went off. The entire sky was lighted. . . ."

Knowing what was likely to happen to any American

women captured by the Japanese, General King ordered all the Army nurses to Corregidor on the evening of the eighth.

"We were told the Japanese had broken through the line," recalled Hook, "[and that] we were leaving in fifteen minutes and should take only what we could carry in our arms. [We] left the hospital at nine and got to Corregidor at three in the morning. All the doctors decided to stay with the patients, even those who had been told to come to Corregidor."

What followed on the next morning, when General King agreed to turn over his twelve thousand American and sixty thousand Filipino troops to the Japanese, was the largest surrender in American history. He surrendered only after being assured by the Japanese colonel handling the surrender that his men would be properly treated. "We are not barbarians," said the colonel. "The troops who have surrendered will be treated well."

What actually happened, however, was something else. It began when an officer from the Japanese General Staff chose at random one of the assembled prisoners, drew his pistol, and exclaimed, "This is the way to treat bastards like these," and shot the man dead.

"After they got us lined up," recalled Harold Feiner, "a Japanese officer gave a soldier an order, and he just walked out and grabbed a man here and he grabbed a man there, an American and a Filipino, and took 'em out to the middle of the field and beheaded 'em. Could of been me. Could of been the man next to me. They went to a man about five men from me and took this poor bugger out and beheaded 'im. And we knew they meant business."

"They'd bayonet an American and laugh," said Norman Matthews. "That affected everybody. You fall into line real quick when you see that happen to someone you know. If anybody argued with a Japanese at that time he was dead in one minute."

And this was only the beginning. Although the Japanese newspaper *Yomiuri Shimbun* headlined the surrender story, "Fiendish American Forces on Bataan Wiped Out!" the fiendishness turned out to be entirely Japanese. As soon as all American and Filipino soldiers had been taken into custody and disarmed, they were herded onto the road and started on a seventy-mile trek to imprisonment at Camp O'Donnell—a trek the world would come to know as the Bataan Death March.

During that march and their subsequent three-and-a-half years of imprisonment, these men were to endure brutalities unsurpassed even by those perpetrated by Hitler's Nazis in Europe, and the brutalities began immediately.

Suffering from malaria and dysentery, weak from starvation, denied food or water, and hanging on only by sheer strength of will, the captives plodded onward footstep by footstep under a blazing tropical sun. There were villages along the dusty road, peopled by Filipinos eager to give help but fully aware they would likely be killed if they were caught at it. As recalled by Major John S. Coleman, Jr., "Most were old women and children. They stood and looked at us with tears rolling down their cheeks. . . ." Philippine Scout Jim Downey said, "They wouldn't let you grab anything the civilians were throwing to you. And the Filipinos that were trying to help, sometimes they'd get shot and sometimes they'd get bayoneted."

As destinations, the villages passed meant nothing. But as markers of survival—as a means of helping a man to hold up—they meant everything. A soldier who had started at Mariveles (as many did) knew when reaching Cabcaben that he had made it for five miles. At Limay he knew had made it for another five. If he could just hold on now and reach Orion without collapsing, he would have survived for yet another five. And he must not collapse. At best that would mean great extra hardship for buddies who would try to carry him along. At worst, it would mean instant death. His Japanese guards did not allow themselves to be inconvenienced by giving aid or transportation to a collapsed prisoner. Generally, they solved the problem by simply bayoneting the man where he fell. Major Coleman "noticed a buck sergeant in front of [him] staggering along and holding to the belt of someone in front of him. He turned loose of the belt and staggered out of the column. The front guard turned and shot at him like someone shooting at a bird, just half aiming.

The bullet hit him in the chest and the sergeant rolled against the curb [where] the guard shot him again. Then the guard rushed up to him and thrust his bayonet through his chest. . . . After seeing this I was determined not to fall out of the column." No matter how thirst-crazed he might be, a prisoner dared not try to get water without permission or even to drink from the slimy puddles beside the road, for that, too, usually meant instant death.

In addition, there were occasional random killings by guards who for no apparent reason would impale a prisoner on his bayonet or behead him with his sword. And it was not uncommon to see alongside the prisoner column a Japanese soldier marching cockily, an American's head stuck on the tip of his bayonet.

It is hard to understand how a people supposedly long and highly civilized could still be committing acts of such medieval barbarity in the mid-twentieth century. It is harder still to understand their doing this not as random acts but as a matter of policy. Japanese historian Saburo Ienaga, however, gives what seems to be as good an explanation as any for the random acts:

> Army draftees were called *issen gorin* ("one sen five rin," or less than a penny). . . . They were expendable; there was an unlimited supply. Weapons and horses were treated with solicitous care but no second-class private was as valuable as an animal. After all, a horse costs real money. A private was worth only *issen gorin*. . . .

> Cruelty toward subordinates was a psychological technique. It provided an outlet for pressure by allowing each rank to shift the oppression to the one below. The oppression snowballed as it rolled down the ranks, till all the tension and abuse landed on the recruits. They were the lowest of the low. . . . Military leaders believed . . . the "skillful" commander could "by treating his men with calculated brutality mold them into a fierce fighting unit in time of war. . . ."

The inevitable side effects of training to breed "vicious fighters" was a penchant for brutality against enemy prisoners and civilian non-combatants. Individuals whose own dignity and manhood had been so cruelly violated would hardly refrain from doing the same to defenseless persons under their control.

That, however, does not explain the atrocities committed as a matter of policy. For this we must to look to those Japanese officers indoctrinated in Bushido, the code of the Samurai that values honor more than life, who believed that anyone so craven as to have chosen surrender over death in battle was of no more value than bugs or worms. It was such officers who informed the prisoners from Bataan that they would not be treated as prisoners of war. Having made themselves "unworthy," they must be considered only as "captives" who deserved nothing, and such food, water, shelter, and medicine as they did receive would come to them not as a "right" but as an act of Japanese benevolence.

The result was treatment so barbaric that it can only be properly understood and described by those who survived it:

> I think it was the third day we stopped at this place where they had a big warehouse. They put us in there and gave us some rice. It was our first meal.
> —Philippine Scout Jim Downey

> My walk lasted nine days, and covered 130 km, about 78 miles. All of our food gathered the previous night was taken from us, and I was not fed again for nine days.
> —George Idlett

> Bataan had lots and lots of artesian wells but they wouldn't let us get any water and they took away most of our canteens. A lot of men would go berserk—wild for water—and go to get a drink at the artesian wells. And if the Japanese were merciful they shot him but most of 'em they bayoneted right in the back while they were drinking.
> —Harold Feiner

> Late in the afternoon we were shoved into a barbed wire enclosure alongside the road. It was already crowded with men, most in bad shape, sick and

wounded and having had no food nor water for some time. There were no sanitary facilities, no nothing. Our addition created a standing-room only situation. Those who died died standing. Many sick and wounded, unable to stand, were trampled to death. Meanwhile Japs were flailing away with sticks, swords, clubs and rifle-butts at the men who were crowded against the barbed wire. . . . Several men were dragged from the enclosure and shot or beaten to death.

—Charles R. Kaolin

They herded us into this warehouse and I never saw anything like that in my life. The feces were piled as high as your ankles all over the place. They had cleared out the dead, and the living had been moved on out. They pushed us into this building, and there was just no way you could sit down or lie down. I saw men there just collapse and die. They were sick, you know, and this will always remain in my mind. This warehouse with this filth.

—Harold Feiner

I was in a shady area when I hear this commotion going on and I heard a woman screaming. I turned around and peeked through the bushes (there was a lot of heavy foliage) and there were three Japanese attacking a young Filipino woman. She had a baby at her breast and a two or two-and-a-half-year-old baby at her side. The children were screaming. She was screaming. They had her up against a tree and were raping her. And we witnessed this. . . . After they finished with the woman they took a bayonet and cut her breast off. Why, I don't know. . . . And I never, never will get that out of my head, what happened to that poor woman.

—Harold Feiner

On the last day's march guards were shouting, clubbing, and having trouble keeping the column moving at a regular pace. The men's feet were swollen to about twice the normal size. Many had cut the strings in their shoes to allow more room and comfort. I saw one major who had cut his shoes into leather strips and the flesh still protruded. . . . Many had dysentery. . . . I saw one man leave the column to defecate and a guard shot him. Some were bayoneted.

—Major John S. Coleman, Jr.

On 16 April 1942 our POW group arrived at San Fernando rail station where we were loaded on old-time railroad boxcars (about 100 persons per car), we had standing room only and a bucket to use for body wastes; it was dreadfully hot, no ventilation at all, and many men—already under terrible stress from the march and hunger and most of all thirst—died on this short train ride. We arrived at a small town named Capote, where we debarked. . . . Next day, 17 April 42, we traveled the remaining seven miles to Camp O'Donnell where, dead tired . . . we each received a cup of rice and a cup of camomile soup (camomile being equivalent to our sweet potato). Then we were assigned to old Philippine Scout bamboo barracks two decks high, split bamboo slats for beds and thatched roofs to ward off the rains. This was the type of shelter all POWs would have during their stay at O'Donnell and at Cabanatuan later on. . . .

—Ray Thompson

And during the following forty-one months that's how it was to be. Abuse, torture, forced labor, tropical diseases, and malnutrition. It was a terrible price they paid. And not until after the war could those who survived Bataan realize how much their defense had bought and how invaluable their stubborn resistance against hopeless odds had been to their country. For they had so delayed the Japanese juggernaut then rolling across the Pacific as to gain priceless time for their nation, so unprepared, to mobilize and arm to beat it back.

THE BATAAN DEATH MARCH

The Japanese were well aware of the propaganda value of pictures showing defeated and captured American troops and made sure that photographers, such as the one at right, were on hand to record this scene at the beginning of what came to be known as the Bataan Death March.

American POWs Samuel Stenzler, Frank Spear, and James Gallagher, their hands tied behind their backs, glare at a Japanese guard as they get a sample of what lies before them on their long march to a prison camp.

American and Filipino prisoners trudge along the rural roads in oppressive tropical heat and humidity, and Japanese soldiers in passing trucks often lean out and hit them with their rifle butts, especially if they're still wearing their steel helmets.

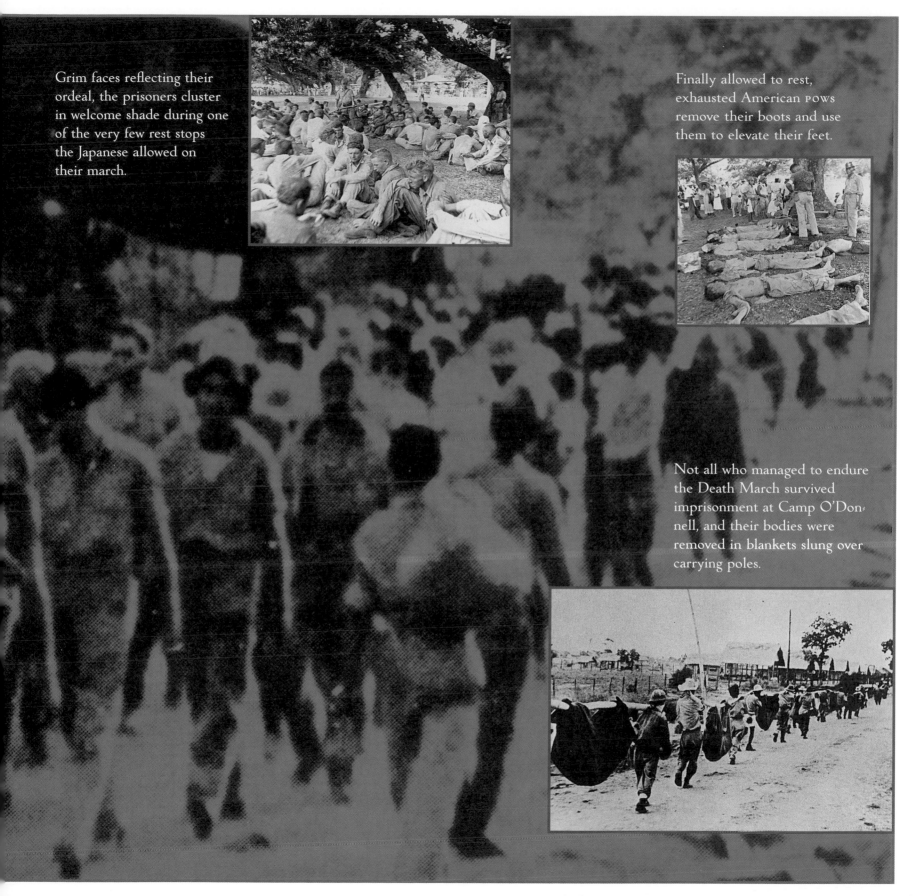

Grim faces reflecting their ordeal, the prisoners cluster in welcome shade during one of the very few rest stops the Japanese allowed on their march.

Finally allowed to rest, exhausted American POWs remove their boots and use them to elevate their feet.

Not all who managed to endure the Death March survived imprisonment at Camp O'Donnell, and their bodies were removed in blankets slung over carrying poles.

SURRENDERING CORREGIDOR

CORREGIDOR ISLAND, one of four fortified islands guarding the entrance to Manila Bay, symbolized the incredible stamina and never-say-die attitude of the underdog American forces against the seemingly unstoppable might of Imperial Japan. At least that was the image portrayed by the U.S. media, which looked for any positive slant on the horrifyingly depressing news of early 1942. What Corregidor amounted to for those Americans and Filipinos stranded there by a U.S. military unable to rescue them was a daily routine of stupefying bombardment and death, and the unavoidable end they knew would most certainly come. To the defenders of Corregidor, the gallant picture portrayed by the American media amounted to a grim struggle for survival, which matched their antiquated World War I vintage weapons against the state-of-the-art might of the forces of Japan.

The staid, massive concrete buildings of Fort Mills at the center of the island were gutted and perforated by the almost incessant shelling. Most of the inhabitants were underground, either in the Malinta Tunnel complex or in various bomb shelters near the island's coastal defense gun emplacements. On May 4 alone, as prelude to their invasion of Corregidor, the Japanese landed sixteen thousand artillery shells on the island in a twenty-four-hour period. The elegant prewar base on Corregidor, complete with golf course, swimming pool, movie theater, immaculately landscaped tropical grounds, bathing beach, and streetcar line, was turned into a barren, blasted, shell-hole–pockmarked wasteland.

The sure sign that Corregidor was expendable had come in March when General MacArthur and his family were evacuated. By the time the Japanese invaded on the evening of May 5, 1942, many of the big coastal defense guns and large mortar emplacements had either been blown up or put out of action. Even though the Japanese landing faced stiff opposition that night, by the next day it became clear that the situation was hopeless. As casualties mounted, Lieutenant General Jonathan Wainwright surrendered the remnants of the U.S. Army Forces in the Far East

(USAFFE), numbering roughly thirteen thousand men and a small group of Army nurses, on May 6, 1942.

Corregidor was again to witness the ravages of intense bombardment and death, but this time during the American invasion to retake the island in February 1945. It was after the recapture of "The Rock" that the true extent of the devastating effects of two all-out bombardments three years apart became clear. Visitors today view Corregidor in virtually the state it was found in after its recapture in 1945. The island, once the bustling administrative center of the American military infrastructure in the Philippines, was left almost totally deserted well into the 1980s. Tourists could visit on day trips from Manila, but little was being done to preserve what was left on Corregidor.

Then in 1986, control of the island was transferred from the Philippine Department of National Defense to the Department of Tourism. The Corregidor Foundation was formed to upgrade the island's infrastructure and to supervise development of what is called the Corregidor National Historical Landmark and Tourism Zone. A hotel was constructed near the west entrance to the Malinta Tunnel, overlooking the Bottomside dock areas. The Corregidor Beach Resort was built where American and Filipino prisoners of war were held in the days following the fall of Corregidor. Funds were secured to clear and help preserve what was left of the ruins of the shattered concrete hulks of the Fort Mills buildings and gun emplacements. Many visitors come out from Manila for the historical day trip and are taken to view the ruined buildings and giant guns in open-sided buses made up to look like cars from the prewar electric trolley that ran to all parts of the island. But others stay at the hotel or beach resort, or spend days hiking and camping all over the island. Corregidor——prewar paradise, shell-torn wasteland of death and defeat, and eventual battered but proud symbol of America's victory— has now settled into its present role, described in a glossy tourist brochure, as an island of "historical treasures and diverse adventures."

OPPOSITE, TOP: The North Dock area on Corregidor before the war. Visitors to Corregidor today usually land at the dock at the center of the photo. General MacArthur's entourage, including his wife and four-year-old son, boarded a PT boat that had pulled up to Lorcha Dock at lower right on March 10, 1942. The general's party was evacuated to Mindanao, and taken from there by airplane to Australia.

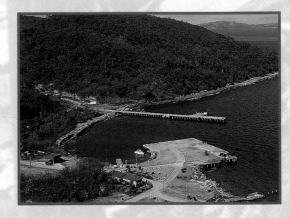

A view of the North Dock area today seen from the top of Malinta Hill. Not much remains of Lorcha Dock at lower right.

OPPOSITE, BOTTOM LEFT: Though battered by bombing and shelling, the remains of Lorcha Dock in this 1978 view show how it withstood the ravages of time for many years after the war.

OPPOSITE, BOTTOM RIGHT: Storm surges and rough seas from passing typhoons have now reduced Lorcha Dock to this state in the late 1990s. To commemorate the departure of MacArthur from this dock, a statue has been erected with the general gesturing toward Malinta Tunnel. The immortal words "I shall return" are emblazoned on the concrete pedestal next to his statue, even though he uttered those words in a speech on his arrival in Australia.

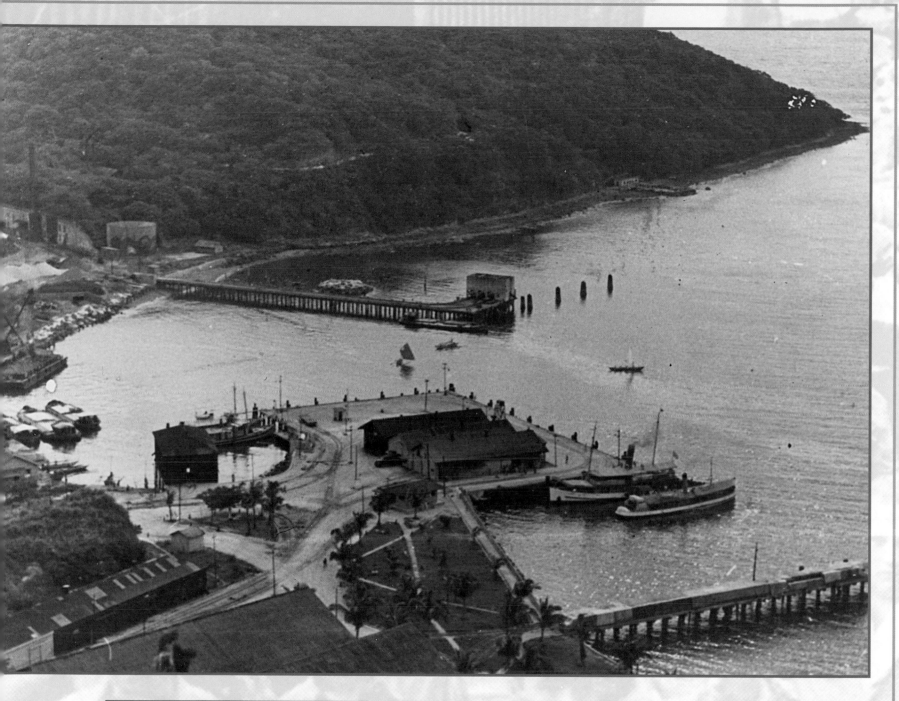

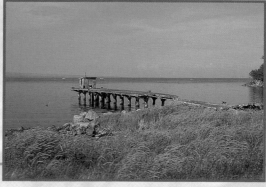

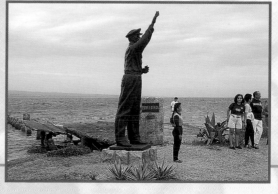

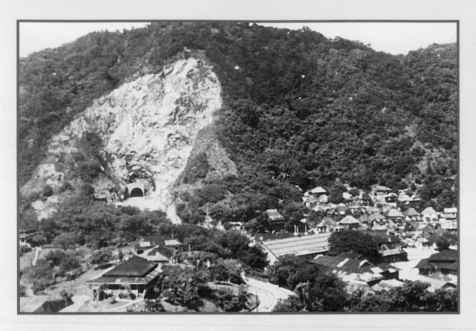

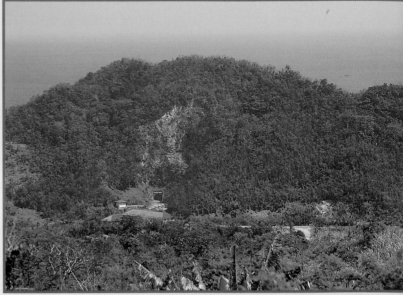

TOP LEFT: Malinta Hill dominates the area called "Bottomside." The landslide-scarred slopes of the old quarry mark the site of the west entrance to the Malinta Tunnel.

TOP RIGHT: A similar view today. All buildings in the Bottomside area were leveled during the war. Today the hotel, a chapel, and several other buildings have been built in the vicinity.

RIGHT: During the 1930s, a complex of tunnels was hewn out of the solid rock of Malinta Hill. The main tunnel passage (the west entrance shown here in a prewar photo) was complete with an electric railway line and had twenty-four laterals branching out from it. This underground facility, including hospital and storage facilities, became known to the world simply as the Malinta Tunnel and was head-quarters of the United States Army Forces in the Far East (USAFFE) after the Japanese shelling made Fort Mills, on the high ground at the center of the island, uninhabitable.

FAR RIGHT: West entrance of the Malinta Tunnel today. The interior of the tunnel's main passage, as well as a number of the laterals and almost all of the hospital laterals, have been restored to their prewar state after numerous explosions inside during the final Japanese defense of the tunnels caused a number of partial cave-ins. One of the more odd commemorative signs on all of Corregidor is placed at the entrance to the lateral that housed island commander General George Moore's office. The sign notes that twenty-five graduates of Texas A. and M. University gathered at that spot on April 21, 1942, for a tradition called the Annual Muster. This event took place only fifteen days before the island fell. The sign goes on to note that twenty "Aggies" (as the school's students are nicknamed) died on Corregidor.

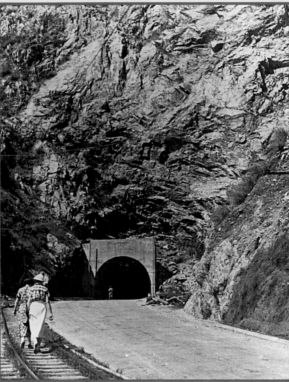

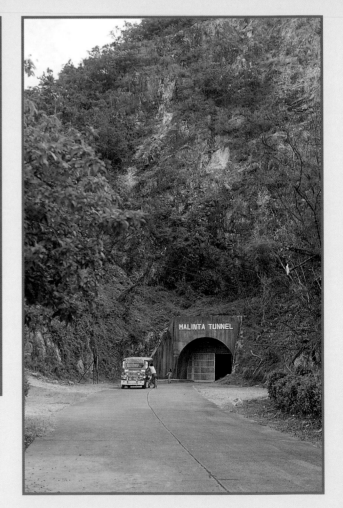

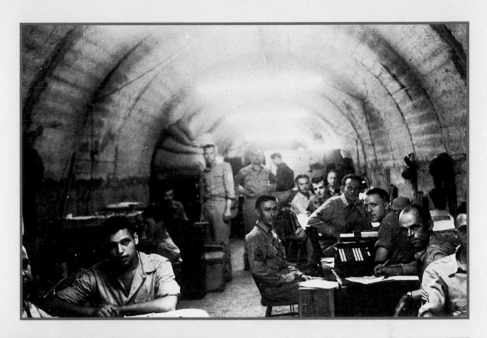

RIGHT: Photo taken during the final stages of the Corregidor siege on May 3, 1942, in the Malinta Tunnel at the entrance to Lateral 12. The finance department is in the foreground, and in the background just out of sight was radio operator Irving Strobing.

BOTTOM: MacArthur and his chief of staff, Major General Richard Sutherland, do not look pleased with their situation in this photo taken at MacArthur's "headquarters" during the siege of Corregidor, near the back of Lateral 3 in the Malinta Tunnel.

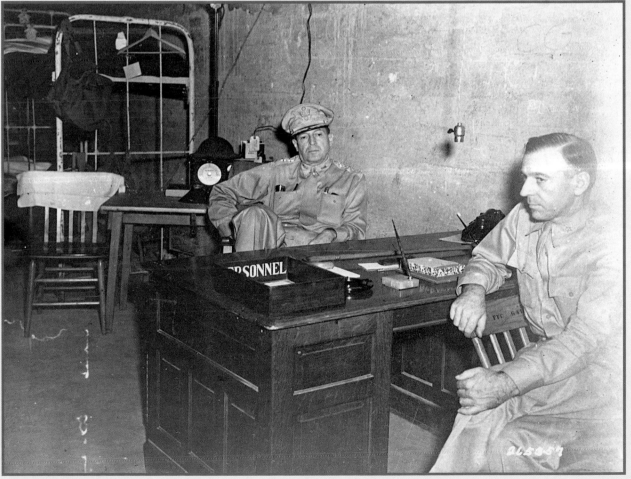

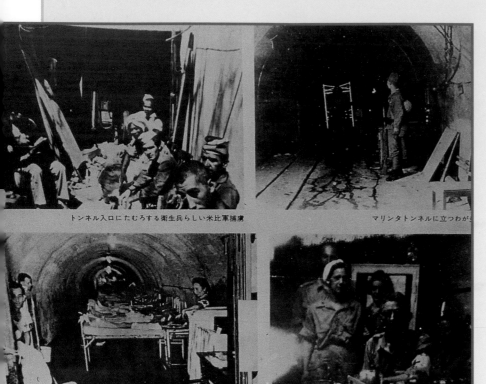

トンネル入口にたむろする衛生兵らしい米比軍捕虜　　　　　　マリンタトンネルに立つわが

LEFT: These photos were taken in the Malinta Tunnel by the Japanese shortly after the fall of Corregidor. The trolley tracks can be seen in the view of the main passage at upper right. One of the hospital laterals is at lower left, and American medical staff, including a couple of nurses, are pictured at lower right. Conditions in the tunnel at this time were recounted in a book by the Belote brothers, James and William, entitled, *Corregidor: The Saga of a Fortress:* "In the tunnel the American and Filipino nurses were not molested, although in anticipation of the worst, they stationed one of their huskier sisters at the entrance to their quarters armed with a large iron skillet. Life for them was anything but pleasant. With nearly a thousand patients to care for, limited to but two slender meals a day, not permitted even to step outside the tunnel for a breath of fresh air, they settled into a numbing, monotonous routine existence. . . . together with the doctors and enlisted medical personnel, the nurses finally left Corregidor in early July to spend the rest of the war practicing their profession under slightly better conditions at the Santo Tomas civilian internment camp in Manila."

BOTTOM LEFT: During the retaking of the Malinta Tunnel by the Americans in 1945, numerous powerful explosive charges were set off by the remaining Japanese, who were killed in the blasts. The concrete lining of the tunnel was seriously damaged. After the war the central shaft of the tunnel was restored along with at least parts of the laterals that branch from the main passageway. Today, the main shaft, shown here, closely resembles its appearance during the war.

BOTTOM RIGHT: Several of the restored laterals now house dioramas depicting aspects of the history of the tunnel. This one, showing the Japanese occupation of the tunnel after the defeated Americans were removed from the island, and the others are part of the "sound-and-light show" inside the tunnel.

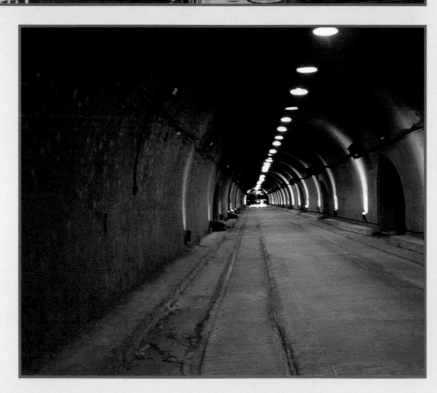

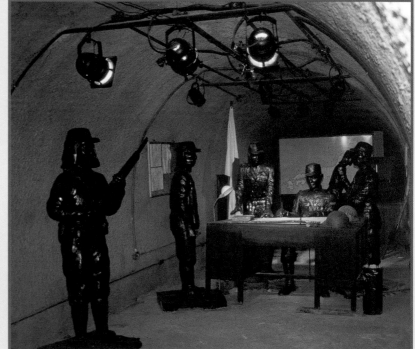

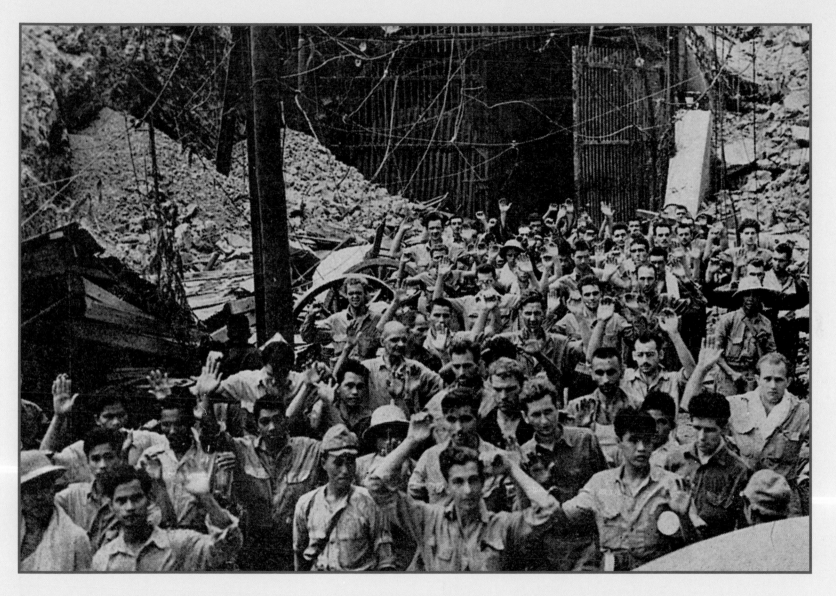

U.S. and Filipino troops, grim-faced and exhausted after the ordeal of the siege, surrender to the Japanese outside the west entrance to Malinta Tunnel in this captured photo taken on the afternoon of May 6, 1942. Radio operator Irving Strobing, at his post near the rear of Lateral 12, sent off a rambling yet poignant "last message" that was widely reproduced in the U.S. after the surrender (". . . definitely against all regulations," recalled Strobing, "but what were they going to do to me?"). Everyone in the tunnel had heard rumors of a Japanese tank approaching.

Immediately they all realized that a tank could drive right through the tunnel, stopping to fire down the length of each crowded lateral as it went. But then word came that the surrender had occurred. General Wainwright, a beloved leader dear to the hearts of all the men who served on Corregidor, had decided to end the now-pointless struggle before more Americans and Filipinos were killed. Strobing remembered, "A Japanese officer and some others walked into the tunnel, and we all had to come out into the main

tunnel for a short surrender ceremony. Then we went out the west entrance [shown in this photo] and we were all just kind of standing around. After a while many of us sat down, but then we saw General Wainwright and his officers go down to the dock. The Japanese were taking them over to Manila for the formal surrender. We were all exhausted from the siege and we hadn't slept much in a few days, but we all got up, stood at attention, and saluted as the general got on that boat. I think every man there was crying, but there wasn't a sound."

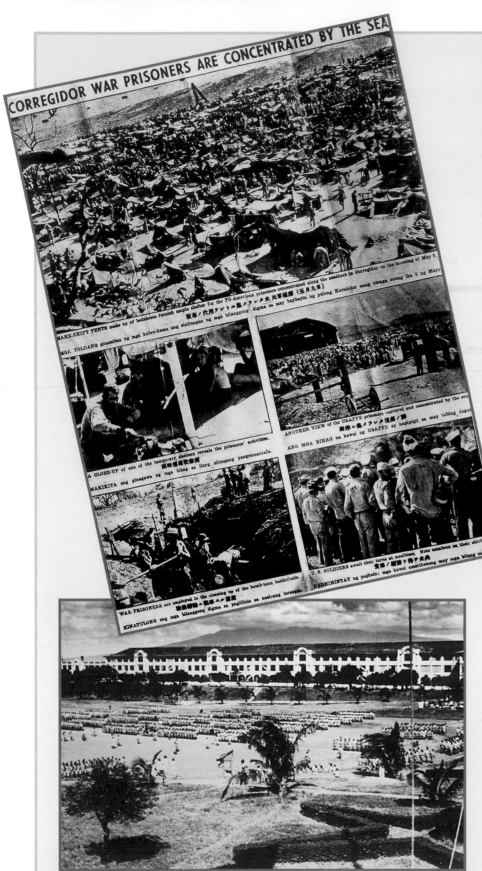

CORREGIDOR WAR PRISONERS ARE CONCENTRATED BY THE SEA

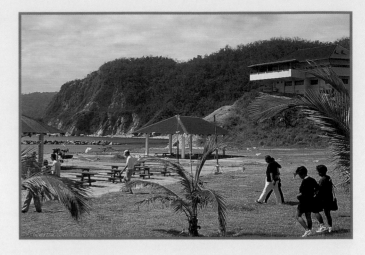

LEFT: For the first couple of days after the surrender of Corregidor, it seemed like the Japanese didn't quite know what to do with the American and Filipino troops they had captured. Irving Strobing recalled, "They didn't have enough food to feed us so they kind of let us scavenge for things to eat." Strobing was taken with several others to care for Japanese wounded. "We were each assigned one wounded man, and we had to sit with them. When mine wanted water I had to give him a drink, or mop his brow, or things like that."

After a couple of days Strobing and the other captives on Corregidor were herded to a large concrete-surfaced space called the Ninety-second Garage area. Here, the Americans and Filipinos began to learn what captivity under the Japanese was all about. In their book *Corregidor: The Saga of a Fortress*, the Belote brothers described the scene: ". . . the Ninety-second Garage area [was] a two-block-sized basin on the south shore just east of Malinta Hill. At one time the area had been the island's seaplane station; later it was converted into the motor pool for the Ninety-second Coast Artillery. For the sixteen thousand miserable Americans and Filipinos it was hellish. Except for the shrapnel-riddled shells of two large hangars, there was no shade at all. Thousands of vicious, biting, blue-black flies swarmed everywhere. The Filipinos, whom the Japanese had segregated from the Americans, arrived first and appropriated one of the two hangars. The other was reserved for five hundred of the officers. The remaining thousands of men found what comfort they could in the open, on concrete and earth. To

escape the painful 'Guam blisters' raised by the relentless tropical sun, they erected little shelters from canvas, blankets, and corrugated sheet iron." These photos, taken from a Japanese English-language newspaper distributed in Manila, show life for the captives much as described by the Belote brothers in their book. The photo at top shows the shelters erected by the men out on the open concrete. After fifteen days in the open, the captives were shipped to Manila and paraded down the streets. This display was designed to provoke scorn from the Filipinos, but had the opposite effect instead as the residents of Manila took pity on the prisoners. The only consolation for the Corregidor captives was that they did not have to suffer the deprivations of a death march, as did their comrades following the surrender of Bataan. After the ill-conceived parade through Manila, most were shipped to the prisoner camp at Cabanatuan, and were later distributed throughout the Philippines and Japan.

ABOVE: Today the Ninety-second Garage area is the grounds for the Corregidor Beach Resort. Picnic shelters and bungalows have been built on the concrete in the foreground where American and Filipino captives suffered in the glaring sun. In the background on the hill overlooking the area is the restaurant and conference facility of the resort.

BOTTOM LEFT: The heart of Fort Mills on Corregidor was the "Topside" area on the high ground at the center of the island. Depicted in this 1933 photo is the Topside Parade Ground. In the background is the massive, concrete "Mile Long" Topside Barracks.

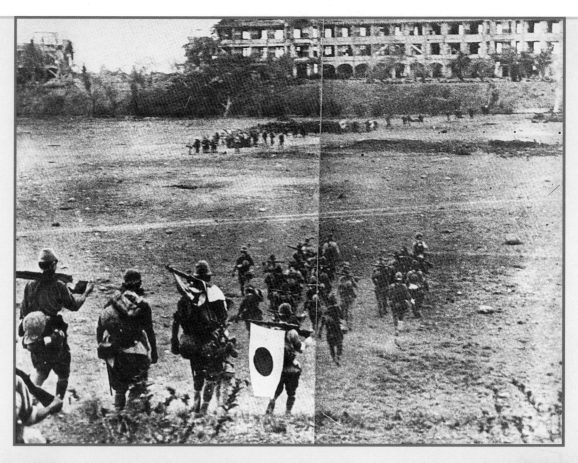

RIGHT: Captured photo showing Japanese troops crossing the Topside Parade Ground after their successful invasion of Corregidor in May 1942. The devastated Topside Barracks can be seen in the background.

BELOW LEFT: The deserted remains of Topside Barracks still look down on the Parade Ground in the foreground. The concrete helicopter pad is a recent addition.

BELOW CENTER: In this photo taken from the Topside Barracks building in 1937, the post headquarters building can be seen at left, and the iron flagpole flying the Stars and Stripes is at center.

BELOW RIGHT: The roofless, bombed-out shell of the post headquarters building today.

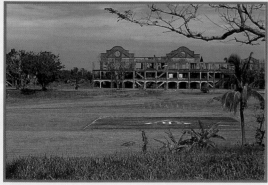

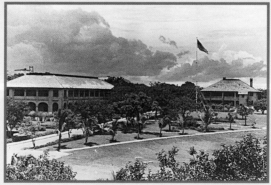

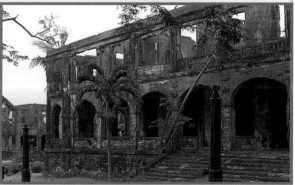

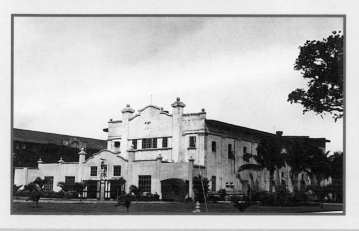

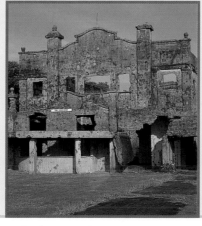

FAR LEFT: The Fort Mills movie theater in early 1941. Close inspection of the marquee on the front of the "Post Cine," as it was called, reveals that the feature attraction was the 1936 Eleanor Powell movie, *Born to Dance.*

LEFT: The remains of the bombard-ment-scarred shell of the movie theater. The thick concrete walls were perforated by the repeated blasts of bombs and shells.

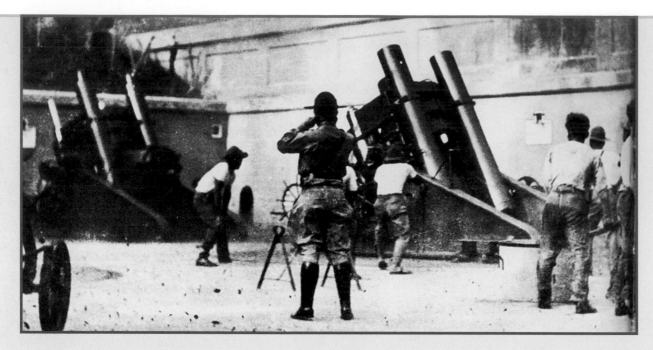

ABOVE: A prewar photo of the M-1908 mortars of Battery Geary. On January 26, 1942, these twelve-inch mortars fired sixteen rounds of seven-hundred-pound shells into Japanese positions on the Bataan Peninsula. This was the first major action by large coastal artillery guns against a hostile force since the Battle of Fort Sumter in 1861. Battery Geary consisted of these four mortars in Pit A, and four older M-1890 mortars in adjacent Pit B. A heavily reinforced concrete magazine separated the two pits. The concrete wall in the background marks the outer wall of the center magazine. After intense shelling, the M-1908 mortars pictured here were out of commission in early May. The older mortars in the far pit on the other side of the magazine were still being fired, but Japanese shelling was gradually eating its way through the concrete wall of the magazine pictured here. The commanding officer of Battery Geary, Captain Thomas Davis, ordered his men to start emptying the magazine of powder charges. The job was only partially completed when, at 4:27 P.M. on May 2 during an extended period of vicious Japanese shelling, a 240-mm shell finally penetrated the weakened concrete wall of the center magazine and ignited the remaining powder charges inside. There was a tremendous explosion that completely destroyed Battery Geary and rained mortars, ammunition, and chunks of concrete down over a large area. Most of the men had taken shelter in a gallery on the far side of the battery. Miraculously, only six men were killed and six wounded of Geary's sixty-man crew. Davis's decision to go against orders and partially empty the magazine had, fortunately, resulted in a still-huge but just barely survivable blast for most of the men.

BOTTOM LEFT: The remains of Battery Geary today. The one-hundred-foot diameter crater at the center of the photo marks the explosion that was ignited in the magazine at the center of the battery. The massive concrete magazine structure was completely obliterated in the explosion, leaving only the grass-covered crater shown here. In the foreground is one of the remaining M-1890 mortars from Pit B. In the background is the remains of Pit A pictured above. One of the thirteen-ton steel mortars from Pit A was launched 150 yards through the air and landed on the golf course. Two others were driven sideways through the wall of the gallery at the far end of the photo; the end of one can be seen projecting out from under the concrete roof of the collapsed gallery at center back. Another mortar from Pit A was thrown about 100 feet and still lies at the side of the road at far center back.

BOTTOM RIGHT: Close-up view of one of two M-1908 steel mortars driven through the concrete gallery wall at left by the massive explosion of Battery Geary.

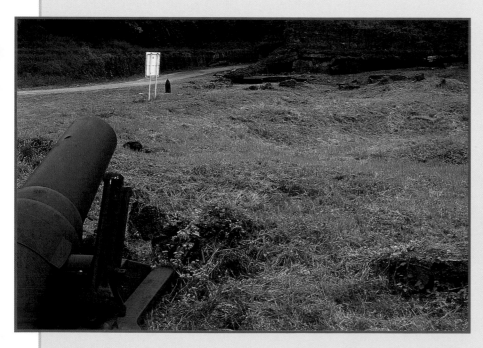

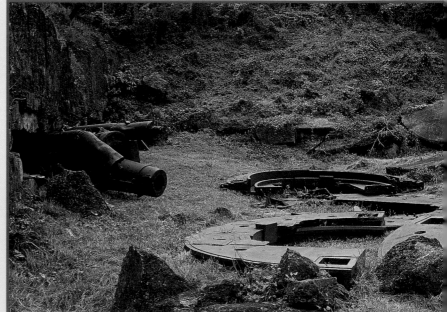

RIGHT: Captured Japanese photo, most likely posed beside the twelve-inch gun of Battery Hearn on Corregidor shortly after its capture in May 1942.

BOTTOM LEFT: Scarred by shrapnel from shells that exploded nearby, the long-range twelve-inch gun of Battery Hearn still points skyward. Designed as a flat-trajectory gun to be used against ships threatening from the sea, it was pressed into service to fire on Japanese land targets on the Bataan Peninsula.

BOTTOM RIGHT: A view of Battery Way shortly after Corregidor was recaptured by the Americans in 1945. During the Japanese invasion of Corregidor the night of May 5 and morning of May 6, Major William "Wild Bill" Massello and his gun crews endured almost

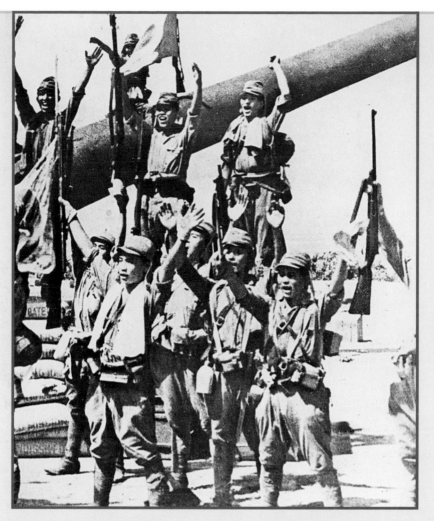

continual Japanese shelling and debilitating casualties to keep firing the only functioning mortar, the one at far right, on the Japanese landing barges and positions on Bataan. The Japanese shelling decimated gun crew after gun crew, but as soon as one crew was hit, another would jump from cover to replace them. By the time the mortar finally quit firing during the middle of the morning of May 6, after the breechlock froze, casualties were over 70 percent. Many men had been knocked unconscious from concussion or were suffering from horrific shrapnel wounds. Massello was still alive, barely, and was in command in the gun pit until the end, though his arm was nearly severed and he had sustained a serious leg wound.

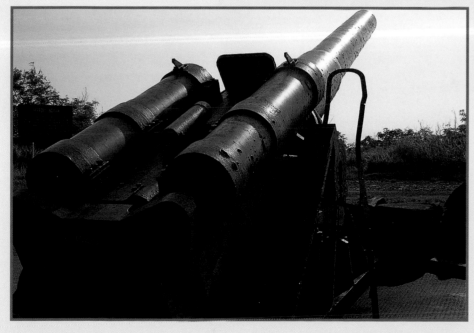

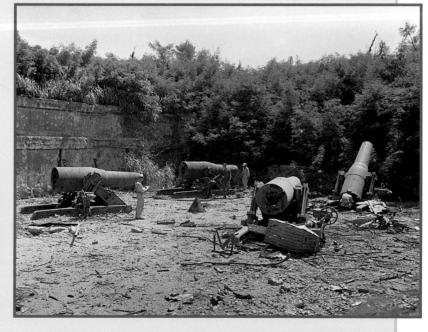

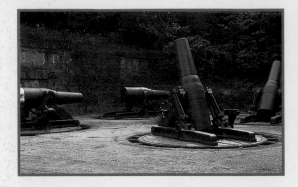

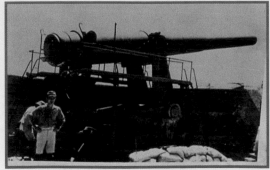

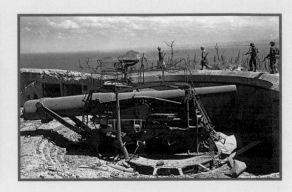

TOP LEFT: A present-day view of Battery Way. The last big gun on Corregidor to fire on the enemy, the mortar at far right, is still pointed skyward in its final position.

TOP CENTER: A captured Japanese photo taken after the fall of Corregidor shows a member of the Japanese occupation forces posed in front of one of the guns of Battery Crockett.

TOP RIGHT: The Japanese did work on some of the American batteries to attempt to |make them operational, but usually with little success. Some repair was done on this gun in Battery Crockett, but it was not in firing condition when the Americans recaptured Corregidor early in 1945.

BOTTOM LEFT: This same gun in shell-scarred Battery Crockett today. This battery was the scene of the amazing ordeal of Captain Lester Fox, a Fifty-ninth Coast Artillery surgeon. As described by the Belote brothers in their book, on April 24 the Japanese started to shell Battery Crockett. Captain Fox was in the battalion aid station, and "... fire had broken out in the hoist room and several men had been wounded, Fox was busy giving aid. More shells crashed through, breaking his leg, but as he recalled it years later, '... I hopped around on my other leg and was able to organize the remaining men in the battery to put out the fires that were threatening the powder magazine.' Still more shells hit, '... ripping off part of my right elbow and producing many soft tissue wounds scattered throughout the right side of my body.' The others fled the compartment, shells continued to explode, '... and I was wounded repeatedly; in the right eyebrow, losing the sight of my right eye, fracturing several ribs, and generally making me very mad.' Although it seems impossible, this tough doctor survived to be carried to the Malinta hospital after the shelling, and from there to pass into captivity as a patient when the Rock surrendered."

BELOW: There are a number of monuments on Corregidor today. This one commemorates the cooperation of American and Filipino soldiers during the siege of Corregidor.

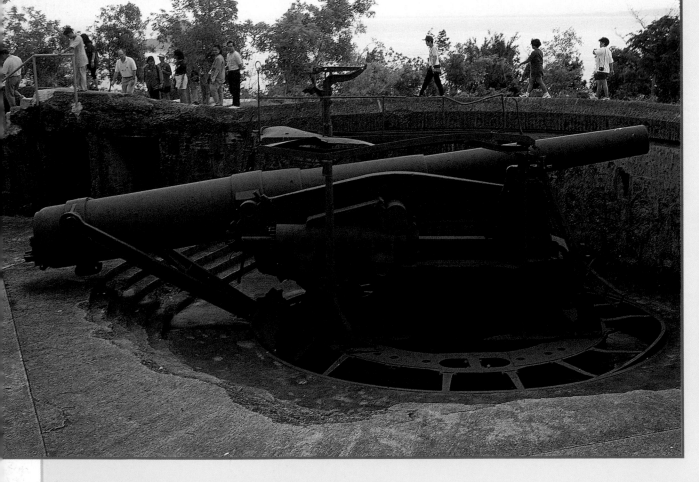

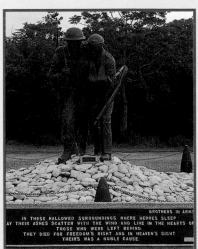

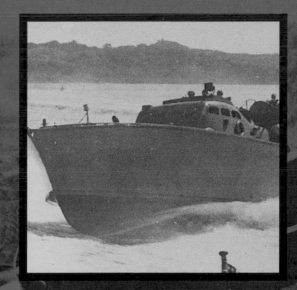

CHAPTER 3

THE LONG ROAD BACK
Invading Guadalcanal

BY MIDSUMMER 1942 Americans on the Home Front were beginning to breathe a little easier. Back in those frightening winter months when every newscast carried word of new defeats, many had come to think we could actually lose the war. Now, however, Americans were beginning to take a different view. The Doolittle Raid on Tokyo, the naval victory in the Coral Sea, and the smashing defeat of Japan's Navy at Midway proved that the enemy was not invincible after all. True, the news from Europe was still all bad, but even so there was growing confidence that victory, though perhaps slow in coming, would eventually be won.

But as the Home Front fears of defeat began to fade, the discomforts of a wartime economy began to grow. To prevent runaway wartime currency inflation, price controls had been imposed on most civilian goods. As a result things that could not be profitably produced within the limitations of imposed "ceiling" prices either were not available or were only found at outlandish prices on the illegal Black Market. No automobiles had been built since January, and until the end of the war none would be. All current inventory had been taken for use by government agencies and the Armed Forces.

Gasoline was rationed, and no car owner whose driving could not be proved essential to the war effort could buy more than three gallons per week. Shoes were rationed, too, as were sugar, meat, butter, and a host of other food and consumer items. And compounding the food problem was the fact that even at the unheard-of wage of twenty dollars per day (which only a year or two earlier had been considered a decent week's income), farm labor was so hard to come by that more than 25 percent of America's commercial fruit and vegetable crops had to be left unpicked and rotting in the field. Accordingly, in cities all across the land people began converting backyards and lawns into Victory Gardens, growing vegetables in window boxes, and home-canning what they produced.

With so many men gone to military service, unprecedented numbers of women were entering the labor force, especially in war production, and "Rosie the Riveter" became the heroine of the day. Rosie would have, however, no more silk or nylon stockings to wear in her off hours. All available silk was needed for powder bags for the Navy's heavy guns, and all available nylon was needed for parachutes and a host of other things. So, when Rosie went dancing at night she painted her legs with a special makeup material that made it appear she was wearing stockings, and with a special pencil she drew a seam-line up the back of each leg.

On the other hand, most people on the Home Front were earning more money than they had ever earned before, and despite the inconveniences of rationing and shortages, most were managing to enjoy it. They flocked to movie theaters to see Greer Garson in *Mrs. Miniver*, Fred MacMurray as Rosalind Russell's private secretary in *Take A Letter, Darling*, Alan Ladd and Veronica Lake in *This Gun for Hire*, and James Cagney in the smash hit *Yankee Doodle Dandy*. And they flocked, too, to record stores to buy Kay Kyser's recording of "The White Cliffs of Dover," the Andrews Sisters' "Boogie-Woogie Bugle Boy from Company B," the Title Spinners doing "Comin' in on a Wing and a Prayer," Sammy Kaye's rendition of "Remember Pearl Harbor" as well as such wartime gems as "Der Fuehrer's Face" by Spike Jones, Teddy Powell's rendition of "Goodbye Mamma. I'm Off to Yokohama." Or, perhaps, Lucky Mellender's or Carson Robinson's rendition of "We're Gonna Have to Slap the Dirty Little Jap," a song optimistically promoted as "one of the best tunes yet written about our scrap in the Pacific."

America's military planners, on the other hand, were not breathing easier. They saw the situation just as columnist Raymond Clapper saw it that summer when he wrote, "Never before has individual freedom hung so precariously in the balance. . . ." In the Atlantic German U-boats were sinking Allied ships faster than they could be replaced—racking up an incredible total of 365 Allied vessels in the first five months of the year alone. In Eastern Europe the German Army, rolling relentlessly eastward, appeared certain to capture Moscow. In North Africa another relentlessly rolling German army had pushed British and Australian forces eastward until their backs were against the Egyptian border.

In the Pacific the Japanese, despite heavy losses at Midway, still had the Allies greatly outnumbered in men and ships and planes and guns. Moreover, the Japanese Zero could outperform any fighter plane the Allies had. As Marine Ace Captain Joe Foss put it, "When you're flying an F4F Wildcat and meet a Jap flying a Zero you're outnumbered."

Now, the Japanese were about to use those superior forces to cut the long Allied supply line to Australia. Should they succeed, no power on earth could prevent them from invading Australia and New Zealand. And those nations, whose fighting men were almost all in North Africa tackling Germans, would surely fall like ripe apples to the Japanese.

As Allied strategists saw it, the key to the Japanese plan of cutting off supplies to Australia must lie in the Solomons, an obscure group of Australian Mandated islands lying about a thousand miles off Australia's northeastern coast. These were not the romantic, carefree Pacific-paradise kind of islands dear to filmmakers and novelists of the time. On the contrary, they were a collection of miserable, malaria-ridden pestholes reeking of tropical rot, of rivers rife with crocodiles, and of land infested with unimaginable numbers of biting insects. As Joe Foss recalled it later, "The island of Guadalcanal was a rude shock for a guy from the plains of South Dakota. . . . There were only two seasons: Wet, hot and steamy and wetter, hotter and steamier. . . . Mosquitoes thick as termites in a woodpile . . . and these buggers were the sticking kind. They'd swarm over your face so thick you had to wipe them off, and before you were done they'd be covering the other side of your face. I think they even got hooked on the repellent we used." Author Herman Melville, a hundred years earlier, must have had a similar experience in the Pacific: "If I were a king the worst punishment I could inflict on my enemies would be to banish them to the Solomons."

Miserable the Solomons may have been physically,

but in that summer of 1942 they were of supreme importance strategically. To successfully isolate and conquer Australia the Japanese had to have them. To prevent that catastrophe the Allies had to have them. And the Japanese got there first. On April 1 they had occupied the island of Buka. On May 3 they took Tulagi, capital island of the Solomons, and there they began constructing a seaplane base. In June the Americans, laying plans to retake Tulagi "and adjacent areas," sent the First Marine Division to New Zealand.

On July 4 Japanese troops landed on the north shore of an island they knew as Gadarukanaru, which the Allies knew as Guadalcanal, and they commenced construction of an airfield that could handle both bombers and fighters. A few days later an American reconnaissance B-17 found and photographed the operation. And at that point the Allies needed to retake both Tulagi and Guadalcanal, and the need went from urgent to imperative. For that field, if the enemy were allowed to make it operational, would provide Japan with the sought-after control of Australia's air and sea-link to the United States on southern New Guinea.

The Solomons invasion plan had its naysayers. Both General MacArthur, now elegantly entitled Supreme Commander, Southwest Pacific Ocean Area (COMSWPOA) and Vice Admiral Robert Ghormley, Commander of the South Pacific Fleet (COMSOPAC), were powerfully opposed. The planned operation was code-named Watchtower, but MacArthur and Ghormley said it should have been called Shoestring, and with good reason. The Solomons were too far away for support by land-based aircraft, and air cover could be provided only by using the Navy's too-few carriers, exposing them to destruction by superior Japanese naval forces, as well as a large force of land-planes from the huge enemy base at Rabaul, some six hundred miles to the north. On top of that, said Ghormley, the United States didn't have enough shipping in the Pacific for execution of such an operation, nor enough supplies to support it, nor naval power to protect it. Moreover, General MacArthur pointed out, the only force presently available for the operation was the First Marine Division now arriving in New Zealand, a division consisting mainly of green troops, untested and, so he believed, undertrained.

President Roosevelt and his Naval chief of staff, Admiral Ernest King, knew the risks but knew also they were caught between the devil and the deep blue sea. To attack the Solomons and fail would be a disaster. But allowing the Japanese to establish bases there would almost certainly lead to catastrophe. So, in a decision much like that of George Washington deciding to cross the Delaware, they ordered Watchtower to proceed with D-Day set for August 1, 1942.

When they cast that die only three weeks remained in which to prepare for the operation—far too little time for any amphibious invasion, and especially for this one, America's first.

The initial problem was with the supply ships. It is imperative that those supporting an invasion must be "combat loaded" so that the things first needed on the beaches are the first to be unloaded. Mortars, howitzers, ammunition, jeeps, trucks, drinking water, food, field kitchens, field hospitals and medical supplies, lumber, mobile repair shops, shovels, tents, blankets, trench diggers, bulldozers, mechanic's tools, field telephones and telephone wire, radios, typewriters, desks and other office supplies, electricity generators, and a thousand other things all must be stowed in the proper order. "Getting ready to send out a troop convoy," wrote Raymond Clapper, "is like trying to empty a dozen mail-order houses at once." And the fantastically complex process of getting it loaded just right, observed a Coast Guard cargo officer, "Is a chess game you cannot win."

But some of the supply ships arriving at Wellington, New Zealand, in early July did not come combat loaded. They would have to be emptied and their cargoes completely reorganized and reloaded in the proper order. It was something skilled longshoremen working long hours could easily accomplish in the two to three weeks remaining before they were to sail for Guadalcanal. But to the disgust and even fury of Watchtower's commanders, the heavily unionized longshoremen of New Zealand refused to work long hours or on weekends, war or no war. As a consequence the Marines, themselves, pitched in to do the job, and by working around the clock did get it done on time.

Another problem was the attitude of some of the operation's key commanders. If a military operation is to succeed, and especially one as risky as this, it needs the wholehearted support of all those who are to lead it. But this one did not have that support. Its overall commander, the brilliant but cautious Admiral Ghormley, even asked to have the operation postponed. When that was denied he proceeded with it as ordered but made no secret of the fact he expected it to fail. And at a fiery commanders' conference held on the aircraft carrier *Saratoga* on July 26, the commander of the battle group, Admiral Frank Fletcher, also made no secret of the fact that he, too, believed the invasion to be an exercise in foolhardiness. In fact, he said, it would so endanger his three aircraft carriers that he would allow them to provide the invasion with only forty-eight hours of air cover before being withdrawn. At that, Admiral Kelly Turner, commander of the transport fleet, exploded. He could not possibly unload all the troops and supplies in fewer than five days, he said. And yet Fletcher was going to leave his cargo ships and transports naked to enemy air attacks for three of those days!

Major General A. A. "Sunny Jim" Vandegrift, commander of the First Marine Division, was just as upset, telling Fletcher that leaving the Marines without air cover on a hostile beachhead would be tantamount to murder.

Finally Fletcher gave in a little bit, but only a little. He would provide air cover for seventy-two hours, he said, but not a minute more. And as he was the senior officer present (Ghormley not attending) that's how the matter was left.

Under cover of darkness on the night of August 6, Admiral Turner's transports and cargo ships and their military escort finally came down into Sealark Channel, soon for good reason to be known as Iron Bottom Sound. They were to have been there a week earlier, but the complications of putting Operation Pestilence together (as the invasion was now known) had proved to be just too great for that schedule. But they were here now, in the narrow waters between the islands of Guadalcanal on the south and Tulagi on the north. Aboard the transport *MacCawley* (the "Wacky Mac" to her men) General Vandegrift, knowing this was to be a shaky operation at best, wrote what he hoped would not be his last letter to his wife: "Our plans have been made and God grant that our judgment has been sound. . . . Whatever happens you'll know that I did my best. Let us hope that best will be enough."

Aboard the transport *American Legion,* war correspondent Richard Tregaskis, here to cover this first American landing of the war, was up and on deck before dawn: "The fact that we had got this far without any action made us feel strangely secure. . . . The thing that was happening was so unbelievable that it seemed like a dream. . . . We were slipping through the neck of water between Guadalcanal and Savo Island . . . and not a shot had been fired. Suddenly I saw a brilliant flash of yellow-green light coming from the gray shape of a cruiser on our starboard bow. I saw the red pencil-lines of the shells arching through the sky, saw dark flashes on the dark shore of Guadalcanal where they struck. . . . I looked at my watch. The time was 6:14."

Now, the invasion beaches on both Guadalcanal and Tulagi begin flashing fire from a preinvasion bombardment by four cruisers, six destroyers, and eighty-four planes from Fletcher's aircraft carriers. With minesweepers bustling about ahead of them the transports were split into two groups. Fifteen of them came to anchor about four miles off Guadalcanal and another four about the same distance from Tulagi, and all began preparing to land men and cargo. But because the landing operations on Guadalcanal cannot tolerate air interference from the enemy seaplane base on Tulagi, at 7:30 two companies of the First Marine Raiders under Colonel Merritt Edson debark to put a stop to that. At eight o'clock they report having landed. At 8:15 Edson radios, "Landing successful. No opposition." Shortly thereafter they are going to find opposition,

and plenty of it. They have, however, neutralized the seaplane base, and that is the important thing at the moment.

Aboard the transport *George F. Elliot* machine gunner Robert Leckie, H Company, Second Battalion, has been on deck since daylight. From below decks the bombardment had sounded so fierce, he wrote, that he expected upon emerging into "that dirty dawn" to "see the world alight." But actually he saw on the distant shore only "a few fires flickering, like the city dumps, to light our path to history."

At seven o'clock whistles had blown, bos'n's pipes shrilled, and Marines, looking like flies crawling a wall, swarmed by the hundreds down cargo nets hanging from the sides of the transports and into the little thirty-six-foot LCPs (Landing Craft, Personnel) that were to take them to the shores of Guadalcanal.

For the men in the boats, most of whom have never faced a military enemy nor heard a shot fired in anger, now is a time of waiting. And suppose for a moment you are one of those troops, untested, waiting tense and dry-mouthed, thinking long thoughts born of a mixed bag of feelings. You are as frightened as you have ever been. You are about to die—to become a tragic, bullet-riddled bundle, bleeding and dying on an unknown beach so very far from home.

At the same time, however, you know you will not die. Having never known a world without you in it, you cannot conceive of one now. Besides, you are a tough, trained, competent warrior—you are a Marine. When you first arrived for training at Parris Island or Camp Pendleton, you were told by your drill instructors that you were nothing. You were, in their oft-repeated phrases, a simple shithead, a miserable piece of human flesh that they would try with little hope of success to train. But what they did with their never-ending assaults on your attitudes, ego, and dignity was to disassemble you as a civilian and reassemble you as a Marine. And when you finally were graduated from their clutches, trained, toughened, and disciplined, you were a Marine. You knew it. They knew it and let you know they did, and sent you forth feeling chesty and proud. They sent you forth feeling you were a tough and able Marine in the best damn service in the best damn country in the world and with a loyalty to the Marines that will last all the rest of your life.

Besides, you are not alone. You are a member of a squad and that squad has become your family. You have learned to rely upon each other and to know that upon the performance of each rests the lives of all. And so, really, your great fear is not of dying but of failing to do your part, of letting your squad-mates down, or of the unbearable disgrace of having them see you cower or flee. And although you may not know it, it is this fear, the fear of failing your comrades or showing cowardice, that has served as the main wellspring of combat courage since the beginning of time, and it will so serve you now.

AUGUST 7, 1942, 8:40 A.M.: Destroyers take up positions marking the line of departure for Guadalcanal invasion boats.

9:00 A.M.: Fire-support group begins pounding the landing beaches. Landing craft start in. When the first wave is thirteen hundred yards off the beach, naval fire stops.

9:10 A.M.: Fifth Marines land on a sixteen-hundred-yard front against no opposition, which is almost disappointing to men who have been so keyed up to meet it. But the Japanese, caught by surprise, have fled—so precipitously as to leave food still on the tables in their mess tents. Unknown to the landing Marines, there were only about five hundred Japanese in the area anyhow, mostly construction workers of the Rikusentai Battalion, together with a few combat troops. Overwhelmingly outnumbered and outgunned they have abandoned everything and taken to the jungle.

Marine units move inland to set up a defense perimeter bounded by three creeks and the beach. On the beach, meanwhile, things are becoming a jumbled mess. Coast Guard and Navy boats are delivering supplies faster than the Marines can handle them. They ask the Navy for men to help clear the mess, are refused, and the situation becomes even more jumbled.

At the huge Japanese base at Rabaul, Admiral Yamamoto knows he simply cannot afford to allow Guadalcanal and its airfield to fall into Allied hands and sends twenty-seven Betty bombers and eighteen Zero fighters to hammer both the beaches and the ships in the sound. On Bougainville Island coast-watcher Paul Mason sees them and radios a report: "Twenty-seven bombers headed southeast." These bombers attack and scatter the transports in the sound but damage none. The destroyer *Mugford*, however, is hit by a bomb that kills twenty-two men, and the destroyer *Jarvis* is hit by a torpedo. American F4Fs from Fletcher's carriers attack and shoot down sixteen Japanese planes while losing twelve of their own. The Japanese lose an estimated fourteen additional planes from fuel exhaustion due to the long range of the attack.

AUGUST 8: On shore the principal action is organizing, taking the airfield—which is done without opposition—setting up defense perimeters, trying to clear the jumble on the beach, trying to move heavy guns through the mud without the proper prime-movers to pull them. Across the sound Marine units have secured the island of Tulagi, and the First Parachute Battalion has captured the tiny island of Gavutu.

Out among the ships, however, things are less peaceful. Determined to nip this invasion in the bud, Yamamoto has sent waves of bombers and torpedo planes to destroy the Marines' sources of supply. Although seventeen of the attackers are shot down, they hit and seriously damage the eight-thousand-ton transport *Barnett* and sink the eleven-thousand-ton transport *George F. Elliot*. Even worse, the intensity of the attack causes Admiral Fletcher to renege on his promise of seventy-two hours of air cover. He seeks and obtains permission to take his battle fleet with its precious carriers out of harm's way and to keep it out until there are enough land-based aircraft on Guadalcanal to protect them. He departs late in the afternoon, leaving behind only six cruisers and eight destroyers to guard the men on the beach.

AUGUST 9: Fletcher's withdrawal has left Turner's transport and supply fleet entirely unprotected from air attacks that are sure to come. Moreover, Turner has already lost one ship, almost lost another, and doesn't intend to lose any more. And so even though the ships are far from being unloaded he, too, takes his fleet out of harm's way, and with it about half the invasion's supplies of food, weapons, ammunition, construction equipment, gasoline, medical supplies, etc., and even some still-unloaded troops.

The worst, however, was yet to come. That night a Japanese force of seven cruisers and one destroyer slipped undetected into Sealark Channel, catching the Allied cruiser force unprepared. In a matter of mere minutes the Japanese inflicted one of the worst defeats in the history of the American Navy. The American cruisers *Vincennes, Astoria,* and *Quincy* and the Australian cruiser *Canberra* were sunk, and the American cruiser *Chicago* and the destroyers *Patterson* and *Ralph Talbot* were badly damaged. One thousand and twenty-three American and Australian sailors were dead; 709 were wounded. The Japanese, on the other hand, lost only 58 dead, had 53 wounded, and suffered slight damage to three cruisers.

Now the Marines on the beaches were truly alone. Unprotected by sea or by air, and with half their supplies —including the entire stock of some essentials—gone with Turner's transports, they had been abandoned and they knew it. And all General Vandegrift could say to them was, "It's now up to us to hold on. Remember, you are Marines."

The one positive thing about the situation was that the departure of the fleets caused Yamamoto to believe the Americans were abandoning their invasion attempt. So, instead of attempting to land massive forces to oppose them, he began sending in small detachments to mop up any American forces remaining on the island.

The Americans meanwhile were struggling to make the airfield operational. And it was a struggle because much of the machinery and equipment they needed was still aboard the departed transports. Nevertheless, with machinery the Japanese had abandoned, the Marines managed to have the airfield ready on August 20 for the carrier *Long Island* to deliver nineteen Marine F4F fighter planes and twelve Marine SBD Dauntless dive-bombers. In a ceremony following their arrival, General Vandegrift broke a bottle of captured sake against a wall of the field's only remaining building; then, he declared, in honor of Marine flier Lofton Henderson who died at Midway, "I christen thee Henderson Field." And because the code name for Guadalcanal was "Cactus," the air units based there became informally known from that time forward as "the Cactus Air Force."

On the next day, August 21, the troops Yamamoto had been sending to "mop up" Guadalcanal—the Ichiki Battalion—finally made their attack. At ten after three in the morning 250 of them charged screaming across a sandbar at the mouth of the Ilu River near the edge of Henderson Field. The Americans, however, were dug in and prepared and in fifty minutes of fierce combat had wiped out the entire group. Meanwhile a Marine battalion crossed the Ilu upstream and by dawn was in position for a flanking counterattack. Then five American tanks crossed the river and joined the action. By afternoon it was all over. All but 2 of the 800 men in the Ichiki Battalion's attack force were dead, and the only other Japanese survivors were 125 men left behind to guard the beach where the battalion had landed.

It was a fantastically lopsided American victory. The U.S. had lost only thirty-five killed (one for every twenty-three Japanese) and seventy-five wounded. But it was more than that. It was a turning point. Up until now the men of the Japanese Army, rolling undefeated in every land encounter across the Pacific, had begun to appear invincible. They had come to believe they could not be defeated. What is more, many among the Allies were beginning to believe it, too. But here, in their first real engagement with Americans since defeating the isolated and starving men of Bataan, Japanese soldiers had not just been defeated, they had been routed and destroyed, and the effect on Western morale was almost incalculable.

It affected Admiral Yamamoto, too. He realized now that he was in for a bigger scrap than he'd bargained for. He was still perfectly confident of being able to recover Guadalcanal and destroy its American occupiers, but it was going to take a lot of force. So he began to plan a massive effort, a "big push," he said, that would be sure to do it.

As the days passed, the Japanese continued to bombard Marine positions and Henderson Field from both the sea and the air. Meanwhile, two Japanese forces, totaling 2,100 men, were making their way toward a designated meeting point behind a hill near the edge of Henderson Field. It was hard going through almost impenetrable jungle, but they did manage to come together on the morning of September 13, the date set for the "big push" attack that was to shove the Marines into the sea. That evening they launched it, slipping stealthily down across a grassy clearing and up onto the reverse slope of a little ridge overlooking Henderson. What they could not know then but were about to find out was that their arrival was anticipated. Commanded by Colonel Merritt "Red Mike" Edson, the First Marine Raiders and the First Marine Parachute Battalion were dug in on the ridge. And, informed of movements in the grass by simple rattles suspended on wires, they were waiting.

At 8:55 Japanese artillery began the bombarding of where they supposed the American positions were. Five minutes later their warships opened up from Sealark Channel, lobbing giant naval shells into Henderson Field and hurling giant flares into the sky over the ridge.

Now Japanese commanders shouted, *"Totsugeki! Totsugeki!"* "Charge! Charge!" and sent their men swarming in waves up the ridge and into a withering fire from the machine guns and point-blank artillery of Edson's men. The Japanese soldiers began falling like wheat before a scythe, but their determination was such and their charge so fierce that they managed to penetrate and nearly overwhelm some Marine positions before being wiped out or driven back.

A half-hour later they attacked again, charging over the bodies of their own dead, and again they were repulsed, but just barely. And so it went until half-past-two in the morning when "Red Mike" finally felt able to telephone to General Vandegrift, "We can hold."

When dawn came to what now was and forever would be known as "Bloody Ridge," it revealed the bodies of 600 Japanese and 40 American dead. The remnants of the Japanese force—about 800 effectives remaining from the original 2,100—were gone, retreating in the direction of Mount Austin. A few fanatics, however, had hung back to die in suicidal charges by small units and individuals. Three of them, in fact, almost got to General Vandegrift before being shot down, almost at his feet.

And the ordeal still wasn't over. Having gotten lost in the jungle, another 800 Japanese led by Colonel Akinosuke Oka hadn't arrived in time for the fight. But they were here now, and like those who preceded them charging in waves that continued until almost every one of them had been killed.

And then it was truly over—a victory to be recorded in the history books as another important turning point in the war. And it was a learning experience, too. What the Americans learned about the Japanese, and would have to face in all combat with them from here on, was that they would fight to the death but never surrender. More often than not, individuals who seemed to be giving up carried concealed grenades for killing both themselves and those to whom they appeared to be surrendering.

What Admiral Yamamoto learned was that as soldiers these Americans were tough, courageous, determined, imaginative, and never to be underestimated—the exact opposite of how they were represented to be in Japanese military training. The wipeout of the Ichiki Battalion at the Tenaru River had suggested that. This debacle proved it. Still, Henderson Field, with its potential for air mastery, simply must not be allowed to remain in Allied hands. Henderson was the key. If it could be retaken and its air threat destroyed, the Japanese fleet would be free to move in and wipe out the United States Navy. In fact, Yamamoto and a number of other Japanese military leaders thought the outcome of the entire war might just rest upon the outcome at Guadalcanal. And with that in mind the admiral began organizing an all-out, do-or-die land, sea, and air attack that would begin a month later, on October 15.

"This operation," Admiral Yamamoto told his officers, "cannot be unsuccessful."

During the weeks that followed, Japanese aircraft and naval vessels continued to bombard American positions on the island and especially Henderson Field. Fighting on land was intermittent and seesawed back and forth with neither side making any great gains. At sea there were sporadic skirmishes as the Japanese attempted to interfere with American convoys bringing in supplies and reinforcements, and the Americans attempted to interfere with the steady stream of Japanese vessels doing the same thing, a supply operation the Americans nicknamed the Tokyo Express. During these exchanges both sides lost several destroyers and a cruiser apiece and had several other ships damaged, but the Americans lost the carrier *Wasp*. All of this, however, was but preliminary to Yamamoto's all-out attack, which because of delays by the Japanese Army he had been forced to postpone to October 23. Meanwhile, he was working at getting the Marines "softened up."

On the afternoon of October 13 Yamamoto sent waves of aircraft that blasted Henderson's buildings and runways with uncanny accuracy. Then, that night, the Japanese battleships *Kongo* and *Haruna* slipped undetected down what was known as the Slot into Sealark Channel and from there opened a bombardment that no veteran of the event will ever forget. For an hour and a half they poured fourteen-inch naval shells—almost a thousand of them—into Henderson and surrounding support areas. "For minutes at a time," wrote Captain Joe Foss, "the roar of explosives was so loud and the pain in my ears so intense I could do nothing but hold my hands over my ears and cringe. Screams pierced the air when someone was hit. Those two hours were indescribable. Unless you've been through it you just can't imagine what it's like. . . . [And] when the ear-ringing barrage . . . finally ceased the screams and sobs we heard were even more terrible."

When it was all over, forty-one men were dead, most

of the aviation gasoline had been burned (the captain of the *Kongo* later said that at one time Henderson resembled a "lake of fire"), only forty-two aircraft were still operable, and the runways were pitted with bomb craters.

Despite its devastating effects, however, the attack turned out to be a mistake on Yamamoto's part, because it brought on a change of American command that was to alter the entire complexion of the campaign. After reading the damage reports the cautious Admiral Ghormley had had just about enough. "Guadalcanal is virtually out of aviation gasoline," he reported to Admiral Chester W. Nimitz at Pearl Harbor: "Japanese warships have attacked every night with impunity. Their bombardments have wrecked the airport installations, destroyed aircraft, killed men, and severely damaged troop morale." If he were to be expected to continue holding Guadalcanal, Ghormley continued, he would have to have every submarine, PT boat, cruiser, and destroyer Nimitz could send to him. On top of that, he would have to have an additional ninety heavy bombers, eighty medium bombers, sixty-five dive-bombers, and two groups of fighters.

Ghormley's memo got results all right, but hardly what he must have anticipated. Frustrated by Ghormley's defeatist attitude and impossible demands, Admiral Nimitz blew up. Then he fired Ghormley and immediately sent pugnacious Vice Admiral William F. "Bull" Halsey to replace him and to try to turn the campaign around.

It was a fateful choice and perhaps the best of Nimitz's distinguished career. Halsey was called "Bull" for good reason. He looked a little bit like a bulldog and fought entirely like one. "Jesus Christ and General Jackson!" he exclaimed upon receiving Nimitz's order. "This is the hottest potato they ever handed me!" He then flew immediately to Guadalcanal. Arriving there on October 18, he asked General Vandegrift, "Are we going to evacuate or hold?"

"I can hold," said Vandegrift, "but I have to have more active support than I've been getting."

"All right," Halsey replied, "I'll promise you everything I've got."

Next, Halsey issued his first General Order. It said, in seven words soon to be repeated on signs all over the area, "Kill Japs. Kill Japs. Kill more Japs." And with Halsey's aggressive attitude reinforcing rather than conflicting with that of General Vandegrift, the previously sagging troop morale went soaring upward.

Meanwhile, on October 15, U.S. carrier aircraft found and attacked a convoy of Japanese troopships attempting to unload men at Tassafaronga Point. Unfortunately, however, before the Japanese transports were forced to flee they managed to land most of their cargoes of supplies and about four thousand men. This brought Japanese strength on Guadalcanal to some twenty thousand. Thus reinforced, Yamamoto, at 9:00 P.M. on October 23, finally launched his all-out attack. It opened with a thundering, debris-showering bombardment of American defenses on Henderson's inland side. A half-hour later the bombardment ceased and the Japanese Army came charging forward. After a period of wild fighting, some Japanese elements actually made it to the very edge of the field, which led their commander, in a burst of foolish optimism, to report to his headquarters that Henderson had been captured. Not only was this report not the fact, it was the very opposite of it; for only minutes after his report was made his entire command was overrun and virtually obliterated by a furious American counterattack.

Yamamoto, however, still believed that Henderson had indeed been taken. And so, assuming that his fleet was now safe from ground-based American planes, he ordered it to search out any and all Allied naval forces it could find in the Solomons area. At almost the same moment, Admiral Halsey was ordering his fleet to search out and engage any Japanese naval forces it could find in the area.

On the night of the 24th the Japanese Army attacked Henderson Field anew. Shouting "Babe Ruth, eat shit!" they charged again and again. Again and again they were mowed down by organized fire from Marines and from soldiers of the Army's Twenty-fifth Division, where even the cooks and company clerks found it necessary to join in. Finally, along about midnight, the battered remnants of the

Japanese force withdrew, leaving three thousand of their dead behind them.

Meanwhile, since the morning of October 24 the American and Japanese fleets had been probing like two blind boxers trying to find each other. At half-past-two on the morning of the 25th the Americans made the first discovery. The pilot of a Catalina patrol plane reported spotting the Japanese fleet and gave its location, then added, wryly, "Notify my next of kin." It was an unnecessary request, however, for after illuminating some of the Japanese ships with flares the slow, lumbering Catalina managed to escape unscathed.

Next morning American air searches again found the Japanese fleet (which had changed course after being spotted), and Admiral Halsey issued an order that even for him had to have set a record for to-the-point terseness. "Attack!" it said. "Repeat, Attack!"

By this time the Japanese had located the Allied fleet and launched an attack of their own. Both the American and Japanese attacks were by air alone and launched so simultaneously that some of the attacking flights actually passed within sight of each other going in opposite directions.

American dive-bombers drew first blood, striking and severely damaging the Japanese carrier *Zuiho*. Shortly thereafter Japanese bombers and torpedo planes found the American carrier *Hornet* and damaged her so seriously that she later had to be sunk.

And so it went on into October 27, the two fleets never coming within sight of each other and trading blows only by air. When it was all over the Japanese had gotten the best of it on paper, but only on paper. They had killed 316 Americans, destroyed seventy-eight American planes, sunk the carrier *Hornet*, extensively damaged the carrier *Enterprise*, the battleship *South Dakota*, the cruiser *San Juan*, and three destroyers. They, on the other hand, had lost no ships at all, although two of their carriers and one cruiser had been heavily damaged. They had, however, lost most of their air cover—one hundred hard-to-replace aircraft along with one hundred even harder to replace experienced pilots. Moreover, the fuel in their bunkers had become critically low. And these two things together forced them to withdraw and leave the field to the Americans.

Having failed in trying to take Henderson Field on land and in destroying the American fleet at sea, Admiral Yamamoto was rethinking the whole business of trying to recapture Guadalcanal. Actually, twenty thousand Japanese were still holding 90 percent of the island, but it was the useless 90 percent, with terrain so rugged and vegetation so hostile as to be in places almost uninhabitable. The Americans held only a little piece of the north shore—but it was the important piece, the only piece fit to accommodate airfields and military installations of any value. But they were holding it so stubbornly and with such unbelievable resourcefulness and determination in the face of all the odds that Yamamoto now concluded the price of further efforts to dislodge them would be far too high.

"We must," he radioed Tokyo, "abandon the effort to recapture Guadalcanal."

The Japanese High Command thought otherwise. On October 29 Yamamoto received a message in which the Emperor expressed displeasure at the way the war in the South Pacific was going. The High Command, far removed from the realities of war and still arrogantly certain of Japanese superiority in all things, including military, ordered him to continue invincibly the campaign against Guadalcanal. And Yamamoto, who, though regretfully, always allowed loyalty to his Emperor to take precedence over his own principles and common sense, promised to "redouble" his efforts to take the island. But now the tide was running against him.

At the end of the month Marine Fighter Squadron 211 and parts of Marine Scout-Bomber Squadron 132 reinforced the Cactus Air Force. A few days later Seabees units landed at Aola Bay, forty miles east of Lunga River, and began construction of yet another airfield. The Marines, now being better supplied, were able to increase their offensive pressure against the Japanese and began pushing them farther and farther back from Henderson and its support areas.

On November 12, six thousand fresh troops of the U.S. Army's 182nd Infantry arrived, and in spite of a Japanese fleet advancing to prevent it, were successfully landed. Consisting of two battleships, a heavy cruiser, and fourteen fast destroyers, the Japanese fleet bombarded Henderson Field, but then during the night was engaged by five American cruisers that had escorted the Army transports in. It was a gutsy thing for them to do, and in the wild, confused melee that followed the Americans were to pay heavily for it. The action lasted only twenty-four minutes. But in those twenty-four minutes (which would find their way into history as the Naval Battle of Guadalcanal) the Americans lost two rear admirals, D. J. Callaghan and Norman Scott, who were killed, the cruisers *Atlanta* and *Juneau* and the destroyers *Laffey, Cushing, Monsson,* and *Barton,* which were sunk, and the cruiser *San Francisco,* which was badly battered. The Japanese, on the other hand, lost only the battleship *Hei* and one destroyer sunk, and had several destroyers damaged by fire.

Meanwhile, in preparation for his next desperate attempt to retake Guadalcanal, Admiral Yamamoto also had reinforcements coming in, eleven troop transports carrying thirteen thousand men of Japan's Thirty-eighth Division together with supplies, plus eleven escort vessels, and with air cover being provided by the carrier *Hiya* lying to the north out of range of Henderson's planes. But again the tides of fortune turned against the admiral. On the morning of November 14 his transports were discovered by planes from the USS *Enterprise* and subsequently were attacked by both land and carrier aircraft.

"Despite the exhausting non-stop battle of the day before," wrote Joe Foss, "we were determined to blow the bastards out of the water." And they did—sinking seven of the eleven well before the day was over.

On the evening of that same day another Japanese battle fleet, consisting of the battleship *Kirishima,* four cruisers, and nine destroyers, was intent upon both protecting such troop transports as were still afloat and in plastering Henderson Field with naval gunfire. To oppose those fourteen ships the Americans were able to send out only six, and four of those were destroyers, which was not quite as inadequate a response as it sounds. For the other two were the huge new battleships *South Dakota* and *Washington*, carrying between them eighteen sixteen-inch guns as opposed to eight fourteen-inchers carried by the *Kirishima*.

At a little after eleven o'clock the two forces met, steaming into and through course and counter-course on a night just as black as the previous one. And just as on the previous evening their meeting turned into a disorganized, flame-filled brawl. The Japanese opened the affair by concentrating all their fire on the American destroyers and in twenty minutes had put all four out of action: the *Preston* and *Walke* sunk and the *Winn* and *Benham* disabled though still afloat.

Chief Electrician's Mate George Behrens was aboard the *Walke:*

> We came upon the Japs between Guadalcanal and Savo Island and fired a star shell. And, why, it looked like the cliffs of Dover out there, only the wall we saw was not rock but the sides of Jap ships. . . .
>
> They started to shoot and we started to get hit. I couldn't raise anybody up forward on the intercom, so I went up to see what was going on. I found the No. 1 5-inch gun turret completely gone. Not a cotton pickin' thing left but the round ring it had sat on. . . . When I started aft the whole bridge started burning like a blowtorch. Everybody up there was dead and I nearly caught on fire. 20-millimeter ammunition was blowing up all over the place.
>
> We started getting shells from both sides. Then we caught a torpedo and the ship broke in two and we didn't stay up very long after that. I was on the back end, which was floating, but when it became clear it was about to sink I jumped off. Then another explosion blew me clear up out of the water and out of my life jacket. Fortunately I didn't lose it because when I came down my arm went back

down through it. But now it had some little had some little holes in it, and since it was an air-inflated jacket I spent the rest of the night and half the next day periodically blowing it up. It kept me real busy.

The battleships *South Dakota* and *Washington*, meanwhile, were heading north to take on the Japanese heavies, the battleship and the cruisers. The *South Dakota*, her maneuvering ability crippled by an electrical problem, soon suffered so much torpedo and artillery damage as to remove her from the action. The *Washington*, however, went on to fight it out with the Japanese battleship *Kirishima*, and in just seven minutes, in one of only four direct battleship-to-battleship shootouts of the entire war, left her sinking. Not only was the Japanese fleet again forced to withdraw, but this action together with that of the previous two nights had destroyed whatever ability it still might have had to protect what was left of its troopship convoy.

George Behrens, who was still in the water at the time, recalls that, "When the sun came up I could see those beached Jap transports and our Air Forces coming over and just bombing the hell out of 'em."

And bomb them they did, to the point that of the twelve thousand men Yamamoto had sent to land on the island only some three thousand or so actually managed to do so. And of the ten thousand tons of supplies that were supposed to be landed, only a pitiful five tons—260 cases of ammunition and 1,500 bags of rice—actually reached the shore.

Meanwhile the DMS (Destroyer-Minesweeper) *Aaron Ward* was cruising the area picking up survivors, including Behrens: "They took us over to a Marine hospital on the beach and put me and another guy out in a doggone tent. . . . When they washed me down with kerosene to remove the oil I'd picked up, they not only found my rear end all shot up but that the impact of that underwater explosion had caused some of my intestine to be hanging out. They poked it back in by using a disinfected screwdriver handle. Then they bandaged my other wounds and gave me a shot for gas-gangrene. And I'll tell you that's a shot you'll never forget!"

He reported seeing some guys there mixing plaster of Paris in an old Japanese bathtub to make casts for broken bones, and on a tree behind the tub they had a sign, "Hollywood Casting Office."

What it all came down to was this: During the past three days the Japanese had lost two battleships, a heavy cruiser, and 11,700 men. Evacuation efforts had saved their destroyers and eleven transports and 7,000 or more men. But their biggest loss was their initiative. Now it was the Americans rather than the Japanese who controlled the seas surrounding the southern Solomons, and Admiral Yamamoto knew the Americans were on Guadalcanal to stay. The Japanese High Command in Tokyo, however, refused to face that fact. Never in the past one thousand years had anyone managed to retake territory Japan had seized, and it was inconceivable that anyone should be allowed to do so now.

Accordingly, on November 30 eight Japanese destroyers set out to deliver supplies and reinforcements to forces about fifteen miles west of Henderson Field at Tassafaronga. This, too, turned out to be a failed mission, but in losing, the Japanese again extracted a price. Met by a far superior force—five American cruisers and four destroyers —they managed to torpedo four of the five cruisers and to sink one of them, the *Northhampton,* and to kill more than four hundred Americans while losing only one destroyer of their own. In early December the Japanese General Staff passed the command of the Southwest Pacific Area to General Hitoshi Imamura. Imamura received his orders from the Emperor himself, who with tears in his eyes asked him to save the suffering soldiers on Guadalcanal. Then, at General Staff headquarters, he was ordered to cooperate with Admiral Yamamoto in first reinforcing the troops on Guadalcanal and mounting an offensive to drive the Americans into the sea.

But it was all to no avail. Continuing an operation the Americans had called the Tokyo Express, Japanese destroyers kept trying to resupply their troops, at this stage by dropping strings of supply-laden oil drums that would then wash ashore or be retrieved by small boats and swimmers. But now that Americans controlled the surrounding seas they were able to prevent much of those supplies from ever reaching shore, while at the same time resupplying and reinforcing themselves with increasing ease.

In early December fresh Army troops arrived to relieve the ragged, weary, and disease-ridden First Marine Division. On December 9 the command was passed from Marine General Alexander Vandegrift to Army General Alexander Patch, and the Marines, having done their job in the face of almost impossible odds, departed for rest and recuperation in Australia.

On that same day General Hyakutake on Guadalcanal radioed General Imamura: "An average of 100 men starve to death daily. This average will only increase. By the time we get two division reinforcements doubtful how many troops here will be alive." Imamura acknowledged the message by recognizing the courage of the men on Guadalcanal as "enough to make even the gods weep," but then asked those starving men to "set His Majesty's heart at ease" by helping to retake the island.

Despite the general's determination and that of the General Staff, however, the handwriting was on the wall and was unmistakable—even though the General Staff never saw Chief Petty Officer Yoshida Kosichi's poem:

> Our rice is gone
> Eating roots and grass
> Along the ridges and cliffs
> Leaves hide the trail, we lose our way
> Stumble and get up, fall and get up
> Covered with mud from our falls
> Blood oozes from our wounds
> No cloth to bind our cuts
> Flies swarm to the scabs
> No strength to brush them away
> Fall down and cannot move
> How many times I've thought of suicide.

The General Staff did, however, see General Hyakutake's radiogram of December 23: "No food available and we can no longer send out scouts. We can do nothing to withstand the enemy's offensive. 17th Army now requests permission to break into enemy positions and die an honorable death rather than die of hunger in our own dugouts."

Now, even members of the General Staff had to admit the situation was hopeless, and after several days of wrangling, finger-pointing, and blame-shifting they asked the Emperor's permission to give up the struggle for Guadalcanal. Reluctantly, on January 31, the Emperor granted it.

The Emperor did not, however, grant Hyakutake's request to destroy the remainder of his army in suicidal banzai charges. He wanted instead to save as much of that army as possible for future service. Accordingly, on dark nights in January destroyers of the Tokyo Express continued running to the island. Now, however, they were not bringing troops in but taking them out. They concealed this action so well, and their rear-guard covered the evacuation with such fierce holding actions, that the Americans thought they were still bringing reinforcements in, and so, themselves, continued to bring reinforcements to contain them. And this, in turn, led to one of the last naval engagements of the campaign, the Battle of Rennell Island.

In the last week of January 1943, Task Force Eighteen —three aircraft carriers, six cruisers, and five destroyers commanded by Rear Admiral Robert Giffen—was hurrying north to meet and protect an incoming convoy of supply ships and transports. In the opinion of the admiral, however, the task force wasn't hurrying fast enough. It was being held back by the aircraft carriers, two of which could make no more than sixteen knots. Feeling more secure in these waters than he should have, he sent cruisers and destroyers racing on ahead, leaving the carriers to catch up later—which, as he was about to learn, was a mistake.

At twilight on January 29, as the task force was steaming just to the north of Rennell Island, Japanese land-based bombers and torpedo planes came sweeping in, but the admiral had no planes to send up to meet them.

"We picked up these bogies," recalled Gunnery Officer Wylie Davis, who was up in the cruiser *Chicago*'s forward fire director at the time:

And the next thing we knew one came in dropping a fish, which fortunately missed us. Came across right over my head, so low he almost took off the top of the foremast. I started back to my battle station in the after fire director up on the aftermast, and we were still just steaming along and taking no evasive action. Then more planes showed up and got four hits on our ship. We caught two amidships and another about two-thirds of the way aft and right under my battle station. None of the people around me got hurt but a lot of us got knocked down, and an enormous column of water soared up and then washed down on us.

The Japs had just knocked the hell out of two engine rooms, and it was a miracle we didn't go down right then, we were so flooded. And it was down there we had all our casualties—about eighty men as I recall, all Engineering people, out of our crew of eleven hundred.

The cruiser *Louisville* took us in tow and towed us all through the night. Next day, in tow, making no more than two or three knots and with an oil slick pointing to us like a great big arrow, we knew the Japs would come back, and they did. In early afternoon they hit us with two more torpedoes, and that was the end of the *Chicago*. Even then, though, by taking about twenty minutes to sink she gave us time to get everybody off.

In early February the Japanese began evacuation in earnest, three times sending whole fleets of destroyers in to take men off the island. Losing only two ships sunk and six damaged from a total of sixty sorties they did very well, so well in fact that when the American pincer movement closed on where the Japanese had been no one was any longer there. All had gone. And so on that day,

February 9, 1943, General Alexander Patch reported to his higher command that the Japanese on Guadalcanal had suffered "total and complete defeat" and that the island was secured.

And so now finally, it is all over, America's first counterthrust of the war, its first amphibious invasion ever, had succeeded. The cost had been high: about sixteen hundred men dead and twenty-six hundred wounded; two aircraft carriers, seven cruisers, fifteen destroyers, three troop transports, a considerable number of PT boats sunk; and 615 aircraft shot down or destroyed on the ground.

But for the Japanese the cost had been infinitely higher. They had managed to evacuate only about twelve thousand men from the island, leaving behind an estimated fifty thousand dead from combat, disease, hunger, and transport sinkings. And that was only part of it. The cost to Japan's leaders in ego, confidence, and "face" had to have been incalculable. They had come into this conflict convinced of their own superiority as a people, as warriors, and with faith in the code of the Samurai. They had come in believing that the Allies, and especially the Americans, were leisure-loving, morally degenerate, and cowardly. But in April's bombing of Tokyo and Yokohama these "cowardly degenerates," led by Colonel Doolittle, had managed to carry off the first successful attack on the Japanese homeland in twelve hundred years. Then in June at Midway the American Navy inflicted upon the unquestionably superior Japanese Navy its first defeat in a thousand years. Now, at Guadalcanal they not only had given the Japanese Army its first whipping in a millennium but also had taken back the first land the Japanese had ever had to give up after seizing it.

What it all came down to was that in losing Guadalcanal the Japanese had lost not only all hope of conquering Australia but their impetus as well. No longer could they roam the Pacific seizing territory almost at will. The day of the invincible Japanese juggernaut was over. From now on it was going to be a different kind of war.

GUADALCANAL

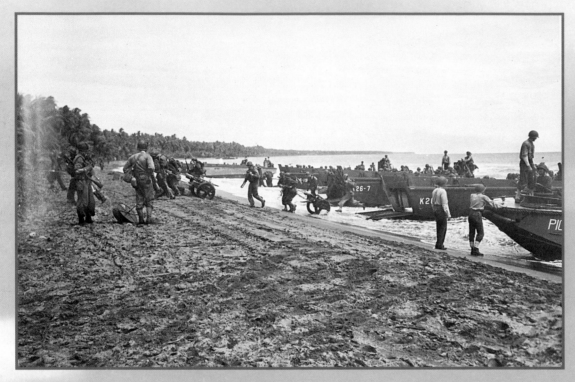

On August 7, 1942, U.S. Marines land on the Guadalcanal beach code-named "Red," actually a black sand beach.

AFTER THE WAR, Guadalcanal and the Solomon Islands receded from American consciousness as the Cold War and other frightening aspects of twentieth-century living aroused new and more vivid fears. Memories of the war in the Solomons were revived briefly when former PT boat skipper John F. Kennedy was elected president. The book describing his escapades in the Solomons, *PT 109,* and a movie of the same name were very popular.

For most Americans today, however, Guadalcanal has become just another obscure island in the South Pacific, in an equally obscure island group that happens to be an independent country called "Solomon Islands." But independence was not automatically achieved when the islands were liberated from the Japanese, for after the war the British returned their colonial administration. Not until 1978 did the Solomon Islands gain independence. The new town of Honiara, which evolved from the American military facilities near Henderson Field, became the capital on Guadalcanal.

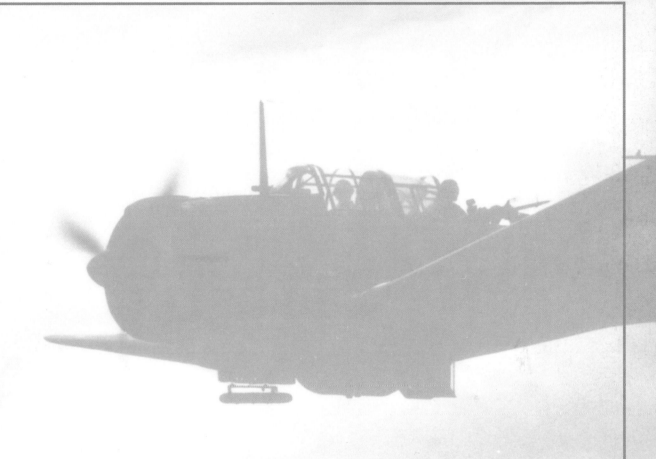

But large-scale tourism, so familiar in some other Pacific island groups after the war, never materialized on Guadalcanal. This may be due in part to the fact that malaria, the scourge of Allied and Japanese troops alike during the war, made a comeback in the Solomons after being almost tamed by a postwar generation of drugs.

Today a visitor would be impressed with the deserted, quiet beaches, ancient rain forests, and green-shrouded jungle mountains, scenery in stark contrast to the sometimes-miserable conditions endured by American and Japanese fighters in 1942. In 2000 these conflicting images were vividly brought to the movie screen in the World War II film *The Thin Red Line,* when parts of the movie were shot on location on Guadalcanal. However, tribal, environmental, and political conflicts have troubled the Solomons in the early twenty-first century, warding off visitors to these islands so rich in World War II history.

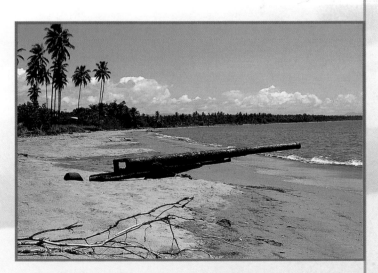

A rusted gun points out to sea at Red Beach.

TICKET TO ARMISTICE

**USE THIS TICKET, SAVE YOUR LIFE
YOU WILL BE KINDLY TREATED**

Follow These Instructions:

1. Come towards our lines waving a white flag.
2. Strap your gun over your left shoulder muzzle down and pointed behind you.
3. Show this ticket to the sentry.
4. Any number of you may surrender with this one ticket.

JAPANESE ARMY HEADQUARTERS

投 降 票

此ノ票ヲ持ツモノハ投降者ナリ
投降者ヲ殺害スルヲ厳禁ス

大 日 本 軍 司 令 官

Sing your way to Peace pray for Peace

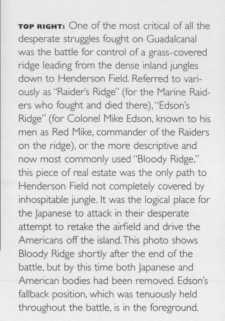

This "Armistice Ticket" was printed by Japanese intelligence officers very familiar with Americans and their customs and dumped in large quantities from airplanes over American positions during the battle for Guadalcanal.

On the other hand, Japanese survivors of later battles had little familiarity with the protocol of surrender, a concept totally foreign to the rank-and-file Japanese soldier.

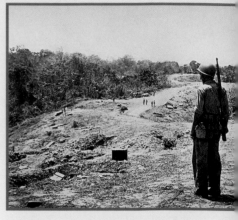

TOP RIGHT: One of the most critical of all the desperate struggles fought on Guadalcanal was the battle for control of a grass-covered ridge leading from the dense inland jungles down to Henderson Field. Referred to variously as "Raider's Ridge" (for the Marine Raiders who fought and died there), "Edson's Ridge" (for Colonel Mike Edson, known to his men as Red Mike, commander of the Raiders on the ridge), or the more descriptive and now most commonly used "Bloody Ridge," this piece of real estate was the only path to Henderson Field not completely covered by inhospitable jungle. It was the logical place for the Japanese to attack in their desperate attempt to retake the airfield and drive the Americans off the island. This photo shows Bloody Ridge shortly after the end of the battle, but by this time both Japanese and American bodies had been removed. Edson's fallback position, which was tenuously held throughout the battle, is in the foreground.

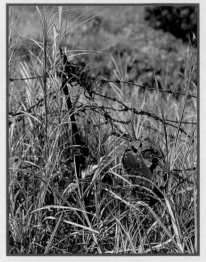

Japanese attackers had this view of the final American fallback positions. Faint outlines of American foxholes are still etched into the sides of the knoll at center. Red Mike and his Raiders were able to hold a line centered on this knoll in spite of numerous horrific, suicidal charges by the Japanese during the night of September 13–14, 1942. If the Japanese could have broken through this American position, their advance to Henderson Field (seen faintly in the distance beyond the knoll) would have been impossible to stop.

CENTER RIGHT: The American defenders on Bloody Ridge hung tin cans filled with pebbles from barbed wire strung around their positions, so Japanese attempts to infiltrate their lines could be heard when the wire was moved and rattled the cans. Some of the barbed-wire defenses remain on Bloody Ridge, and a bullet-riddled tin can still hangs from the strands, grim testimony to the intensity of the fire on the ridge during the battle.

BOTTOM RIGHT: American memorial placed on Bloody Ridge near the scene of the last positions held by Edson's men. The plaque describes how the Americans held off the Japanese attackers during the long night of September 13–14. Visitors are asked not to take artifacts from the grass-covered hills of the Ridge, but, instead, to place recovered relics near the monument. In this photo an American helmet and two mortar shells rest on the memorial, and various other pieces of rusting battle debris lie in the grass at the foot of the monument.

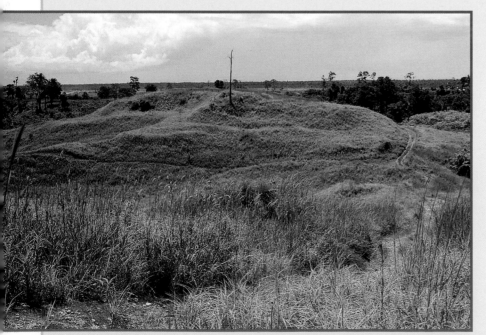

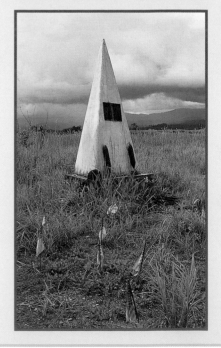

TOP LEFT: Henderson Field, named after a Marine flyer (Lofton Henderson) killed at the Battle of Midway, became a bustling hub of aerial activity in the Solomon Islands. The original control tower, built shortly after the airfield was secured from the Japanese, gave way to the "new" tower on the right in this 1943 photo.

TOP RIGHT: The skeletal remains of the "new" World War II tower remain at Henderson Field. Postwar facilities were built adjacent to the old tower. In 1998 the Japanese government funded a $20 million international terminal building nearby, which a Japanese contractor built. This marked the first significant Japanese construction effort at the airport since 1942 when they did the initial work on the airstrip that the Americans subsequently captured, expanded, and named Henderson Field.

BOTTOM: Among the many planes that flew from Henderson Field to battle the Japanese were B-17s. These planes became famous in the European theater and also played an important part in the Pacific war, especially in the early stages. Favorites of pilots and ground crews alike, the B-17s were durable and reliable like no other U.S. heavy bomber in World War II. Paul Meehl, a B-17 crew chief who lived in Colorado until his death in 1988, recalled that "the plane could fly itself." Here, a B-17 based at Henderson Field is on a bombing run over Japanese-held Gizo in the northern Solomons in October 1942. Smoke from Gizo can be seen in the distance.

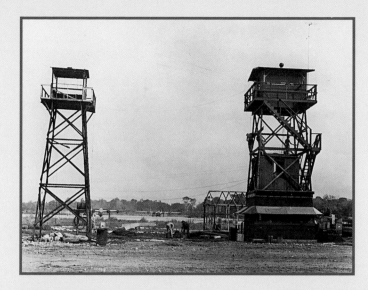

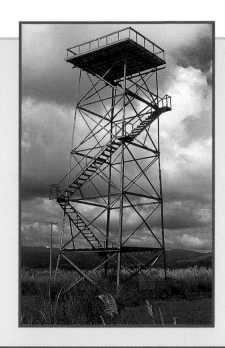

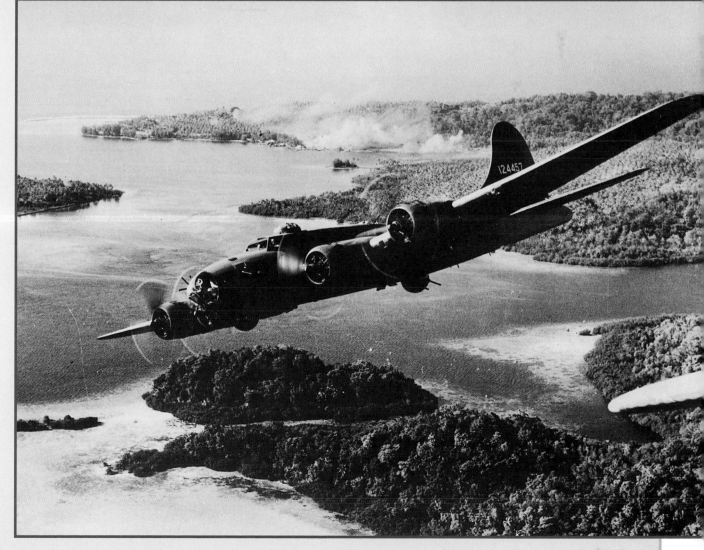

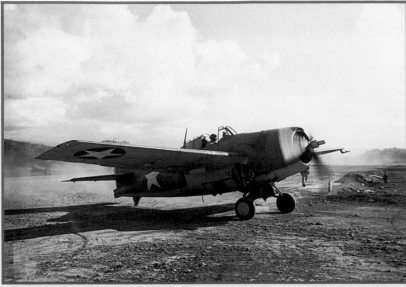

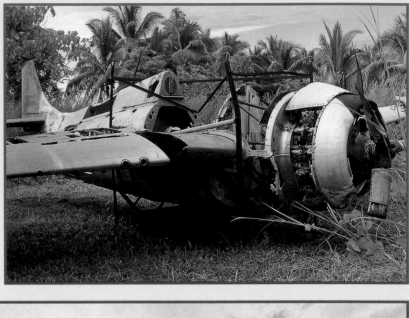

One of the invaluable Grumman F4F Wildcats of the Cactus Air Force (as Americans on Guadalcanal named their defending air contingent) returning to Henderson Field from a raid on Japanese positions in December 1942.

RIGHT: The wreckage of this F4F Wildcat was found near Henderson Field and is on display at Vilu, Guadalcanal.

RIGHT: While Americans held the area around Henderson Field, the Japanese repeatedly landed troops and supplies farther up the coast. This resupply and reinforcement effort came to be called the "Tokyo Express" by Americans. On occasion, U.S. planes were able to intercept the Tokyo Express and damage or sink transports before they were able to unload, which was what happened in mid-November 1942 when several were caught by what Americans called the "Buzzard Patrol." Eleven Japanese transports carrying about thirteen thousand reinforcements were nabbed north of Guadalcanal by U.S. planes. In the subsequent bloody carnage, the jam-packed ships were bombed and strafed, and Japanese troops died by the thousands in this wholesale slaughter. Some American pilots were literally sickened by the sight. Four transports finally limped to Guadalcanal later that night, and the damaged hulks were beached to unload the remains of their troops and supplies. Only about three thousand men out of the original twelve thousand were landed. Roughly two thousand were rescued from the shark-infested waters around Guadalcanal, but the rest were either dead or went missing. The next morning American planes, ships, and artillery finished off the beached ships. In this picture, two of those transports burn in the distance on the Guadalcanal shore.

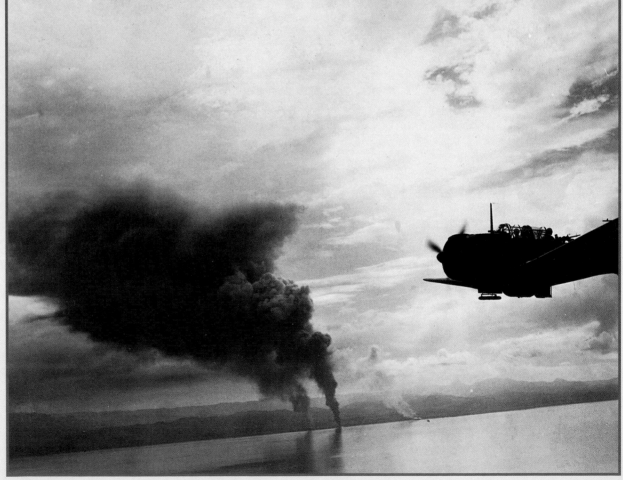

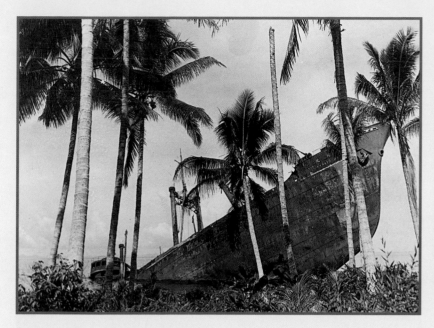

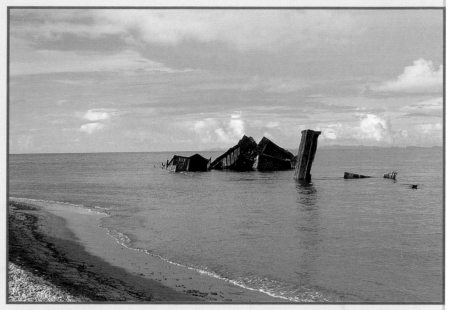

One of the heavily damaged Japanese troop transports beached after being caught by the Buzzard Patrol on November 14, 1942.

This same beached ship today has become an attraction for snorkelers and divers. Only the stern section below the water line and parts of the forward section protruding above the water remain. Salvagers sheared off most of the ship above the waterline after the war.

Another victim of the Buzzard Patrol, this Japanese transport lies abandoned after being destroyed by U.S. planes, ships, and artillery on November 15, 1942.

By the time this photo was taken in the late 1970s, salvagers had left very little of this ship behind. Today even fewer traces can be found.

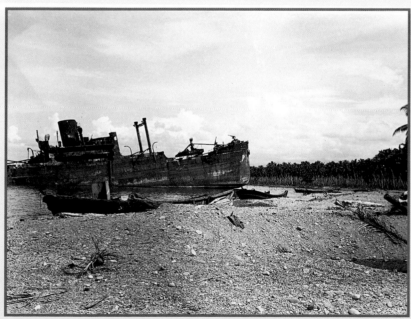

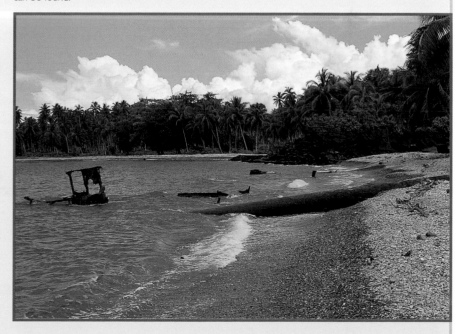

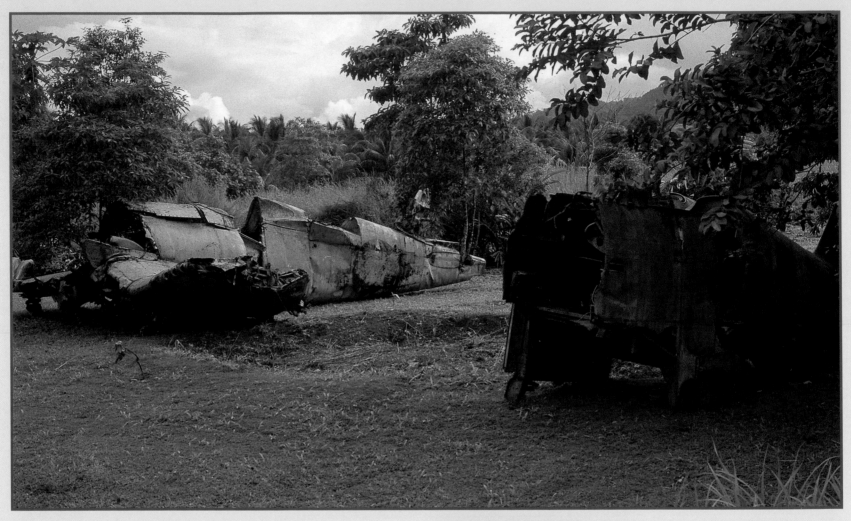

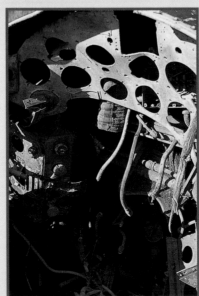

ABOVE: American planes were heavier and more sturdily built than their Japanese counterparts. Consequently, wrecked hulks of U.S. planes are more frequently discovered where they crashed in the jungle, while only scattered pieces of Japanese planes can usually be found. The remains of these two American aircraft were discovered in the jungles surrounding Henderson Field. The plane at left is a Corsair fighter, its distinctive gull wings clearly identifiable. Note also the faded outline of the American star at the rear of the fuselage. Tropical weather, heat, and humidity strip the paint off the old wrecks, but the aluminum skin and structure show little deterioration. Unfortunately, in the first twenty or so years after the war, the aluminum in such wrecks made salvage a lucrative proposition, and many relics disappeared forever. World War II plane wrecks are now extremely valuable due to their rarity and historical significance and are prized exhibit items for overseas museums and collectors. A number of South Pacific countries have now made it illegal to export World War II wrecks, since such artifacts are considered part of their historical heritage.

LEFT: The cockpit of the wrecked Corsair in the picture above. When the plane crashed into the jungle the impact destroyed many of the cockpit instruments. However, close inspection shows that the gun switch at the left is still in the "on" position, indicating that this plane was probably shot down while engaging the enemy.

A wing from a downed Japanese airplane clearly shows the outline of the Rising Sun insignia.

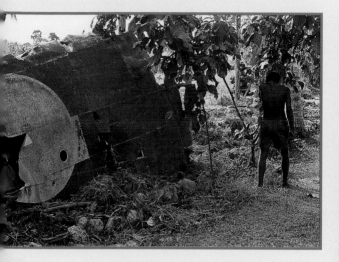

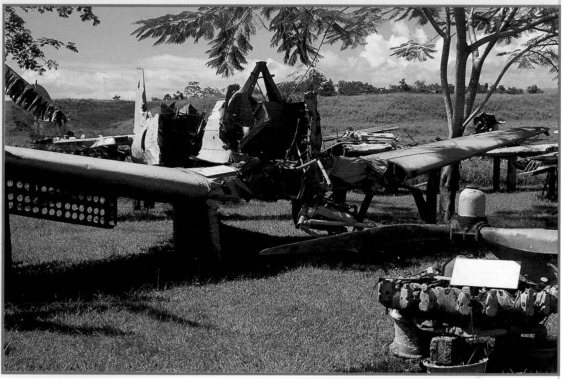

TOP RIGHT: This American SDB Dauntless dive-bomber was shot down and crashed into the jungle near Henderson Field and is now one of the war relics on display at Betikama on Guadalcanal. The hills in the background are literally mounds of American equipment covered with earth. When the war ended, vast amounts of matériel were buried here and elsewhere on Guadalcanal. Locals describe how huge holes were excavated, vehicles and equipment of all kinds were driven in, bulldozers covered this equipment with earth, then another layer of equipment was driven in on top of the first, and the process was repeated until the number of layers built up formed the low hills seen in this photo today. Several relics have been "mined" from the mounds and are on display in this collection.

BOTTOM RIGHT: War relics collected from all over Guadalcanal are exhibited at Vilu. Japanese canteens, guns, and helmets can be seen in this photo. A number of the helmets are riddled with multiple bullet holes. Guides explain that U.S. soldiers and Marines would sometimes fire rounds from their rifles into the helmeted heads of dead enemies abandoned by retreating Japanese, graphic evidence of the intensity of emotion during the battle.

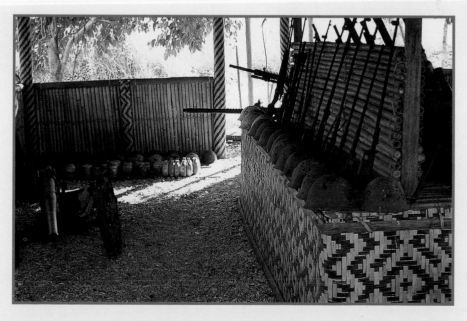

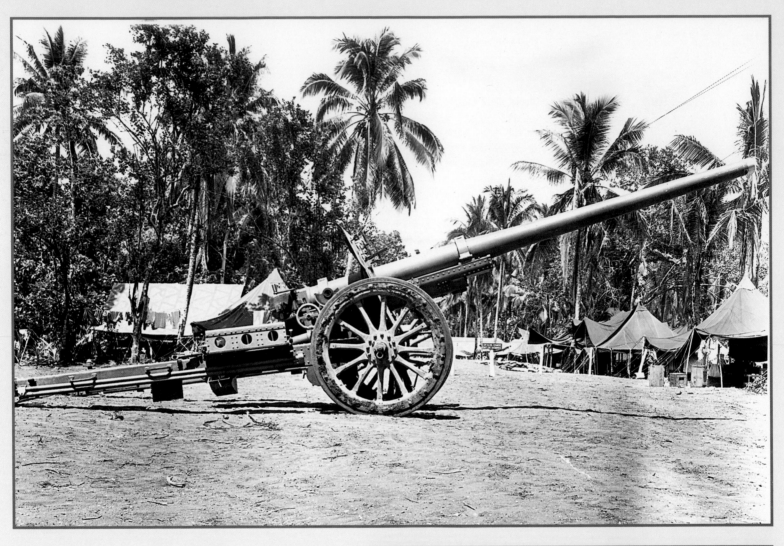

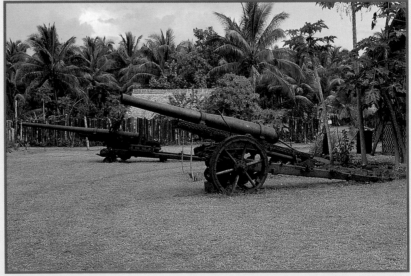

ABOVE: Japanese artillery pieces were known to the Americans by the generic term of "Pistol Pete." This particular Pistol Pete was captured during action near Kokumbona, Guadalcanal.

RIGHT: A Pistol Pete on display as part of the war relic collection at Vilu, Guadalcanal.

TOP LEFT: A large staging area for amphibious tracked vehicles known as LVTs or, more affectionately, "Alligators," was located on Guadalcanal. The area became known as "Alligator Flats."

TOP RIGHT: A World War II Alligator rests in a field near the former Alligator Flats.

BOTTOM LEFT: Local guides stand in the center of Alligator Flats, where abandoned and overgrown Alligators peer out from under their mantle of jungle foliage.

BOTTOM RIGHT: George Behrens on the destroyer *Walke,* about two months before the ship was sunk by the Japanese on November 14, 1942, between Savo Island and Guadalcanal.

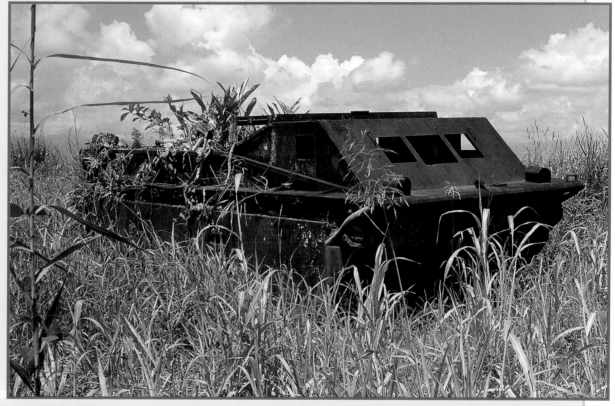

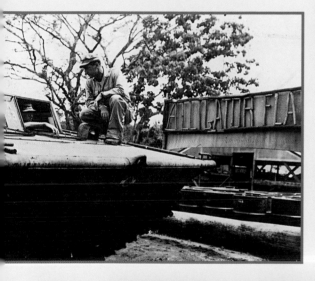

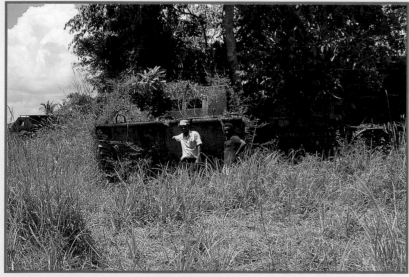

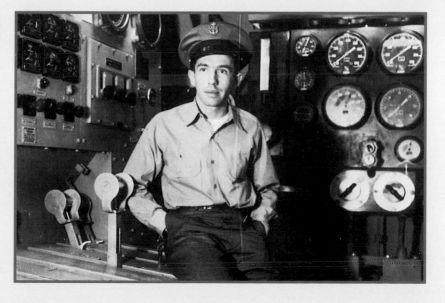

SOUVENIR MANIA

There seems to have been an almost insatiable desire to collect war souvenirs on Pacific islands, particularly anything associated with the Japanese military. Favorite items were Japanese flags and weapons, such as those proudly displayed by Colonel Evans F. Carlson and his Marine Raiders on Guadalcanal in early 1943. Today, such souvenirs come to light in boxes found in attics or at estate sales. Others are handed down to descendents or, in some cases, are donated to museums.

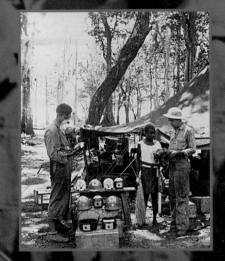

To take advantage of the brisk trade in war souvenirs Bob Weeks (at the right) set up a little stand outside his tent on Guadalcanal. Prospective buyer twenty-three-year-old Joe Andrejka checks out the mementos, some adorned with a genuine Rising Sun added at no extra charge. Meanwhile Weeks bargains for more items with a local islander.

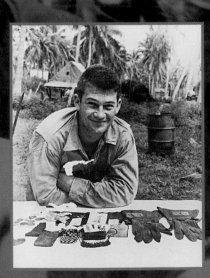

Philip Leeds was shot down by a Japanese Zero and lost in the jungles of Guadalcanal for eighteen days in 1943. When he finally showed up back at the airstrip, his fellow pilots were not so much amazed that he had survived and walked out of the jungle after being given up for lost, but that he somehow ended up with priceless souvenirs taken from a Japanese pilot he encountered in the jungle.

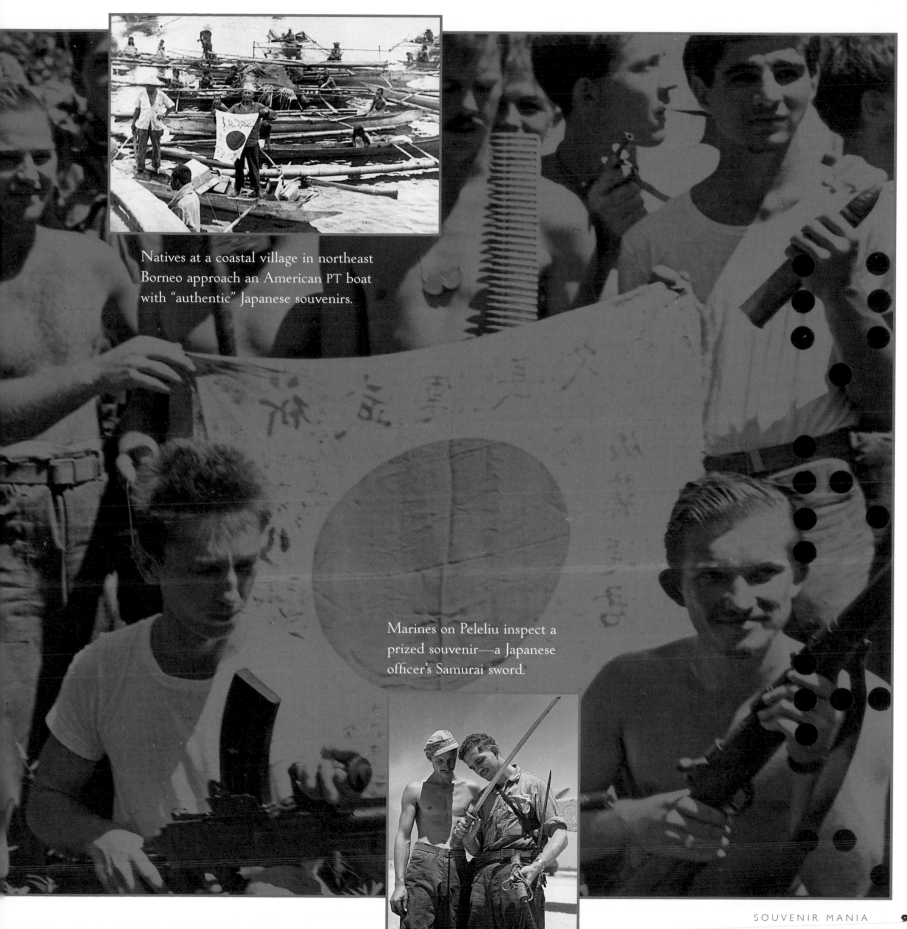

Natives at a coastal village in northeast Borneo approach an American PT boat with "authentic" Japanese souvenirs.

Marines on Peleliu inspect a prized souvenir—a Japanese officer's Samurai sword.

PT BOATS were basically large plywood speedboats that could rocket through the water and, in theory, get close enough to launch torpedoes and sink much larger ships. The resounding bass roar of their three Packard engines reminded the crews of finely tuned engines in the hot rods they had recently parted with at home. A contemporary artist likened the crew and their PT boat to a modern-day knight on a charging steed, lance poised to unseat the enemy. Most skippers and crews scoffed at this romantic image, but such an appeal was tangible to many young males, and the boats were indeed hot and fast. Plus the mostly easy-going camaraderie between officers and men, and the underdog David vs. Goliath role they often played, made service in PTs memorable to most who served in them. What PT boat crews seldom discussed was the shared danger that bonded crews together. When under fire from the larger ships they were supposed to sink, they manned a death trap. Well-heeled, college-age males were particularly attracted to PT boat service by the lure of being able to command a Navy boat shortly after being commissioned. The ranks of PT boat skippers were filled with future overachievers like John F. Kennedy.

One of the first PT boat bases in the Solomon Islands, tiny Tulagi Island, was hastily built in the early stages of the war against the Japanese. From Tulagi, these torpedo boats made forays against Japanese convoys and barges bringing reinforcements and supplies to Guadalcanal and other islands in the Solomons. Tulagi had been the British capital of the Solomon Islands since 1895, and it lay opposite Guadalcanal, tucked up close to the much larger Florida Island, across what was to become known appropriately as Iron Bottom Sound (for the many ships sunk there during the war). When the Japanese occupied the British Solomon Islands, they took up residence at

Tulagi in the old colonial buildings. Since the island afforded no suitable flat ground, the Japanese began construction of an airfield on Guadalcanal. Consequently, Guadalcanal became the main objective of the American invasion. The fight for Tulagi was brief but initially more fierce than on neighboring Guadalcanal. Out of the main Japanese force of about a thousand men stationed on Tulagi, all but twenty-seven taken prisoner (and a few who swam to neighboring Florida Island) were killed in three days of intense fighting in August 1942. After it and the adjoining islets of Gavutu and Tanambogo were secured, Tulagi became not only a PT boat base but a staging area and anchorage for larger ships.

Later to become one of Tulagi's most famous denizens, future President John F. Kennedy first tasted combat while skippering a PT boat based there. James Michener, writing about life on Tulagi and the escapades of the torpedo boats in *Tales of the South Pacific*, describes Tulagi's PT boats in somewhat less glamorous terms than those used by the media of the day: "They were rotten, tricky little craft for the immense jobs they were supposed to do. They were improvised, often unseaworthy, desperate little boats. They shook the stomachs out of many men who rode them, made physical wrecks of others for other reasons. They had no defensive armor. In many instances they were suicide boats. In others they were like human torpedoes."

Indeed, PT boats left their mark on men who served on them. One of the most common legacies was impaired hearing. The very reason these torpedo boats were often successful—their powerful Packard engines—was exactly what left the men who served on them with lifelong disabilities. Al Hahn was a motor machinist mate (engineer or "motor-mac") who operated and literally lived with the Packard engines below deck. He, like many other motor-macs, lost most of his hearing in one ear and had impaired hearing in the other. This could have been expected for men who were so close to the engines, but other crewmembers often suffered similar ailments. David Levy, a PT boat skipper who was based with Kennedy on Tulagi, also experienced lifelong hearing impairment from the roar of the Packard engines. However, most of the men on the PT boats didn't realize their hearing was being destroyed until it was too late. Al Hahn recounted, "As we got close to the end of the war we all spent a lot of time sitting around playing cards. The other guys started to notice that the motor-macs we played cards with all talked real loud. One day, someone asked me why I talked so loud when we played cards. I said I didn't think I talked louder than anyone else. Then we started comparing notes, and the engineers from the boats in the other squadrons all talked loud, too. They tested a few of us, and we were all losing our hearing. It was too late to do anything about it by then. The war was just about over."

For the men endangering their lives on the PT boats in World War II, hearing impairment was the least of their problems at the time. Enemy bullets and shrapnel could easily cut through the thin plywood hulls. PT boats in the Solomons were often assigned the task of "barge hunting," destroying the barges in which the Japanese would ferry about thirty to forty troops. The PT boats had the firepower advantage when they closed in on the barges, but rifle fire from the enemy troops would often kill American sailors because the PT boats had no armor to protect them.

PT boats were sometimes also sent out to harass and hopefully sink much larger Japanese ships, and it was on such a mission that Kennedy's boat, PT 109, was rammed inadvertently and sunk in the dark by an onrushing Japanese destroyer. Although two of his men were killed, Kennedy swam with the survivors to

a nearby islet and managed to arrange their rescue in an exploit that would later help propel him into the White House. However, at the time he was less than proud that he allowed his boat to be rammed and sunk, and he endured the inevitable ribbing. One of his fellow PT boat skippers, David Levy, recalled, "Sure we let him have it. We all gave him a hell of a time in a good-natured way. He was supposed to sink Japanese ships, not get in their way and be sunk himself. He knew it, too, and really never said anything about it. He would just as soon have forgotten the whole thing." Kennedy was much more proud of his subsequent activities on PT 59. But Kennedy's father recognized the media value of the PT 109 story and exploited it for all it was worth. In fact, Robert Donovan, author of the highly successful book *PT 109*, recalled, "Kennedy hated to have the PT 109 story be his legacy from the war. He tried long and hard to talk me out of writing the book." In spite of Kennedy's wishes, it was the story of PT 109 that immortalized him in the American media pantheon of war heroes.

After the war Tulagi reverted to a quiet island whose main industry is a Japanese fishing operation. It is a pleasant ride by inter-island trader ship across Iron Bottom Sound from Guadalcanal. Few traces of the old PT boat base are left to remind the visitor that the roar of Packard engines once echoed between Tulagi and nearby Florida Island as these famous torpedo boats left on their treacherous missions.

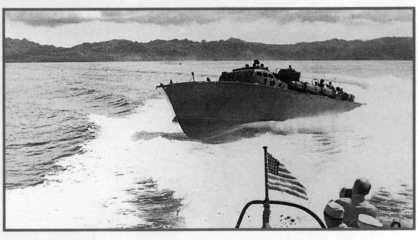

PT 59 shows off for the cameras near Tulagi. Guadalcanal is in the background. David Levy, at the controls of PT 59 in this photo, later turned this boat over to John F. Kennedy after PT 109 was rammed and sunk. In this boat Kennedy later pulled off a daring evacuation of some trapped Marines from under the noses of the Japanese. He thought that such an audacious incident with a positive outcome would be the war story that could be used in his future political career. Instead, his father focused on the more dramatic media value of the PT 109 incident, and, to Kennedy's chagrin, PT 109 was forever associated with him in his rise to political power.

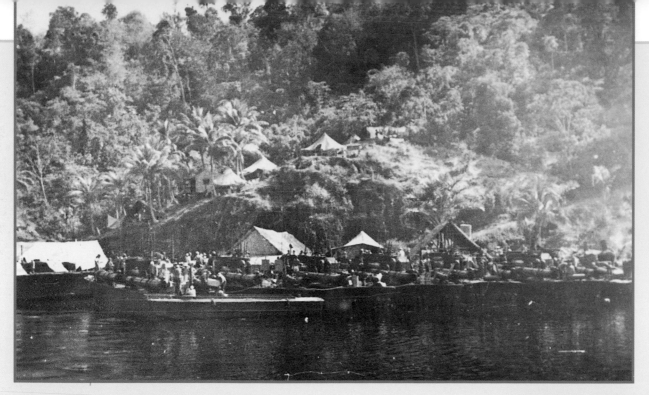

BELOW: An inter-island ship approaches the government wharf on Tulagi after cruising across Iron Bottom Sound from Guadalcanal.

BOTTOM: A souvenir Japanese flag found at Tulagi Island. David Levy, twenty-two-year-old skipper of PT 59, is standing second from left. He created a stir in his hometown when he sent this flag back to his twelve-year-old cousin in late 1942.

Approaching Tulagi in late 1942, one could see at least eight PT boats tied up at the dock. Tents are perched on the jungle-enshrouded hillside in the background.

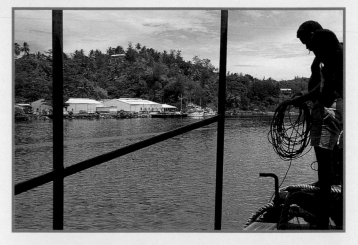

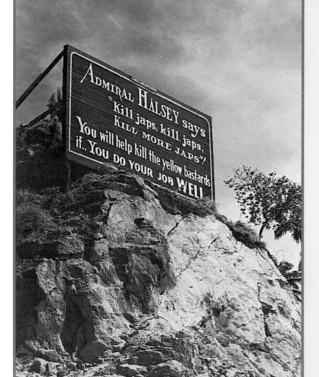

LEFT: Many Americans who passed through the Solomons during the war did not stop at Tulagi, but they do remember the infamous billboard looming over the Tulagi ship anchorage. Admiral Halsey ordered this sign to be erected shortly after he took command in October 1942.

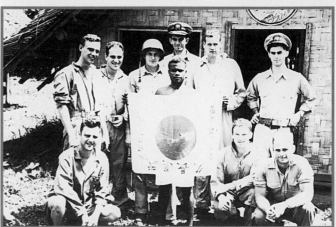

RIGHT: The plywood construction of the PT boats was no match for enemy projectiles. This PT boat has been damaged by a Japanese shell that passed through the deck and hull without exploding. If it had detonated, the boat would surely have been destroyed.

BELOW: This is just one of the many PT boats that came to grief while battling the Japanese Imperial Navy. Sailors inspect the wreckage of a PT boat that washed up on a Guadalcanal beach.

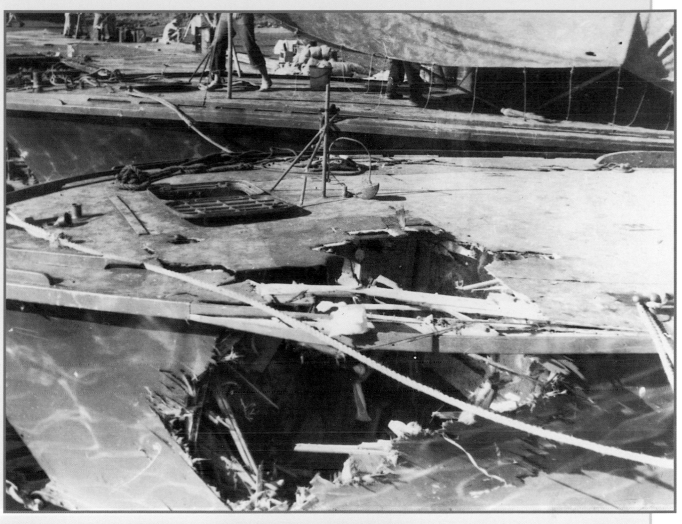

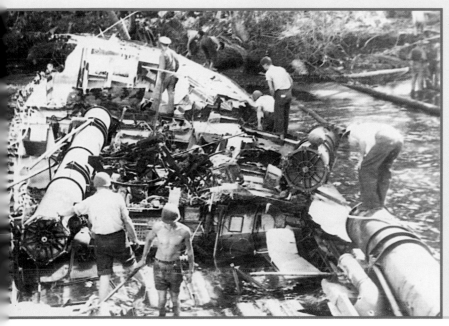

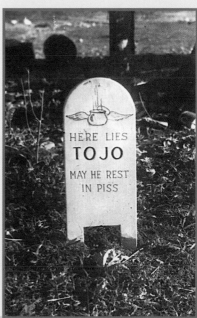

A PT boat skipper photographed this urinal that saw action in the Russell Islands northwest of Guadalcanal.

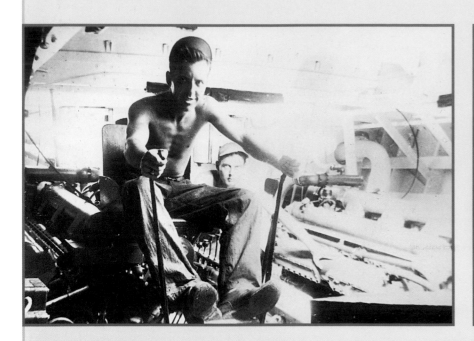

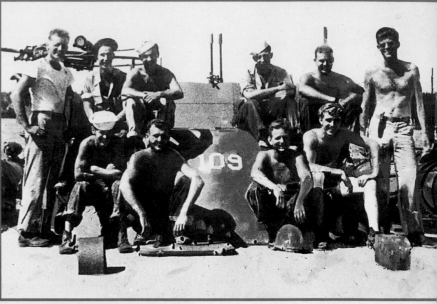

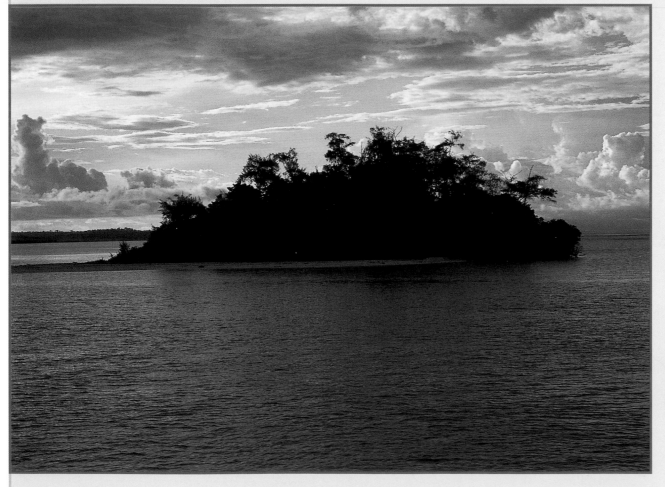

TOP LEFT: Motor-mac Al Hahn at the controls in the engine room of a PT boat. Two of the Packard engines are visible in the photo.

TOP RIGHT: John F. Kennedy and crew aboard PT 109 at Tulagi Island.

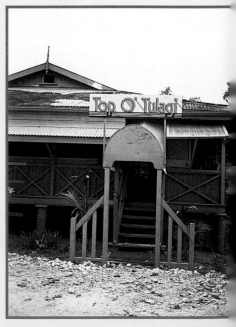

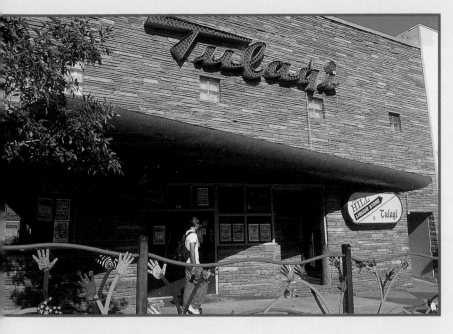

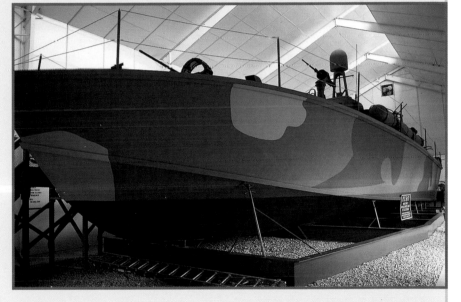

MUNDA AND THE EVOLUTION OF AN ISLAND BASE

A FAMILIAR sequence was repeated time and again during World War II on islands all over the Pacific. The Japanese would begin this process by starting construction of an airstrip. They would clear jungle, palm trees, and underbrush, dredge coral from the reefs, and crush, spread, and finally water the dazzling white surface with saltwater. This type of rudimentary airstrip would then become a strategically important target for the Allies. Shelling, bombing, and strafing attacks would be followed by an amphibious landing and bitter fighting, leading inevitably to a change of possession and the airstrip in the hands of the Allies. Then Navy Seabees or Army Air Forces engineering battalions would repair and vastly enlarge the original Japanese facility using the same coral construction technique. Even while construction was continuing, aircraft would arrive and begin flying missions to support the next island invasion. Pilots and support personnel arriving first would live a rustic existence in hastily erected tents while sturdier facilities were being constructed. Soon the ubiquitous Quonset huts and wood-frame military buildings would appear and give the place more of a permanent feeling.

Tales of terror and heroism would circulate around the base as pilots engaged the Japanese in the air and strafed and bombed them on the ground. There were shot-up planes coming back, wounded and dead pilots, crashes, and mangled bodies to be removed from wreckage. There were air raids and bombing attacks from the Japanese, or the nuisance night bombings by single Japanese planes collectively dubbed "Washing Machine Charlie" for the syncopated sound a single airplane engine would make in the dark tropical night. Amidst all of this, USO entertainers would appear, and then vanish just as suddenly, on their peculiar island-hopping tours.

As the fighting moved farther away, the base would turn to logistical support and become a transit point for planes and personnel moving forward to island bases closer to the fighting. There were fewer shot-up combat planes and more transport and cargo planes. Those who were wounded in fighting near the base were shipped home, and soon the hospital held wounded mostly brought in from battles many miles distant.

Then the fighting was thousands of miles away, and the base would begin to wind down. The final phase was the "roll-up" of the base, the rapid process of closing down a facility that may have accumulated a rich history in valor and suffering but was of no more use in the fight against Japan. Seemingly permanent buildings that had replaced the earlier tents suddenly were dismantled and carted away. In a matter of weeks an entire base could be rolled-up, leaving only concrete slabs and foundations and long, empty acres of the white coral runways and taxiways, with discarded equipment piled in dumps in the jungle or cast into the ocean. Relentless tropical vegetation would almost immediately begin to reclaim shell-scarred and bomb-blasted terrain, and much of what remained was covered with green in a couple of years.

Local villagers, displaced at first to avoid the fighting and then kept away from the base for security reasons, would slowly move back and build modest houses, sometimes using the few scraps of material left behind. Some of them would have fought with or worked for the outsiders who built the base, and their memories would be the only local record of what had happened. The foreigners who fought, lived, and suffered there would never forget the base even though they now lived in countries thousands of miles away and would probably never return. For the rest of their lives, these men would retell incredible stories of their experiences to anyone who would listen back home, and nurses who had worked in the hospitals on those islands would remember horribly injured men and their heartbreaking suffering.

Usually the most visible surviving legacy of such bases is the coral runway, and many of these would continue to serve as a connection to other islands near and far. Small planes still land on the old World War II coral surfaces on some outlying islands, while other island countries, in upgrading their airport facilities, have been able to pave directly over the old coral surface without having to do anything to prepare it for a modern-day asphalt covering. Yet these bases, and most of what went on there, are forgotten now, lying on islands that the vast majority of people living today have never heard of. Munda, on New Georgia in the Solomon Islands, is typical of one of these bases.

When the Japanese were pushed off Guadalcanal after bitter jungle fighting that lasted until February 1943, they decided to establish a defense perimeter farther north in the Solomons. This line would pass through New Georgia Island, and a key anchor of this line would be the airstrip they were constructing at Munda near the eastern end of New Georgia. Allied coast-watchers first noticed that the Japanese were constructing an airstrip there in early December 1942. The Japanese devised an ingenious system to attempt to camouflage the airstrip as they worked on it, stringing cables from trees out across the cleared area and tying the tops of palm trees to the cables. From the air, the Japanese reasoned, the whole construction site would appear to be a coconut plantation. The Americans were not fooled, however, and the first U.S. naval bombardment of the construction area occurred in early January 1943. As in the case of Guadalcanal, capture of this airstrip became imperative for the Americans, both to keep it from being used by the Japanese and to make it available for the Americans, New Zealanders, and Australians who would assist in pushing the Japanese farther north.

After a series of battles fought to secure bases northwest of Guadalcanal and as a prelude to the fight for Munda, U.S. Army and Marine forces landed east of the Munda airfield in July and began a tortuous slog through dense jungle. The unbelievably thick green foliage seemed even worse than on Guadalcanal. Hidden Japanese bunkers were everywhere. The rain, mud, and insects made it a thoroughly miserable experience for almost everyone involved. It wasn't until early August that the Americans wrested control of Munda's cratered coral runway from the Japanese. While skirmishes continued in the jungles around the airstrip, crews of Seabees began work on repairing and expanding the facility the Japanese had begun. Only one week after Munda fell, American fighter planes were landing on the renovated Munda airstrip, and for the next two months Munda would become the busiest airstrip in the Solomons as planes based there struck Japanese positions farther north.

Frank Walton described life at Munda: "One entire end of the island had been leveled by bombs, artillery, and Naval gunfire. A few splintered stumps were all that remained of a huge coconut grove. Wrecked airplanes lay all around, pushed to one side if they interfered with the work on the strip, otherwise left where they were . . . everywhere there was activity. Bulldozers worked in the glare at one end of the runway, lengthening and widening it. Trucks buzzed around. Aircraft landed and took off regularly . . . ; It was hot, steamy. A foul odor pervaded the air. Flies were having a field day: there'd been no time yet to bury the dead Japanese."

The famous "Blacksheep Squadron," headed by Greg "Pappy" Boyington, was based in Munda during this period. Quonset huts on concrete slabs quickly replaced tents, and Bob Hope legitimized the airfield with a stop on his USO tour of the Solomons. As the fighting continued to move farther north, the airstrip at Munda gradually became a quiet rear area.

After the war and into the early twenty-first century, a visitor arriving at Munda by plane landed on the giant wartime runway. Tufts of grass covered most of the original coral surface, but small inter-island airplanes used only a fraction of an airstrip built to accommodate heavy bombers. Even though the network of roads, taxiways, and aircraft parking areas have been reclaimed almost totally by the dark green jungle, the nearly impermeable coral taxiways could still be uncovered in many places by simply rolling up the overlying vegetation like a giant carpet.

Since it was kept clear of encroaching vegetation, the runway was the only obvious trace of anything that went on during the war at Munda. But local guides can show visitors dumps of wartime matériel looming eerily out of the shady, wet greenery. Landing craft, cut in thirds with acetylene torches by the Americans after they had outlived their usefulness, are stacked like giant building blocks in the jungle. Vehicles peer out from the foliage, and guides point out piles of unexploded shells and bombs that, if disturbed, can blow up unexpectedly. In spite of the danger, locals still try to salvage explosives from the dumps to use in fishing and occasionally get killed by setting off ammunition. If the old shells can be detonated in the lagoon, stunned fish rising to the surface make an easy but obviously risky haul for villagers. A few of the inhabitants old enough to remember tell stories of the Japanese, Americans, New Zealanders, and Australians who lived and fought in and around Munda. Nothing is written down, and no local record will remain when the eyewitnesses pass away.

In April 2001, the Solomon Islands government issued a press release announcing plans to "upgrade Munda airport to international standards." A combination of international loans and grants totaling about $1 million is projected to pay for "further development . . . intended to help the growing tourism industry . . . which includes diving and game fishing." For the first time since the war, construction equipment is slated to be rolled out again at Munda.

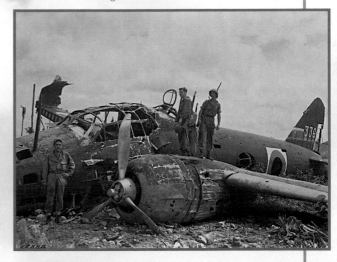

U.S. troops pose beside the wreck of a downed Japanese Betty bomber near the airstrip at Munda shortly after its capture on August 6, 1943.

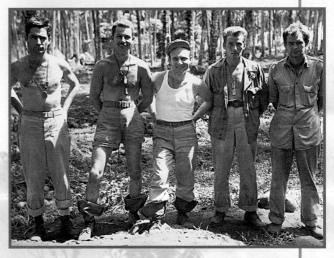

The close-in jungle fighting around the airstrip at Munda produced many episodes of desperation and sheer terror. Just such a situation involved these five Army soldiers. Left to right they are Sergeant A. Demers, Corporal G. Kramer, Lieutenant N. Kliebert, Sergeant H. Ashton, and Sergeant K. Dietlin. They alone held off an all-night assault by an estimated three hundred machete- and bayonet-wielding Japanese soldiers bent on annihilating a group of American wounded on a trail near Munda in August 1943.

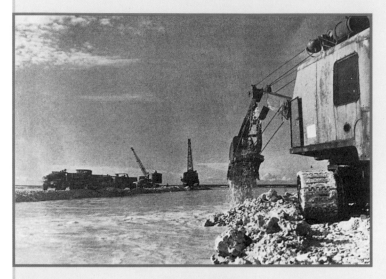

TOP LEFT: Coral is actually a collection of industrious living organisms that, over time, have built up reef communities around virtually every island in the tropical Pacific. To build an airstrip, living coral was dredged from the reefs, crushed, spread over the ground, steamrollered, and watered down with saltwater. The living coral organisms would continue to grow for a time, bond together, and form an almost impermeable, concrete-like surface. James Michener writes in *Tales of the South Pacific*, "If, as some Navy men have suggested, the country ought to build a monument to the Seabees, the Seabees should, in turn, build a monument to Coral. It was their staunchest ally." No doubt engineer aviation battalions and their Japanese counterparts would also agree. The first step in the construction of a coral airstrip was to dredge live coral from the fringing reef surrounding the island.

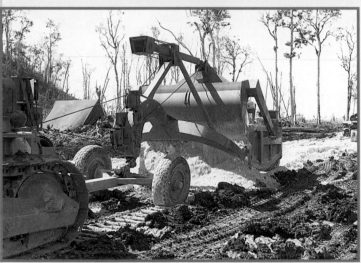

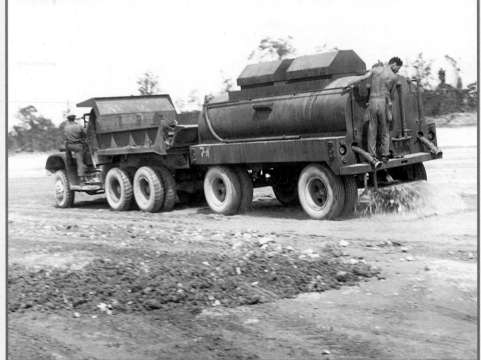

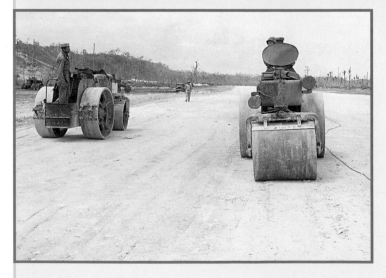

CENTER LEFT: Next the coral was hauled to the cleared site and spread over the ground. At Munda the original Japanese coral airstrip was resurfaced and expanded, with newly cleared areas such as the one shown here covered directly with crushed coral. Depending on the underlying surface, steel matting sometimes was laid down before the coral was spread, thereby giving a more stable foundation in areas prone to poor drainage.

BOTTOM LEFT: After the coral was spread, steamrollers compacted the surface.

ABOVE: The critical step in the process was the frequent soaking of the freshly spread and compacted live coral with seawater from the lagoon. This allowed the living coral organisms to continue to grow for several more days and bond together to form a near-permanent paved surface.

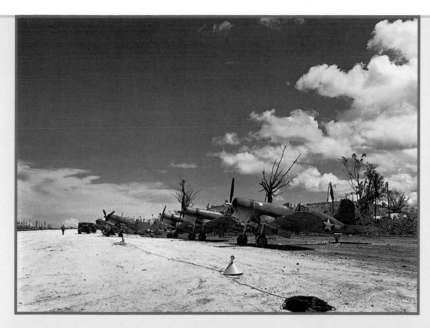

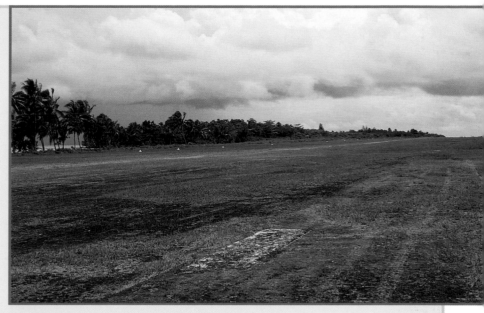

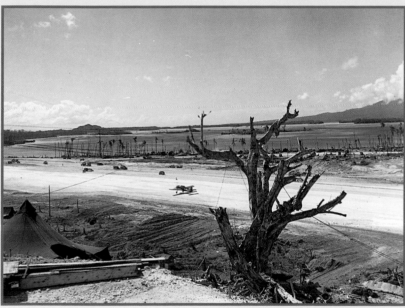

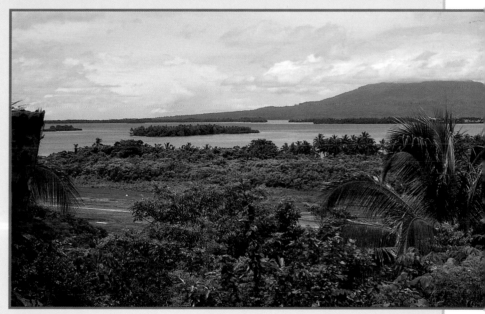

TOP LEFT: The finished product. These Corsairs have just landed on the recently completed, blinding-white coral airstrip at Munda in 1943.

TOP RIGHT: Grass grew over much of the original wartime coral airstrip at Munda, but it was still in use by inter-island aircraft in the early twenty-first century.

CENTER LEFT: The runway at Munda is in use even as Seabee construction crews continue to expand the width to accommodate heavy bombers. Looming in the distance at background right is the island of Rendova, which was an active PT boat base at the time this photo was taken in the latter part of 1943.

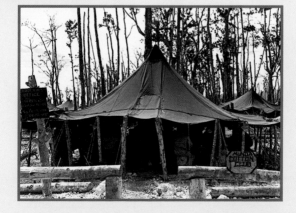

Intense aerial and naval bombardment during the battle to secure the airstrip virtually cleared the area of the normally lush jungle vegetation, a situation that would be repeated in many island bombardments to follow.

CENTER RIGHT: A late–twentieth-century view of the Munda runway, which is barely visible through the dense vegetation that has regrown to surround the airstrip. Rendova Island is in the distance.

BOTTOM: A tent city immediately sprang up around the Munda airstrip after its capture. Here, the chaplain's office doubles as the "Munda Cotton Club."

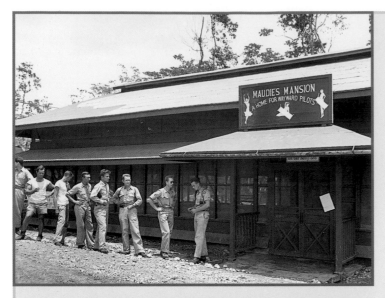

TOP LEFT: Frank Walton described his first meal at Munda in September 1943: "A sign over the mess-hall door read: 'Maudie's Mansion—A Home for Wayward Pilots.' We crunched along the rolled coral floor, sat on splintery mahogany benches at long, rough mahogany tables, ate fly-covered Spam and beans with dehydrated potatoes, and drank warm chicory. . . ." This photo of Maudie's Mansion, known for the scantily clad (and totally unclad) women on the sign above the entrance, was taken in October 1943. Note that essential details have been discreetly covered up for the benefit of this photo. These men have lined up at the front door of Maudie's in the midday heat to wait for lunch to be served.

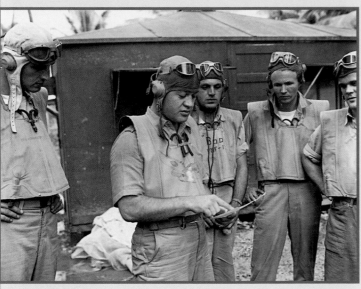

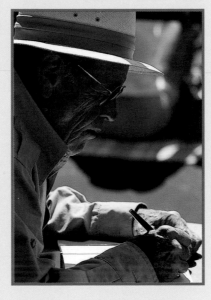

CENTER LEFT: Munda had the distinction of playing host for a time to Greg Boyington's famous Blacksheep Squadron. The Blacksheep came to symbolize the brash, irreverent, but highly successful type of flier that the public at home loved to identify with. Boyington, a wizened thirty-year-old (compared to the other pilots who were in their early twenties), was dubbed "Gramps" by the pilots and "Pappy" by the media. The bad-boy image of Boyington and the Blacksheep Squadron was more a media invention than anything else, but the legend lived right on through to the 1970s when a television show was created to perpetuate the myths, much to the chagrin of the veteran pilots of the squadron. In fact, the Blacksheep were highly trained professional fliers. They seldom went out alone to do personal battle with the

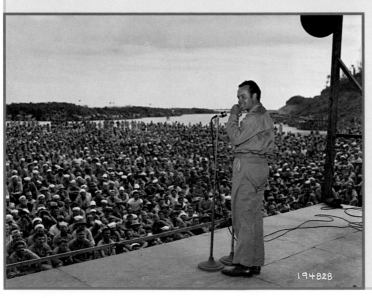

Japanese, as legend says they often did just to be ornery. They frequently flew as part of extensively planned and coordinated missions with U.S. Navy, Army Air Forces, and New Zealand Air Force fighter squadrons based in the Solomon Islands. Here, at Munda, Boyington briefs his pilots before a mission.

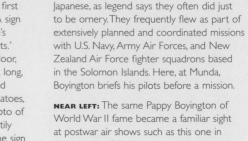

NEAR LEFT: The same Pappy Boyington of World War II fame became a familiar sight at postwar air shows such as this one in Colorado in 1984. He toured from air show to air show in a van (with his personalized Medal of Honor license plates) and sat for hours patiently autographing copies of his popular 1958 best-seller *Baa Baa Blacksheep.* People lined up and waited for the chance to get an autograph and say a few words to an American legend, the leader of the hell-bent-for-leather Blacksheep and a Medal of Honor winner. For these people there was always a certain fascination with actually coming face-to-face with a man who shot down twenty-eight Japanese aircraft. For many who didn't experience World War II at any greater depth than in a theater or in front of a TV, Boyington embodied much of what World War II in the Pacific seemed to be about—danger and adventure on exotic tropical islands. He had the reputation of an exuberant maverick not afraid to defy authority, always improvising with his band of skilled pilots, and continually confounding the more conventional Japanese. Most fans of the 1970s TV series loosely based on his exploits didn't know that he was shot down shortly after sending his twenty-eighth enemy aircraft crashing in flames into the tropical ocean. Then he narrowly missed being killed by an American bombing raid on the Japanese base at Truk while he was being held there as a POW. For the rest of the war he suffered the privation of Japanese camps until his eventual release. In the years that followed, he never seemed to come across anything he was quite as good at as shooting Japanese Zeros from the sky. Perfectly adapted for war, he seemed ill at ease in other occupations. When once asked if he ever wanted to return to the Pacific islands where he became famous, he replied: "I had some chances, but I never really wanted to go back. I guess I saw enough of them when I was there the first time. Those islands are too damned hot anyway!" He will get no more chances to visit the jungle-shrouded airstrip at Munda, or the palm-lined runway at Vella Lavella where he and the Blacksheep had their picture taken in Boston Red Sox baseball caps lined up on the wings of a Corsair. Greg Boyington died on January 11, 1988, in California at the age of seventy-five.

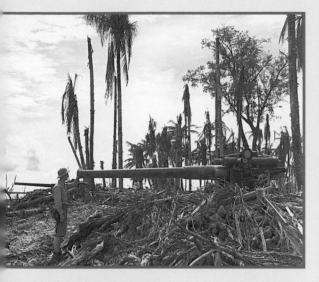

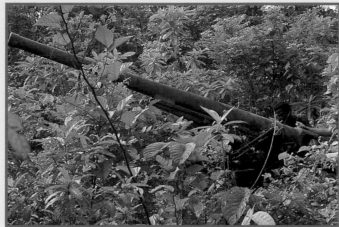

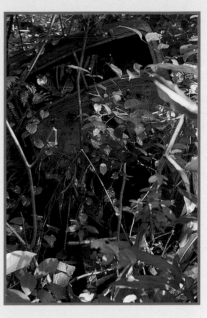

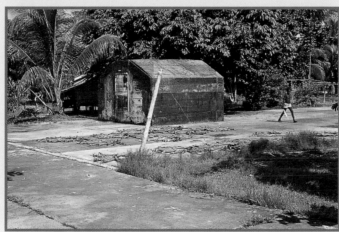

ABOVE: U.S. trucks were abandoned by the score and remain in overgrown dumps surrounding Munda.

OPPOSITE BOTTOM LEFT: If, suddenly, a USO troupe would appear, everyone who could take a break would crowd around to see who had shown up. In this case Bob Hope entertains the troops at Munda on August 5, 1944. There is no shortage of space to accommodate the audience since the stage has been set up on the runway, seen stretching off into the distance in the background.

TOP LEFT: These Japanese naval guns had shelled Munda for a week during the fight for the airstrip, and they became a favorite attraction for anyone who passed through Munda. Inevitably, they were nicknamed "Pistol Pete" by the Americans.

ABOVE LEFT: American landing craft no longer needed were cut into thirds and piled up in this jungle dump near the airstrip at Munda.

TOP CENTER: Though it is a difficult hike through the jungle that has grown up around Munda, this particular "Pistol Pete" is still a local attraction for visitors.

ABOVE RIGHT: Almost all the structures built for the base at Munda were dismantled after the war. What remains are concrete foundations or floor slabs, such as this one said to be the remains of the base PX. The large concrete structure was the vault where the payroll was kept.

RIGHT: What had been the busiest airstrip in the Solomon Islands was quickly abandoned by the Allies after the war. In this 1946 photo, the once-bare, bomb-blasted Munda has already begun to re-vegetate. Today, only the airstrip at the center remains clear of prolific jungle growth.

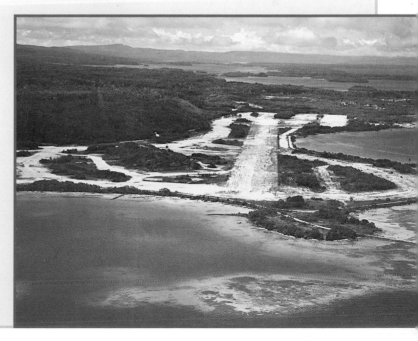

BORA BORA, THE ISLAND PARADISE

I wish I could tell you about the South Pacific. The way it actually was. The endless ocean. The infinite specks of coral we called islands. Coconut palms nodding gracefully toward the ocean. Reefs upon which waves broke into spray, and inner lagoons, lovely beyond description. I wish I could tell you about the sweating jungle, the full moon rising behind the volcanoes, and the waiting. The waiting. The timeless, repetitive waiting. —**James Michener**, *Tales of the South Pacific*

THERE WERE numerous bizarre aberrations to the "war" in the Pacific where men were stationed on remote islands with nothing much to do but wait. Of all of these island outposts, Bora Bora in French Polynesia was unusual. On this island the U.S. had established its first advance base after the attack on Pearl Harbor, an operation code-named Bobcat. Since it was the first of what would be many bases set up on islands across the Pacific, the operation ran into numerous difficulties. Fortunately, the island was thousands of miles from the fighting, and lessons learned on Bora Bora concerning logistics and supplies were usefully applied to subsequent operations.

However, for the men stationed on Bora Bora, logistics and supply were the furthest things from their minds. Navy Lieutenant James Michener, future Pulitzer Prize winner, was sent to Bora Bora to investigate a possible rebellion of Naval personnel stationed there. Anticipating a mutinous situation, Michener was amazed to learn that the men were not demanding to be shipped home. On the contrary, they were threatening to rebel if someone tried to send them home! Stationed on a fantastically lush tropical island many miles from where blood was being shed, most of the men had the interesting living arrangement of being boarded, if that is the right word, by local families. This in itself, would seem irregular in a military setting, but there was more of course. The fringe benefit the sailors were ready to rebel to preserve, the situation they wanted to keep secret from the Navy and their families back home, the reason they were ready to mutiny rather than be sent home, was that they were sleeping with the beautiful Polynesian daughters of their host families, with the sanction and encouragement of

their commanding officers and the parents of the girls. Lieutenant Michener was assured that the sailors worked dutifully on their various tasks around the island by day, like road-building or setting up the occasional coastal defense gun. At night, however, while a handful remained on duty at the base, the rest returned to their girlfriends and their obliging host parents in villages scattered along the coast of the island. In a characteristic understatement, Michener noted in his memoir, The World is My Home, "It was a well-run base marked by an unusual degree of happiness."

Michener went on to describe the living arrangements. "It seemed as if each man stationed on Bora Bora had his own hut. In many cases it was built for him by the men of the girl's family because they approved of her association with the Americans who could bring food and other necessary items to the place. . . . I found the little houses both clean and practical: a bed of coconut matting, a table, a chair, nails to hang the sailors' clothes so they would be neat, and not much else, for living took place out of doors or at the naval base; the hut was for night affairs only, including sleeping."

Though he was supposed to write a critical appraisal of the situation on Bora Bora, Michener gave the place a glowing report and promised to keep the names of the sailors a secret. He even found it hard to leave the island himself when the time came to go. He, too, had become enchanted with this idyllic version of war the sailors had found for themselves on Bora Bora. In his memoirs, Michener concludes, "In the long years ahead whenever anyone would ask: 'Michener, you've seen most of the world. What was the very best spot of all?' My answer would invariably be 'Bora Bora.'"

"To put it quite simply, Bora Bora is the most beautiful island in the world."—James Michener, *The World Is My Home*.

BELOW: Work on Bora Bora consisted of any number of duties to take up the daylight hours, including numerous low-key road-building projects. The Seabees in this photo have been assigned the task of taking a landing boat out to one of the small islands—called *motus*—on the circling reef to dig up coral gravel for a road around the island.

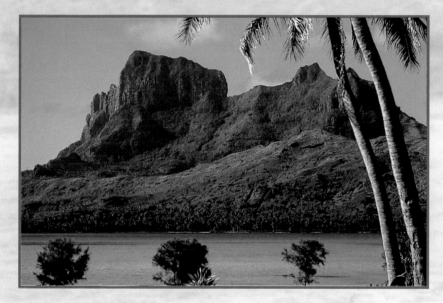

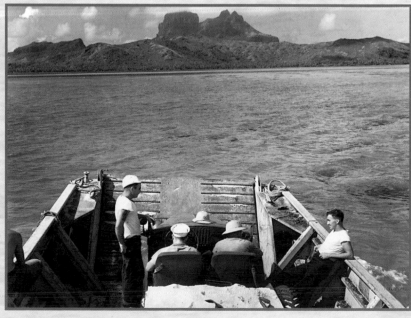

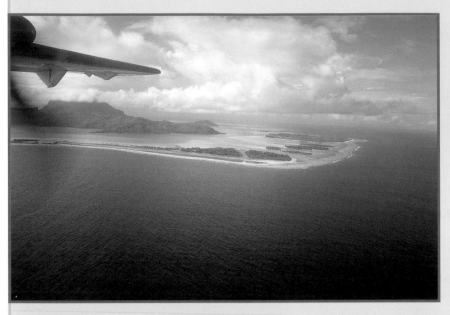

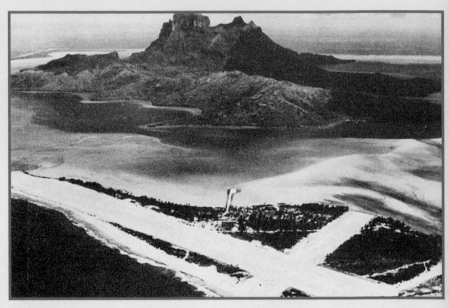

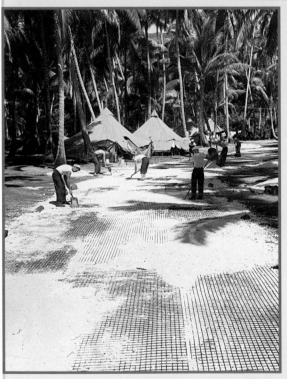

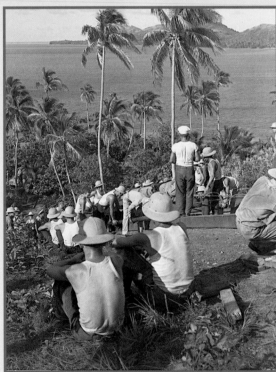

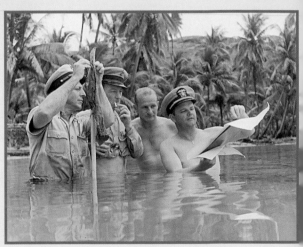

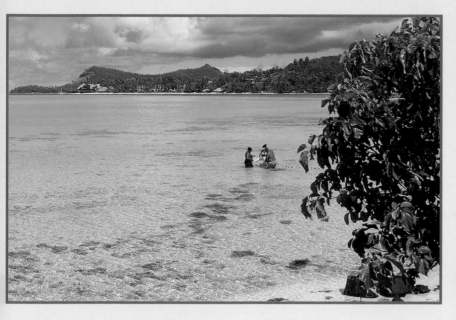

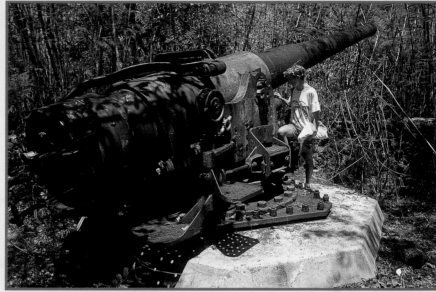

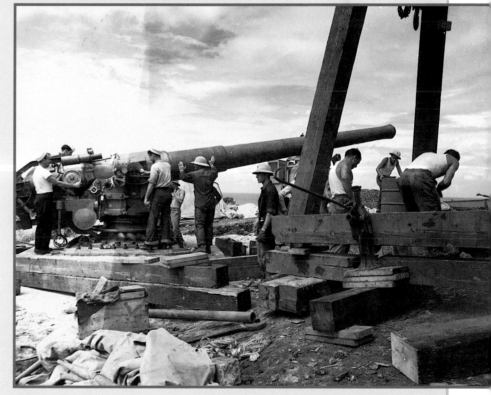

OPPOSITE TOP LEFT: One of the first jobs for the Seabees on Bora Bora was to build an airstrip, which is still in use today.

OPPOSITE TOP RIGHT: This was the first and only coral airstrip at that time in all of French Polynesia. In *The World Is My Home,* Michener described his wartime arrival at Bora Bora: "The airstrip for the island was unique: a long, beautiful coral pathway, wide enough to accept a DC-3, built of shimmering white coral that almost blinded the eye. It was located not on the island itself, which was too hilly to permit a strip, but far out on the fringing reef. Landing at Bora Bora was the best possible introduction to the island; when I first came, as we flew in low over the dark Pacific, I saw to my left the towering basaltic pillar from the old volcano and the lime-green beauty of the lagoon, then there was a sudden drop and the crunch of tires on the packed coral. I was in the heartland of Polynesia."

OPPOSITE BOTTOM LEFT: Once the airstrip was completed, the sailors were kept busy during the days with such tasks as leisurely road-building under the palms.

OPPOSITE BOTTOM CENTER: In addition to building the airstrip and working on roads that circled the island, one of the most arduous jobs on Bora Bora was to install eight coastal defense guns on low hills overlooking the lagoon. One of these seven-inch guns is hauled up a steep slope by sheer brute force.

OPPOSITE BOTTOM RIGHT: The sparkling, warm, clear water of the lagoon at Bora Bora now attracts tourists from all around the world. In 1943 these men enjoy the 85-degree water while holding a "staff meeting."

ABOVE LEFT: It is not just the tourists who enjoy the warm, placid waters of the lagoon at Bora Bora. Here, several of the Polynesian locals fish in the shallow, clear water.

ABOVE RIGHT: Today, several of the World War II coastal defense guns are still in place.

RIGHT: Tropical foliage has now nearly obscured the open views of the surrounding lagoon that were so critical when this gun was installed during the war.

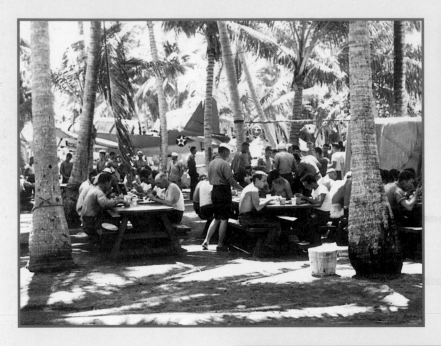

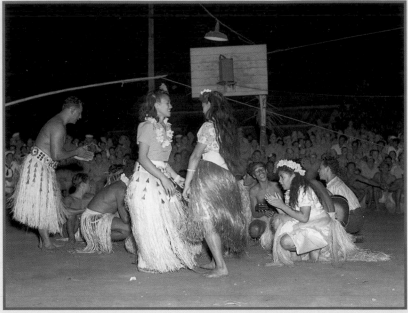

ABOVE LEFT: Work for the sailors on Bora Bora everyday ranged from physical labor to menial tasks around the base, but no matter what the assignments were, lunchtime was always a pleasant interlude that seemed to evoke the atmosphere of a tropical summer camp. Here, Seabees sit down to the midday meal at picnic tables set among the swaying palm trees. In the background is a seaplane pulled up on dry land for maintenance. The Inshore Patrol Squadron arrived at Bora Bora on February 17, 1942, and started air operations the following month.

ABOVE RIGHT: For the sailors the real attractions on Bora Bora were the young women of the island shown here performing a traditional Polynesian dance for the American contingent (seen seated in the background).

RIGHT: Today tourists flock to Bora Bora for the beauty of the lagoon and the beaches. This is the scene at one of the island tourist resorts called Hotel Bora Bora.

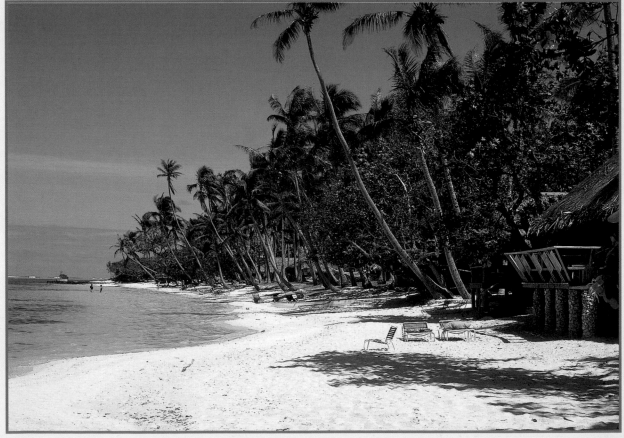

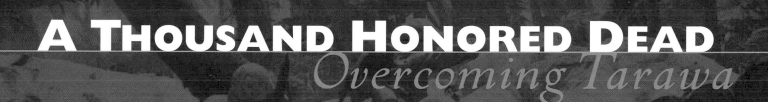

CHAPTER 4

A THOUSAND HONORED DEAD

Overcoming Tarawa

THE DRUMS HAVE ROLLED

THE BELLS HAVE TOLLED

THE FINAL MASS IS SAID

WE LEAVE BEHIND,

ON TARAWA, A THOUSAND

HONORED DEAD

—*Captain Earl J. Wilson*

THE GILBERT ISLANDS, lying some twenty-five hundred miles southwest of Hawaii, are a chain of coral atolls—surf-washed reefs that enclose quiet lagoons studded with green islets—which from the air resemble jade necklaces floating upon a blue-green sea. These were the tropical isles of romantic South Seas movies—of sun and sea and palm trees, dreamy and placid. Living was easy, with one day just about like the next. But in early 1942 when Japanese naval forces came to occupy islands that had been ruled by Britain, the living was easy no longer.

The Japanese first murdered the Gilberts' eleven white residents and then impressed the native men into slave labor. Using them along with their own troops and laborers press-ganged from Japanese-occupied Korea, they set about fortifying various of the islands and transforming one of them into what they intended to be an impregnable fortress.

Their purpose was threefold: First, to link the Gilberts into a defensive chain intended to protect and forever preserve Japan's newly conquered empire in the western Pacific. Second, to create another base from which Japanese planes could hammer supply lines that connected the United States to the South Pacific and Australia. And finally, the Gilberts were to become a military bear-trap—a "Waylaid Attack," its commanding officer called it, where they could inflict upon the Americans a defeat so one-sided and slaughter so terrible that they would have no heart for further assaults upon Japanese strongholds, and they might even consider negotiating a peace. The islet the Japanese chose for their stronghold lay in the southwest corner of Tarawa Atoll, and its name was Betio. Seen from above, Betio resembles a long, slim bird lying on its side, back to the sea on the south, stomach to the lagoon on the north, its short-beaked head to the west, and a long, slender tail curving to the southeast. And extending from the belly of the bird like a long sticklike leg, a fifteen-hundred-foot pier crosses the reef to link the island to navigable waters in the lagoon.

Betio is tiny, measuring no more than two and a quarter miles tip to tip, one-third of a mile across at its fattest, and its area of 291 acres is a mere one-third that of New York City's Central Park. But tiny as it is, the Japanese managed to cram into it 106 machine-gun pillboxes (some spaced only fifty feet apart), fourteen light tanks dug into the sand with their cannon aimed seaward, thirty-eight heavy guns ranging up to five and one-half inches in bore, and, at each end of the island, a pair of giant eight-inch coastal defense guns.

To protect all this deadly hardware and the troops manning it, they built dozens of bunkers, blockhouses, and hardened gun emplacements with concrete roofs as thick as five feet and walls as thick as ten, then covered and surrounded them with protective layers of coral gravel and coconut logs. And as if that weren't protection enough, they converted Betio's surrounding reef into a lethal maze of barbed wire, steel antitank "hedgehogs," underwater barriers of coconut logs, and underwater mines.

To man this formidable bastion they brought in 4,836 battle-hardened troops of the elite Sasebo and Yokohama Imperial Landing Force—Japan's best, and volunteers all—led by Rear Admiral Keijo Shibasaki. And when at last the physical installations were completed and the troops all in place, the admiral surveyed the result and found it good. "A million Americans," he declared, "could not take this island in a hundred years!"

The American commanders, meanwhile, had been pondering how best to seize the initiative in the Pacific and to begin acting instead of reacting. After their attack on Pearl Harbor, the Japanese had needed only five months to take control of more than 12.5 million square miles of new territory, and with the exception of Guadalcanal and a few tiny American and Australian toeholds on New Guinea and New Georgia, they still held all of it. Thanks to the naval battles of Coral Sea and Midway and the recapture of Guadalcanal, the enemy juggernaut had been slowed and perhaps even stopped. Now Western leaders were ready to try taking back some of that lost territory.

From beginning to end the Allied Pacific strategy was shaped largely by two strong-minded men—Admiral Chester W. Nimitz and General Douglas MacArthur—each jealously protective of his own authority and branch of service, each with a different solution for the problem, and each competing for the ear of another strong-minded man—President Franklin D. Roosevelt—in hopes of getting his own solution approved.

MacArthur believed in what he called "leapfrogging" or "island-hopping": advancing on Japan by stair-stepping up the great chain of enemy-held islands stretching from the Solomons and New Guinea northwest to the Philippines and then northeast to Japan itself. The Army would, of course, command and execute the operation, and the Navy would, as assistant, supply ocean transportation and offshore artillery fire, and protect the Army's beaches from offshore attack.

Admiral Nimitz, too, believed in island-hopping—but of a different kind. Instead of climbing the stairway of islands from the bottom he wanted to slash into and through the middle of it—to seize an island on the Japanese perimeter, then another farther in, and then another, until Japanese forces to the south wouldn't any longer need to be fought. Cut-off and isolated, they would simply "die on the vine." These operations, naturally, would be directed and executed by the Navy, and the Army would assist by serving as a sort of military janitor, mopping up and occupying what the Navy and Marines had won.

Guadalcanal, had been the latter sort of operation—won by the Marines, mopped up and occupied by the Army. Since then, General MacArthur, with Navy support, had continued to work at his brand of island-hopping. But by mid-1943, with the Pacific war already eighteen months old and the recapture of Guadalcanal a whole year in the past, his results had been less than impressive. At least, that is how the people back home saw it. Daily newspaper maps and commentary reminded them that, aside from a few islands in the Solomons and a few fragile Allied footholds on New Guinea, the Japanese still controlled the whole Pacific Ocean west of Midway and north of the Coral Sea—all of which had been seized more than a year before—and the home folks were becoming impatient and more than a little frightened. "Japan can be the most powerful military nation on earth," exclaimed an August 1943 issue of *Life* magazine, "quite possibly too strong to be conquered even by the U.S. and Britain."

As for MacArthur's island-hopping, *Life* bitingly observed: "Guadalcanal . . . is about 3,000 miles from Tokyo.

During one full year of desperate fighting we have advanced [from there] to the tip of New Georgia, a distance of approximately 200 miles. Assuming we do as well in the future . . . we shall be able to make a bloody landing in Tokyo 14 years hence, in the summer of 1957. After that we can proceed to the conquest of Japan."

Admiral Nimitz and his boss, Chief of Naval Operations Admiral Ernest J. King, also were concerned about the slow Allied progress, as was the president himself. So, in the summer of 1943, President Roosevelt agreed that Admiral Nimitz should now try his brand of island-hopping. As might be expected, General MacArthur was not pleased. Later he wrote in his memoirs: "Admiral King claimed the Pacific as the rightful domain of the Navy . . . as almost his own private war. . . . He resented the prominent part I had in the Pacific War [and] had the complete support of Secretary of the Navy Knox [and] the support in general principle of President Roosevelt. . . ."

The general's objections notwithstanding, the die had been cast, and as his first objective—the initial chunk to be wrenched from the enemy's protective rim—Admiral Nimitz chose the Gilbert Islands. Invasion date: November 20, 1943.

It would be a new kind of gamble—the sort of amphibious attack in which the defenders hold all the aces. In fact, few such operations had been attempted in modern times, fewer still had succeeded, and the Americans had yet to make one at all, or, at least, not one like this stacked up to be. The possibility had been foreseen way back in 1920 by future general and commandant of the Marine Corps John LeJeune. With remarkable clairvoyance he and Marine Major Pete Ellis not only had anticipated an action of this kind but that it would involve recovering islands seized by Japan. As a result, practice for such an operation had been a part of Marine Corps training for the past twenty years. But that's all it had been, practice. This would be for real.

So far, the Americans' only amphibious invasion experience had been at Guadalcanal and in MacArthur's recent landings on New Georgia and New Guinea, and under much different conditions. Those were large islands with room to operate in an organized way. Room to expand a beach-head into a secure operating base for those support systems—supply, repair, medical, etc.—essential to a successful operation. At Guadalcanal, moreover, the initial landing had been unopposed—something extremely unlikely here.

These landings would be a quite different proposition—more difficult to plan, more dangerous to execute, and with a whole lot of untested kinks to be worked out. The little coral-strip islets of the Gilberts had no "interior." There, the beach was the island and the island was the beach. Period. Attacking troops would be totally exposed to hostile fire from rifles, machine guns, artillery, mortars, grenades—whatever the enemy chose to throw at them. They would be eyeball-to-eyeball with an enemy shooting from hardened emplacements barely an arm's length away, and their only armor, as an old Marine saying had it, would be their khaki shirts. And as if that weren't enough, their vital support operations would not be behind the battle line but within it, entangled in it, interfering with it, and just as vulnerable to enemy fire.

Under such conditions any amphibious attack should surely fail—foundering in its own blood. Indeed, the only similar major attack of modern times had done just that. Made at Gallipoli by the British in World War I, it had cost seventy thousand casualties and accomplished nothing. But the planners of the Tarawa operation figured they had a foolproof answer—the destructive power of modern bombing planes and naval gunnery focused upon one small target. Concentrating their firepower upon tiny Betio they must surely pulverize the enemy's defenses and so demoralize and decimate his troops as to make the invasion itself little more dangerous than a walk in the park.

"We're going to pound that place with Naval shellfire and dive-bombers," declared Major General Holland M. "Howling Mad" Smith, commander of the Marine Fifth Amphibious Corps. "We're going to steamroller it until Hell wouldn't have it." "We do not intend just to neutralize it," said Admiral Harry Hill, commander of Navy Task Force Fifty-three. "We do not intend just to destroy it. Gentlemen, we will obliterate it!"

On November 13, 1943, the "obliterating" began. Swarming up from bases on the islands of Canton, Baker, and Funafuti, heavy bombers of both the Army and Navy commenced bombing Betio round-the-clock. Five days later, planes from eleven Navy aircraft carriers joined in. A day after that ships of Navy Cruiser Division Five spent the day slamming eight-inch shells into the island.

Then, on the evening of that day—November 19, 1943—the bombing stopped and the guns fell silent. On Betio, Japanese troops creeping cautiously from their shell-battered bunkers saw silhouetted on the moon-sparkled sea the dark outlines of dozens of ships approaching from the west. What they were seeing, although they could not have known it then, was a portion of the greatest battle fleet ever assembled up to that time: ten battleships (three of them sunk at Pearl Harbor but resurrected and now thirsting for revenge), sixteen aircraft carriers, eighteen cruisers, fifty-two destroyers, and dozens of cargo ships and other auxiliary vessels. And, twelve transports carrying the nineteen thousand men of the Second Marine Division.

November 20: Shortly after midnight the transports move in near the entrance to the Tarawa channel and heave to. Along with them are several vessels of a brand-new type. Designed specifically for this kind of operation, they are called Landing Ship–Tanks by the Navy, Large Slow Targets by their crews, and LSTs by everyone. And they are slow. Rated to cruise at eleven knots, sometimes they do well to make nine. Shaped like a decked-over bathtub with a boxy little superstructure perched on one end, the LST is 327 feet long, 50 feet wide, flat of bottom, and shallow of draft. It is designed to run its nose up against or even onto a beach where, by opening its two tall bow doors and dropping a hinged ramp, it can deliver men and machines onto the shore, sometimes without even wetting their feet. By the same process LSTs can launch amphibious landing craft at sea, allowing them to drive directly from the hold, over the ramp, and into the water. The LSTs are sluggish, lumbering ugly ducklings. And they are to become one of the most valuable Allied vessels of the entire war.

Now the ponderous wheels of the invasion machine begin to turn. LST bow doors swing open, ramps drop, and "amtracs" (Amphibious Tractors) roar and clatter from the holds to swim for a time in six-tractor holding-circles in the sea. Known also as "Buffaloes," the amtracs are simply open-topped, floating steel boxes fitted with cleated caterpillar treads that propel them over rough ground and obstacles on land and through water when afloat. The Buffaloes, too, are new—so new that today will be their first test in battle.

Cargo booms swing, davits are cranked out, and each ship begins lowering its thirty-odd landing craft into the water. These craft are of two types, both also new designs developed especially for such operations as this. Like the amtracs, they are floating, open-topped boxes. Unlike the amtracs they are propeller-driven and can operate only in water. The LCVPs (Landing Craft–Vehicle–Personnel), thirty-six feet long and made of plywood, are intended primarily for troops, although they can carry jeeps or other small vehicles. The LCMs (Landing Craft–Mechanized), fifty feet long and made of steel, are designed to transport trucks and tanks as well as men. Both are flat bottomed and shallow of draft, and both have flat bows that drop to become ramps when discharging Marines and cargo on the beach.

3:00 A.M.: The invasion troops are awakened and given the Marine's traditional precombat breakfast—a meal loved by the men but hated by the surgeons who soon may be trying to repair shot-torn intestines stuffed with it.

"We ate early that morning and we ate good," said amtrac driver Sergeant Karl Leffler. "Steak and eggs. Worst thing they could feed you before combat, but I guess they wanted to be sure our last meal was a good one."

It has been a hot and restless time for troops trying to sleep in the transports' holds. In iron ships that have been baking under a tropical sun in these pre–air conditioning days, the living spaces tend to remain insufferably hot all through the night. *Time-Life* correspondent Robert Sherrod finds it this way on the transport *Zeilin*, where: "We jumped out of bed swimming in sweat. . . . Nobody took more than 15 minutes to eat his steak and eggs and fried potatoes and drink his two cups of coffee, but everybody was sweat-soaked before he had finished."

3:55 A.M.: All landing craft are in the water now—hundreds of them—puttering round-and-round in lazy, six- or seven-boat circles near their mother ships (like elephants circling at a circus, someone has said)—and Boat Group

officers begin hailing them in for loading.

It is not a simple operation to get five thousand men down cargo nets and into the right boats at the right times. To the uninitiated it would appear to be disorganized bedlam. Whistles are blown. Orders are shouted. Other orders, preceded by "Now hear this!" echo metallically from ships' PA systems. Hundreds of sweating, nervously wisecracking Marines jostle their way toward debarkation stations, jamming ladders and companionways that have become too small because the men, loaded with packs and rifles and battle gear, have become too large. But it is not chaos. Mission planners have cranked out thousands of pages of charts and instructions telling each unit and vehicle where to go when, and what to do when they get there. Each platoon leader knows where his men are to disembark. Each boat operator knows where to come alongside to pick them up and what position in which assault wave he is to take up after he has them.

5:10 A.M.: The first three waves are loaded, and still no interference from shore. Then, just when it appears the enemy really has been "obliterated" the defenders open up with big guns, sowing the wind and reaping the whirlwind. For what the Japanese get in return is a crashing, smashing, flaming bombardment that veterans of that morning still remember with awe.

"We were sitting out there, bobbing around like a cork in a fishpond," said amtrac driver Leffler, "when all the battlewagons and cruisers suddenly opened up."

With a "great thud in the southwest," wrote correspondent Sherrod, "the first battleship . . . raised the curtain on the theater of death." Then all join in and the western sky flickers with orange and yellow flame stabbing like summer lightning from the guns. Their shells, heated white by friction with the air, sail through the predawn darkness like slow comets, rattling and rumbling as they go.

The island disappears under a mass of winking explosions and writhing flames from which bursts one enormous, volcano-like eruption. *Maryland*'s giant guns have found and destroyed the ammunition stores of the Japanese big guns on Betio's west end, with an explosion so violent that the guns themselves are destroyed along with their blockhouses.

5:45 A.M.: It is light enough now for pilots to see ground targets. The Naval bombardment ceases in order to allow carrier planes to work over whatever the big guns may have missed. But there has been a mix-up. The planes don't come, and the Japanese take advantage of the lull to resume their fire. Their big eight-inchers are gone, but they have plenty of other artillery left, and now that they have light enough to choose their targets, they go to work on the transports.

On the *Zeilin* Corporal Eddie Owen sees splashes and thinks they are porpoises until, "a shell suddenly screamed through the rigging." Robert Sherrod sees them, too, "not more than fifty yards from our stern," and he says to Major Howard Rice: "Those boys need some practice!" Retorted Rice, "You don't think that's our own guns doing that shooting do you?" This is dangerous business. The transports must be preserved at any cost. None has been hit so far, but only through sheer luck. Now they hoist anchor and steam out to sea, their landing craft bobbing after them like chicks following mother hens.

Again the American warships answer the Japanese by opening fire, and again the island disappears in flame and smoke.

6:10 A.M.: At last the carrier planes arrive, and once more the ships cease fire to let them do their work. At the same time the battleships are moving in, some to within a mile of the island. After ten minutes of bombing and strafing the planes leave, and the battleships begin a selective short-range shelling meant to find and destroy individual enemy batteries.

Meanwhile, all troops of the first five assault waves have been loaded into their boats, and because the boats are out on the open sea they are having a most unpleasant time of it. In Sherrod's Fifth Wave boat: "Half a barrel of water comes over the bow every minute. Every one of its thirty-odd men is soaked before we chug half a mile." On top of being wet, many are seasick and vomiting, and all are trying more or less vainly to shelter rifles, radios, telephones, and other vital hardware from the drenching spray. But even though miserable physically, most are comfortable mentally—optimistic and expecting an easy day. That's what they've been told to expect. A milk-run. A pushover. And

having seen the island blasted by three thousand tons of bombs and shells in just the past two hours—ten tons for every acre—a mere supplement to all the bombing of the past week, the men believe it. Sergeant Jack Lent said he felt "kinda sorry for the Japanese. I thought we were wipin' em out." Private Robert Lewis "thought the island was gonna be sunk." "Most of us believed we could practically run up on the island and take it over," said Private First Class Mickey Franklin.

But then, they didn't yet know what Japanese Chief Petty Officer Tadeo Onuki knows. "They shell us 24 hours a day," he writes in his diary, "but with little effect."

At seven o'clock the minesweepers *Requisite* and *Pursuit* make the first American penetration of Tarawa lagoon, steaming in through the channel and right into trouble. Their orders are to sweep a path for the landing craft and then to lay down a protective smokescreen. But they immediately find themselves under such heavy enemy fire that they call for help. Destroyers *Dashiell* and *Ringgold* respond, sailing into the lagoon and unleashing their five-inch guns at the guns firing from shore. *Ringgold* takes two hits. Both, fortunately, are duds. Seeing the flash of the guilty gun, *Ringgold's* gunnery officer shoots back, blowing up the offending gun along with its ammunition.

That done, things quiet down in the lagoon, and the landing craft begin churning in through the channel and taking their assigned assault-wave positions. Having both land and water capabilities, amtracs will make up the first waves. They would make up all if there were enough of them, but there are not. There are only enough for the first three waves, and while still out at sea they were loaded with men transferring from LCVPs.

"We got our troops," said Sergeant Leffler, "fifteen or twenty I think a tractor would carry, fully equipped—that's in addition to the four or five crew members. Then we took off for the lagoon and the Line of Departure. Exactly when we went in I don't recall." A minesweeper at each end marks the Line of Departure, about three miles from the beach. But there is confusion among the boats. It is taking them longer than planned to get into position, and H-hour, originally set for 0830, has to be set back to 0845, and then to 0900.

Meanwhile, those amtrac drivers who have managed to get into position are having a hard time staying there. "It was tricky," said Leffler. "Like operating a caterpillar —one lever to control the right tread and another to control the left. To stop you had to pull 'em both back, and to keep position on the Line you had keep working those levers all the time."

During the delay there is a wind shift that would make a smoke screen useless, and the screen is canceled.

8:37 A.M.: At last all amtracs are in position. Drivers gun their engines, treads spin and churn, and the first three waves, carrying three Battalion Landing Teams, begin foaming toward the beach. On the right, the Third Battalion, Second Regiment (3/2), heads for the strip of beach lying under the "beak and throat" of bird-shaped Betio. This will be known as Red Beach One. In the center, the Second Battalion (2/2) aims for the belly of the bird to the right of the long pier —Red Beach Two. And on the left, the Second Battalion of the Eighth Regiment (2/8) also churns toward the belly of the bird, but to the left of the pier—Red Beach Three.

An offshore wind blows smoke and dust into the faces of the Marines and again they are soaked by spray, but for the first two miles this is their only discomfort. Then, at the beginning of the third and final mile they arrive at the war. It begins as a spattering of rifle and cannon fire that grows ever heavier. By the time they have reached the reef—a quarter- to a half-mile out, depending on location —it has become what Marine historian Robert Leckie will remember as, "a volcano of flame and sound . . . amtracs blowing up, amtracs beginning to burn, amtracs spinning around, slowing and sinking."

Now, the really bad news. The water over the reef is not as it is supposed to be. The attack was scheduled for a period of neap tide—a low-water time leaving a maximum of dry beach between the water and a four-foot coconut-log sea-wall extending all along Betio's north side, but at the same time, or so the experts have calculated, leaving enough water

on the reef to allow all landing craft—LCVPs and LCMs as well as the amtracs—to run their cargoes of men and equip-ment all the way to the beach. What the planners did not and could not know was that capricious Nature would choose this particular time to overlay the predictable neap tide with an unpredictable Pacific freak called a "dodging tide." The result is water too shallow for the LCVPs and LCMs. Thanks to their caterpillar treads the amtracs can wallow across the reef, but they are far too few for the job—only eighty-seven to begin with, and that number shrinks each time one is found by an enemy shell. And the dodging tide is making a problem for them, too: "If you didn't time yourself to come in between the breakers," said Leffler, "they'd pick you up and bring you in like a surfboard. If you're on the leading edge and slanted down your bow will hit the reef and it'll flip you over. That's what hap-pened to some of 'em. Got caught at the wrong time and flipped over on the reef." Marine combat correspondents will report later that because the defenders were still dazed from the last bombardment, their first fire was not as effective as later, and the first three waves got in with "relatively few casualties." As far as the men in the boats are concerned, however, the defenders have not been dazed nearly enough, and their fire is incessant and deadly.

"We see [the Marines] coming in their landing craft," Tadeo Onuki writes in his diary. "They probably think we have been overcome by the bombing and shelling, but we have not."

The commander of the amtrac battalion, Major Henry Drewes, is killed when his tractor takes a direct hit. The commander of Battalion 2/2, Lieutenant Colonel Her-bert Amey, is killed also when his tractor becomes entan-gled in barbed wire and then is hit as the occupants leaped out to make a dash to the beach. "He went down like a Marine," said Corporal Robert Mobert: "With bullets swishing all around us he raised his pistol and said: 'Come on men. . . . The bastards can't stop us!' [Then] he was killed. . . . He was a real man."

9:10 A.M.: Men of Battalion 2/8 begin landing on Red Beach Three and taking cover behind its low, log seawall.

Two minutes later the first amtracs of Battalion 2/2 crawl up on Red Beach Two. One minute after that two companies of Battalion 3/2, led by Major Mike Ryan, begin landing on Red Beach One.

Leffler's amtrac carries the troops to Red Beach Two, "between a long pier and a Japanese privy hangin' out over the water. We never got hung up or lost our traction on the reef. Got up to the sand and the troops jumped out. The beach was so tiny that when our tractor's nose was against the log seawall our rear treads were still in the water, and so crowded we had a helluva time keeping from running over people." Even with this abnormally low tide there is an average of only twenty feet or so between water and log seawall, and where Marines hold any beach at all that twenty feet is all they hold.

9:15 A.M.: Marines are on all three beaches now, but just barely.

Correspondent Sherrod lands on Red Two just in time to see an enemy soldier caught in the stream of a flamethrower: "[He] flared like celluloid . . . dead instantly but the bullets in his cartridge belt exploded for a full 60 seconds. . . . It was the first Jap I saw killed on Betio. The first of four thousand. Zing, Zing, Zing the cartridge-belt bullets sang. We all ducked low. Nobody wants to be killed by a dead Jap."

9:17 A.M.: The fourth, fifth, and sixth waves begin their run to reinforce those already on the beaches. They are, however, mostly in LCVPs and LCMs rather than amtracs. Because they are and because the "dodging tide" continues to work for the Japanese, this is about to become one of the bloodiest mornings in the history of the Corps.

Striking the reef, boats lurch and grind and ground themselves to become sitting targets for Japanese gunners. Their ramps drop, their troops pile out and begin wading toward a shore that in some places is as much as a half-mile away. Exploding shells throw up geysers of water. Machine-gun bullets whack and whistle as they lash the water and ricochet from it. Men begin to go down. Some fall to enemy fire. Some step into potholes invisible in the shell-roiled water and drown there, too burdened by packs and equipment to climb out. Still others become entangled in barbed wire and are shot down before they can tear themselves free.

Lieutenant Roy Thaxton and his platoon, heading to Red Beach One, "were sitting ducks. . . . Hiking across that 600 yards of water was the most devastating thing any of us ever experienced in our lives. We just literally had to wade into the muzzles of their guns. By the time we made it we'd lost over half our people."

While wading the endless yards to Red Beach Three, Private First Class Carroll Strider wryly remembers an officer earlier saying: "We'll need only two men. One with a piece of chalk and one with a rifle. One to shoot 'em and one to mark 'em down." But that was then and this is now. Now, "so many bullets were popping all around that it sounded like there was one every square inch." He remembers also a letter in his pocket—a letter in which his mother quotes Psalms 91:7:

> A thousand shall fall at thy side,
> and ten thousand at thy right hand;
> but it shall not come nigh unto thee.

And the psalm is prophetic, for in Strider's case that's just how it will be.

Coast Guard Bos'n's Mate Carl Jonas will always remember his LCVP running aground, "in an exploding no-man's land six to eight hundred yards from the nearest shore. . . . the circle of the beach dotted with motionless shapes. . . . In the water more specks, a few moving toward the shore but the bulk moving out . . . heading for us. We realized with a shock that they were the wounded."

On Red Beach One, Major Ryan radios the flagship: "Boats held up on reef, right flank Red 1. Troops receiving heavy fire in water." Lieutenant Commander Robert McPherson sees them from a Kingfisher scouting plane overhead, "Tiny men, their rifles held over their heads, slowly wading beachward. I wanted to cry."

Bos'n Jonas and his crew manage to free their boat from the coral and load it with wounded: "They lay below the gunwale, reaching up like the men in Italian primitive paintings of the damned in hell. . . . A few died in the boat. The rest just lay there."

As the morning wears on, the action, growing ever more disjointed and confused, is best told by its radio and telephone communications:

10:10 A.M.: Elements of 2/8 on Red Beach Three report advancing a few hundred yards inland to the edge of the airport.

10:30 A.M.: Unidentified sender to Major General Julian C. Smith aboard the flagship *Maryland:* "Have landed. Unusually heavy opposition. Casualties 70 percent. Can't hold."

10:45 A.M.: Commanding officer on Beach Red Two to Colonel David Shoup, now ashore in charge of combat: "Stiff resistance. Need half-tracks. Our tanks no good."

11:05 A.M.: Colonel Shoup sees what is happening to Battalion 3/8, trying to wade in from grounded LCVPs to reinforce the troops on Red Beach Three and telephones the commander there: "Third battalion is landing to your rear and catching hell."

A fortunate few do still get to come in amtracs. On its first trip to the beach the amtrac battalion lost so many tractors that, "After that," said Leffler, "we were on our own and just helping out where we could. We didn't have time to think and we weren't guided or instructed. Somebody in a grounded Higgins boat would yell, 'Hey! Over here!' and we'd go. We knew we had to get those fellows in there. First day we made about five trips. Only casualty was our tractor's crew chief. He got shot sideways through his nose."

11:58 A.M.: Commander of 2/2 on Red Two to Colonel Shoup: "Situation bad. We need help."

12:03 P.M.: Commander of 3/2 on Red One to Colonel Shoup: "Under fire from large caliber guns on west coast. Need air support."

12:29 P.M.: Battalion 2/8, trying desperately to hold and enlarge the tiny inland enclave it has taken, telephones Colonel Shoup: "Resistance stiffening. Request strafing."

And, five minutes later: "We have enemy tanks to our front."

1:30 P.M.: 3/8's attempt to reinforce 2/8 on Red One has been a disaster and Colonel Shoup radios General Smith: "The Third Battalion of the Eighth Marine Regiment approached the reefs and, upon grounding, was met with a hail of machine-gun, rifle, and anti-boat gunfire which inflicted heavy casualties and completely disorganized the unit. To escape . . . they drifted west and waded through the water, landing on both sides of Betio's pier [Beaches Red Two and Red Three]. This unit was absorbed mainly by the Second Battalion of the Eighth Marine Regiment."

1:30 P.M.: Still no good news anywhere. The sun is high and blistering hot. Drinking water is almost gone. Blood plasma is gone. Ammunition is low. Some fifteen hundred Marines are on the beaches now, most of them still pinned down behind the seawall and so crowded that an incoming mortar shell cannot help but find flesh. A Navy pilot flying overhead reports that the beaches are "cobblestoned with helmets." The bodies of some two hundred Marines bob in the lagoon now, and a stench of death seeps into the air.

All the division's battalions but one have been committed, and the issue is still in doubt. Heroic attempts are made to break out of the beachheads and they meet with some success, but far from enough. As Tadeo Onuki sees it: "It appears we have broken the landing attempt. Landing craft are running aground and enemy soldiers are falling right and left under our thundering fire."

As the hot, stinking hours pass, messages continue to tell the story.

1:45 P.M.: Unidentified to Colonel Shoup: "Reserve teams unable to land. Is there another beach where we can land?"

1:50 P.M.: Commander of 3/2 on Red One to Colonel Shoup: "Anti-boat guns holding up reserves. Troops are 400 yards away from Jap guns on right."

3:00 P.M.: Two companies of the Second Regiment's Third Battalion have been on Beach Red One for the past six hours, but the rest of the battalion is still bobbing around in boats in the lagoon, unable to land. Now its commander radios General Smith: "I am out of contact with my assault units." The general replies, unsympathetically: "Land at any cost, regain control of your battalion and continue the attack."

When at last darkness comes the situation is this:

AT SEA: The aircraft carrier *Independence* has taken an aerial torpedo and, surrounded by a protective bevy of destroyers, is limping south to Funafuti for repairs. The dauntless battleship *Mississippi* has suffered a gun-turret explosion killing ninety-three and wounding nineteen. The destroyer *Ringgold* has been damaged by enemy fire, and the destroyer *Dashiell* has been seriously damaged by grounding.

On Shore: Five thousand Marines have landed, or tried to, and of these almost one-third now are dead or wounded. Beaches Red Two and Red Three are joined at the base of the pier to form a continuous strip, but Red Two's right and Red One's left are separated by a six-hundred-foot gap occupied by enemy gunners. On Red Beach Two the Second Regiment's Second Battalion has managed to widen its ground somewhat, pushing as much as 150 yards inland in some places. On Red One, however, the troops have only what they started with—twenty feet of sand between seawall and sea.

In the Lagoon: General Smith's last reserve, the First Battalion, Eighth Regiment, is bobbing around in landing craft, as is a part of the Third Battalion. They will remain there throughout the night. They don't want to remain there, and one Guadalcanal veteran is heard to cry out: "For Christ's sake, let us in! What can they be thinking in there, seeing these boats in the water, needing our help, and us sitting here like we was back home!" But those are the orders, and in the Marines, orders are to be obeyed.

7:00 P.M.: General Smith to Colonel Shoup: "Hold what you have. Develop contact between your battalions. Clear isolated machine guns still holding out on beach. Prepare to meet counterattack."

10:00 P.M.: Colonel Shoup to General Smith: "Have dug in to hold limited beachhead. Second Battalion, Eighth Marine Regiment, holds left flank. Second Battalion, Second Marine Regiment, and First Battalion, Second Marine Regiment, hold Red Beach Two. No word from Third Battalion, Second Regiment. My command post, center of Red Beach Two."

It is an eerie night for the men on the beach: splintered palms weirdly silhouetted against a moonlit sky; sputters of rifle fire breaking out and then dying away only to break out again, especially in the neighborhood of the long pier; groans and delirious mumblings of the wounded; obscene invitations and insults called out by the enemy in preposterously mangled English; scary coral rustlings that could be (and often are) made by an enemy trying to sneak in with knife, gun, or grenade.

And it is a busy night. The very first landing of the day, made by a scout-sniper platoon led by Lieutenant W. D. "Hawk" Hawkins, was to secure the long pier and thus prevent its use by the enemy as a base for crossfire on incoming Marines. And the pier, running from shore to the deep water of the lagoon, might also, if taken and held, provide a way of landing men and supplies from vessels much larger than landing craft. Hawkins's men did take the pier and did hold it, but Japanese artillery has kept it unusable all through the day. Now, a few small supply boats have reached it under cover of night, but the men unloading the boats are all too visible on the pier's moonlit white coral surface, and enemy gunners are giving them fits. "We would drop when a man was hit," said Sergeant Gene Ward, "freeze until the firing ceased, then move forward. . . . I had . . . the suspicion that it wasn't really happening."

Four amtracs make it to the beach during the night, bringing ten disassembled heavy howitzers and ammunition—guns critically needed, which by dawn already will be assembled and in action.

The night would be busier still if Admiral Shibasaki could have his way. He has planned a night counterattack—a banzai charge with which he had hoped to kill every Marine on the beach—but his communications are so messed up that he can't get the charge under way.

The Americans' communications are messed up, too, and no one group knows much about the actions or condition of any others. All they know is, they are thirsty, hungry, tired, frightened, and all too many of them are hurt. But they know, too, that against all odds they have held, and are holding still.

November 21: At the first light of dawn General Julian Smith sends his last reserves, the First Battalion of the Eighth Regiment under Colonel Elmer Hall, to reinforce the beleaguered troops on Red Beach Two. Because very few amtracs are still operable, nearly all of these troops must go in LCVPs, and because the dodging tide is still working its mischief they will be forced to wade into the teeth of enemy fire for a quarter-mile or more across a reef now cluttered with the wreckage of LCVPs, LCMs, amtracs, a few tanks, and the hulk of a small, sunken Japanese freighter.

All is quiet at first. Then all hell breaks loose. During the night dozens of enemy snipers and machine gunners have sneaked out to infest the wreckage, as hermit crabs infest empty conch shells on a beach. Lurking there, hidden and silent, they wait until the wading Marines are well out on the reef and committed. Then they begin a slaughtering crossfire never to be forgotten by those who survive it. Platoon Leader Al Tidwell had forty-one men when he started, but "By the time I got to the beach & had roll call . . . eighteen had been killed goin' in."

As Sergeant Gene Ward will recall it:

When the ramp went down the men spilled out into
chin-deep water. Almost at once some were
hit. . . . I became aware of the wasp-like sound
of the bullets and the sharp slap they made
hitting the water around me. . . . Every fourth
or fifth bullet was a tracer and you could see
'em coming. They blazed and hissed like angry
fireflies. . . . Like others around me I kept only
my eyes and right hand, which clutched my
carbine, above water. . . . [When] the water shallowed
I wormed along on my belly. . . . coral
cuts badly and my hands and wrists were bloody but I
felt nothing. . . . [A man] up ahead a few yards . . . was
hit in the chest and his blood
stained the water. A moment later a bullet hit
just in front of my chin. . . . I lurched up and
made the beach . . . falling twice. . . . [It] was
strewn with dead Marines. I picked my way between
the bodies and threw myself down beside
a battered amtrac. I was dead beat. . . . All of us
lay prone, as still as the dead men around us.

And a Marine combat correspondent watching the beach will describe seeing: "Men fighting back tears of blind rage to see these boys go down. A man would fall, get up and stumble a few more feet before he went down again. You could see him fighting to hold his head above the water and to get up on his feet. Some of them crawled on their elbows. Some hung on the barbed wire entanglements and drowned. There are no foxholes in the water."

After a time, Colonel Hall radios Colonel Shoup that his remaining waves are "laying off." His reason: "Impossible to land vehicles and equipment because of heavy enemy fire."

8:52 A.M.: Colonel Shoup to flagship: "Imperative you land ammunition, water, rations and medical supplies on Red Beach Two and evacuate casualties."

Then, a few minutes later: "Situation doesn't look good."

9:22 A.M.: Colonel Shoup to General Smith: "Making every effort to occupy north and west ends of island."

10:50 A.M.: Battalion 3/2, trying to move from behind the seawall and advance to the north and west, has been pinned down by enemy troops dug in so completely as to be invisible. "We could only see gun blasts from between coconut logs," said Lieutenant Thaxton, "so that's what we shot at." And the battalion commander calls for help from bombers and tanks.

11:14 A.M.: Navy bombers hit a Japanese fuel dump, and the very island shakes under an explosion that sends smoke and flame roiling and billowing hundreds of feet into the air.

11:30 A.M.: Colonel Shoup to General Smith: "Situation is still critical."

NOON: Nature relents at long last. The dodging tide dies away. Water rises in the lagoon, and soon LCVPs and LCMs are able to cruise all the way to the beaches. A stream of men and supplies begins to flow in, and, mercifully, a stream of casualties begins to flow out.

It is another hard day for the men on the beaches—another day in hell. Again, tired and hungry and thirsty, they bake under a blazing sun. Again many continue to fight despite painful and sometimes frightful wounds. The air is heavy with dust and smoke. The sick-sweet stench of rotting flesh grows ever stronger. The sound of gunfire—the crackle of rifles, the crump and boom of heavier stuff, and the sharp Toongg! of mortars firing—goes on, incessant and unbroken, and more bodies add to those already littering the land and bobbing lazily in the lagoon.

But the men are beginning to get supplies now, and they are beginning to make progress. Victory is no longer in doubt, just the price of it.

Early Afternoon: Battalion 3/2 finally succeeds in advancing from Red Beach One. Together with units of 2/2 it captures Green Beach—the short southwest end of the island comprising the "face" of the bird—and secures a strip of beach 150 yards deep. This prompts a team of Marine combat correspondents on the scene to report that: "At 12:35 P.M. on the second day of battle the tide turned definitely in favor of the Marines [and as] the afternoon wore on they butchered their way across Betio. . . . It was essential and costly. . . . Occasionally it required six to seven hours to cover fifty to a hundred yards, so stiff was the resistance."

And signs of eroding Japanese morale begin to appear. Seventeen in one dugout alone are found to have committed hara-kiri, and others are being found elsewhere.

4:00 P.M.: Optimistic for the first time, Colonel Shoup radios General Smith: "Our casualties heavy. Enemy casualties unknown. Situation: We are winning."

By nightfall things look better still. The boundaries of beaches Red Two and Red Three have been pushed almost halfway across the island, and Marines hold two narrow corridors entirely across it, cutting the enemy forces in two. And Marine units are now firmly established along the face of the bird on Green Beach.

Colonel Shoup ends his day by radioing General Smith: "Our troops dishing out hell and catching hell. Pack howitzers in position and registered for shooting on tail of Betio. Combat efficiency: We are winning."

And then he says to his staff: "This is the damndest crap game I ever got into."

November 22: The third day is pretty much a repetition of the second, except that now there is no slaughter in the lagoon and the Marines on shore are advancing on all fronts. Slowly and painfully, but advancing. Steeped in the code of the Samurai, the Japanese continue choosing to die rather than surrender, and they try to take as many Marines as possible with them when they go. They tie themselves into the tops of palm trees and snipe from there until killed. They hide in camouflaged spider-holes, so no Marine knows when he may fall to the bullet of an unseen sniper.

Admiral Shibasaki's big command blockhouse has so far managed to withstand everything the Americans can throw against it. Now, an offshore destroyer blasts it with eighty rounds of five-inch shells, but still to no avail. Inside, however, the admiral realizes the end is near and sends the Japanese High Command a final message: "Our weapons have been destroyed and from now on everyone is attempting a final charge. May Japan exist for 10,000 years." Then, unable to face defeat and capture, he commits hara-kiri.

Chief Petty Officer Tadeo Onuki also knows the end is near, but like the others is determined to fight on as long as he can: "Our forces have lost much food and ammunition and are no longer a match for the enemy. But in spite of all, our soldiers courageously fight and shake the guts of the Americans."

Noon: Commanding General Julian Smith arrives from the flagship and takes direct control of operations on Betio.

4:00 P.M.: General Smith radios Corps Commander Holland M. Smith: "Situation not favorable for rapid cleanup of Betio. Heavy casualties among officers make leadership problems difficult. Still strong resistance areas. Progress slow and extremely costly."

7:00 P.M.: The Marines now occupy the main part of Betio, including the airstrip. Upon seeing the situation map, correspondent Keith Wheeler writes: "It looks as though the Marines are winning on this blood drenched, bomb-hammered, stinking little abattoir of coral sand."

And it is true, but it is not over. There is a nasty little pocket holding out between the left flank of Red One and the right flank of Red Two, and there still are many Japanese in the tail of the Betio bird, and none of them is ready to give up.

When darkness comes, the Second and Third Battalions of the Eighth Regiment and the First Battalion of the Sixth are holding a line across the island at the western tip of the airfield. Shortly after dark they are startled to hear "B'NZAI, B'NZAI!" and "Malines! We come to dlink your brood!" screamed by hundreds of Japanese swarming out of the tail area in a desperate suicide attack.

The attack lasts an hour—a wild, confused hour of enemy soldiers madly charging into Marine lines with guns, bayonets, sabers, and hand grenades. When it is over, First Battalion's Lieutenant Norman "Hard Tom" Thomas phones his command post: "We need reinforcements. Another attack like that and the line may break."

His commanding officer, Major William K. Jones, replies, "I can't, now. You've got to hold." Jones does, however, send the tank *China Gal* with water and ammunition for the men on the line. He also requests and gets Naval and artillery fire on the Japanese positions—fire that will be continued throughout the night.

11:00 P.M.: Again, waves of fanatical, banzai-screaming Japanese charge the line, one even leaping into Thomas's command post, where "Hard Tom" first slugs and then shoots him. This time, however, the Marines are ready and the charge is stopped cold.

NOVEMBER 23, 4:00 A.M.: Again the Japanese in the tail of the island come shrieking out in what will be their last, largest, and most desperate charge. This one, too, will last for an hour—a wild, savage, hand-to-hand hour in which Marine casualties are heavy and Japanese casualties are nearly total.

5:00 A.M.: Thomas telephones Major Jones: "It's over. We stopped them. Please send stretcher-bearers to evacuate the wounded."

Later in the morning the Third Battalion of the Sixth Regiment, accompanied by several tanks, pushes on down the island's tail. In the process they will find and capture the severely wounded Tadeo Onuki, one of only seventeen Japanese to be taken alive in the entire Tarawa operation. Onuki will write in his diary: "I wait in our bunker for the time we will make our last charge. Suddenly our bunker becomes a fiery hell. Inside it is completely burning. Gradually I become conscious. I am pressed under something heavy and cannot move. I am pressed under the charred bodies of my fellow soldiers. When I get out I cannot believe it. I just stand as in a dream."

Four-and-a-half hours and 475 dead Japanese later the battalion arrives at Betio's tip-end. And now, except for the cleanup of isolated enemy snipers, it *is* all over.

At a little past noon Ensign W. W. Kelly lands the first American plane, a Navy F4F, on Betio's airstrip. At twelve minutes past one, General Julian Smith announces to all units on the island and all the ships offshore that the battle for Betio is completed.

More than a thousand Americans and nearly five thousand Japanese have died in the battle, and their bodies lie fly-infested and bloating under the tropical sun. But now it is over, and a few days later its survivors are evacuated for much needed rest, recreation, reorganization, and reoutfitting. They leave behind, in the words of Associated Press Correspondent Richard Johnson: "blasted, shell-torn beaches . . . scarred blockhouses . . . splintered, topless coconut trees [and] the sweet, sickening smell of death." And they leave, also, the beginnings of a cemetery in which will appear this epitaph:

> To you who lie within this coral sand, we who remain pay tribute to a pledge that in dying thou shalt surely not have died in vain. But when again bright morning dyes the sky and waving fronds above shall touch the rain, we will remember.

And remember they will. Fifty years later, to the day, a group of them will return—Roy Thaxton, Carroll Strider, Al Tidwell, Jack Lent, Robert Lewis, and Mickey Franklin, among many others. Gray-haired and grandfatherly, they will stand at attention, choking back emotion or openly wiping away tears, as the "Marine Hymn" is played, and they dedicate to their fallen comrades of a half-century earlier a monument inscribed:

"Follow Me"
2nd Marine Division
United States Marine Corps
Battle of Tarawa
November 20, 1943
To our fellow Marines who gave their all
The world is free because of you
God rest your souls
1,113 killed 2,290 wounded
The Central Pacific Spearhead
To World Victory in World War II
Semper Fidelis

THE AFTERMATH of the seventy-six-hour battle for Betio Island, part of Tarawa Atoll, presented as gruesome a scene as had yet been witnessed in the Pacific in World War II. Since the whole island of Betio is less than a mile in area, the incredible carnage was concentrated onto a very small battlefield. Dead bodies were everywhere. Stiffened corpses of Marines killed as they tried to wade into the beach still hung life-lessly on barbed-wire entanglements offshore, or washed ashore in groups on the churned-up sand of the beaches. The torn and mutilated corpses of luckless Japanese defenders littered the cratered landscape. Many of the American dead were never to be found or were buried hastily in shell holes, and most Japa-nese bodies were simply covered over in mass graves.

To this day this tiny island in Tarawa Atoll remains one mass grave with probably over five thousand bodies entombed there for all time. At least most of them will remain there permanently. Today when a foundation or trench is dug, human remains are often uncovered and some are identified. A 1974 excavation for a water pipeline on Betio uncovered an amtrac that had been buried for thirty-one years. Inside, incredibly preserved in the fuel oil that leaked from the vehicle when it was hit, were the skeletons of two American Marines as well as their personal effects, which included toothbrushes and aspirin. One of the Marines was wearing dogtags, and he was identified as Private Henry Verhaalen. After thirty-one years Private Verhaalen was no longer "missing in action." Another trench excavation in 1987, just behind Red Beach Three, uncovered a complete skeleton of a Japanese soldier who was found seated in the buried pillbox he died in, dressed in his uniform, a water can at his side, and a Swiss watch on his wrist.

The captured Japanese airstrip on Betio was renamed Hawkins Field by the Americans in honor of a Marine in the assault waves named Dean Hawkins. "The Hawk," as he was known, frankly confided to his friends that he would win a Medal of Honor but would not survive the war. In the initial stages of the invasion, he undertook the dangerous task of assaulting Japanese pillboxes with grenades and explosives. After knocking out a number of them and being wounded several times, he finally was killed. His premonition proved to be true, and he was posthumously awarded the Medal of Honor.

As subsequent and even bloodier island invasions would occupy the world's attention, Tarawa, despite initial media furor over the shocking numbers of casualties, was surprisingly and quickly forgotten. A second, larger airstrip was built on another of the islets and named Mullinix Field. After the war, when the U.S. abandoned Tarawa and the atoll was turned back over to the British, Mullinix Field became the airstrip used to this day. Hawkins Field, like the rest of ravaged Betio, slowly began to revegetate.

Today visitors fly past little Betio on the final approach to Mullinix Field, now named Bonriki Inter-national Airport. The old coral surface of the wartime runway only recently was covered by asphalt paving.

From the air the islet of Betio itself appears to be a verdant green paradise, a startling contrast to the desolate, bomb-blasted, body-strewn horror of 1943. Tall palm trees sway in the breeze, and inviting white sand beaches ring the island, the same beaches where corpses of American Marines washed ashore after being cut down by Japanese machine guns. On closer inspection from the ground Betio turns out to be the crowded commercial center of the independent nation of Kiribati (pronounced Kiribas). It is estimated that perhaps as many as twenty-five thousand people now live on Betio, and sanitation for this many inhabitants is an ongoing problem. Hawkins Field, the objective of the landings in November 1943, is mostly covered with palm trees or tin-roofed huts. Only one area of the old whitened coral airstrip is still clear, and it is used for a soccer field. Main roads on the little island parallel the old taxiways, and one very straight road traces almost the entire length of the wartime airstrip, marking its south side.

In spite of the population density of Betio, remnants of the profound devastation of the battle are inescap-able. The giant concrete bunkers built by the Japanese, still showing pockmarks from shellfire of many calibers, will remain for years to come, silent testimony to the Japanese engineers who designed the "bomb-proof" structures. Some of the American amtracs, or what's left of them, still lie just offshore in the shallow water where they were destroyed during the battle. They are slowly disintegrating and are now barely recogniz-able. One of the American tanks that tried to come ashore rests in the shell hole just off the beach where it was put out of action by Japanese fire.

A barefoot stroll along the narrow white sand beaches where Marines were pinned down and killed by a hail of Japanese bullets is less dangerous today but still can be a bit hazardous to visitors—treads of amtracs and assorted pieces of jagged, rusting metal and trash may still inflict modern-day bloodshed on the sands of Tarawa (as was the case for one of the authors). The coconut log seawall where Marines took cover (if they made it in alive from the landing craft) has now been reconstructed with concrete, but is surprisingly similar to what was originally built by the Japanese. The famous pier where Marines took shelter on their wade in over the reef was replaced by a larger, longer version after the war. In 2000 a new Japanese-funded $22 million port facility changed the landscape all around the vicinity of the old pier. This major construction project also altered parts of the adjoining invasion beaches that, up till then, had remained essentially unchanged from the day the Marines landed fifty-seven years earlier.

The giant gun emplacements the Japanese built and the rusting barrels of the big guns have been left mostly undisturbed since the shelling ended. Only the natural erosion of the shifting sand shorelines, the inevitable ravages of rust, and the hand-painted Kiribati graffiti have altered their appearance. More recently a new preservation effort on Betio resulted in protective paint jobs on the eight-inch guns.

The arrival of any American on Tarawa today is unusual, and visits by veterans are even more rare. Yet, a Japanese delegation of Bereaved Relatives visited almost annually for many years. On the site of the old U.S. war cemetery, just behind Red Beach Two, the Japanese erected several monuments during the 1980s and 1990s commemorating the defenders who died there. In June 1987 a causeway was dedicated linking the islet of Betio to the neighboring island of Bairiki and paid for by the Japanese. Named the "Nippon Causeway," the 3.4-kilometer sea road is said to have cost the Japanese government around $10 million. Although the last traces of the American amtracs are rusting away in the sparkling tropical waters around Betio, the legacies of the "defeated" Japanese, from the Nippon Causeway to the new port facility to the blasted concrete bunkers, will long remain as monuments to the ironies of twentieth-century warfare.

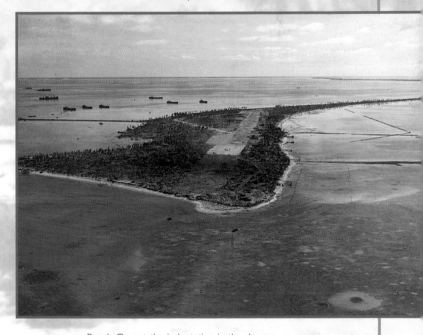

The tiny islet of Betio was devastated by the U.S. invasion, but the American bombardment purposely spared the Japanese airstrip as much damage as possible, to allow its use by U.S. aircraft soon after the battle. The western end of the island is in the foreground, and other islets of Tarawa Atoll can be seen in the distance. The invasion beaches are along the shore at the left of the photo, with Red

Beach One at the indentation in the shoreline, Red Beach Two just this side of the pier, and Red Beach Three just beyond the pier. Seabees and aviation engineers extended the airstrip, named it Hawkins Field, and then abandoned it at the end of the war. Today more than twenty thousand people live there, and the entire airstrip has been reclaimed except for a short stretch used for a soccer field.

Aerial view of Betio in the late twentieth century. New piers have been constructed near the site of the old one made of coconut logs (marked by the dark streak in the water to the right of the newer pier). The new port facility, finished in 2000 after this photo was taken, has significantly altered the area around the base of the pier, and the old runway of Hawkins Field has almost totally vanished, except for the part used as a soccer field at right center. The west end of the runway (right) is covered with grass and brush. Red Beach One is in the right foreground where there is a shoreline indentation. Red Beach Two is to the left between Red Beach One and the pier. Red Beach Three is just to the left of the pier. A change in water color from light or mottled to dark blue marks the edge of the coral reef in the foreground. Between the edge of the reef and the island beaches, the water depth varies between one and six feet, depending on the tide. It is across this long, exposed stretch, roughly eight hundred yards, that many of the invading Marines had to wade in the face of murderous Japanese machine-gun and mortar fire.

OPPOSITE TOP LEFT: Landing boats of the Marine assault waves approach Betio on November 20, 1943. Betio itself is obscured by smoke and fires from the terrific naval and aerial bombardment. A Kingfisher scouting plane carrying Lieutenant Commander Robert McPherson can be seen over the invasion beaches in the distance. From his vantage-point he monitored the initial invasion waves.

OPPOSITE TOP RIGHT: Postwar Betio seen from a distance—clear water, quiet, white sandy beaches, and swaying palm trees—is more appealing than the glimpses stolen by Marines who peered over the front of their landing craft only to see a bomb-blasted roaring inferno and a pall of smoke. Before the completion of the Nippon Causeway in 1987, visitors approached Betio as the Marines did in 1943, from the water. Now visitors can

drive a rental car or take an island bus from the airport to Betio.

OPPOSITE BOTTOM LEFT: Grim-faced Marines in one of the later waves, fully aware of the deadly carnage being dealt out onshore, contemplate their fate as they head in to the invasion beaches on Betio.

OPPOSITE BOTTOM RIGHT: A Higgins boat of one of the later waves unloads near the coconut log pier well out from shore. These men were able to use the cover of the pier to increase their chances of survival during the eight-hundred-yard wade in to the beach. Note the total disregard of enemy sniper and machine-gun fire shown by the two men on top of the bullet-swept pier. This phenomenon was witnessed many times by incredulous war correspondents as some men put their lives totally in the hands of fate.

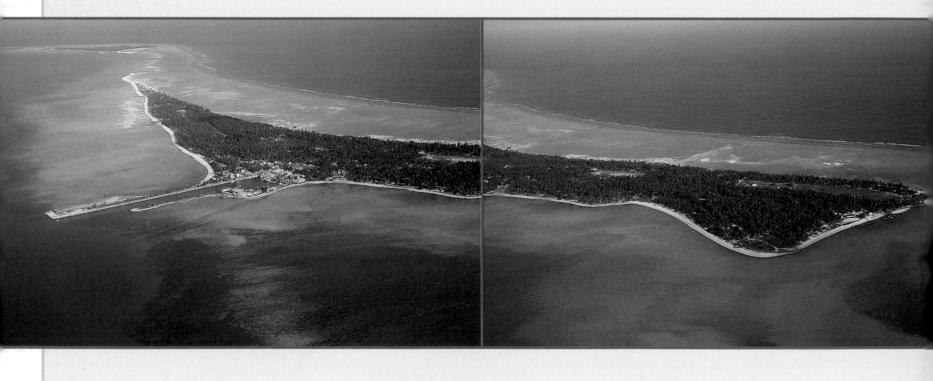

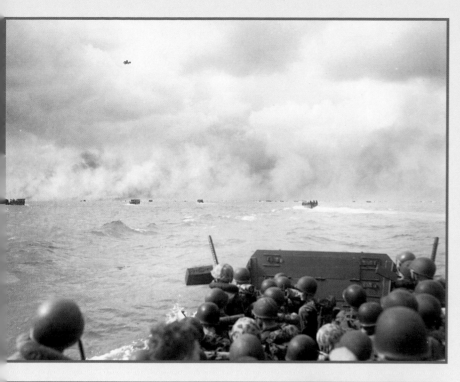

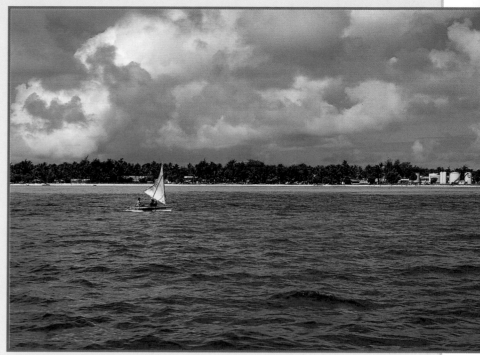

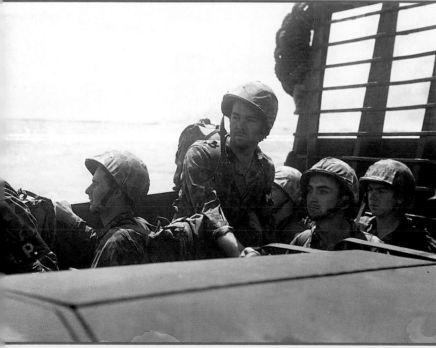

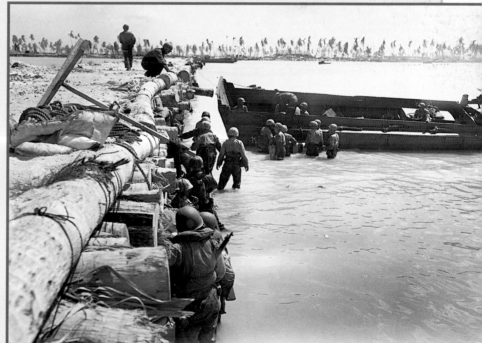

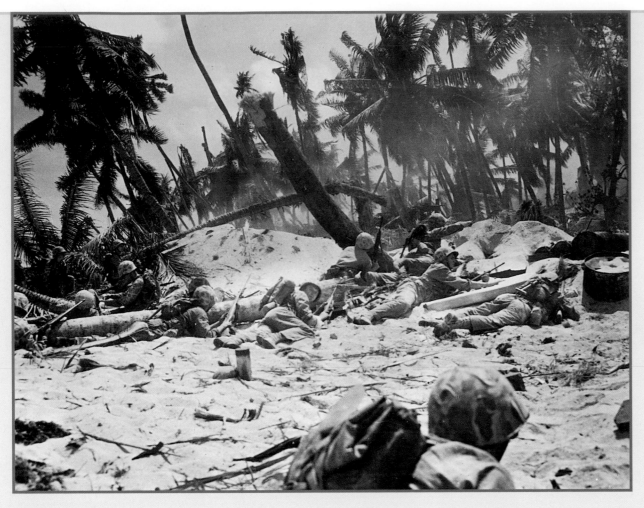

a Japanese shell, and a towel has been placed over his wounds to protect against flies.

OPPOSITE TOP: Some of the Japanese "bomb-proofs" were huge concrete blockhouses covered with sand so as to resemble large hills. These Marines, led by Sandy Bonnyman, are storming one such bunker, which was actually the power-generating station for the island. They are firing at Japanese soldiers counterattacking from the other side at point-blank range. The counterattack was beaten back, but Bonnyman was killed shortly after this photo was taken. He was posthumously awarded the Medal of Honor.

OPPOSITE BOTTOM LEFT: A view in the 1990s from roughly the same location shows the remains of the Japanese power plant, its former sand covering now almost entirely cleared away. No signs mark the structure, and there is no indication that a Medal of Honor was earned atop this former Japanese strong-point, which sits abandoned amidst vegetation that threatens to overgrow it, surrounded by the urban development of Betio. A postwar concrete foundation is in the foreground, and the police station is just out of the photo to the left.

OPPOSITE BOTTOM CENTER: Many of the Japanese defenders on Betio chose suicide rather than surrender. The technique used here was to remove a shoe, place the rifle to the head, and pull the trigger with the big toe.

OPPOSITE BOTTOM RIGHT: One of only seventeen survivors of the Japanese garrison of almost five thousand men on Tarawa.

ABOVE : Around noon of the first day this group of Marines is pinned down by sniper fire. A squad leader points to where he thinks the sniper is hidden.

BELOW LEFT: As the invasion waves pile up on the small beaches, some men decide to advance, their faces tense and drawn, their bayonets fixed and rifles at the ready. Other men, dazed and shocked, unable or unwilling to deal with the bloody maelstrom swirling around them, have removed their helmets and sit stunned and exhausted on the beach.

BELOW CENTER: These Marines have shed their packs and most of their gear, leapt up over the seawall (the photographer is peeking the camera above the top to take this photo), and are advancing into a hail of Japanese bullets.

BOTTOM RIGHT: Harried and tense corpsmen under fire evacuate a seriously wounded Marine from the battlefield by boat. This man has had his shoulder ripped open by

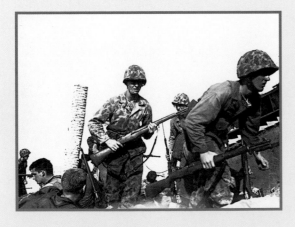

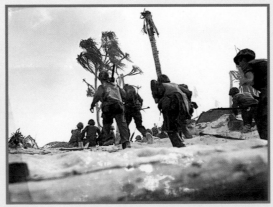

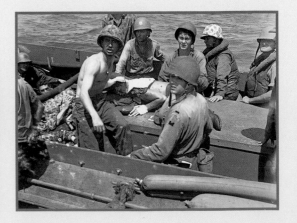

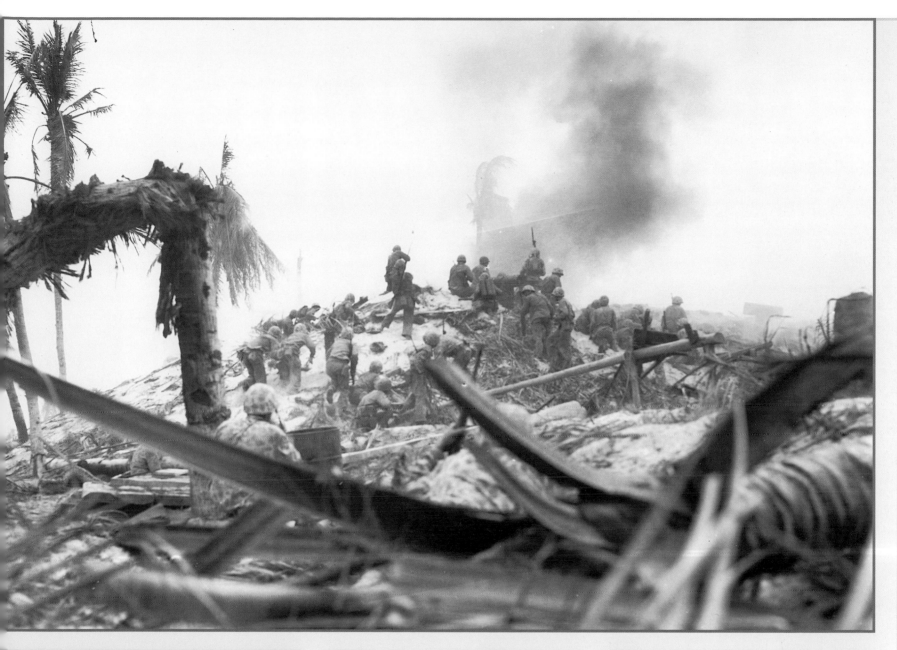

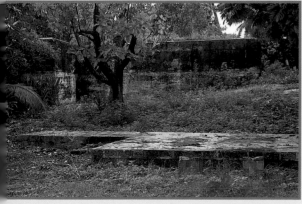

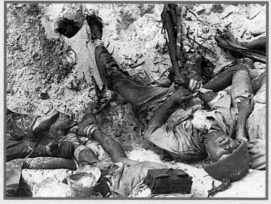

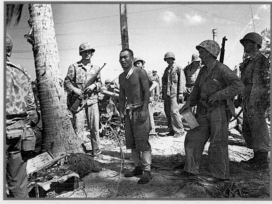

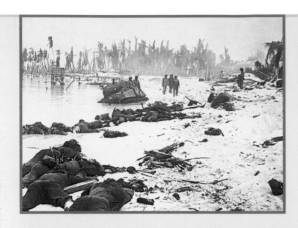

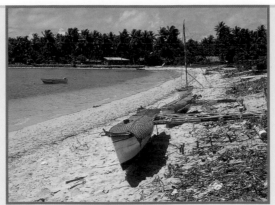

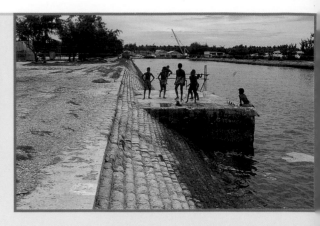

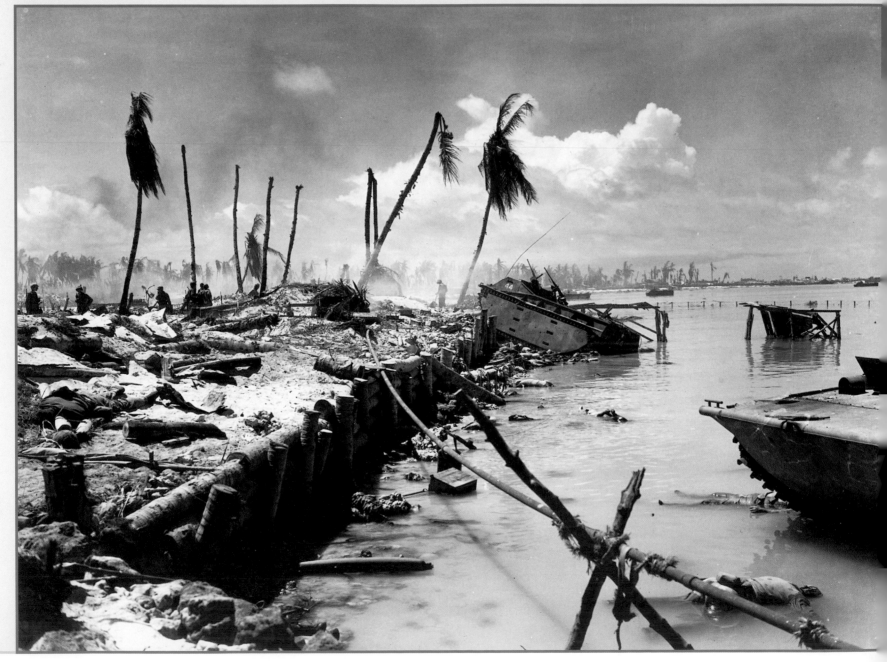

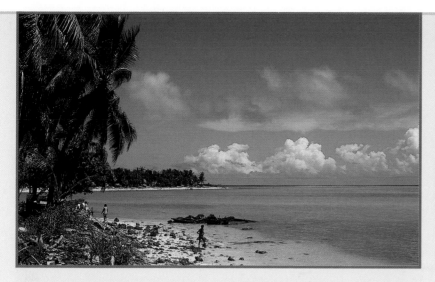

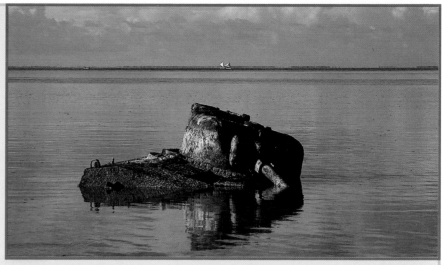

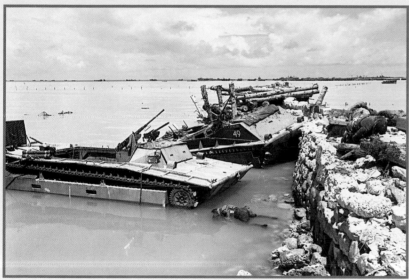

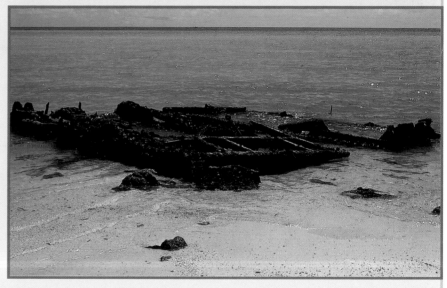

OPPOSITE TOP LEFT: As the remnants of the Japanese defenders were driven to the eastern end of the island on the third day, the invasion beaches were left littered with bloated American corpses washed ashore with the tide. Most of these Marines on Red Beach One were killed wading toward the island under a murderous hail of Japanese machine-gun fire.

OPPOSITE TOP CENTER: Red Beach One in the early 1990s, with Kiribati outrigger canoes pulled up on the white sand. This area has since been turned into a dump for the estimated twenty-five thousand people living on Betio.

OPPOSITE TOP RIGHT: Children play along the edge of the postwar concrete pier prior to the construction of the new port facility.

OPPOSITE BOTTOM: Red Beach Two from the base of the pier, photographed as the battle

still rages on the eastern end of the island. The amtrac at center was disabled as it tried to crawl up over the coconut log seawall, which provided the only shelter from Japanese machine-gun fire in the early stages of the battle. Marines crouching in the wall's lee had to decide whether to stay put or risk death by leaping up and over the top to face a hail of Japanese bullets. The intersection of Red Beach Two (foreground) and Red Beach One (in the distance) is just behind the amtrac at center. Note the dead Marines in the water.

TOP LEFT: The child on the beach is in the area formerly marking the division of Red Beach One (in the distance) and Red Beach Two (in the foreground). A strong-point of Japanese fortifications, pillboxes and machine-gun nests to the left inflicted heavy casualties on Marines as they waded in to the beaches

from the right. When this photo was taken in the mid-1990s, the deteriorated remains of two amtracs could still be seen rusting at water's edge behind the child.

TOP RIGHT: This U.S. tank lies offshore just where it was disabled during the invasion. It was one of the tanks that was to land on Red Beach One during the initial phase of the battle, but boats ferrying the tanks couldn't make it across the reef because the water was too shallow. Off-loaded at the edge of the reef the tanks had to be driven in to the beach some twelve hundred yards through the shallow water. Upon reaching the shore the tank drivers found they had either to drive over the dead and wounded Marines that littered the narrow sandy strip or to maneuver parallel to the beach just offshore to reach a gap in the seawall blown by engineers. Most chose the

latter alternative. Of the six tanks that tried to weave between shell holes in the reef and the dead and wounded in the water, only two made it to shore. This one drove into a shell hole and remains there to this day.

BOTTOM LEFT: Two of the amtracs used by the first waves of the invasion force lie abandoned near a small coral rock pier at the junction of Red Beach One and Red Beach Two on Betio. The body of a dead Marine floats in the shallow water near the amtrac in the foreground.

BOTTOM RIGHT: These same two amtracs survived well into the 21st century where they were abandoned under heavy fire during the invasion. The small coral rock pier that formerly was to the right of these vehicles was hauled away for construction material elsewhere on the island.

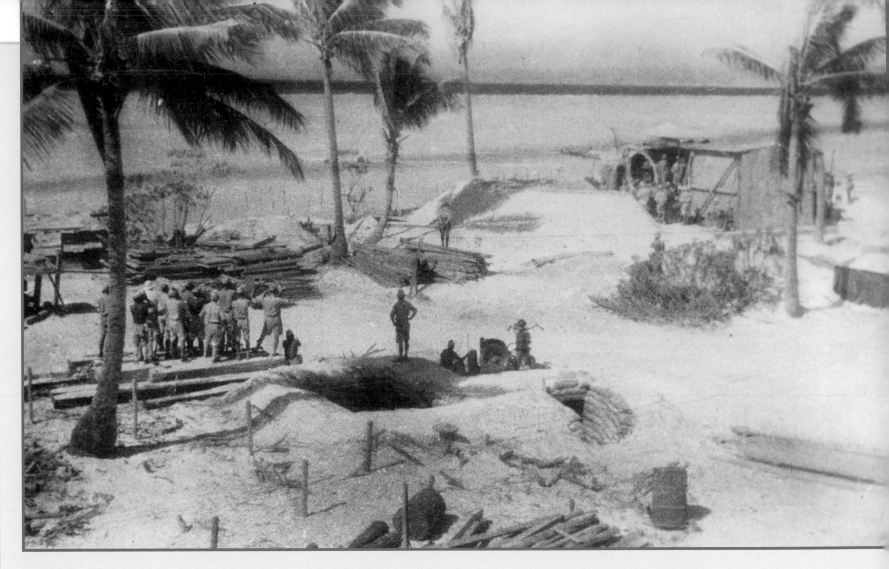

ABOVE: One of the eight-inch guns at the western end of Betio (right) is aimed out to sea for gunnery practice in this Japanese photograph taken in mid-1943. The Japanese expected the American assault to come from the open sea, but American forces actually chose to land on the more sheltered lagoon side.

BOTTOM LEFT: Two Marines pose on top of one of the tanks put out of commission in a shell hole just off Red Beach One.

BOTTOM CENTER: The Japanese had installed a variety of novel defenses on Betio, including a number of steel rifle shelters. The one in

this photo was blasted in the naval bombardment when a large-caliber shell exploded next to it, leaving the shell hole and dead Japanese soldiers.

BELOW: A remarkably intact Japanese steel rifle shelter near the eastern end of Betio.

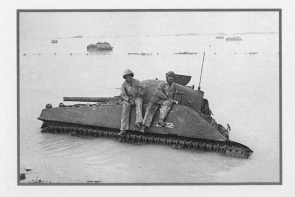

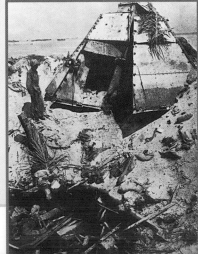

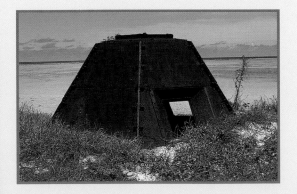

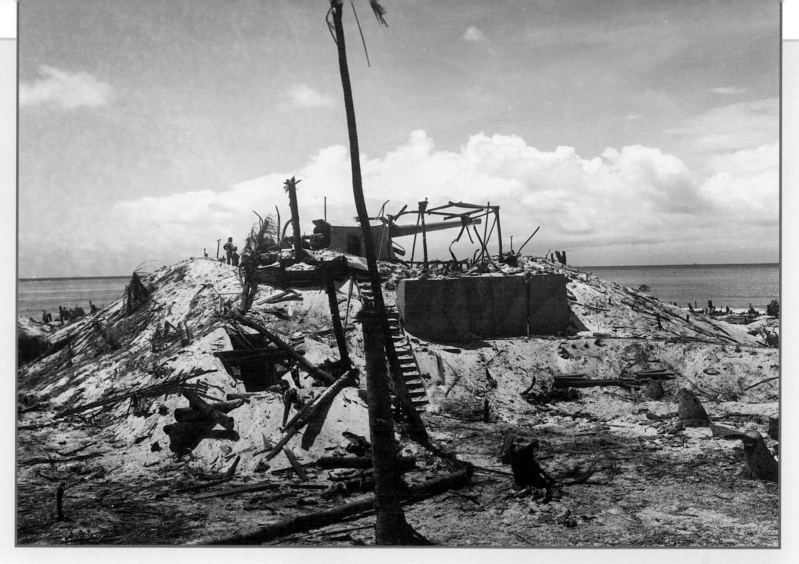

ABOVE: This same gun emplacement after the battle had ended. A direct hit by the battleship *Maryland* ignited the ammunition stored inside the emplacement, resulting in a massive explosion during the predawn bombardment. The palm trees that shaded this end of the island have almost been totally decimated by shellfire.

RIGHT: The remaining eight-inch gun at the west end of the island sits atop its massive concrete fortifications, now much exposed after the years have eroded a good bit of the sand that used to almost cover the emplacement. The other eight-inch gun, behind and below this one, has fallen victim to erosion. Ocean waves and currents have changed the shape of the shoreline on this end of the island, causing the lower gun to fall into the water.

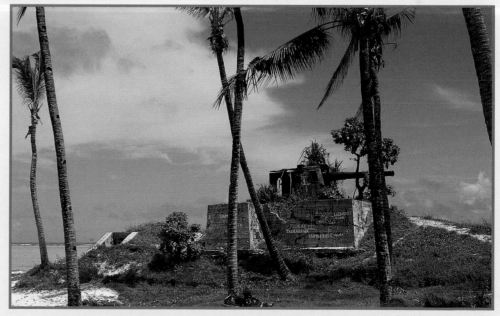

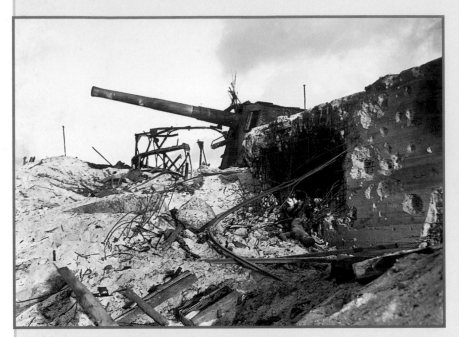

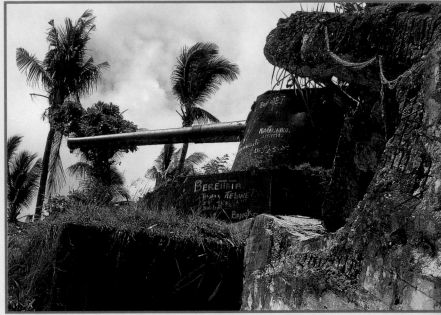

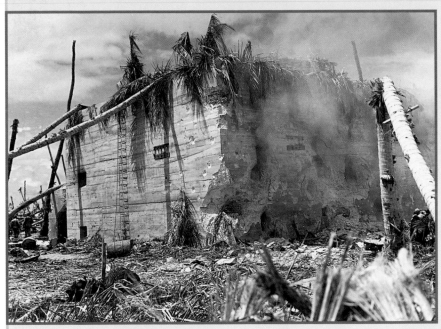

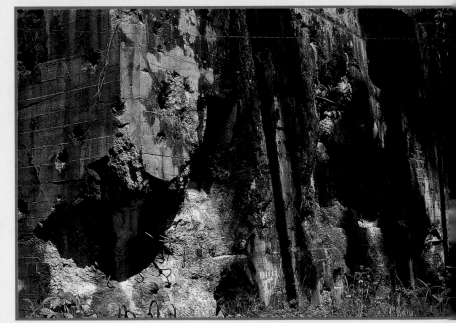

TOP LEFT: The direct hit from *Maryland* that detonated the magazine beneath the eight-inch gun at right blew a hole through the four-foot-thick reinforced concrete wall at the center of the picture.

TOP RIGHT: The dents in the thick steel plating of the gun housing caused by impacts of American shells are still visible. This gun has since been painted as part of a restoration project for war relics.

BOTTOM LEFT: One of the most impressive Japanese concrete blockhouses on Betio was Admiral Shibasaki's headquarters, located about one hundred yards inland from Red

Beach Three. This photo was taken shortly after the blockhouse was "neutralized" by the Marines. Its thick, concrete walls clearly show the effects of point-blank shelling by a destroyer close in. That shelling, and fire from almost any other weapon available to the Marines, was ineffective in penetrating the thick walls. Finally on the third day of the battle, Marines were able to kill Japanese machine gunners operating from the roof,

and engineers set explosive charges to blow open a steel entry door. Those inside either killed themselves or were immolated by flamethrowers and burning fuel poured through the opening.

BOTTOM RIGHT: Close-up view of the seaward side of Shibasaki's blockhouse still clearly shows the effects of point-blank shelling by an American destroyer.

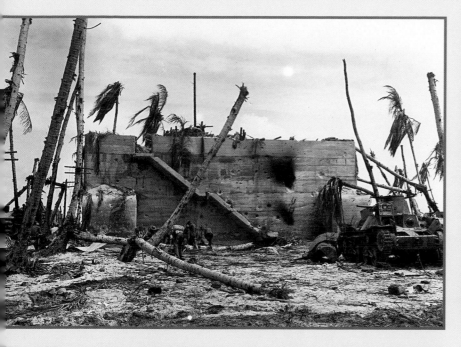

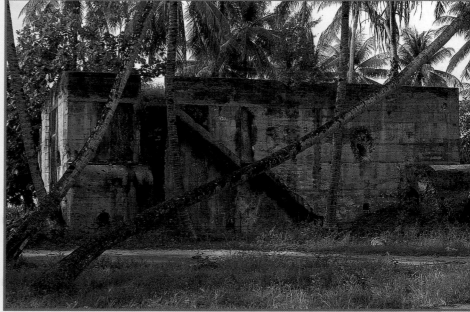

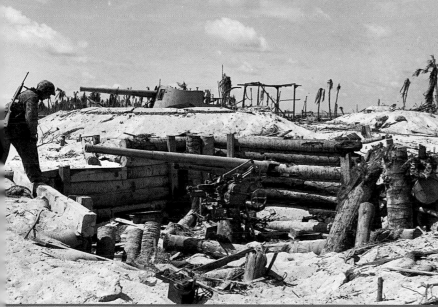

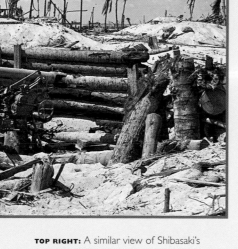

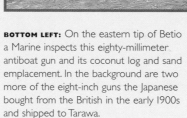

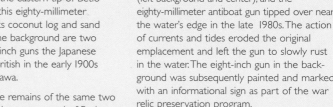

TOP LEFT: The rear view of Shibasaki's command blockhouse. Stairs lead to the roof where Japanese machine gunners were able to have a clear shot at Marines who tried to advance near the structure during the first two days of the battle. Note the blackened shell-marks in the concrete walls, and the remains of a Japanese light tank at right.

TOP RIGHT: A similar view of Shibasaki's command blockhouse today shows that its appearance is little changed from World War II. Visitors can climb the stairs to the roof and get the same panorama of Betio that Japanese machine gunners had in 1943. Today the blockhouse itself is deserted but is surrounded by dwellings and businesses nearby.

BOTTOM LEFT: On the eastern tip of Betio a Marine inspects this eighty-millimeter antiboat gun and its coconut log and sand emplacement. In the background are two more of the eight-inch guns the Japanese bought from the British in the early 1900s and shipped to Tarawa.

BOTTOM RIGHT: The remains of the same two eight-inch guns at the eastern end of Betio (left background and center), and the eighty-millimeter antiboat gun tipped over near the water's edge in the late 1980s. The action of currents and tides eroded the original emplacement and left the gun to slowly rust in the water. The eight-inch gun in the background was subsequently painted and marked with an informational sign as part of the war relic preservation program.

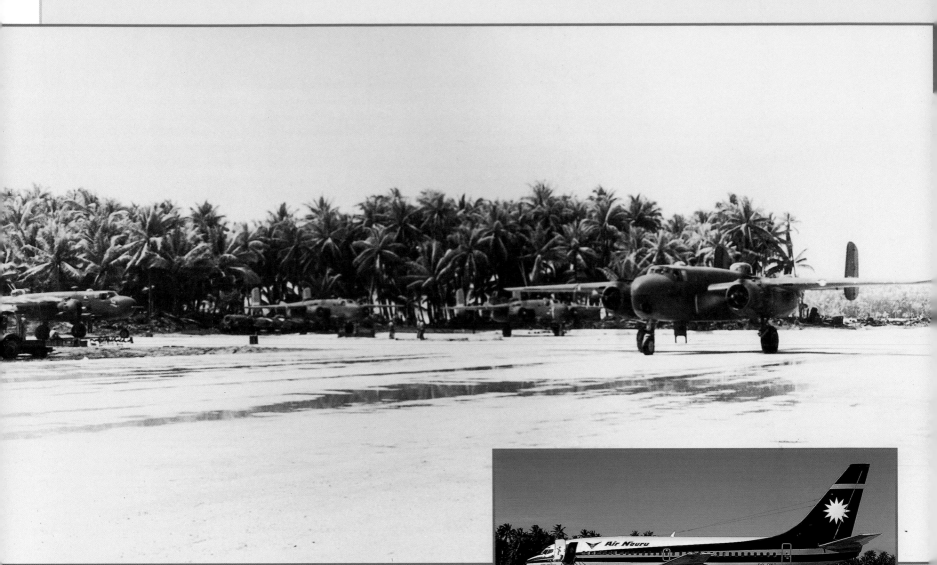

ABOVE: Shortly after the Americans occupied Tarawa, a second airstrip was built on another island in the atoll. Sometime in 1944 a B-25 taxis out on this coral runway named Mullinix Field.

RIGHT: Passengers on arriving international flights today land on the former Mullinix Field, now called Bonriki International Airport. Air service to Tarawa is infrequent and notoriously unreliable, but Kiribati has tried to address these problems by upgrading the runway to facilitate better service. This photo was taken before asphalt paving covered the original coral surface in the 1990s.

OPPOSITE TOP LEFT: The Marshall and Gilbert Islands Bereaved Families Association erected this Japanese memorial, one of several on Betio, in November 1982 on the site of the old U.S. war cemetery. Gilbert Islands was the former name of modern Kiribati. The U.S. Second Marine Division memorial is located farther inland. As was the case with most island battlefield cemeteries in the Pacific, the bodies of American servicemen were disinterred after the war and returned for reburial to the States. An inscription in English on the back of the monument reads, "In memory of those gallant men who fought and died on the Gilbert Islands during World War II. May they sleep in peace." It is estimated that roughly five thousand bodies, Japanese and American, remain buried on Betio to this day. Another Japanese memorial nearby, a small stone slab, has inscribed on it a poem that captures the emotions felt by relatives who still come to visit the faraway island where loved ones died in 1943. The words in English appear above the Kiribati language translation, with the Japanese characters on the other side:

Where have you gone, my dear,
In this lagoon?
Standing on sand with my soles burning,
I feel your soul coming.

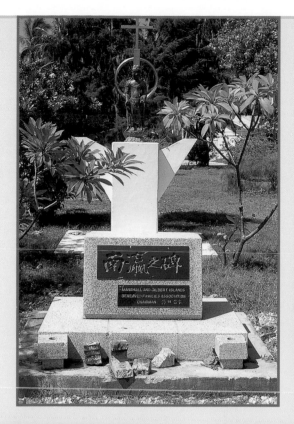

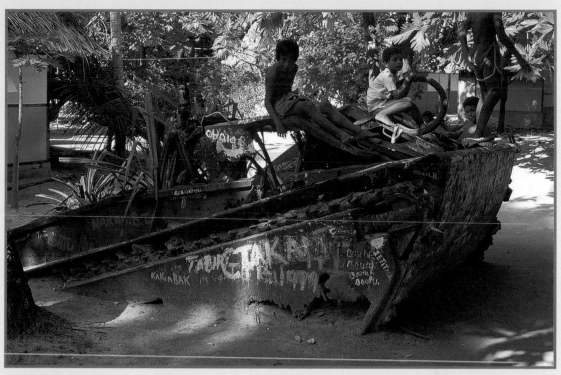

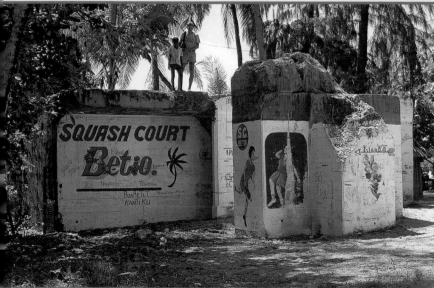

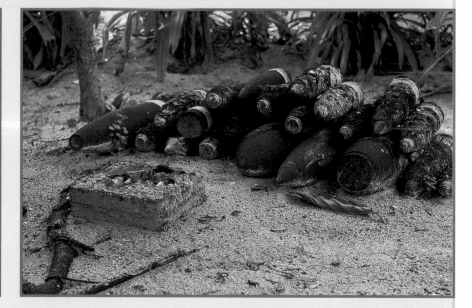

TOP RIGHT: This Marine amtrac rearing out of the ground just inland from Red Beach One has become a graffiti-covered piece of playground equipment for these children. This particular amtrac is the best preserved of any that remain on Betio today. Of several theories as to why this amtrac ended up in this position, one explanation is that as it maneuvered up and over the seawall at the edge of the beach in one of the initial invasion waves, it was hit by artillery and driven into a shell hole where it has remained ever since.

BOTTOM LEFT: One of the massive concrete bunkers, said to be the personal quarters of the island commander and formerly covered with sand by the Japanese, had most of its roof blown off during the battle. With the sand and debris cleared away, it was used as a squash court in the 1980s. Subsequently repainted in more staid colors, the bunker was then used as part of the facilities of the neighboring Marine Training School, an organization that prepares students for careers in the merchant marines.

BOTTOM RIGHT: As on most Pacific islands where intense fighting occurred, unexploded and potentially lethal shells are still turning up. This stack of artillery shells was collected near the police station on Betio, just behind Red Beach Three. The box at front left contains rusted but still neatly packed antitank shells.

EVENTS AT SEA

A long-standing tradition in the Navy was the equator-crossing ceremony. Every gob or landlubber who had never previously traversed the equator (or didn't have a card to prove it) was subject to initiation, a time-honored practice under the general heading of "Neptune Parties." The ceremonies varied from ship to ship, but all involved some degree of humiliation. Initiates, called "pollywogs," were usually presented a summons (shown here) to appear before the "High Court of the Raging Main," which consisted of "shellbacks" dressed up as various denizens of the briny deep like King Neptune and Davy Jones. Punishments handed down to the hapless pollywogs often included dressing in ridiculous clothing, being smeared with oil or ripe garbage, or being swatted or hazed in a variety of ways.

The goal of the initiation was the Shellback Card, which would ensure that this never happened again. Many a Pacific veteran carried such a card for years. Another variant of travel tribulation in the Pacific was to enter the "Realm of the Golden Dragon" by passing over the International Dateline in mid-Pacific. Additionally, one could become a "Short Snorter" by crossing the equator by air, or by simply making a long transoceanic flight. Each passenger on the plane would pass around a "Short Snorter Bill," a U.S. dollar bill, that everyone onboard would sign.

Subpoena and Summons Extraordinary
The Royal High Court of the Raging Main

Region of the South Seas } ss
Domain of Neptunus Rex

To Whom May Come These Presents
Greetings and Beware

WHEREAS, It having been heralded by Mother Carey's chickens that the good ship USS Wm. P. BIDDLE., bound southward of the Equator, is about to enter our domain; and

WHEREAS, The aforesaid ship carries a large and loathsome cargo of landlubbers, beach-combers, guardo-rats, sea-lawyers, lounge-lizzards, four-flushers, cross-word puzzle bugs, bridge sharks, San Diego shieks, asphalt arabs, and other foul creatures of the land, falsely masquer-ading as seamen, of which low scum you are a member, having never appeared before us; and

WHEREAS, THE ROYAL COURT of the RAGING MAIN will convene on board the good ship Wm. P. BIDDLE on the 13th day of March at longitude ....; and,

WHEREAS, An inspection of our Royal Muster shows that it is high time your sad and wandering nautical soul appears before OUR AUGUST PRESENCE;

BE IT KNOWN, That we hereby summon and command you Charles D. McNeal Now a ...... Pollywog .... to appear before the Royal High Court and Our August Presence on the aforesaid date at such time as may best suit OUR pleasure, under penalty of eternal pickling.

You will accept most heartily and with good grace the pains and penalties of the awful tortures that will be inflicted upon you to determine your fitness to be one of our Trusty Shellbacks and answer to the following charges:

CHARGE I. In that you have hitherto wilfully and maliciously failed to show reverence and allegiance to our Royal Person, and are therein and thereby a vile landlubber and polly-wog.

CHARGE II. Failing to feed his Majesty's subjects the proper amount of food.

Disobey This Summons Under Pain of Our Swift and Terrible Displeasure. Our Vigilance is Ever Wakeful, Our Vengence is Just and Sure.

Given Under Our Hand and Seal.

Harry Moore,
DAVEY JONES
Clerk

NEPTUNUS REX
Ruler of the Raging Main

Ancient Order of the Deep
This is to certify that
Rex A. Smith
has been gathered into our fold and duly initiated
as a
TRUSTY SHELLBACK
having crossed the Equator and invaded my Realm aboard
U.S.A.T. "HALEAKALA"
on
at Latitude 00° 00' 00", Longitude 167° 30' West.
Davy Jones   Neptunus Rex
His Majesty's Scribe   Ruler of the Raging Main
Attested by:

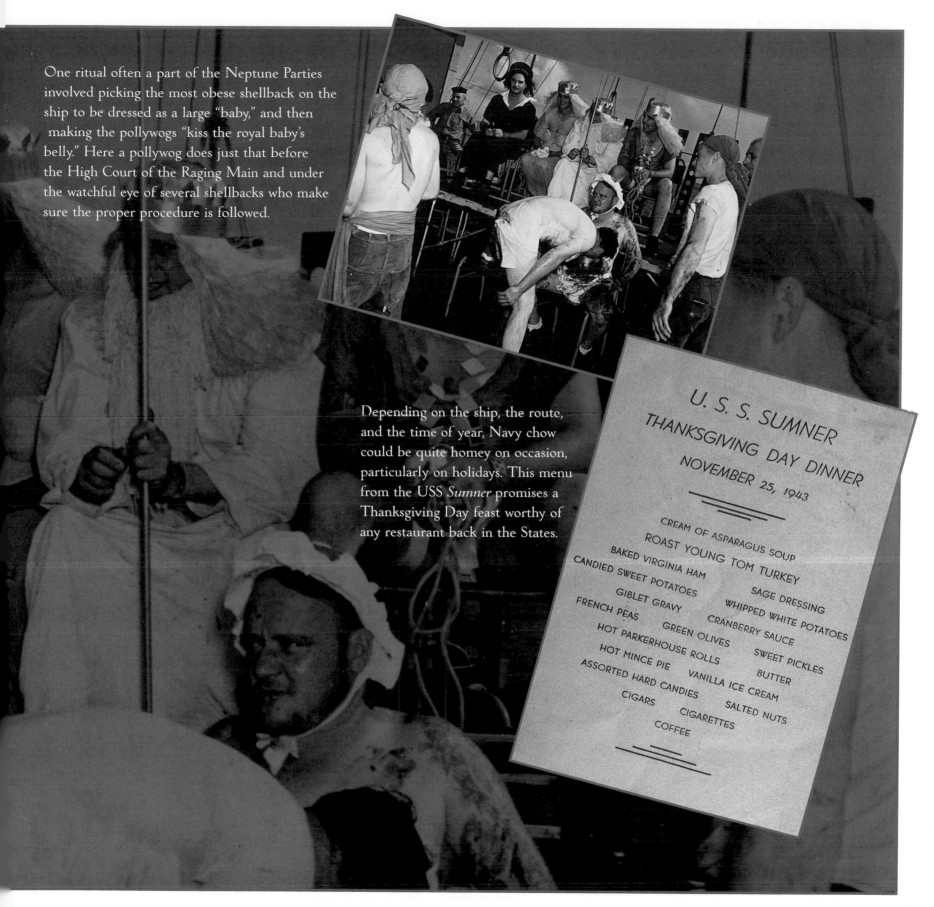

One ritual often a part of the Neptune Parties involved picking the most obese shellback on the ship to be dressed as a large "baby," and then making the pollywogs "kiss the royal baby's belly." Here a pollywog does just that before the High Court of the Raging Main and under the watchful eye of several shellbacks who make sure the proper procedure is followed.

Depending on the ship, the route, and the time of year, Navy chow could be quite homey on occasion, particularly on holidays. This menu from the USS *Sumner* promises a Thanksgiving Day feast worthy of any restaurant back in the States.

U. S. S. SUMNER
THANKSGIVING DAY DINNER
NOVEMBER 25, 1943

CREAM OF ASPARAGUS SOUP
ROAST YOUNG TOM TURKEY
BAKED VIRGINIA HAM
CANDIED SWEET POTATOES   SAGE DRESSING
GIBLET GRAVY   WHIPPED WHITE POTATOES
FRENCH PEAS   GREEN OLIVES   CRANBERRY SAUCE
HOT PARKERHOUSE ROLLS   SWEET PICKLES
HOT MINCE PIE   VANILLA ICE CREAM   BUTTER
ASSORTED HARD CANDIES   SALTED NUTS
CIGARS   CIGARETTES
COFFEE

AFTER TARAWA, the Americans continued their push across the western Pacific in early 1944. Ahead lay the Mariana Islands of Saipan, Tinian, and Guam. They presented themselves not only as heavily defended obstacles held by thousands of Japanese soldiers, but as essential bases for the Air Forces' new superfortresses —the B-29s. These silver giants, revolutionary airplanes by World War II standards, were designed to mete out devastation by aerial bombing on a previously unimaginable scale. With a wingspan of over 140 feet and a fuselage 100 feet long, the B-29 was the largest and heaviest production airplane built up until that time. As the first B-29s became available in 1944, they flew long-range missions over Japan and other targets in Southeast Asia from bases in India and airstrips in China. But the logistics were nightmarish, the missions were perilous, and the B-29s had engines with a propensity for catching fire. The Marianas would afford better bases from which truly effective large-scale bombing raids of Japan could be mounted.

The American military juggernaut was honed to a deadly level of combat efficiency by mid-1944, from experience gained in island invasions beginning with Guadalcanal, Bougainville, Cape Gloucester, and Tarawa and continuing all the way across the tropical western Pacific through Kwajalein, Eniwetok, and the Admiralty Islands. In a two-month period in 1944, first Saipan and then Tinian and Guam were overrun by tens of thousands of American fighting men. The combat was bitter and intense, and the sheer number of men on both sides that were locked in a deathly struggle churned out casualties that made previous Pacific invasions pale in comparison. The fighting on Saipan piled up about 3,000 American dead, with nearly 11,000 wounded. Roughly 600 of the Japanese defenders survived; the remaining 29,400 or so perished on the island. In one massive banzai charge at Tanapag on Saipan, more than 4,000 Japanese troops were cut down. In the subsequent invasion of Guam, over 2,000 Americans and nearly 17,000 Japanese were killed, with at least 5,000 Americans wounded and only about 1,200 Japanese taken prisoner.

A number of cornered Japanese military and civilian personnel chose to leap to their deaths from cliffs on Saipan and Tinian. These suicides, relatively few compared to the number who did surrender, were nevertheless perceived to characterize the Japanese penchant for choosing death to surrender. The Saipan and Tinian suicides, horrible as they were, became an indelible symbol of illogical Japanese fanaticism that burned itself into the American consciousness. Those images propelled the American war machine headlong toward Okinawa and Japan. No conceivable alternative seemed possible. It was believed that total annihilation was the only answer for a people the Americans viewed as insanely fanatic.

Shortly after the fighting ended, Seabees and Army engineer aviation battalions got to work quickly on expanding the existing Japanese airfields and building new facilities at an astounding rate. Aslito Airfield on Saipan was renamed Isley Field in honor of an American aviator shot down over the island. The first B-29 arrived at Saipan in October 1944, and the massive North Field complex on Tinian, featuring four parallel 8,500-foot-long runways, began receiving B-29s in December 1944. Several months later two more runways at West Field on Tinian were completed. By February 1945, the sprawling North Field base on Guam was ready for its first B-29. Nearly one quarter of a million men ended up stationed on Guam, many involved in some way with the B-29 operations at North Field, Northwest Field, Agana Field, and Harmon Field. Hundreds of Saipan-, Tinian-, and Guam-based B-29s proceeded to methodically reduce sixty-five Japanese cities to ashes.

The sheer magnitude and scale of the aerial operations in the Marianas are even now hard to comprehend. It became routine to fill the skies with several hundred B-29s on grueling missions characterized by up to seventeen hours of flying over open ocean to and from Japan. A total of 414 planes were lost in the Pacific during the course of delivering almost 170,000 tons of bombs over Japan. Each B-29 usually had a crew of eleven men, and multiplying that by the hundreds of planes in each raid, with its inevitable percentage of casualties, the numbers of men killed and injured reached above three thousand.

Those numbers would have been even higher had it not been for dedicated air-sea rescue operations.

Another factor that proved significant in saving lives of aircrews was an island, Iwo Jima. This barren volcanic wasteland lay midway between the B-29 bases in the Marianas and Japan. After its capture, roughly twenty-four hundred B-29s made emergency landings there, saving the lives of an estimated twenty-six thousand men. This was cited as justification enough for the gruesome expenditure of over six thousand American lives to capture the island. In spite of intensive rescue operations and the option of using Iwo Jima as an emergency landing base, many airplanes would simply vanish without a trace over the vast ocean wastes.

The direct involvement of aircrews was supported by ground crews, maintenance men, reserve troops, naval personnel, and thousands of others in the military who were required to keep the bombing effort going. The B-29 annihilation of Japan added up to a scale of military operation unmatched on any of the other Pacific islands during the war.

Today only Guam remains a U.S. military island. Andersen Air Force Base (formerly North Field) was headquarters to Air Force B-52s that bombed Vietnam in the late 1960s and early 1970s. Isley Field, now named Saipan International Airport, is a commercial facility and international point of access for thousands of Japanese tourists who peacefully invade Saipan annually. The sprawling North Field complex of runways on Tinian, where the *Enola Gay* took off for the world's first atomic bomb attack, is now abandoned. The old coral, asphalt-topped runways are still clear for the most part, but the taxiways and hardstands have mostly disappeared beneath a layer of vegetation. Other than the old airstrips, the legacies from World War II seen today on these islands are the debris left over from the initial invasions in June and July 1944. Tourist development and relentless tropical vegetation have altered or covered much of what is left from the war. Only the long-abandoned runways on Tinian still evoke the memory of gleaming B-29s roaring off into the tropical night loaded with the deadly means of destruction for the cities of Imperial Japan.

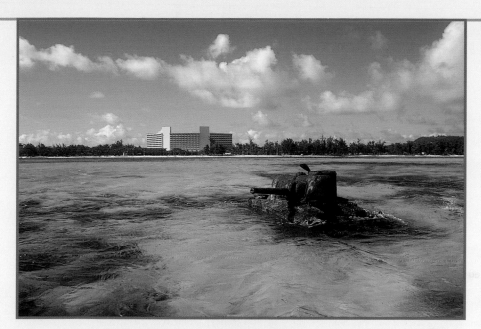

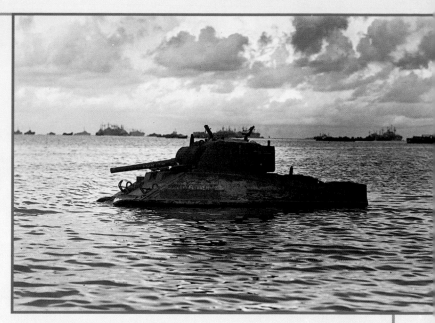

This U.S. medium tank is one of three still remaining in the waters off the invasion beaches of Saipan. It belonged to the Fourth Marine Division. On D-Day, the Japanese were sweeping the landing beaches with fire from their prepared positions on Afetna Point. Today this former World War II Japanese stronghold is now occupied by the Japanese tourist hotels in the background. The tanks were desperately needed by the Americans to assist the troops pinned down on the beaches. Of fourteen tanks, six were unloaded under heavy fire from shore at the edge of the reef. They were intended to crawl to the beach through the presumably shallow water. The water proved deeper than expected, and only one tank made it to its objective. Of the five that didn't, three are left today, eerie reminders of the beginning of the end of Japanese rule on Saipan.

One of the American medium tanks that did not make it to the beach during the Saipan invasion was nicknamed "Flivver," and the inscription on the gun barrel reads "B there I time."

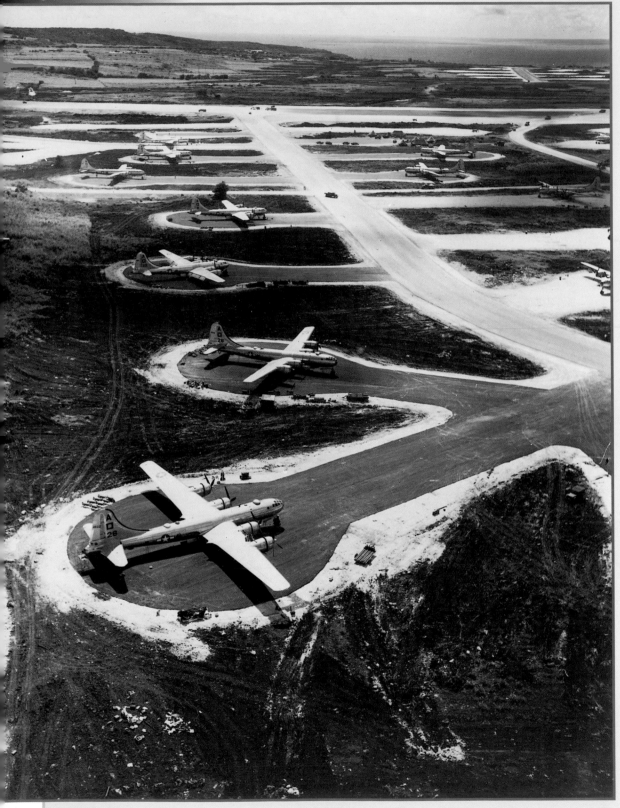

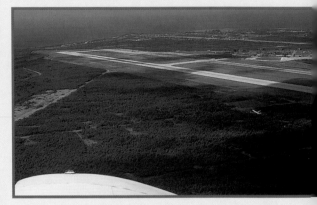

LEFT: Construction crews built two parallel runways and added miles of taxiways and numerous hardstands at Isley Field on Saipan for the brand-new, gleaming silver B-29s.

BELOW: The two original World War II runways of what is now Saipan International Airport are easy to distinguish. More difficult to make out but still evident is the complex of aprons, taxiways, and B-29 hardstands, several of which can be seen in the foreground of this photo. In the distance the remains of another World War II runway can be seen. This was Kobler Field, long since abandoned and now the site of a real-estate development known locally as Koblerville.

OPPOSITE TOP LEFT: Nine days after the invasion of Europe by the Allies, U.S. forces landed on the beaches of Saipan. In the first twenty minutes of the invasion, eight thousand troops and seven hundred amtracs surged ashore. Unexpected ocean currents caused entire units to land on the wrong sections of the beach. This resulted in chaos and deadly congestion as the Japanese mortars and artillery not silenced by U.S. Naval gunfire wreaked havoc among the troops crowded at the water's edge. In this photo, Marines in the first wave take cover to wait for the following three waves to arrive.

OPPOSITE TOP CENTER: Fourth Marine Division veteran Fred Everett stands on the beach where he came ashore on Saipan. "There was a lot of confusion," Everett recalled in 1995. "The driver of our LVT wanted to put us ashore at the wrong spot. We knew where we were supposed to be, but we had to pull a gun on him to make him take us to where we wanted to land."

OPPOSITE TOP RIGHT: Marines inspect the remains of a Japanese light tank.

OPPOSITE BOTTOM: Of the many shattered hulks of Japanese light tanks abandoned during the battle of Saipan, one was preserved next to the coast road.

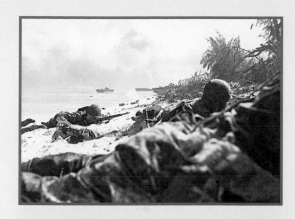
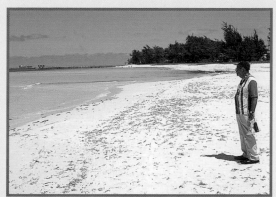
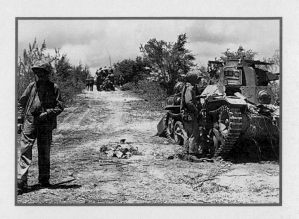
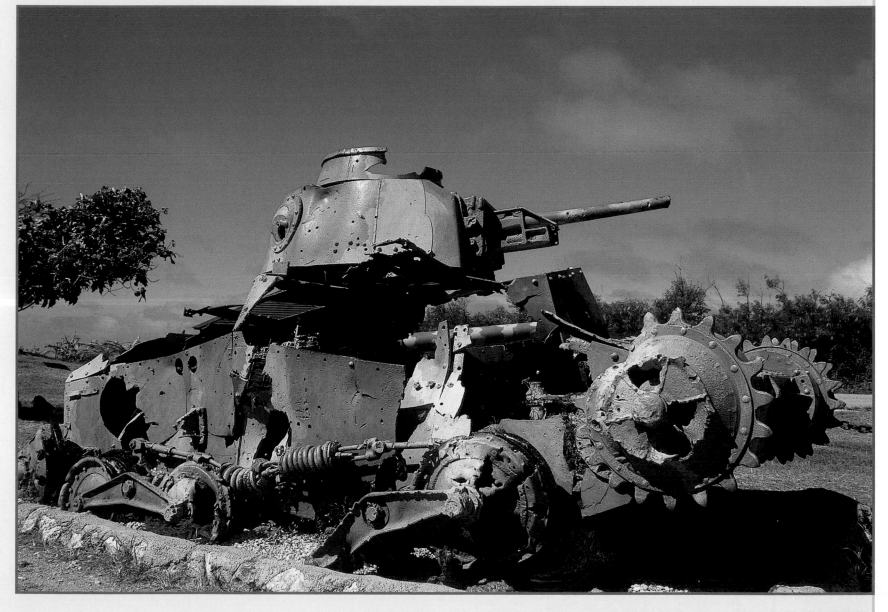

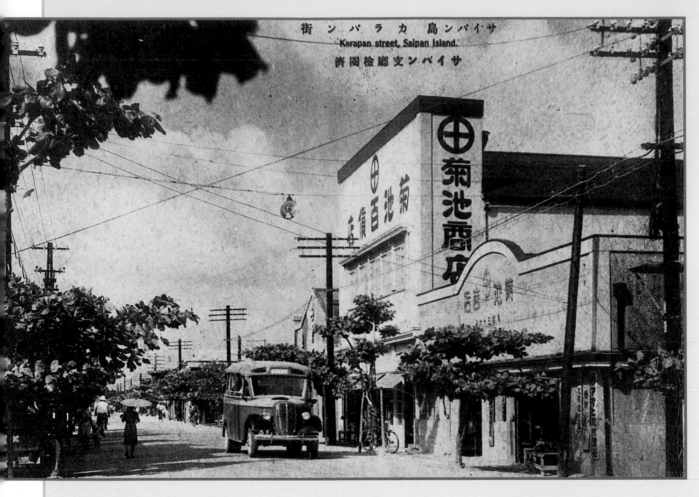

街ンバラカ島パイサ
'Karapan street, Saipan Island.'
済閲検廳支ンパイサ

菊池百貨店
菊池商店
菊池商店

Garapan is a bustling resort town filled with Japanese tourists. The tree-lined streets remain, but now tourist shops crowd the streets, and hotels loom along the beaches in the background.

OPPOSITE TOP LEFT: The remains of this Japanese bunker overlook a beach used for swimming by U.S. servicemen in the background.

OPPOSITE TOP RIGHT: The same bunker circa 1990. When the Japanese originally emplaced a six-inch naval coastal defense gun inside, the ocean literally lapped at its walls at high tide. Today, the shifting sands of Micro Beach in front of the Hyatt Regency Hotel nearby have left the old bunker about fifty yards inland. The gun inside is long gone, but the bunker's proximity to one of the finest white-sand beaches on Saipan has given it a life after the war. For a time it was the "Bunker Bar," a popular place to stop and have a drink while at the beach. When this photo was taken, it was a windsurfing shop catering to the Japanese tourists staying at the nearby hotel.

OPPOSITE CENTER LEFT: This was the scene the morning after the Tanapag banzai charge, thought to have involved the largest number of Japanese troops of any other such charge that occurred during World War II in the Pacific. As Japanese units overran American positions and penetrated farther south along the coast, rear area reserve troops, cooks, clerks, and wounded picked up anything that could shoot and mowed down the onrushing Japanese. Before the charge was over, more than four thousand Japanese troops had been killed.

ABOVE: The period of Japanese rule on Saipan (the "Japanese Time," as locals still refer to it) began in 1914 and ended with the American invasion in 1944. The Japanese had developed Saipan into a thriving center for sugar cane production during this era. Garapan, the prewar capital of the Marianas, had a population of fifteen thousand Japanese, and this prewar postcard depicts a typical street scene in the capital. The town had bus service, street lights, and tree-lined avenues.

BOTTOM LEFT: The same street in Garapan after the American invasion.

BOTTOM RIGHT: The same street in Garapan around 1990. After the war the ruins of the prewar capital were bulldozed, and today

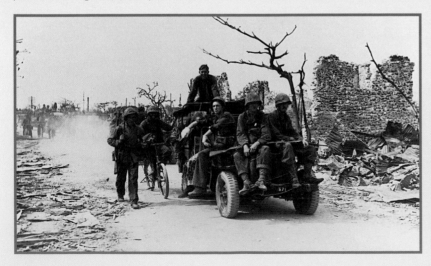

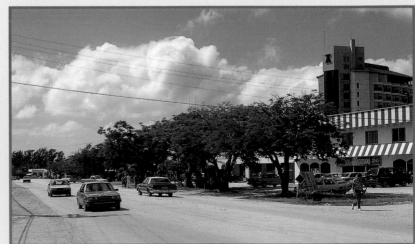

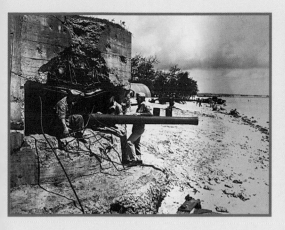

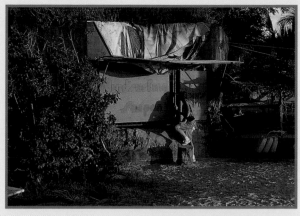

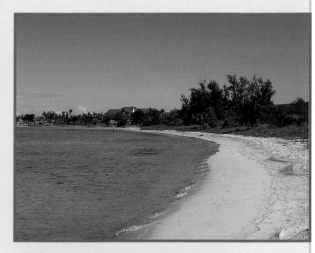

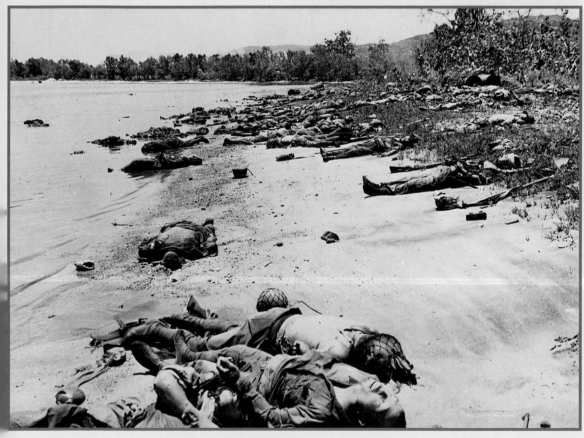

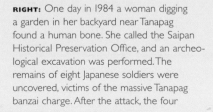

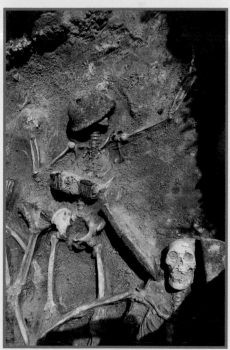

RIGHT: One day in 1984 a woman digging a garden in her backyard near Tanapag found a human bone. She called the Saipan Historical Preservation Office, and an archeo-logical excavation was performed. The remains of eight Japanese soldiers were uncovered, victims of the massive Tanapag banzai charge. After the attack, the four thousand or so bodies were quickly buried in mass graves by the Americans. These Japanese soldiers were still wearing their helmets and ammunition belts when they were covered over with sandy soil. The man at upper left was an officer, as evidenced by his Samurai sword scabbard still at his left side.

Imposing cliffs tower over the churning blue ocean at the northern tip of Saipan where, in the closing stages of the battle for that island, hundreds of Japanese jumped to their deaths. These shocking and well-publicized suicides formed an indelible impression in the minds of American military planners.

Robert Sheeks, a Japanese language officer with the Second Marine Division at Saipan, recalled the events surrounding the Japanese suicides:

go out on day or night patrols I find some.' And he said 'Let's go see D-3, David Shoup.' He was a real hero and leader at the time. We went to see Col. Shoup, and he starts off, 'Sheeks, OK, I hear what you say, how many are there?' That was his manner, bottom line. So I said, 'Well, sir, I would guess that there are several hundred.' He responds, 'So how many have you seen?' I answered, 'Well, maybe 15 or 20.' He says 'Well maybe there are 15 or 20 out there!' 'No, sir,' I say,

an article written by Robert Sherrod in *Time* magazine (see *Time*, 8/7/44). It had in it a headline something like 'suicide for 20 million—will all the Japanese fight to the last man, woman, and child?' So at the time I was writing a little article about Saipan and what happened to the civilians, and I especially wanted to correct this impression that we were up against a mass suicide of everybody based on what happened on Saipan. Of course it's very dramatic if you see 100 or 200 people, including families, jump off

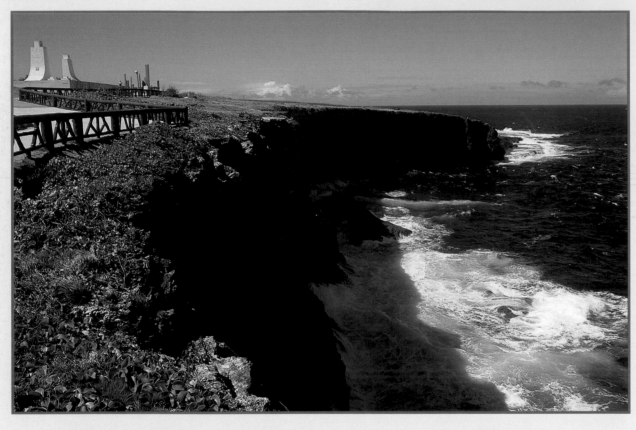

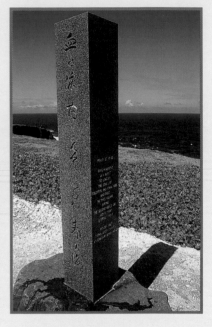

This is one of the many Japanese monuments placed at the top of the cliffs. Erected in 1987, the inscription reads in part, "... to console the souls of soldiers and civilians who died on this island during the Second World War and to pray [for] eternal peace."

"There was a great deal of publicity about the Japanese who had committed suicide, and the impression was widely spread that all the Japanese had killed themselves by jumping off the cliffs. Since my job was to round up Japanese, I was very much involved in the mop-up operation and getting Japanese civilians, and military, and paramilitary out from fortifications and caves in which they took refuge. I was very conscious of how many people were still out in the boondocks. I was thinking in terms of hundreds and hundreds, so I told my commanding officer, who was Col. Tom Colley, that I believed that there were many Japanese who had not been captured or killed. So he said 'How many do you think?' And I replied, 'I think probably hundreds.' 'What do you base it on?' he asked. And I said, 'Well, every time I

'there are a lot.' So after that on patrols and mop-up and so on we got something like 7 or 8 thousand more and there were still more out there. I don't know how many we ended up with totally in the prison camp, I think we probably had well over 10 or 12 thousand. These included Japanese, Chamorro [Saipan natives], and Carolinians [natives of the Caroline Islands to the south]. So anyway, I felt that the impression that people had of all the Japanese committing suicide was misleading. It scared even tough young Marines into shooting because they didn't want to take chances that they might be blown up by a desperate Japanese. I had gone around to units and talked about the importance of taking prisoners, and most of the reaction was, 'yeah, you go out and take 'em!' Anyway, then out came

a cliff one after another. You think the world is coming to an end, but the world's not coming to an end, it's one or two hundred people jumping off a cliff. There's a difference. So the way I wrote the article, I took a little sideswipe at Sherrod and *Time* magazine for writing something that possibly could be misleading. Anything that anyone wrote that went out had to go through the military censor. The censor called me and said, 'Hey, Sherrod's a great friend of the Marine Corps, and we don't want to write stuff like this, do we?' And I said, 'Well, I'm not writing it about him. I'm writing it about facts compared to the impressions.' And he said 'I think you better cut out all this section on the suicides.' So I said OK, otherwise it wasn't going to get published. It was finally published, by Lt. Robert Sheeks, USMCR."

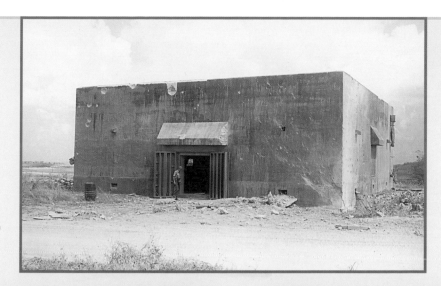

RIGHT: This Japanese concrete blockhouse near Aslito Airfield, one of a number of large fuel-storage bunkers built before the war, bears the scars of the U.S. bombardment.

CEMTER LEFT: This same blockhouse is one of the first sights visitors to Saipan see as they leave the former Japanese Aslito Airfield, which became the American Isley Field, then Saipan International Airport, for the drive to the beachside hotels.

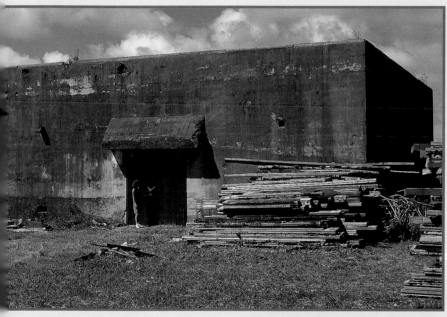

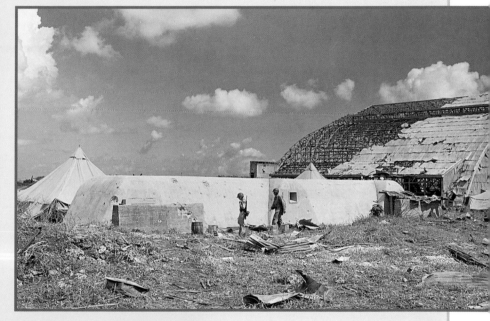

CENTER RIGHT: American soldiers inspect a Japanese-built concrete bomb shelter near Aslito Airfield. The remaining shell of one of the Japanese hangars is in the background.

RIGHT: The remnants of one of the Japanese air raid shelters at Saipan International Airport today.

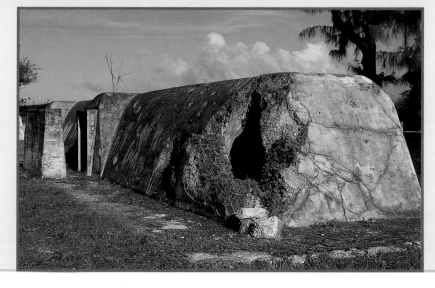

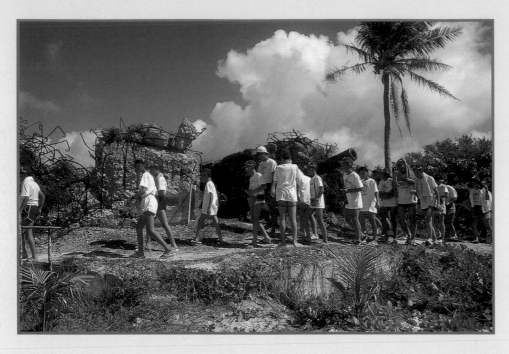

Japanese school children on holiday in the Marianas file past the broken and twisted carcass of a Japanese World War II gun emplacement on tiny Managaha Island just off the coast of Saipan. Now a popular and scenic spot for day trips from the main island, Managaha was taken by the Americans in the closing days of the Saipan campaign. In a fifteen-minute period before the landing commenced, U.S. artillery units rained 900 105-mm and 720 75-mm shells on Managaha, an island about the size of a city block. After this barrage the Americans met little resistance from the fifteen dazed and shaken Japanese soldiers left alive. Only one American was wounded during the mini-invasion.

Though Garapan was mostly leveled by American bombardment, the ruins of a few of the Japanese structures remain. The hospital, shown here, was in good enough shape to be used by the Americans as a field headquarters and hospital during the battle for the island.

The ruins stood for years in much that same condition (as seen here in the late 1980s), until in 1997 the shell of the old hospital was remodeled to house the Commonwealth Museum of History and Culture.

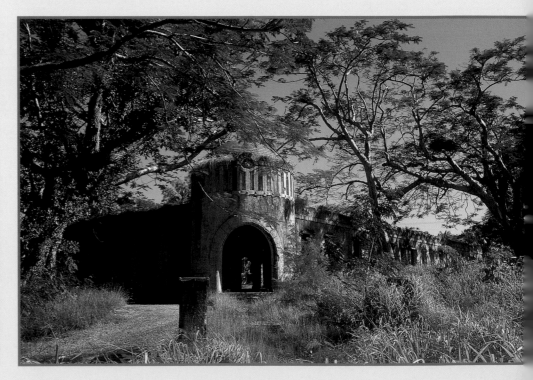

The next U.S. objective after Saipan was nearby Tinian. The Japanese expected the Marines to land on the beaches near Tinian town in southern Tinian. They felt certain that a large force (over fifteen thousand Marines would land on the first day alone) could not negotiate the narrow beaches of northern Tinian. But after a feint toward southern Tinian, the Marines landed their large force on two beaches less than two hundred yards in length. Such restricted beach area required quick movement inland and efficient logistical support. The Japanese were effectively fooled, and the Tinian operation proceeded with the fewest casualties of any of the Mariana invasions. During the nine-day operation, 389 Americans were killed and 1,816 were wounded. More than 5,000 Japanese were killed, and 252 were taken prisoner. Of the Americans killed, forty-three died on the battleship *Colorado,* and nineteen perished on the destroyer *Norman Scott.* These ships were hit by accurate six-inch shellfire from Japanese shore installations near Tinian town during the initial diversionary maneuver. The six-inch guns were of the same British vintage as the eight-inch batteries encountered the previous year on Tarawa. As with the guns on Tarawa, the British guns were purchased by the Japanese in the early 1900s during a period of more friendly relations. In addition to the usual mines and beach defenses, there were a few other more unorthodox hazards for the U.S. landing forces. The Japanese apparently had heard of the American penchant for souvenir hunting and had placed various desirable items, such as cases of Japanese beer, watches, and other collectibles, in the landing-beach area wired with explosives to kill curious Americans. However, it seemed odd to the Americans that such prime items would be left lying around in the open, and demolitions experts defused the "bait."

BOTTOM LEFT: In 1995 on the Tinian beach where he and fellow Fourth Division Marines came ashore, Fred Everett performs a ritual repeated by many veterans on return visits to Pacific island battlefields: he loads up a plastic bag with beach sand to take home as a memento.

BOTTOM RIGHT: Everett stands next to a Marine amtrac unearthed in 1995 near the Tinian invasion beaches.

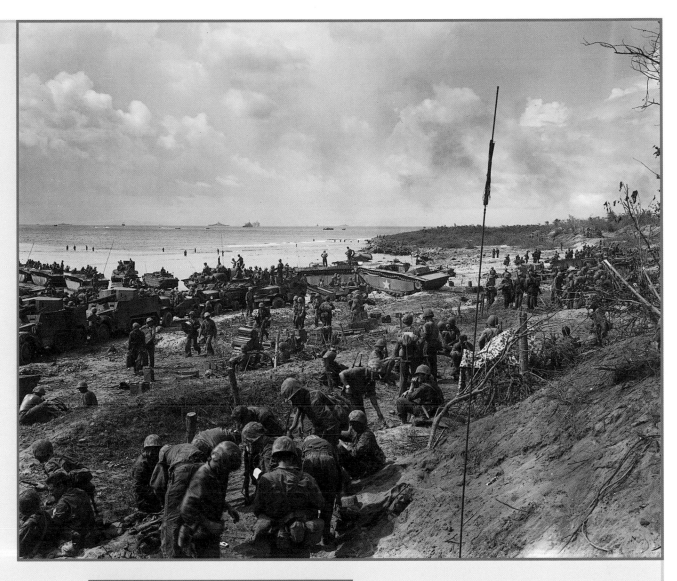

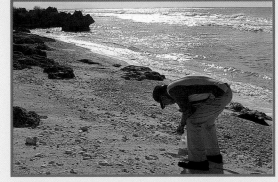

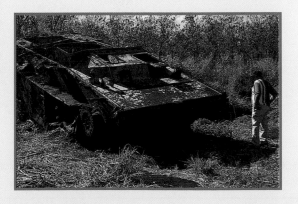

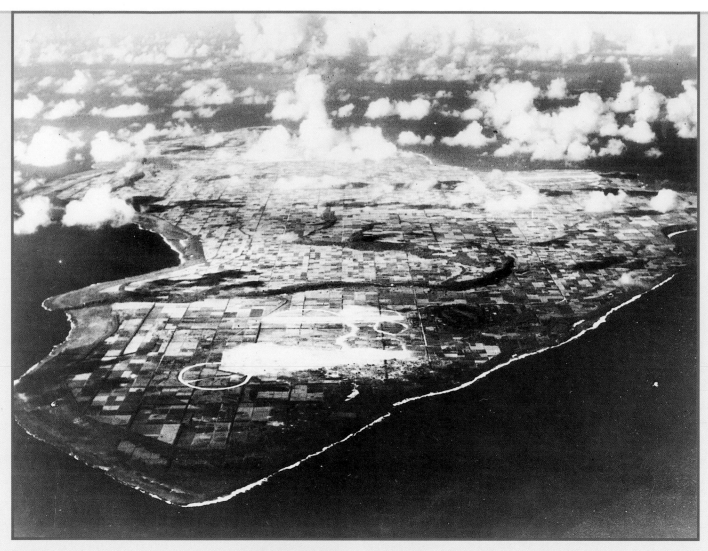

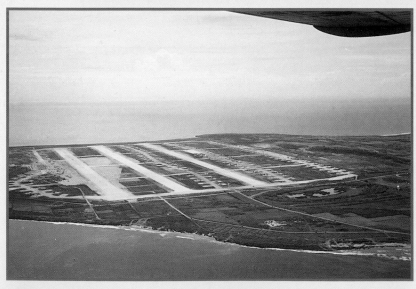

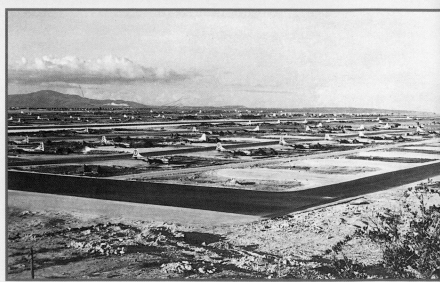

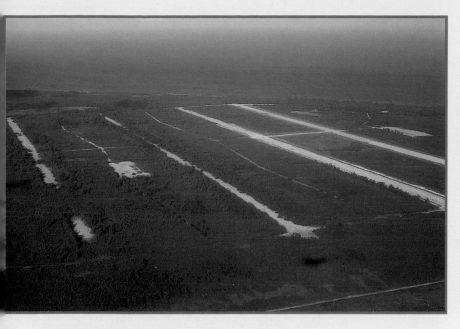

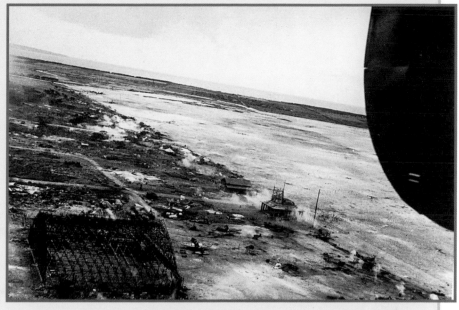

OPPOSITE TOP: This preinvasion photo of Tinian shows the progress of Japanese construction at the Ushi Point Airfield (in the foreground), nestled among the extensive sugar cane fields (nearly the entire island was under cultivation for sugar cane).

OPPOSITE BOTTOM LEFT: By early 1945 the former Ushi Point Airfield was almost unrecognizable. The four parallel eighty-five hundred-foot runways are in various stages of completion in this photo taken from the west. Numerous hardstands and taxiways are also being built to accommodate the fleet of

B-29 Superfortresses. The original landing beaches are in the center foreground. Both the *Enola Gay*, leaving for Hiroshima with the world's first tactical atomic bomb, and *Bock's Car*, departing for Nagasaki with the second, took off from Runway A at left in the short space of three days.

OPPOSITE BOTTOM RIGHT: B-29s stretch as far as the eye can see in this 1945 view of North Field on Tinian. Mt. Tapotchau looms in the background on neighboring Saipan.

TOP LEFT: An aerial view of Tinian taken from the east shows the vast North Field complex and how the ubiquitous *tangan-tangan*, seeded from the air by the U.S. after the war to revegetate the island, threatens to engulf the runways. The two at right (Runway A is at far right) are kept clear by the U.S. military. They lease the northern two-thirds of the island for infrequent exercises. Even though some of the taxiways, hardstands, and runways are disappearing beneath the *tangan-tangan*, nearly all of the coral asphalt surfaces remain in excellent condition, an amazing fact considering that literally no maintenance has been done since the war.

TOP RIGHT: Aerial view of Japanese facilities at the Ushi Point Airfield on Tinian under fire during a preinvasion raid. Note the smoke coming out of the flight operations building at lower right.

BOTTOM LEFT: The Army Air Forces used the bombed-out, cast-concrete hulk of the Japanese flight operations building and built a wood-frame control tower on top.

BOTTOM RIGHT: The flight operations building still stands at the airfield today, but the control tower the Americans added on top was dismantled shortly before the field was abandoned.

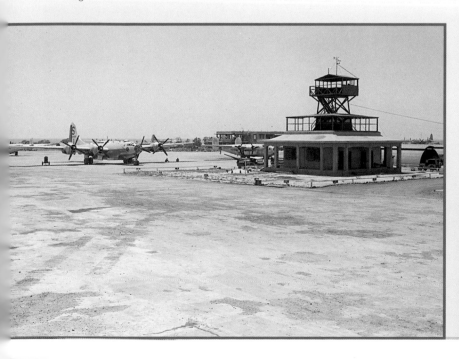

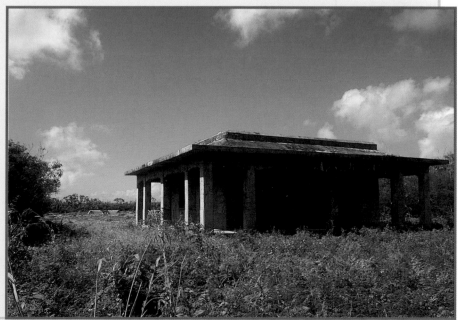

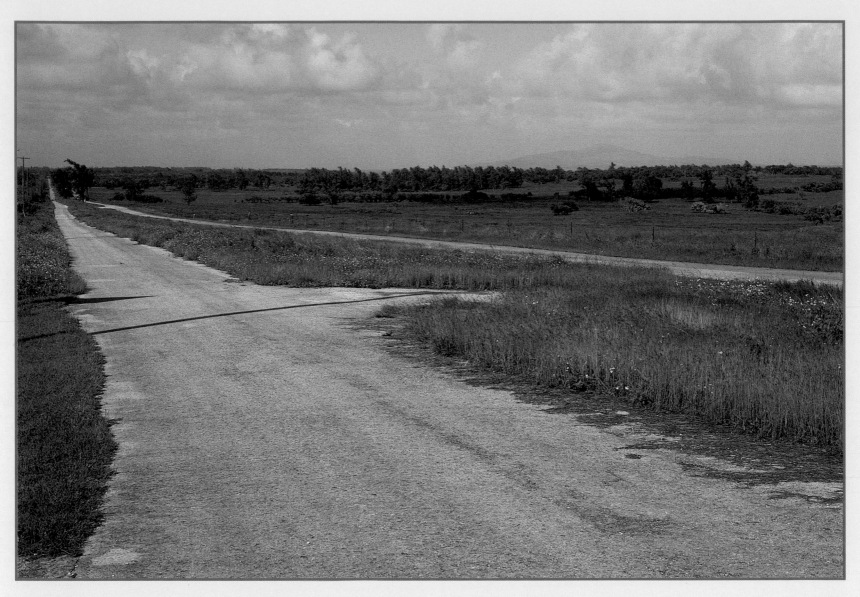

Tinian was reputedly the world's premier sugar cane producer before the war, and the island was literally covered by sugar cane fields. A railroad ran to all parts of the island and connected even the more remote areas to the main town. Over eighteen thousand Japanese lived in the bustling little metropolis that boasted a theater, stores, schools, and temples, but this entire town was reduced to rubble by the Americans in the preinvasion bombardment. After the island was secured, a vast complex of roads and runways was built and laid out like New York's Manhattan Island, complete with the names Central Park, the Battery, and the Village. The two main north-south arteries on the island were four-lane highways. One was 8th Avenue and the other, pictured here, was called Broadway. Broadway and 8th Avenue once handled hundreds of vehicles daily. Trucks carrying bombs and cargo lumbered from the wharves in the south of the island (the Village) to the sprawling air bases at West and North Fields. After the war the military facilities were dismantled, the runways and roads were abandoned, and a small number of locals were repatriated. Today the population has passed the one thousand mark, and the most significant development since the construction projects of 1945, the Tinian Dynasty Hotel and Casino, was opened in 1997. Funds for a new runway to be built over 8th Avenue were allocated in 1999. The rest of the old coral asphalt roads, highways, and runways remain in remarkably good condition. This legacy is a monument to the amazing endurance of American World War II construction.

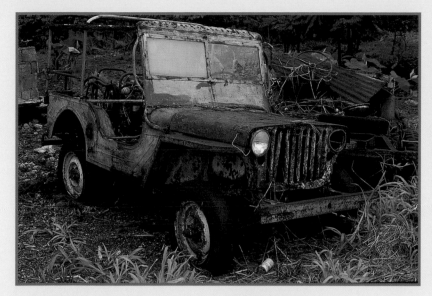

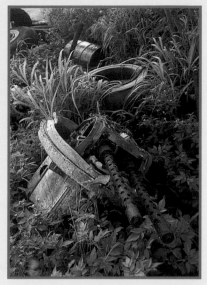

Given the hundreds of B-29s on Tinian during the war, surprisingly few traces of the planes are left on the island today. In the years following the departure of the Americans, scrap merchants stripped the island clean of most remaining wrecked planes or parts. Locals helped cut huge wing and fuselage sections into smaller pieces with axes, making it easier to haul the scrap by truck to the wharf. Visitors are hard-pressed to find any physical remnant of the B-29s whatsoever. These few relics rested near the tarmac of one of the World War II runways from West Field, which was used on into the early twenty-first century. They are now on display in front of the small terminal. In the foreground is a B-29 remote-control gun turret. Several large B-29 tires can be seen in the background.

Abandoned American jeeps lie rusting in a field on Tinian in the late 1980s. A number of old American vehicles left after the war were still driven on the highways of Tinian by local islanders for years.

When the Americans abandoned Tinian after the war, they tore down and removed virtually every one of the hundreds of structures they had built. Only a few Quonset huts and this group of wood-frame buildings, said to have been the island commander's quarters, remained in the late 1980s. The directions to get to these buildings, as given by local school teacher Joe Connolly, went something like this: "Take Broadway north to 42nd Street. Take a right and go past 2nd Avenue and look on your right." Those directions would make sense if you were on Manhattan, but there are no street signs on Tinian today. Only the locals know the street names. Visitors can get a good idea of the island layout from a map of wartime Tinian at its peak development affixed to the Seabees monument outside town. All one has to do is find it. Just take 8th Avenue north to 86th Street.

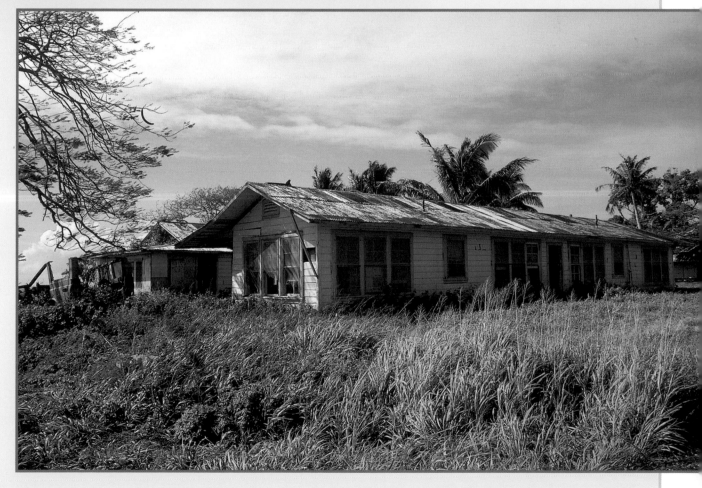

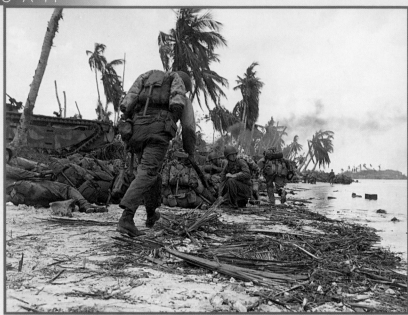

LEFT: Marine landings on Guam took place at two locations on the west coast on July 21, 1944. This was the scene at one of the beaches near Agat.

BELOW: The same gleaming white sand beach today lies just off the nearby coast road as it winds toward the undeveloped beauty of southern Guam. This invasion beach bears no trace of its violent World War II history, of the men cut down as they jumped from their amtracs under a rain of Japanese fire, or of the explosions of Japanese mortars among the Marines huddled for cover at the water's edge.

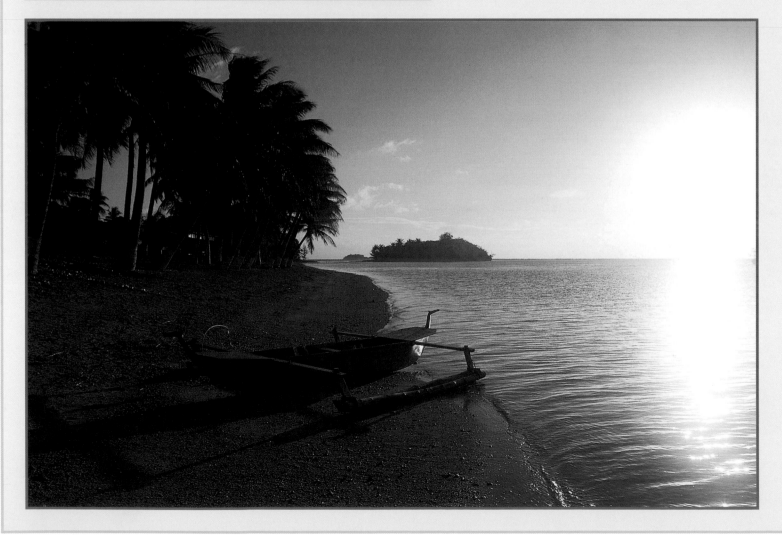

RIGHT: The other landing beach, at Asan, shown here, was subjected to sixteen days of naval shelling prior to the landings. Most of the disabled amtracs in the shallow water over the offshore reef struck landmines as they moved toward the beachhead during the initial phase of the battle.

BELOW: Today the beach at Asan is the centerpiece of the War in the Pacific National Historical Park. The visitor center is just out of the picture to the left. Operated by the U.S. National Park Service, the visitor center and the invasion beaches at Asan comprise one of a number of sites of historical interest from World War II on Guam.

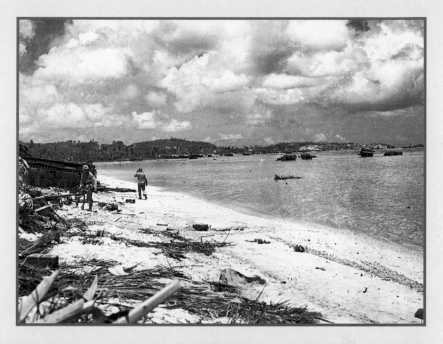

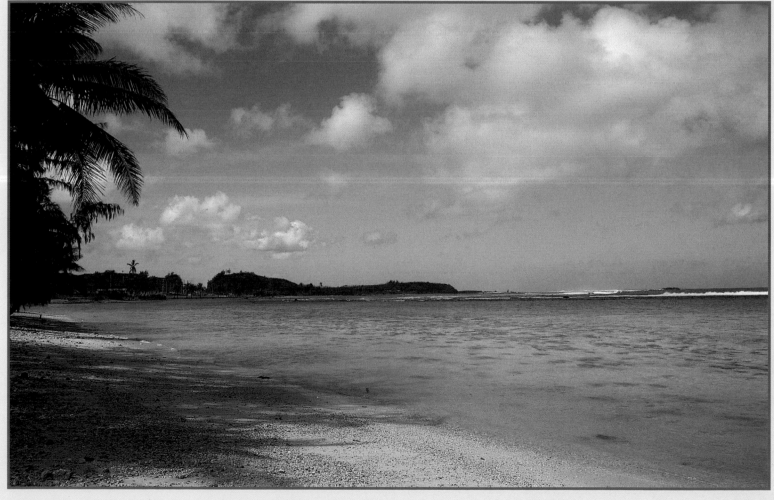

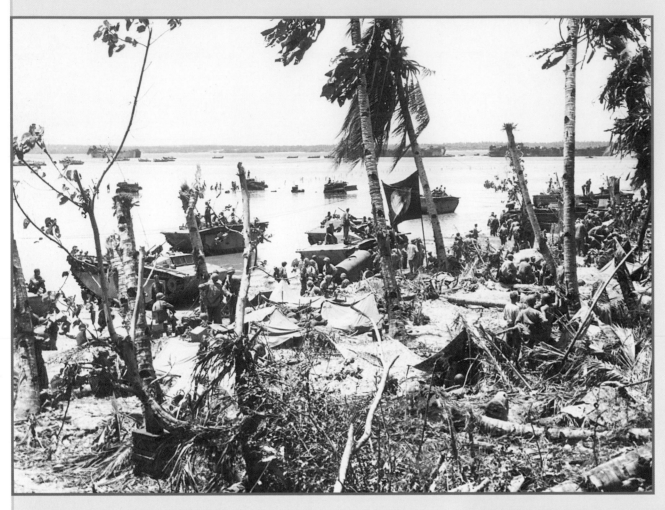

LEFT: Marines and equipment pour ashore at Gaan Point near Agat.

BOTTOM LEFT: The same scene at Gaan Point today. The site is now preserved and maintained by the War in the Pacific National Historical Park.

BOTTOM RIGHT: A Japanese gun and the flags of the U.S., Japan, and Guam mark this former Japanese stronghold at Gaan Point near the center of the Agat invasion beaches.

BELOW: World War II–vintage 6 oz. Coke bottles frequently wash up on beaches in the Marianas where Americans were based, for thousands of Cokes were dumped into the ocean as preparations were made to leave the islands. Many of the bottles were full and are sometimes found today still unopened. The place on Tinian where the bottles were dumped is now referred to by locals as "Dump Coke."

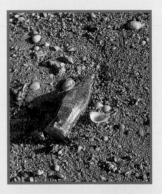

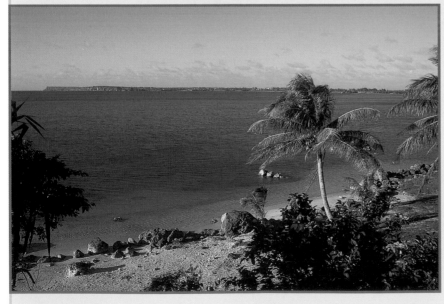

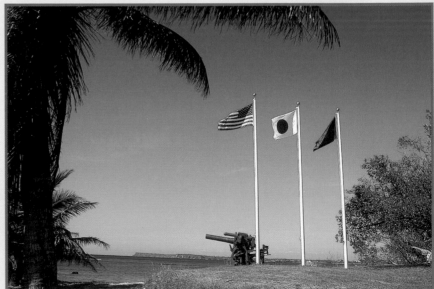

RIGHT: In the late 1980s, wooden crosses marked the crest of Bundschu Ridge, which rises steeply behind the Asan invasion beaches in the distance. This topographical feature was named onboard ship during an invasion planning meeting en route to Guam. Its namesake, Captain Geary Bundschu, and his unit were assigned the task of securing the heavily defended ridge. In the early stages of the landing, American troops struggling over the reef to the beaches in the background were showered with mortar shells and gunfire from the entrenched Japanese positions on the ridge. Desperate attempts to move up the steep face were met with a rain of steel from the Japanese above. The Americans finally fought their way to the summit, but in the process Captain Bundschu was killed on the ridge that bore his name. It was near this spot that Jim Milliff, a young Marine who landed on the beach below a few days earlier, won a Silver Star medal in a somewhat unorthodox way. As he tells it, "We came in on the beach by Asan Point and up Bundschu Ridge, and we were eventually dug in on a hillside close to there, three of us in a foxhole. In the middle of the night we saw 10–12 Japanese coming up the road in front of us. I reached for my rifle but it was wrapped in a poncho to keep it dry and I couldn't get it out in time. All of a sudden a Japanese officer charged right up to our hole with his sword above his head. As he started to swing it down to take my head off, I was calmly thinking I would parry the blow with my left hand like I'd been taught. But I just jumped up and grabbed the sword with both hands, yanked him off balance and yelled for someone to shoot him. Elkhorn had a .45 pistol and took a shot but hit me in the hip! I kicked the Japanese officer up in the air and then someone shot him." At this point in the story Milliff points out the scars plainly evident on the palms of his hands nearly sixty years later. He still has the Japanese sword that put the scars there, as well as the American .45 slug they dug out of his hip.

BELOW: Similar view from Bundschu Ridge shortly after the landing.

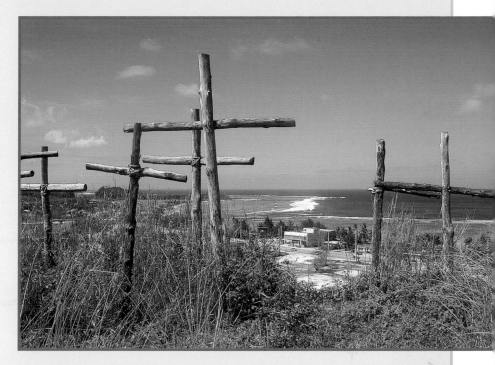

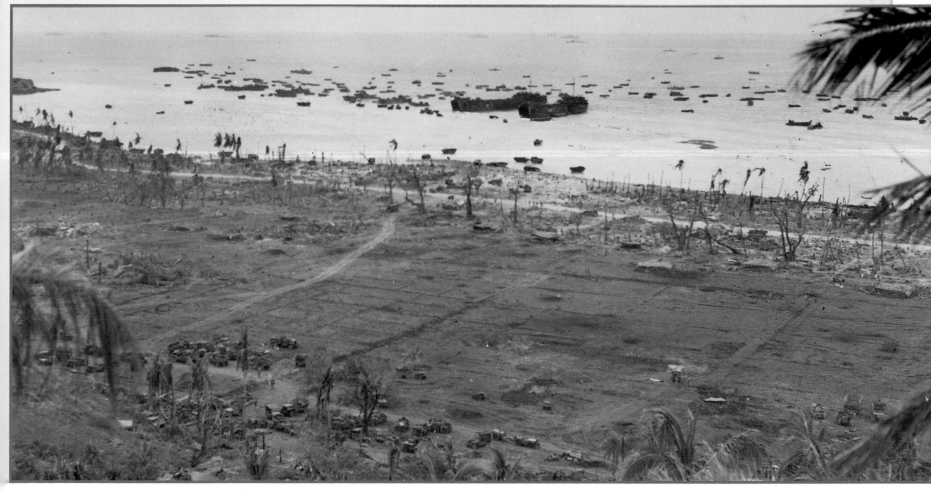

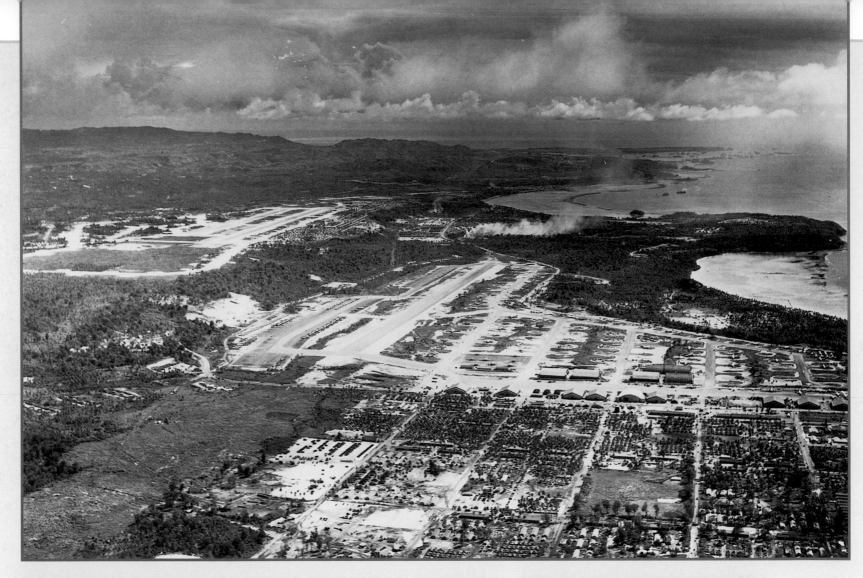

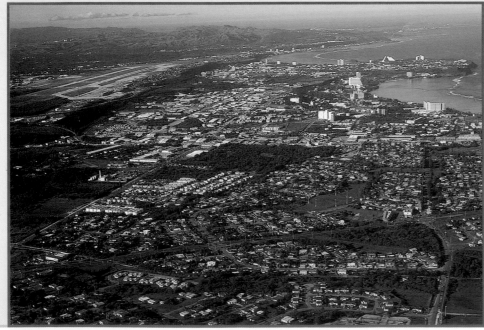

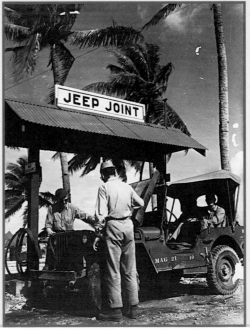

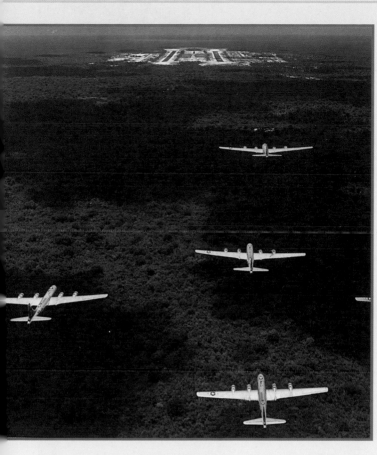

OPPOSITE TOP: After the fighting on Guam ended, the sprawling B-29 facilities and airstrips Agana Field (left) and Harmon Field (right) were quickly built.

OPPOSITE BOTTOM LEFT: Today Agana Field has become Guam International Airport, Harmon Field has turned into a commercial development complex, and Tumon Bay at right is home to the thriving Guam tourist industry with its high-rise hotels, shops, and white sand beaches.

OPPOSITE BOTTOM RIGHT: Though most traces of the fighting and subsequent B-29 base development have disappeared, many veterans who passed through Guam will never forget the most famous filling station in the Pacific, the "Jeep Joint."

ABOVE: By early 1945 Army engineer battalions and Seabees had blasted a huge airfield complex out of the jungles of northern Guam. These B-29s are approaching the distant parallel runways of North Field.

RIGHT: North Field was renamed Andersen Air Force Base after the war and is the only World War II air base still in active military use in the Marianas.

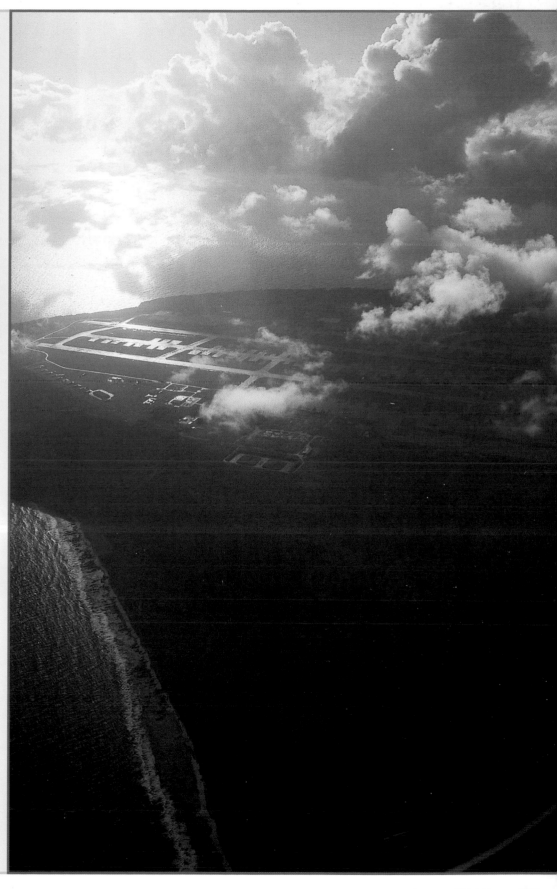

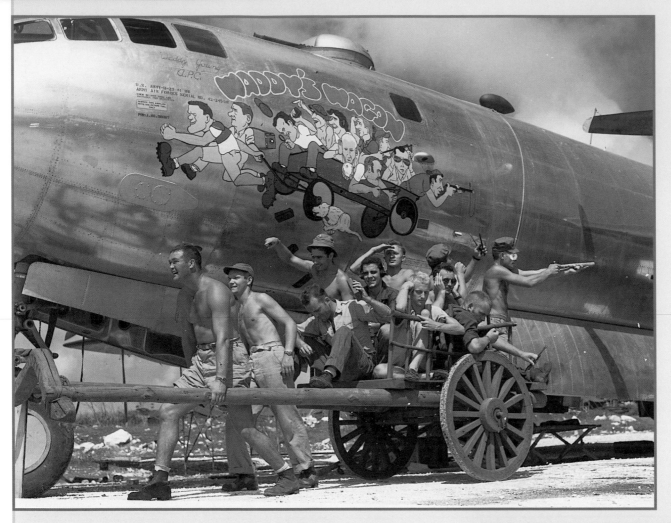

LEFT: As B-29 operations began on Saipan, the daily life-and-death drama of combat and all that went with it soon began to unfold. The crew of *Waddy's Wagon* poses here beside the nose art caricature on their B-29. Piloted by Captain Walter "Waddy" Young (left), former All-American football star and collegiate wrestling champion from Oklahoma, this aircraft was the fifth B-29 to take off from Saipan on the initial Tokyo bombing mission, and was the first to return from that mission. Luck ran out for *Waddy's Wagon* and her crew on January 9, 1945, when the plane ditched in the ocean after leaving the formation to "ride herd" on another B-29 disabled by two Japanese fighters that had rammed it. The next day the only trace of either plane to be found by search crews was a nacelle door floating in the empty ocean about four hundred miles from Japan.

BOTTOM LEFT: The large-scale, prewar Japanese development of Saipan included massive concrete blockhouses and buildings at the airport. This structure, complete with massive bomb-proof iron doors and window coverings, was the flight operations center for Japanese aviation at Aslito Airfield. It later was put to the same use by the Americans after they captured the airstrip and named it Isley Field.

BOTTOM RIGHT: Today the World War II flight operations center sits next to the modern terminal facility for Saipan International Airport.

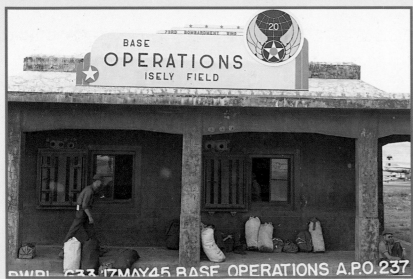

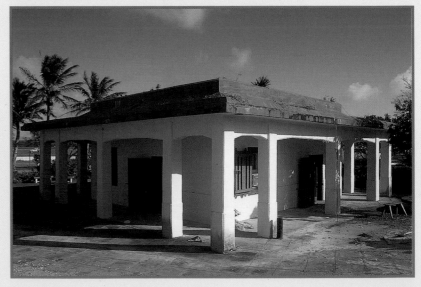

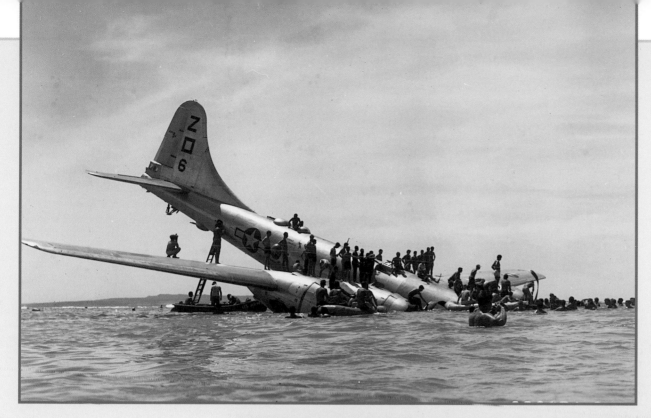

This B-29, named *Draggin' Lady* by her crew, lost power in two engines and tried to return to Isley Field. That effort failed, and the plane nosed into the water just short of a beach where a group of men had been watching the big plane lurch toward them. As the plane hit the water, the men on shore swarmed out to help rescue the crewmen inside. A number of the crew were brought to shore, but three were trapped in the submerged nose of the plane and drowned before the frantic efforts of men chopping through the fuselage could free them. The plane was later hauled to shore and scrapped.

The strange, the sad, and the bizarre became everyday occurrences as the missions flown from Saipan rolled on. This particular B-29, or what's left of it, made it back from a mission over Japan with only two good engines on the left side. Cannon fire disabled two engines on the right side, causing one of the propellers to spin off and slash a hole into the fuselage. The crew was still able to fly the crippled plane fifteen hundred miles back to Saipan at about five hundred feet above the ocean. Seventeen hours after they had taken off, they slammed down on the runway at Isley Field. The plane immediately lost hydraulic pressure and careened out of control down the runway with no brakes. It veered to the left, slammed into a parked B-29, and broke in two where the runaway propeller had perforated the fuselage. As the remnants of the giant airplane ground to a stop, the dazed crew emerged from the wreckage, and later posed for this photo.

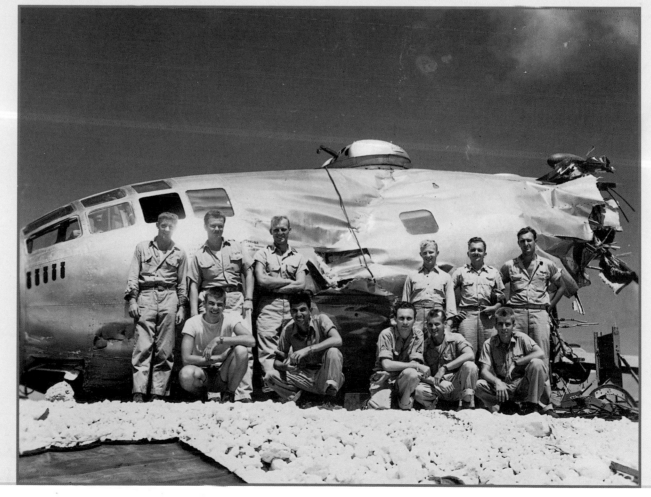

FOR EVERY AIRSTRIP built on an island seized from the grip of the Japanese, many more were constructed on islands far from the fighting. These rear-area bases were of vital importance as stepping-stones for airplanes and ships traversing the Pacific's broad expanse. Men and women stationed on these islands had plenty of time to savor the languid climate of the tropical Pacific, secure in the knowledge that the closest they would get to bloodletting was when fights broke out after volleyball games. Most of the time the chief enemy was boredom and that "middle of nowhere" feeling prevalent on tropical isles that truly were in the middle of nowhere. Today some of these islands are tourist meccas. Others have shrunk back to the obscurity they enjoyed before the war.

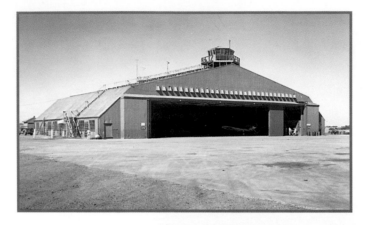

LEFT: The combination hangar and control tower at the Nadi airstrip in early 1945.

BELOW: The old World War II hangar, minus control tower on the roof, in 1984. The next year, when a hurricane destroyed this building, the materials were salvaged to rebuild a Methodist church in a nearby village.

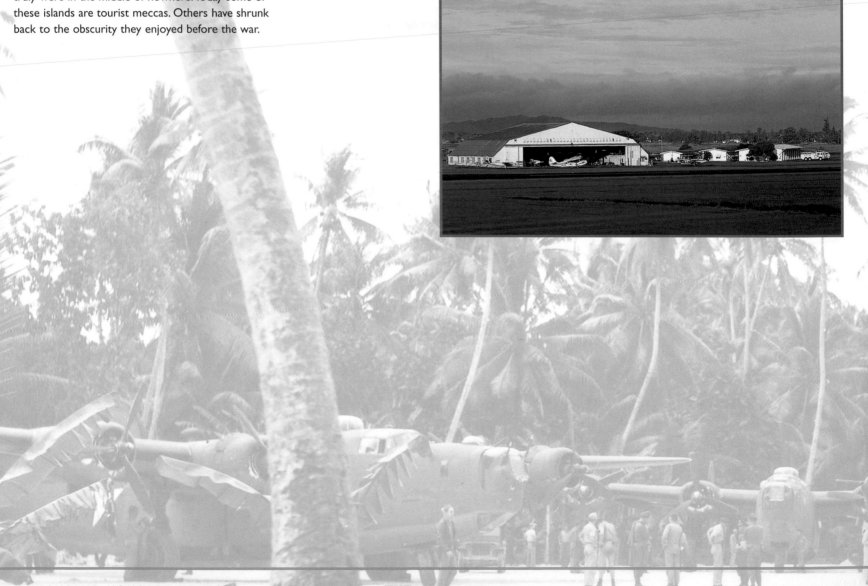

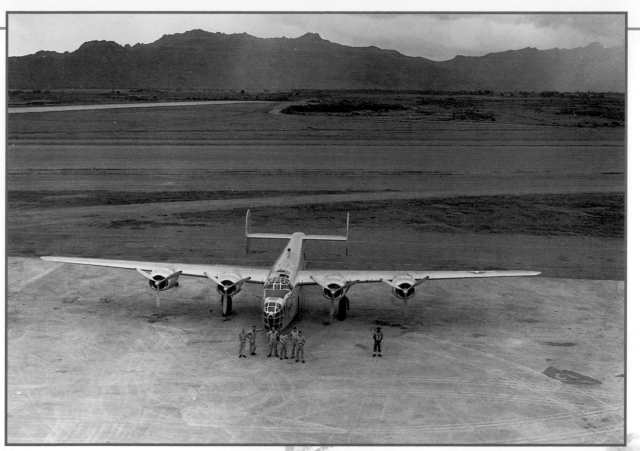

LEFT: The Americans built a large airstrip and base near Nadi on the western coast of the island of Viti Levu in Fiji. Like similar support bases at Noumea and Espiritu Santo, this field was a stopover point for airplanes on their way to the Solomons or New Guinea. In this photo, the crew of a B-24 Liberator bomber poses in front of their aircraft. Note the Fijian guard standing apart at right. A typical adventure for crews with a layover in Nadi was to forage the surrounding countryside for pineapples and watermelon to carry on the next leg of the flight.

BELOW: Today Nadi is a major international airport and point of access to the independent country of Fiji. Though political difficulties engulfed the country in 1987 and again in 2000, Fiji is still one of the most heavily visited island countries in the southwestern Pacific.

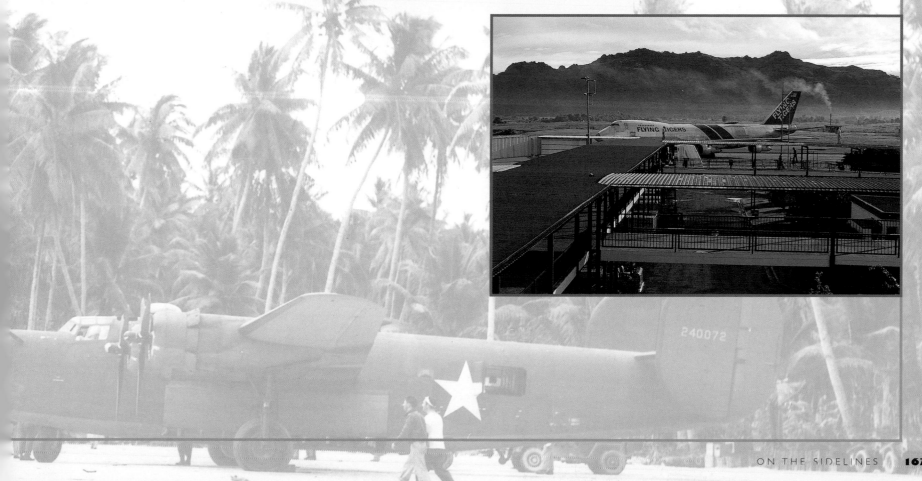

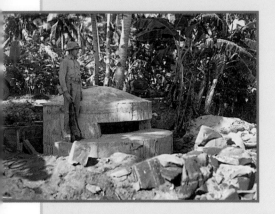

LEFT: The island of Tutuila in American Samoa, more popularly known as Pago Pago (one of the villages on Tutuila), became a stopping place for Allied ships carrying various war-related cargoes. There was a large PX, and stateside beer was available in the afternoons. The Marines who used the island for jungle training had a chronic fear of catching what the Samoans called *mumu*, known to American doctors as elephantiasis. Concrete pillboxes such as this one ringed the island and were manned by Marines, even though the nearest Japanese soldier was almost two thousand miles away.

RIGHT: This photo of the so-called Marine Airfield was taken shortly after its construction in 1942. The island of Tutuila afforded little flat ground, so the Seabees had to build the majority of the coral runway out into the shallow water of the lagoon. The edge of the coral reef is clearly seen where the waves are breaking at the bottom of the photo. There the depth of the water goes from about three to five feet in the lagoon near the runway to about one thousand feet deep just beyond the edge of the reef.

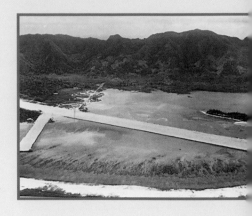

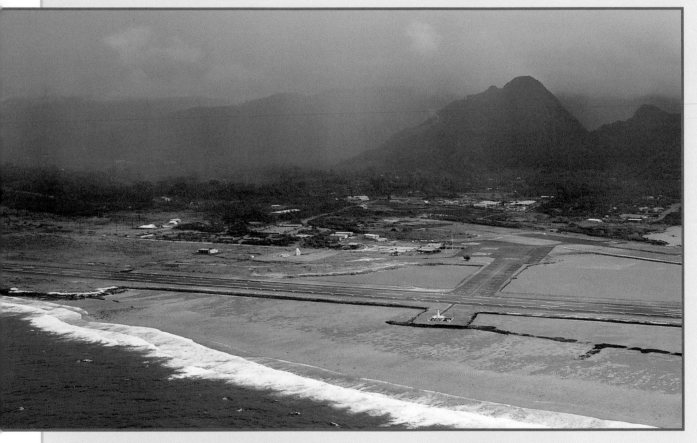

LEFT: The Navy had established a coaling station to take advantage of the deep-water bay at Pago Pago years earlier. In the mid-thirties, Pan American Airways attempted to use the bay as a refueling stop for its Clipper flying boats on their way to New Zealand from Hawaii. The landing was particularly tricky, because sheer cliffs soaring about fifteen hundred feet up from the edge of the water ring the bay. In spite of the difficulties, a number of hair-raising landings were completed by the Pan Am Clippers. However, after taking off from Pago Pago for New Zealand in 1936, Pan Am's senior pilot and the rest of his crew were killed. Apparently they had encountered mechanical difficulties, and the flying boat exploded in mid-air as the pilot attempted to return to Pago Pago. Shortly thereafter Pan Am came up with another route to New Zealand that bypassed Pago Pago. Pan Am was to experience another tragedy at Pago Pago when in 1974 one of its Boeing 707s crashed while trying to land in a rainsquall. All but a handful of passengers were killed. In this photo taken in the late-1970s, the post–World War II reef runway (foreground) can be seen connecting with the old wartime crosswind runway, which is now used as a tarmac and taxiway. The main World War II runway, disused at this time, can be seen in the background. It has since been resurfaced and connects with the end of the reef runway out of the picture to the right.

FAR LEFT: To sailors weary of the endless expanse of water, Pago Pago Harbor's craggy peaks adorned with brilliant green vegetation were a welcome sight. There were other sights that were even more welcome. Clarence Cook, a member of the Navy armed guard on the Victory ship *Hastings*, recalled the scene as his ship pulled up to the dock, "There were topless Samoan girls standing on the dock welcoming the ship, and this got us to cheering since we'd been at sea a long time. They were waving their wraparound *lavalava*

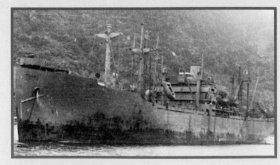

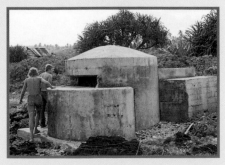

skirts at us. Then we really started cheering when we got close enough to the dock to see that they didn't seem to be wearing much underneath." Here, the *Hastings* weighs anchor in Pago Pago Bay. This Victory ship and others like it, and their sister Liberty ships, hauled cargo to ports around the world throughout the war. When this photo was taken in April 1945, the *Hastings* was carrying tons of ammunition; it was, in effect, a floating bomb.

Another hazard for Americans in Pago Pago was a deadly Samoan drink called *tuba,* made from fermented coconut juice. Americans would barter for the beverage and consume heartily, exceeding in quantity but not in treasured quality the rationed stateside beer at the PX. Cook shuddered in later years when recounting his *tuba*-related brush with death on Pago Pago. "Two Marines, drunk on *tuba,* were driving their jeep around the dock area like maniacs one day. They damned near ran me over. I barely was able to jump out of the way at the last minute. I would have died right there on the dock at Pago."

OPPOSITE BOTTOM RIGHT: Concrete pillboxes built during the war still wait for the Japanese invasion that never came.

BELOW: The formidable vegetation-covered mountains, which made the landing of Pan Am flying boats so hazardous in the 1930s, ring Pago Pago Bay. Years ago a cable car apparatus that swung high above the waters of the bay, seen in this photo from the late

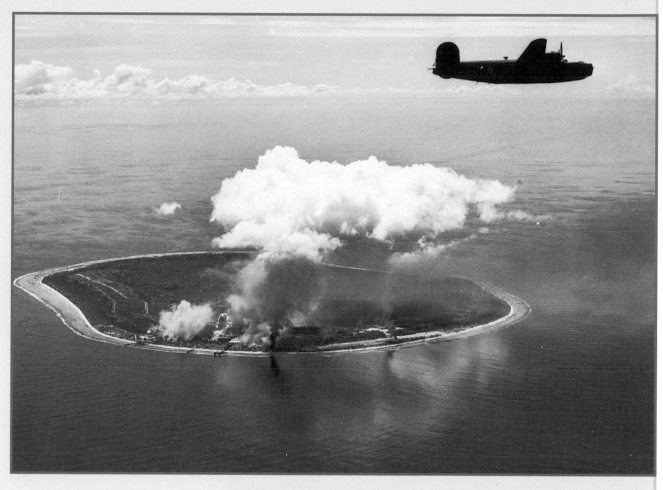

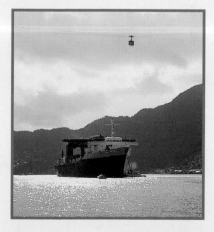

1970s, was built with U.S. aid money to enable construction of a TV transmission tower on one of the steep-sided mountains to the right. Tragedy once again struck Pago Pago in 1980 when a Navy airplane buzzing a holiday crowd hit the cable, lost control, and crashed into the Rainmaker Hotel, directly behind where this photo was taken, killing six crewmen aboard

the plane and two tourists in the hotel. Luckily most of the hotel residents were in town about a half mile away attending a celebration.

ABOVE: A B-24 Liberator flies above Japanese-held Nauru Island during a bombing raid on April 21, 1943. This B-24 raid was staged through Funafuti from Hawaii on what was one of the longest air operations of the war. The objective was the phosphate facility on Nauru, which itself at one time was covered almost entirely with a layer of phosphate. The Japanese occupied Nauru at the beginning of the war and fully expected an Allied invasion to retake the island.

RIGHT: The gray area now covering most of Nauru is the limestone moonscape left after the phosphate was strip-mined. Though profits from the mining operation made tiny Nauru a wealthy nation, the island's phosphate supply is nearly exhausted and Nauru's future is uncertain. The environmental damage from the mining operation is the subject of ongoing lawsuits.

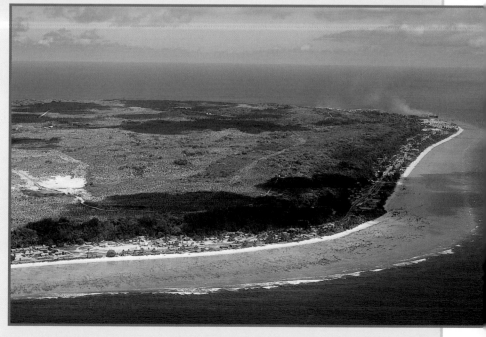

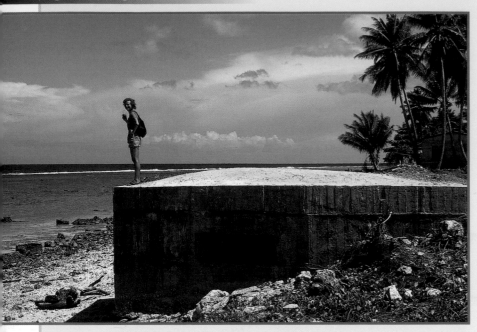

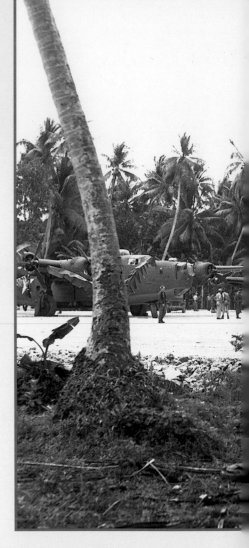

The Japanese fortified Nauru with numerous concrete bunkers such as this one. But the Allies never invaded, choosing instead to bomb the island's facilities and circumvent it. In the Allies' island-hopping strategy, numerous Japanese-held islands were left to this fate.

Lying at about nine degrees south latitude between Fiji and Tarawa, Funafuti was perceived by planners to be an important island base for support of the invasions in the western Pacific. In early October 1942 American forces peacefully landed on the island to a friendly reception from the local islanders. The British government representatives on the island were two New Zealand soldiers who, fearing the possibility of Japanese occupation, were understandably pleased to see Americans arrive on the scene. On other islands in the Gilbert and Ellice group that were occupied by the Japanese, the handfuls of New Zealand military and other Allied personnel were rounded up and sent to the Japanese base at Tarawa. Later, all were beheaded when the U.S. invasion of Tarawa was imminent. A monument to their sacrifice stands today in the midst of a local cemetery on Tarawa.

At Funafuti Atoll, the Americans chose the islet of Fongafale for the airstrip. It was the only islet in the atoll long enough for a heavy bomber runway. Within a month planes were landing, and a tent city sprang up beside the airstrip beneath the feathery shade of the tall palm trees.

The biggest event to hit Funafuti (it even merited media coverage in *Life* magazine) was when the Seventh Army Air Force used the island as a staging base for bombing raids on Nauru and Tarawa in April 1943. The plan was for twenty-two B-24 Liberator bombers to fly from Hawaii to Funafuti. Then they were to bomb the Japanese-held phosphate plants on Nauru, return to Funafuti, and for good measure bomb the Japanese airstrip at Tarawa before flying back to Hawaii. According to plan, twenty-two B-24s arrived at Funafuti from Hawaii in mid-April and bombed the phosphate plants on Nauru to the northwest on April 20. However, the enraged Japanese sent nine bombers from their base at Tarawa to bomb the B-24s at Funafuti in retaliation. They struck in the middle of the night on April 21. Tiny Fongafale Island afforded little protection for aircraft or men, and two American planes were totally destroyed, a number were damaged, and six men were killed. Only twelve B-24s were able to fly the next day to bomb Tarawa.

After the excitement of the Nauru raid, things calmed down a bit until the buildup for the Tarawa invasion began. The protected lagoon of Funafuti Atoll became a major staging and refueling area for invasion support ships. Rex Alan Smith took part in the dredging of Te Buabua Channel in October 1943. "We spent almost two months dredging that channel to thirty-five feet to allow crippled ships to have an easier passage into the protected lagoon, so they wouldn't have to use the natural dangerous and shallow Teava Fuagea Channel. Then when the crippled carrier *Independence* came limping into Funafuti she used Teava Fuagea anyway!"

Early in November 1943, Funafuti became the advance headquarters of the Seventh Army Air Force. Shortly before the Tarawa invasion the Japanese staged a couple of more air raids on Funafuti, this time from their airstrip on Nauru. Smith recalled watching one of the air raids from the deck of the *Sumner* anchored in the lagoon. "There were at least eight battleships and a whole lagoon full of ships getting ready for the Tarawa invasion. It was a moonlit night and the Japanese couldn't help but see us. The order was put out to all ships not to open fire, so we wouldn't attract any attention. The raid lasted from about 3 A.M. to 6 A.M. and was intermittent. I remember feeling the concussion of distant exploding bombs through the deck, and seeing big fireballs going up over on the airstrip. All was quiet in the lagoon, though. Then all of a sudden the Army ship *MacKenzie* down the lagoon opened up with all of its guns, tracers spraying into the air in all directions. It was the damnedest sight! You know, some poor bastard never gets the word." Luckily for the *MacKenzie,* the Japanese planes concentrated exclusively on the airstrip. Smith added, "The scuttlebutt going around the fleet the next day was that the Japanese damaged fourteen planes, wounded two men, and killed a dog." The wreckage of a C-47 transport plane destroyed on the ground in that raid still sits beside the runway where it was bulldozed the day after the raid. When the Tarawa landings finally occurred, some of the casualties were brought to the hospital at Funafuti, and the Japanese runway on Betio in the Tarawa atoll became a forward base for the Allies.

As 1943 drew to a close, Funafuti became a stopover for ships and planes heading for bases farther north and west. There was a bit of excitement in May of 1944 when the "Lone Eagle" Charles Lindbergh stopped over as he island-hopped his way westward to islands closer to the fighting. He was a civilian consultant working to improve the

performance of the F4-U Corsair fighter, but he later flew about fifty combat missions and shot down at least one Japanese plane. But all that happened far from Funafuti. When the end of the war finally came, the U.S. abandoned the airstrip and returned the atoll to British jurisdiction.

In 1978 Funafuti became the main island of the newly independent country of Tuvalu. Today the chief legacy from the war, as on so many other remote Pacific islands, is the old coral airstrip. Infrequent flights from Fiji to the south and Kiribati to the north land on the massive runway, which is ludicrously large for the small twin-engine aircraft that use it now. For a time in the early 1980s, a World War II–vintage Grumman Goose twin-engine seaplane serviced the outer islands of Tuvalu. Two of the atolls, Nukufetau and Nanomea, were also U.S. bases with coral airstrips built

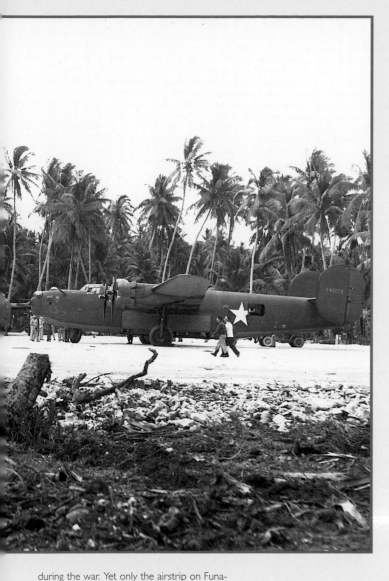

during the war. Yet only the airstrip on Funafuti is kept clear and used by aircraft, and the old Goose no longer operates in Tuvalu. Access to the outer islands is now as it was before the war—by occasional ship.

The largest industry today on Funafuti is stamps. It turns out that Funafuti and the country of Tuvalu live on in the hearts of stamp-collectors around the world. Since no one really heard of Funafuti during the war (except for the men who passed through, and sometimes they weren't sure where they were), Funafuti may be one of the few islands in the Pacific that is better known now, at least among one segment of the population. Tuvalu has taken an active role in the global-warming debate, since the country is entirely made up of low-lying atolls. There are concerns that sea-level rise could submerge the entire country before the end of this century.

ABOVE LEFT: B-24s from Hawaii crowd into an aircraft parking area cleared among the palm trees on Funafuti.

ABOVE: Seventh Army Air Force personnel pose beside a bomb wistfully inscribed "Bing Crosby to Seventh Air Force to Tojo." Note the various forms of nonstandard attire, which actually became a kind of informal island dress code: no shirts, cutoff shorts, loafers from home, and various kinds of caps. The heat and humidity were so severe on most Pacific islands, and the distance from headquarters so great, that men were allowed to dress in almost any way that afforded a measure of comfort.

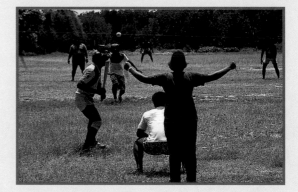

RIGHT: Before the old grass-covered World War II coral runway was paved over with asphalt, it was used as an informal park and athletic field. Here it is used as a softball field in the 1980s.

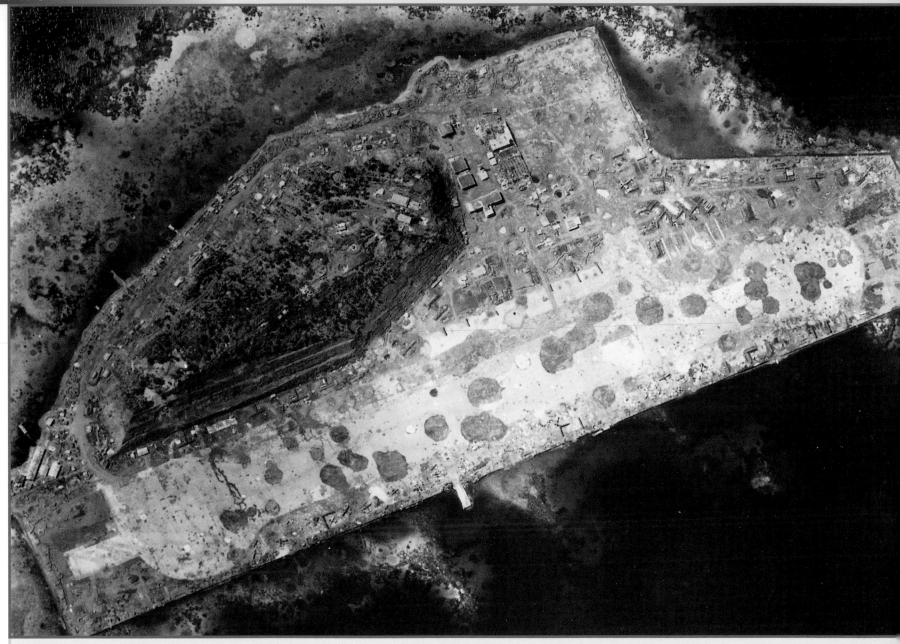

Truk Lagoon has become a world-renowned scuba-diving destination, famous for its coral-encrusted fleet of sunken Japanese ships. Before that, Truk was notorious for ships very much above the surface, since early in the war Truk was an important air and naval bastion for the Japanese. Instead of invasion, Truk was designated to be leapfrogged as part of the Allies' island-hopping strategy, but

Truk was severely disabled in a devastating raid by U.S. carrier aircraft on February 17–18, 1944. Roughly two hundred Japanese planes were destroyed, and the forty-one ships sent to the bottom set a record for total tonnage sunk in a single action that would stand for the rest of the war. Today Truk is known as Chuuk, part of the Federated States of Micronesia.

ABOVE: The Japanese developed extensive port facilities and airfields on the islands then known as Truk. This aerial view of the bomb-cratered airfield on Eten shows damage from American bombing raids. The T-shaped concrete structure at upper center is the headquarters building.

RIGHT: One of the original coral airfields built by the Japanese during the war was still used for overseas flights such as this one in 1978. The sensation of landing in a fully loaded Continental Air Micronesia 727 on the short coral airstrip—really the equivalent of an aircraft carrier deck to a large commercial jet—will not soon be forgotten by anyone who experienced it. The runway was subsequently paved over with asphalt and lengthened.

FAR RIGHT: The massive concrete Japanese communication center on Moen is now used as a high school.

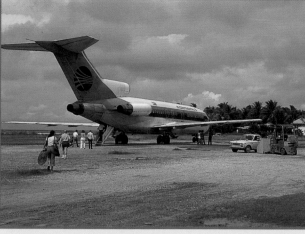

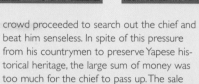

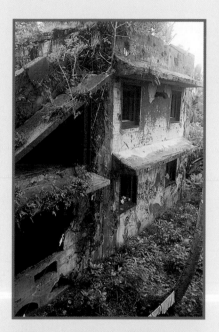

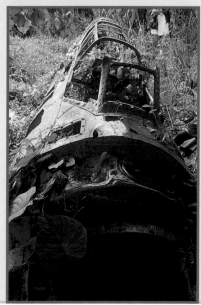

TOP LEFT: Overgrown with vegetation and difficult to get to today, this is the remains of the headquarters building on Eten.

BOTTOM LEFT: Though Chuuk, as it is now known, is famous for scuba diving on the Japanese ships and planes, there is at least one plane wreck on land. This Japanese reconnaissance plane was shot down and crashed on the island of Moen, and it rests in the backyard of a private residence.

CENTER RIGHT: After the American raids on Truk, a number of the Japanese aircraft that survived the destruction were flown to their base on Yap to the west, but most were caught on the ground in subsequent Allied air raids. The remnants of a number of these planes, such as the one shown here, remain on Yap, still parked where they were disabled in 1944 near the old Japanese airstrip. This Zero shows the damage inflicted by American bombs that exploded nearby. One wing is crumpled, another blown off; the engine is separated from the front of the plane, and the fuselage is riddled with shrapnel holes. Disintegrating remains of four Zero fighters are left today, along with pieces of several others that miraculously survived the postwar scrap hunters. More recent threats, now common to many Pacific islands, are wealthy private collectors in search of increasingly rare World War II relics. In the mid-1980s on Yap a Japanese collector attempted to buy the remains of five other Zeros from a local chief. Even though it is nominally illegal to remove any war relic from the island, there were sufficient loopholes in the law at that time to allow export of war relics under certain conditions. Local people heard about the impending sale and protested to the local historical preservation officer and other high government officials. The government disapproved of the sale but was powerless to stop it and advised the people to settle the matter in the "traditional" Yapese way. The crowd proceeded to search out the chief and beat him senseless. In spite of this pressure from his countrymen to preserve Yapese historical heritage, the large sum of money was too much for the chief to pass up. The sale went on and the planes were shipped to Japan. Attempts were then made to close the loopholes in the law in the face of increasing pressure on local landowners from overseas collectors to sell the few remaining Zeros.

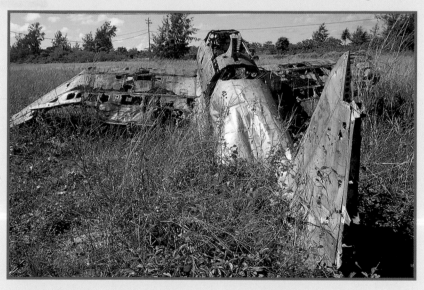

BELOW: The old Japanese runway on Yap, abandoned today, was used for domestic flights from Guam (Continental Air Micronesia 727s) until a new airstrip was built nearby in the early 1980s.

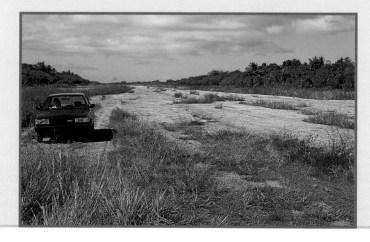

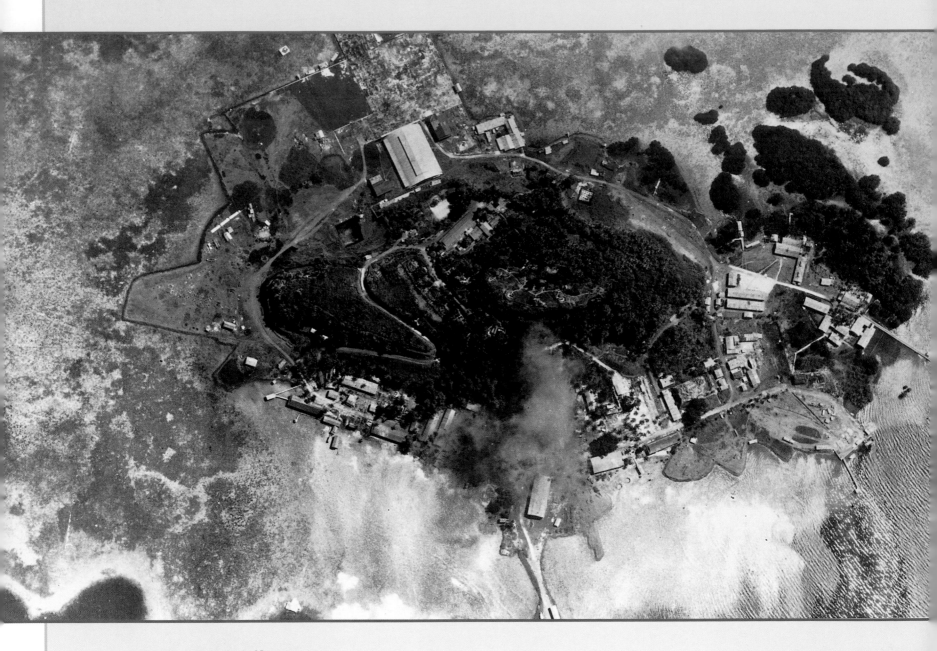

The Japanese-held island of Ponape was
leapfrogged by the Americans after the
Marshall Islands to the east were invaded.
As on many islands in the Pacific, the Japanese had fortified Ponape in anticipation of an
invasion that never came. Today Pohnpei, as it
is now known, is part of the Federated States
of Micronesia. The Japanese built this seaplane
facility on tiny Lenger Island offshore from the
main island. This was what the facility looked
like in February 1944, before American bombers leveled everything on the island.

An aerial view today shows the remains of the large seaplane ramp near the top of the island. For a visitor willing to hack through the dense jungle growth that now covers the island, there are also remnants of numerous fortifications, coastal defense guns, an underground network of elaborate concrete-lined tunnels, and the wreckage of a large hangar. An American bomb caved in the front part of the hangar—the huge crater can still be seen beneath the crumpled metal framework brought down in the blast. Pieces of a Japanese float-plane pinned under the wreckage are discernable in the jumbled mass of twisted iron. Bomb craters are evident all over the island, but the tunnel complex holding the fuel storage system is still intact. A local islander named Alonso Ladore, who was eighteen years old at the time of the American raids, tells of forced Japanese labor and hard times after the island was cut off. He remembers the U.S. Naval ships offshore shelling the island, and the planes that rained destruction from the sky. "We didn't mind the planes. You could always see them and run and hide if they came to bomb. But the ships! They were far away, and when they shot the shells would explode all over the place, and the people didn't know when or where to hide."

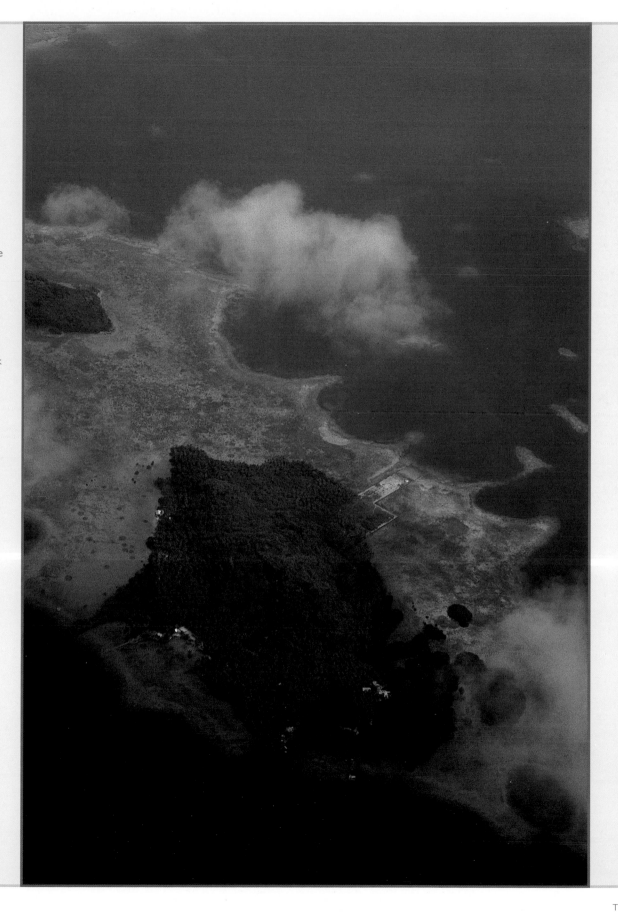

PELELIU: THE UNNECESSARY SACRIFICE

IN SEPTEMBER 1944 the battle for Peleliu, in the Palau group of islands east of the southern Philippines, was to be, in the opinion of First Marine Division Commander Major General William H. Rupertus, "a fast one, rough but fast; we'll be through in three days; it might take only two." Until his dying day, Rupertus almost certainly regretted he ever uttered those words. Peleliu was definitely rough, but not fast. The battle lasted almost two months and cost America nearly nine thousand killed, wounded, or missing. About ten thousand Japanese died on Peleliu, and most remain entombed in caves sealed beneath the island's surface. The American dead, initially buried in a large cemetery just behind the invasion beaches, were moved to other cemeteries in the U.S. shortly after the war.

Eventually some of the original Palauan residents returned to Peleliu to find their villages leveled and the island a wasteland of blasted terrain, with tons of live ammunition that made (and still make) walking off the main tracks a hazard. Now they inhabit the northern part of the island, having left the rest relatively untouched since the Americans departed—deserted, overgrown, silent.

The struggle for Peleliu was one of the most gruesome, bitter, and horrific fights in World War II, which was due in part to the confined terrain of the battleground—only a few square miles of a small island. The Marines seized most of that area in the first few days. The real agony of Peleliu would take place in the ridges of the island interior, the steep, jagged limestone gorges and pinnacles that the Japanese had honeycombed with caves and tunnels. The Americans referred to this complex of nightmarish terrain collectively as "Bloody Nose Ridge," or later the "Umurbrogol Pocket," but each individual topographic feature had its own macabre, ferocious fight. Hundreds of lives were consumed at objectives known to the Americans as "the Horseshoe," "Hill 300," "the Five Sisters," "the Five Brothers," "Old Baldy," and "Walt Ridge." All of these battles were fought tunnel by tunnel, cave by cave, and all lay within an area equivalent to a few city blocks. In this confined space thousands of combatants on each side fought to the death. As Peleliu veteran Gene Sledge said in a "Dateline NBC" interview in 1995 about the fierce fight between the Americans and Japanese, "We were like two scorpions in a bottle, and no scorpion lets another get near it."

The irony of Peleliu, an irony especially bitter for surviving veterans of both sides, is that two days before the invasion Admiral Halsey had decided that the capture of Peleliu was "unnecessary to support the seizure of the Philippines." Earlier strategy sessions had envisioned MacArthur's drive to recapture the Philippines as starting in the far south of those islands.

The Japanese air base on Peleliu would be a threat to MacArthur's right flank, and the Marines were to secure that flank by invading Peleliu, with the Army taking neighboring Angaur. However, in a series of carrier-based air raids in the central Philippines in mid-September 1944, when Halsey's planes met minimal Japanese resistance, the central Philippines seemed ripe for the picking. MacArthur could move up his schedule and invade Leyte directly. If there was to be no fiercely contested invasion of the southern Philippines, the threat that Peleliu posed was minimal, and the impending invasion unnecessary.

There was only one problem. The invasion fleet, carrying the First Marine Division and the Army's Eighty-first Infantry Division, was already en route to Peleliu and Angaur, and the Peleliu landing was only two days away. With the wheels set in motion, only quick decisions by the top American leaders, Nimitz and MacArthur, could change the course of events. MacArthur, extremely anxious to retake the Philippines, readily agreed to move up his timetable for invading the central Philippines. But for reasons no one at that time or ever since has been fully able to understand, Admiral Nimitz did not cancel the Peleliu invasion. As Harold Stassen, former Minnesota governor, future GOP presidential hopeful, and Nimitz aide during the war, related in 1989, "The invasion of Peleliu was a

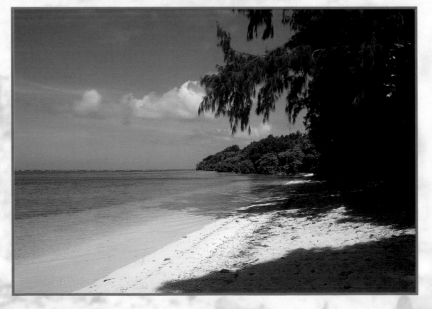

In the southern islands of the Palau group, the Japanese had built an airstrip on Peleliu and heavily fortified the island in anticipation of an American invasion. They first expected the Americans to attack in mid-1944, but the landing did not occur until September, after the Marianas had been secured. This respite gave the Japanese commanders, Colonel Nakagawa and General Murai, extra time to prepare their complex network of deadly defenses. By the time the Marines invaded on September 15, 1944, the Japanese had prepared a tortuous maze of caves and tunnels with multiple entrances and exits. Some had guns and cannon emplaced to rain down fire on the invasion beaches. And a number of amtracs carrying the first waves ashore were hit by accurate Japanese shellfire from these caves, most of which were not damaged by

the preinvasion bombardment. Instead of the relatively easy sweep from the beaches to the airfield that had been envisioned, Marines were met with a maelstrom of artillery, mortar, and machine-gun fire at the water's edge. Lucky Marines who made it safely onto the beach were pinned down by intense Japanese fire.

Eugene B. Sledge (author of *With the Old Breed: At Peleliu and Okinawa*) describes his arrival in an amtrac in the second wave to land on Peleliu: "Our amtrac came out of the water and moved a few yards up the gently sloping sand. 'Hit the beach!' yelled an NCO moments before the machine lurched to a stop. The men piled over the sides as fast as they could. I followed [my friend] Snafu, climbed up, and planted both feet firmly on the left side so as to leap as far away from it

terrible mistake, a tragedy that was needless and should not have happened."

Nimitz took the reasons for his decision with him to the grave when he died in 1966, but many disillusioned Peleliu veterans still would like an explanation. As J. M. Kerr noted in a 1995 "Dateline NBC" interview, "It was classed as a military mistake and was hushed up, covered up. Today you can interview 100 people on the streets of any town in the U.S., and I doubt if you could find one who knew what Peleliu Island was— never heard of it." The Marines had been told that Peleliu was necessary to cover the southern Philippines invasion, but well before Peleliu was secured they got word that MacArthur had already invaded the central Philippines. "The war had passed it by," said veteran Sledge on "Dateline NBC." "The attitude of most of my buddies was what the hell are we doing here— we were supposed to take this island so it would be possible for them to take the Philippines.... I can understand how Viet Nam veterans feel because I fought at Peleliu, which was pointless."

The battle formally ended on November 27, 1944, two days after the Japanese commanders Major General Kenijiro Murai and Colonel Kunio Nakagawa committed suicide in their last bastion near the center of the island, a cave deep in a cliff the Marines had dubbed "China Wall." Yet it wasn't until nearly three years later that the last Japanese defenders finally surrendered. On April 21, 1947, Lieutenant Tadamichi Yamaguchi and twenty-six of his men crawled out of a complex of deep caves untouched by the hostilities. Fifty years after the battle ended, Yamaguchi returned to Peleliu to revisit the old battlefields, joining a number of American Marine and Army veterans on a similar mission. Looking back on it in 1995, on "Dateline NBC," Yamaguchi reflected on his decision to hold out for nearly two years after the war ended: "We couldn't believe that we had really lost. We were always instructed that we could never lose."

Today Peleliu is known mainly to visitors as a reference point in locating prime dive sites for the ever-increasing numbers of scuba divers who flood into Palau. Though almost all tourists stay near Koror, the capital of the Republic of Palau, about twenty-five miles north of Peleliu, the real attractions are the reefs that wind amidst the Rock Islands. Lying between Koror and the big island of Babeldaob in the north and Peleliu and Angaur in the south, the Rock Islands are a complex of squat, green, vegetation-capped limestone knobs scattered amongst some of the most spectacular coral reefs to be found anywhere in the Pacific. Except for the occasional history buff or day-trippers looking to spend a day of rest between dives, a good percentage of visitors to Peleliu are divers who pull their dive boats up for lunch at the old abandoned Camp Beck Dock near Orange Beach Three.

Nearly sixty years have passed since the battle for Peleliu, and the island continues to represent danger and sometimes death. But now it is in the context of the modern scuba-diving world. A particularly spectacular dive site dubbed "Peleliu Wall" lies just offshore from the southern tip of Peleliu, what the Americans referred to as the southwest promontory, near Ngarmoked Island. The edge of the coral reef drops off hundreds of feet straight down into the dizzying blue depths. If divers bother to look up before they start a dive on Peleliu Wall, they have a clear view, not more than 150 meters away, of the jungle-covered site where Marine Private First Class Arthur Jackson won the Medal of Honor by personally destroying thirteen Japanese emplacements and bunkers and killing roughly eighty-five Japanese defenders. There is no marker commemorating that achievement, only thick green foliage covering the chaotic sharp edges of the limestone rocks that were the killing fields. Few today even know that a battle took place on this verdant green island. Though the mention of Peleliu does evoke images of desperate, sudden death for many visitors, it is the death of a few scuba divers who were swept away by surging currents in 1994, not the nearly twelve thousand human beings who killed each other there in 1944.

as possible. At that instant a burst of machine gun fire with white-hot tracers snapped through the air at eye level, almost grazing my face. I pulled my head back like a turtle, lost my balance, and fell awkwardly forward down onto the sand in a tangle of ammo bag, pack, helmet, carbine, gas mask, cartridge belt, and flopping canteen. 'Get off the beach! Get off the beach!' raced through my mind.... My legs dug up the sand as I tried to rise. A firm hand gripped my shoulder. 'Oh god,' I thought, 'it's a Nip who's come out of a pillbox!' I couldn't reach my kabar [knife], fortunately, because as I got my face out of the sand and looked up, there was the worried face of a Marine bending over me. He thought the machine-gun burst had hit me, and he had crawled over to help. When he saw I was unhurt, he spun around and started crawling rapidly off the beach. I scuttled after him. Shells crashed all around. Fragments tore and whirred, slapping on the sand and splashing into the water a few yards behind us ... machine-gun and rifle fire got thicker, snapping viciously overhead in increasing volume." This photo (opposite page) shows the beach Sledge landed on. Like most Pacific island beaches, the scale is small— only a few hundred meters of sand where thousands of Marines poured ashore. And also, as with most Pacific beach battlefields, it is almost impossible to visualize the maelstrom of exploding shells and machine-gun fire that made such small spaces so extremely deadly. The only sounds a visitor hears today are the soft wash of the crystal-clear, warm water on the white sand and the occasional birdcall from the dense foliage that presses in on the beach and swallows up nearly all traces of combat.

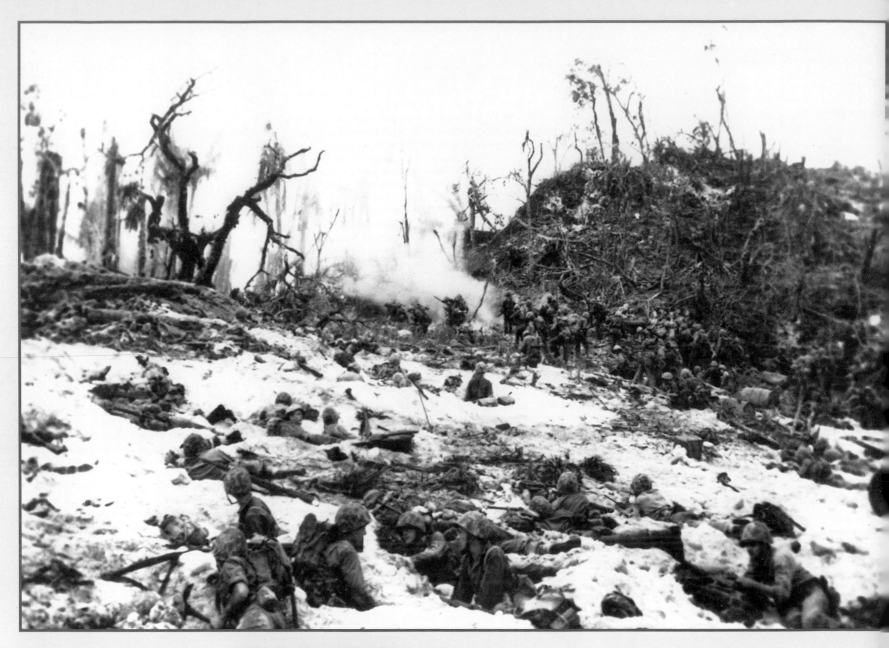

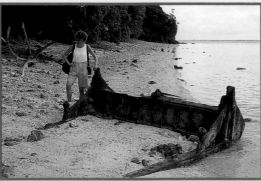

ABOVE: Just after landing, Marines are pinned down on the southern end of White Beach Two. The Americans called the limestone hill at right the Southern Promontory, and a number of Japanese bunkers and caves in this ridge had to be assaulted by Marines. The plume of smoke and the charging Marines at center back mark the struggle for a Japanese bunker at the base of the ridge.

LEFT: The remains of an American amtrac emerge from the sand on White Beach Two today. In the background, almost totally swallowed up by the jungle, is the seaward edge of the Southern Promontory. A visitor taking a short walk inland along the base of that overgrown limestone ridge can still find the bullet-scarred remains of the large concrete bunker being stormed in the photo above.

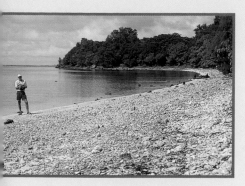

ABOVE: Perhaps the fiercest fighting on the invasion beaches of Peleliu on D-Day took place at the northern end of White Beach One, shown in this photo. Today the small scale of the White invasion beaches strikes a visitor. They only total about four hundred yards, but at one end was the Southern Promontory, with fire directed from bunkers aimed to the north, and on the northern end was the feature Marines dubbed "the Point," shown in this photo. Inexplicably, the Point had not been shelled in the preinvasion bombardment. Fire from the undamaged Japanese gun emplacements, and in particular from a large, rock-covered concrete bunker containing a forty-seven-millimeter antitank-antiboat gun, swept south along the length of White Beach One in the foreground.

BELOW: This section of White Beach One is swarming with men and supplies being unloaded in relative safety on the afternoon of D-Day, after nearby gun emplacements had been destroyed. Yet only several dozen yards farther down the beach in the background is the Point. When this photo was taken, Captain George Hunt and the survivors of his unit were stranded on the Point, cut off from the rest of the Marines on the island.

BELOW RIGHT: Captain Hunt and K Company, Third Battalion, Fifth Regiment, of the First Marines had assaulted the Point in the initial landing, but theirs was to be one of the most agonizing experiences of the first couple of days on Peleliu. Violent fighting decimated Hunt's men as soon as they landed, but they slowly took control of the Point by methodically assaulting each Japanese position and emplacement in turn. Finally they were able to storm the troublesome bunker containing the forty-seven-millimeter gun that had killed dozens of Marines on the beach in front of it. Today this bunker dominates the north end of White Beach One as it did in 1944, its three-foot-thick concrete roof still covered with coral rock. This photo was taken from behind the bunker, and the blackness in the foreground is the rear exit that leads out of the caved-in remains; White Beach One is bright in the sunshine in the distance. Bill Ross, in his book, *Peleliu, Tragic Triumph,* describes what took place here: "Willis, moving swiftly in a low crouch, dropped a smoke canister just outside the emplacement's aperture. Its dense cloud covered the approach of a corporal armed with a powerful rifle grenade launcher. The Marine took careful aim and fired the missile straight at the gun barrel. The direct hit blew the cannon to smithereens and triggered a thunderous, flaming blast of stacked artillery shells. A choking curtain of acrid smoke swept the interior of the bunker. Screaming Japanese, many with uniform afire from head to foot, groped to escape the inferno through a rear exit [shown in this photo]. The ones who made it were slaughtered by waiting Marines positioned for that specific purpose." With the fall of this bunker at around 10:30 A.M. on D-Day, only Hunt and about thirty-four of his men remained unhurt. The rest lay dead or wounded on the jagged limestone and coral rocks of the Point. Then their ordeal really began. They had to endure repeated Japanese counterattacks while cut off from the rest of the Marines who were only a couple of hundred yards away farther down White Beach One. Somehow they held on. Finally, two days later, relief arrived. Hunt (who later wrote a book about his experience called *Coral Comes High*) and 78 survivors left the Point, all that remained of 235 who began the assault. There is no marker or plaque to commemorate their sacrifice. Only the shrapnel-scarred concrete of the Japanese bunker suggests that a battle ever occurred there.

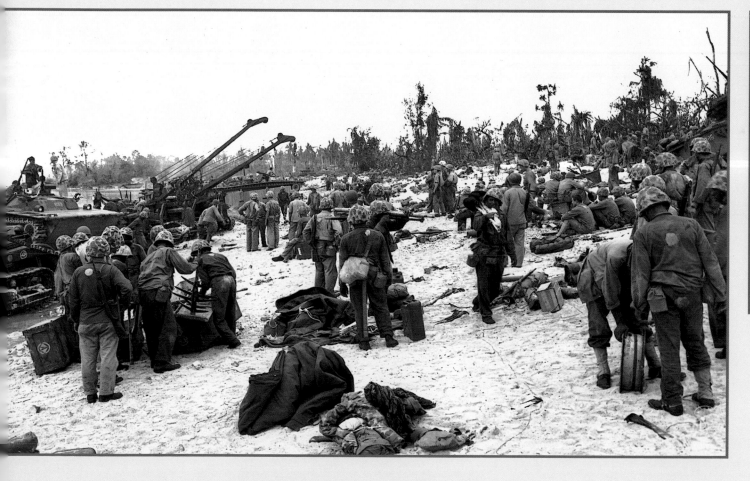

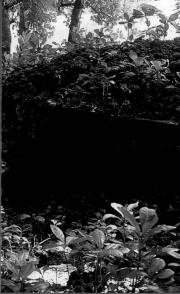

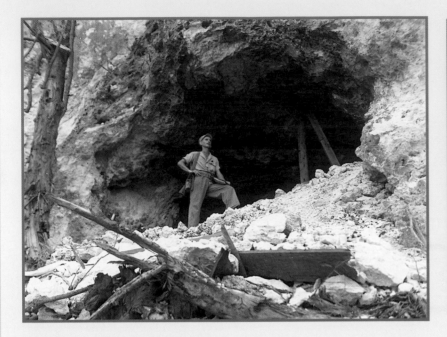

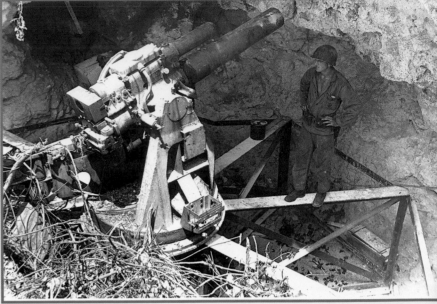

ABOVE LEFT: The Japanese had a new plan for their defense of Peleliu. Instead of leaving their positions and repeatedly charging the U.S. lines as they had in earlier Pacific island battles, they settled themselves into the complex of caves they had blasted out of the island's almost impervious limestone hills. This calculated strategy, to be visited upon Americans again on Iwo Jima and Okinawa, was designed with one objective in mind: kill as many Americans as possible before being killed themselves. Such a philosophical outlook, itself part of the Japanese military training, was accepted without question by the defenders. One of the few

Japanese survivors, Tadamichi Yamaguchi, told "Dateline NBC," "There was nothing we could do. It is the Japanese tradition to say that we must fight until the very end until we die." This not only amazed and enraged the Americans but, in turn, went against their own fundamental belief structure. As Marine veteran Tom Quinn put it for the same "Dateline NBC" segment, "I was never taught to expect to die, only expect to win."

In preinvasion aerial photos, the ridges behind the Japanese airfield looked like innocuous wooded hills. When stripped of vegetation by bombardment, the "hills" turned out to be

a nightmare of solid rock escarpments hiding a labyrinth of Japanese caves. In this photo a Marine stands in the opening of one of the Japanese caves that has just been cleared.

ABOVE RIGHT: Japanese artillery pieces, such as this two-hundred-millimeter naval gun, were emplaced in the caves of Peleliu and were rarely knocked out by American bombing or shelling. They continued to inflict heavy casualties until silenced one by one by small rifle squads scrambling up the sharp limestone escarpments.

BELOW LEFT: This same gun has been turned to point out of the mouth of the tunnel and is

a featured stop on battlefield tours of Peleliu.

BELOW RIGHT: Today some of the Japanese caves and tunnels have been opened, but visitors are constantly reminded that Peleliu is literally an uncleared battlefield, complete with rusted, unstable live ammunition. Here in the "1000-Man Tunnel" visitors can still find Japanese beer and sake bottles strewn about with other discarded items such as this canteen, as well as unexploded shells and mines. Visitors are warned to be especially wary of Japanese grenades, considered to be the most potentially hazardous of all the ordnance left behind on Peleliu.

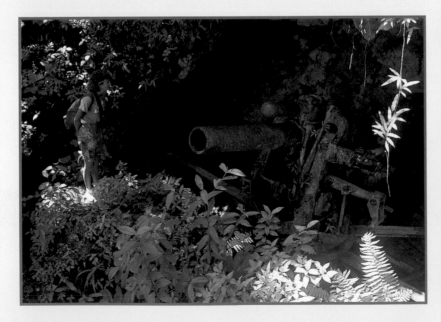

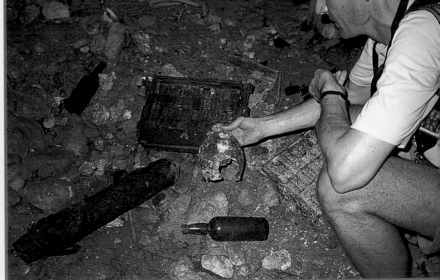

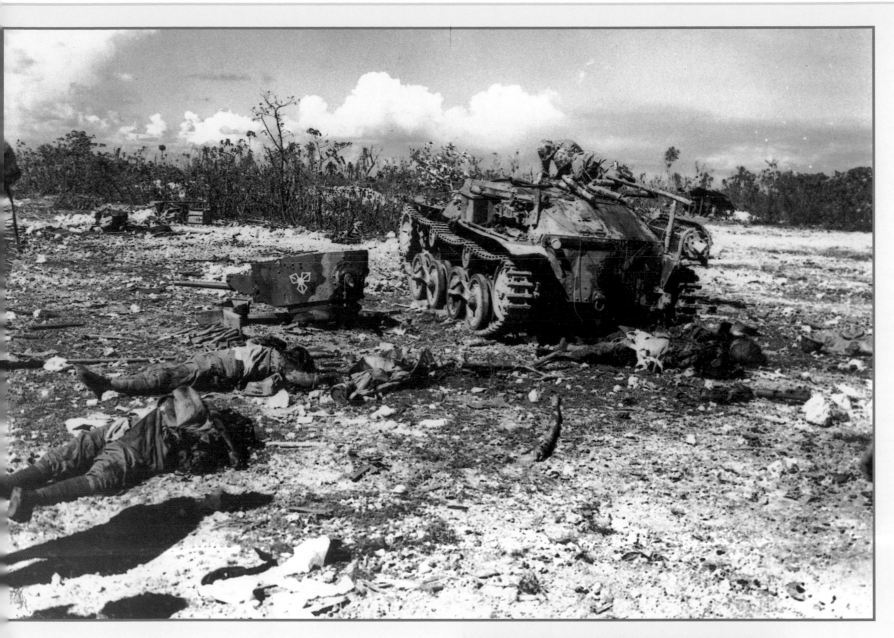

ABOVE: There were no chaotic banzai attacks on Peleliu and few counterattacks at all, but one of those few came on the afternoon of D-Day. A number of Japanese light tanks and several hundred troops attempted an organized counterattack across the airfield right toward the heart of the American front lines just inland from the invasion beaches. But what started as a well-coordinated counterattack soon disintegrated into something akin to a cavalry charge. The tanks suddenly opened their throttles and headed for the American lines at full speed. The Marines immediately opened fire on the onrushing tanks, and destroyed them one by one. The supporting troops, left behind by the speeding tanks, were slaughtered. Curious Marines inspect the remains of one of the Japanese tanks destroyed in the frantic counterattack here. The bodies of the Japanese tank crew lie where they were gunned down after trying to escape.

RIGHT: Only one of the Japanese tanks from the doomed counterattack on D-Day is left on Peleliu today. Though impossible to verify, it closely resembles the turretless tank in the photo above.

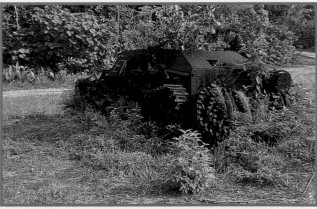

All that remains of the American airbase on Peleliu is a portion of the old World War II coral airstrip kept clear for small aircraft like the one at left. The photo is taken roughly in the direction of the charge of four Marine infantry battalions on D-Day +1.

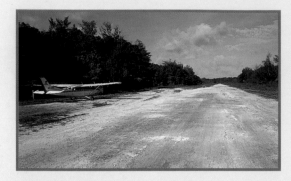

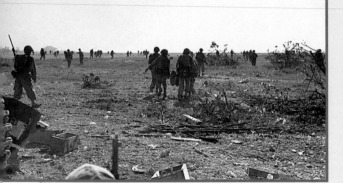

The charge was an old-fashioned frontal assault on Japanese positions on the far side of the airfield. As shown in this photo taken in the relative safety of the south edge of the airfield, the entire area in 1944 was a clear field of fire, a blinding white expanse of crushed coral. As seen in the distance, the Marines charged across the wide-open spaces under a rain of artillery and machine-gun fire. Gene Sledge participated in the charge (running roughly the length of what now remains of the airfield shown here) and described it in his book, *With the Old Breed: on Peleliu and Okinawa:* "We moved rapidly in the open, amid craters and coral rubble, through ever increasing enemy fire. I saw men to my right and left running bent as low as possible. The shells screeched and whistled, exploding all around us. . . . we were exposed, running on our own power through a veritable shower

of deadly metal and the constant crash of explosions. For me the attack resembled World War I movies I had seen of suicidal Allied infantry attacks through shellfire on the Western Front. . . . Japanese bullets snapped and cracked, and tracers went by me on both sides at waist height. This deadly small-arms fire seemed almost insignificant amid the eruption of shells. Explosions and the hum and the growl of shell fragments shredded the air. Chunks of blasted coral stung my face and hands while steel fragments spattered down on the hard rock like hail on a city street. Everywhere shells flashed like giant firecrackers. Through the haze I saw Marines stumble and pitch forward as they got hit. I then looked neither right nor left but just straight to my front. The farther we went, the worse it got. The noise and concussion pressed in on my ears like a vise. I gritted my teeth and braced myself in anticipation of the shock of being struck down at any moment. It seemed impossible that any of us could make it across." But many Marines, including Sledge, did make it across, and the airstrip was in American hands.

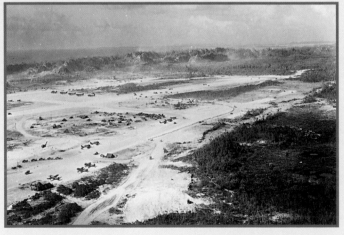

The treacherous limestone rock formations on Peleliu run from behind the airstrip almost to the northern tip of the island. The arduous task of blasting the Japanese from the estimated five hundred caves that honeycombed these ridges lasted almost two months. But the initial objective, the airstrip built by the Japanese, was captured after the first week. In this photo the runway is in use while Army engineer and Seabees construction crews make improvements even as the fighting rages in the blasted and barren limestone escarpments a short distance away in the background.

OPPOSITE TOP: After the airfield area was secured, the Marines advanced into the nightmarish valleys and gorges of the limestone ridges of Peleliu. Here, Marine infantrymen and tanks advance cautiously into a valley they named the Horseshoe, a ring of limestone ridges honeycombed with Japanese caves and gun emplacements. Americans named the hill on the right Walt Ridge after Lieutenant Colonel Lew Walt who led an early attempt to capture it. Before the battle, the Japanese had called it Higashiyama. On the left is Five Brothers, and just out of the photo on the left, above where this photo was taken, is Five Sisters. Note the Marines taking shelter behind the tank at the front of the column. It has just fired at a Japanese position on the ridge to the left where smoke is rising. The photographer is standing on the spot where the First Marine Division monument is located today.

The horror of Peleliu was a combination of incredibly fierce and suicidal fighting and the abominable conditions of the battlefields in and around the deadly limestone ridges. Sledge described his impressions of the Horseshoe in his book: "The sun bore down on us like a giant heat lamp. . . . occasional rains that fell on the hot coral merely evaporated like steam off hot pavement. The air hung heavy and muggy. Everywhere we went on the ridges the hot humid air reeked with the stench of death. Japanese corpses lay where they fell among the rocks and on the slopes. It was impossible to cover them. Usually there was no soil that could be spaded over them, just the hard jagged coral. The enemy dead simply rotted where they had fallen. . . . it is difficult to convey to anyone who has not experienced it the ghastly horror of having your sense of smell saturated constantly with the putrid odor of rotting flesh day after day, night after night. . . . Added to the awful stench of the dead of both sides was the repulsive odor of human excrement everywhere. It was all but impossible to practice simple elemental field sanitation on most areas of Peleliu because of the rocky surface. . . . digging into the coral rock was nearly impossible. Consequently, thousands of men, many suffering with severe diarrhea, fighting for weeks on an island two miles by six miles—couldn't practice basic field sanitation. . . . Added to this was the odor of thousands of rotting, discarded Japanese and American rations. At every breath one inhaled hot, humid air heavy with countless repulsive odors. . . . Shattered trees and jagged rocks along the crest looked like stubble on a dirty chin. Most green trees and bushes had long

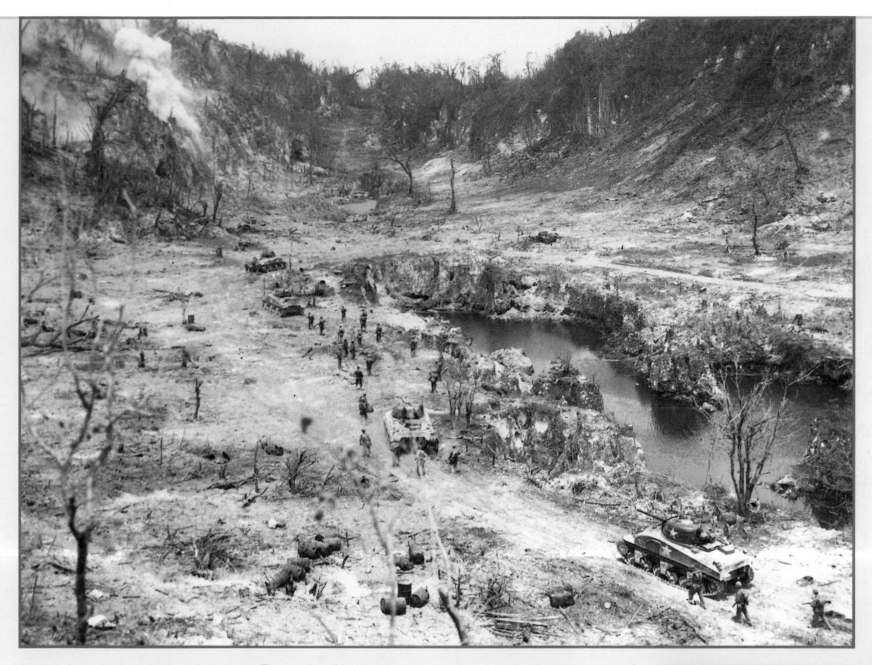

since been shattered and pulverized by shell-fire. Only the grotesque stumps and branches remained. . . . the overwhelming grayness of everything in sight caused sky, ridge, rocks, stumps, men, and equipment to blend into a grimy oneness. Weird, jagged contours of Peleliu's ridges and canyons gave the area an unearthly alien appearance. The shattered vegetation and the dirty-white splotches peppering the rocks where countless bullets and shell fragments had struck off the weathered gray surfaces contributed to the unreality of the harsh landscape."

RIGHT: The same view of the Horseshoe today. The incredibly luxuriant vegetation has concealed most of the deadly contours of Peleliu's limestone ridges and gorges. During a ceremony on the fiftieth anniversary of the Peleliu invasion, Walt Ridge, at right, was renamed Pope Ridge in honor of Everett Pope. He calls the ridge "my hill," and rightfully so. He won the Medal of Honor when he led a desperate charge to the top, and then had to spend the next twenty-four hours trying to

get back down alive. He and the survivors of the charge were cut off and slowly annihilated on the exposed summit of the ridge. During his visit to Peleliu on the fiftieth anniversary, Pope commented to "Dateline NBC": "On D-Day we landed with 230 in the company. When we got [to the ridge] we had 90 left, so 90 of us started up the hill and only 8 of us came down." It was two weeks before the Marines retook the hill and retrieved the bodies Pope was forced to leave behind.

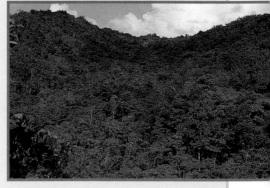

RIGHT: A napalm canister is loaded onto this Marine Corsair fighter. These planes would take off from Peleliu's airstrip, fly for about thirty seconds, drop the napalm canisters on a designated target in the ridges, and return to the airstrip to repeat the process, surely the shortest missions of the war in the Pacific.

FAR RIGHT: One of the authors inspects the rusted hulk of an armored LVT and the remains of a "used" napalm canister that was found amidst the ridges of Peleliu.

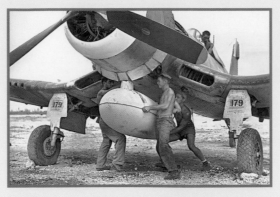

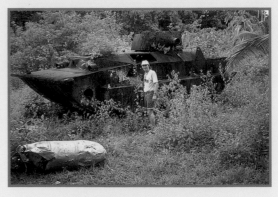

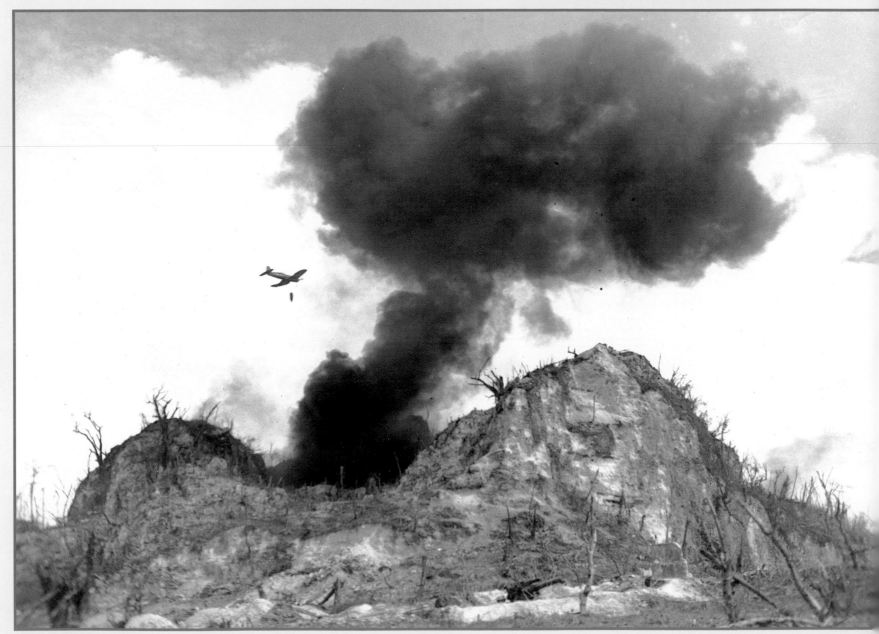

OPPOSITE BOTTOM: A Corsair fighter drops a napalm canister on Japanese positions between topographic features dubbed the Five Sisters (left) and Hill 300 (right). The Marine memorial is now located on the cleared shelf at the base of Hill 300, and visitors can climb steps to the summit of the Five Sisters to visit the Army memorial.

TOP LEFT: Hill 300 today looms menacingly over the First Marine Division memorial, erected by a group of veterans for the fortieth anniversary of the battle.

TOP RIGHT: A Japanese monument has been constructed near the base of the Five Sisters. A sign nearby directs visitors to a trail leading to the caves in China Wall where the last Japanese command post was located. The plaque lists all the Japanese units that served on Peleliu, but there were few survivors from any of these outfits.

BOTTOM: This monument to all who fought and died on Peleliu was erected by the U.S. Army shortly after the battle ended. For nearly fifty years it was silhouetted on the summit of one of the Five Sisters as shown here, silently overlooking the horrific killing ground of Peleliu's ridges. Visitors could climb a series of steps and finally an iron ladder to reach the monument. For the fiftieth anniversary of the battle, a wooden observation platform was constructed around the stone obelisk. Visitors today have a much easier climb up a series of concrete and wooden stairs to reach the viewing platform.

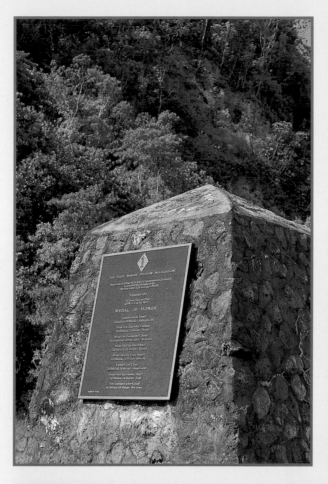

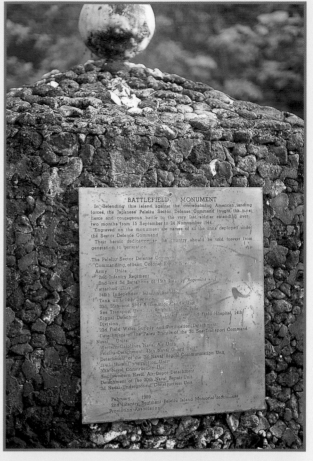

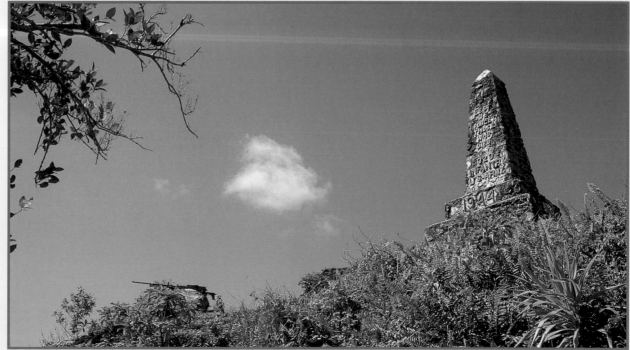

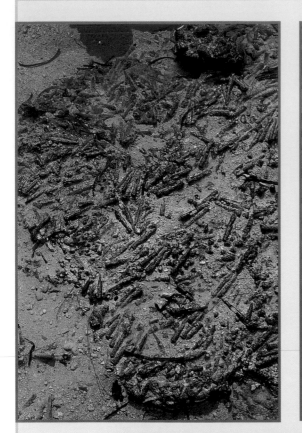

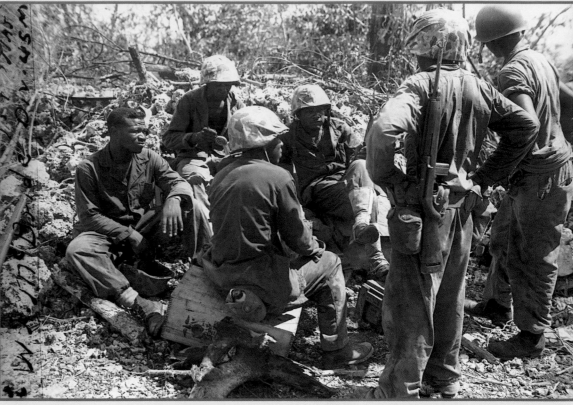

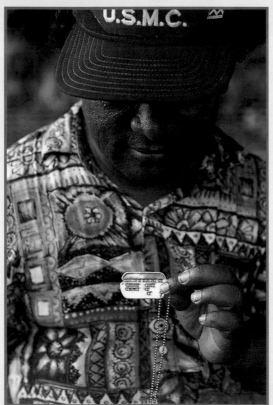

TOP LEFT: A pile of rifle bullets, left behind on White Beach One during the battle, remains there to this day, solidified in the coral sand into a rocklike mass.

TOP RIGHT: Black Marines performed heroic service on Peleliu as ammunition loaders, drivers, and stretcher-bearers. In some cases they were pressed into service to fight with frontline units.

BOTTOM LEFT: Tangie Hesus, a battlefield guide on Peleliu, shows an American dog tag he found in the sand of White Beach One.

BOTTOM RIGHT: The Americans turned Peleliu into a support base that was home to a number of fighters and bombers. The legacy of that operation is the World War II airstrip, still in use today, and piles of aircraft scrap left when the island was abandoned after the war. Though facilities were constructed on Peleliu to qualify it as a major base, it was never fully utilized. Mostly Peleliu served as a refueling stop for planes heading somewhere else. After the war the base was rapidly dismantled, and the relentless vegetation quickly covered most traces of what had taken place on the island for those fateful, now mostly forgotten, months during 1944.

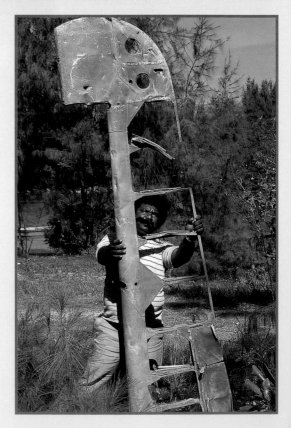

The moment of death on Peleliu. A Marine, hit by sniper fire, receives morphine from a corpsman as the last flicker of life slips away.

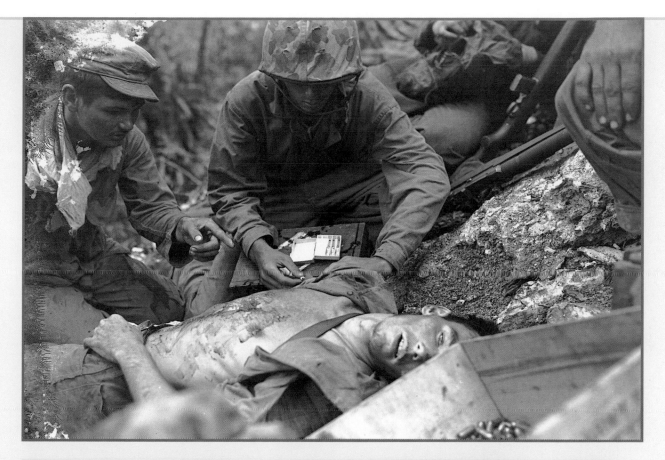

MASH unit surgeons on Peleliu, stripped to the waist in the intense heat, patch up Austin Shofner. This wound was just one more close call for someone who had a series of incredible experiences in the Pacific war. Captured at Corregidor, he spent eleven months in captivity before he led a ten-man group in the first and only American escape from a Japanese POW camp. His group brought first news of the details of the Bataan Death March to the outside world. Shofner stayed on in the Philippines six more months, leading guerrillas in a series of raids. One involved the rescue of five hundred prisoners about to be executed. He then returned to the Marines and led assault groups at Peleliu and later at Okinawa. MacArthur awarded Shofner the Distinguished Service Cross for his actions in the Philippines, and he went on to earn the Silver Star and Legion of Merit. He survived the war, retired from the military in 1959, and died at age eighty-three in 1999.

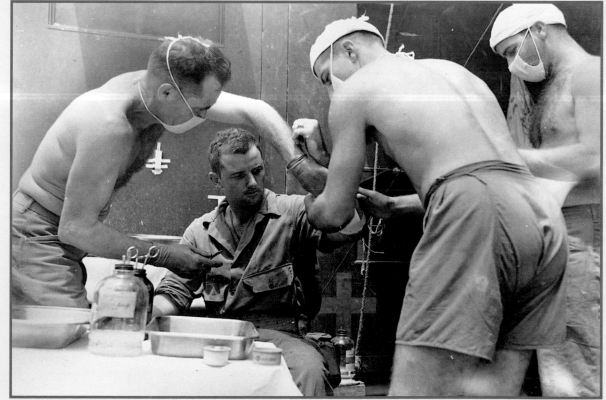

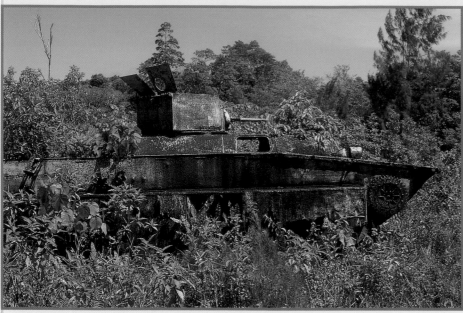

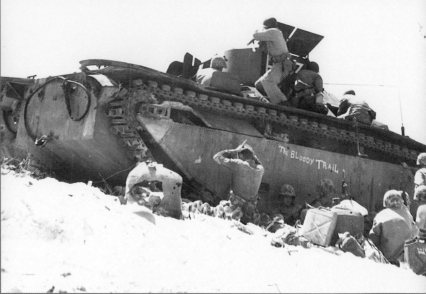

This armored amtrac—an LVT(A)1— was knocked out of action on Peleliu during the battle and today rests below a cave containing a Japanese artillery piece.

Marine infantrymen fire at Japanese from behind the shelter of an LVT(A)1 amtrac with the name The Bloody Trail.

A jeep is used to demonstrate the combat unloading capabilities of an LVT4 amtrac. The back door opened to allow men and vehicles to disembark.

The back door to this LVT4, which was disabled during the battle for the island, remains permanently open.

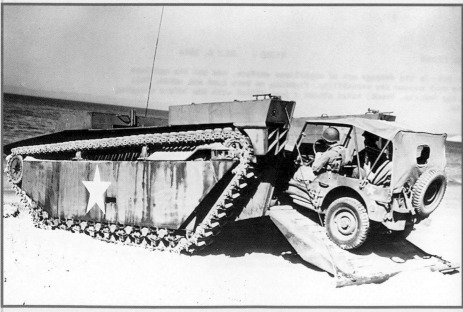

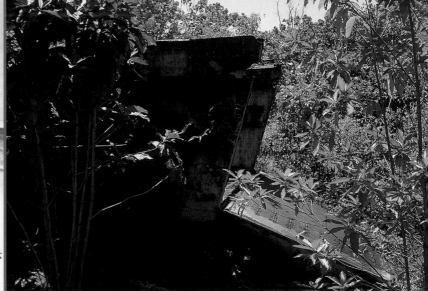

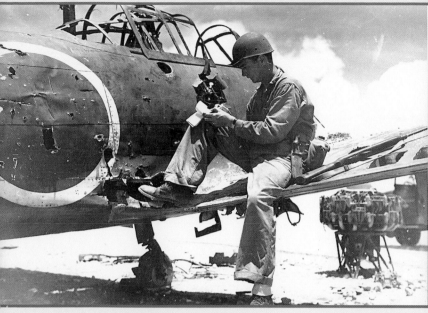

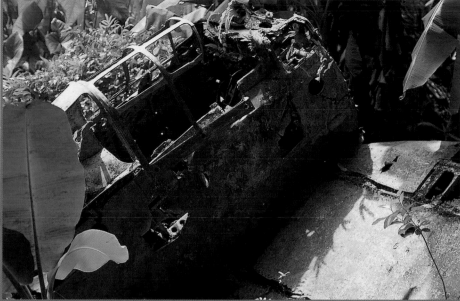

One of the reminders of Japanese operations on Peleliu before the American invasion, this Japanese Zero wreck rests near the old airstrip.

The only identifiable Japanese aircraft wreck on Peleliu today is this Zero near the airstrip, possibly the same one pictured to the left.

A dazed Marine is led down from one of Peleliu's ridges after a very close call. A Japanese sniper's bullet pierced his helmet (which he is holding in his right hand) and grazed his head. This man had been trying to place a charge of dynamite in the entrance of a Japanese cave when he was hit.

The terrific strain of the intense fighting on Peleliu is etched on the face of this Marine.

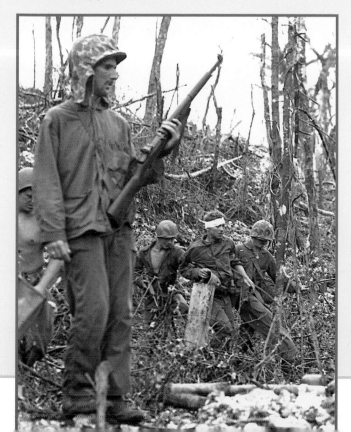

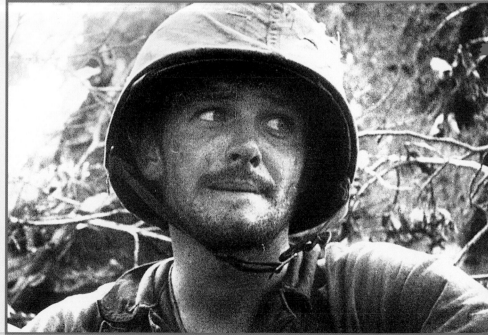

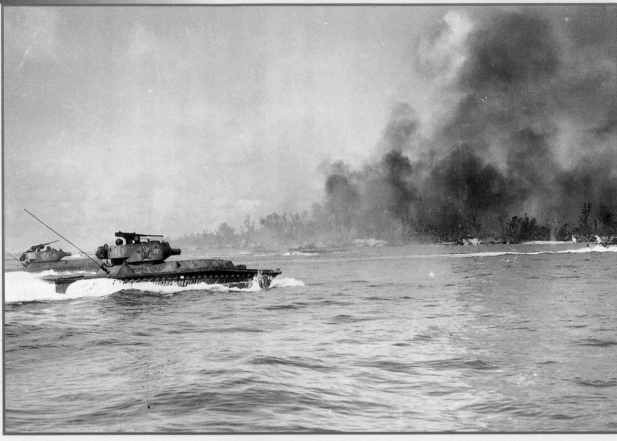

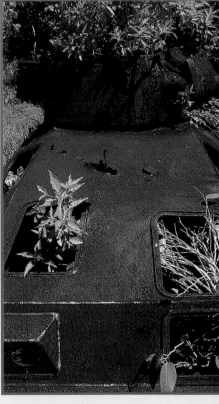

TOP LEFT: Amphibious LVT(A)4 tanks, part of the U.S. Army invasion force, churn toward the beach of Angaur.

TOP RIGHT: The Japanese shell that ripped through this American amphibious LVT(A)4 tank remaining on Peleliu can be traced by a track torn in the iron armor.

BOTTOM LEFT: Overrun by American infantry units of the Army while the campaign on nearby Peleliu was grinding on, Angaur was quickly turned into a formidable airbase with a coral runway capable of handling heavy bombers. In this December 1944 photo, B-24s of the 494th Bomb Group are parked along the taxiways. The southeast tip of Peleliu is just out of the picture at top left.

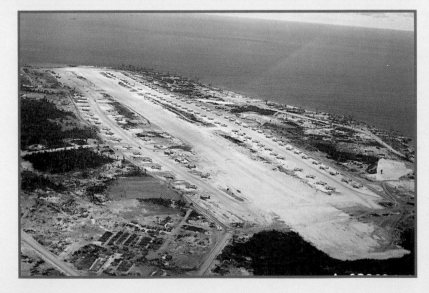

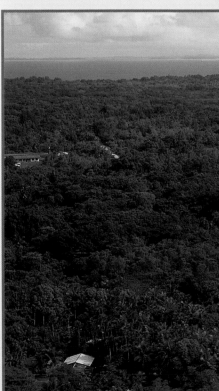

BOTTOM CENTER: A similar view of the Angaur airstrip today. As on Peleliu, almost all of the vegetation cleared by the Americans for the base proper has grown back. But like the runways on Tinian in the Marianas, the Angaur runway today remains clear and in excellent condition. The eighty-five-hundred-foot-long strip of pavement, suitable for heavily loaded B-24s and occasional B-29s, is barely utilized by the present-day air traffic that consists of a daily flight by a light plane from the main Palau airport near Koror farther north.

RIGHT: Angaur became a staging point for the drawn-out bloody battle on neighboring Peleliu. Here, on September 21, 1944, supplies are unloaded on one of Angaur's beaches. Steel pontoons extend from the beach to assist the unloading.

BOTTOM RIGHT: The rusting remains of the temporary pontoon docks are all that are left to indicate that this Angaur beach was a major unloading area for supplies.

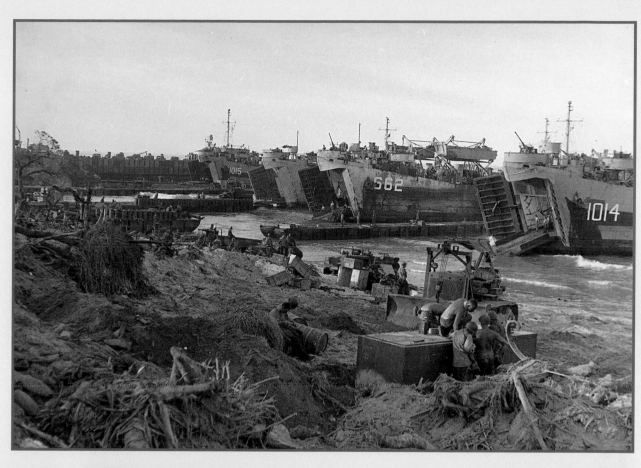

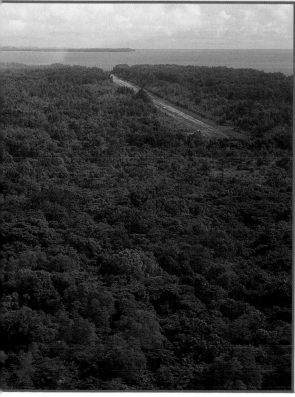

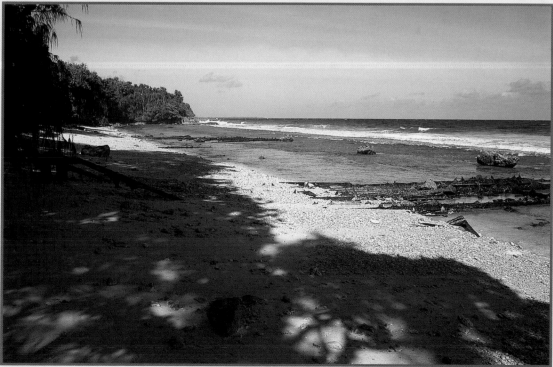

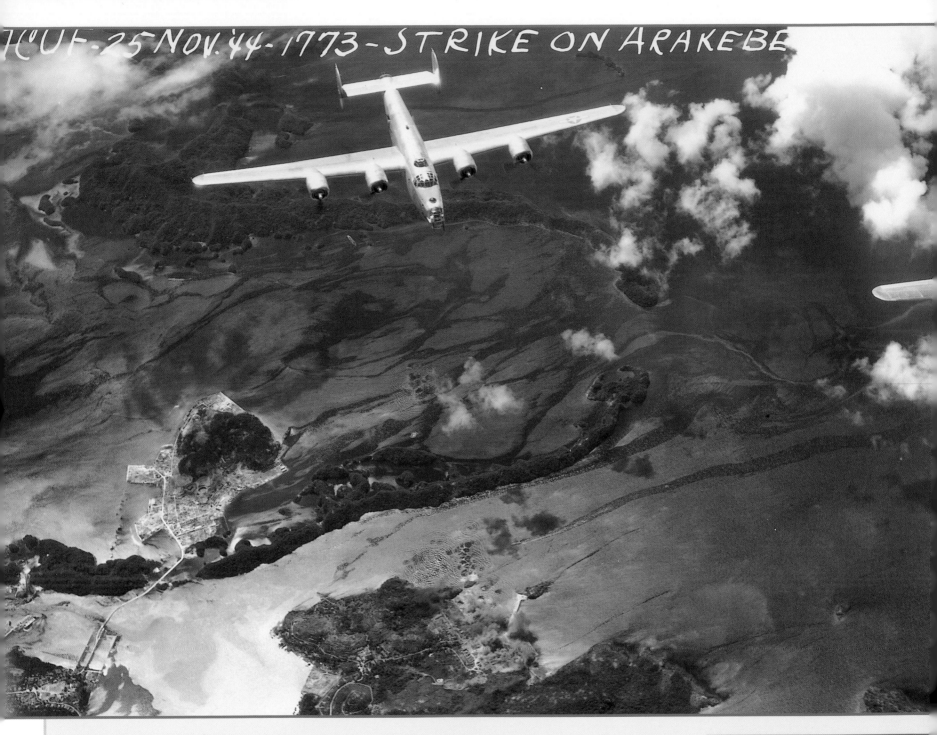

ICUF-25 NOV. '44 -1773 - STRIKE ON ARAKEBE

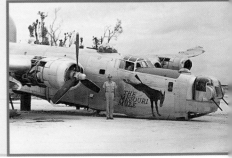

A B-24 from Angaur bombs the Japanese seaplane base on Arakabesang Island near Koror in the northern part of Palau. Koror is now the capital of the Republic of Palau and the center of tourist activity for the island group. The Japanese seaplane base, seen amidst exploding bombs in the bottom center of this photo, is now the site of the Palau Pacific Resort, one of the starting points for dive trips into the famed Rock Islands.

RIGHT: This B-24 lies wrecked and abandoned on Angaur. Posing beside it is its former pilot, Colonel Lawrence Kelly of Grover, Missouri (thus the name *Missouri Mule*). This plane was the first to take off from the airstrip at Barking Sands, Kauai, on October 4, 1944, for the start of the journey to Angaur. Then on April 10, 1945, Colonel Kelly was at the controls of *Missouri Mule* on a raid over

the Philippines when Japanese ack-ack shot away the landing gear. He successfully belly-landed his stricken plane on the runway at Angaur, but the plane was a total loss. As can be seen in this photo, it was cannibalized for parts (both engines on its left side have been removed, and the back of the plane has been jacked up to facilitate the further removal of parts).

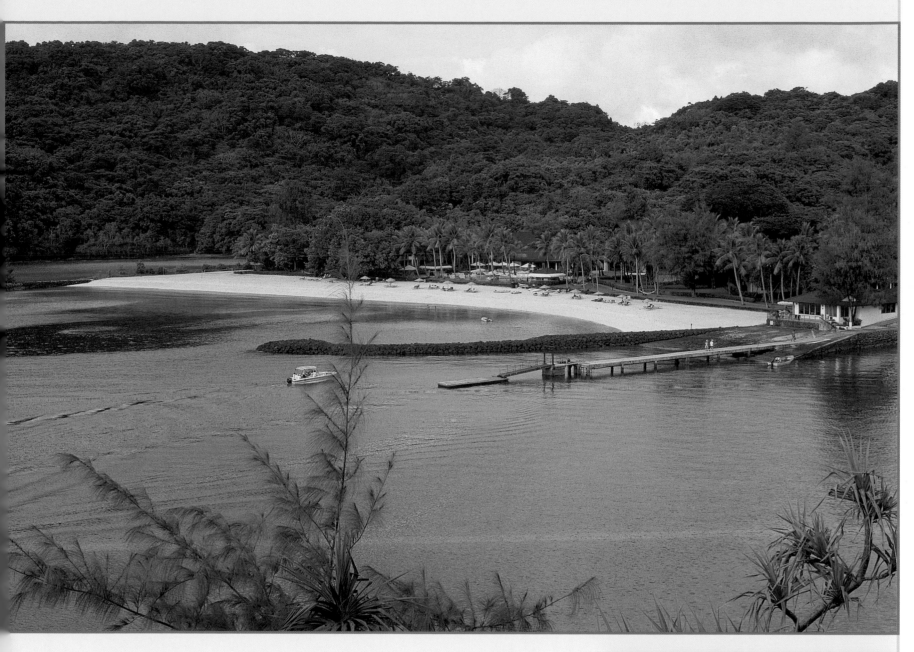

The site of the Palau Pacific Resort today, built on the remains of the old Japanese seaplane base. Note the concrete seaplane ramp with a modern small-boat dock built atop it at right.

RIGHT: One plane wreck identifiable as a B-24 remains on Angaur today amidst a jumble of parts of airplanes in the area called "the boneyard" where the *Missouri Mule* was abandoned near the airstrip. The B-24 bomber lies on its left side, the cockpit at right, the nose section peeled off at left. Not visible in this photo, behind the cockpit section is a massive piece of wing with part of its aluminum skin missing, revealing the thick, rubber, self-sealing gas tanks. A large propeller, rusted and bent, is propped up against a tree out of the photo to the left. A piece of fuselage with a fading American star insignia lies near another wing section with a huge landing gear strut still in the down position. A gun turret and a piece of fuselage lie next to each other. Pieces of abandoned airplanes loom out of the dark-green light of the jungle, haunting remnants of scenes long past—sweating men cursing the heat and humidity as they climbed into sweltering cockpits, the roar of finely tuned piston engines echoing over the lush island, gleaming planes lifting off into the tropical skies, some to return, some simply to vanish and never be found. A few are discovered years later. In 1988 the remains of a Navy pilot were found with the pieces of his wrecked fighter on a nearly inaccessible island north of Angaur. His rusted revolver was nearby, and with his dog tags was the St. Christopher medal he wore around his neck for good luck, something he obviously ran out of on a long-forgotten day in 1944.

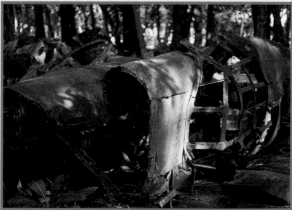

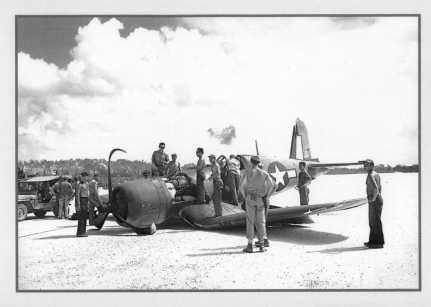

LEFT: Aftermath of a Corsair belly landing on Peleliu.

BELOW: This wreck of an American Corsair fighter, shown here in the late 1990s, lies near the B-24 wreck shown earlier. It is said that the plane crash-landed on the reef near the shore in 1944 before the airstrip was completed. It was hauled out of the water and moved to its present position in the jungle where it has rested since the war. Even though it is against the law to remove war relics from the islands of Palau, wealthy outsiders are constantly applying pressure on locals to sell all or part of World War II aircraft wrecks such as this one. In 1988, pieces of this plane were moved to a nearby site in an illegal attempt to ship them to Australia.

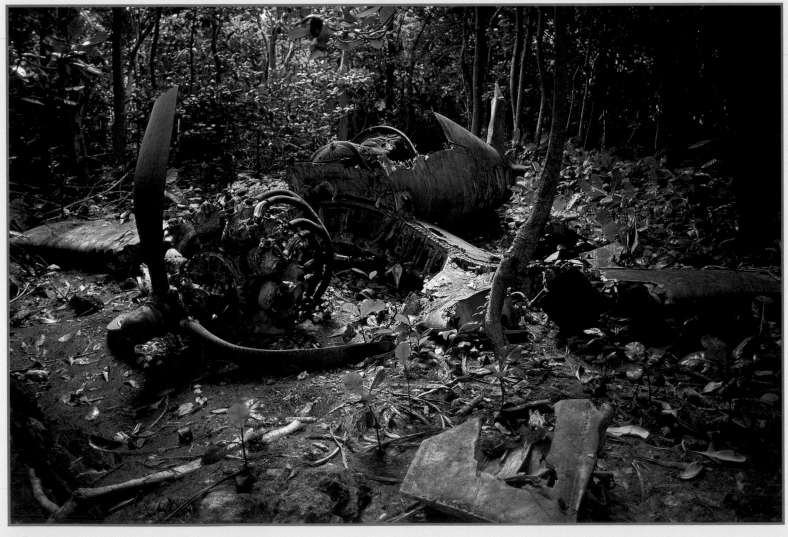

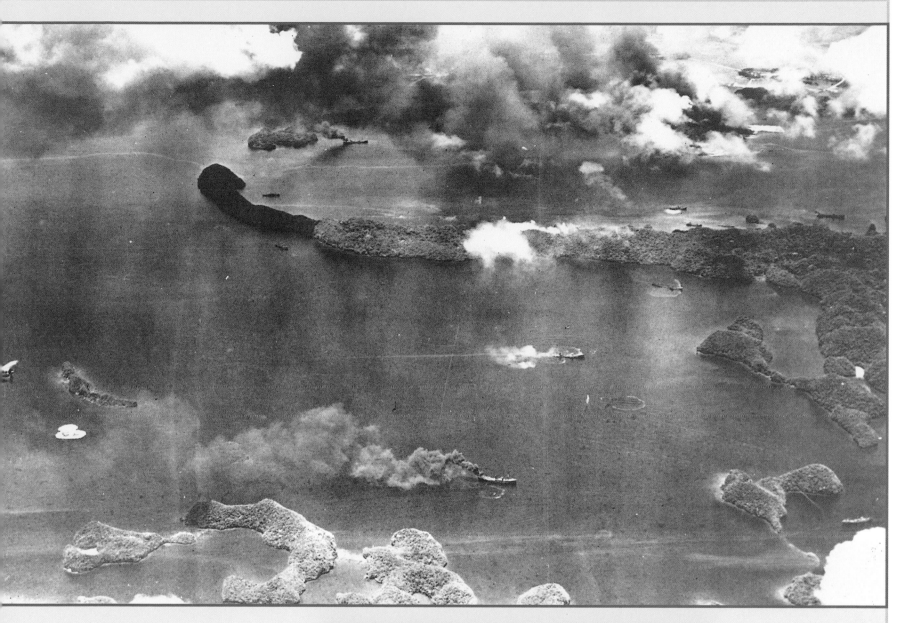

ABOVE: During an American air attack on Japanese shipping, the fabled Rock Islands of Palau become a hunting ground. As part of this carrier raid in March 1944, American F6Fs (one can be seen at left) attack Japanese ships near the harbor of Koror, north of Peleliu.

RIGHT: Today speedboats skim between the Rock Islands carrying divers to world-renowned scuba diving and snorkeling spots.

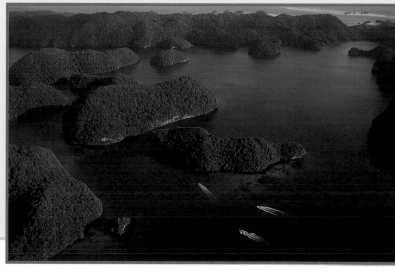

SUBMARINES

A U.S. Navy submarine heads for the open sea, leaving behind the protected confines of the submarine base at Midway. Many of the subs reported lost at sea were last seen departing this mid-Pacific stop-off point. A number of submarines and all men aboard still remain unaccounted for; they simply vanished into the depths, never to surface again.

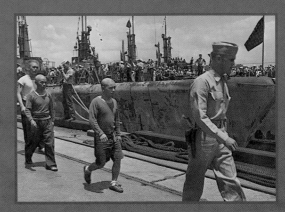

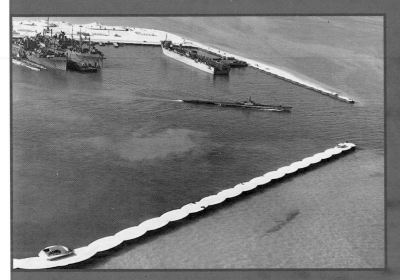

The usual mission for submarines in the Pacific was to sink enemy ships, and they alone sent more than five million tons of Japanese shipping to the bottom. Another important function, particularly late in the war, was to pull Allied fliers out of the drink when they were shot down or ditched at sea. Here, a U.S. submarine surfaces literally in the shadow of enemy territory as the Japanese island of Kyushu looms in the background. The object of this rescue, in the circled life raft, is Captain Roy Jacobson, an Air Force pilot shot down on a fighter sweep over Japan.

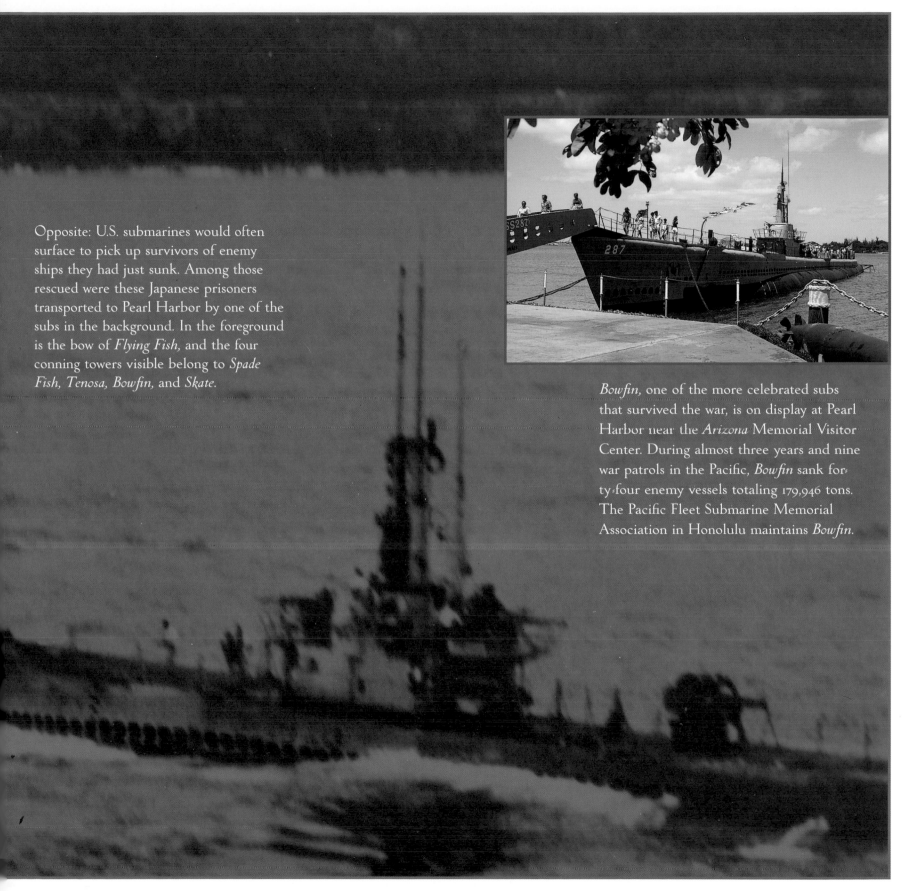

Opposite: U.S. submarines would often surface to pick up survivors of enemy ships they had just sunk. Among those rescued were these Japanese prisoners transported to Pearl Harbor by one of the subs in the background. In the foreground is the bow of *Flying Fish,* and the four conning towers visible belong to *Spade Fish, Tenosa, Bowfin,* and *Skate.*

Bowfin, one of the more celebrated subs that survived the war, is on display at Pearl Harbor near the *Arizona* Memorial Visitor Center. During almost three years and nine war patrols in the Pacific, *Bowfin* sank forty-four enemy vessels totaling 179,946 tons. The Pacific Fleet Submarine Memorial Association in Honolulu maintains *Bowfin.*

STEAMY, LANGUID, and traditionally over-romanticized images of the South Seas depict the islands as strange mixtures of unique circumstances and evocative tropical surroundings. The vast majority of American men and women in the Pacific were not directly involved in the fighting, and the war for them consisted of monotonous day-to-day living on island bases. Both the Allies and the Japanese were not only geographically far from home, but found themselves in foreign cultural and climatological environments. However, this odd existence was livened up with as many familiar amenities from home as could be mustered, in addition to organized or improvised entertainment of almost any kind. If, on any given day, one were to step off a plane on a typical Pacific island rear-area base, the scenes pictured here would be those a visitor most likely would encounter.

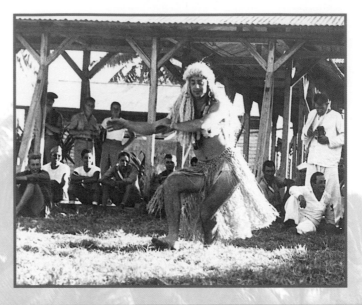

LEFT: A proud tradition of the South Pacific is making visitors look silly. Shown here upholding that tradition is Lieutenant (junior grade) Joseph "Hoot" Gibson doing his interpretation of the hula.

BELOW: Enterprising airmen soon realized that aircraft wing tanks could be fashioned into small sailboats, and a "regatta" for some of these craft was organized on Palau, started by a shot from a .45 pistol.

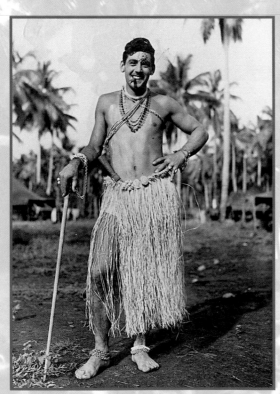

Like good tourists, American servicemen were usually up to the task of blending in with the local environment to better experience the authentic flavor of the South Seas. In this photo, twenty-five-year-old Corporal Luigi Greasso models his conception of what native dress is all about in the Solomon Islands.

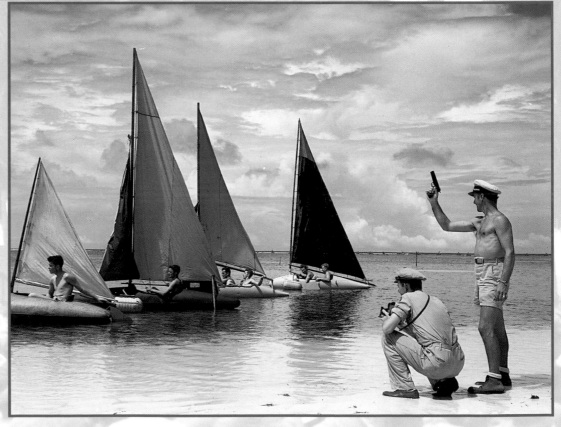

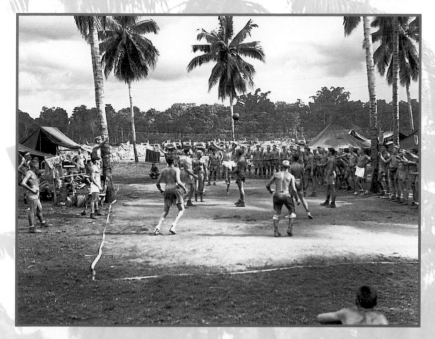

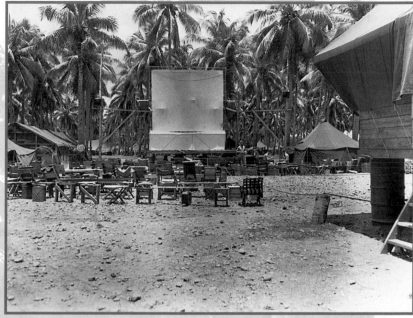

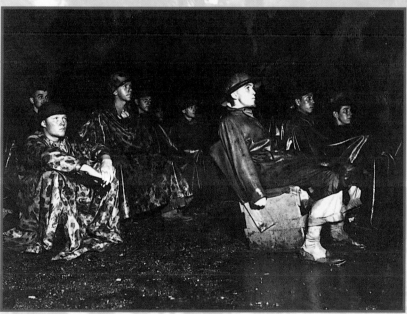

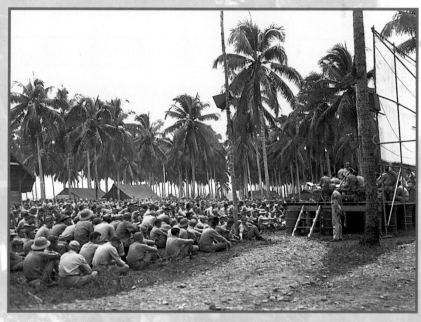

TOP LEFT: This hotly contested volleyball match on Guadalcanal was played for tremendous stakes—an entire team's beer ration.

TOP RIGHT: Movies were shown on a regular basis whenever conditions permitted, and most Pacific island theaters were of the open-air variety. This one on Guadalcanal boasts innovative seating made of scrap materials.

BOTTOM LEFT: Open-air theaters did have their drawbacks, particularly when it rained. These men sat through a tropical downpour to watch a movie on Guadalcanal, even though, as they reported, it was hard to hear the soundtrack as the rain drummed on their helmets.

BOTTOM RIGHT: Touring USO acts usually started off with big-band music to liven up the crowd before the show went on. Here the band warms up an evening audience waiting to see Randolph Scott and Joe De Rita on Guadalcanal during January 1944. Note the movie screen behind the stage and the projection booth at far left.

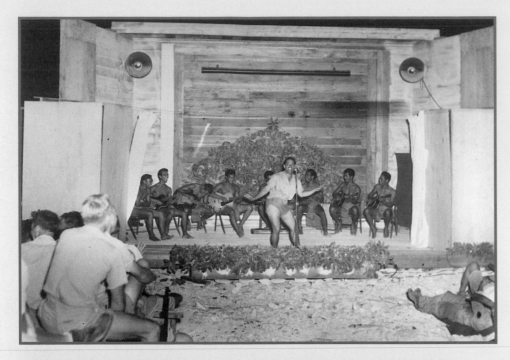

LEFT: Underwater demolition crew by day, entertainers by night, the "Royal Taxi Cab Hawaiians" perform for a captive audience on Canton Island in 1943.

BELOW: The dancing "Chorines" from the all-Marine show *Pacific Panics* perform one of their intricately choreographed routines on Guadalcanal in April 1944.

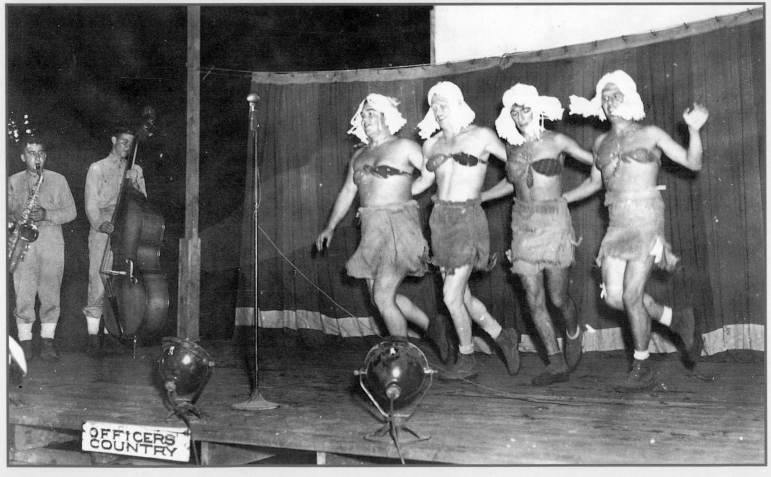

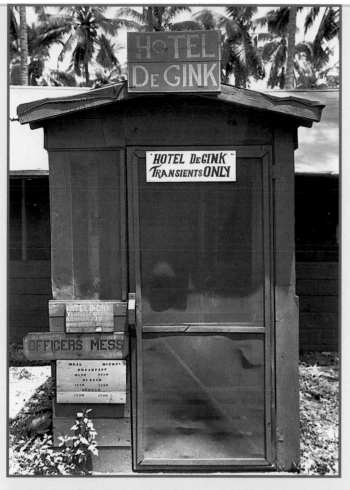

LEFT: ". . . Lieut. Bus Adams, SBD pilot . . . was nursing a bottle of whiskey in the Hotel De Gink on Guadal. He was sitting on an improvised chair and had his feet cocked up on a coconut stump the pilots used for a footrest. He was handsome, blond, cocky. He came from nowhere in particular and wasn't sure where he would settle when the war was over. He was just another hot pilot shooting off between missions." This was how James Michener introduced readers to life in the legendary Hotel De Gink on Guadalcanal in *Tales of the South Pacific*. This photo depicts the entrance just off the main highway near Henderson Field that greeted officers in 1944 on their way to the Hotel De Gink's mess hall. The enlisted men's entrance was on the side. Resident pilots and other men passing through Guadalcanal could stay at the De Gink and dine in this sumptuous facility. Prices ran twenty cents for breakfast, thirty cents for lunch, and forty cents for dinner.

BELOW LEFT: Killing time between missions inside the Hotel De Gink on Guadalcanal in 1943 was a familiar activity replayed in tents and Quonset huts on islands all over the Pacific. The stuffy heat brought on an understandable urge to strip down for comfort, and the cots are covered with mosquito netting. But more oppressive than the heat were the idle hours of waiting.

BELOW RIGHT: A common solution to the personal hygiene problem, this shower on Guadalcanal was improvised by hoisting a water-filled drum overhead with a block and tackle.

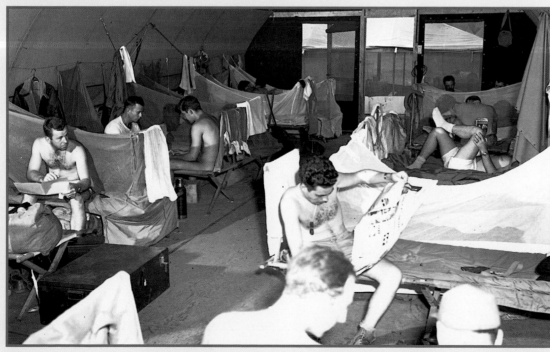

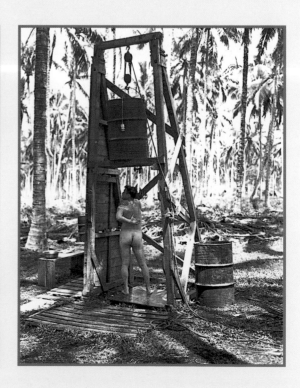

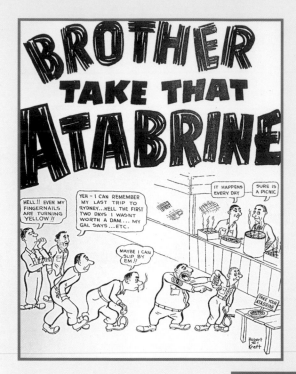

here!' He slapped the fly of his pants. . . . 'You're nothin' but a burned-out wreck.'" This flier was included in training material handed out to recruits.

RIGHT: Malaria control units such as this one were formed to try to keep down the numbers of disease-transmitting mosquitoes. After the war parts of New Guinea and the Solomons were still malaria problem areas. Travelers to those destinations were advised to take a new and very effective malaria drug called chloroquine, and such measures helped beat malaria back to a low ebb in the mid-1970s. Then so-called chloroquine-resistant strains of malaria appeared and malaria cases began to increase again. New drugs have been introduced since then to attempt to combat this persistent South Pacific menace, but malaria in some areas has returned to World War II levels.

BELOW: This sign was one of many on malaria-infested Guadalcanal, reminding everyone to be sure and take the "mandatory" yellow pills.

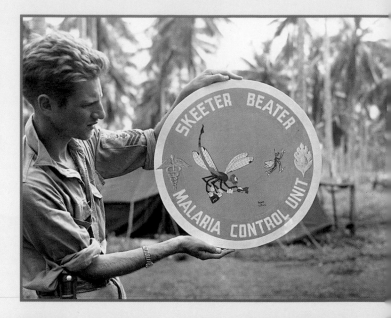

ABOVE: "It was the atabrine that gave Joe his worst trouble. He hated the little yellow pills and wasn't sure they did any good. . . . But all the same everyone had to take his atabrine tablets daily. That was not so bad until you began to turn yellow. Then you got worried." This is how James Michener describes one of his character's feelings toward atabrine in *Tales of the South Pacific*. If anything was more capable of inflicting devastating casualties than actual combat on many tropical islands, it most certainly was disease in general and malaria in particular. The drug atabrine had been devised to keep the mosquito-borne disease in check, and its effectiveness was hotly debated at the time, but there were many who became convinced that it did some good. Harlan Wall, an Army artilleryman in New Guinea, took his atabrine religiously and turned yellow along with all the rest of the men. He recalls, "You know, all the guys I saw who took atabrine never got malaria, but it seemed like the ones who did catch it were the ones who didn't take their pills." This is at least a passably convincing testimonial. Perhaps of more concern to some men were the rumors that atabrine caused impotency. In *Tales of the South Pacific,* Michener recounts a scene where just such a rumor was being repeated: "'As I got it straight from a doctor . . . all this atabrine does is keep malaria down. It don't show on you, see? You're yellow, and it doesn't show. But all the time malaria is runnin' wild! Down

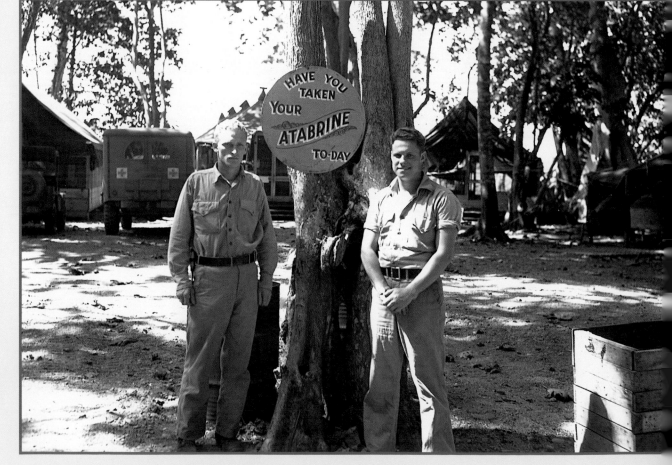

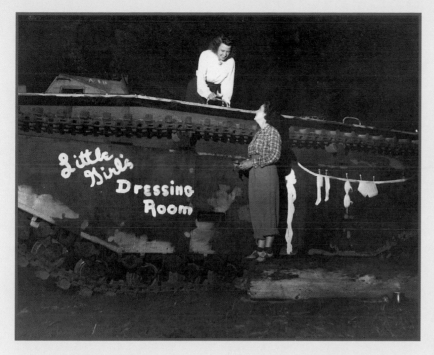

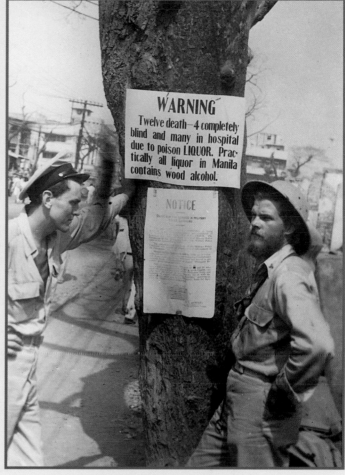

ABOVE: Though very few American women were stationed on Pacific islands near the beginning of the war, more arrived as the fighting moved closer to Japan. About six weeks after these nurses had arrived on Guadalcanal in 1944, a beach excursion was organized for them. A few of the men anticipated the need for a dressing facility at the beach, so an amtrac was provided for that purpose and appropriately labeled.

RIGHT: Even after islands would become rear areas, there were hazards. This sign in Manila warns of poisoned liquor.

BELOW LEFT: Danger of invasion had long passed, but barbed wire adorned the beach at Waikiki in Hawaii for most of the war.

BELOW RIGHT: Taking advantage of the island breezes, these Seabees in the Admiralty Islands have constructed windmill washing machines.

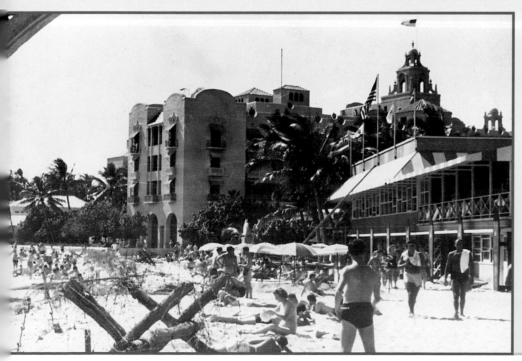

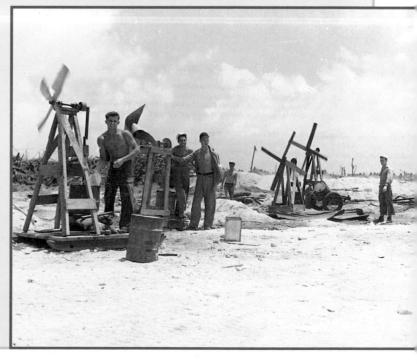

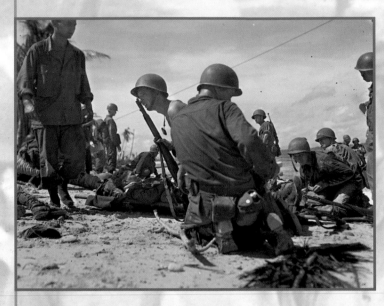

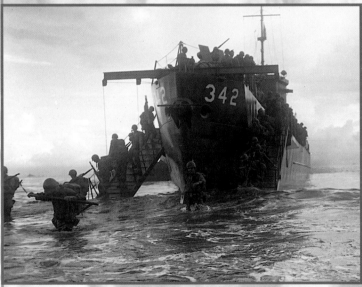

TOP: As Admiral Nimitz surged across the central Pacific, General MacArthur was driving toward the Philippines via a leapfrogging campaign up the northern coast of New Guinea. This photo depicts a scene that was played out time and again in numerous landings during the New Guinea campaign. American soldiers hit by Japanese snipers' bullets receive treatment on the beach during the Wakde Island invasion in May 1944. After emergency dressings are applied, Coast Guard–manned landing craft transfer the wounded to assault transports anchored offshore. Wakde Island became a base of operations for General George Kenney's Fifth Air Force, and planes from the airstrip there played a key role in subsequent battles farther up the coast. In a typical imaginative tactic of the Fifth Air Force, instantaneously fused thousand-pound bombs were dropped on the Japanese defenders of Noemfoor Island, which resulted in a virtually bloodless landing for U.S. infantry units. After several days of fighting, the three Japanese-built airfields on that island were under Allied control. Lying sixty miles west of nightmarish Biak Island, scene of a much more bloody and protracted campaign, Noemfoor was used to provide air cover for the next leapfrog up the coast: the invasion of the Vogelkop Peninsula.

BOTTOM: Allied troops meet no resistance as they disembark in the early morning hours on yet another New Guinea beach, this one at Arara near Sarmi. After months of grueling jungle fighting on the Kokoda Track and in the Finisterre Mountains, Australian Army units subsequently undertook the task of clearing out pockets of Japanese resistance while the Americans leapfrogged farther toward the Philippines. This area today is in Papua (formerly Irian Jaya) on the Indonesian side of the border that divides the massive island of New Guinea. Papua New Guinea, east of the border, has been an independent country since 1975.

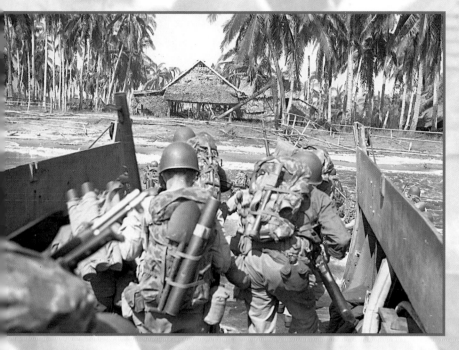

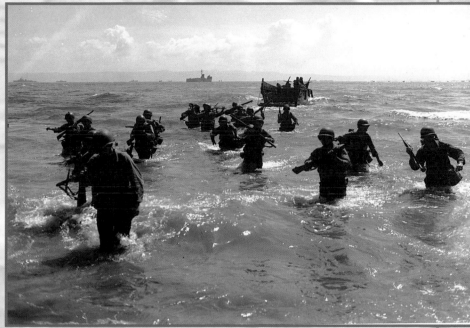

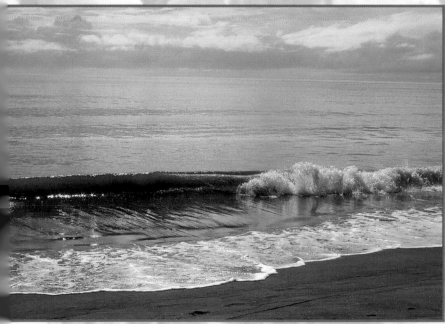

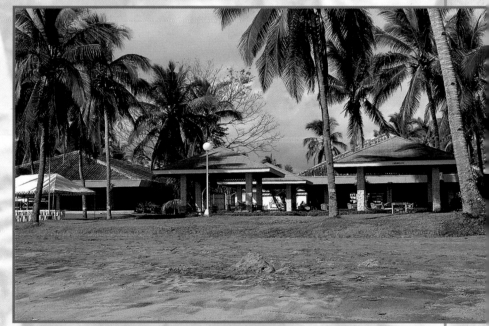

TOP LEFT: U.S. Army troops finally storm ashore on the beaches of the Philippine island of Leyte on October 20, 1944. Though fighting was intense in certain spots, overall resistance was light. Much more severe combat awaited the Americans farther inland.

TOP RIGHT: GIs land on Red Beach under fire.

BOTTOM LEFT: Gentle waves today wash the black sands of Red Beach, which attracts visitors from all over the central Philippines.

BOTTOM RIGHT: Visitors now to Red Beach on Leyte can stay in the MacArthur Park Beach Hotel shown here. U.S. Army troops who landed on this beach overran the Japanese defenders dug in on what are now the hotel grounds. Several hundred meters north of the hotel is where MacArthur dramatically waded ashore, an event now commemorated by a memorial park.

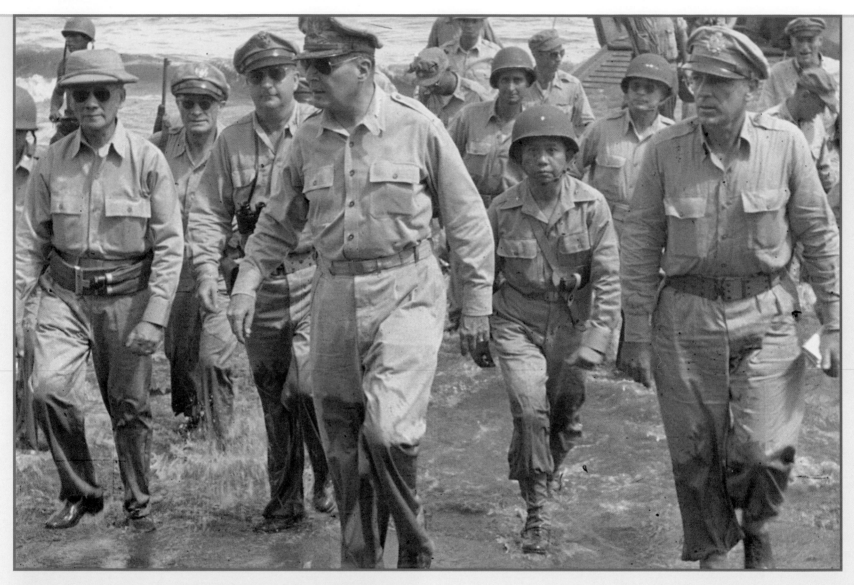

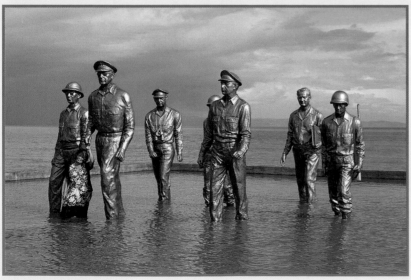

ABOVE: General MacArthur makes good on his vow to return to the Philippines. Here he wades ashore at Red Beach at Palo just south of Tacloban during the Leyte landing on October 20, 1944.

LEFT: MacArthur's return to the Philippines is immortalized in these twice-life-sized gilded statues that commemorate his wading ashore. In this photo the woman is striking a pose popular with Filipino tourists. Nearby government guards allow a certain amount of this activity before shooing visitors out of the reflecting pool.

OPPOSITE TOP LEFT: The ubiquitous image of the general with his trademark corncob pipe is incorporated into the logo of the MacArthur Park Beach Hotel, as seen on one of the hotel vans in the late 1990s.

OPPOSITE TOP RIGHT: Leyte landings also took place on Blue Beach at Dulag, about twenty kilometers south of Red Beach. An interesting monument on Hill 120 just inland from Blue Beach commemorates the landings. Here a concrete statue of a GI climbs a concrete palm tree to raise the American flag.

OPPOSITE CENTER LEFT: As soon as the Tacloban area was secured, MacArthur set up his headquarters in the Price Mansion in the middle of Tacloban. The owner, Walter Price, was a successful American businessman before the war, who was imprisoned at Santo Tomas in Manila with other civilian internees. His Filipino wife had been tortured by the Japanese and fled into the jungle. Used earlier by the Japanese as an officers club, the house was well known to them. When they discovered that MacArthur was there, their air raids targeted the mansion frequently. The general's aides worried for his safety and suggested he move his headquarters to a more secure location. As usual, MacArthur refused, saying he liked the broad porches, which were well suited for his pacing. In spite of several near misses, the mansion survived the war virtually unscathed and remains today, part office and part museum, in the middle of bustling Tacloban.

CENTER RIGHT: It seems like the image of MacArthur wading ashore on Leyte crops up everywhere in the Philippines, as in this bas relief next to the old Commonwealth Building in Tacloban. It was here on October 23, 1944, that MacArthur restored Philippine civilian government, with Tacloban as capital until the liberation of Manila.

BOTTOM LEFT: At the top of Hill 120 is an Army monument with a unique oversized concrete replica of a GI helmet as its center-piece. A small entrance at the back enables visitors to take shelter from Leyte's frequent passing showers.

BOTTOM RIGHT: Though initial Leyte landings were relatively bloodless for Americans by the standards of Pacific-island invasions, civilian casualties were quite high. This monument in Dulag commemorates Filipino casualties suffered during the prelanding American bombardment.

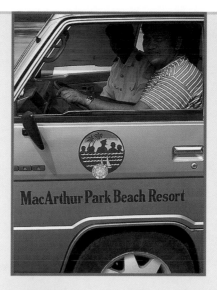

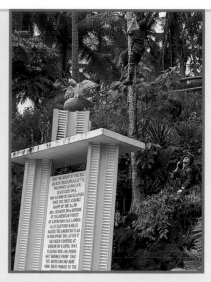

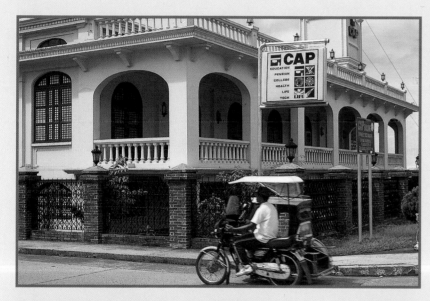

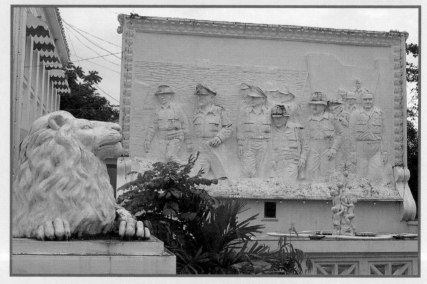

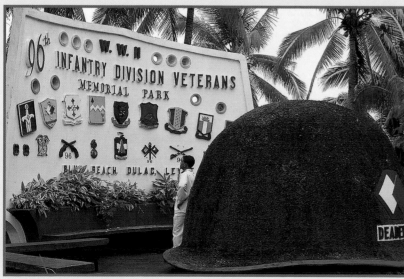

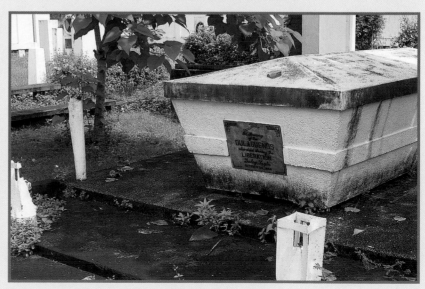

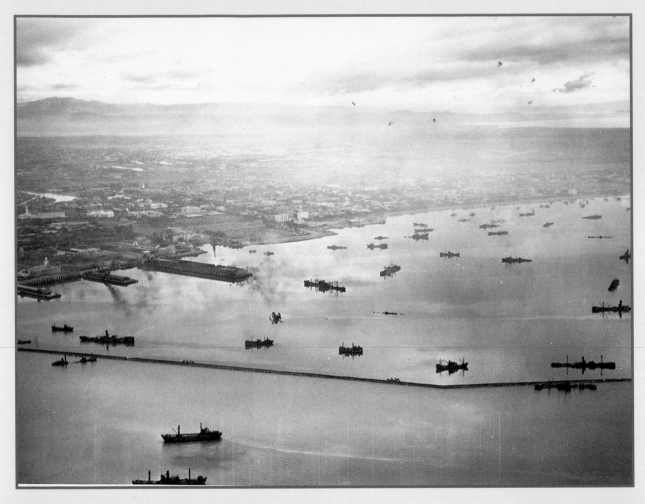

LEFT: At the end of 1944, MacArthur was poised to assault the island of Luzon in his quest to recapture the Philippines, and by early 1945 U.S. forces were churning toward Manila. This photo, taken during an air raid just before fighting reached the outskirts of the city, shows the roughly fifty sunken or immobilized Japanese ships cluttering Manila Bay.

BELOW LEFT: When the Japanese overran the Philippines in 1942, they interned more than four thousand Allied civilian prisoners within the precincts of Santo Tomas University. In this captured Japanese photo the internees are assembled on the grounds.

BELOW RIGHT: After the liberation of the Santo Tomas internees in the early stages of the battle to retake Manila, GIs make friends with two girls who had been imprisoned.

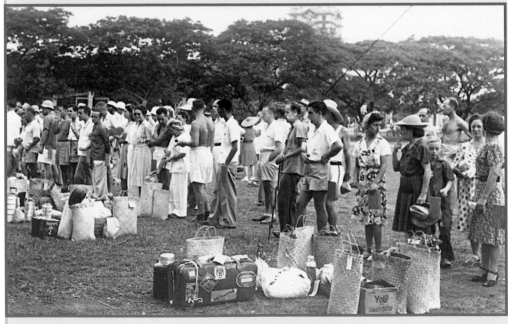

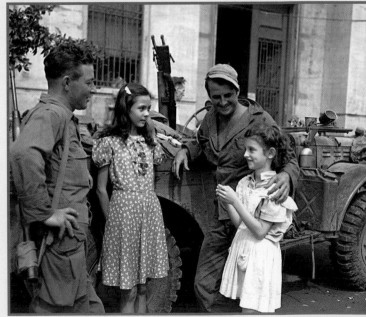

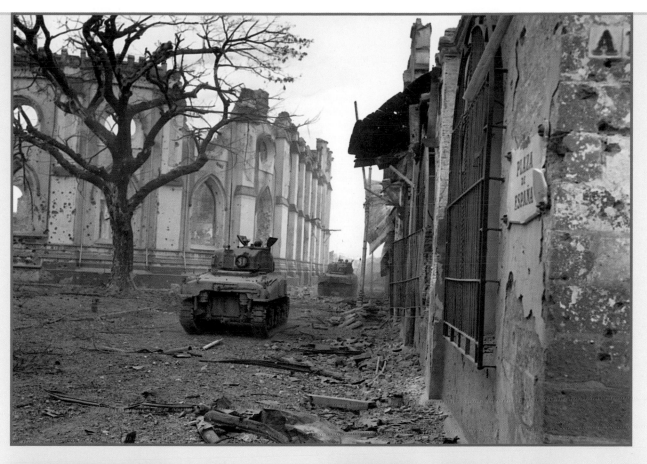

RIGHT: The commander of Japanese forces in the Philippines, General Tomoyuki Yamashita, the "Tiger of Malaya," who had been a war hero to the Japanese in the early years of conquest, claimed until the day he was hanged as a war criminal on February 23, 1946, that he categorically ordered the evacuation of Japanese forces from Manila in the face of the advancing American Army. It was only when it was too late, he maintained, that he discovered fanatical Japanese sailors and marines under the command of Admiral Iwabuchi had either not received his evacuation orders or had ignored them—they planned to fight to the death in the streets of Manila. Regardless of the details, the outcome was that the Americans virtually had to destroy Manila to defeat the remaining Japanese defenders. The GIs steadily fought their way through the streets during February 1945, and the Japanese gave ground grudgingly, burning buildings and killing civilians as they retreated street by street. They finally fell back behind the walls of the old city of Intramuros in the heart of Manila, taking with them four thousand Filipino civilians as hostages. The Americans made the decision that they would blast their way into the ancient city, and incessant shelling preceded their assaults. At one point the Japanese released several hundreds of hostages, who were mostly women and children. Male hostages already had been executed by the Japanese and were found later by the Americans. More than one thousand Japanese finally died in Intramuros, but it has been estimated that about one hundred thousand Filipinos perished in the retaking of Manila. The city of Manila, and the old fortress of Intramuros, were left in devastated ruins. In this photo taken on February 23, American tanks move through the streets of Intramuros to assist in blasting the dug-in Japanese defenders from their positions. The remains of the Manila Cathedral are at back left.

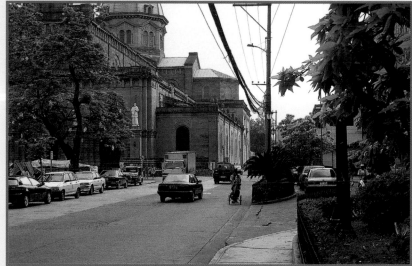

ABOVE: A photo taken from the same vantage point today. The Manila Cathedral, one of twelve churches in Intramuros before the war, was rebuilt after the war and stands at back left in this photo.

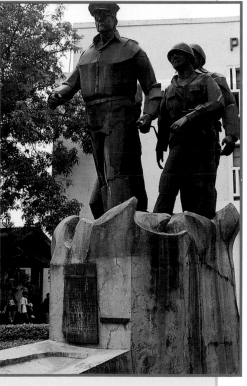

RIGHT: These statues stand just inside the south gate to Intramuros today, a larger-than-life reminder to Manila residents and tourists alike of the enduring presence of MacArthur and of his return to liberate the Philippines.

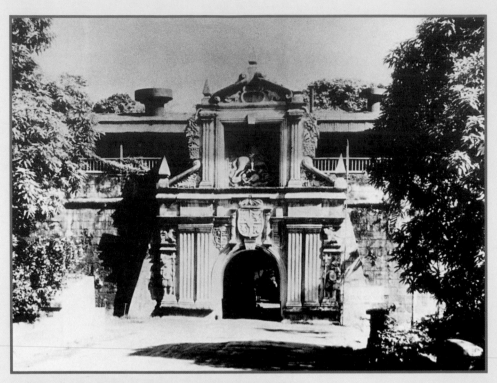

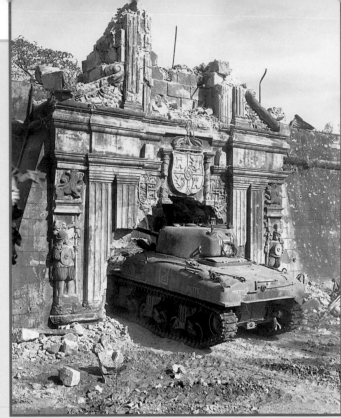

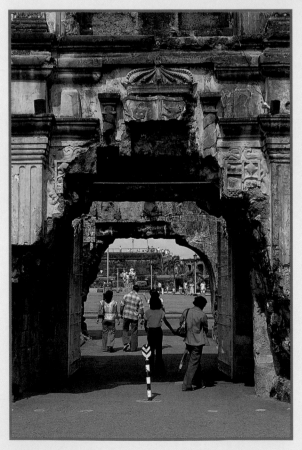

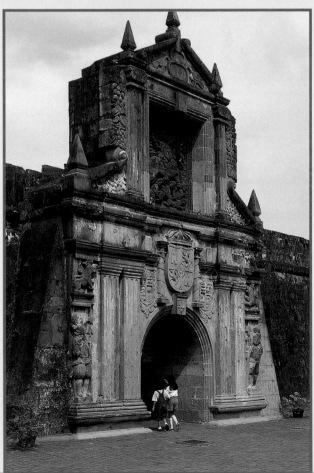

TOP LEFT: Old Fort Santiago, built in one of the corners of the walled city of Intramuros, was first begun by the Spanish in the late 1500s. The fort's old main gate, shown here before the war, epitomized the colonial Spanish influence.

TOP RIGHT: During the final stages of the fight for Intramuros, the Americans had to blast their way into Fort Santiago, thus "enlarging" the old gate, shown here as an American tank rolls through.

BOTTOM LEFT: Restoration of much of Manila continued for years after the war ended. Visitors to Fort Santiago passed for several decades through the old gate in the state it had been left after the battle. This photo was taken in 1978.

BOTTOM RIGHT: Finally in the 1980s the old gate was restored to its prewar elegance.

OPPOSITE TOP LEFT: Restoration of damaged buildings in Manila continues, but war-ravaged remains such as these could still be found in sections of Intramuros in the late 1990s.

OPPOSITE TOP RIGHT: On a street corner cleared of rubble, this monument has been erected to commemorate the sacrifice of the estimated one hundred thousand Filipinos killed during the battle for Manila.

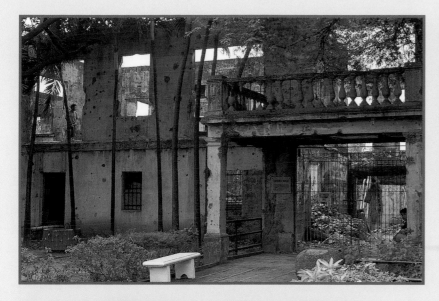

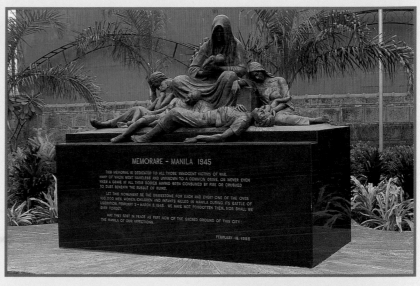

Within the memorial text:

MEMORARE - MANILA 1945

THIS MEMORIAL IS DEDICATED TO ALL THOSE INNOCENT VICTIMS OF WAR,
MANY OF WHOM WENT NAMELESS AND UNKNOWN TO A COMMON GRAVE, OR NEVER EVEN
KNEW A GRAVE AT ALL THEIR BODIES HAVING BEEN CONSUMED BY FIRE OR CRUSHED
TO DUST BENEATH THE RUBBLE OF RUINS.

LET THIS MONUMENT BE THE GRAVESTONE FOR EACH AND EVERY ONE OF THE OVER
100,000 MEN, WOMEN, CHILDREN AND INFANTS KILLED IN MANILA DURING ITS BATTLE OF
LIBERATION, FEBRUARY 3 - MARCH 3, 1945. WE HAVE NOT FORGOTTEN THEM, NOR SHALL WE
EVER FORGET.

MAY THEY REST IN PEACE AS PART NOW OF THE SACRED GROUND OF THIS CITY:
THE MANILA OF OUR AFFECTIONS.

FEBRUARY 18, 1995

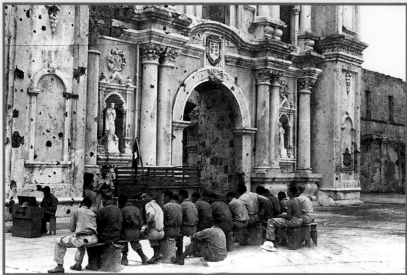

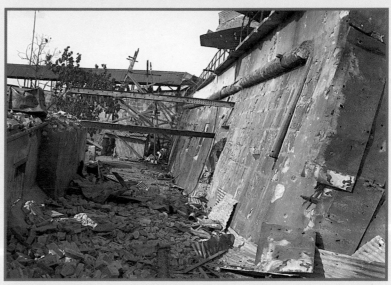

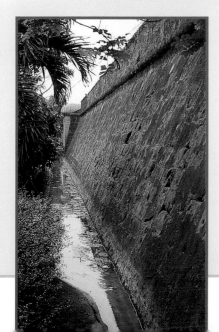

CENTER LEFT: A group of black servicemen gathers for religious services outside the bombed-out shell of one of the twelve prewar churches in Intramuros.

CENTER RIGHT: The sturdy city walls of Intramuros proved difficult to breach during the fight for the city.

BOTTOM LEFT, RIGHT: Now the city walls have been restored to their prewar state, and in areas where the old moat proved wide enough, a golf course has been built.

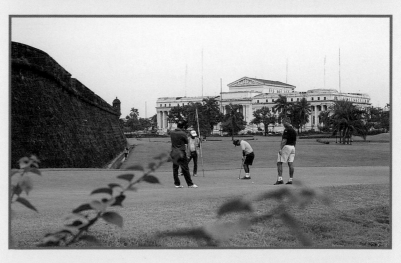

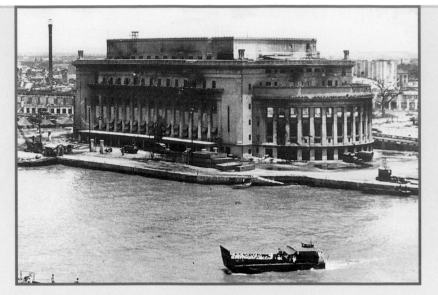

RIGHT: In the battle for Manila, every major building became a mini-fortress that had to be stormed. The Manila Post Office, shown here after the battle ended, was the scene of some particularly bitter fighting.

BELOW Like many other landmarks in Manila, the Post Office was restored after the war and is still in use today.

OPPOSITE TOP LEFT: Before the war, the elegant Manila Hotel was the center of high society and the residence of visiting dignitaries. General MacArthur and his family lived in a specially built suite on the sixth floor, which was known throughout the Philippines for its beautiful furnishings. MacArthur, a notorious pacer, walked miles on his balcony that overlooked Manila Bay before being forced to flee to Corregidor. Then the Japanese commander was said to have taken up residence. During the retaking of Manila, the hotel became another fortress to be stormed. MacArthur had heard that his suite was still intact, but as the battle for the hotel raged from floor to floor, the general was horrified to see his suite, with many of his belongings still inside, burst into flame. In a final act before dying, the Japanese set the building afire. This is the smoking ruin of the Manila Hotel shortly after it was liberated.

OPPOSITE TOP RIGHT: After liberation the front part of the old hotel was restored to its prewar grandeur, but the back part was demolished for a multistory annex. Today, only part of the MacArthur family penthouse suite remains in its original condition, seen here in this present-day photo as encompassing the five arched windows at center-top, with MacArthur's favorite balcony still overlooking Manila Bay. The old suite has been enlarged and is today the premiere accommodation for visiting dignitaries to Manila. Ordinary guests can book the "MacArthur Suite" for the going rate of $1,000.00 per night. The suite is decorated with photos highlighting the general's career, and on one wall is a glass case showing his many medals, which his wife donated to the hotel after his death. A number of the old medals, on display in a similar case before the war, have returned to their original location. They were hastily swept into a towel by Mrs. MacArthur and taken along to Corregidor when the MacArthurs were forced to leave Manila during the Japanese invasion. The medals constitute a few of only a handful of the general's personal effects that survived the ultimate destruction of the suite during the recapture of Manila.

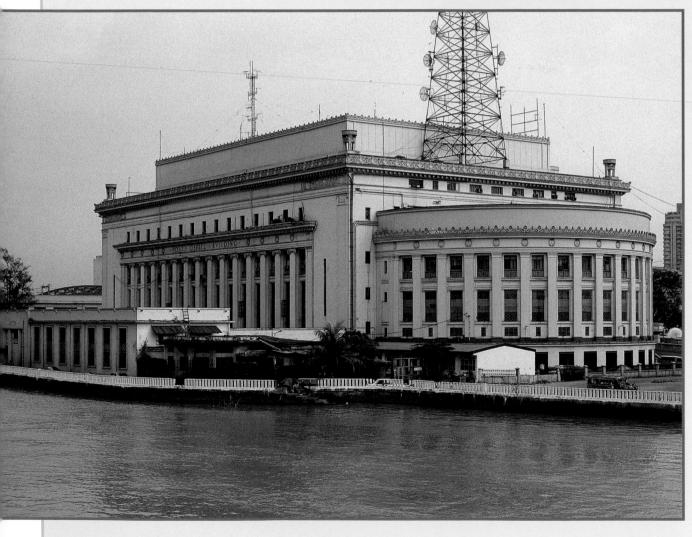

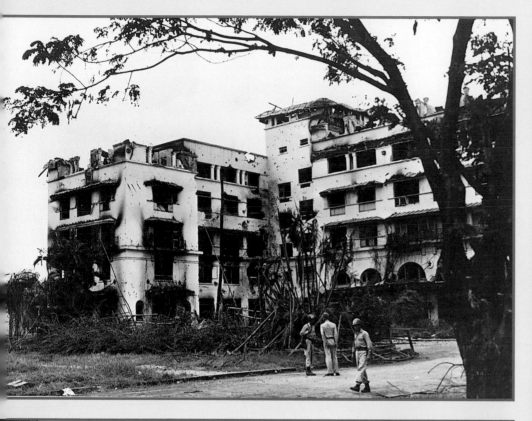

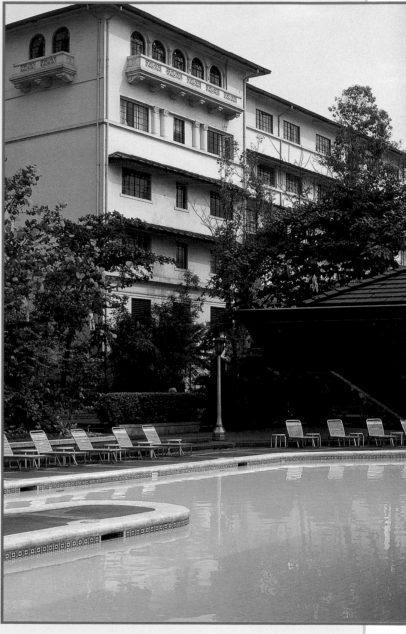

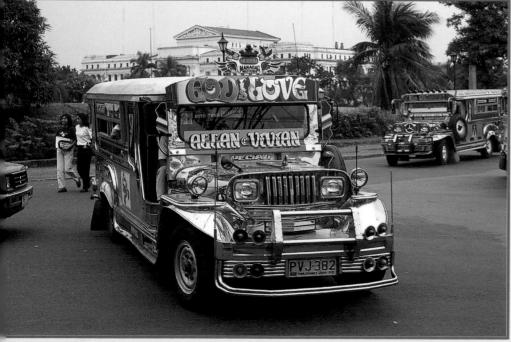

LEFT: Certainly the most visible legacies from the war are the ubiquitous "Jeepneys" that are a popular form of mass transit in the Philippines today. Originally customized surplus American jeeps, the Jeepneys now have evolved into an art form all their own that barely resembles the original World War II models.

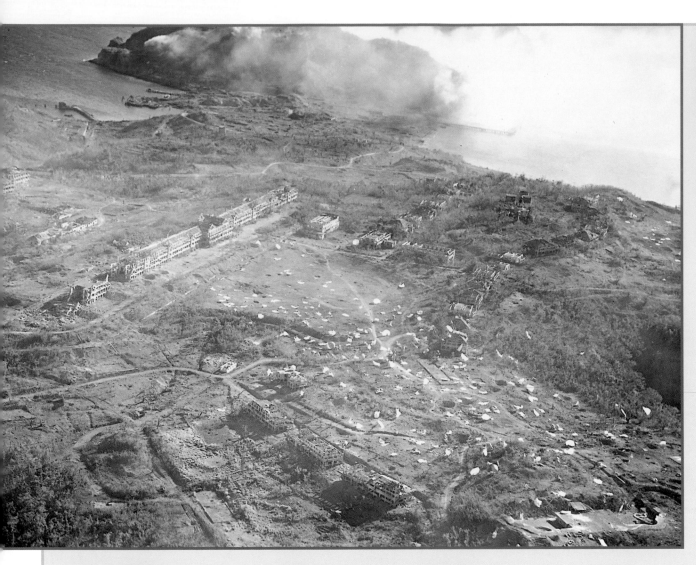

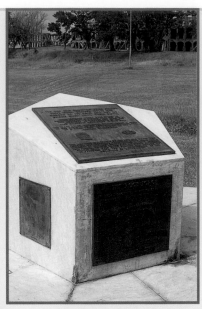

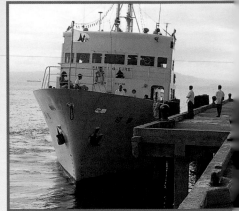

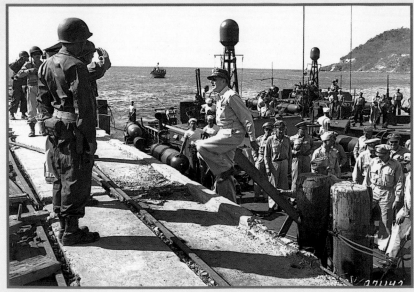

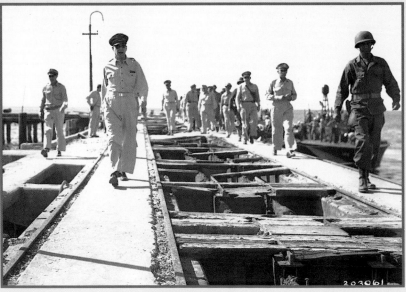

MacArthur wanted badly to see the Malinta Tunnel, where his headquarters was in the final stages of the battle for Corregidor. The west entrance was closest to South Dock, and the general's entourage went there first. An account of the visit from a 1945 issue of *Coast Artillery Journal* describes what was found: "It was partially closed by a landslide and smoking lightly. All semblances of the former road and electric railway approaches had disappeared. The bald face of the cliff into which the tunnel had been constructed showed the effects of air and artillery action."

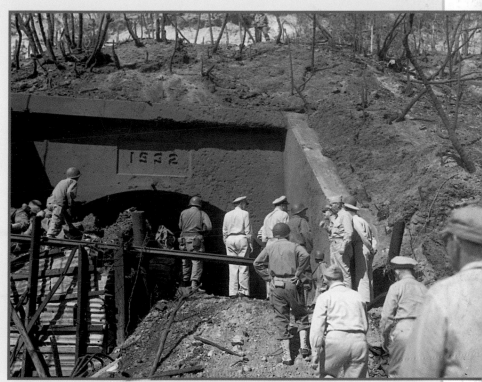

OPPOSITE TOP LEFT: The island fortress of Corregidor was recaptured by the Americans in February 1945. The invasion began with a spectacular airdrop of 2,050 Army paratroopers dubbed the "Rock Force." This aerial view of the Topside drop zone shows traces of the white parachutes draped over the parade ground area, and the bombed-out skeletons of the old Fort Mills buildings. The low level of the jump and the small, treacherous drop zone resulted in a number of paratroopers landing in Japanese positions, on cliffs, or in the ocean.

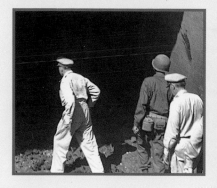

OPPOSITE TOP RIGHT: Today this monument to the Rock Force paratroopers stands on the scene of the Topside drop zone, the old parade ground. Nearby is the Pacific War Memorial commemorating all of the battles that took place in the Pacific. Other memorials on Corregidor include a Japanese memorial, a Philippine memorial, and a statue of a Philippine woman to commemorate the role of the Filipina in the struggle to liberate the Philippines.

OPPOSITE CENTER RIGHT: Part of South Dock has been reconstructed and today serves as a landing point for some of the boats carrying tourists from Manila.

OPPOSITE BOTTOM LEFT: Though fighting still raged on Corregidor, MacArthur could not wait—he had to return in spite of the danger. Here he steps from PT 373 on March 2, 1945, and sets foot on Corregidor's South Dock. It was less damaged and marginally safer from sniper fire than Lorcha Dock on the north side of the island, from which he left in 1942. He was evacuated three years earlier on a PT boat (PT 41, piloted by Medal of Honor winner Johnny Bulkeley) and deliberately chose to return on a PT boat.

OPPOSITE BOTTOM RIGHT: MacArthur strides down the remains of South Dock.

Proceeding on the road around Malinta Hill, the party came to the east entrance. In spite of warnings that Japanese defenders had recently detonated explosive charges to commit suicide inside the tunnel, MacArthur strode straight into the east entrance (shown above), the same entrance he had entered daily to get to his office in Lateral 3 during the siege. Debris from the explosions and Japanese bodies littered the main tunnel shaft. The account of his visit continues: "The situation was tense as General MacArthur walked deeper into the tunnel, pausing amid a heap of some 200 charred skeletons of Jap defenders. He glanced at a pile of 12-inch seacoast gun shells, still hot. He surveyed the scene with a calculating glance, kicked aside some Japanese food near his feet, peered deeply into the darkness of the inner main shaft, turned and walked out."

TOP RIGHT: While MacArthur was inside the Malinta Tunnel, his entourage waited nervously outside.

RIGHT: A tour group waits to enter the east entrance of the Malinta Tunnel today. This is the starting point of the "Sound and Light Show" inside the tunnel that depicts the history of the battles for Corregidor.

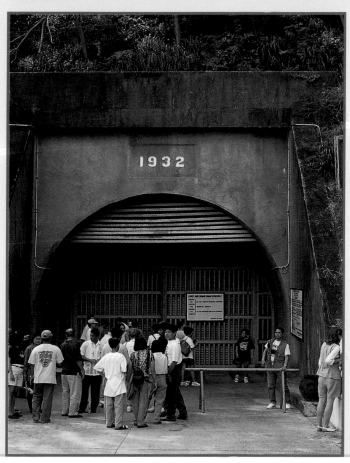

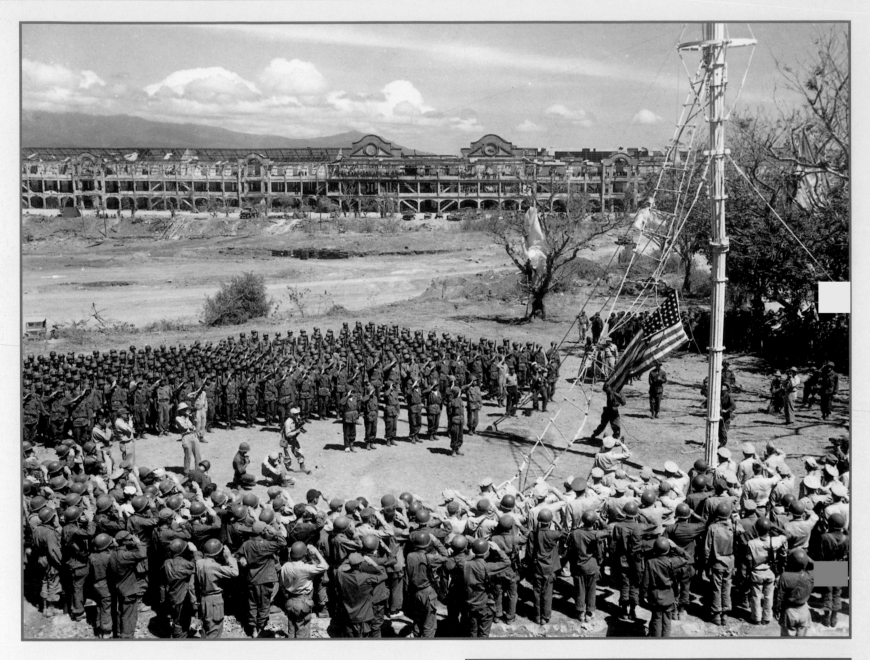

ABOVE: The culmination of MacArthur's return to Corregidor was the raising of the Stars and Stripes on the historic steel flagpole, a mast from an old Spanish warship. It had stood over the Fort Mills area on Topside for decades. In the ceremony pictured here, MacArthur intoned the words, "I see that the old flagpole still stands. Have your troops hoist the colors to its peak, and let no enemy ever haul them down."

RIGHT: The old steel flagpole still stands on present-day Corregidor, along with the ruins of the concrete buildings of Fort Mills.

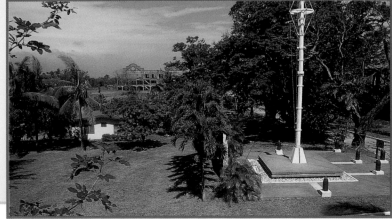

CHAPTER 5

UNCOMMON VALOR A COMMON VIRTUE

Securing Iwo Jima

THE STARK, APPALLING, BRUTAL, TRAGIC FACT

WAS THAT OF ALL THE MARINES WHO LANDED

ON IWO, NEARLY THIRTY PERCENT WERE

CASUALTIES, BUT THE AVERAGE LOSSES OF

ASSAULT UNITS, THE TROOPS WHO FOUGHT

ON THE FRONT, WERE SIXTY PERCENT.

— *Bill Ross,* Iwo Jima: Legacy of Valor

THE BARE FACTS that describe the battle for Iwo Jima are, as such things tend to be, a simple, straightforward, faceless accounting of figures. But such statistics are incapable of standing for one of the most shamelessly brutal battles of World War II, fought on what was and still remains the most bizarre of all the Pacific island battlefields. Three U.S. Marine divisions, the Third, Fourth, and Fifth, took thirty-six days to extinguish the fierce Japanese resistance and to secure a small, 7.5-square-mile island. Nearly six thousand Marines died, and over seventeen thousand were wounded, a casualty toll that still holds the record in Marine Corps history. Twenty-seven men earned the Medal of Honor on Iwo, twenty-two Marines and five Navy men. Fourteen were awarded posthumously. Just over one thousand of the defending Japanese survived, though only 216 prisoners were captured during the battle itself, many of them Koreans from a labor battalion. In the two months after the battle officially ended, U.S. Army troops captured over eight hundred Japanese and killed another 1,602, increasing the total to more than twenty thousand Japanese deaths on Iwo. Most of the dead remain entombed in the caves and tunnels where they fought to the death.

Behind those bare statistics, numbers that can be summarized for any battle, was a degree of annihilation and terror that matched and possibly exceeded any other fight in the Pacific. This was because the battle took on the unique characteristics of Iwo itself. Virtually every square foot of the island was fortified or could be brought under fire. There was no room to maneuver, no place to hide, no safe "rear area." There was no chance for flanking movements, no tactical options other than simple, brutal frontal assault. The island had no scenic, historical, or cultural significance, and no indigenous population. It was simply a battlefield from one end to the other. Most of what little scrub vegetation had struggled to grow in the sulfurous, coarse, volcanic sand was pulverized by the preinvasion bombardment. The island was stripped bare, cleared, and set up like a giant stage for human carnage—thousands of men killing each other, day after day, without letup, for thirty-six days.

Ask almost any U.S. Marine Corps veteran who fought on Iwo Jima to describe the island, and the answer almost invariably is "Hell." Surely almost any veteran of any campaign could describe the battlefields he fought on as hell, but, unlike most, Iwo Jima (which means "sulfur island") literally fits the description. It was and is a steaming volcanic seamount covered with gray-black, pumice-like coarse sand, and it reeks of the smell of sulfur. The lifeless volcanic cone of Mount Suribachi looms menacingly at one end of the island. Add seventy thousand hostile men jammed into the confined island area of a few square miles, locked in mortal combat, firing rifles, mortars, heavy artillery, and machine guns at each other, and Iwo Jima surely reminded more than one veteran of Dante's Inferno.

Iwo's hell-like geography was in stark contrast to most of the other Pacific island battlefields. Exotic jungles like those of Guadalcanal and Bougainville, though hellish to fight through, were green and lush and wildly beautiful in their own way, and environmentalists struggle today to help save what remains of those old-growth rainforests. Americans who fought on coral atoll and small-island battlefields such as Tarawa, Kwajalein, and Saipan, could at least imagine the stunning natural beauty of their white sand beaches, blue lagoons, and waving palm trees, even though at the time the islands were churned up by shellfire and their palm trees shredded by shrapnel. The recovered natural beauty of many of these formerly remote and unknown Pacific outposts has today made some of them tourist attractions that feature plush tropical resorts. But there were no rain forests, white sand beaches, or palm trees on Iwo, and there still aren't. It was and is an alien lunar landscape, an island that seemed to be designed for nothing else but killing, and it remains a nearly deserted, barren, haunted place to this day.

Though seemingly isolated, remote, and of little significance to anyone, Iwo was put on center stage by the logistics of Pacific warfare. It happened slowly but inexorably. Soon after the bloodbath of Tarawa, former ambassador to Japan Joseph Grew said: "The Japanese will not crack . . . even when eventual defeat stares them in the face. Only by utter physical destruction or utter exhaustion of their men and materials can they be defeated." By 1944, experience not only had led American military planners to believe

Grew was absolutely right, but also to realize that until Japan's home islands had been bombed and bombed heavily, the Japanese could never be forced to surrender. However, the vast distances of the Pacific and the range limitations of existing bombers had made such attacks pretty much impossible until late 1944. By then America had captured from the Japanese the islands of Guam, Tinian, and Saipan, mainly for the purpose of putting to deadly use the capabilities of a new bomber—the B-29. The Boeing Aircraft Company was by then mass-producing the huge, long-range bomber it had been developing since the beginning of the war.

Guam, Saipan, and Tinian lay roughly fourteen hundred miles south of Tokyo. When delivering a five-ton bomb load the B-29 had a round-trip range of about thirty-two hundred miles, meaning that, on paper at least, heavy bombing of Japanese cities and their war industries had become not only possible but practical. Major General Curtis E. LeMay was sent to Isley Field on Saipan in January 1945 to head the Twenty-first Bomber Command and prepare it for the bombing of Japan. Because of news about Japanese atrocities coming from freshly liberated areas of the Philippines, and the unbelievable cruelties inflicted by the Japanese on prisoners in the infamous Bataan Death March, LeMay took to the job with fierce enthusiasm. "Up to now we've just been swatting flies, "he exclaimed, "but now we can go after the whole manure pile."

It only took a few B-29 missions to Japan to show that what had been practical on paper was not turning out to be practical in the air. There were many problems, one being that the brand new B-29 was still a cranky airplane plagued by as-yet-unfixed "bugs." At high altitudes, for instance, its engines were prone to overheat and occasionally to blow a cylinder head or catch fire. There were other difficulties, by far the worst of which was fuel consumption. In theory a B-29 flying from Isley Field could return home from bombing Tokyo with 15 or 20 percent of its fuel still in its tanks. It could, that is, if its engines behaved themselves throughout the trip and if it had not suffered severe battle damage. But fuel consumption was made much worse by an unexpected factor. The B-29s

were having to contend with and, in fact, were the first American planes to have encountered hitherto unknown rivers of high-altitude, high-velocity air that were to become known as the jet stream. Flowing at speeds of well over 150 MPH and occasionally as much as 200 MPH off the east coast of Asia, the jet stream played havoc with bomb runs over Japan. Using excessive fuel to battle the winds all too often made the difference for a B-29 and its ten-man crew between getting home from a raid or disappearing forever beneath the sea.

The upshot was that at the end of February, and after eight B-29 raids on Japan, General LeMay was moved to remark, "This outfit has been getting a hell of a lot of publicity without having accomplished a hell of a lot in results." LeMay then switched to low-altitude incendiary raids to avoid the jet stream as well as to improve bombing results. But the twin problems of fuel consumption and damaged planes not being able to make it back to their bases did not go away. Additionally, the B-29s were being attacked on their way to and from Japan by enemy planes based on a godforsaken little island about halfway to Japan. On the maps it was marked "Iwo Jima." But even before the B-29s started bombing Japan, the military planners had anticipated the need for an emergency stopover base for bombers and crews that were in trouble. Without such a place many crippled B-29s would go down in the sea. Accordingly, well before the first B-29 had even arrived in the Marianas, the site for that emergency base had been chosen —that same little barren, sulfur-reeking, Japanese-owned island called Iwo Jima. Miserable as it was otherwise, Iwo Jima's location made it ideal for the purpose, and an operation to take it from Japan was already in the planning.

But the Japanese, too, had realized Iwo's value to the Americans and had sent General Tadamichi Kuribayashi with twenty-one thousand men under him to see that it wouldn't be taken. The Americans were determined not to have a repeat of Tarawa where hundreds of Marines died because preliminary shelling and bombing that was supposed to have knocked out the enemy's capacity to resist seemed only to have made him stronger. The Americans bombarded Iwo Jima off and on for months before invading it, and that was simply preparatory to an intensive three-day bombardment prior to the invasion.

Unlike Peleliu, there was little debate about whether or not to invade Iwo. But unlike Okinawa to follow, there was slim choice of tactics. There was little doubt that the American strategy would involve the steep beaches on the southeastern shore, the only practical avenues for landing. The defending Japanese knew this and also knew that frontal attack against prepared, dug-in positions was the Americans' only option.

As necessarily obvious as the American strategy was, the Japanese defense was just as straightforward. General Kuribayashi ordered his men to tunnel and dig in for a fight literally to the death. They hollowed out an interlocking system of tunnels, caves, and chambers—some as much as seventy feet below the surface—spacious enough to hold Kuribayashi's entire command. Iwo Jima was less an island than it was an earthen battleship. Following the tactics on Peleliu, Kuribayashi dictated there would be no dramatic banzai charges that squandered Japanese lives. The Japanese would defend the island from their tunnels and caves to the last man. The stage was set for carnage on a frightening scale.

At dawn on February 19, 1945, some fifty thousand Marines on transports lying off Iwo Jima had little inkling of what lay in store for them. They downed their standard prebattle breakfast of steak and eggs, then boarded landing craft and headed for the beach. Overhead they could hear the *whishhhh* and *shhhooshh* of shells from battleships, cruisers, and destroyers, which during the past three days had fired twenty-two thousand rounds of high-explosive shells into the island and were still at it when the troops started for the shore.

Sergeant Milo Cumpston of landing team 3/28 remembered it thus: "The destroyers and battleships were laying back of us, and their shells were going *shhh, shhh, shhh* over our heads. You'd hear the guns banging away out at sea, then from the island you'd hear *boom! boom! boom!* and see red flashes and pieces of island flying up in the air. With all this bombardment we figured it'd take us only two or three days to take the place." And as the first landing waves went ashore it did begin to seem that way. Thus far the

invaders' greatest discomforts had been trying to protect rifles from salt spray breaking over the bow and staying out of the way of seasick Marines. "In a landing craft," said Cumpston, "there's always guys pukin'."

The next discomfort turned out to be lightweight black volcanic sand. Charging off the boat ramps men sank into it over their boot-tops and sometimes even over their knees. From the water's edge the sand rose in a series of terraces that ranged from five to eighteen feet high. While men were struggling up the terraces, the beaches were soon cluttered and obstructed with wheeled and tracked equipment, half-tracks and tanks and the like, that couldn't climb the walls of sand at all. And because Iwo had no surrounding reef, the sea swells traveled right in to the beach where all too often they would cause a landing craft to broach-to and wind up blocking the way for other craft like a stranded whale. But all this was secondary to the relatively eerie calm on the island. There was some shelling and small-arms fire, but nothing like what the Marines were expecting.

Though there were over twenty thousand Japanese on Iwo Jima that morning, the Americans rarely caught sight of a live Japanese soldier. Marine veteran Frank Didier recalled, "The problem was you never saw any of them. You wouldn't think there was a person on the island."

"We went in on Green Beach," recalled Cumpston, "and there was no firing—I couldn't figure out why in the hell the Japs weren't firing on us." But when Cumpston and his team topped the second terrace, he didn't have to wonder any longer. General Kuribayashi had planned it that way: let the Marines get ashore and become exposed and bogged down at the top of the terraces, and then let them have it. And at a little after 10 A.M., with the entire first wave landed and the beaches crowded with men and equipment, the Japanese gunners opened fire.

"After we got up the second terrace we started getting the shit shot out of us," recalled one veteran. "Mortars started coming in, then they started laying a barrage in there on us and we just dug holes and stayed there. Wasn't a good place to be, but trying to walk or run through that rain of fire would have been worse. The sand, the ash, you'd sink clear up to your damn knees in it. It was porous-type stuff and the big problem was walking. When a shell would explode in it, the sand became a kind of shrapnel, and a lotta guys were getting hurt that way."

Much later, in a letter to his father, Robert Kunkel described it more poetically: "The noise was overpowering. Rifle fire whined, artillery boomed, and men screamed! The stench was overwhelming; all the common battlefield odors, plus the pungent scent of sulfur fumes which rose from the gaps in the rocky terrain."

At first all was confusion. Shells falling, sand and body parts flying, men huddling in sandy shell-pits or trying with their bare hands to dig some kind of sheltering hole. Then training began to take over. To the casual observer it still would have seemed like chaos, but actually it was developing a kind of order. Marines were cross-trained, first to be combat riflemen, then specialists of one kind or another. So, now men began to move. Flamethrower and demolition men began attacking pillboxes. Tanks and bull-dozers that had managed to struggle up the terraces began attacking blockhouses and pillboxes. Men fighting their way forward from the beach were meeting stretcher-bearers with wounded men moving past them. And among all this were medics giving emergency aid to the badly wounded and chaplains giving comfort when they could or admin-istering last rites.

As for Cumpston and his crew, they were clearing paths through minefields. "We'd work three abreast with about twelve feet between the two outside guys. As we crawled ahead, probing for mines with our K-Bar knives the two outside men would unroll ribbons to leave a clear trail for men, tanks, trucks, or whatever. And in all our mine-clearing work we never once had one go off accidentally."

Though progress was being made, casualties were heavy. Some Marines numbered their time on Iwo not in days but hours or even minutes. Fourth Marine Division veteran Mike Michel described what happened shortly after he landed in one of the first waves on the far right. "I was runnin' up across the beach. We had four guys killed right away by a shell. I got up on to the third terrace and ran right into the face of a machine gun. It blew the head right

off of the guy right next to me." He paused for a long moment, and went on. "I was carryin' a 60-mm mortar, and when I got shot, I was runnin' with the mortar, and I got hit right in the mortar tube. It hit me in the chest and knocked me back into a shell hole, and my chest hurt so I put my hand up there and I looked down and it was covered with blood. I thought, oh shit, I've been shot in the chest. So I pulled my jumper open, and there was no blood under-neath. When that bullet hit, it exploded, and I got it in both hands, and in my forehead. It was all fine shrapnel. The mortar tube saved my life. It did destroy the mortar —you couldn't fire that thing! I dropped it and looked up and a Jap was comin' right at me. I had a carbine. I think he took about eight rounds before I stopped shooting. I don't know if the first one killed him or not. Don't ask me why he was comin' at me. There were a lot of strange things that went on on those beaches. He probably wanted to make sure I was dead." Michel was taken off Iwo and out to a hospital ship off shore. He returned to Iwo fifty years later to walk on the beach where a mortar tube saved his life.

The intensity of the machine-gun fire and shelling took a fearful toll on the thousands of Marines who struggled through the coarse sand up the beach terraces toward the Japanese airfields. John Sbordone was a platoon leader on Iwo. "We landed at about 10:30 or so, later on in the morn-ing," he said. "We got out OK and started running up the terraces. We were all loaded down and the sand was real soft, so after about two hundred yards we were tired so I thought we should rest. I said, 'Down, men,' and we all laid flat. Then we started to get shelled. The man right next to me had his legs blown off. I figured we couldn't stay there, so I said, 'Let's go' and we started running up the terraces again. After another few hundred yards we got to the edge of the airfield No. 1. There wasn't anyone else around, so I called my commanding officer on the radio and asked where we should go into the line. He asked me again to confirm we were at the edge of the airfield, and then he said, 'Hell, you are the front line!' I said, 'Where the hell is everybody?' I guess they were all dead or wounded."

Bullets and artillery were not the only concerns. In

addition to the hundreds of mines being attended to by Cumpston and his cohorts, there were buried artillery shells and aerial torpedoes with the detonators facing upward, with the intention of stopping tanks. Dale Plummer was in one of the tanks the Japanese had in mind when they planned their defenses. He recalled, "The tank ahead of us hit a mine and stopped. We tried to go around it and hit a buried aerial torpedo. I was told that our turret was blown fifty feet in the air, and the tank flipped over. I don't remember it. I came to on another tank going to the rear. I wish we'd had more blades [bulldozer-like blades attached to the front of some tanks] on the tanks. That way, if you hit something you ruin the blade but the tank is OK. If we had had one of those on our tank, I'd have four crewmen alive today." Plummer was the sole survivor of his tank crew.

Marines landing on the left had their orders: get across the island's narrow neck in front of Mount Suribachi and seal the enemy-infested, gun-bristling mountain off from the rest of the landing areas. And, astonishingly, it took only an hour and a half after H-hour to do just that. There were heavy casualties on the way, with so many ordinary young men rising to extraordinary accomplishment that, in the words of Fifth Marine Division historian Howard M. Connor, "Every yard of their advance made another hero."

Among these was Corporal Tony Stein. As his company advanced, Stein kept the area in front of it sprayed with bullets from an air-cooled machine gun he had salvaged from a wrecked plane. When they became pinned down by enemy machine-gun and mortar fire, he leaped up and deliberately exposed himself so that resulting enemy fire would locate guns to be dealt with. When the Marines again started to advance, Stein charged ahead, neutralizing one enemy pillbox after another, and he killed at least twenty Japanese soldiers in the process. When his ammunition was exhausted, Stein ran back to the beach for more. He made eight such trips, on each one taking time to help a wounded Marine to the beach. When his company finally was forced to fall back, Stein covered its retreat with rapid fire even though his weapon was twice shot out of his hands. And it was then that his luck ran out. His day's work had won him the Medal of Honor but it was awarded posthumously.

By nightfall of D-Day at Iwo, the Marines had secured a beachhead a thousand yards wide. It was expensive real estate, bought by twenty-four hundred Marine casualties, six hundred of them dead and more dying. Or, put another way, 11 percent of all casualties the Marines took on Iwo were suffered between dawn and dusk of the first day.

The conquest of Iwo Jima settled into a slow, grim process of destroying pillboxes and blockhouses and neutralizing caves, one after another, day after day. By the end of D-Day+3, the Marines had Mount Suribachi cut off and entirely surrounded, and enemy resistance from its slopes and caves was largely neutralized. On D-Day+4 a forty-man patrol made its way to the top of Suribachi where, at 10:35 A.M., a group of them, including Hal Schrier, Boots Thomas, Hank Hansen, and Chuck Lindberg, were photographed raising the first American flag to wave from the highest point on Iwo Jima. It was also the first American flag to fly over any land directly administered by Tokyo. Sixteen-year-old Private First Class James Roberson had chosen to stay out of the picture and on guard, which turned out to be fortunate. When an infuriated Japanese soldier suddenly rushed out of hiding to interrupt the proceedings, Roberson and his BAR saw to it that he did not. Then a Japanese officer emerged from the same cave swinging a sword with only half a blade, but he was quickly dispatched. The cave actually held quite a few more Japanese, but swift work by the Marines with grenades and flame-throwers ended any further threats from that source.

When the flag was raised, men near Suribachi cheered, and ships offshore sounded their whistles. No one on Iwo who saw the flag-raising will ever forget the feeling. "I saw the first small flag from where I was," remembered Bill Hastings who was in the front lines facing the Japanese about a mile north of Suribachi. "Us guys didn't say a word. Well, in the first place we were up where we would have been shot if we'd have made a loud noise, but we all felt, well, I don't know, a thrill, a sense of pride, patriotism."

That afternoon the first flag was replaced by a larger one. Associated Press photographer Joe Rosenthal went along on the trip to Suribachi's summit and took a picture of the flag going up. He didn't know it at the time, but instantly he made the six men in the photo famous, and along the way became famous himself.

Most postwar-generation Americans, if asked, cannot tell you what happened on Iwo Jima, let alone point it out on a map. But there are a few who recognize "the Picture" (Rosenthal's flag-raising photo), or some who have visited "the Memorial" near Arlington National Cemetery modeled after the photo. These reminders of Iwo have been passed down to us from that single event on the fifth day of the battle. The photo of the second flag-raising became the most celebrated image of World War II.

After the surge of elation from the flag-raisings, the grim reality of what faced them started to sink in for every Marine on the island. Though the Japanese strategy of killing as many Americans as possible before being killed became clear early in the fight, there wasn't much the Marines could do about it. They had to endure the shelling and almost constant enemy fire, attack straight ahead into the Japanese guns, and methodically kill the defenders, starting in the south of the island and ending in the north. "You'd kind of go forward until someone got shot, and hopefully you could hear where the shot came from, or you'd see a rifle barrel stickin' up," remembered Bill Hastings. "Then the word was passed, 'give this guy some cover, he's goin' to go up.' So everybody who had something to shoot was shootin,' not indiscriminately, because we only carried eighty rounds of ammunition. We had to measure it off. Say there's one cliff with a hundred or so caves. Where's the shootin' going to come from? So you concentrated on the cave you were interested in. If fire comes from the others and our guys get shot, they just get shot. You'd try to get in any way you could, side, front, just any way to get there."

Since every square foot of Iwo could be brought under fire, and given the close proximity of American and Japanese forces on the small island, stress and vigilance went hand in hand to rob exhausted men of sleep. "After you don't sleep for three or four days at a time, you're too numb to get scared. You're just numb," noted Bill Hastings. "You then respond from training. Your mind is gone, everything is gone, but you are still doing your job as a result of your training. No way could you sleep, 'cause they'd jump in the

foxholes with you. They were good infiltrators at night and, I mean, you sleep you die! That's all there was to it. I went four days at one point without sleep. We were physically fit, but we were numb and groggy. On other islands you could pair off and one guy could sleep while the other kept a lookout, but not on Iwo Jima."

For the veterans who fought there and somehow survived, the battle of Iwo Jima usually does not bring to mind sweeping maneuvers or stunning triumphs. They usually remember Iwo as a collection of events, of things that happened to them, things that occurred in a slow-motion blur of danger and death, day after day of fighting, monotonous in its consistent horror, repeated frontal assaults, and friends killed and wounded. They almost always can name the exact number of days they spent on the island, one way to quantify their almost unimaginable experience. Chuck Lindberg, one of the Marines who raised the first American flag on Mount Suribachi, recalled, "I was carrying a flamethrower. It was risky. I lasted eleven days. I got shot on Hill 362A. I was carried off; I was doped up so bad, arm all shattered."

As if the stress of combat wasn't enough, some men had additional experiences that added to the horror. "My job ended up bein' carryin' bodies. So that's what I done," remembered Frank Didier. "We had to pick up the dead Marines and carry them back to the cemetery. We'd also have to collect the body parts. It was not too hard. If anything were around, we'd pick it up and put it together. Usually in most places there'd be one part here, and another a ways away, see. So you could pretty much tell which one they went to."

Yet, as in any battle, there were moments of sheer incongruity that relieve the stress, if only for a short time. "One day we were coming up to a cave that had a kind of wooden door in front of it," Bill Hastings recalled. "I saw a Japanese soldier run into the doorway and close the door behind him. I thought there may be more in there so I decided to blow it shut. I took a big lump of C-4 explosive, and you know I hadn't worked with it much, and I plastered it on the door and blew it up. It was a lot bigger explosion than I had expected. And then I looked up and Japanese money was coming down out of the sky! I figure there must have been a safe with the payroll just inside the door to that cave, and I blew this Japanese money all over the island!" Hastings kept some of the bills, his only souvenirs from Iwo.

And then there were ghoulish things that added to the surreal, otherworldly realm of Iwo. Stephen Nisbet remembered such an encounter. "One day there was a kind of lull and a guy with pliers came up to where our squad was dug in, looking to collect gold teeth from Japanese bodies. He came over to one that was close to me and I could see what he wanted to do. I told him to get the hell out of there. 'But there's a Jap there,' he says. So I say, 'Yeah, but he's our Jap so get the hell out of here.' I was just amazed that with all that was going on and needed to be done, some guy had time to go around doing stuff like that."

One day in particular stands out in the memories of many Marine veterans because of an event that gave Iwo's battle-weary Marines a dramatic illustration of why they were fighting. On March 4, D-Day+13, pilot Raymond Malo and his crew, flying in the B-29 named *Dinah Might*, became victims of one of the eccentricities of the B-29: a troublesome fuel system. As they neared Iwo on their way back from a bomb run over Japan, they still had plenty of fuel in reserve tanks but most of it couldn't be accessed. Iwo was not yet ready for B-29s, and Malo was ordered not to try to land there. The only runway under American control was too short, had barely been graded, and its north end was under fire by Japanese guns. Malo and his crew, however, found no difficulty in deciding between the possibility of a court-martial for disobeying orders or going down in the sea. The weather was bad and they had no radar, but navigator Bernard Bennison managed to find Iwo anyhow. Now it was up to Malo and his copilot to get their sixty-ton monster safely down on a four-thousand-foot airstrip, about half the length of runways they flew off of in the Marianas. Even by using all the tricks in the book—coming in at a speed dangerously close to stalling, dropping the plane onto the runway rather than landing, then throwing on full flaps and full brakes—they still were going to run out of runway had Malo not at the last minute kicked the plane into a screeching half-ground loop, shearing off a telephone pole with his wing just short of the north end of the runway. That did the job. Then to escape Japanese shells exploding close to where their landing was finally stopped, *Dinah Might* quickly had to taxi to the south end. Any Marine within sight of that runway never forgot the incongruous sight of the huge, gleaming silver B-29 suddenly appearing from the leaden sky and making an impossible landing in an area that was still being fought over. It most certainly drove home the reason they were there, and maybe, somehow, made the horrific fighting worthwhile. The fuel transfer problem was soon fixed, and the plane, barely able to take off on the short runway, resumed its trip back to the Marianas.

Very few Marines made it through Iwo unscathed. Most who survived had at least one close call where death was barely avoided. Those who survived their wounds consider themselves lucky. Those who got off Iwo without a single wound consider themselves extremely lucky. Being with survivors of Iwo is like talking with a group of lottery winners. They all consider themselves extremely fortunate to be alive. "I got blasted in the pack—my pack was shot off," said Frank Lipere. "Then I was running port arms, you know, holding the rifle in front of my chest, and the bullet just took my rifle and broke it in half. The rifle saved my life. That's how lucky I am."

Bill Hastings made it all the way through to the end of the battle with only what he considered a minor wound. "I only got knifed lightly," he said in a matter-of-fact tone with no hint of irony. "I went into a cave, and I stepped over some bodies, and after I stepped over one, he was still alive. He got up behind me and I was just able to see him out of the corner of my eye, my peripheral vision, you know, just in time for me to swing around. He hit my hand with the knife, but I had a .45 in my other hand, so I won and he lost. But I did get wounded four times on Saipan. What can you say?"

Some veterans remember odd details they associate with being wounded. "I don't know how it come about, but I had found a No. 10 can of grapefruit. I was carrying that damn thing back, and I had my rifle, and when I got hit I didn't lose either one," remarked Frank Didier. "I felt a sharp sting here and I looked and my pants were torn, and the guy alongside me didn't even know that I was hit. The bullet went right through my butt and there was a hole the size of a silver dollar where it came out. It barely missed my spine and my hip. I could put my finger in the hole and feel my hip bone."

Admiral Nimitz declared Iwo "officially secured" early on March 19, but there would be bitter fighting for the rest of that day and for eight more days after that. There would be over one thousand more American casualties before it was really ended. Frank Lipere was still alive and fighting near the end and remembered Nimitz's announcement. "When they said the island was secure, we were fighting another ten days or so, and they were still killing Marines. The big joke was, 'This island is secure?'"

Combat on Iwo was straightforward, gruesome, gory work with few surprises except one right at the end. There was a frenzied banzai charge in the early morning hours of March 26, an event not totally unexpected, given that it featured some of the last surviving defenders. The well-organized, ruthless killing from their tunnels and caves was at an end. The surprise was that their charge was not directed against the attacking Marines. Their targets were sleeping fighter pilots in tents next to one of the airstrips, some distance away from the endgame unfolding at the far north end of the island. Other tents in this rear area held Marine shore parties, supply troops, and Seabees. After four hours of confusion and mayhem, airmen, ground crew, Marines, and Army troops finally crushed the attack as dawn broke. Among the American casualties were nine Marines killed and thirty-one wounded, forty-four pilots killed and eighty-eight wounded. Amidst the fallen Americans lay 196 dead Japanese. Only eighteen were taken prisoner, and most of them were only captured because they were too seriously wounded to continue killing Americans. First Lieutenant Harry Martin played a key role in organizing the Marines who beat back this last Japanese attack. He died in the fight and had the distinction of winning the final Medal of Honor of the twenty-seven awarded on Iwo.

Milo Cumpston, the Marine with the Fifth Pioneer Battalion whose job it was to clear Japanese mines, played an unexpected role in stopping this final banzai charge. The evening before, he and his corporal, Albert Abbotellio, had laid out some mines they had to get rid of somehow, and they planned to detonate them in the morning. But during the night, after the Japanese first attacked the pilots and Seabees, the next stop was the Fifth Pioneer Battalion tents. On their way, they ran right through the mines. When Cumpston and Abbotellio heard explosions close by, their first thought was that some animal had stumbled into the field and set off their mines. But the next morning they found 13 dead Japanese strewn about where the mines had been. It happened that the main attacking force had been decimated by Cumpston's "discarded" mines. Turning back from their planned route and returning down the ravine they had come through, they ran into Marines, Air Force men, and assorted Seabees who had been in hot pursuit. Between Milo's mines and the aroused rear-area Americans, this final banzai charge on Iwo was obliterated.

As a result of this action, the Twenty-first Fighter Group was the only USAAF unit that fought as infantry during World War II. The banzai charge against the pilots and Seabees was the last gasp of the Japanese, and the next day the battle for the island was finally over. Two weeks later, the surviving pilots would again climb into their P-51 Mustangs and begin shepherding B-29s on raids against the Japanese mainland. These missions were so hazardous that a pilot needed to fly only fifteen to complete his tour of duty.

Anyone who survived was lucky indeed, but nothing can erase the fact that the casualty rate was horrific. Jack Rasmussen returned on the fiftieth anniversary of the battle to the beach on Iwo where he landed and read from a faded sheet of typewritten paper he brought with him. "This is my roster. There are about two hundred men in a company. There were a few survivors in the headquarters company and mortar platoon. This is the first platoon here. OK, here's Lieutenant Smith, missing in action. This next one, killed in action, Bob Carroll, a real good friend of mine, wounded in action, died of wounds. Haralson, killed in action. Lingle, killed in action. Gryczan, combat fatigue. Dumis, combat fatigue. This next one, Hillman, he lived. He's a coach in Illinois. He's a good friend of mine even now. He got a chest wound. This next guy was 'Frenchy' LaSalle. He got wounded but it must have been a flesh wound because he came back to duty. Ken Jarrell, he was in my squad. He was the first one to me when I got hit . . . wounded in action. Bonesteel was one who didn't get hit. . . . So there were two guys out of forty in our platoon who didn't get hit, Brubaker and Bonesteel. But then there was more than that because we had replacements. So they say, how can you get over 100 percent casualties? Well, this is the way you can do it. You see, these guys at the bottom here were replacements. You see they were all privates. Probably just out of boot camp. Then what do you tell them when they show up on Iwo? You tell them, don't shoot Marines. Shoot Japs. Keep your butt down. But then they get killed or wounded and they are gone and they never knew anybody."

Given the fear, terror, and inexplicable experiences, scenes that in their wildest imaginations they could never have expected to see, how did men make it through Iwo and keep their sanity? Of course some didn't. Someone who saw a lot of combat fatigue cases on Iwo was Army chaplain John Vayhinger. "There were several types of combat fatigue," he remembered. "There was the psychological: they'd be sullen, staring, have extreme agitation, and have very sensitive nervous reflexes. Then there was 'concussion,' where there was actual brain damage, and they had mental symptoms. It seemed to me that about 50 percent recovered within two months, 90 percent recovered within two years, and there were some who never recovered."

Even some of those who considered themselves mentally intact after Iwo had problems, as Vayhinger related. "One night after I got home I woke up and I had my forearm behind my wife's neck, and I was pushing with the palm of my other hand on her forehead. I was trying to break her neck like we'd been taught in training. I had been having a nightmare and she'd grabbed me to try and wake me. I had to tell her, "Never touch me when I am having a nightmare!"

Many Iwo veterans had similar experiences after they got home. "I had problems with bad dreams for about a year when I got back," recalled Bill Hastings. "Or there'd be a loud noise or something like that and I'd duck into the gutter or into a door; you know, just crazy things. I went immediately into college, and they kept havin' beer parties and stuff. Boy, I would go to these parties, and while I'd be there I would have a sudden feeling that I had to get out of there—these people are jammed up too much, they're too close together. It kind of ruined it. You know on Iwo if you got ten or fifteen guys bunched together, you got a mortar on top of you."

And these feelings sometimes don't go away, they lie submerged and can be triggered again years later. Two of Bill Hastings's buddies phoned him and tried to talk him into going along for the fiftieth anniversary return trip to Iwo. "A couple of the guys called and asked me to go with them, guys that I had been with there, and I says, bullshit, why do you want to go back there for? Well, OK, they wanted to go back, so I say, OK, I'll go with you. And I must say I agreed to go only because the guys wanted me to be with them. I would never go back on my own. And immediately as soon as I said yes, I started having flashbacks, and every day, once or twice a day, something would just happen or I'd see something, just at home or anyplace else, and boom, I'd get a flashback. It would be an image, something dangerous or somebody gettin' killed, or something like that." Hastings continued to have flashbacks during his visit to Iwo in 1995. The frightful images slowly faded back into the recesses of his mind during the following year. He said he won't go back to Iwo, and he hopes the flashbacks don't return.

Some Iwo veterans had certain mental attitudes that helped them survive the strains of combat. Jim Westbrook made it all the way through Iwo without being wounded, and described his mental approach. "Every night on Iwo I said to myself, I made it through today, now if I can just make it through tonight. And the next morning, I would think, well, I made it through the night, now if I can just make it through today, and so on all the way through. That's how I made it." Others had unique spiritual experiences. John Sbordone was with Jim Westbrook on Iwo, and he also survived without major injury. "I'm not a real religious person or anything, but I had a feeling on Iwo, a real spiritual closeness, that I would make it through," he recalled. "I have never felt that way before or since, but it made me believe that I was going to make it through, and I did."

Bill Hastings had an even more dramatic spiritual experience on Iwo. "About the fourth or fifth day I'm layin' on the beach," he remembered. "And I'm on this beach and artillery shells are crossing right overhead, and way in the middle of the night it got to worrying me that they were going to collide right over my head. You know, what a stupid thing to worry about. But it got to bothering me and I really got scared. And all of a sudden, I didn't ask, it just came, a big booming voice from up there someplace, and it said, 'You are chosen, do not fear.' And I relaxed, and I haven't been afraid since. I'm not a nonreligious person, I'm just kind of in the middle. But you know, after that, every time we were asked to do something, which was constantly, nobody would want to do it unless I was with 'em. They thought I was going to come through. I still have this feeling. For some reason, I can't explain it, but whenever we were asked to do something they would say, well Hastings has to go with us."

To the few who have made the trip back today, Iwo looks just like it did in the old World War II photos, a barren, deserted, sulfurous killing field, essentially devoid of value since the Japanese signed the surrender on the deck of the USS *Missouri* in Tokyo Bay. But for a few months in 1945, it was one of the most important pieces of real estate in the Pacific. And it will remain exactly that to the veterans who survived. They will carry Iwo with them to their dying day.

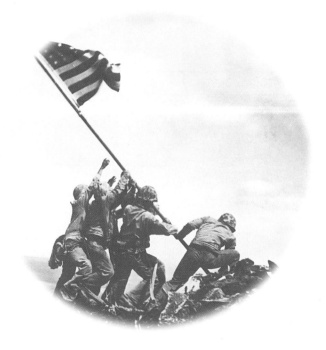

IWO JIMA lives on not only in the minds of the men who fought there, but survives almost undisturbed since 1945 in the middle of the Pacific Ocean. In one of the supreme ironies of World War II, Iwo Jima has returned to its status prior to the American invasion: a fortified Japanese military installation and air base, off limits to most outsiders. Consequently, of all the Pacific island battlefields, Iwo Jima is the most difficult to visit. How did this happen? Following World War II, the United States administered the island until 1968, when there was no longer any real justification for holding onto Iwo, except for the Coast Guard LORAN navigation station way up on the north end. The station was finally turned over to the Japanese Coast Guard in October 1993, ending an American presence on the island that began with the invasion on February 19, 1945. The airfield on Iwo Jima is now operated by the Japanese military as it was before the invasion. The difference today is that U.S. Navy Carrier Air Wing Five conducts carrier landing operations and other exercises from time to time on Iwo, and other U.S. military units sometimes use the island for training.

A visit to Iwo today almost always requires hooking up with a group of veterans for an infrequent tour that has the permission of the Japanese government. The first of these special veterans' tours was for the fortieth anniversary of the battle in 1985. At that time there were still regular U.S. military flights into Iwo to keep the LORAN station going, and the vets flew in on a U.S. military aircraft. After the Japanese regained control of the island in 1993 and regular U.S. military supply flights stopped, a group tour using chartered commercial jets was allowed back on Iwo to commemorate the battle's fiftieth anniversary in 1995. It was a big deal. More than seven hundred people (including over four hundred veterans) from both the U.S. and Japan flew in on Continental Airlines charter jets for a one-day visit. A couple of more plaques were added to the memorial erected during the 1985 visit, and there was a moving ceremony. Japanese and American survivors of the battle sat near each other and listened to the widow of the Japanese commander, General Kuribayashi. She gave a lilting, sad speech in Japanese, her strained, high-pitched voice echoing over the old battlefield where her husband lies entombed in an unknown tunnel somewhere on the north end of the island, still at his post where he died fighting the Americans.

Since then there have been a few more groups allowed to visit the island on day trips, but Iwo remains just about as stark and inhospitable as it was in 1945. There is no hotel, no ground transportation, and few amenities beyond the air base facilities on the site of old airfield No. 2. Military trucks had to be landed on the beaches of Iwo to haul the seven hundred visitors around the island the day of the fiftieth anniversary commemoration. Some of the scrub vegetation in the center of the island has grown back, but the bleak, gray-black, coarse-sand beach terraces still march up from the surf line, and the stark skyline of Mount Suribachi still glowers over the south end of the island.

Shortly after Iwo was secured, the Americans built a network of roads, including one that switchbacks up the steep sides of Suribachi. On its summit are several markers and memorials, American and Japanese. One was erected on the site of the U.S. flag-raisings. There is a small plaque nearby commemorating Bill Genaust, the combat cameraman who was standing with Joe Rosenthal when the second flag was raised. As Rosenthal shot the most famous still photo of World War II, Genaust was filming a color motion picture of the same scene. Genaust was killed on Iwo a few days later. Nearby are monuments dedicated to the kamikaze pilots who died during the battle for Iwo Jima and two other memorials to the Japanese war dead.

The view from the summit is very familiar to anyone who has looked at photos taken from that spot during the battle. The island has scarcely changed in appearance, though veterans marvel at the scrub grass and stunted bushes that have regrown over the center of the island, where there was nothing but bomb-pulverized volcanic material in 1945. The pervasive stench of sulfur everywhere is particularly noticeable on the summit of Suribachi.

The flags were actually raised on one lip of the volcanic cone. If you turn and look the other direction from the angle Rosenthal took his picture, there is a silent, steaming volcanic crater that plunges away from the summit, all streaked with yellow and orange mineral residue. At the summit a visitor doesn't have to try hard to picture the scene of the second flag-raising, since that photo has become perhaps the most recognizable image to come out of World War II. Iwo does, then, have an indelible image attached to it, unlike the other Pacific battles (except that of Pearl Harbor,

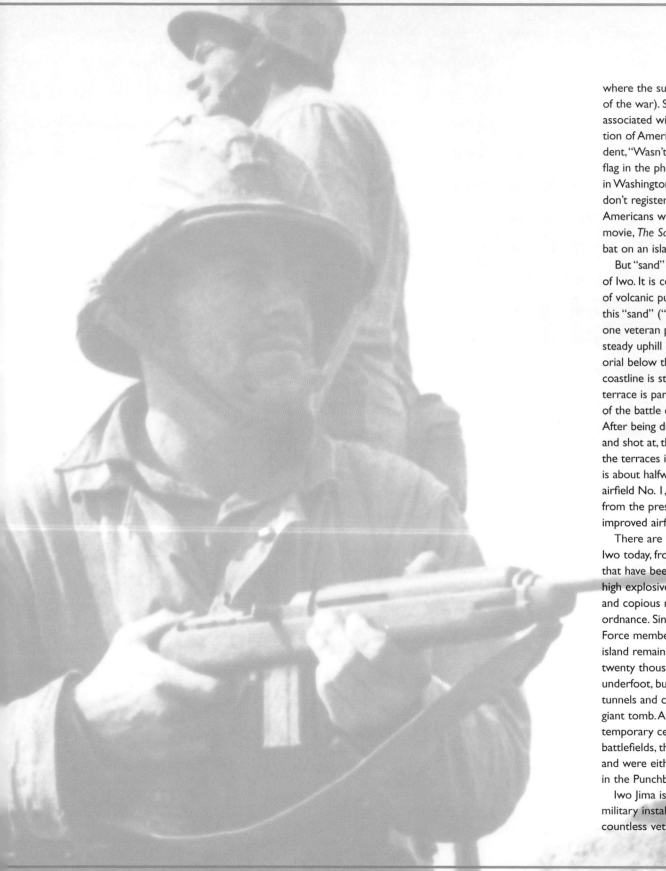

where the sunken *Arizona* still evokes powerful images of the war). So Iwo Jima has a chance at least of being associated with a Pacific battle by the younger generation of Americans. In the words of one high school student, "Wasn't Iwo Jima the place where they raised the flag in the photo, the one they made the statue out of in Washington?" If "the Picture" and "the Memorial" don't register in the collective consciousness, some Americans will at least remember the John Wayne movie, *The Sands of Iwo Jima,* and its depiction of combat on an island somewhere in the Pacific.

But "sand" is a misnomer for what covers the surface of Iwo. It is composed of gray-black, lightweight pellets of volcanic pumice. Visitors struggle to churn through this "sand" ("like climbing through a pile of wheat," as one veteran put it) and become quickly winded by the steady uphill climb from the surf line toward the memorial below the now-abandoned airfield No. 1. The coastline is still a series of terraces, and each successive terrace is part of that steady, steep uphill climb. Photos of the battle cannot convey the difficulty of this climb. After being dumped on the beach while being shelled and shot at, the Marines then had to fight uphill over the terraces into heavy direct fire. The battle memorial is about halfway up the climb from the surf line to airfield No. 1, along the east coast road that runs from the present-day airfield (a vastly expanded and improved airfield No. 2) to Mount Suribachi.

There are many remains of the battle to be seen on Iwo today, from uncovered tunnels, numerous caves that have been reopened after having been sealed by high explosives in 1945, bombed-out concrete bunkers, and copious numbers of dangerous unexploded ordnance. Since there are only a few Japanese Defense Force members stationed there now, by and large the island remains deserted. The corpses of most of the twenty thousand Japanese defenders lie somewhere underfoot, buried where they died in their countless tunnels and caves. For the Japanese, the island is one giant tomb. American dead were buried in several temporary cemeteries, but, as on other Pacific island battlefields, the bodies were removed after the war and were either sent home to relatives or reinterred in the Punchbowl Cemetery in Honolulu.

Iwo Jima is still there, off limits, a fortified Japanese military installation and tomb, and the subject of countless veterans' nightmares.

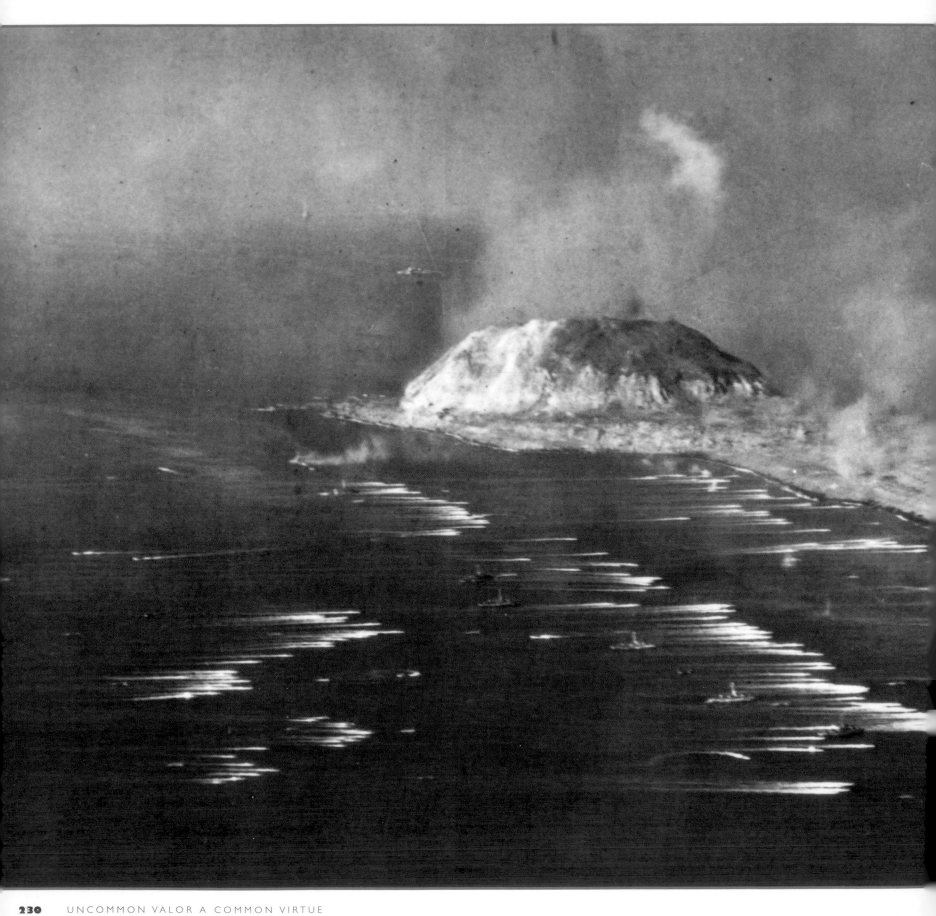

UNCOMMON VALOR A COMMON VIRTUE

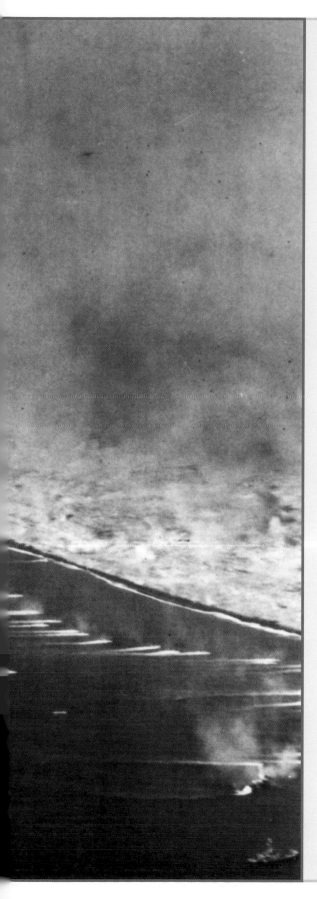

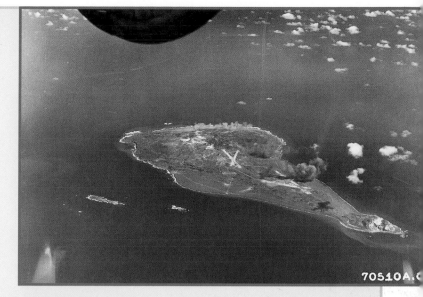

70510A.

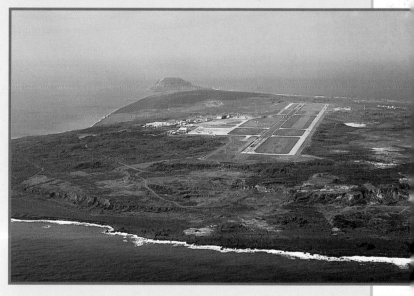

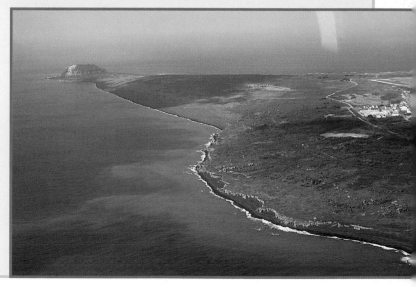

LEFT: The volcanic wasteland island of Iwo Jima was invaded on February 19, 1945, after it was decided that the island's airfields would prove invaluable for use in bombing the Japanese home islands. Iwo Jima lived up to its promise, providing fighter bases for protecting the B-29s over Japan. Even more important, nearly twenty-three hundred B-29s made emergency landings on Iwo Jima. Those landings saved the lives of an estimated twenty-five thousand men, far exceeding the cost of the nearly six thousand American lives needed to secure the island. This photo was one of the first of the Iwo Jima landings released to the media. The waves of amtracs carrying the invasion force can be seen heading in to the beaches. Mount Suribachi looms in the background.

TOP RIGHT: Aerial view of Iwo Jima looking from the southwest, taken by a crewman on a B-24 during a preinvasion bombing raid. Mount Suribachi is at lower right. The invasion beaches extend up from Suribachi on the right-hand (eastern) shore. The initial objectives of the invasion were Mount Suribachi and airfield No. 1, the southernmost of the two airfields, now abandoned. Farther toward the north is airfield No. 2, which has been expanded and is still in use today.

CENTER RIGHT: Aerial view of Iwo Jima today taken from the north end of the island looking south. The old airfield No. 2, now vastly expanded, is the only airstrip still in use today.

BOTTOM RIGHT: Of all the Pacific island battlefields, Iwo Jima is perhaps the least changed from its wartime appearance.

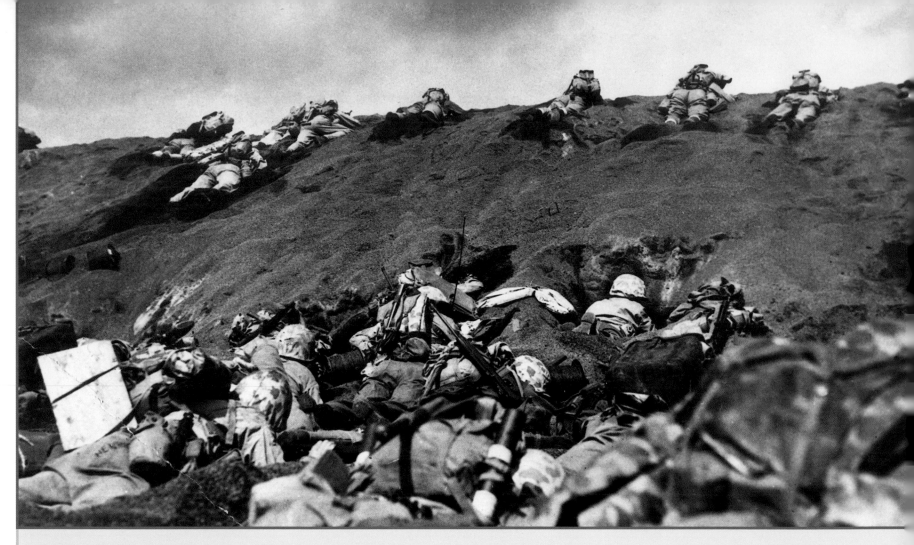

ABOVE: Upon landing, the Marines faced porous, coarse volcanic sand, steep beach terraces, and heavy Japanese fire. These Fifth Division Marines are pinned down just as they have landed.

BELOW LEFT: The gray-black sand and the beach terraces are virtually the same today. On the fiftieth anniversary this Marine veteran is scooping a souvenir sample of the sands of Iwo Jima to take home with him.

BELOW CENTER: Marines flattened on the beach by enemy fire from in front of them also had to contend with Japanese guns aimed at them from the heights of Mount Suribachi in the background. From the angle of the photo, the cameraman is certainly pressed very close to the beach.

BELOW RIGHT: Mount Suribachi looms over the invasion beaches, little changed from 1945.

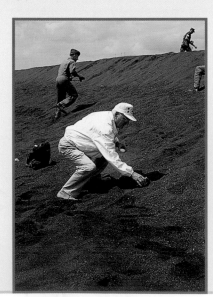

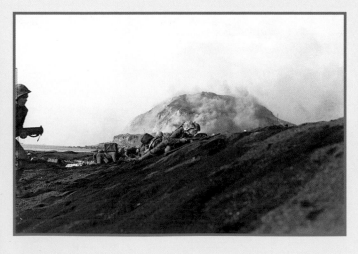

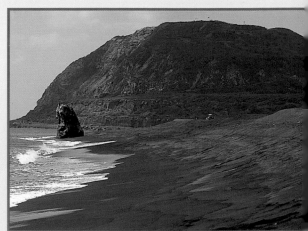

RIGHT: The enemy fire was so intense that Marines were pinned down immediately after coming ashore, even as more men and equipment pressed in behind them. These Fourth Division Marines are temporarily stalled midmorning of D-Day.

BELOW: With enemy fire coming from ahead and from Mount Suribachi on their Left, these Fourth Division Marines faced a steady uphill climb toward airfield No. 1 straight ahead of them.

RIGHT CENTER: Those same invasion beaches on the fiftieth anniversary, with U.S. Marine veterans pinned down by TV film crews.

RIGHT BOTTOM: After a visit to the invasion beaches, present-day visitors are usually surprised by the climb back up to the coast road that runs just below the elevation of abandoned airfield No. 1.

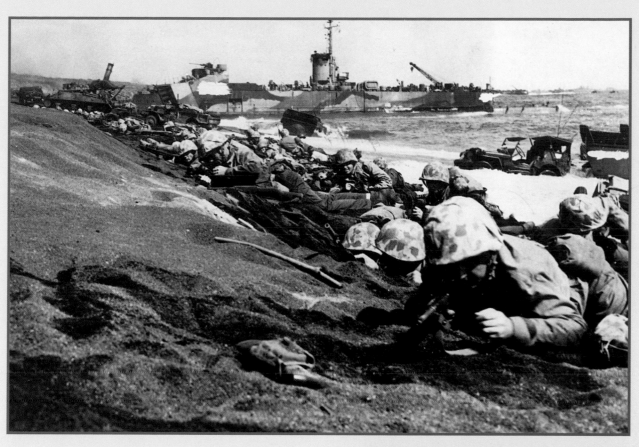

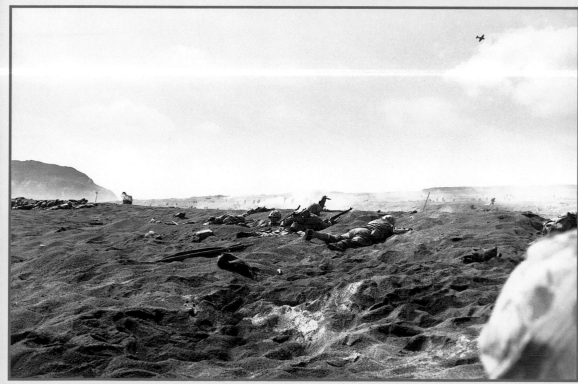

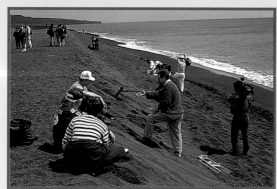

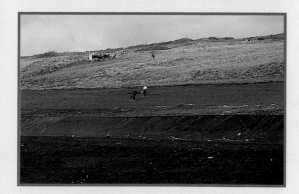

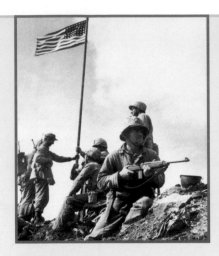

An American patrol fought its way to the top of Mount Suribachi four days after the initial landing and raised a small U.S. flag as fighting raged on the beaches and barren volcanic no-man's-land below. Here is the scene photographer Lou Lowery captured on the top of Suribachi just after the first flag was raised at 10:35 A.M. Chuck Lindberg, standing at back right, ended up being the only member of either flag-raising team to live to see the twenty-first century.

RIGHT: Even though the first flag could be seen from the landing beaches, it was judged to be too small, and a second patrol was sent to the top of Suribachi later that morning with a larger flag. Photographer Joe Rosenthal and movie cameraman Bill Genaust were standing next to each other, and both captured the scene four hours after the first flag-raising. This photo of the second flag-raising became one of the most memorable images of World War II. Even though the two flag-raisings occurred four days after the initial landings, bitter fighting continued for more than a month, until all but 216 of the twenty thousand Japanese defenders were dead.

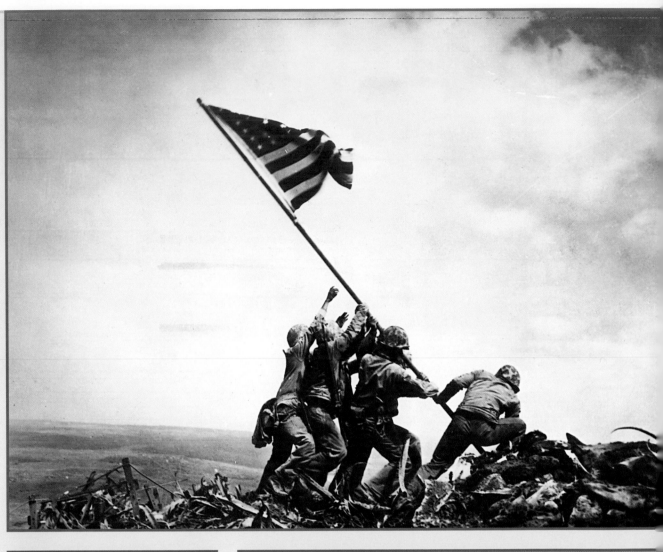

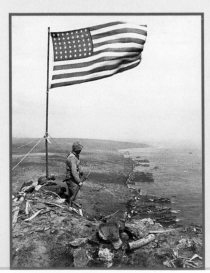

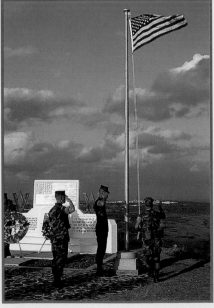

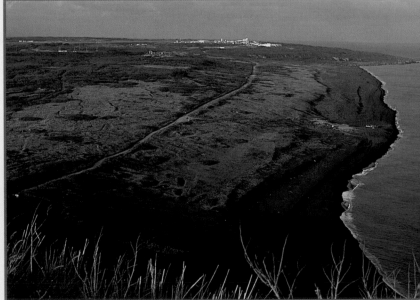

OPPOSITE BOTTOM LEFT: With the battle raging on in the grueling American drive toward the north end of the island, the U.S. flag flew from the summit of Mount Suribachi as more troops and equipment were unloaded on the beaches below.

OPPOSITE BOTTOM CENTER: Today, a number of monuments stand atop Mount Suribachi. Americans erected this one in late 1945 on the site where the two flags were raised. On the fiftieth anniversary of the battle, this Marine honor guard commemorated the flag-raisings of February 1945.

OPPOSITE BOTTOM RIGHT: Though some of the scrub vegetation has grown back and the landing craft have long since departed, little else has changed this view of the landing beaches from the summit of Suribachi.

RIGHT: The fighting moved inland and turned northward, leaving dead Marines (such as the one in the foreground) and abandoned equipment on the beaches.

BELOW LEFT: With no safe "rear area" on Iwo, and since artillery could rain down at any time, there was never a good time to do it, but parties of Marines, including Frank Didier, were formed early on to start collecting the bodies.

BELOW RIGHT: The beaches today are clear of wreckage, but the steep slope and volcanic pumice sand are the same.

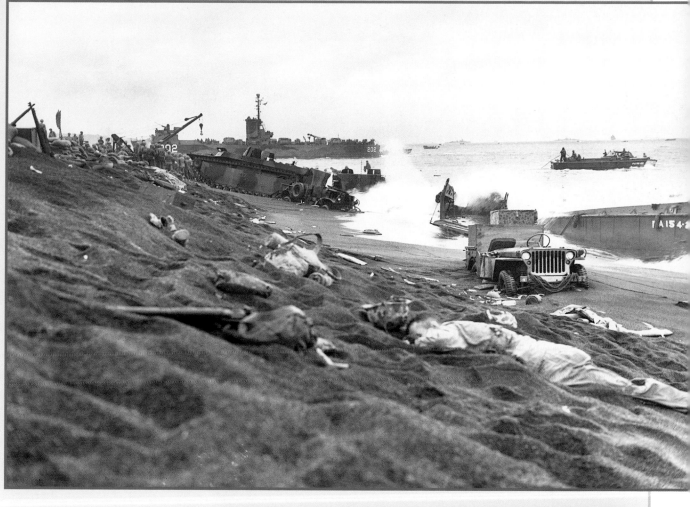

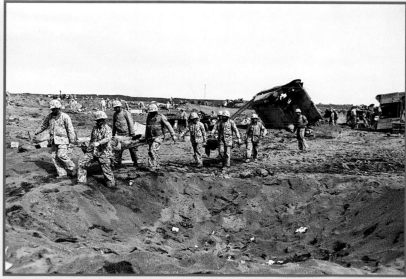

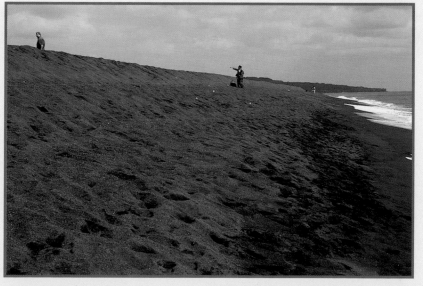

RIGHT: On March 4, while the fighting continued just north of airstrip No. 1, this B-29, *Dinah Might,* became the first of the big bombers to make an emergency landing on Iwo. The crew had a problem transferring fuel from one tank to another coming back from a mission over Japan and they were running short on gas. Instead of ditching in the ocean, they decided to set the plane down on four thousand feet of freshly graded runway. Prior to that, Marine artillery spotter planes, like the one in the foreground, had been able to use part of the runway. It was quite an occasion, and anyone who could get away from duties around the airstrip ran over to

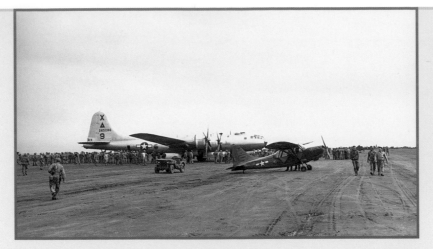

take a close-up look at the reason they were fighting for the island. The problem fixed, the plane gunned the engines on the far south end and barely made it off the ground, using all of the four thousand feet of completed runway. On April 12, 1945, this same plane made another emergency landing on Iwo. One crewman was left behind to supervise repairs while the others were flown back to the Marianas. Though the crew dodged the proverbial bullet with not one but two life-saving emergency landings, all but the one left on Iwo were killed on combat missions within six weeks. *Dinah Might* survived the war and ended up being scrapped in Arizona.

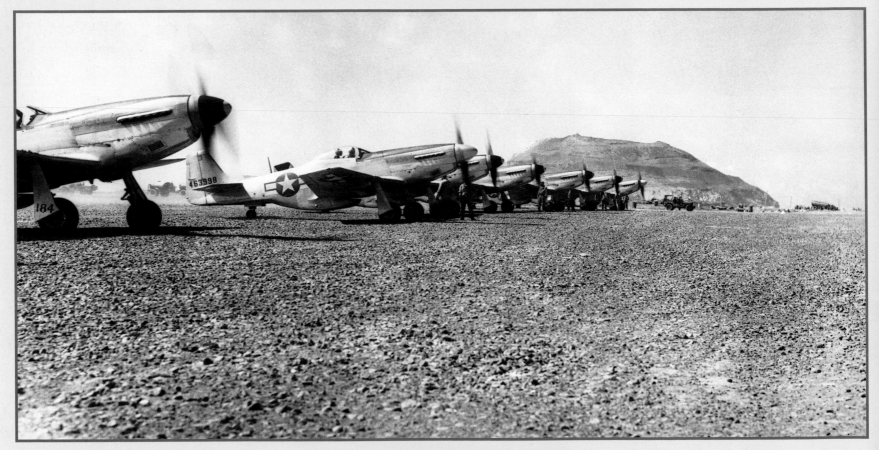

ABOVE: By mid-March, airfield No. 1 was home to P-51 fighter escorts, seen here warming up before flying a mission. Iwo provided the capability for the B-29s to have fighter escort over Japan. This view, looking south, shows Mount Suribachi in the distance. The new road being constructed to the summit can be seen switchbacking up the side.

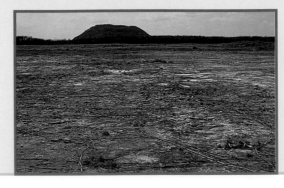

LEFT: The Americans developed and used both Japanese airfields (sometimes referred to as Motoyama No. 1 and Motoyama No. 2, their Japanese designations) for the rest of the war. Airfield No. 1, shown here, was subsequently abandoned after the war in favor of the larger available area for runways and base facilities provided by airfield No. 2, which is still in use today.

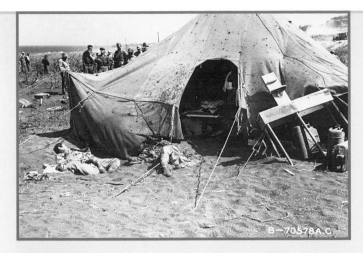

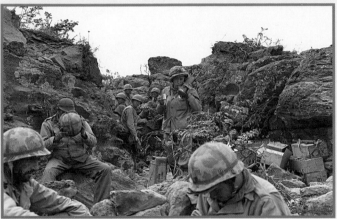

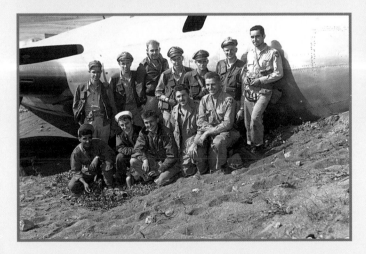

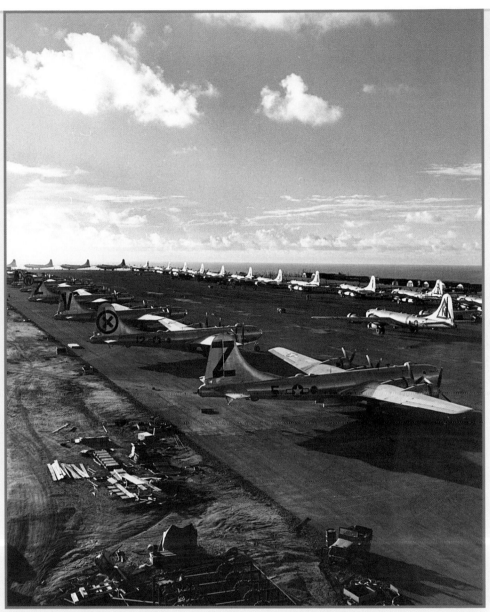

TOP LEFT: Aftermath of the final organized Japanese attack of the battle. Several hundred of the remaining Japanese defenders stormed an area near airstrip No. 2 and killed sleeping fighter pilots in their tents in the early morning hours of March 26. Here, two of the attackers lie where they fell. The one on the right held a grenade to his chest and pulled the pin. Before the chaos and confusion was over, the

Twenty-first Fighter Group had lost forty-four pilots killed in action, and the remains of nearly three hundred Japanese littered the tent area.

CENTER LEFT: Command post of the Twenty-eighth Marines on the north end of Iwo near the end of the battle. The Americans were driven from this location the day before, but fought back to reoccupy the position. These were the men who paid the price to save endangered air crews.

BOTTOM LEFT: With two engines knocked out over Tokyo, this crew crash-landed their B-29 on Iwo. Someone computed that all the crewmembers on all the B-29s that made emergency landings on Iwo totaled nearly twenty-five thousand lives saved.

ABOVE: When there was a big firebomb raid over Japan, you could count on plenty of emergency landings on Iwo. By morning, this would be a typical scene. Scores of B-29s from many different groups (indicated by the variety of tail markings) would land overnight. Many simply had run low on fuel. Others limped in with battle damage, some with engines shot out, still more with various mechanical malfunctions or wounded who needed emergency medical attention. The Marines had paid the price, but scenes such as this proved that it had been worth it. There were 2,251 emergency landings on Iwo by war's end.

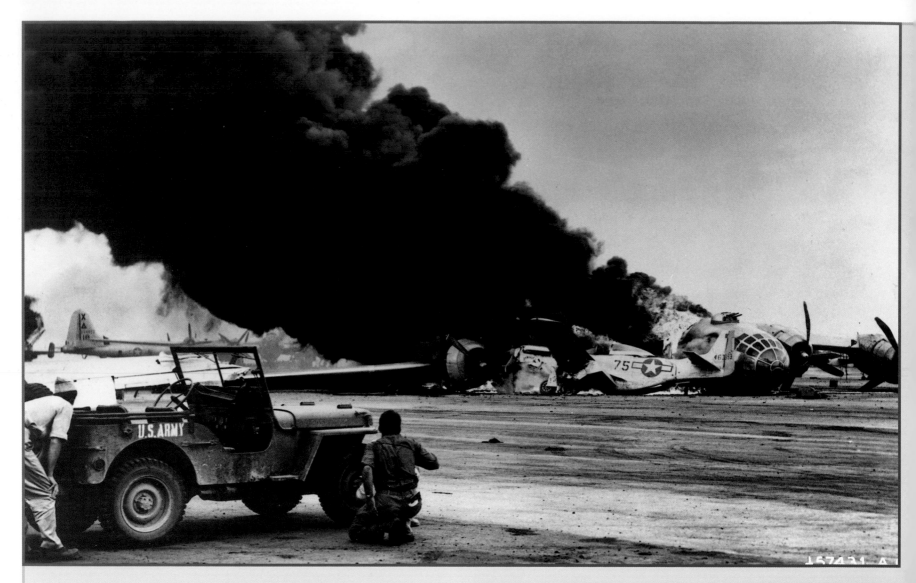

ABOVE: Believe it or not, the entire flight crew of this B-29 walked away from this crash. Survivor Rueben Best told the story: "I was on my first mission to Japan as a B-29 waist gunner. We were hit over the target and the plane in front of us blew up. We lost the rudder and the two engines on the left side, and limped to Iwo to make an emergency landing. We made two passes at airfield No. 1 and our pilot was having trouble controlling the drift of the plane. We would be all over the place on our approach, and people on the ground were worried we would drift into the tents and P-51s parked next to the runway. On our last approach, someone on the ground made the decision to drive a D-8 bulldozer onto the runway to 'stop' us. Our pilot couldn't believe his eyes but by then we were too low and couldn't pull up. He tried to skip the plane over the bulldozer but we clipped it and skidded into a row of P-51s

next to the runway. That's just what they were afraid we would do, but it was their bulldozer that caused us to crash! The plane broke apart as we slid to a stop. My knee was hurt, but as the plane started to burn I crawled out through a break in the fuselage. The guys up front got burned, and they put me in a hospital on Iwo. Our pilot had trouble with that bulldozer decision for a long time. I still can't believe they did such a stupid thing. My left leg was a mess, and they shipped me to an Army hospital on Saipan. But they thought my leg was in good enough shape to give me a helmet and gun, and they almost sent me to fight as infantry on Okinawa! That didn't interest me much, so I got a chaplain to intervene and finally got sent back to Tinian to be a gun instructor."

RIGHT: B-29 waist gunner Rueben Best sets foot on Iwo Jima in 1995 for the first time in

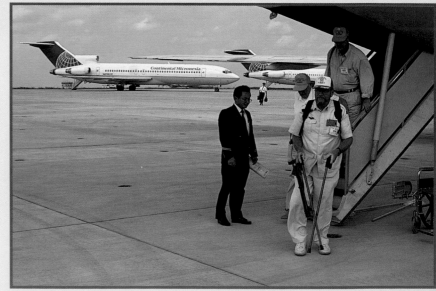

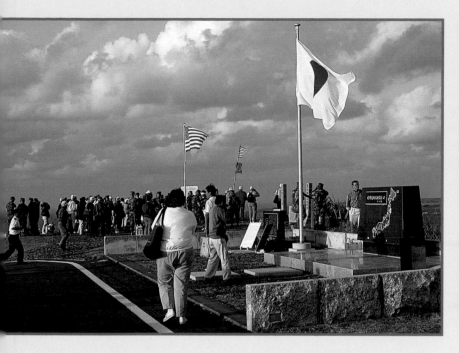

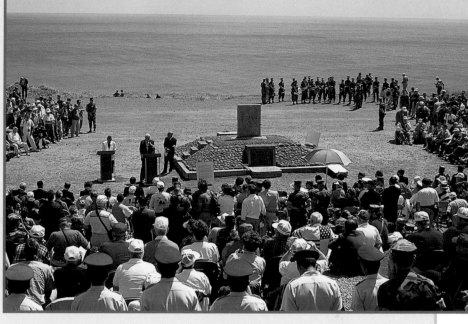

fifty years. His knee, injured during his crash landing on Iwo, continued to bother him after the war until he finally had knee replacement surgery in 1994. He walked onto the runway on Iwo in 1995 with the help of canes, but he was alive. One of the Marine veterans on the trip asked if he thought his first and only mission was unlucky. "Bad luck?" Rube replied with a smile. "Well, if it hadn't been for Iwo I probably wouldn't be here at all, so maybe that was good luck."

ABOVE LEFT: The fiftieth anniversary of the battle for Iwo Jima saw one of the largest

collections of Americans on the island since World War II. This was the scene on the summit of Mount Suribachi as Army, Navy, Air Force, and Marine veterans, each with some specific tie to Iwo and many accompanied by spouses or adult children, crowded around the Japanese memorials (foreground) and the U.S. memorial (background) on the spot where the two flag-raisings took place.

ABOVE RIGHT: American and Japanese veterans participated in the fiftieth anniversary rededication of a memorial above the invasion beaches first erected on the fortieth anniversary.

BELOW LEFT: A U.S. veteran inspects a recently opened Japanese tunnel. A combination of live and spent ammunition and other artifacts lay scattered near the entrance. Iwo is honeycombed with such tunnels, the vast majority of which remain sealed, untouched since the war.

BELOW CENTER: Veterans who visited Iwo on the fiftieth anniversary brought an assortment of mementos with them. Some wore their green Marine Corps shirts, some with rips or holes, reminders of the wounds that were their tickets off the island. One Marine

veteran wore his old dress blues. Homer Cross, standing here on the beach he landed on fifty years before, brought a unique reminder of how lucky he was. A Japanese bullet entered and exited his helmet but only grazed his skull.

BELOW RIGHT: Marine veteran Jack Rasmussen brought a different kind of remembrance to Iwo, a roster of his company listing all the names, most with the notation "wounded in action" or "killed in action." Out of forty men in his platoon, only two walked off Iwo unharmed.

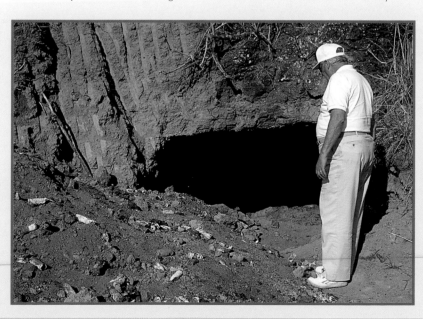

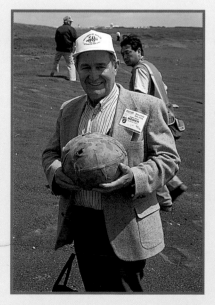

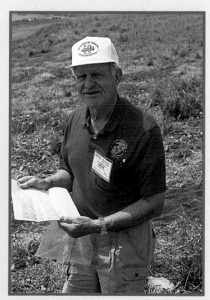

ONE OF THE IRONIES of the Pacific war was that very few Americans could actually communicate with the Japanese, even though tens of thousands were locked in deadly contact with them. Two small groups of Americans eventually would provide the only practical avenues of communication. Ethnic Nisei, first-generation descendents of Japanese immigrants and themselves U.S. citizens, were often recruited as interpreters from the detention camps where many Japanese-Americans were rounded up after the war started. They became the main Japanese language interpreters for the U.S. Army and were mostly enlisted men. Recruited from a camp in Minnesota, Army interpreter Minoru Hara, in an interview for the 1989 film, *The Color of Honor* by Loni Ding, recalled that, "When I left the camp there must have been a lot of people saying I'm a stupid fool, especially when I'd had [U.S. Army sentry] guns pointed at me several times. Yet, I volunteered. This is the only country I have." Army Intelligence first set up a secret school in an old warehouse at the Presidio in San Francisco (it was subsequently moved to Minnesota), teaching the Nisei volunteers contemporary Japanese and Japanese military language.

The Marines, on the other hand, relied mainly on caucasian Japanese Language Officers. Some "JLOs," as they were called, had studied Japanese or other oriental languages in college. Others were missionary kids who had grown up in Asia and were already fluent in either Japanese or Chinese. But many had no prior knowledge of Japanese, and almost all had to receive special training. Much as the Army had done in San Francisco, the Navy set up a Japanese language school at the University of Colorado in Boulder. Bob Sheeks, a JLO graduate of the school at Boulder, recalled that "they were looking for anyone who had experience in oriental language to take a crash course in Japanese. I told them my interest was in Chinese. They said that was not their priority, but they were desperate for people to learn Japanese, so I said OK."

The Nisei volunteers, most of whom had grown up speaking Japanese at home, had an obvious advantage when it came to being interpreters. But there were other problems in sending ethnic Japanese into a war zone where the mentality of American combatants was to kill any Japanese they saw. As Manny Goldberg, an Army Intelligence officer who worked with the

Nisei interpreters, recalled in *The Color of Honor,* "One thing I was afraid of was that the Marines were gonna shoot at our boys because they shot at anything that moved that looked Oriental." Harry Fukuhara, a volunteer from an internment camp at Gila River, Arizona, remembered one solution to this problem in the film, *The Color of Honor:* "When it came time for a landing we all were assigned a bodyguard. It was very tough for them because they had to stay with us twenty-four hours a day. We slept in the same foxholes, ate together, even went to the latrine together, and when we were working they were always nearby. A couple of times I was mistaken for a Japanese soldier. On New Britain all of a sudden this one soldier looked up and aimed his rifle at me. I started talking to him, and the more I talked the more he got confused!"

JLO Sheeks, who had grown up in China, was recruited while studying at Harvard, and he had a particular motivation to fight the Japanese in the Pacific. "I hated the Japanese. I had seen what they had done in China. The Japanese were cruel, bestial. The Japanese soldiers were horrible at times. One could stomach their arrogance, but the needless torture—a lot of it was private torture. They would capture the servants of foreigners who had left and would torture them to find out where valuables were hidden. They would torture them to death.... I hated them. So I get in this Japanese language training [in Boulder] and who is training me but Japanese Americans, some of the nicest people I'd ever met, respectable, decent, and kind, and good teachers. They were doing more for the war effort than I ever did in the Marine Corps reserve, training us to go out and fight people of their same ancestry, and taking painstaking efforts and doing all of this in spite of the fact that they had relatives who were dispossessed and sent into camps and losing their family's life savings in California. When I saw Japanese films that had been confiscated for training, and I read about Japanese history and culture, I thought, hey, the Japanese aren't so bad except for these militaristic totalitarian types. So pretty soon I was willing to keep hating Tojo and the Emperor but not every Japanese."

Though Sheeks and other JLOs had enlightened attitudes toward the Japanese, most other Marines were usually not so inclined. "A major task, curiously, was to lecture to as many Marines as possible about

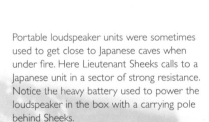

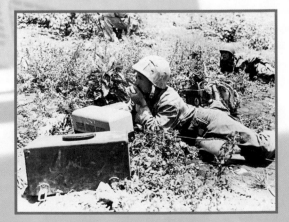

Portable loudspeaker units were sometimes used to get close to Japanese caves when under fire. Here Lieutenant Sheeks calls to a Japanese unit in a sector of strong resistance. Notice the heavy battery used to power the loudspeaker in the box with a carrying pole behind Sheeks.

the need and importance of taking prisoners alive," Sheeks said. "The reasoning had to be cast in terms of saving Marine lives, but the attitude of many was that of skepticism, like, 'To hell with catching Japanese for the intelligence unit. It's safer and our job to kill the enemy first.' Also, our boys were so influenced by stories of how treacherous the Japanese were, that they were even nervous about the possibility that women and children would carry grenades and blow up any American near by."

While educating Americans about capturing enemy Japanese alive was a concern for the white JLOs, a great fear for the Nisei interpreters was being captured alive by the Japanese. After his battalion was cut off during a pitched battle with the Japanese, Technical Sergeant Howard Furamoto described, in *The Color of Honor,* what interpreter team leader Bob Honda did next. "After we'd survived numerous banzai charges, he went around to each interpreter in his group and said to them, 'If it appears we're going to be captured, I'm saving a bullet for each one of you rather than have you be captured and tortured.'"

The duties of the Army and Marine interpreters nominally centered on interrogating prisoners and translating captured documents. However, another role for interpreters soon emerged. They were put in the position of actually trying to save enemy lives by convincing Japanese to surrender.

The Pacific war was often characterized by differences in cultural attitudes and behavior, and this was especially true in regard to surrender. After taking part in the Tarawa invasion, Bob Sheeks noticed, "the Japanese did not know how to surrender. It was apparent to me that we could have obtained more prisoners had they known a bit more. The Japanese top brass had indoctrinated the troops that no Japanese in all of history ever surrendered. In case any one was captured they wouldn't be Japanese any more. They were not imbued with our common knowledge that you use white flags, raise your hands above your head, etc."

Sheeks and a few other JLOs decided to remedy this situation in hopes of getting more Japanese to surrender, although they were unsure at first of how their efforts would pan out. "The whole idea at the time seemed outlandish to most Marines, as everyone was convinced that no Japanese would surrender,"

Sheeks said. One of their first attempts was at Saipan. "Methods included the design and printing of 'surrender passes,' and of instructions on surrender procedure," Sheeks recalled. "The whole effort was very amateurish and almost a private venture initiative of several JLOs. I also improvised methods of 'delivery' of the leaflets, methods that were informal to say the least. There was no provision for such activity, but some friends who were aerial spotters for artillery agreed on an 'old-pal' basis to eject leaflets out of planes on call. They would heave bundles out over certain map coordinates over Saipan, and later Tinian. It was crude, but it worked surprisingly well and got good results." Since the official policy of the Marine Corps was to kill Japanese, Sheeks and the other JLOs had to devise such surrender stratagems on their own, with little support, initially, from higher levels. "As there were no official funds available," Sheeks remarked, "the only financial source for the work was the Division's recreation budget, from which funds were diverted to pay for leaflets and loudspeaker equipment for voice beaming to Japanese in fortified emplacements and caves."

The "voice beaming" turned out to be a practical solution to a problem in communicating first encountered at Tarawa. "You could try shouting, but shouting in a foreign language is not easy, and there is a lot of other noise going on anyway during a battle. We realized that if you had a loudspeaker, you could be farther back, behind an obstacle, and your voice could still be heard." This idea was not well supported early on by the Marine brass, and the JLOs again had to improvise. "We got the speakers from the recreation department and mounted them on jeeps," Sheeks recalled. "Ours worked very well on numerous occasions. Our goal or expectation was never to get a mass exodus, but I felt we were doing well if we could get ten or fifteen people out at a time."

Yamauchi Takeo, a member of the Forty-third Division of the Japanese Army, was in a cave in the far north of Saipan near the end of the battle. He recalled, in H. and T. Cooks' book, *Japan at War,* that ". . . the Americans began to broadcast surrender advice over loudspeakers. . . . 'Japanese forces! Throw down your arms! We will protect the honor of those who have fought hard and who give themselves up. We have water. We have food.' Their Japanese was a little shaky.

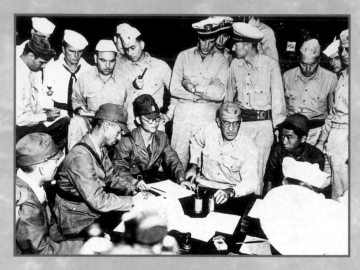

Army Nisei interpreter Sergeant Larry Watanabe (seated at right in baseball cap) translates the Japanese surrender proceedings on Wake Island on September 4, 1945. Japanese Wake Island commander Rear Admiral Shigematsu Sakaibara (later executed for war crimes) signs the surrender document, while Brigadier General Lawson Sanderson (seated to the right of Watanabe) and Colonel Walter Baylor (in back row with pipe, the last man to leave Wake during the siege in 1941 and the first American to set foot back on the island in 1945) look on.

Whenever possible, JLOs enlisted the aid of people who had already surrendered to convince others to come out. Here two Korean laborers have agreed to try to talk a group of Japanese soldiers in a cave in the cliffs in the distance into surrendering. One young Japanese finally came out under heavy fire from his comrades. Then the surrendered man went back and convinced the rest to surrender.

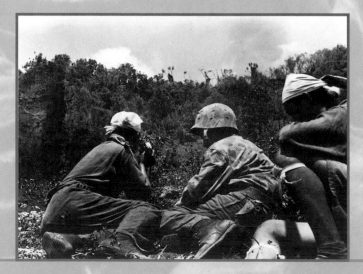

That was the first time I heard an American call to surrender." He feared being shot by his fellow soldiers if he tried to give himself up, but later surrendered successfully and survived the war.

In spite of prior expectations to the contrary, thousands of Japanese civilians and military surrendered on Saipan and Tinian. "It would not be an exaggeration to say that the combination of leaflets, loudspeaker, and patrol work greatly increased the number of Japanese civilians and military who were saved from unnecessary death," said Sheeks. "Unquestionably American lives were also saved, as there were instances in which a person who surrendered supplied valuable information about fortified emplacements and caves still being manned by resisting troops. Occasionally the resisters were induced to surrender. At other times the fighting continued, but we had the advantage of knowledge about exact locations, weapons, fire lanes, safe approaches, number of enemy, etc."

However, despite the best efforts of the JLOs, surrender was just not an option for some Japanese. "I could sometimes converse at fairly close quarters with troops who would not surrender nor allow civilians with them to come out," Sheeks remarked. "I was all for trying the next day again, but the military imperative was to push on. So out came the grenades, satchel charges, and flamethrowers. It was heartbreaking at times, but wonderful if we were successful in getting them to surrender peacefully."

Sheeks went on to describe an unsuccessful attempt. "One time right at the edge of the Marpi airport [on Saipan], there was a vertical hole in the ground. I don't know why it was there; maybe it was a natural formation, almost at the edge of the airstrip. Some guys were walking along with me doing our work, and they heard something and said to me, 'There are some Nips down there.' And sure enough I could see two of them sitting down there in this hole. So I started talking to them. I tried the usual spiel, come on out, the war is over, you will be given food and medical treatment, we have a camp, and so on, and that we couldn't allow them to stay there, we had orders, we don't want to hurt you, please put down your weapons and come on out. They were apathetic. They sort of mumbled to each other, and then suddenly I saw, or half saw, a kind of quick motion, and I figured, uh-oh, they are going to shoot

or something. These other guys were sort of looking down, so I instinctively pushed them back and sure enough the Japanese blew themselves up. And that's not the only time that happened. They just blew themselves up. So we went back and looked down there, and what a mess."

Cross-cultural communication differences could run both ways, and Bob Sheeks encountered just such a situation at Tinian. "We captured a Japanese petty officer who was extremely helpful at great personal risk in working with me to get Japanese out of caves and to surrender. After several days of really heroic help from him, an irate Japanese soldier who refused to surrender shot him. Fortunately the petty officer was not killed, but his forearm was shattered. Our commander, Colonel David Shoup (later to become Marine Corps Commandant), heard about this and was curious to know why a Japanese would do what he did, helping me to get Japanese to surrender. It made no sense to him at all. So I was to conduct an interview by Shoup with this Japanese enigma, which I did. It was a very strange conversation indeed. Colonel Shoup had the bluntest of questions, which pained me. For example, 'Ask this Jap why he is a traitor.' Shoup wanted simple answers and was impatient with complex replies. The fact of the matter was that the Japanese was an educated man, independent of thought, and very brave. He thought well of what I was trying to do. He had seen that surrenders were being handled with some dignity and no brutality. He felt that death was a senseless choice for those who had fought as well as possible, and was especially senseless for innocent civilians. Colonel Shoup remained mystified and said to me afterward, 'We are wasting time. We will never know what makes these Nips tick!' Shoup was a terrifically able and effective commander, and a powerful fighting Marine leader. The Japanese petty officer happened to be an intelligent, humanistic person, keeping his dignity in a situation of utter and devastating defeat. It was a mismatch of minds, with no communication. Language was not the barrier."

First Lieutenant Robert B. Sheeks was later awarded the Bronze Star for his work in effecting enemy surrenders on Saipan and Tinian, becoming, as he put it, "one of the very few persons who was decorated during the war in the Pacific for saving enemy lives!"

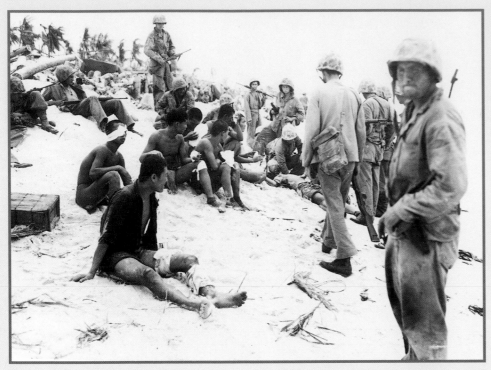

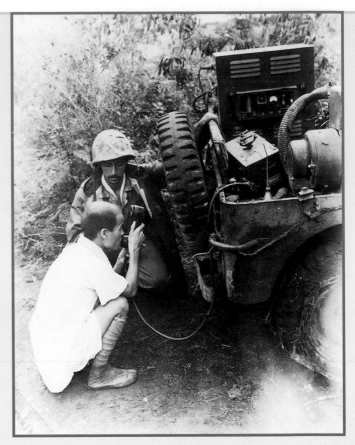

ABOVE: Japanese Language Officer Bob Sheeks (kneeling at center back) with a Japanese prisoner at Tarawa. "They were collecting a few prisoners and we had MPs who were bringing them along to the beach," he recalled. "I tried to interrogate quickly the ones who were dying to see what they knew before they died, and then I helped out with the others and got them water and cigarettes. Eventually these prisoners went out to a ship, and my job was to accompany them to Pearl. I questioned them en route, and they later proved useful in helping to identify structures in aerial and submarine recon photos."

ABOVE RIGHT: JLO Sheeks (in helmet) assists a Japanese civilian to broadcast surrender appeals from a jeep-mounted loudspeaker (at right) during the Tinian campaign.

RIGHT: One of the makeshift jeep-mounted loudspeakers used to talk the Japanese into surrendering during the Marianas campaign.

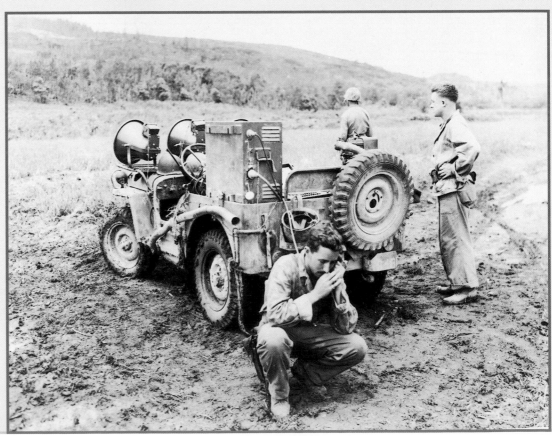

A lost child uses a portable loud-speaker held by JLO Sheeks to call out to her parents who are holed up in a cave with a group of Japanese civilians and soldiers. It was the end of the day and the anxious Marines in the trucks needed to get back to the security line. The little girl wanted to stay, pleading in Japanese, "Just one more try."

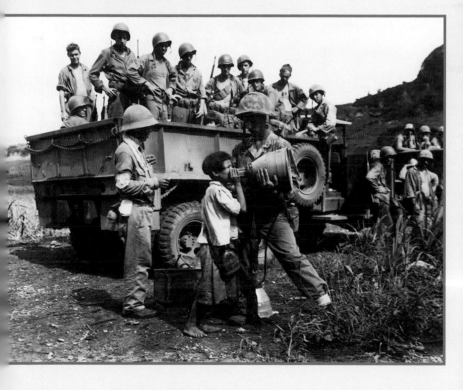

RIGHT: The payoff. A Japanese soldier and little girl have just been talked into surrendering. Suspicious Marines in the background are not fully convinced.

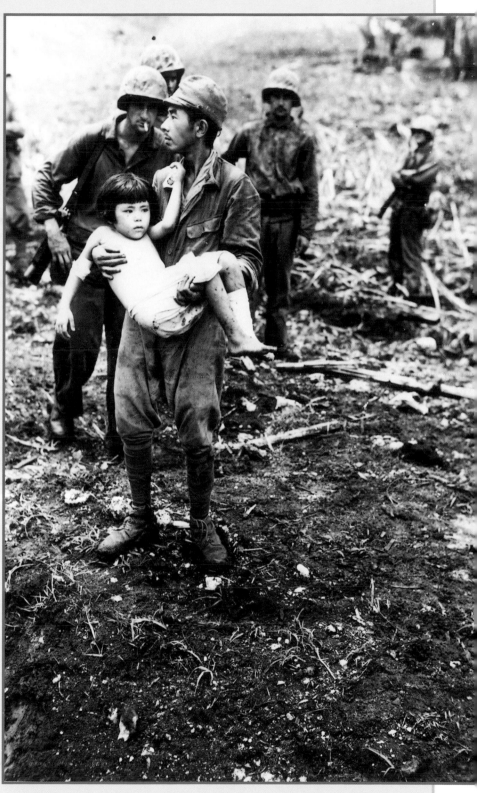

AS WORLD WAR II swept through Europe, many large civilian populations were devastated and brutalized. In the Pacific as well, war had traumatic though less-publicized effects on native populations. Since many islanders had little if any previous contact with the outside world, some of the cultural and societal impacts of the war were understandably life altering. So-called "cargo cults" either were reinforced or sprang up from scratch on several islands, and some have survived to this day. These cults arose to help islanders deal with the sudden, unfathomable appearance of large numbers of white men with incredible amounts of "cargo"—machinery, vehicles, and amazing goods of all descriptions—that natives had either only seen before in limited examples or not at all. Some islands lightly colonized before the war experienced massive intrusions of foreign men and matériel. Many islands were fortified by the foreigners, and a number were subsequently blasted with high explosives of all types and invaded. Some became bases where airstrips were built and airplanes materialized seemingly out of thin air to land on them. To islanders unfamiliar with twentieth-century mechanized society, all of this was quite baffling and intriguing.

Some islander populations were displaced from their ancestral villages to make way for the outsiders and their bases. Other islanders became scouts or provided labor for the armies. They proved invaluable aides in the tropical jungles in a climate that was taxing for both Allied and Japanese forces. Still others were killed or injured in the bombing and fighting, or were brutalized or otherwise became victims of atrocities. Whatever the degree of exposure, the delimited topography of most islands made it impossible to completely escape what was going on.

After the war Pacific islanders built up oral histories of their wartime experiences, and only recently has a concerted effort begun to record these spoken accounts. As with participants from Allied nations and Japan, the war was usually the central event in the lives of those who experienced or witnessed it. On many of the islands, the war also marked the beginning of a more extensive involvement with western societies and economies, and the end of living in traditional isolation.

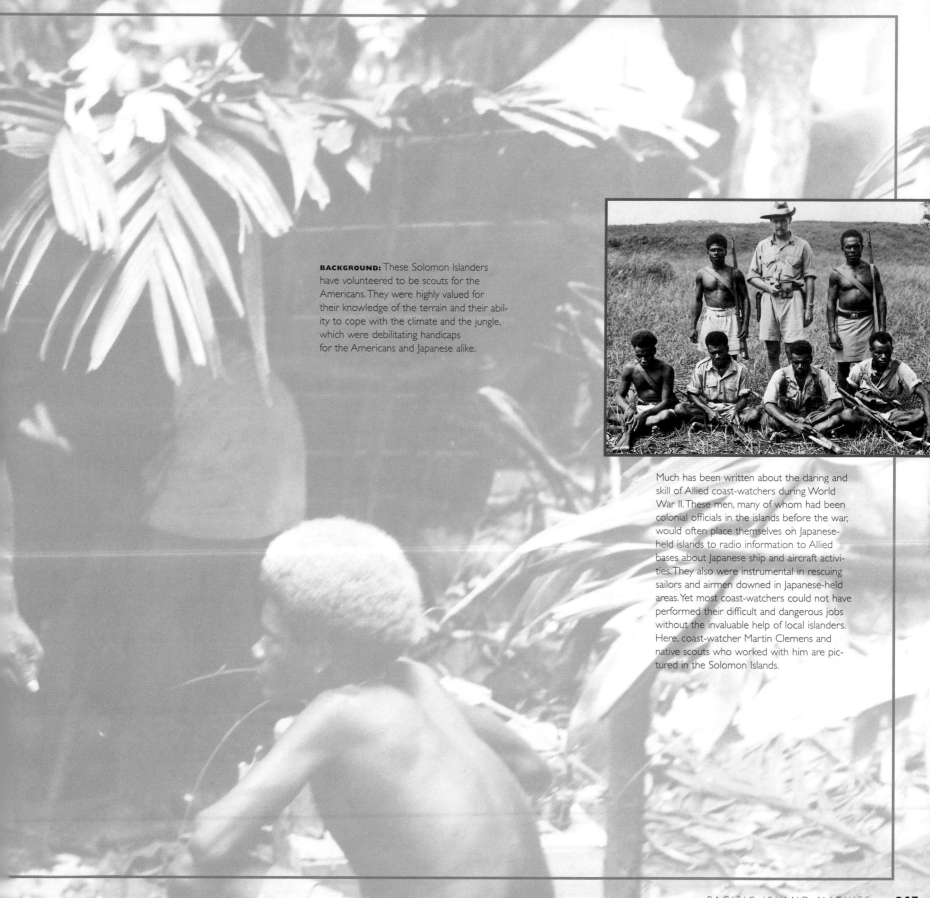

BACKGROUND: These Solomon Islanders have volunteered to be scouts for the Americans. They were highly valued for their knowledge of the terrain and their ability to cope with the climate and the jungle, which were debilitating handicaps for the Americans and Japanese alike.

Much has been written about the daring and skill of Allied coast-watchers during World War II. These men, many of whom had been colonial officials in the islands before the war, would often place themselves on Japanese-held islands to radio information to Allied bases about Japanese ship and aircraft activities. They also were instrumental in rescuing sailors and airmen downed in Japanese-held areas. Yet most coast-watchers could not have performed their difficult and dangerous jobs without the invaluable help of local islanders. Here, coast-watcher Martin Clemens and native scouts who worked with him are pictured in the Solomon Islands.

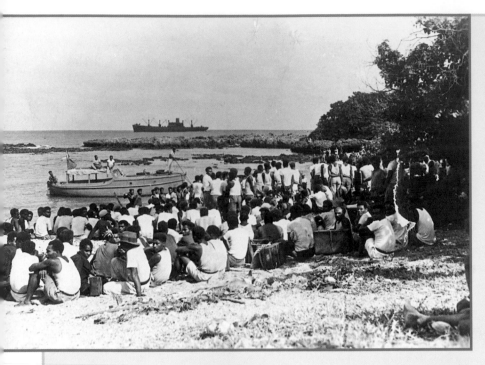

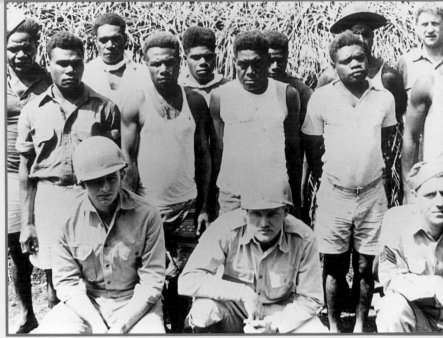

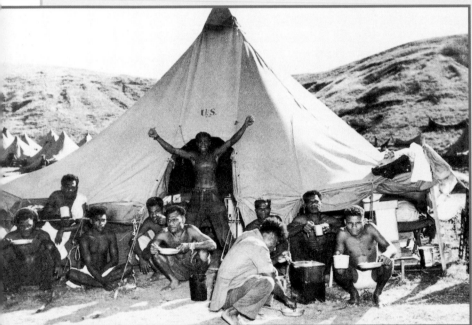

TOP LEFT: A more common islander experience was to perform labor either for the Japanese or later the Allies. In the New Hebrides (now the independent nation of Vanuatu), men were extensively recruited from several different islands to work for the Americans on Efate and Espiritu Santo. This photo shows islanders waiting on the beach on Tanna Island in 1942 to board the ship in the distance, the USS *Cape Flattery,* for the trip to Efate to begin work.

TOP RIGHT: On Efate these men from Tanna Island pose with several of their American supervisors. Many returned to their home island after the war and became part of the "John Frum" cargo cult, one of a number of cults that sprang up in the Pacific. The Tanna group believes there was an American named John Frum who came to the islands with much cargo. Before he left after the war, Frum was supposed to have promised the people of Tanna that one day they too would have all the cargo he possessed if they strictly adhered to their old pre-European customs.

LEFT: Island laborers in a U.S. Army camp on New Caledonia.

OPPOSITE TOP LEFT: Tuk Nauau, shown on Tanna Island in 1976, was a young man when he worked for the Americans on Efate during the war. He typified John Frum cargo cult members in that he believed this American would return to Tanna if the islanders adhered to their traditional customs, including wearing native attire. Tuk was anxious to find out if visitors were American, for if they were, he encouraged that photos be taken. He reasoned that John Frum would see them some day in America and realize that the people of Tanna were maintaining their customs. Frum might then be convinced to return as promised and give the islanders much cargo. Note the American quarter around Tuk's neck and the nonfunctional pocket watch hanging from his hip. Tuk explained that such small items were given to him by Americans during the war, and should John Frum happen to see him in a photo wearing these items, it will be remembered that Tuk is a "friend of man America." Tuk asked occasional American visitors if they thought John Frum would return. An American anthropologist studying the John Frum people always answered that oft-asked question with the reply, "Who knows what the future may bring?" Since the war, the John Frum cult on Tanna has become a politically unifying force to be reckoned with. Its adherents played a significant role in the tumultuous birth of the new nation of Vanuatu in 1980.

OPPOSITE CENTER LEFT: This former native coast-watcher, who introduces himself congenially as Falavi, is pictured in a 1981 photo in his home on Vaitupu, an atoll in the Ellice Islands (now the country of Tuvalu). During the war Falavi was educated in a New Zealand mission school on the island of Beru southeast of Tarawa. As a teenager he was paralyzed from the waist down by polio, but in spite of his handicap he distinguished himself as one of the best students at the school. Two New Zealanders who manned the shortwave radio on the island and monitored Japanese military activities in the area recruited him to assist them as a coast-watcher when the war began. One day a group of Japanese soldiers landed on the island and demanded that all westerners give themselves up, but the New Zealanders operating the radio had already fled to the bush. Apparently the Japanese knew of their coast-watching activities and threatened to kill an islander every hour until the New Zealanders appeared. Upon hearing this news, the Kiwis gave themselves up and, along with twelve other Europeans living on the island (including two nuns), were taken to the Japanese base on Tarawa. They were later beheaded in 1942. Before leaving Beru, the Japanese smashed the radio to make sure there could be no further communication with the Allies.

Falavi witnessed all that had occurred, and immediately after the Japanese left with their prisoners he decided to try to repair the radio. Soon he had it working again and made contact with an Allied base. After some initial confusion as to why an islander was operating the radio, the Allied base on Funafuti to the southeast realized they had a valuable resource on Beru. It didn't take the Japanese long to surmise that someone still must be broadcasting their activities from Beru, and they returned periodically to search for the radio. And when they did, Falavi's friends would carry him (and the radio) to a hiding place in the bush, where he was able to avoid capture by the Japanese. His radio reports on Japanese military movements became invaluable as the Americans prepared to invade Tarawa. Falavi was later awarded the King George Medal by the British for his service to the Allied war effort.

BOTTOM LEFT: A number of local islanders had worked at the sprawling Japanese naval base on Dublon Island at Truk (now Chuuk, one of the Federated States of Micronesia) before and during the war. Kimiuo Aisek, shown here on Dublon in the early 1990s, was one of them. In 1944 he was seventeen years old and employed by the Japanese Navy piloting a small launch back and forth from a dock on Dublon to the Japanese cargo ships anchored in the lagoon. He also witnessed the attacks on Truk by U.S. carrier–based airplanes. Asked to recall those events, he smiled and replied softly, "I was scared." Many ships were sunk, the thriving Japanese base was devastated, the adjoining town where many Japanese civilians lived was obliterated, and many people were killed or injured by the initial and follow-up bombings. After the war Kimiuo was one of the few people on Truk who took visitors to Dublon, showed them the overgrown remains of concrete foundations, and told exactly what the Japanese had built and where. He made sure to point out one of the few remaining buildings from the Japanese base on Dublon. "It was the pharmacy. It was part of the hospital where they did medical experiments on captured American pilots," he said. "I heard about this during the war from some Japanese friends of mine. They said it was bad. They experimented on the Americans, then bayoneted a few and beheaded the rest, and said that those things were done on direct orders from the head surgeon." Captain Hiroshi Iwanami, former fleet surgeon and command-

ing officer of the naval hospital on Dublon, was tried and executed after the war.

Kimiuo was a product of the prewar Japanese period. He learned Japanese in school and looked back fondly on how neat and orderly the Japanese kept the island, the town of Dublon, and their base. After the bombings in 1944, conditions deteriorated at Truk when the Japanese started to confiscate food from the locals as their supplies ran out. As Kimiuo put it, "Things were very good before February 1944. After that, no good."

After the war, Kimiuo witnessed heartbreaking scenes as Japanese men who had been based at Truk were segregated from their local wives as part of the process of repatriating naval personnel back to Japan. "The Japanese were given a choice," recalled Kimiuo. "Either leave alone or take along kids from the marriage, but the local wives must stay." Occasionally years later, elderly Japanese tourists returned to see where they lived and worked in the 1930s and '40s. Some of the men asked about certain Trukese women, either former wives or girlfriends. They also wanted to see where the town of Dublon once stood. Today there is nothing but jungle and a few roads, the ruins of the old civilian hospital above the town, a few concrete foundations, one of the rusted fuel-oil tanks by the docks, and a couple of piers. "Some of them weep," Kimiuo said. "They see there is nothing left of the naval base or the beautiful little town."

Kimiuo not only helped load and unload the Japanese ships at Truk lagoon before the raids, he saw them attacked and sunk and remembered where they went down. Subsequently a pioneer in locating and exploring the sunken Japanese fleet, he was instrumental in bringing sport scuba diving to Chuuk and in establishing its reputation as one of the premier wreck-diving locations in the world. Kimiuo passed away in 2000.

FAR RIGHT: Milton Siosi, shown here in this 1976 photo, was an eighteen-year-old scout for the Americans during the campaign to capture Munda. A lifetime resident of Munda, Milton proudly displays faded tattoos on his left arm of a winged American insignia and a guitar, both souvenirs of his days spent fighting alongside the Americans. He possessed an interesting ability to "smell out" Japanese who were otherwise invisibly concealed in jungle machine-gun nests. He says the Japanese soldiers always had a distinctive smell that was easy for him to

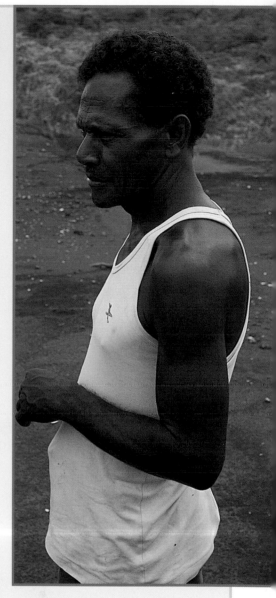

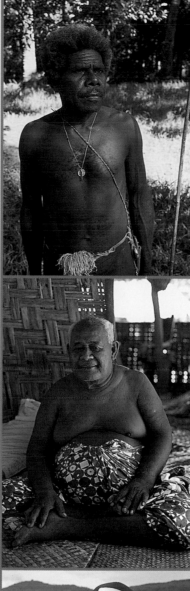

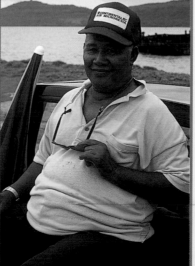

detect. To Milton, Americans also had their own identifying smell, so he would often creep out far ahead of them to literally sniff out the enemy.

Quite a number of men in the Munda area had direct experience with the fighting. One, a deaf-mute named Poka, used animated sign language to explain to visitors how he was able to kill a downed Japanese pilot. After the pilot had struggled to shore from where his plane went into the water, he aimed his service revolver at Poka and ordered him to climb a palm tree and bring down a coconut to chop open for a drink. Poka complied. After he came down with a coconut, the Japanese pilot turned his back to sit on the beach. Poka seized the opportunity and smashed the pilot's skull with the coconut.

The Carriers

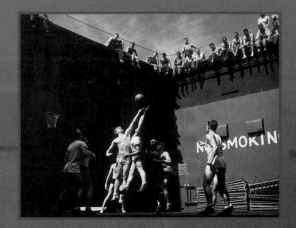

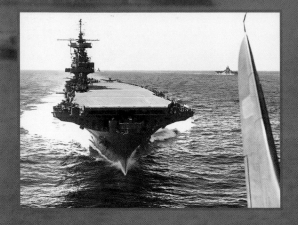

Short of actual combat, most excitement on aircraft carriers centered on the launch and recovery of airplanes. USS *Enterprise* is seen from a SBD Dauntless dive-bomber shortly after takeoff, and in the right background is the carrier *Lexington*.

Memories for many veterans of the Pacific war do not center on any particular island but on the countless hours spent at sea. Most hours were passed with work duties mixed with free time, recreation, and boredom—and occasional moments of terror and death. In this 1944 photo taken aboard the carrier *Monterey*, a future president of the United States plays basketball. The jumper at left is young Gerald R. Ford.

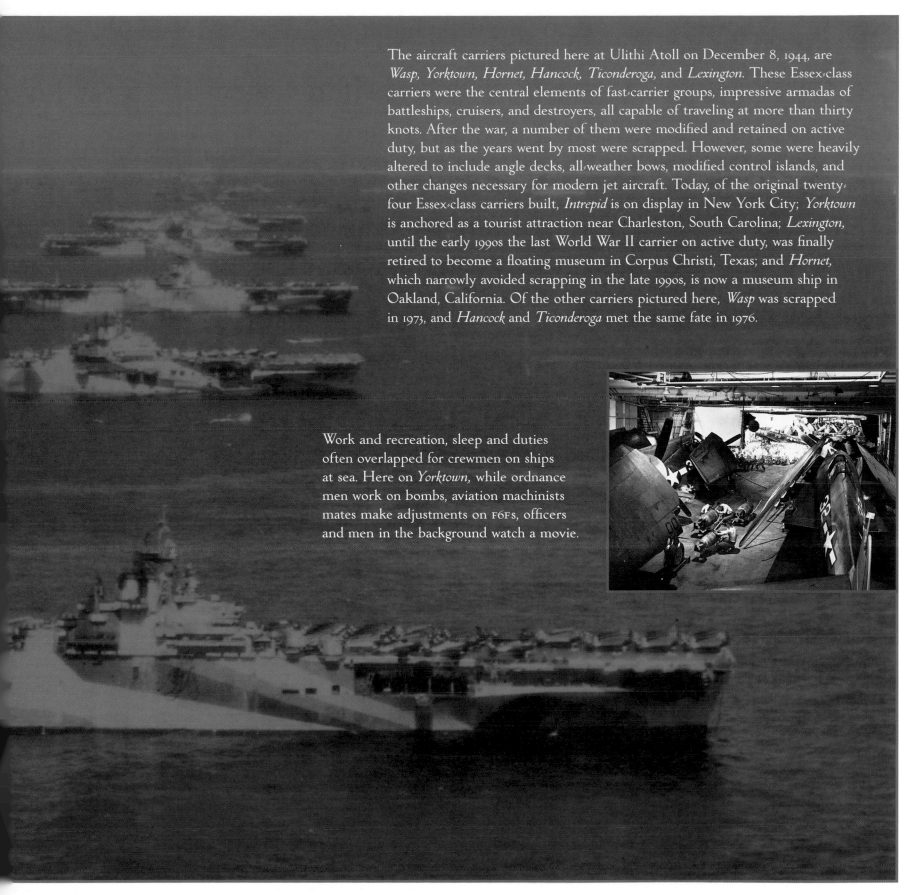

The aircraft carriers pictured here at Ulithi Atoll on December 8, 1944, are *Wasp, Yorktown, Hornet, Hancock, Ticonderoga,* and *Lexington.* These Essex-class carriers were the central elements of fast-carrier groups, impressive armadas of battleships, cruisers, and destroyers, all capable of traveling at more than thirty knots. After the war, a number of them were modified and retained on active duty, but as the years went by most were scrapped. However, some were heavily altered to include angle decks, all-weather bows, modified control islands, and other changes necessary for modern jet aircraft. Today, of the original twenty-four Essex-class carriers built, *Intrepid* is on display in New York City; *Yorktown* is anchored as a tourist attraction near Charleston, South Carolina; *Lexington,* until the early 1990s the last World War II carrier on active duty, was finally retired to become a floating museum in Corpus Christi, Texas; and *Hornet,* which narrowly avoided scrapping in the late 1990s, is now a museum ship in Oakland, California. Of the other carriers pictured here, *Wasp* was scrapped in 1973, and *Hancock* and *Ticonderoga* met the same fate in 1976.

Work and recreation, sleep and duties often overlapped for crewmen on ships at sea. Here on *Yorktown,* while ordnance men work on bombs, aviation machinists mates make adjustments on F6Fs, officers and men in the background watch a movie.

WHAT WAS TO BE one of the most frightening and gruesome battles of the Pacific war began inauspiciously enough on April 1, 1945. On that sunny Easter Sunday morning, thousands of Americans charged ashore on the Japanese island of Okinawa, almost without firing a shot. At the time, most of the world's attention was directed toward Europe, where the war in that theater was drawing to a close. But the situation on Okinawa was soon to turn ugly, and eighty-two terrifying days were to pass before this final land battle of World War II would lurch to a close.

The men fighting there were outraged that the world was virtually ignoring the horrific trench and bayonet warfare playing out in the blasted, oozing, rain-soaked, nightmarish hell that was Okinawa. Off-shore the support ships were being subjected to an unbelievable onslaught of grimly determined kamikaze pilots who attacked in swarms day after day, an assault that continued virtually unabated for

The fine weather encountered on D-Day soon turned cold and rainy, transforming the island into a muddy nightmare. To many who fought on Okinawa, the desolate, rain-soaked landscape brought to mind photos they had seen of World War I battlefields. William Manchester, a U.S. Marine who was seriously wounded on Okinawa, describes his first view of the battlefield in his memoir, *Goodbye Darkness:* "I had chosen a spot from which the entire battlefield was visible. It was hideous, and it was also strangely familiar,

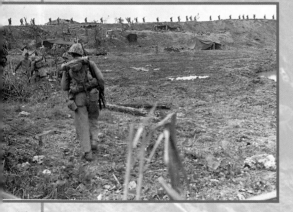

resembling, I then realized, photographs of 1914–1918. This, I thought, is what Verdun and Passchendaele must have looked like. The two great armies, squatting opposite one another in mud and smoke, were locked together in unimaginable agony. . . . It was a monstrous sight, a moonscape. Hills, ridges and cliffs rose and fell along the front like gray stumps of rotting teeth. There was nothing green left; artillery had denuded and scarred every inch of ground. Tiny flares glowed and disappeared. Shrapnel burst with bluish white puffs. Jets of flamethrowers flickered here and there, and new explosions stirred up the rubble."

the duration of the battle. The large civilian population of Okinawa suffered along with the Japanese and American combatants. Estimates are that over 150,000 civilians, about 108,000 Japanese, and nearly 7,400 Americans were killed on Okinawa. More than 30,000 Americans were wounded, and about 240 are still listed as missing in action. Some American veterans of the ordeal even now find it difficult to come to grips with what they experienced there and will forever remember the incomprehensibe atrocities witnessed in the blood and mire and stench of Okinawa. Names like Kakazu Ridge, Wana Draw, Sugar Loaf Hill, and Shuri Castle still make veterans shiver but provoke no response in most Americans today. Most Okinawans have tried to put behind them the horrors of those three months in 1945, and rapid economic development has now covered many of the World War II battlefields with housing and industrial construction. The old Shuri Castle, destroyed during the battle, was restored after the U.S.-built University of the Ryukyus was relocated from its sacred site when the island was handed back to Japan in 1972.

There is a large number of monuments on the island (at Mabuni alone, in the Okinawa War Memorial Park, every prefecture in Japan has a memorial to its own soldiers who died in the battle). Yet in 1985 Okinawans requested that veterans invited to a special memorial ceremony not wear any type of military symbol. In June of 1987 a twenty-five-foot-high memorial was dedicated by American and Japanese veterans groups, and more of them were dedicated on the fiftieth anniversary in 1995. This amazing outpouring of emotion, manifested by the largest number of memorials on any Pacific island involved in the war, is almost totally lost on the rest of the world. The nightmarish battles on Okinawa were fought in relative obscurity, and regretfully the world remembers little of those last brutal, hand-to-hand encounters of the war. Charles Leonard, a U.S. Marine wounded during the battle, laments, "The last battle was the easiest to forget—except for those who were there."

BELOW: Soon the detritus of battle was scattered across the desolate killing grounds of the Okinawa hills and ridges. A Marine Corps photographer, moving over the Sugar Loaf Hill battlefield after the fighting had ended, found this Marine helmet torn by shellfire. Inside the helmet liner was an Easter card with the inscription "To my son. . . ."

RIGHT: Manchester has vivid memories of the weather on Okinawa. "Torrents blew in from the East China Sea for three straight weeks, day and night, and no one who has not fought under such conditions, or even worked under them, can possibly envisage how miserable they are." Most veterans who fought at Okinawa can identify with these two Marines crouching miserably in their water- and mud-filled foxhole manning their mortar.

OPPOSITE TOP LEFT: Yet, as bad as it could be to settle into a disgusting, muddy foxhole where the only possible reward was relative safety, there were never any guarantees. Examining the aftereffects of an all-too-common occurrence on Okinawa, a Marine inspects what is left of a foxhole that, before a direct hit from a Japanese shell, had sheltered an eighty-one-millimeter mortar crew. One American died instantly, and two others were seriously wounded. The only identifiable remains are a shrapnel-filled mortar tube and canisters, a GI boot, and a ravaged helmet. The response of a veteran viewing this photo: "What can you do—if your number's up it's up."

OPPOSITE TOP RIGHT: Marines fought in the mud, slept in the mud, and, here, lined up for chow in the mud.

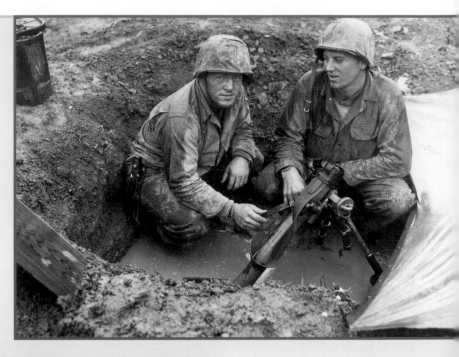

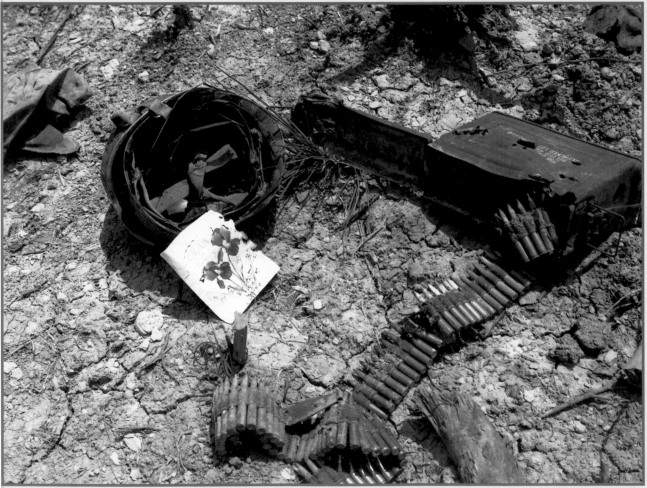

OPPOSITE CENTER LEFT: A visitor to Okinawa today has even greater difficulty imagining what went on there in 1945 than on other Pacific islands where more remains from the battles. Okinawa was and is now part of Japan, and there is little to remind anyone that Americans ever fought on the island. The monuments placed by American veterans' groups are few and difficult to locate. The overwhelming majority of memorials are for Japanese, usually commemorating countrymen and women who died either in battle or by suicide. Today urban development on Okinawa has engulfed many of the old battlefields. Often, the place names assigned by the Americans to features on their maps during battle, though immortalized in the Valhalla of Marine and Army history, are either not in use by Okinawans now or have been altered in various ways. One of the first major battles on Okinawa was fought on and around what the Americans knew as Kakazu Ridge. Today the town of Kakazu lies at the foot of what is now called Kakazu Hill. This scenic viewpoint at the top of the hill overlooks urban development in the area that was formerly barren battlefield, and a park surrounds the base of the hill. On the horizon in the distance can be seen the next objective for the Americans after Kakazu: Maeda Ridge.

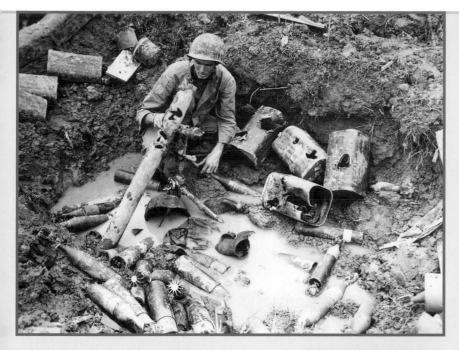

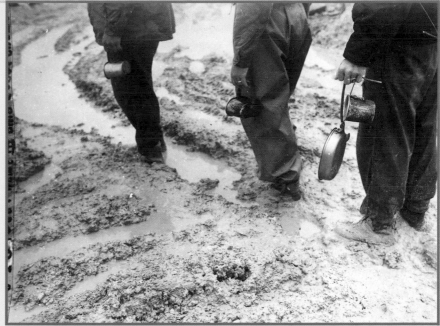

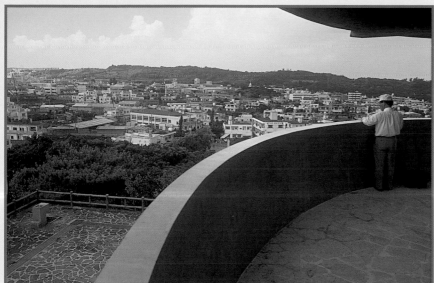

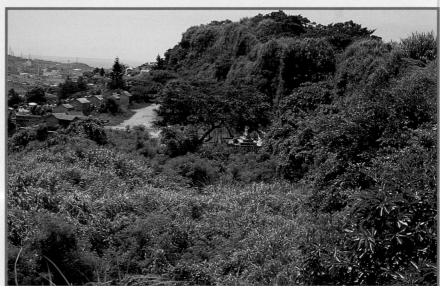

CENTER RIGHT: Another Okinawa landmark made infamous by heavy loss of life on both sides was Sawtooth Ridge, part of the Urasoe-Mura escarpment. Also called Maeda Ridge, it is today flanked by modern concrete tombs. In 1945 Desmond Doss, medic and conscientious objector, was the only American soldier left unharmed on top of the ridge after a vicious Japanese counterattack. Under heavy fire, he lowered fifty of his wounded comrades down this cliff to safety, and in the process won the Medal of Honor. Later he was badly wounded.

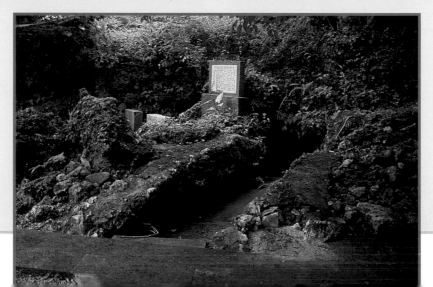

LEFT: Like most battlefields on Okinawa, there are no historical markers on Maeda Ridge to tell what happened to Americans who fought and died there. Only visitors who bring their own documentation know the story of Desmond Doss. The few clues that anything unusual happened here are the Japanese memorials and several markers outside old cave entrances like this one paying tribute to the Japanese defenders who died inside.

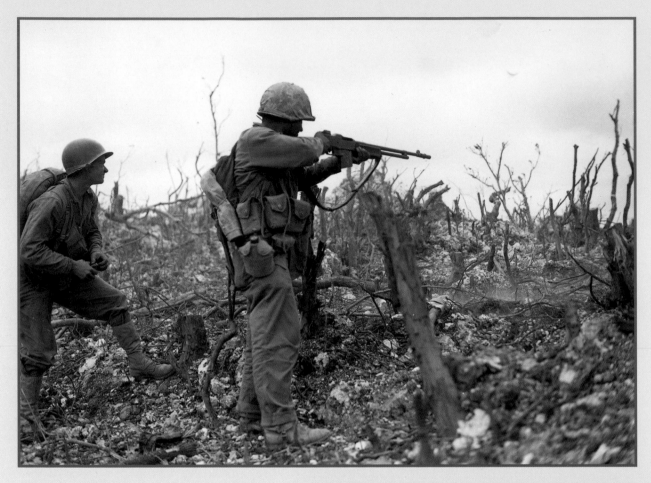

me wonder what it was like to be in a quiet place. We had been under and around plenty of 'heavy stuff' at Peleliu, but not on nearly so massive a scale or for such unending periods of time as at Wana. The thunderous American barrages went on and on for hours and then days. In return, the Japanese threw plenty of shells our way. I had a continuous headache I'll never forget. Those thunderous, prolonged barrages imposed on me a sense of stupefication and dullness far beyond anything I ever had experienced before. It didn't seem possible for any human being to be under such thunderous chaos for days and nights on end and be unaffected by it—even when most of it was our own supporting weapons, and we were in a good foxhole. How did the Japanese stand up under it? They simply remained deep in their caves until it stopped and then swarmed up to repulse each attack, just as they had done at Peleliu."

BELOW: Only after close examination of topographic and modern road maps can a visitor find what was known to Americans as Wana Draw (in the foreground) and Wana Ridge (rising in the background). What was Wana Draw is now Sueyoshi Park. There are no historical markers to indicate the importance of this battlefield, and locals display only blank looks when asked about Wana Ridge or Wana Draw. The outskirts of Naha press in from the left, roughly at the entrance to what was once

ABOVE: This is a typical combat scene on another Okinawa battlefield whose name is famous in the annals of the U.S. Army and Marine Corps: Wana Ridge. Wana Ridge and Wana Draw, at its base, became increasingly familiar names on Okinawa as determined Japanese resistance there held up the American advance for days, with terrific loss of life on both sides. Amidst the blasted, barren, and muddy terrain, the Marine at left readies a hand grenade to throw into a Japanese cave, while the Marine at right prepares to fire on fleeing Japanese. Eugene Sledge, a U.S. Marine who fought on Okinawa, describes how this battlefield was prepared for such assaults by the infantry in his book, *With the Old Breed: at Peleliu and Okinawa:* "Our massive artillery, mortar, naval gunfire, and aerial bombardment continued against Wana Draw on our front and Wana Ridge on our left. The Japanese continued to shell everything and everybody in the area, meeting each tank-infantry attack with a storm of fire. A total of thirty tanks, including four flamethrowers, blasted and burned Wana Draw. Our artillery, heavy mortars, ships' guns, and planes then plastered the enemy positions all over again until the noise and shock made

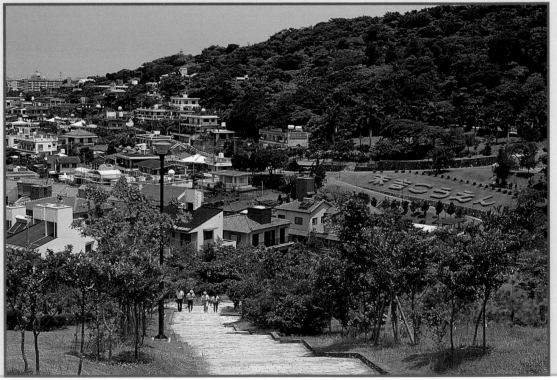

known as Wana Draw, where Eugene Sledge had a close call in 1945: "We eased up to the edge of the draw to cross in dispersed order. An NCO ordered three men and me to cross at a particular point and to stay close behind the troops directly across the draw from us. The other side looked mighty far away. Japanese machine guns were firing down the draw from our left [to the right in this photo], and our artillery was swishing overhead. 'Haul ass, and don't stop for anything 'til you get across,' said our NCO. . . . We left the field and slid down a ten foot embankment to the sloping floor of the draw. My feet hit the deck running. . . . The Japanese machine guns rattled away. Bullets zipped and snapped around my head, the tracers like long white streaks. I looked neither right nor left, but with my heart in my throat raced out, splashed across the little stream, and dashed up the slope to the shelter of a spur of ridge projecting out into the draw to our left. We must have run about three hundred yards or more to get across. . . . We glanced back to see where the two new men were. Neither one of them had made more than a few strides out into the draw from the other side. One was sprawled in a heap, obviously killed instantly. The other was wounded and crawling back." Sledge's sprint started out on the far side of the photograph at the base of Wana Ridge, roughly where the shrubbery is shaped to spell the park's name,

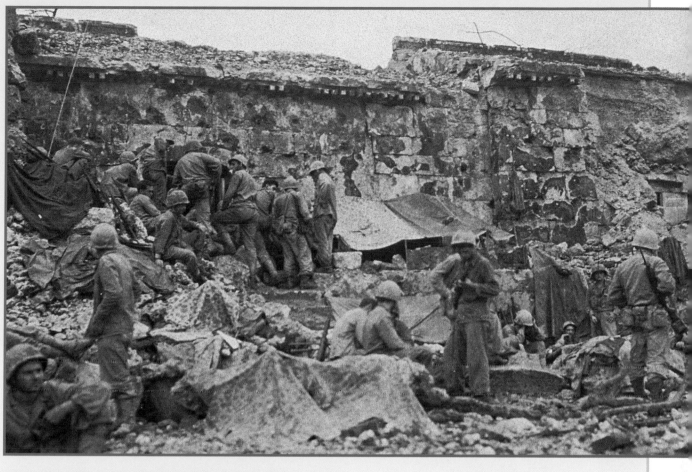

then crossed the stream hidden at the bottom of the valley, and ended up just to the left of the concrete steps in the foreground that now descend to the stream.

ABOVE: One of the premier landmarks on Okinawa, the center of ancient Ryukyuan culture, was Shuri Castle. Its prominent strategic position at the top of a central massif of high ground, and its use as headquarters by the Japanese high command, doomed the ancient edifice to destruction. Here members of the First Marine Division take shelter behind what is left of part of the Shuri Castle complex.

LEFT: In the 1950s the University of the Ryukyus was built on the site of old Shuri Castle by the American occupation administration. After the island was handed back to Japan in 1972, the university was finally moved, and the entire Shuri Castle complex, part of which is shown here, was restored to its prewar appearance. Just to the left and down the side of the hill is the entrance to an underground complex of tunnels used as headquarters by the Japanese commander, Lieutenant General Mitsuru Ushijima, during the defense of Okinawa.

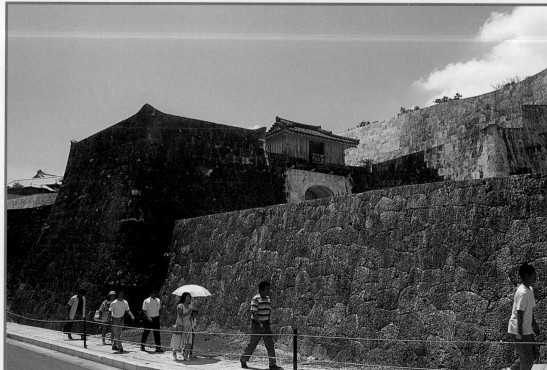

RIGHT: Another famous battlefield, at least famous to the Americans who fought there, was Sugar Loaf Hill and the adjoining complex of rounded bluffs given the names Half Moon and the Horseshoe by the U.S. forces. These low hills overlooked the city of Naha from the north and were turned into heavily fortified defensive positions by the Japanese. William Manchester described them: "There the hills stood, piled in great weighty, pressing, heaped, lethal masses, oppressive beyond words for us who studied the maps and knew that one way or another the peaks must be taken." In a battle that would become a turning point in the fight for Okinawa, the Americans repeatedly hurled themselves for more than a week, in mud and rain, against these seemingly innocuous hills. When it was over, 2,662 Americans and an estimated 4,000 Japanese had been killed or wounded. This 1945 view of the barren no-man's-land of Sugar Loaf Hill looks south across the area where attacking Marines were cut down by Japanese fire.

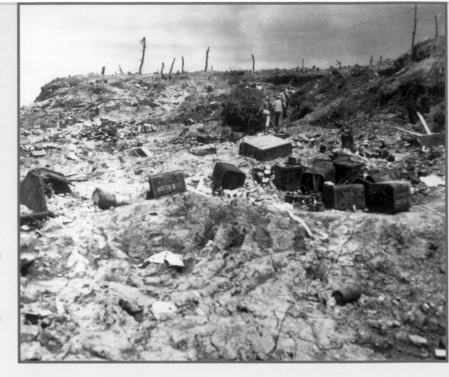

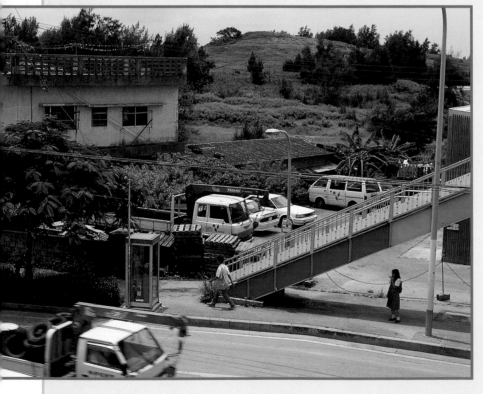

LEFT: William Manchester personally experienced the desperate struggle for these hills: "In one charge up Half Moon we lost four hundred men. *Time* reported after a typical night: 'there were 50 Marines on top of Sugar Loaf Hill. They had been ordered to hold the position all night, at any cost. By dawn, 46 of them had been killed or wounded. Then, into the foxhole where the remaining four huddled, the Japs dropped a white phosphorous shell, burning three men to death. The last survivor crawled to an aid station.' In another battalion attack, all three company commanders were killed. . . . The infantry couldn't advance. Every weapon was tried. . . . none of them worked. If anything, the enemy's hold on the heights grew stronger. The Japanese artillery never seemed to let up, and every night Ushijima [the Japanese commander] sent fresh troops up his side of the hill. We kept rushing them, moving like somnambulists, the weight of Sugar Loaf pressing down on us, harder and harder." During the course of this desperate struggle, there were many instances of incredible courage under fire. One was that of Major Henry Courtney, described by Manchester, ". . . he rallied what was left of his battalion at the base of Sugar Loaf, asked for volunteers to make 'a banzai of our own,' and led them up in the night through shrapnel, small-arms fire from Horseshoe and Half Moon, and grenades from Sugar Loaf's forward slope. Reaching the top, he heard Japs lining up on the other side for a counterattack.

He decided to charge them first, leading the attack himself, throwing hand grenades. His last cry was, 'Keep coming—there's a mess of them down there!'" Only fifteen survivors finally came down from the summit after that charge, and Major Courtney was not among them. He was posthumously awarded the Medal of Honor.

After the war the Sugar Loaf Hill area was turned into a housing development for U.S. forces on the island. That housing project was abandoned and then razed in the late 1980s, and the developing city of Naha began to swallow the entire area. This view looks south toward what was left of Sugar Loaf Hill in 1993. It is across this ground that the Marines attacked and were repulsed repeatedly. Much of the area subsequently was excavated and bulldozed, leveling most traces of the Horseshoe and much of Sugar Loaf Hill itself. At the eleventh hour in 1994, a grassroots movement on Okinawa, in collaboration with the U.S. Sixth Marine Division, saved the remains of Sugar Loaf Hill. By that time it had been bulldozed and shoe-horned into retaining walls as part of planned urban development. Sugar Loaf Hill today stands as an odd concrete-girdled sentinel amidst relentless urban development, its formerly menacing neighbors Horseshoe and Half Moon now barely distinguishable amidst the streets and buildings, and the din of shelling and gunfire has been replaced by the noise of traffic flowing in and out of Naha on the nearby highway.

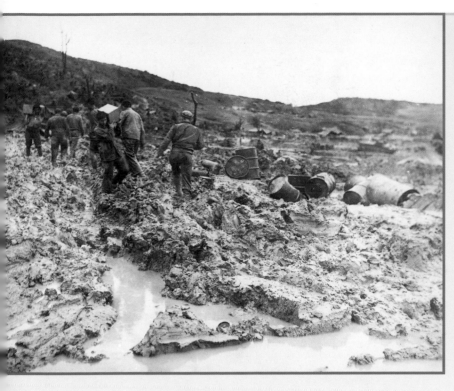

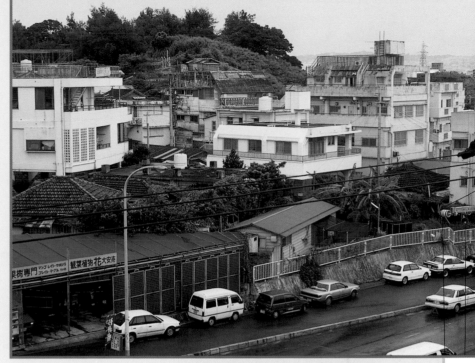

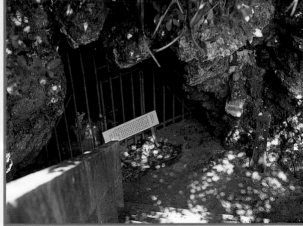

ABOVE: Eugene Sledge arrived on Half Moon shortly after it had finally been taken from the Japanese. "Taken" was a relative term since Japanese troops were still holding out in caves on part of the forward slopes of Half Moon. Sledge describes the scene: "It was the most ghastly corner of hell I had ever witnessed. As far as I could see, an area that previously had been a low grassy valley with a picturesque stream meandering through it was a muddy, repulsive, open sore on the land. The place was choked with the putrefaction of death, decay, and destruction. In a shallow defilade to our right, between my gun pit and the railroad [now Highway 330], lay about twenty dead Marines, each on a stretcher and covered to his ankles with a poncho—a commonplace, albeit tragic, scene to every veteran. Those bodies had been placed there to await transport to the rear for burial. At least those dead were covered from the torrents of rain that had made them miserable in life and from the swarms of flies that sought to hasten their decay. But as I looked about, I saw that other Marine dead couldn't be tended properly. The whole area was pocked with shell craters and churned up by explosions. Every crater was half full of water, and many of them held a Marine corpse. The bodies lay pathetically just as they had been killed, half submerged in muck and water, rusting weapons still in hand. Swarms of big flies hovered about them. . . . The mud was knee deep in some places, probably deeper in others if one dared venture there. For several feet around every corpse, maggots crawled about in the muck and then were washed away by the runoff of the rain. There wasn't a tree or bush left. All was open country. Shells had torn up the turf so completely that ground cover was nonexistent. The rain poured down on us as evening approached. The scene was nothing but mud; shellfire; flooded craters with their silent pathetic, rotting occupants; knocked-out tanks and amtracs; and discarded equipment—utter desolation. The stench of death was overpowering. The only way I could bear the monstrous horror of it all was to look upward away from the earthly reality surrounding us, watch the leaden gray clouds go scudding over, and repeat over and over to myself that the situation was unreal—just a nightmare—that I would soon awake and find myself somewhere else. But the ever-present smell of death saturated my nostrils. It was there with every breath I took. . . . Not long after [we] took over Half Moon, several of us were on a work party, struggling through knee-deep mud to bring ammo from the rear up to the mortar positions." This photo shows just such a work party near Half Moon.

ABOVE RIGHT: Today the vegetation-covered summit of Half Moon (in the background) rises above the suburban development of Naha. This photo was taken from the eastern slopes of what was formerly Sugar Loaf looking across what had been a railroad line, now Highway 330 in the foreground leading to Naha at right. Gene Sledge's mortar position would have been just behind the white building at left. Though the battles for Half Moon, Sugar Loaf, and the Horseshoe were crucial turning points in the fight for Okinawa, with tremendous loss of life on both sides, only Peace Memorial Park on the bulldozed remains of Sugar Loaf Hill marks what had been one of the most desolate battlefields in the entire Pacific war. Engulfed by the chaotic Naha suburbs of Daido and Asato, Half Moon is the least topographically altered of the three original hills. Though recognizable as a strategic feature, it is hard to imagine that it could have warranted the tremendous loss of life required to secure it.

LOWER RIGHT: The fighting on Okinawa relentlessly ground on from the battles around Shuri and Naha in May to successive bloody struggles to the south for reinforced ridges and hills with names like Yuza Dake, Yaeju Dake (called the Big Apple by the U.S. Army), Hill 95, and Kunishi Ridge. The mere thought of those dreaded ridges can send chills down the spines of veterans, but none of them has any meaning to most present-day Okinawans. The Japanese defenders were literally driven south to the sea, and resistance ended at Hill 89 near Mabuni. It was here, outside the entrance to one of a network of caves that was the final headquarters of the Japanese high command, that Lieutenant General Mitsuru Ushijima and his chief of staff, Lieutenant General Isamu Cho, committed ritual suicide on June 22, 1945. Hill 89 is now known as Mabuni Hill to visitors who climb down stairs from the summit to view the spot, shown here, where the two Japanese commanders met their final end. It is a simple opening in the cliff face with a spectacular view of the Pacific, the final barrier to their retreat.

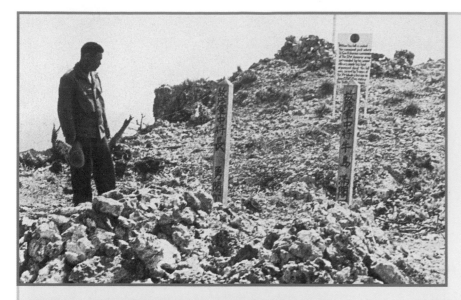

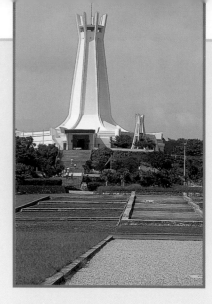

TOP LEFT: As the U.S. Army overran the summit of Hill 89 and clambered down the far side, they found the bodies of Ushijima and Cho, which were carried back to the summit and buried in the shallow graves shown here.

CENTER LEFT: Today the graves are marked by this impressive monument that is a major attraction for Japanese tourists who make the pilgrimage to the manicured summit of Mabuni Hill.

BOTTOM LEFT: The entire Mabuni Hill area has been turned into a vast World War II shrine to commemorate the Japanese who died on Okinawa and elsewhere in the Pacific. Over forty-five large monuments, such as this one, have been built to honor the war dead from every prefecture in Japan. Among others, there are also monuments to Japanese dead from the Sixty-second Army Division, a "Davao Monument," and a "Bougainville Island War Hero Memorial Monument" to honor Japanese who died in those battles. In 1995 the Cornerstones of Peace memorial was dedicated. It consists of 1,200 black granite slabs listing every person who died during the battle for Okinawa: 12,281 Americans, 110,000 Japanese soldiers and Okinawan conscripts, and more than 150,000 Okinawa civilians.

TOP RIGHT: The centerpiece of the many Mabuni war monuments is the Peace Hall (shown here), a tower built in 1978 to house a forty-five-foot-high statue of Buddha. Okinawans today say that ghosts of the war dead inhabit Mabuni Hill.

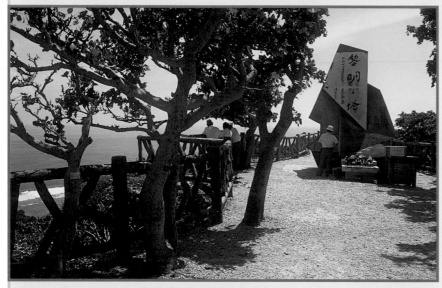

OPPOSITE TOP LEFT: One of the major tourist attractions in all of Okinawa is in the south of the island at Himeyuri. Tourists gather to peer down into a cave, shown here, where 167 high school girls (trainee nurses) and their teachers committed mass suicide on June 19, 1945, rather than surrender to U.S. forces who had overrun the area. Also known as the "Cave of the Virgins," the site includes a meditation area, shrine, gift shop, and manicured gardens to cater to the busloads of Japanese who visit. Another major attraction just south of Naha is the subterraneous tunnel complex called the "Old Japanese Navy Underground Headquarters." Visitors descend into the elaborate network of tunnels and read from the tourist leaflet that about four thousand Japanese naval personnel and their commander, Rear Admiral Minoru Ota, committed mass suicide on June 13, 1945, rather than surrender. General Ushijima had tried to convince Ota and his men to retreat to southern Okinawa, but Ota chose suicide in the tunnels for himself and his men. Visitors can view the death poem Ota scrawled on the wall of his headquarters tunnel—"How could we rejoice over our birth but to die an honorable death under the Emperor's flag." The tourist leaflet goes on to say, "We earnestly urge you to kindly express your sympathy for those Japanese comrades who died heroically for their homeland. . . ."

OPPOSITE TOP RIGHT: One of the Japanese suicide rocket bombs captured on Okinawa is suspended from the ceiling of a Smithsonian Institution Air and Space Museum warehouse in the 1980s.

OPPOSITE BOTTOM: As bad as the fighting was on land, there was little respite for those offshore on ships. An incredible rain of human destruction from the skies—the kamikazes—faced Allied sailors during the Okinawa campaign. Japanese airmen were willing to offer their lives on the chance they could take some of the enemy with them. Kamikaze attacks resulted in 34 ships sunk and over 350 damaged. U.S. casualties at sea from the kamikaze attacks amounted to ten thousand men. In addition to the conventional kamikaze aircraft hurtling toward U.S. ships, the Japanese devised several other new wrinkles. One was the *Ohka*, or "cherry blossom," manned rocket bomb. Carrying more than a ton of explosives in the nose, these craft were released from bombers near the target and guided by a single pilot wedged into the tiny cockpit. Frightening in concept, they were relatively ineffective in practice. Of the eight hundred manufactured, about fifty were used on suicide missions, and only three actually exploded on target. This is a photo of one of several *Ohka* found on Okinawa by American troops.

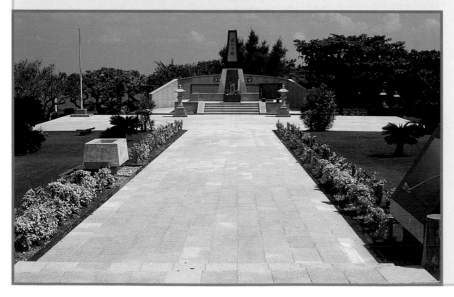

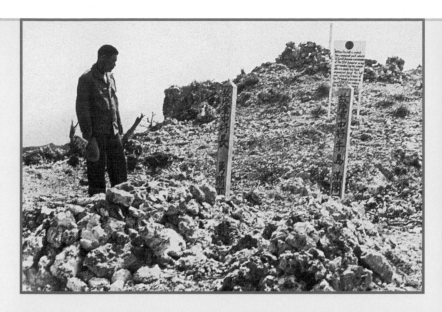

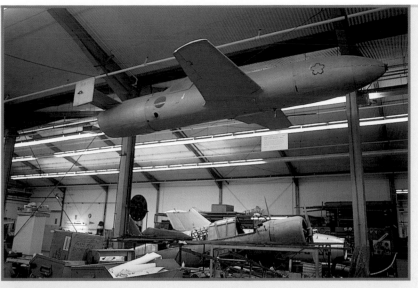

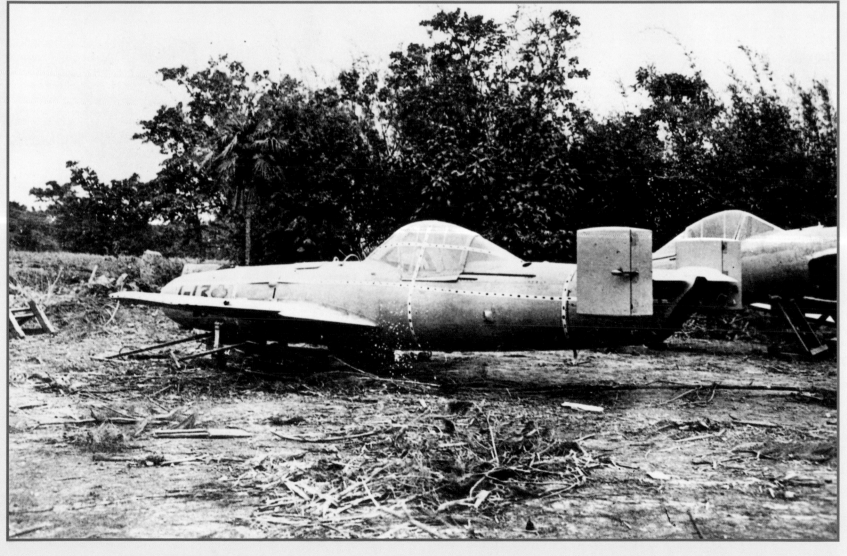

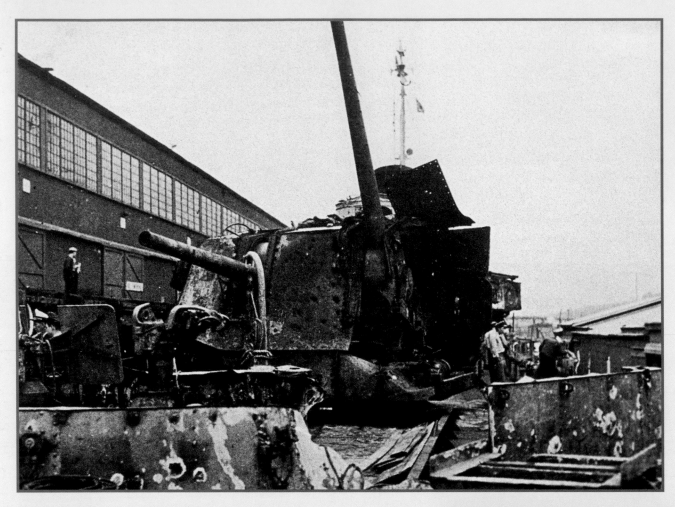

second heroic effort, the crew saved the ship again, this time from the scrap yard. In 1981, thanks to the efforts of the crew and others, *Laffey* became a museum ship at Patriots Point near Charleston, South Carolina. It lies just astern of fabled World War II Pacific veteran the carrier *Yorktown*, another namesake of a ship that was sunk in 1942, during the Battle of Midway. This photo of the rear five-inch gun mount was taken after *Laffey* had just returned to Port Angeles in May 1945, about a month after her ordeal near Okinawa. One Japanese kamikaze ricocheted off the top of this turret, two crashed into it directly, and a bomb exploded on the deck nearby. The seven-man crew of the five-inch gun, as well as gunners on other gun mounts in the foreground, were killed, and others were severely wounded.

BELOW: *Laffey* at Patriots Point, South Carolina, today. The rear five-inch gun turret was repaired and shows no evidence of the catastrophes that took place in and around this area near the stern of the ship. Veterans of *Laffey's* crew still volunteer and perform restoration and maintenance on the ship. One crewman, Jim Spriggs (in cap at left), was on hand the day this photo was taken in 2000.

ABOVE: Of all the tragic and heroic stories to come out of the kamikaze attacks on American ships at Okinawa, the ordeal of the destroyer USS *Laffey*, the namesake of a destroyer that went down at Guadalcanal in November 1942, was one of the most amazing. Posted to Radar Picket Station One north of Okinawa, *Laffey* was one of a group of ships that were the early warning system and first line of defense against the swarms of kamikazes headed south from Japan. The Japanese pilots were intended to dive their planes into American carriers and battleships, but many ended up crashing into the first American ship they saw, the destroyers and other ships on the radar picket line. On the morning of April 16, 1945, about fifty Japanese kamikaze planes headed toward *Laffey*. Of those, a mind-boggling twenty-two planes singled out the small ship for attack. Some were shot down either by *Laffey's* guns or U.S. Corsair fighters trying to help fend them off. But five Japanese planes crashed directly into *Laffey* and erupted in

tremendous explosions. Another one glanced off the top of the rear gun turret, while two more struck the ship's mast as they careened past out of control. Even one Corsair hit the ship's radar antenna as it chased down a Japanese plane. Bombs from three additional planes exploded on *Laffey's* decks, and damage was inflicted from three more planes whose bombs exploded near *Laffey* as they were shot down and hit the water. The ship was left a burning, wrecked hulk, with thirty-two dead and seventy-one injured, nearly one third of the crew. But the survivors somehow kept the ship afloat, and after temporary emergency repairs at Okinawa, *Laffey* limped back to Port Angeles near Seattle for a complete makeover. The heavily damaged ship was first put on display, and about ninety-three thousand civilians toured the scorched and devastated vessel. *Laffey* was repaired, returned to active duty, and finally decommissioned in 1975. She then faced the seemingly inevitable fate of being scrapped. But in a

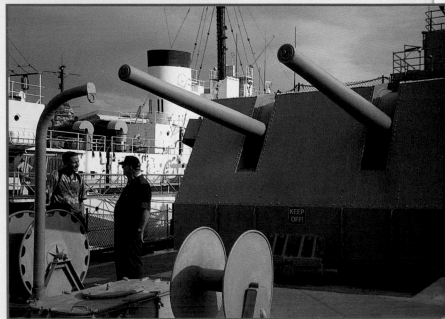

CHAPTER 6

ENDING THE PACIFIC WAR
Bombing Hiroshima and Nagasaki

SURE WE ALL CHEERED WHEN WE HEARD THEY DROPPED

THE BOMB. BUT WE WEREN'T CHEERING BECAUSE ALL THOSE

PEOPLE DIED. WE WERE CHEERING BECAUSE WE KNEW THEY

COULDN'T TAKE SOMETHING LIKE THAT BOMB, AND THEY

HAD TO SURRENDER. I WASN'T GOING TO HAVE TO BE

IN THE INVASION. I WAS GOING TO MAKE IT HOME.

—*Harlan Wall, Infantryman, U.S. Sixth Army*

President Roosevelt had to have known he was in failing health, but he seemed not to have considered that Fate might, at any time, terminate his presidency and thrust Harry Truman into his place. The apparent fact that he never allowed Truman to learn anything at all about "the Bomb" or the enormous multi-billion-dollar supersecret Manhattan Project, which for the past three years had been working to produce it, was almost inexplicable. In spite of recent speculation to the contrary, this almost unbelievable state of affairs appears to have been the case. When the other dignitaries attending Truman's swearing-in ceremony had filed out of the room, Secretary of War Henry L. Stimson lagged behind to speak to the new commander in chief privately. During the days of the Truman Committee, Stimson had lived in fear that relentless probing for waste in the defense program would somehow lead to discovery of that most massive and most secret of all the war's financial sinkholes, the Manhattan Project. But now that Truman was president, Stimson realized it was imperative that he know of the "immense secret project" that appeared to be about to "give the country a new explosive of almost unbelievable power." But even then the secretary was so vague that on the following day Senator James F. Byrnes, who had been Truman's closest friend in the Senate, felt it necessary to stop by and fill him in on more of the details. Though Roosevelt had never told Truman anything, for at least two years he had been telling Byrnes and six other congressional leaders everything about the Manhattan Project.

The project's senior physicists, together with the secretary of war and top American military commanders, had been debating for the past year or more how best to use a weapon that could vaporize an entire city and everyone in it. So far they had not managed to reach a consensus. Some felt that it would be a weapon too horrible to be used in any case. A few among the scientists thought that exploding the thing might start a chain reaction that "could destroy the entire world." Byrnes, himself, was of the opinion that mere possession of such a weapon, whether used or not, "ought to put us in a position to dictate our own terms at the end of the war." In any case, the final decision was now President Truman's.

On May 8 the war in Europe finally came to an end, making it even more imperative that Japan must soon be defeated. But as one historian put it, the question was no longer whether Japan would be defeated but whether that country could be made to surrender. On shore on Okinawa, one Marine would later recall, "The struggle for survival went on day after weary day. To those who entered the meat grinder itself the war was a nether world of horror from which escape seemed less and less likely . . . time had no meaning. Life had no meaning."

Offshore things were about as bad. Day after day masses of Japanese suicide planes were hammering at the fleet supporting the invasion. Hundreds fell to antiaircraft fire and to American fighter planes but others got through, sinking some ships and turning others into flaming coffins for many of their men. The destroyer *Aaron Ward,* even after taking seven hits from kamikazes, still had not sunk, but in the words of one observer, it was only "a floating junk pile." Another destroyer, the *Laffey,* was attacked by twenty-two Japanese kamikaze aircraft in less than one hour and left in a similar state. In early May the aircraft carrier *Bunker Hill* was reduced by kamikazes to a burned-out, still-floating shell, with one of every three of her crew dead, wounded, or missing.

Moreover, the Japanese were now busily organizing an invasion defense plan code-named *Ketsu-Go.* Its aim was to immerse the invading forces in so bloody a combat hell that they would be forced to accept a negotiated peace that would leave the Japanese homeland and government relatively intact. And American Intelligence, being able to read much of Japan's encoded military mail, was assembling a pretty good picture of *Ketsu-Go.* It would make use of some five thousand kamikaze aircraft and six thousand explosive-laden suicide boats, many of which, together with the necessary explosives and fuel, were already assembled. Potential invasion beaches were being covered by heavy coastal artillery entrenched in deep caves and tunnels. By summer 1945, Japan had, at home, an army of over two million officers and men as well as the National Volunteer Force of militia officially put at twenty-eight million. On top of that, there were plans for guerrilla warfare against any invaders who might actually secure a toehold ashore.

Taken all together, said Colonel Takushiro Hattori of the Imperial General Headquarters, this would enable Japan to inflict upon invading forces such a "staggering blow" that they would be forced "to comprehend the indomitable fighting spirit of the Japanese . . . and to recognize the difficulty if not impossibility of subduing the Home Islands." What it all came down to, it seemed, was that although there was no chance Japan could force the Allies into accepting such a peace, there was every chance she could force them into experiencing the greatest bloodbath in the history of warfare.

Against this background the seven-member Interim Committee set up by Truman to examine all the possible options for using the atomic bomb carried on its deliberations. Secretary Stimson characterized the members' duty this way: "It is our responsibility to recommend action that may turn the course of civilization. In our hands we expect soon to have a weapon of wholly unprecedented destructive power. Today's prime fact is war. Our great task is to bring this war to a prompt and successful conclusion. We may assume that our new weapon puts in our hands overwhelming power. It is our obligation to use this power with the best wisdom we can command."

If the bomb were not used, the alternative was to invade Japan, and the Joint Chiefs, of course, had been planning for this eventuality. Based on the Yalta guarantee that Anglo-American forces would receive full support from the Red Army, and assuming a November 1 landing on Kyushu and a midwinter invasion of Honshu, Secretary Stimson later recalled that he was informed that "such operations might be expected to cost over a million American lives. . . ."

General MacArthur was to point out that thus far Americans had been fighting isolated island garrisons cut off from reinforcements. The vast mass of the Imperial Japanese Army, between five and six million troops, with thousands of tons of ammunition stowed underground in caves, had never been defeated in battle and they were being brought home from China and elsewhere to defend the sacred soil of Dai Nippon. He added, "Unless the Japanese islands were to be blockaded and the people left to starve—the least humane of all solutions—that force must be met and defeated." MacArthur predicted the greatest bloodletting ever. He expected to take fifty thousand casualties just in establishing that November 1 beachhead. Over five thousand kamikazes were known to be waiting in underground hangars, preparing to take down an equal number of naval vessels with them. Finally, MacArthur warned Washington, ". . . the Japs might fade into the mountains to fight as guerrillas," which could lead to "a ten-year war with no limit on casualties." Historian and Pacific veteran William Manchester later noted, "The Japanese said over their radio time and again that 100 million Japanese were willing to die for their homeland."

The B-29 incendiary raids, massive and terrible as they were, seemed not to have shaken the Japanese will to resist. The overnight raid of March 9–10, 1945, burned down 25 percent of the city of Tokyo, amounting to over 267,000 buildings. More than 83,000 Tokyo residents died that night, nearly 41,000 were injured, and one million were made homeless. But the knock-out blow to Tokyo occurred two months later in two raids a night apart. On the night of May 24–25, 520 bombers, the largest number of B-29s to fly on a single mission over Japan, dropped 3,646 tons of bombs on the city. They came again on the night of May 25–26—464 giant, silver B-29s dropping 3,253 tons of incendiaries in a strong south wind and 50 percent humidity. Among other places, they hit the Yasukuni Shinto shrine to the war dead, the central markets, Tokyo Station, the old American Embassy, the Imperial Hotel that Frank Lloyd Wright designed, the Kabuki Theater, the Water Ministry, the Navy Ministry, the Army General Staff Headquarters, the war minister's official residence, the Ministry of Greater East Asia, and Keio University. The Imperial Palace also burned even though it was not a target—the wind-driven flames could not be kept from it. Said a survivor:

It was like a fireworks display. . . . Blazing petroleum jelly, firebrands and sparks flew everywhere. People were aflame, rolling and writhing in agony, screaming piteously for help, but beyond all mortal assistance. . . . I saw roofs flying in the air and a huge flaming telephone pole being spun by a tornado. . . . It was the longest night of my life.

The destruction was so extensive that the Americans would no longer consider Tokyo a target worthy of B-29s. Since the B-29 raids apparently had not moved the Japanese closer to surrender, the option of invasion was very much still on the table. Planners were now considering what such an invasion would face, and what it would take to succeed. An April 1945 study by the Joint Chiefs concluded invasion of Kyushu (first set for October 1 and later set back to November 1) would require thirty-six divisions —1,532,000 men—and that casualties would be heavy.

Japan had at home 2,350,000 officers and men organized into fifty-three infantry divisions and twenty-five brigades, two tank divisions, four antiaircraft divisions, and a national volunteer militia estimated at twenty-eight million, all for employment in *Ketsu-Go*. But there were severe shortages in Japan: fuel, ammunition, food, everything. The Japanese had, however, been stockpiling for defense, and by summer 1945 they figured their reserves as 100 percent of the ammunition, 94 percent of the fuel, and 164 percent of the rations required. They had about five thousand eighteen-foot *Shinyo* attack boats each capable of carrying up to a ton of explosives for use in ramming ships of the invasion fleet. By the end of June 1945 Japan had produced two thousand aircraft especially designed for kamikaze service. Earmarked for use against an invasion were additional thousands of Navy planes and anticonvoy and anti–task force bombers. On the whole, the Japanese High Command was pretty confident of their prospects. After all, on Okinawa, two-and-a-half Japanese divisions had held out against an American force five times that size for a hundred days.

As Americans had discovered on Iwo Jima, Okinawa, Saipan, and other islands, the Japanese were regular moles when it came to digging interconnecting caves, tunnels, and underground artillery positions. And in Japan, the hills behind potential invasion beaches were honeycombed with such structures. The High Command directed the Army to continue fighting even though there might be nothing to eat but grass and dirt and no place to sleep but open fields. An Army spokesman called upon the troops to give their lives, "slaying several enemy soldiers with one," to "break the enemy's will to fight." They were exhorted by Colonel Hattori to "inflict a staggering blow against the first wave of enemy invaders" and thus demonstrate the iron determination of the Japanese Army and people and the impossibility of conquering the home islands.

Meanwhile, some Americans were seeking ways to demonstrate the terrible new weapon to Japanese warlords without having to use it on innocent civilians. The idea was that a huge, impressive, unimaginable explosion would frighten Japan into surrendering, thus circumventing the need for either an invasion or an atomic bomb drop on a populated area. A number of scientists who had worked on the bomb petitioned to have it demonstrated "in an appropriately selected uninhabited area." Counter arguments, however, prevailed. A demonstration left open the possibility that the bomb-carrying plane would be shot down, that the bomb would fail to explode and thus encourage rather than discourage further resistance, that the bomb-carrying plane would even go down for some other reason—mechanical failure, weather, etc.—before the announced demonstration, thus making it appear the U.S. had been bluffing. And not least, if the bomb proved of lower than theoretically calculated force, the Japanese, masters of deception themselves, might conclude that by massing and dropping a huge explosive load in one bomb, the U.S. had faked the whole thing.

Some argued that such a demonstration was pointless because the moral issue had already been rendered moot. As the central tenet of the Japanese bombing campaign, General LeMay had instituted a policy of systematic total destruction of Japanese cities by firestorm, with associated massive civilian casualties. Killing thousands of Japanese civilians in a single night was now routine. The only difference would be that one plane with one bomb could accomplish in an instant what hundreds of planes and thousands of incendiary bombs could do over the course of an evening. These people argued, cynically but with the weight of blunt fact behind them, that it was no longer a question of whether to kill and maim, but how you did it.

As a final consideration, the Americans had no bombs to spare. Apart from the one rigged on the tower in the Alamogordo desert for the test shot code-named Trinity, there were just two more, bearing the names Little Boy and Fat Man.

Military advisors, meanwhile, not knowing about the new weapon, were pressing President Truman to let them proceed with, in his words, "existing plans for the invasion of the Japanese home islands." All of these circumstances pointed toward a decision Truman would have to make, and led to a May 31 meeting chaired by Stimson at the Pentagon. Participants in that meeting signed off on a final report summarizing the deliberations of the Interim Committee and one other group Truman had commissioned to study the matter of using the bomb, taking into account military, moral, and humanitarian factors. Their joint recommendation was to use the bomb as soon as possible and direct it at a dual target—a military installation near other buildings more susceptible to damage—and to drop the bomb without warning. In conclusion, they wrote, "We can propose no technical demonstration likely to bring an end to the war. We can see no acceptable alternative to direct military use."

Acting on that advice, on July 24 President Truman gave tentative approval to dropping the bombs: "The 509th Composite Group, 20th Air Force, will deliver its first special bomb as soon as weather will permit after about 3 August, 1945, on one of the targets: Hiroshima, Kokura, Niigata and Nagasaki. . . ." It was not an easy decision. As Stimson put it, "The decision to use the atomic bomb was a decision that brought death to over a hundred thousand Japanese. No explanation can change that fact and I do not wish to gloss it over. But this deliberate, premeditated destruction was our least abhorrent alternative."

The president then made a broadcast to Japan offering, in exchange for unconditional surrender, "a new order of peace, security and justice," of "freedom of speech, religion and thought," and of "new industries and participation in world trade relations." The reply, when it came, was from the premier, Admiral Baron Kantoro Suzuki. Truman's offer, he said, was "beneath contempt."

In preparation for probable success in developing an atomic bomb, in September 1944 the 393rd Heavy Bombardment Squadron had been detached from the 504th Bombardment Group to form the nucleus of a new group to deliver it—the 509th Composite Group, which was activated at Wendover Field, Utah, on December 17, 1944. After extensive and secret training to drop a single large, heavy bomb, they moved to their forward island base, Tinian, home to hundreds of B-29s jam-packed onto that relatively small island. With the arrival of the 509th, Tinian would forever be associated less with devastating fire-bombing raids launched from there than with the storied atomic bombs.

On Tinian the 509th compound was shrouded in secrecy, surrounded by barbed wire fences, and armed guards. Men assigned to the 509th soon became familiar with endless kidding and criticism because all they did was train; they never flew combat missions over Japan. Over and over they heard the chant,

Into the air the secret rose,
Where they're going nobody knows.
Tomorrow they'll return again,
But we'll never know where they have been.
Don't ask us about results or such
Unless you want to get in Dutch.
But take it from one, who is sure of the score,
The 509th is winning the war.

The first operational atomic bomb was dubbed Little Boy, not because of its size—it was huge—but apparently due to its svelte, somewhat conventional appearance in comparison to the second bomb, Fat Man. Little Boy was ferried to Tinian in parts. Its first shipment of active material arrived on July 26, 1945, on the cruiser *Indianapolis*. The odd and unusually heavy secret cargo was rumored to be enough gold to buy Japan out of World War II. Three days after unloading the mystery cargo at Tinian, the *Indianapolis* was torpedoed and sunk on its way to the Philippines. Of the twelve hundred men aboard ship, only nine hundred or so survived the sinking, and about three hundred were eventually rescued from the sea. Meanwhile on Tinian the rest of the active material for the first atom bomb arrived on July 28 and 29 aboard planes flown from the U. S.

As the B-29 crews from the 509th trained in secrecy on Tinian, another secret operation was under way to ensure the bombs' delivery. A group of scientists and technicians worked on Project Alberta in air-conditioned buildings a short distance to the northwest of the northernmost runway on Tinian, where the *Enola Gay* and *Bock's Car* would take off for Japan with the bombs. The men involved with Project Alberta were given the task of performing the final assembly and loading of the two bombs, a somewhat problematic task due to their large size.

Normal bomb-loading of a B-29 simply meant hauling bombs on trailers to where the plane sat on the tarmac, lifting the bombs into the bomb bay, and attaching them with shackles to the bomb-release switches controlled by the bombardier. But the atomic bombs were too large to roll under the fuselage of a parked B-29. They had to be lowered into pits, which the B-29s were backed over, and the bombs were cranked up into the bomb bays with hydraulic lifts. Two especially designed pits were constructed on Tinian by the Seabees, one for the Little Boy bomb destined for Hiroshima, and the other for the Fat Man bomb that ultimately hit Nagasaki. Identical pits were constructed on Iwo Jima halfway to Japan. In case of mechanical problems en route, the bomb-carrying plane could unload the weapon into the Iwo pit, to be reloaded onto an alternate B-29 standing by. Nothing was left to chance.

The primary target for the first bomb was Hiroshima, a city that grew up in the late sixteenth century around a nobleman's castle. After the Meiji Restoration in 1868, which restored the Emperor to supremacy and created a centralized government, it became a military base and remained so during World War II. In fact Hiroshima had been developed into the headquarters for defending the whole western half of Japan. For that purpose a vast underground communications complex was being constructed inside Mount Futaba. From this command center, Field Marshal Shunroku Hata and his staff of nearly four hundred men, a veritable "best and brightest" of the surviving command structure, had orders to deliver Japan from the inevitable invasion and save the Empire from defeat. In anticipation of the final battle to come, men and supplies continued to be crowded into a city already a frantic center of military-industrial activity. Preparations for invasion proceeded around the clock at Mitsubishi works near the dockyards and at Toyo Industries with manufacturing facilities for rifle parts. Along with many smaller factories, workers were urged to maintain a frenetic pace of production.

Troops drilled daily on the vast grounds of stately Hiroshima Castle, which housed regional and divisional Army headquarters. More than forty thousand men were stationed there, along with training facilities, a hospital, and storage depots. Earlier that spring Hiroshima's airport had been expanded to accommodate the increased military air traffic. In preparation for either firebombing or invasion, roughly sixty thousand civilians had been evacuated, leaving about 280,000 inhabitants by early August.

Back on Tinian the waiting was finally over for the 509th. The bomb preparation crews of Project Alberta had finished their work by the afternoon of August 5. They gently eased Little Boy onto a trailer for the short ride from the assembly building to the nearby, specially designated hardstand, lowered the bomb into the pit, and backed a newly christened B-29 over it. The plane, *Enola Gay*, would from that day symbolize the dawn of nuclear warfare. A hydraulic lift whined and strained as the heavy bomb was lifted up into the bomb bay. Then the plane was taxied to another hardstand some distance away to await its departure for Hiroshima that night.

Hours later, the crew of the *Enola Gay* headed to their plane after a midnight briefing and found the entire area lit with bright lights and teeming with photographers, reminding pilot Colonel Paul W. Tibbets of a "Hollywood premiere." Before they left, the crew was asked to pose for numerous pictures. Though a camera plane was designated to take photos as part of the three-plane Hiroshima attack force (an instrument plane to monitor blast effects, a camera plane to take photos, and the *Enola Gay*), tail-gunner Bob Caron was handed a camera at the last minute and told to shoot all the exposures on the roll. It was August 6, and the timetable studied at the crew briefing went off like clockwork:

1:37 A.M. Three weather B-29s take off to scout conditions over selected target cities—Hiroshima primary, with Kokura and Nagasaki secondary.

2:45 A.M. *Enola Gay* takes off. A short time later two B-29s with scientific instruments do the same. They will rendezvous with Tibbets over Iwo Jima.

7:25 A.M. Weather plane *Straight Flush* radios weather satisfactory for bombing primary target.

8:09 A.M. *Enola Gay* begins the bomb run. Escorts *The Great Artiste* and *Number 91* fall back and circle for taking readings and photos.

8:15 A.M. *Enola Gay* drops the bomb. *The Great Artiste* drops three parachute packs of instruments.

8:16 A.M. *Pika!!* And clocks in Hiroshima stop at 8:16 forever.

Enola Gay banked steeply away from Hiroshima in a maneuver all 509th crews had practiced many times before. The mushroom cloud roiled up over the devastated city, and Bob Caron was asked to describe what he saw from his prime vantage point in the tail-gunner's seat. On the ground below approximately seventy thousand people were already dead, with twice that number injured. He busily snapped photos with the camera handed to him just before takeoff, trying to shoot around the aluminum framework of the windows in his tail-gun perch. In between photos, Caron spoke into his interphone. Fellow crewman Jacob Beser captured his words on a wire recorder, documenting for posterity the first eyewitness account of an atomic bomb exploding over a city:

A column of smoke rising fast. It has a fiery red core. A bubbling mass, purple-gray in color, with that red core. It's all turbulent. Fires are springing up everywhere, like flames shooting out of a huge bed of coals. I am starting to count the fires. One, two, three, four, five, six . . . fourteen, fifteen . . . it's impossible. There are too many to count. Here it comes, the mushroom shape that Captain Parsons spoke about . . . It's like a mass of bubbling molasses. The mushroom is spreading out. It's maybe a mile or two wide and half a mile high. It's nearly level with us and climbing. It's very black, but there is purplish tint to the cloud. The base of the mushroom looks like a heavy undercast that is shot through with flames. The city must be below that. The flames and smoke are billowing out, whirling out into the foothills. All I can see now of the city is the main dock and what looks like an airfield. There are planes down there.

When *Enola Gay* returned to Tinian the crew quickly discovered that their mission was no longer a secret. A crowd of pilots and ground crews surrounded the plane, and Colonel Tibbets was immediately awarded a medal by General Carl "Tooey" Spaatz. Despite the excitement, there was to be no celebration for the crew of *Enola Gay* just yet. They were whisked away to debriefing. Brigadier General Thomas F. Farrell, representing the Manhattan Project, sat in and listened as the crew described what they experienced. He made notes that he sent to the War Department. Among them:

Sound—not appreciably observed.

Flash—not so blinding as [Trinity] because of bright sunlight. First there was a ball of fire changing in a few seconds to purple clouds and flames boiling and swirling upward. . . . All agreed light was intensely bright and white.

Cloud rose faster than [Trinity] reaching thirty thousand feet in three minutes. It was one-third greater diameter. It mushroomed at the top, broke away from column and the column mushroomed again. Cloud was most turbulent. It went at least to forty thousand feet, flattening across its top at this level. It was observed from combat airplane three hundred sixty three nautical [miles] away with airplane at twenty five thousand feet. Observation was then limited by haze and not curvature of the earth.

Blast. There were two distinct shocks felt in combat airplane similar in intensity to close flak bursts. Entire city except outermost ends of dock areas was covered with a dark gray dust layer, which joined the cloud column. It was extremely turbulent with flashes of fire visible in the dust. Estimated diameter of this dust later is at least three miles. One observer stated it looked as though whole town was being torn apart with clouds of dust rising out of valleys approaching the town. Due to dust visual observation of structural damage could not be made.

Judge and other observers felt this strike was tremendous and awesome even in comparison with [Trinity].

Farrell went on to consider the possibility that the atomic bomb blast could be mistaken by the Japanese for a "huge meteor," which indicates the concern high-ranking officials had that the bomb could be written off by the Japanese as a fluke, natural or otherwise. A second bomb had to be dropped as soon as possible to prove that the first was no accident.

Meanwhile in Japan, there was understandable confusion and shock as to what exactly had occurred at Hiroshima. The first announcement that something unusual had happened was by Tokyo Rose saying three planes, not the usual hundreds involved in the firebomb raids, had bombed Hiroshima. An hour later the Tokyo government announced that train service to Hiroshima had been suspended. The 6 P.M. broadcast by NHK (Japan Broadcasting Corp.) said simply, "Hiroshima was attacked by B-29s this morning at 8:20. The planes have turned back after dropping incendiary bombs. The damage is being investigated."

The next day Radio Tokyo announced, "As a result of the wanton attack a considerable number of houses [in Hiroshima] were demolished and fires were caused to start at several points. . . ." That same day Domei News Agency gave the first indication that what happened at Hiroshima was unprecedented. "By employing the new weapon designed to massacre innocent civilians, the Americans opened the eyes of the world to their sadistic nature. What caused the enemy to employ such bestial tactics revealed how thin a veneer of civilization the enemy has. . . ."

However, the Japanese military chose to play down the bomb and continued to incite people to resist to the end. On August 8 Japanese Navy officers declared Hiroshima had been hit by "an electron incendiary" bomb. An Army weapons specialist knowingly declared it to be a "sulfuric acid bomb." General Hata, commander of the Western District Army and himself a survivor of the blast, reported to Tokyo headquarters that "defensive measures against the bomb were possible"; that "burns sustained by survivors wearing light clothing were relatively light"; and that the fires were so intense because the bomb exploded at a time when much of the population was using fires to cook their breakfast.

Since the U.S. only had two atomic bombs ready to go in early August, the strategy was to drop them as rapidly as possible to give the strong impression that they were churning off some relentless assembly line. Indeed, that assembly line was functioning at top speed, but after the first two bombs there would be a delay of several weeks in preparing a third. That sense of urgency, plus the forecast of an impending stretch of bad weather in the western Pacific, drove the men of Project Alberta to work at top speed to ready the Fat Man bomb.

Everything was proceeding fairly smoothly in the huts of Project Alberta as the assembly continued, or at least as smoothly as could be expected when assembling an atomic bomb. But midmorning of August 8, with the bomb-loading scheduled for that afternoon and takeoff later that night, and only two days after the Hiroshima bomb had been delivered, the men of Project Alberta were temporarily interrupted by a bizarre event. Eyewitness Harlow Russ, a civilian engineer, later wrote in his book, *Project Alberta: The Preparation of Atomic Bombs for Use in World War II*:

In order to prevent an overcrowded condition inside the assembly building, a number of assembly team members who were currently unoccupied had gone outside the fenced area to rest and cool off under the trees. It was a hot day with very little breeze; the tide was in and the sea, outside the reef, was calm. Suddenly the team members outside the enclosure observed a ship that had appeared about a mile away to the north. One of them came inside the building to report it and we immediately called the security force and asked for special agents to help protect the area. Then a number of us, including a guard who neglected to bring a weapon, ran down to the edge of the cliff to get a better view of the ship. It approached us rapidly, sailing along the coast just outside of the reef. It appeared that the ship had rounded the north end of the island through the Saipan Channel. It was an ominous-looking vessel, diesel powered, 150 feet long, with a deck five feet above the waterline, a small superstructure, and masts. It was painted entirely black. It was flying a tattered American flag, but it had no identification markings. As it came closer we could see swimmers, clad in shorts, diving from the deck into the water, one every hundred feet or so and heading for shore, where they were soon hidden from view by the cliffs. We could see clearly that they were not Americans. By the time we had reached our vantage point on

shore, perhaps 30 people were in the water, and others were still diving as the ship passed our position. As the ship passed us, one of the guards on the embankment opened up with his machine gun, firing over our heads into the water just ahead of the ship. The ship immediately swung to sea, circled, and headed back north, picking up swimmers as it went. Because of the rough nature of the coast we could not see whether any of the swimmers had reached shore, or if any were left behind by the ship. Just before the ship disappeared around the north end of the island, two of the security agents arrived in a jeep. They drew their snub-nosed revolvers and rushed down to join us at the shore. We waited and watched but the ship did not reappear.

Russ maintains that he has never heard of any official account of this incident. He and his Project Alberta teammates, already strung tight with the tension and pressure of their nerve-wracking work, came up with the somewhat implausible explanation that surviving Japanese holdouts in the jungles on Tinian, noting the flurry of activities in the bomb-assembly areas on the north end of the island, had associated the unusual activity there with the single-bomb destruction of Hiroshima. They had alerted the commanders on the still-occupied nearby Japanese islands of Aguijan or Rota, and a Japanese commando raid was then launched to target the A-bomb assembly and loading areas. It seemed like a wild story, but that was the best they could come up with, and nobody had a better explanation.

Whatever the truth about the mysterious black ship, there were no further distractions, and all preparations were completed one way or another. The bomb was ready to load onto the designated B-29 named *Bock's Car* on the afternoon of August 8. The bomb was covered in graffiti just before it was hauled to the bomb-loading pit, with various sentiments intended for the Japanese victims. Harlow Russ later recalled what he wrote on the bomb:

Sappy Jappy started scrappy, Bombed Pearl Harbor,
Pretty crappy. Jappy have reached end of scrappy,
bomb will knock Jappy slappy happy.

The bomb was lowered into its designated pit about
fifty meters from where the Hiroshima bomb was loaded
only three days before. *Bock's Car* was backed over the pit,
and Fat Man was lifted into its tight space in the bomb bay.

Later that night just before 2 A.M. on the morning of
August 9, and with much less fanfare, *Bock's Car* lifted off
from Tinian on its way to the primary target of Kokura.
Nagasaki was listed as the alternate, to be bombed only
if there was some problem at Kokura. As smoothly as everything had gone for *Enola Gay*, the opposite was the case
for *Bock's Car*. Even before takeoff it was discovered that
one of the fuel tanks could not be tapped. It was quickly
decided to proceed, to avoid having to unload the bomb and
reload it onto an alternate aircraft. Major Charles Sweeney,
the pilot, who had flown the instrument observation aircraft over Hiroshima, figured that if everything went as
smoothly as on the Hiroshima mission, the extra fuel in
that tank would not be used.

But things did not go as planned. Even as the bomb
was being loaded that afternoon, the weather was threatening around Tinian, and it got even worse after *Bock's
Car* took off. The three planes of the attack force missed
the rendezvous over Yakoshima, an island off the southeast coast of Kyushu. Only two showed up, and after waiting about forty minutes, Sweeney headed to Japan with
only one plane accompanying him, the instrument aircraft
The Great Artiste. By the time they reached Kokura thick
haze and cloud obscured the city. Sweeney tried three different bomb runs, all in vain, and fuel was running low. A
hasty decision was made that would have tremendous
consequences for the people of Kokura and Nagasaki. In
the instant of that nervous decision by Sweeney and weap-
oneer Fred Ashworth, made at thirty thousand feet over a
city marked for destruction, aboard a plane loaded with an
armed atomic bomb, the people of Kokura were saved and
thousands in Nagasaki were doomed.

Nagasaki, called by some the "San Francisco of Japan,"
with its scenic bay, bustling port, the mixture of European
and Japanese buildings clinging to the hills rising from
the waterfront, its rich history of European contact and
commerce, was also covered with clouds by the time
Bock's Car came overhead. Even with only one bomb run,
there would be barely enough fuel to make an emergency
landing on Okinawa, the closest Allied air base, nearly five
hundred miles to the south. Against all orders, Ashworth
ordered a radar bomb run. The aiming point, directly in
the center of the downtown area of the city, was obscured
under a layer of low clouds as the crew attempted to get
a fix on radar. At the last minute bombardier Kermit Beahan spotted a break in the clouds about three miles north
of the center of the city, in the mixed industrial and suburban district of Urakami. This predominantly Christian
neighborhood was the location of the Urakami Cathedral,
the largest Christian church in Asia. The Urakami district
was also home to the Mitsubishi steel works, as well as
the torpedo works where those used at Pearl Harbor were
manufactured. The clouds over Nagasaki were a mixed bless-
ing. Instead of exploding over the downtown area, the bomb
detonated about five hundred meters above the ground at
11:02 A.M. over the northern edge of the city in a broad valley whose sides confined the effects of the blast to a smaller
area than at Hiroshima, even though the explosive force
of the Nagasaki bomb was considerably greater.

At least fifty thousand and perhaps as many as seventy thousand people died, including a number of Allied
POWs at Branch 14 of the Fukuoka POW Camp. Imprisoned
at the camp were Koreans, Chinese, Taiwanese, Christian
missionaries, and about two hundred British, Dutch, and
Australian POWs. The POWs were used as slave labor in the
war industry plants in Nagasaki, most in the Mitsubishi
steel works. A number survived the blast and subsequent
fires. On his way to Nagasaki that previous June, one of the
Australians, Murray Jobling, had narrowly escaped death
when an American submarine torpedoed the POW ship he
was on. Then a year later he somehow survived the atomic
bomb. After being knocked down by the concussion of the

blast, Jobling recalled in an interview for the Nagasaki Atomic Bomb Museum: "I saw one of the Dutchmen trapped under a big beam [from a collapsed building at the steel works]. His mates couldn't get him out and the fire was coming close. He was yelling that he didn't want to burn. I reckon they killed him so he wouldn't be burned alive. That was my first look at a casualty, the first of many."

Meanwhile in the air above, Fred Ashworth recalled in a 1996 interview for *Air Classics* magazine, "The only thing on my mind was where had the darn thing gone off? What did Beahan line up on to drop the bomb?" But the crew on *Bock's Car* had a more pressing problem, namely their dwindling fuel supply. After circling the mushroom cloud once, Sweeney headed the plane straight to the emergency landing field at Okinawa. He barely had enough fuel to bull his way into the landing pattern on a direct approach, and landed just as fuel ran out. Copilot Fred Olivi, in a 1999 interview for *Fly Past* magazine, remembered, "Just as we turned off the active runway the number two engine quit, out of gas."

Ashworth still didn't know exactly where the bomb had gone off. "When we landed at Okinawa, I got all the people who had gone in for a look together in order to figure out where the bomb went. We looked at our target maps and decided that it had gone off in the Urakami River Valley."

Back at Nagasaki in that same Urakami district, the ensuing chaos after the blast and subsequent fires left the surviving POWs free to roam. A group of them went up into the hills above Nagasaki the first night. Jobling recalled, "It was an incredible sight. The whole valley was on fire from end to end."

Three parachute-borne blast gauges (dubbed "Bang-meters" by the scientists on Tinian) were dropped over Nagasaki from the instrument plane, *The Great Artiste*, at the same time as the bomb was released. They were designed to transmit the primary and reflected shock-wave signals back to recording equipment on the plane. They drifted to the ground to the east of Nagasaki where they were recovered intact. Inside one was a handwritten letter (with carbon copies inside the other two gauges) from three of the Project Alberta physicists, Luis Alvarez, Bob Serber, and Phil Morrison. The idea, hatched in the Tinian officers' club late in the evening of August 8, was to try to shorten the war by sending a personal message to a former physics professor colleague of theirs at Berkeley, Ryokichi Sagane, who was then at the University of Tokyo. In his autobiography, *Alvarez: Adventures of a Physicist,* he stated that the letter "would appeal to him to inform the Japanese military that, since two atomic bombs had been dropped, it was obvious that we could build as many more as we might need to end the war by force." Alvarez wrote a draft, Serber and Morrison edited it, and Alvarez wrote out the revised version with two carbon copies and signed it. They then rushed to tape the letters inside the bangmeters before the mission.

When the letters were found, they were delivered to the military. Apparently they were "discussed at length," according to Alvarez. Curiously, Sagane was never contacted and finally saw one of the letters only after the war ended.

The shock and horror of two atomic bombs was the final impetus for the Emperor to accept surrender, and he recorded a radio address to inform the Japanese people. His voice, never before heard by most people in Japan, emanated eerily from radios all over the country. It was one more surreal moment for the Japanese, added to months of firebombing, atomic bombs, and the prospect of foreign occupiers. But the sound of the Emperor's voice brought home to all Japanese that this was indeed the end of the Pacific war, something that they must accept.

When word spread to island bases around the Pacific that the Japanese had finally given up, it was almost as if, in unison, one giant sigh of relief was let out of tens of thousands of lungs. The sense of dread and impending doom surrounding the planned invasion was suddenly lifted. As they found out about the unbelievable new bomb that had somehow gotten the Japanese to surrender, thousands of men realized that, quite literally, they had dodged the proverbial bullet. Harlan Wall, an infantryman in the U.S. Sixth Army, waiting in the Philippines to join the impending invasion waves on the shores of Nippon, remembered, "Sure we all cheered when we heard they dropped the bomb. But we weren't cheering because all those people died. We were cheering because we knew they couldn't take something like that bomb, and they had to surrender. I wasn't going to have to be in the invasion [of Japan]. I was going to make it home."

All over the Pacific, impromptu celebrations broke out. Al Hahn, on a U.S. Navy PT boat in the Philippines, instigated his own: "We had just started working on our boat, changing the engines and getting it ready for the invasion of Japan. That night the radioman and I were left to watch the boat while the rest of the crew went to watch the movie. I was down in the crew quarters reading. The radioman was fiddling with the radio, trying to get some music. About 80 percent of what those radios picked up was static, so he was spending a lot of time trying to find something to listen to. He finally found a broadcast that said a big new kind of bomb had been dropped on Japan, and that it looked like the war was going to be over. He yelled to me and I came up to listen, and sure enough it sounded like it was going to be the end of the war. So now all the other guys were at the movie and we were the only two who knew this, and we wondered what to do. Then we remembered we had a mortar and some star shells in the boat, so we got those out and started firing them right over to where the movie was being shown. So up went these star shells, and when they burst they lit up the whole area. Well they all thought there was an air raid or the Japanese were invading so they come running back to the boat yelling and all fired up and wanted to know what was going on. We told them to come down and listen to the radio, and then they all found out. There was a lot more yelling then. We were all very happy to hear that it looked like the war was over, and we weren't going to have to go in on that invasion." Scenes like this were repeated on hundreds of islands and ships all over the Pacific. Though many thousands had died in Japan, many more thousands would live and make it home. There was a sudden, startling real-

ization they would now make it through a war they had given themselves little hope of surviving.

September 2, 1945, was the long-awaited day that the Japanese surrendered to the Allies. Since MacArthur commanded the Allied land forces and Nimitz the naval forces, the big question was, Who should chair the ceremony? After much debate, a compromise was worked out. MacArthur would officiate at the ceremony, but the surrender would be signed on a Navy ship, the USS *Missouri*, named after Truman's home state.

MacArthur boarded *Missouri* at 8:05 A.M., and the Japanese surrender party came aboard at 8:55. An eyewitness to the events of that day later recounted,

> Sunday was the day of formal surrender. A destroyer took us off the Bund in Yokohama in the early morning and we climbed aboard the U.S.S. *Missouri* in the bay. The U.S.S. *Iowa* lay to one side, the U.S.S. *South Dakota* to the other. An old flag with 31 stars hung from one of the *Missouri*'s turrets, the same flag that Commodore Perry had brought to Tokyo Bay when he opened Japan to the West 92 years earlier. At the very top of the mainmast was the same flag that flew over the Capitol on December 7, 1941.

> The *Missouri* was heavy with people . . . the crush held everyone erect, each of us allotted two square feet of tiptoe space. . . . We thought it was the last war ever and wanted to watch.

The weather had been poor, with clouds and rain the previous day, but almost as if on cue the weather cooperated. Journalist Theodore H. White later wrote, "The skies had lightened, the rain of Saturday had stopped, and the clouds above the ship were breaking up." The sun tried to come out, and in the distance the summit of Mount Fuji "sparkled in the sun." The stage was set. All that was left was to sign the papers and end it once and for all.

The ceremony was solemn and brief. After the signing, MacArthur's deep baritone voice intoned, "Let us pray that peace be now restored to the world, and that God will preserve it always." Then turning to the Japanese delegates General Yoshijiro Umezu and Foreign Minister Mamoru Shigemitsu, he said, "These proceedings are closed."

"There was a buzzing in the distance," White recalled, "then a rumble, then the deafening tone of thousands of planes converging. . . . Four hundred B-29s came low, low over the *Missouri* and fifteen hundred fleet planes rose above, around them and on their wings. They dipped over the *Missouri*, on to Yokohama, inland over Tokyo, then back out to sea again." The war in the Pacific was over. But its legacy would live on in the memories of all participants and their descendants, its detritus etched into exotic tropical landscapes of scattered island archipelagoes all across the world's largest ocean, on through the twentieth century, into the twenty-first century, and undoubtedly beyond.

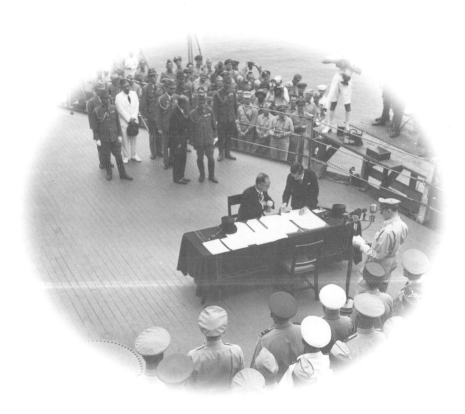

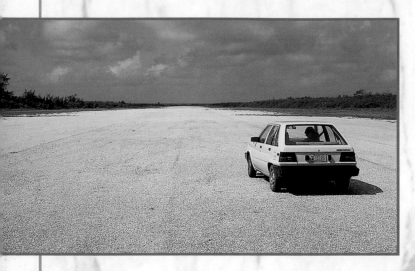

The Pacific war had an ending no one really anticipated. The reality of atom bombs was something that even physicists had trouble visualizing. Yet, part of this surreal endgame was played out on the island of Tinian in the summer of 1945, and visitors today can trace the beginning of the final journey of the atomic bombs from Runway A (shown here), where both *Enola Gay* and *Bock's Car* took off.

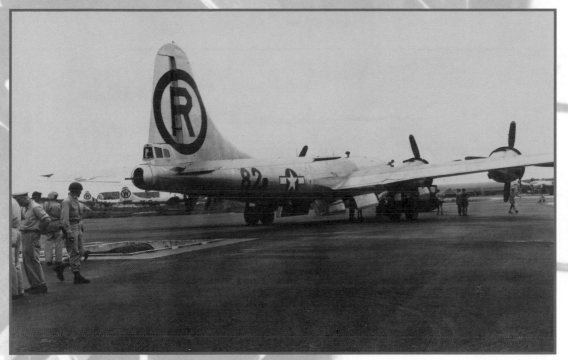

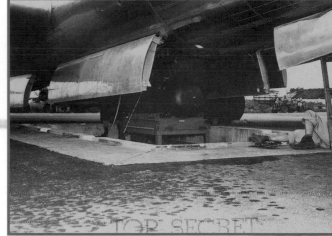

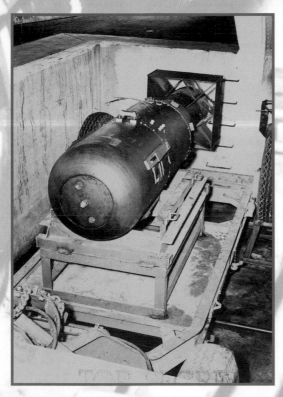

Before the planes could take off, the bombs had to be cranked up into the bomb bay, and this presented a problem. The B-29 fuselage at the bomb bay didn't offer enough clearance above the tarmac to allow the huge bombs and necessary equipment to be positioned underneath. So two specially designed pits were dug on Tinian by the Seabees, one for the Little Boy bomb destined for Hiroshima and the other for the Fat Man bomb, its ultimate target Nagasaki. The first photo here, one of a series declassified in 1999, shows *Enola Gay* backing up over the bomb pit. Once the plane was properly positioned, the tarp covering the bomb was removed (photo at left), and Little Boy was raised into the plane's bomb bay by hydraulic lift (top right photo). An identical pit was constructed on Iwo Jima, halfway to Japan. In case of mechanical problems en route, the bomb-carrying plane could lower the weapon into that pit and have it reloaded into an alternate B-29 standing by at Iwo.

BELOW: Today on Tinian the Y-shaped hard-stand where the atomic bomb pits are located is kept clear of the voracious vegetation that almost covers the island. Visitors can view the two bomb pits, each now appropriately marked with explanatory plaques and filled with coral gravel and plantings. This one is called "Atomic Bomb Pit Number I" and was used to load the Hiroshima bomb. The photo was taken from about the same angle as one showing the bomb being hoisted into *Enola Gay*'s bomb bay on the afternoon of August 5. The plane was then taxied to its hardstand some distance away to await its 2:45 A.M. departure for Hiroshima.

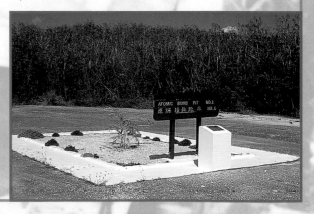

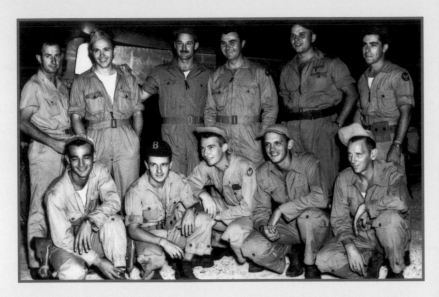

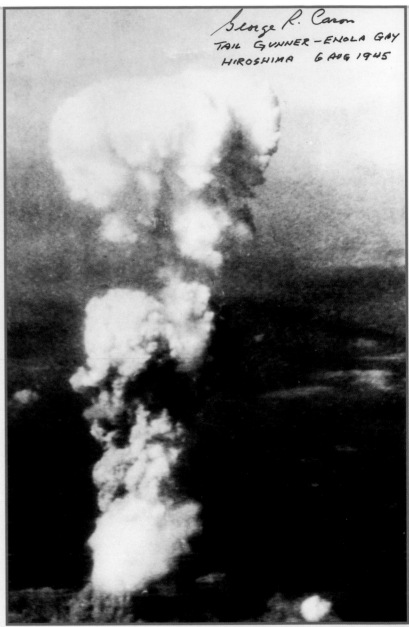

George R. Caron
TAIL GUNNER—ENOLA GAY
HIROSHIMA 6 AUG 1945

ABOVE: The crew of *Enola Gay* headed to their plane after a midnight briefing and posed for numerous pictures, including this group photo. Although one of the three-plane Hiroshima attack force was designated camera plane to take the official photos, *Enola Gay* tail-gunner George "Bob" Caron (wearing a Brooklyn Dodgers cap and crouched second from left in the front row) was handed a camera at the last minute and told to shoot all the pictures on the roll.

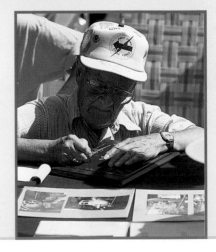

BELOW LEFT: Colonel Paul Tibbets, head of the 509th and pilot for the first atomic mission, waves to the photographers just before departing in *Enola Gay*. Not only that, he was also trying to wave people away from the giant B-29 propellers so he could start the engines.

RIGHT: About six hours after takeoff, as *Enola Gay* banked away from Hiroshima and as the mushroom cloud roiled up over the devastated city, Bob Caron took this shot from his prime vantage point in the tail-gunner's seat. He had struggled to get a clear shot with his camera, but the gun-sight and window framing in his cramped battle station were in the way. "I asked Colonel Tibbets to bank the plane a little to the left so I could get a better shot out my emergency exit window. He did, and that's the picture they printed." Of the twenty-seven exposures on Caron's roll, this picture was destined to become one of the most famous from World War II. So what happened with the camera plane and the trained photographers who were supposed to take the "official" photos? "Apparently none of their pictures turned out," said Bob with a smile. Ironically, an amateur photographed the first atomic bomb detonation over a city, with a camera handed to him almost as an afterthought.

FAR RIGHT: Bob Caron retired to Denver, Colorado, and made appearances on the air-show circuit, selling autographed prints of his famous photo, as well as plaques of an *Enola Gay* image, one of which he is engraving with his autograph at a Colorado air show in 1994. The crewmen of the atom bomb planes themselves became symbols of atomic warfare, and to ward off unwanted attention Caron

had to have an unlisted telephone number and only a post office box for an address. The 509th still has reunions, but usually not in conjunction with the rest of the B-29 veterans. Always separate from the other crews on Tinian, that's how they remain. A number of the 509th crewmen were interviewed for a spate of documentary films to commemorate the fiftieth anniversary of the bombings in 1995, and they became quite familiar to TV viewers fifty years after the fact. Bob Caron, amateur photographer extraordinaire, did not live to see the fiftieth anniversary of the day he took his famous photo—dying a little more than two months short of August 6, 1995.

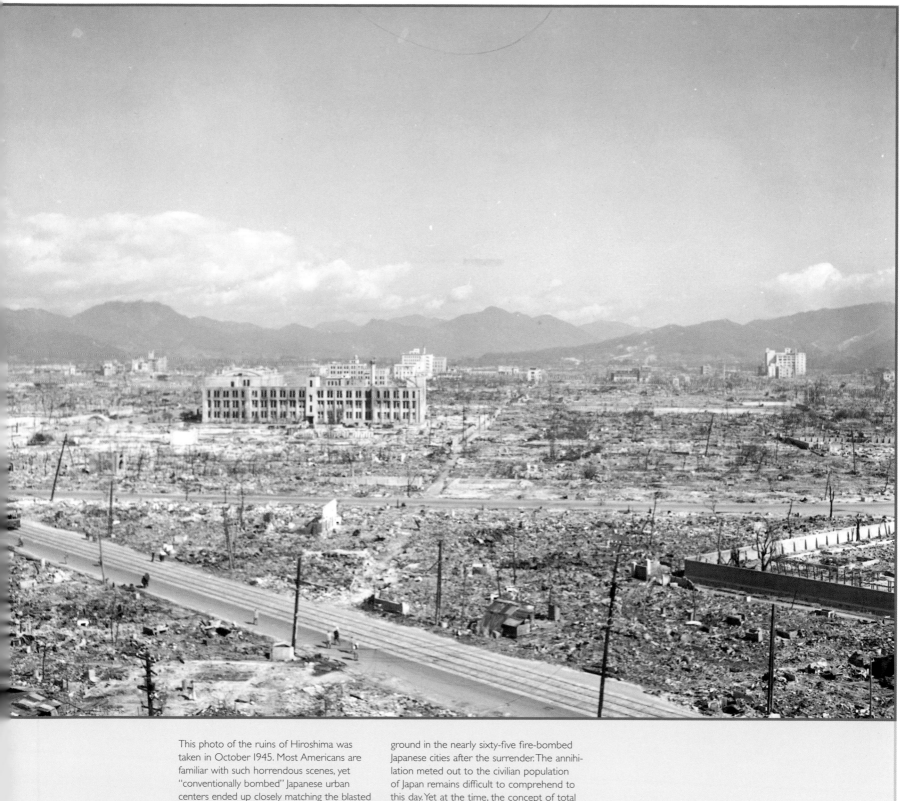

This photo of the ruins of Hiroshima was taken in October 1945. Most Americans are familiar with such horrendous scenes, yet "conventionally bombed" Japanese urban centers ended up closely matching the blasted wastelands of Hiroshima and Nagasaki. Even the aircrews and Air Force planners were unprepared for what they saw on the ground in the nearly sixty-five fire-bombed Japanese cities after the surrender. The annihilation meted out to the civilian population of Japan remains difficult to comprehend to this day. Yet at the time, the concept of total war had been developed to a fine art, and any stratagem thought to bring the war with Japan to a quicker close was put to use.

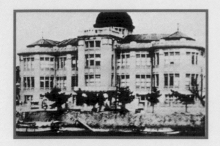

A prewar photo of the Hiroshima Industrial Promotion Hall, destined to become the enduring symbol of the atomic bombing of Hiroshima.

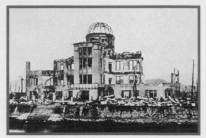

ABOVE: The ruins of the Industrial Promotion Hall shortly after its destruction by the Little Boy atomic bomb in August 1945.

BELOW: The Atomic Bomb Dome is the most visible relic today of the destruction of Hiroshima. Lying across the river from Peace Memorial Park, the shattered building is left in ruins to symbolize the atomic devastation of the city. As the twenty-first century began, the remains of the former Industrial Promotion Hall had undergone two "reinforcement projects," one in 1967 and another in 1990, to structurally stabilize the ruins. The historical marker in the foreground is like others placed around Hiroshima near points of interest dating from August 6, 1945. This one has a photograph taken before the bombing and a short history of the building in English and Japanese. Another marker noting the exact location of ground zero, or the "hypocentre" as the Japanese refer to it, is just behind and to the right of the Atomic Bomb Dome, on a quiet side street about two hundred meters away. It was roughly nineteen hundred feet above that point that Little Boy detonated at 8:16 A.M., August 6, 1945. The contrast of the ruined city and the modern city are no more apparent than here, where the baseball stadium for the Hiroshima Carp looms a couple of blocks behind the Atomic Bomb Dome (one of the stadium's light standards can be seen rising above the left side of the building in this photo). In a peaceful park, where a large museum houses many gruesome artifacts from the bombed city, and a Memorial Cenotaph shelters an eternal flame dedicated to the spirits of the victims, visitors are often reminded of the vitality of modern-day Hiroshima as loud cheers and rhythmic chanting from thousands of fans at the nearby baseball stadium echo over an area that was once ground zero.

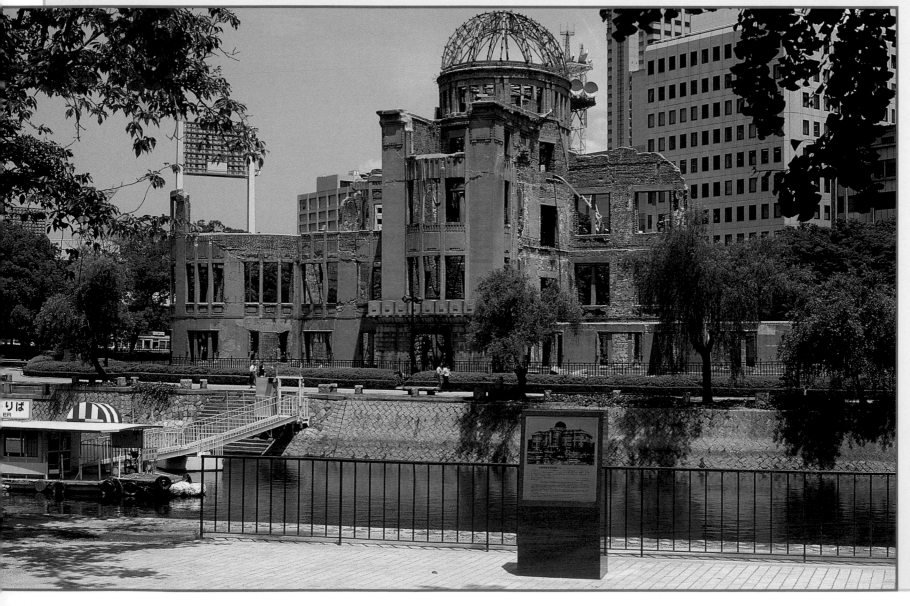

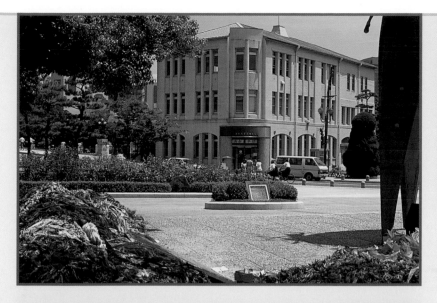

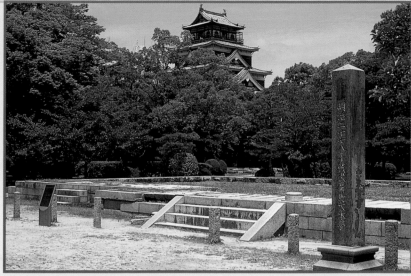

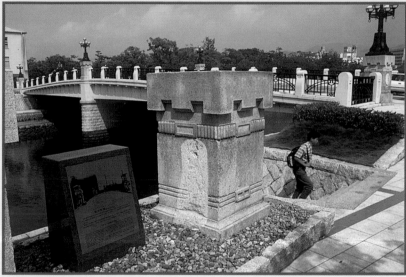

TOP RIGHT: Hiroshima Castle was the center of a vast military complex. Within the extensive castle grounds, and encircled by a huge moat, were forty thousand men as well as divisional and regimental Army headquarters for the defense of all of southern Japan, an infantry training school, a hospital, civilian defense headquarters, the headquarters of the dreaded *Kempei Tai* (secret police), and a number of U.S. POWs. The castle itself was over four hundred years old and rose sixty feet above the various facilities on the grounds. Located only about nine hundred meters from ground zero, the entire castle complex was completely destroyed. It is thought that the largest single group of Hiroshima casualties occurred here, with over a 90 percent casualty rate. In one group alone, three to four thousand soldiers and one American POW out in the open on the parade ground were incinerated instantly by the blast. After the war Hiroshima Castle itself was reconstructed and is shown here

rising above the remaining foundations of one of many military buildings once dotting the castle grounds.

LEFT: Next to the tourist office is the Motoyasu Bridge, shown here. The short two-hundred-meter walk from Peace Memorial Park in the background to the ground zero marker behind this view takes visitors over this bridge. It survived the blast and has been rebuilt only in recent years. Several of the original bridge railing posts have been put on display (foreground) to show how the stone was scorched by the blast of the explosion, while parts shielded by the railing attachments remain their original light color.

BELOW: Interspersed among the modern buildings of downtown Hiroshima is the old Bank of Japan, a surviving veteran of the atomic attack. Though all buildings surrounding the bank were leveled or burned, incredibly it was only slightly damaged by fire in one corner of the structure.

TOP LEFT: Though virtually every wood-frame building within a half-mile radius of ground zero was flattened, a number of reinforced concrete buildings were left standing, or at least their exterior shells were. Most were damaged and gutted by fire, but several survive to this day, including this one about three hundred meters from ground zero in Peace Memorial Park. Before the war it was the Fuel Hall, an office building for the government's fuel administration. All people in the building at the time of the explosion died, except for one man who survived in the basement. The building interior was reconstructed after the war, and it now houses the tourist office for the Peace Memorial Park. In the right foreground is the Children's Peace Memorial with hundreds of strands of multicolored paper cranes heaped around it. The memorial is

dedicated to Sadako, a ten-year-old girl who died from leukemia due to radiation exposure from the blast. She believed that if she could fold 1,000 origami paper cranes, she would survive. She died before she could complete her task, having folded only 644 cranes, but children from her school folded the remaining 356. All 1,000 paper cranes were buried with her. Meanwhile, word spread across Japan of her struggle, and people from all over the country started to send paper cranes to Hiroshima tied together in long strands. The paper crane has now become a symbol of the atomic bombings and the rebirth and hope for the future of Japan. Any site in Hiroshima or Nagasaki associated with the bombings is typically festooned with strings of multicolored paper cranes—thousands of them—placed by civic, religious, or school groups.

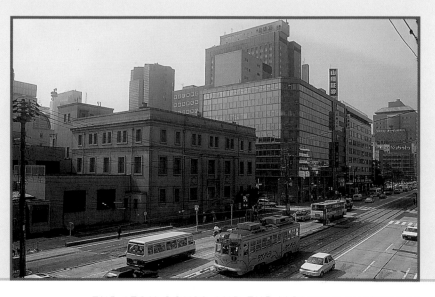

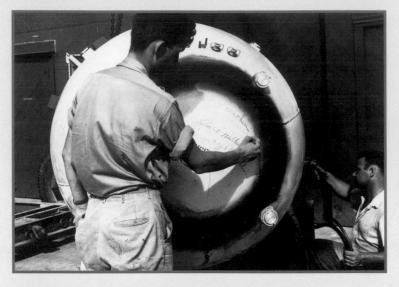

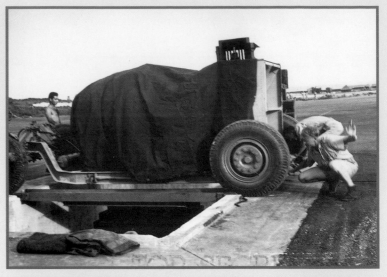

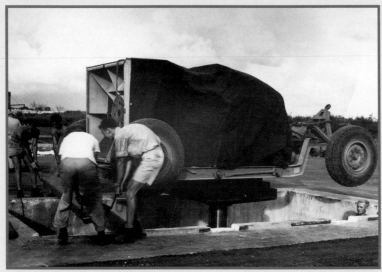

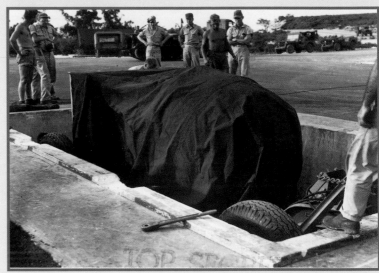

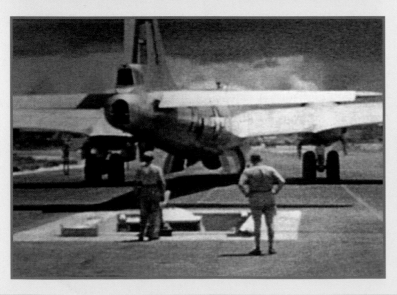

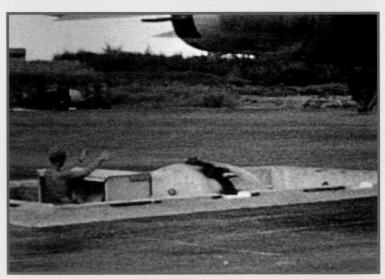

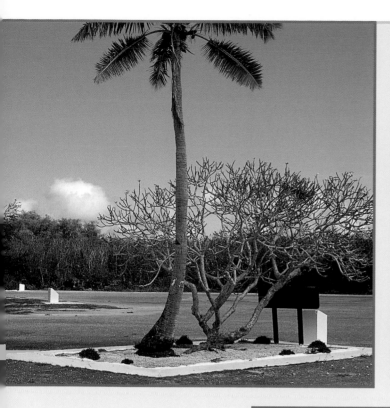

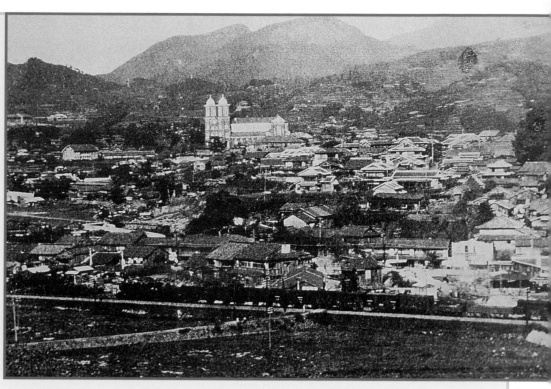

OPPOSITE TOP LEFT: A member of the Project Alberta team autographs the Fat Man bomb bound for Nagasaki as another crewman spray-paints the seals on the metal casing.

OPPOSITE TOP RIGHT, CENTER LEFT AND RIGHT: It was no easy task maneuvering an atomic bomb into a pit. First, the bomb on its trailer was rolled across the pit on steel beams. Then the hydraulic hoist in the pit lifted the bomb trailer and rotated it 90 degrees in line with the pit. Finally the hoist slowly lowered the trailer and bomb down into the pit.

OPPOSITE BOTTOM LEFT AND RIGHT: With the bomb safely positioned in the pit, the B-29 *Bock's Car* was then backed over it.

TOP LEFT: A similar view of Atomic Bomb Pit Number 2 on Tinian today. Like the Hiroshima bomb pit (in the far background just to the right of the white car), the Nagasaki pit has been filled with coral gravel and plantings.

TOP RIGHT AND BOTTOM: This prewar photo shows the Urakami residential area of Nagasaki, with the Urakami Cathedral in the background. Ground zero was roughly in the center of the first photo. This entire area was flattened and the cathedral destroyed, as seen in the second photo. About seventy thousand people died, including a number of Allied POWs at Branch 14 of the Fukuoka POW Camp.

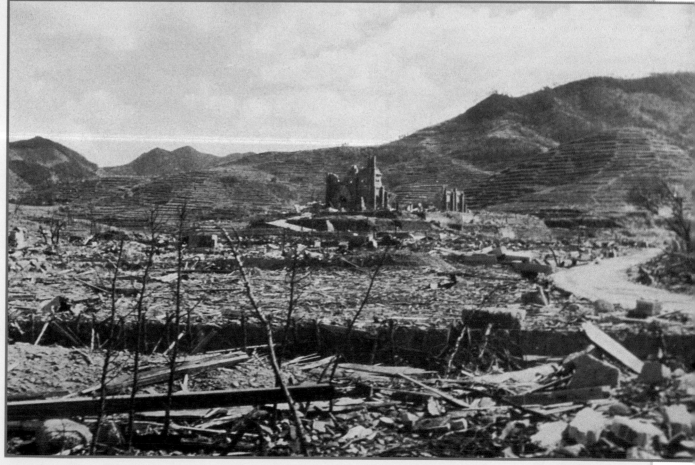

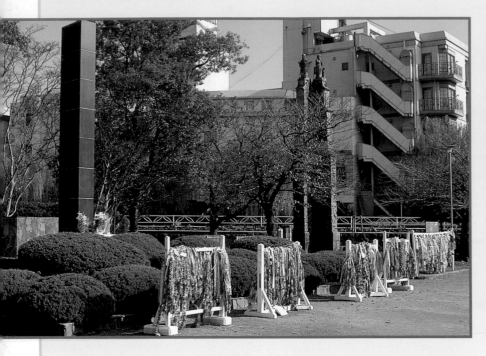

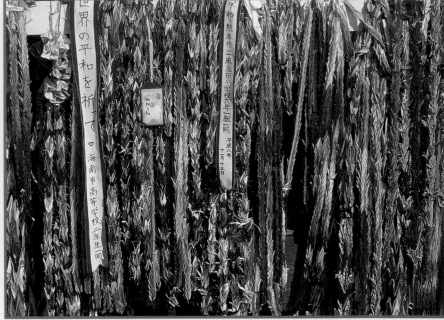

ABOVE LEFT: At 11:02 A.M. on August 9, 1945, the Fat Man atomic bomb exploded about five hundred meters above the black obelisk at left, obliterating the Urakami district, destroying the Mitsubishi steel works and torpedo works, and ravaging the Urakami Cathedral. A part of the ruined cathedral, salvaged when it was reconstructed after the war, has been erected to the right of the marker in the peaceful setting of Hypocentre Park, set amidst the rebuilt, bustling, modern-day Urakami district. Each morning at exactly 11:02 A.M. chimes echo across the site of ground zero, a daily reminder of what happened nearly sixty years ago. On the side of a hill outside this picture is the Nagasaki Atomic Bomb Museum, which houses collections of artifacts and burned and torn clothing of victims moved from the old museum nearby. A large part of the museum is dedicated to atomic survivors all over the world, the human detritus from years of varying degrees of exposure to the effects of atomic weapons construction or testing.

ABOVE RIGHT: As at Hiroshima, strands of thousands of paper cranes are placed in front of the hypocentre marker and on other memorials solemnizing the atomic bombing.

BELOW LEFT: The Urakami Cathedral has been rebuilt on the same spot and was designed to resemble the original structure with its two imposing bell towers. Dedicated in 1981 by Pope John Paul, the cathedral is guarded in the foreground by scorched and blackened statuary from the first cathedral.

BELOW RIGHT: About one hundred meters north of Hypocentre Park on a hill overlooking the Urakami district is Nagasaki's Peace Memorial Park. Amidst the fountains, quiet walkways, sculptures placed by countries around the world, and the large central sculpture in the background, are the foundations of the Urakami Branch Prison that stood on the site the day of the blast. All 134 people in the prison were killed, including guards. The four-meter high, quarter-meter thick surrounding wall was leveled, and the wooden buildings in the prison compound were flattened and burned, leaving only the concrete foundations seen here today.

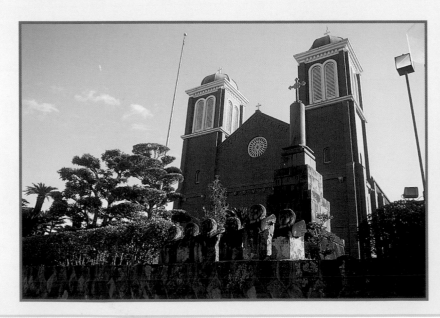

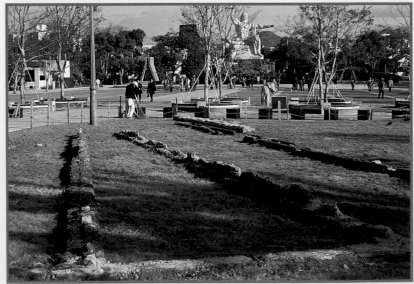

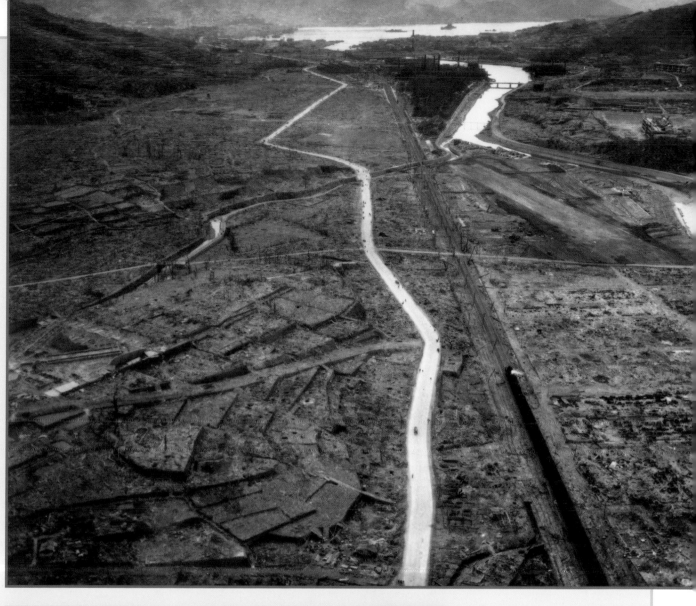

RIGHT: Aerial view of the Urakami district of Nagasaki taken in October 1945. Ground zero is near upper center to the left of the main street just below its intersection with the canal. Downtown Nagasaki is built around the bay at the top of the photo and escaped relatively intact. The Mitsubishi steel works lie in ruins next to the river above the center of the photo in the distance. Note the train in the foreground heading toward downtown Nagasaki. Today, visitors staying at downtown hotels take this same rail line to visit the Urakami memorials and museum. The ruins of the Urakami Branch Prison can be seen as the angled foundations at center far left, the present-day site of Peace Memorial Park.

BELOW: On the side of a hill leading to a shrine stood a stone torii that was partially destroyed by the blast. Photos of this torii came to symbolize the devastation of the Nagasaki bomb.

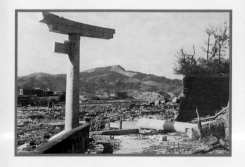

RIGHT: Visitors today find the torii just as it was left in 1945. The shock wave from the bomb, which detonated at right background, knocked down one support column (lying at right foreground) and half the top cross-member. The other support column was twisted on its pedestal and rotated about 30 degrees, yet somehow remained standing. About fifty meters behind where this photo was taken are the remains of the shrine. Incredibly, two giant camphor trees perched on the shrine platform, scorched, burned, and stripped of all foliage by the blast and seemingly dead at the time, are still alive. Somehow, the trees revived and grew around the old dead and broken trunks and limbs, enveloping the old trees in new growth. Their fresh green outlines now tower above the rebuilt shrine. Parts of the old dead trunks are still visible among the new growth, a poignant symbol of the death and rebirth of Nagasaki.

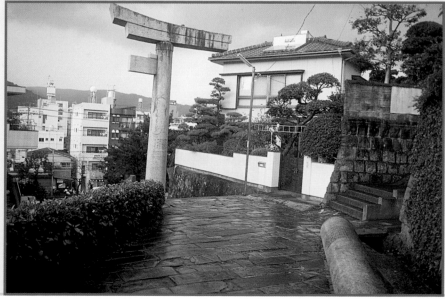

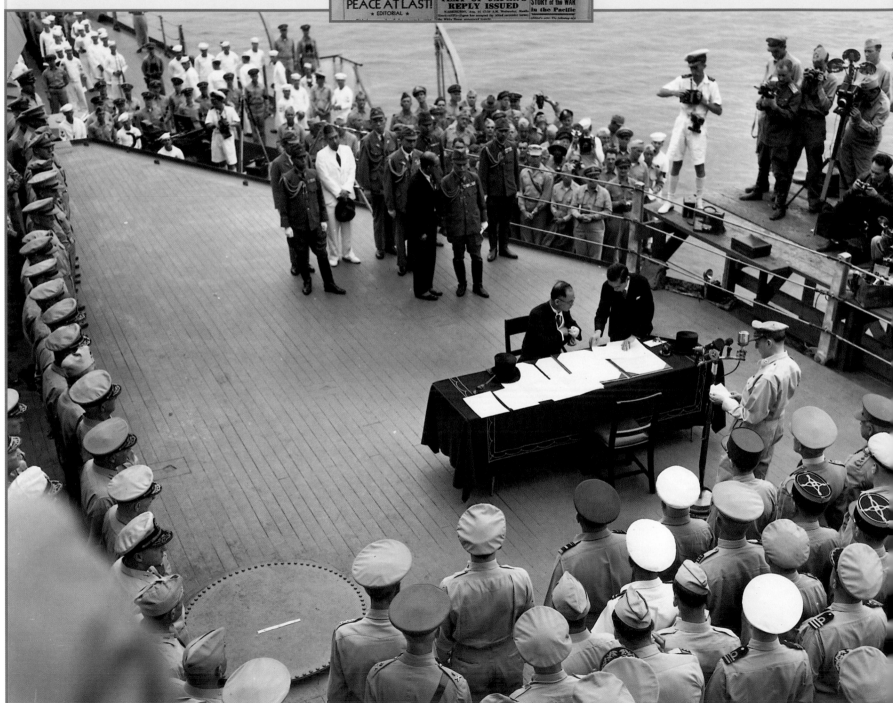

RIGHT: Headlines around the world trumpeted the Japanese surrender. This was the front page of a Philippine newspaper.

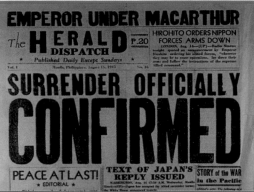

EMPEROR UNDER MACARTHUR

The **HERALD** DISPATCH P.20

Published Daily Except Sundays

HIROHITO ORDERS NIPPON FORCES ARMS DOWN

SURRENDER OFFICIALLY
CONFIRMED

PEACE AT LAST!
EDITORIAL

TEXT OF JAPAN'S REPLY ISSUED

STORY of the WAR in the Pacific

BELOW: On September 2, 1945, General MacArthur (at microphone) conducts the surrender ceremony aboard the USS *Missouri* in Tokyo Bay as high-ranking Allied officers look on. The first to sign the surrender document is Japanese Foreign Minister Mamoru Shigemitsu. Behind him stands General Yoshijiro Umezu, the Japanese Army chief of staff, and other members of the Japanese delegation.

TOP RIGHT: The most popular tourist attraction for years in Bremerton, Washington, was the USS *Missouri*. The stately old battleship was tied up in mothballs next to several aircraft carriers of similar vintage. Visitors were permitted to climb aboard *Missouri* and view the site of the Japanese surrender, which was marked with a plaque embedded into the deck planks and carefully roped off to prevent careless visitors from treading on it. In 1986 *Missouri* was taken out of mothballs, given a facelift, and sent back to active duty. In this 1988 photo, the refurbished World War II battleship glides slowly through the ship channel at Pearl Harbor. Three sister-battleships, *Iowa*, *New Jersey*, and *Wisconsin*, also reentered service in the 1980s. The USS *Iowa* suffered an explosion in the No. 2 gun turret that killed a number of sailors during a training exercise in 1989. The four old World War II battleships ended up playing an active role in the Gulf War in 1991. *Wisconsin* was said to have fired some of the first shots (actually Cruise missiles) of Operation Desert Storm. After their Gulf War experiences, the four ships were again retired, with *Missouri* being decommissioned in 1992.

BELOW: Today visitors can stand where MacArthur received the Japanese surrender, and get a close-hand look at the plaque embedded in the deck to mark the spot.

BELOW RIGHT: The grand old battleship, symbolic of the end of World War II, was saved from being scrapped and became a floating museum at Pearl Harbor, anchored roughly where the USS *Oklahoma* capsized and sank on December 7, 1941. *Missouri's* bow is aimed at the sunken battleship that symbolizes the beginning of World War II, the USS *Arizona*.

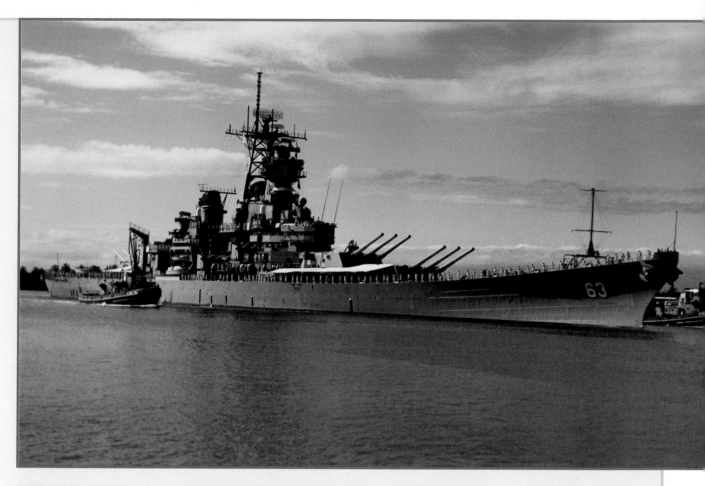

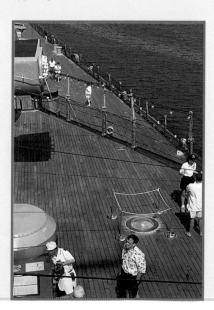

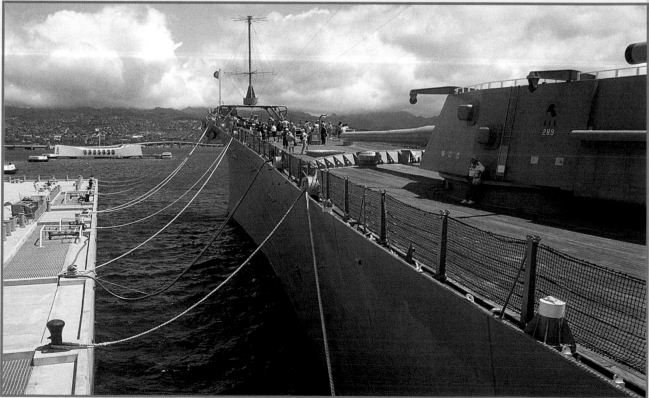

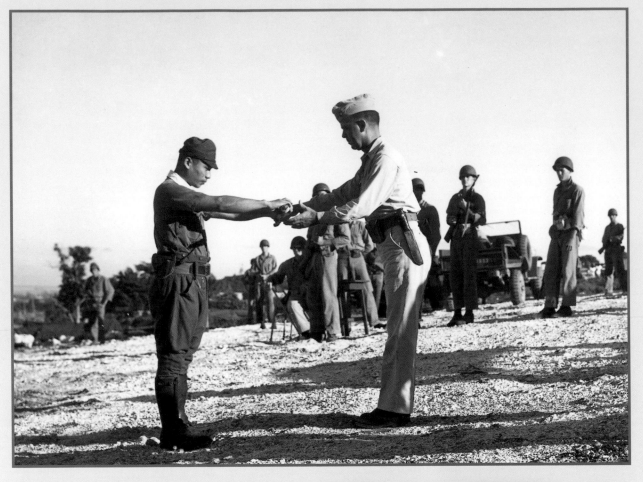

TOP: Japanese Captain Sakae Oba, who led a group of forty-six holdouts after the war ended, is shown here surrendering his Samurai sword to Colonel Howard Kurgis at Saipan on Saturday morning December 4, 1945.

BOTTOM LEFT AND RIGHT: Guy Gabaldon, shown here talking to a Japanese civilian on Saipan in 1944 and in front of his house on Saipan in 1995, was an eighteen-year-old Marine private when he splashed ashore during the Saipan invasion. "I hit the beach right in front of what is now the Diamond Hotel," he recalls, referring to the Japanese tourist resort built on the formerly heavily defended Afetna Point. Raised by Japanese-speaking parents, Gabaldon became familiar with the language. He would sneak out into the jungles of Saipan at night alone, and walk back to camp in the morning with Japanese civilians he had talked into surrendering. The Marine Japanese Language Officers did not officially sanction his activities, but he was effective in his own offbeat way. Hollywood made a movie in 1960, titled *From Hell to Eternity,* about his wartime exploits. In 1980 he moved back to Saipan with his ethnic Japanese wife who was raised in Mexico. "I think I am the only World War II Saipan campaign veteran now living here," he says with a smile. How was it to move back to the scene of his exploits? "Very strange," he says slowly. Then he holds up his wrist and points to a concave depression covered with scar tissue. "One of Oba's men did this to me." Six months after Saipan fell, Gabaldon was out on patrol trying to track down the recalcitrant Japanese captain and his men. Suddenly, shots rang out through the jungle, and he fell to the ground clutching his shattered wrist. After having survived the Saipan landing under fire, after enduring the bitter campaign to take the island, after surviving the landing and campaign to take neighboring Tinian, after talking Japanese civilians into surrendering, he was shot by a renegade band of Japanese holdouts on a supposedly "secure" island. "Yeah, Oba and some of his men showed up here a few years ago," says Gabaldon. "They stayed in one of the big Japanese hotels. Look around here. Japanese tourists everywhere. Big expensive Japanese hotels. The Japanese are buying up all the land to build more hotels." He pauses, and then says slowly, "Who the hell do you think won the war?"

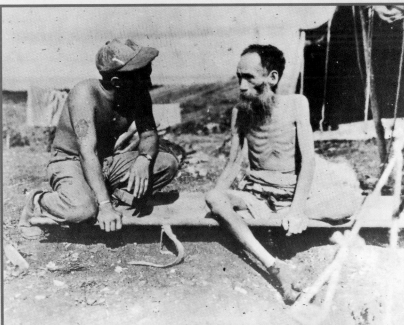

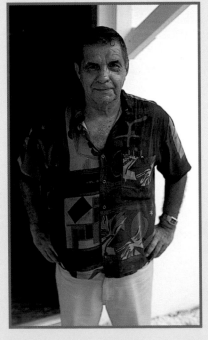

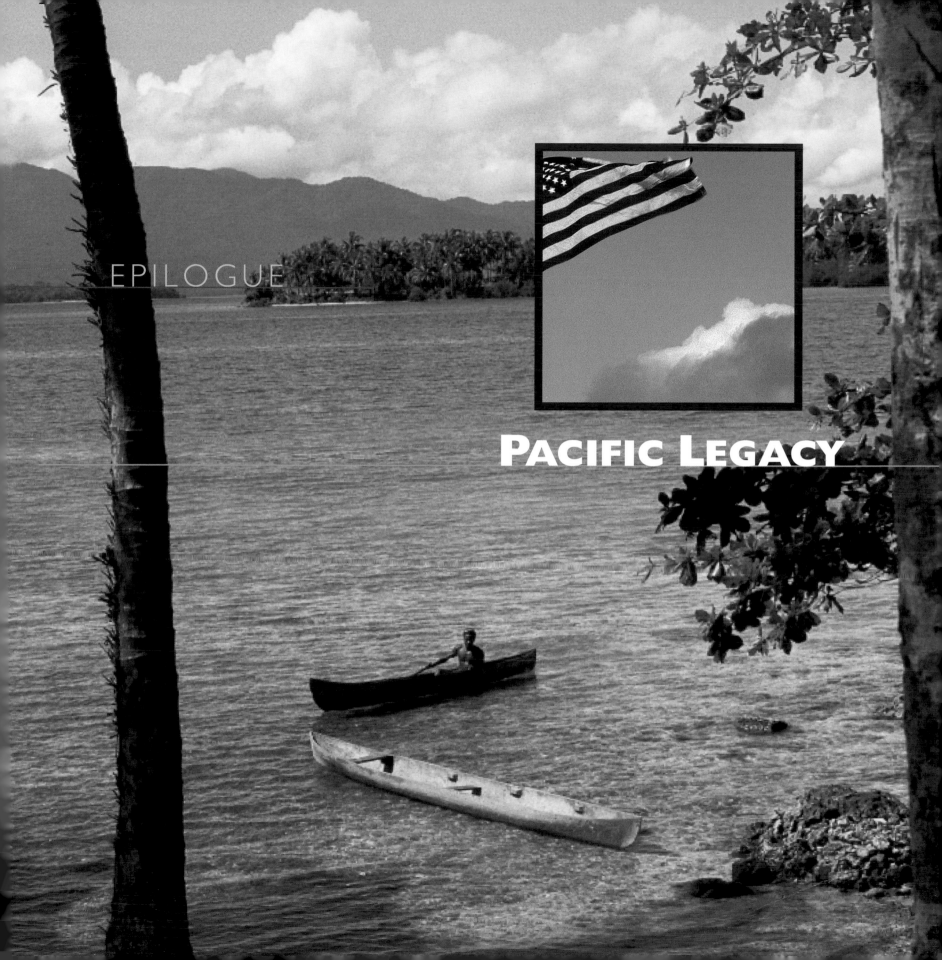

EPILOGUE

PACIFIC LEGACY

TO THOSE WHO WERE THERE on the deck of the USS *Missouri* that September day in 1945, the signing of the surrender documents appeared to bring the war in the Pacific to a close. Of course it did that on one level. But the Allied commanders and even the Japanese knew it wasn't really over yet. Scattered across the far-flung Pacific islands were armed Japanese garrisons that had purposely been bypassed, and many Japanese were still holding out on islands supposedly "secured" in the island-hopping invasions. They all would have to surrender, a group at a time, or individually, island by island.

It didn't take too long before stories of singular surrenders started to emerge. On Guam a Japanese trooper who knew some English, twenty-one fellow soldiers, and an eighteen-year-old geisha girl were hiding out in the jungles. Then in late October 1945, they somehow came across the September 17 issue of *Life* magazine, which featured a photo of the USS *Missouri* surrender ceremony. It was only then they realized, with a shock, that the war had been over for almost two months. Hastily composing a surrender note, they tacked it to a tree near a road, and waited to be contacted. When no one had noticed the note in eight days, they tore it down, rushed out into the road, flagged down a passing truck, and surrendered to the startled driver. On one side, the note read, "The War end! Comes peace in the world! We are join!" The reverse side begins, "We had been lived in this jungle from last year, but now we known by this book [*Life* magazine] that the War end."

Unlike some Japanese holdouts who retreated to remote caves, others were quite aggressive in their efforts to survive. Captain Sakae Oba was the leader of one of these groups. Until he finally surrendered on Saturday morning, December 4, 1945, Captain Oba and forty-six other Japanese soldiers and sailors had played a high-risk hide-and-seek game with American patrols in Saipan's jungles and caves for almost seven months after the island fell to the Americans. Oba's men were notorious for surprise ambushes and various other harassing tactics that continually frustrated American troops. After surrendering, Captain Oba returned to Japan and settled in Nagoya. In 1984 he and about twenty-seven of his men returned to Saipan for a reunion in one of the postwar luxury hotels that catered to Japanese tourists.

Among the groups of Japanese holdouts on islands all across the Pacific, perhaps none were as well provisioned as those on Peleliu. Numerous efforts were made to smoke them out of their hidden and well-supplied cave, but all to no avail. Finally Rear Admiral Michio Sumikawa, wartime chief of staff of Japan's Fourth Fleet and a witness at war crimes trials on Guam, was brought to Peleliu to see if he could get the holdouts to give up. First Sumikawa posted photos of the surrender ceremony, taken almost two years earlier, near where it was thought the holdouts' cave was located. Then, using a bullhorn, he broadcast a surrender appeal that echoed over the old shell-scarred, precipitous, jumbled ridges of the island where so many had died. He hoped he could persuade his countrymen that the war was over, and it worked. Shortly after his bullhorn broadcast, on April 21, 1947, more than twenty months after VJ Day, Lieutenant Tadamichi Yamaguchi and twenty-six of his troopers finally came out of their hiding places to surrender. They were fit and well fed, having lived off a large store of supplies deep in their underground command post, which they supplemented with pilfered goods spirited away at night from the American base.

But these were not the last of the Japanese holdouts, not by a long shot. More than a quarter of a century later, in January 1972, fifty-six-year-old Sergeant Shoichi Yokoi walked out of the jungle on Guam and surrendered. Unaware that the war had ended, his Japanese Army uniform long since in tatters, he had lived for decades in a jungle cave in a remote part of Guam with two fellow soldiers. They died in 1964, leaving Yokoi to make it on his own for another eight years. It took the convincing of two local people, who spotted him while fishing, and what he later said were the supernatural urgings of his dead comrades, to get him to finally surrender. He was repatriated to Japan, married nine months later, and returned to Guam on his honeymoon, this time to stay in one of the large Japanese tourist hotels. He subsequently wrote two books, became a pacifist, and ran for a seat in Japan's upper house of Parliament in 1974 (and lost). But after all this he still was not satisfied with how things turned out. He was quoted as saying, "I'm not happy with the present system of education, politics, religion, just about everything." The old, disenchanted soldier of Imperial Japan, who lost twenty-seven years of his life in the limbo of a jungle hideout, died of a heart attack in 1997 at age eighty-two.

Yet Yokoi was still not the last Japanese holdout. Two years later, Second Lieutenant Hiroo Onoda finally emerged from his remote hideout in the Philippines on March 9, 1974. A Japanese tourist had made contact with him in the jungles of Lubang Island the previous month and helped arrange his surrender. Onoda refused to believe the war had ended and would only surrender himself on orders from his commanding officer. Fortunately that officer was found and flown to the Philippines, where he convinced Onoda that the time had come to surrender. Onoda subsequently wrote a book about his experiences entitled, *No Surrender: My Thirty Year War.*

There also were reports, some as late as 1986, of local people on Vella Lavella in the Solomon Islands sighting elderly Japanese men in loincloths scurrying around in the remote jungles of their island. It was thought the last of the Japanese garrison on Vella Lavella surrendered in the mid-1960s. Yet, perhaps a few very elderly holdouts remain, lost deep in a tropical island jungle, still dedicated until their last breath to the now-quaint and somewhat nostalgic notion in today's Japan of the Emperor as god.

Some people who had second thoughts about using the A-bombs to end the war changed their minds when the full scope and horror of Japanese atrocities came to light. It was widely known during the war that the Japanese were ruthless and brutal. Accounts filtered out about the Rape of Nanking and the Bataan Death March, and these stories were repeated in tents and Quonset huts all over the Pacific. "We were told never to be taken alive," recounts John Beddall, a radioman/gunner with the Forty-first Bomb Group flying B-25s out of Makin Island, north of Tarawa. "They told us that if we were over a Japanese island and were hit, just push the controls over and nose it in. You'd be doing yourself a favor. They'd kill enlisted men outright and torture and then kill officers. Our colonel crash-landed near the shore of one of those islands. We saw four out of the five crew make it out into a raft. A PBY went to pick them up but the Japs beat them to it. No trace was ever found of those guys. They were killed and dumped somewhere."

Allied POWs were beaten, starved, mistreated, tortured, and killed on islands and POW camps all across the Pacific. And if that wasn't bad enough, the infamous Unit 731 performed biological warfare research and medical experiments on Allied POWs and Chinese civilians, who were collectively called *"maruta"* (logs) by the Japanese. Thousands died in various bizarre medical and bacteriological experiments.

As horrific as Unit 731's mission was, virtually no one associated with it ever faced a war crimes trial. Their shrewd leader, Ishii Shiro, convinced American interrogators that the studies his group conducted had produced data that were of great value to the emerging field of biological warfare. MacArthur recognized the importance of the Japanese data and struck a deal that received approval from the highest levels of the U.S. government, all the way up to Truman it is thought. In exchange for the "research data," the Unit 731 doctors, technicians, nurses, and staff were never to be brought to trial. The U.S. held up its end of the bargain and obtained exclusive access to the ghastly results of human experimentation. This was much to the chagrin of the Soviets who also wanted this rare data. To this day there is little known about the details of Unit 731. Most of what has come to light has emerged since the early to mid-1990s as aging participants either provided deathbed confessions, or felt a need to address their guilt by "testifying" to what they saw and did.

Guilt played no part in the successful postwar careers of many of the Unit 731 doctors. With their U.S.-guaranteed immunity, many went on to become leaders in government labs and universities, with distinguished achievements built on the appalling experiments of the war. A group of them, recognizing the need for blood supplies during the Korean War, founded what later became Green Cross, a prosperous and prominent international pharmaceutical company.

The ambiguity of the concept of "war crime" was no more evident than in the case of Unit 731. However, there was no shortage of more conventional war crimes to prosecute after the Pacific war. In almost every area occupied by the Japanese military forces, stories emerged of terrifying and brutal treatment of civilians and POWs alike. Typical of the abuse meted out to POWs was what occurred in the Japanese Naval Hospital at Truk. During war crimes trials held on Guam in September 1947, a gruesome tale was told about the activities of Captain Hiroshi Iwanami, former fleet surgeon and commanding officer of the hospital. Under his direct supervision, several doctors placed tourniquets, which weren't removed for seven hours, on the arms and legs of selected American POWs. Two of the POWs immediately died from shock. Four others were subsequently injected with streptococcus bacteria that caused death by blood poisoning. The dead POWs were then dissected, their heads severed and boiled, and saved for specimens. Iwanami was sentenced to death, and eighteen of his cohorts from the Truk hospital received prison sentences of ten years or longer.

Some atrocities were more obscure, like the case of the roughly five thousand Korean laborers on Tinian the Japanese executed shortly before the American invasion. There is a memorial on the island to those little-known victims of war, whose bodies were burned in brick furnaces near where the memorial, now almost completely overgrown with thick jungle vegetation, was erected.

These tales and others came to light as a result of a series of grisly war crimes trials held in the Pacific by Allied countries that had come up against the Japanese code of Bushido in action. In addition to the trial of the twenty-five high-profile "major" Japanese war criminals from 1946 to 1948 in Tokyo (Hideki Tojo and his associates), the U.S., Britain, Australia, Netherlands, France, Philippines, and China held a total of roughly 2,240 trials, with nearly 5,700 accused, over 4,400 convicted, around 1,000 executed, and 1,000 acquitted. As the trials dragged on into the late 1940s, there was political pressure to speed them up, since the former Allies felt a need to move ahead with their new ally in the Pacific, the modern nation of Japan. But before it was over the U.S. alone tried over 1,400 defendants in 474 trials in Yokohama, China, Manila, and various Pacific islands. While the Nuremberg trials had captured the attention of world media, the Japanese war crimes trials, held in a variety of locations, some not particularly accessible to the mass media, went on mostly in obscurity.

Next to its start at Pearl Harbor, the atom bombs at the end of the Pacific war probably left the most far-reaching legacy. Modern museums at Hiroshima and Nagasaki document the horror on the ground. But what about the planes that dropped the bombs? For better or worse, *Enola Gay*, the most famous of all the B-29s, became an icon of atomic warfare. After the war it was acquired by the Smithsonian Institution and initially sat outside to become a home for birds and other wildlife. Then it was disassembled and stored in a warehouse for years. Efforts were finally begun in the 1980s to restore the cockpit and fuselage. It was intended that those parts of the plane were to be prominently displayed at the Smithsonian Air and Space Museum to commemorate the fiftieth anniversary of the atomic bombings and the end of the war in 1995. The display was originally meant to show not only the restored fuselage of *Enola Gay* but also burned and scorched relics from Hiroshima. However, the proposed exhibit commentary left veterans feeling that there was an overemphasis on the suffering of the Japanese without adequate context for why the U.S. used atomic bombs in the first place. The controversy raged for months. Finally it was decided to do away with the original script and have the display focus on *Enola Gay* itself, the restoration process, the facts associated with the airplane and its mission, and a short video with interviews of crew members. Even then there were protests and incidents inside the museum after the display opened in the summer of 1995. On one day in July three protesters were arrested after pouring human blood and ashes on the old airplane. More than fifty years later, *Enola Gay* still remained a symbol of atomic warfare in all its facets—from the airplane itself, representing the technology that made the delivery of atomic bombs possible, to the human story of the crews who trained and flew the plane, to the aftermath and all its horrors. *Enola Gay* is now slated to be the centerpiece of the new Smithsonian Air and Space facility at Dulles

International Airport outside Washington, D.C. *Bock's Car,* the plane that barely returned from its ill-fated mission over Nagasaki, has rested quietly for decades at the Air Force Museum in Dayton, Ohio, as its more famous sister plane draws most of the attention in the nation's capital.

Meanwhile, back on Tinian out in the western Pacific, where B-29s once lumbered off the long, specially built runways to firebomb Japan, and where *Enola Gay* and *Bock's Car* took off with their atomic cargo, a "tent city" was built on one of those old runways in 1999 to hold Chinese nationals who were caught attempting to enter Guam illegally on modern-day versions of the old POW hellships. Later that year, after the would-be Chinese immigrants were sent back to China, plans were announced for a $12.3-million runway to replace one of the B-29 airstrips that had served as the Tinian municipal airport for years. It had been used mainly by small planes ferrying day-trippers from nearby Saipan to look at the Atomic Bomb Pits at the north end of the island. But local developers had big plans for nearly deserted Tinian. A casino and resort hotel were built in the late 1990s, and a new runway was needed to handle wide-body jets bearing mostly Asian tourists to jump-start a tourism industry on the little island. With mostly gambling on their minds, few of the new visitors would likely be aware of the momentous events that took place there in 1945. At the other end of the atomic bomb pipeline, five of six historic buildings at Los Alamos, New Mexico, which had housed support services for the construction of the atomic bombs, were destroyed, ironically enough, by a raging wildfire in May 2000.

And what of the ill-fated USS *Indianapolis,* the ship that delivered components of the first atomic bomb to Tinian? Two torpedoes from a Japanese submarine sank it while en route to the Philippines shortly after leaving Tinian. The initial blasts killed 300 men, but only 317 out of the 900 who went into the water survived the dehydration, hallucinations, and shark attacks that lasted five days. It was the Navy's worst maritime disaster. But the Navy had completely lost track of the ship, and when it didn't arrive on schedule it wasn't missed. By pure chance a Navy plane on routine patrol finally spotted the survivors in the water.

A call for help was radioed, and soon a PBY from Peleliu, piloted by Adrian Marks, arrived on the scene. He was under orders only to drop rafts. But when he made a low pass and saw the pathetic state of the survivors, he decided to make a dangerous open-sea landing in twelve-foot swells on what he later called a "sun-swept afternoon of horror."

After the hair-raising landing, Marks and his crew immediately realized they couldn't take off again with all the men in the water surrounding his plane. So he taxied the seaplane around, first picking up men who were alone or in small groups. When inside the PBY was filled to capacity, he shut off the engines and tied men to the outside. By the time night came, he had fifty-six survivors in or on his plane. It wasn't until the next morning that a Navy destroyer, *Cecil J. Doyle,* arrived and took the survivors off the PBY. The plane, too damaged to take off, was sunk on the spot. Twelve days later Japan surrendered, ending the war in the Pacific. Adrian Marks, the pilot who went against regulations to save the lives of fifty-six men, was awarded the Air Medal from Admiral Nimitz himself, and he died on March 7, 1998, at the age of eighty-one.

Though the captain of the *Indianapolis,* Charles Butler McVay III, survived the ship's sinking, he was subsequently court-martialed for "hazarding his ship by failing to zigzag," a tactic sometimes used to avoid submarine attack. McVay's conviction was handed down against the objections of many of his surviving crewmen and in the face of testimony from Mochitsura Hashimoto, commander of the Japanese submarine that sank *Indianapolis.* He insisted that he would have spotted and torpedoed the ship even if it had been zigzagging. The United States lost hundreds of ships during the war, but McVay was the only captain court-martialed in connection with the sinking of his vessel. Twenty-four years after his court-martial, wracked with guilt and depression, McVay shot himself to death with a Navy-issue .38-caliber revolver.

But it didn't end there. Years later many of the *Indianapolis* crew still maintained that their captain was made a scapegoat, that the Navy was more at fault for losing track of the ship, thus leaving the sailors to suffer and die. During the 1990s the old Japanese submarine commander

Hashimoto, whose testimony didn't save McVay at his court-martial, joined the survivors' fight to clear McVay's name. But these efforts weren't enough to sway either the Navy or Congress. Then one day in 1997 things took a fateful twist in the unlikely and diminutive form of twelve-year-old Hunter Scott of Pensacola, Florida. He innocently popped a video of the notorious 1975 shark movie *Jaws* into his VCR and was terrified by the movie. That was no particular surprise, of course, but what would turn out to be significant for *Indianapolis* survivors and McVay's family was Scott's fascination with the deranged shark hunter Quint, played by Robert Shaw. Quint's haunting obsession to kill sharks was the consequence of surviving five days in the water after the sinking of *Indianapolis* and seeing his shipmates killed in repeated shark attacks. Scott then launched an obsession of his own, researching the story of the sinking and the fate of Captain McVay, and interviewing survivors for a history fair project. It just didn't seem right to Scott that McVay was court-martialed, and he even contacted U.S. Representative Joe Scarborough, a Florida Republican, who initiated efforts in Congress to clear McVay's name.

Finally, due to the combined efforts of the surviving crew, Hashimoto, and young Scott, on October 31, 2000, Congress and President Clinton exonerated McVay of any wrongdoing. Congress stated that the Navy withheld critical information and assistance that could have saved *Indianapolis* and its crew, and that McVay was not responsible for the ship's sinking or for the massive loss of life that followed. "The American people should now recognize Captain McVay's lack of culpability for the tragic loss of the USS *Indianapolis* and the lives of the men who died as a result of the sinking of that vessel," the resolution states. Hashimoto didn't quite live to see his old foe exonerated—he died the week before at the age of ninety-one.

As ships from the Pacific war go, two of the most notable have now been united in Hawaii. At a Pearl Harbor dedication in 1999, the ship made famous for the signing of the surrender documents, the USS *Missouri*, was docked just off the sunken bow of the USS *Arizona* to form the "bookends of World War II," two ships that will always be associated with the beginning and the end of the Pacific war.

But it's the sunken hulk of *Arizona*, still sheltering the remains of crewmen who didn't make it out on December 7, that continues to haunt visitors and veterans alike, and USS *Arizona* crewman Lewis Robinson was no exception. He never forgot the day he somehow survived and so many of his shipmates didn't, and he was finally reunited with them on December 7, 2000. He became the sixteenth *Arizona* survivor whose mortal remains had been interred to that point by divers in the submerged and rusted hull of the old battleship, and he wasn't the last. Two more former *Arizona* crewmen who had passed away were reunited with their shipmates in the sunken hulk on the sixtieth anniversary of the attack on December 7, 2001. More will certainly follow.

Another man who could never shake the specter of *Arizona* and the other sunken ships of December 7, 1941, was Admiral Husband Kimmel, commander of U.S. Naval Forces on that fateful day. The Navy made him a scapegoat for the Pearl Harbor disaster, and he carried that stigma to his grave. But his family has continued to fight for his exoneration. Based on evidence that started to turn up in the mid-1990s, his sons have argued that Roosevelt and other high government officials knew of the plans for the Japanese attack but did not warn Kimmel or the Army commander, General Walter Short. The last surviving son, Edward Kimmel, well into his seventies, carried on into the twenty-first century the struggle his two older brothers had started. Kimmel vowed, "to fight the damned thing to the very end."

Remains of sunken ships from World War II across the Pacific have become more and more popular as sport scuba diving has made them accessible to a growing number of enthusiasts. The Japanese ships in Truk lagoon and more recently at Kwajalein and Palau are favorites with divers. And as time goes on, more come to light. In May 2000, a scuba-diving crew hired by crewman Larry Tunks, a survivor of the sinking, found the USS *Perry*, a destroyer sunk in 1944 by a mine near Angaur in southern Palau. Of the eight crewmen who died, six are likely still entombed in the sunken hulk, and one of them was Tunks's closest friend. When the divers returned to the surface to report that they had found his old ship, Tunks was there. "It was a pretty emotional minute. There's a lot of hurt there," he said. Though it lies at 240 feet, it is one of only a few U.S. warships sunk in combat in the Pacific accessible to scuba divers. Another, the USS *Houston* lies near Java in Indonesia, and the USS *Arizona* can be viewed only from the surface. Others that have been located in Iron Bottom Sound near Guadalcanal or other locations are too deep for diving, and many more remain undiscovered.

A real bonanza for scuba divers was the opening of Bikini lagoon to sport diving in 1996. Though the people of Bikini are still not allowed to return to live permanently on their atoll because of lingering radioactivity from postwar atomic testing, divers on short visits do not run the risk of adverse health effects. The Bikini Atoll Council manages the diving concession to provide an economic base for a possible future resettlement of their island. Of the twenty-one ships sunk during nuclear testing, ten are divable, including the legendary U.S. aircraft carrier *Saratoga*, and Yamamoto's former flagship during the attack on Pearl Harbor, the battleship *Nagato*.

After the surrender in 1945, *Nagato* was sailed to Bikini from Japan by an American crew. At times it was touch and go whether the huge ship would even make it to Bikini. After midcourse repairs at Eniwetok, crewman Fred Herschler recalled the final sprint to Bikini. "The great monster managed to cruise at 13 knots, the best speed we ever got out of her. We made the [final leg] alone without any help and managed to drop the anchor at our assigned spot all by ourselves." The former pride of the Japanese Navy survived the blast from the first bomb test, but the second sunk her on July 26, 1946.

Bob Gohr logged ten wartime landings on the windswept deck of the USS *Saratoga* in November 1944, and he returned to see his old ship underwater in 1997. But a more meaningful reunion was arranged in 1999 when he celebrated his seventy-fifth birthday on the deck of *Saratoga* in one hundred feet of water. Of his return to *Saratoga* in the waters of Bikini lagoon, Gohr wrote, "although the ship's island structure has seen better days, you can still get into the navigation bridge. The five-inch turrets before and after the island are still intact, as are many of the forty-millimeter quad mounts on both sides of the ship. Swimming through the hangar deck is like trying to move through a very long pile of trash. But there are the remains of two SB2C Helldivers and a TBM Avenger." With advances in underwater exploration technology, shipwrecks from World War II, legacies of final and violent combat sinkings, will continue to come to light. The discovery of the USS *Yorktown*, sunk during the pivotal battle of Midway, received much media attention in June 1998. Former *Yorktown* crewman Bill Surgi was watching video monitors in the research vessel when underwater cameras suddenly revealed the outlines of his old ship 16,650 feet deep in the Pacific. He had last seen *Yorktown* as it disappeared beneath the waves in 1942. It was an emotional moment for Surgi, who spoke for all his crewmates, "It was home. I was coming home, in a way."

And it's not only old ships that are found. Some of the participants, the long-ago-disappeared MIAs of the Pacific war, continue to be discovered where they died. Almost any excavation near Tanapag on Saipan turns up remains of the Japanese who were killed there in the biggest banzai charge of the war. Those and any other Japanese bodies from World War II found anywhere in the Pacific are cremated and the ashes returned to Japan. American MIA remains are identified and returned to their families for burial.

On Tarawa, during construction projects, human remains are routinely discovered, including those of L. P. Gilmore, USN, uncovered by a road construction crew during November 1999. Found with his body was his identification necklace, water container, and boots. Remote crash sites of long-forgotten aircraft regularly turn up in the rugged mountains of Papua New Guinea. A scene replayed several times a year took place in April 2000, when the remains of eight B-17 aircrew were recovered from a remote, jungle-shrouded crash site by a team of experts and returned to the U.S. Army's Central Identification Laboratory (CILH) in Honolulu. DNA and other tests enabled identification of the bodies, and the remains were returned to their families. The plane and crew were on a bombing mission to Bougainville when they flew into bad weather and then a mountain ridge, in that order. In April 2001, the CILH announced they had examined about three hundred crash sites in Papua New Guinea and identified eighty-five former American MIAs.

Finding and finally identifying remains of combatants from the Pacific war is always a bittersweet experience for everyone involved. The sadness and mystery of the long-ago disappearances are replaced with the numbing certainty of the details of their final moments. Mason Yarbrough was one who finally came home in 2000. His family buried him beside his parents on a cold December day in Missouri. The last they had heard of him was a terse message from the military: "killed in action, body not recoverable." His return journey finally ended after he had lain in an unmarked grave on an atoll in the Pacific since August 1942. He was one of nineteen of "Carlson's Raiders" who died in the ill-advised "raid" on Butaritari Atoll. The Marine Second Raider Battalion, led by Colonel Evans Carlson, was trying to draw the attention and therefore the resources of the Japanese, in order to slow the buildup of their defenses and to divert reinforcements from Guadalcanal, which was just then being invaded by the First Marine Division. The raid was a stretch even in the planning stages, but it went ahead anyway.

Two hundred and twenty members of Carlson's crack commando unit, including the president's son, Major James Roosevelt, were landed on what was then known as Makin Island by two submarines on August 16, 1942. From the start things went wrong. The landing was attempted in a driving rainstorm in high surf, and units were quickly separated. Chaos and confusion reigned. In the process of killing about eighty Japanese defenders, the Raiders were pinned down, and at one point Carlson considered surrendering. But finally they were able to extricate themselves, barely making it back to the submarines, but having to leave their dead behind. It was only later, when they took a count of survivors on the two submarines, that they realized they had left as many as thirty behind, all assumed to be "killed in action, body not recoverable." Indeed nineteen had died, including the first enlisted Marine awarded the Medal of Honor in World War II, Sergeant Clyde Thomason. The islanders buried the Raiders with all their gear in an unmarked grave.

But not all the missing Marines had died on Makin. In the chaos and confusion of the raid, some of them had become separated from Carlson's main group and couldn't make it back to the submarines in time. They hid out for a couple of days as best they could on the tiny island, but were inevitably captured on August 30. It was learned after the war that nine of the missing twelve Raiders were taken to Kwajalein Atoll and beheaded. After the Japanese surrender, war crimes investigators tracked down the Japanese commander who ordered the executions, and he was tried and hanged. Yet it remains a mystery where the executed Raiders were buried, and the search for their remains on Kwajalein continued into 2001.

For some of the surviving Raiders, it never sat right that they left their dead comrades behind, and in the late 1990s, surveys of Makin/Butaritari were undertaken to find their final resting place. It was a small island, but big enough to confound early efforts to discover the bodies. A break came when the search team interviewed islander Bureimoa Tokarei who, as a teenager, helped bury the Raiders. Though in his eighties and in poor health, he steered them to a landmark he insisted was near the gravesite. He was right. The missing Marines who died on Makin were finally found right where Tokarei said they were. As the bodies were carefully uncovered, the recovery team found the undisturbed remains of nineteen Marines and one islander, gas masks, ammunition, fifty-five live grenades, and twenty-two old dog tags etched with the fingerprints of their owners.

It was time to take the Marines home, and residents were astounded to see a giant C-130 transport plane set down on their little grass airstrip one day in 1999. Out stepped a full-dress honor guard, and the remains of the Marine Raiders were solemnly carried to the plane. A weeping Tokarei asked to have his photo taken beside the containers holding the bodies he helped bury, then helped recover. He sang the "Marines Hymn," the only song he knew in English.

For almost everyone who served on Pacific islands during World War II, souvenirs were a near obsession. Anything Japanese brought premium prices at the time, but after the war those cherished relics were mostly relegated to boxes in garages and attics. Now, as Pacific veterans head down the home stretch, some of these souvenirs end up being donated to museums such as the small, unassuming repository of

World War II relics on Peleliu, which now contains all kinds of items donated by Marine and Army veterans who fought there. Eyeglasses, family photos, and other personal effects taken from Japanese bodies, and pistols, flags, and swords are most common. Some more esoteric items have been donated—such as the handset from the radio found in a Japanese command post.

Occasionally, the families of the original Japanese owners are located, and souvenirs are returned. One such story began on December 7, 1941, when twenty-eight-year-old Lieutenant Fusata Iida was leading the Japanese attack on the Kaneohe Naval Air Station. His Zero was heavily damaged by antiaircraft fire, and he tried to crash into a hangar. The plane couldn't make it, and he came down next to a road just as Sam Chun was driving past on his way to the base. He ran to the wreckage, pulled the pilot's body from the shattered cockpit, and quickly saw there was nothing he could do—Lieutenant Iida was dead. On impulse, Chun removed Iida's brown leather flight helmet, hoping to return it to the pilot's family some day. Chun didn't live to do this. He died in 1967. Finally in 1999, Elfreida Tsukayama, Sam Chun's daughter, located the Iida family in Japan. On December 7, 1999, Tsukayama returned the faded leather helmet to a member of Lieutenant Iida's family in an emotional ceremony at the old Kaneohe base, now a Marine Corps facility. Tsukayama and Iida, after a tearful embrace, agreed that "yesterday's enemy became today's friend."

Not all souvenirs from the Pacific war promote such a peaceful sentiment. Typically, Pacific war veterans leave behind boxes of undocumented World War II relics for relatives to find and sort through after they are gone. In the summer of 1999 Stephen Chabot came across just such a box of souvenirs from his late uncle, Milton Barrows, a former Navy Seabee who had been on islands all over the Pacific during the war. Among the usual souvenirs, such as a Japanese helmet, mess kit, and uniforms, was a steel canister in a cardboard casing. It was about the size of a soft drink can and had interesting Japanese writing on it. Since he couldn't make sense of it, he tossed the canister aside to continue going through the rest of the box. But he had an uneasy feeling about it, so a couple of days later he called

the police to determine if it was dangerous. The police took one look at the odd object, immediately evacuated Chabot's house, and called in the bomb squad. The mysterious canister was a live Japanese mortar shell, so they carefully removed it for detonation in a remote spot. A supervisor for the Rhode Island state bomb squad said that that same week he had recovered two other Japanese mortar rounds brought back from the Pacific. In 1998, 30 of the 170 calls to the bomb squad in Rhode Island involved military explosives. With the passing of the World War II generation, some of their legacies from the Pacific war are deadly reminders of what they saw and experienced, and curious family members could become unwitting victims decades later.

The legacy and sad fates of the "comfort women" continue to resonate into the twenty-first century. Thought to number as many as two hundred thousand mostly impressed sex slaves from China, the Philippines, and other countries under Japanese rule during the war, they carried on their fight for reparations from the Japanese government. It took until 1992 before the Japanese government would even acknowledge the existence of the practice of conscripting women for military brothels, which stretched from garrisons in Asia all across the Pacific. Only in 1993 did the government issue an apology to the women who were forced to provide sex for Imperial soldiers. Then in 1996 Prime Minister Hashimoto expressed "sincere apologies and remorse" as Japan made its first payment from a private fund to compensate some of the comfort women. However, that wasn't sufficient for most of them. They believed that government funds should be appropriated for compensation, and that only then would the Japanese government be forced to accept ultimate responsibility.

In hopes of persuading Japan to provide additional government funds and to apologize individually to the now elderly victims, some of the former comfort women from all corners of the wartime Japanese Empire—Korea, the Philippines, China, Taiwan, Indonesia, and East Timor—relatedstories of brutality and rape in a mock trial of the government that was arranged in December 2000 by international women's groups in Tokyo, the heart of old Imperial Japan. The tribunal concluded that culpability for the Army's comfort stations went all the way up the line of command to Hirohito himself. The tribunal's decision was symbolic rather than binding, but it called attention to the persistent nightmares of these now elderly or ailing women, more legacies of the Pacific war.

Aging veterans who return to the islands and battlefields where they either fought or were imprisoned marvel at the "anonymity" of places they personally find so hard to forget. However, those who make the long trip to far-flung Pacific outposts discover that most islands have markers and memorials commemorating the World War II sacrifices of the Allies or local people. They are usually surprised to see large numbers of Japanese memorials, some of them just small family markers commemorating a relative who left for a distant island never to be heard from again.

As the twentieth century drew to a close and the next century began, echoes of the great Pacific war continued to appear in the media. On October 1, 1997, newspapers carried a story about the only Japanese pilot to bomb the U.S. mainland during World War II. He had died of lung cancer at the age of eighty-five. In September 1942, Navy pilot Nobuo Fujita dropped a bomb from his submarine-launched airplane on the suburbs of Brookings, Oregon. In 1962 he was invited back to Brookings by the city council and forgiven for his action.

In another newspaper account, in September 2000, one of the most famous Japanese fighter pilots to survive the war, eighty-four-year-old Saburo Sakai, collapsed and died at dinner with a group of American military officers at Atsugi U.S. Navy base in Japan. He shot down sixty-four Allied planes, was seriously wounded, and was one of only three from his prewar unit of 150 pilots to survive the war. He became a gracious symbol of reconciliation between Japan and its former enemies, traveling widely and trading combat stories with some of the pilots he once dueled with in the skies over the Pacific. A Zero he is reputed to have flown in combat is on display at the Australian National War Memorial in Canberra.

On a 1983 visit to the U.S., Sakai met the man who nearly shot him out of the sky over Guadalcanal years earlier.

Harold Jones later told reporters, "I thought he was gone. His cockpit exploded in orange flames, and his head went back against the headrest." Sakai was indeed very nearly gone. He lost an eye in the explosion and could barely see with his remaining eye through the blood running down his face. His Zero went into a seven-thousand-foot plunge that put out the flames, but by then he was barely conscious, only his right arm responded properly, and he was more than five hundred miles away from his base in New Guinea. Somehow he was able to hang on and to nurse his damaged plane back to base. This flight and his survival became the stuff of legend in Japan. But with only one good eye, he was posted back to the home islands, relegated to training duties, and thought his aerial combat days were over. However, in the last desperate weeks of the war, he returned once more to the violent skies, this time against the Americans over Iwo Jima. He survived these dogfights, too, even though by then the Zero was far outclassed by subsequent American designs.

After the war Sakai's famous flight of survival from Guadalcanal to New Guinea was immortalized in a painting displayed in his hometown in Japan. To Harold Jones, the man who believed he had shot Sakai out of the sky, he presented a piece of the silk scarf he used on his survival flight to wipe blood out of his good eye. He wrote ten books based on his wartime experiences from notes in his detailed journals.

From these notes, U.S. records, and other pilots' accounts, it was determined after the war that Sakai had come close to altering the course of later history with one of his wartime aerial attacks. One day in June 1942, Texas congressman Lyndon B. Johnson, on a "fact-finding mission," was being flown around New Guinea in a B-26 named *Heckling Hare*. Sakai dived on the plane and shot out the right engine but couldn't quite bring it down before it ducked into a cloud. Johnson, of course, survived to become president of the United States after the former Solomons PT boat skipper John F. Kennedy was assassinated in 1963.

Yet, like Shoichi Yokoi, the Emperor's lost soldier on Guam, Sakai felt uneasy about postwar Japan. Shortly before his death, he spoke out at a news conference. "We were ordered to go die for victory. Who gave the orders for that stupid war? The closer you get to the emperor, the fuzzier everything gets." Earlier he had been quoted as saying, ". . . we were following his orders. . . . after the war, the emperor should have quit, shaved his head and retired to a temple to take responsibility." He felt he spoke for many Japanese veterans who believed that Hirohito never accepted responsibility for the events of the Pacific war.

The man who not only played a big part in defeating Hirohito but also brought him and the rest of Japan into the postwar world, General Douglas MacArthur, died in 1964, but his wife Jean lived to the age of 101 and passed away in January 2000. She was an eyewitness to some of the great events of World War II, from the initial Japanese attacks in the Philippines, to the siege of Corregidor that she and her young son endured with her husband, to their escape by PT boat and evacuation to Australia, to final American victory in the Pacific, to the rebuilding of postwar Japan. She was buried at the MacArthur Memorial in Virginia next to her husband, returned to him in death, again side by side as they were throughout World War II.

Another legacy from the Pacific war has contributed heavily to present-day political strife on Guadalcanal in the Solomon Islands. The indigenous people of that island had come to resent the presence of natives of the nearby island of Malaita who stayed on after they came to work for the Americans during World War II. Finally in 2000, guerrilla groups were formed to drive the Malaitans out, and the violent ethnic conflict brought about near-total political and economic collapse. Some of the instruments used in the conflict were frightening tools of war left behind decades earlier. Militia groups on both sides of the conflict made use of American munitions from the battle for Guadalcanal in 1942. Long hidden but not forgotten ammunition dumps furnished a virtually limitless supply of .50-caliber machine-gun bullets. Homemade weapons were built to accommodate the old ammunition, which decades later was still in good enough condition to be fired from makeshift guns and kill people.

Less violent but culturally significant literary and film legacies of the Pacific war also continued on into the twenty-first century. The postwar writing careers of several authors were launched by books based on wartime experiences in the Pacific, and the legacies of veterans James Michener, Leon Uris, and James Jones, among others, have taken the form of reincarnations of their work in subsequent plays and films.

Leon Uris, who joined the Marines at age seventeen and participated in the Tarawa invasion, based his 1953 book *Battle Cry* on his experiences in the Pacific. He sold the screen rights to the book and then wrote the screenplay for the 1955 movie of the same name. He went on to become a best-selling author of such books as *Exodus* and *Trinity*.

James Michener's *Tales of the South Pacific*, drawn from his Naval experiences in World War II, won the Pulitzer Prize for fiction in 1948. Rogers and Hammerstein went on to create a hit Broadway musical based on the book. *South Pacific* opened April 7, 1949, at the Majestic Theatre, ran for 1,925 performances, and won the Pulitzer Prize for drama. That was followed in 1958 by a popular musical version filmed on Kauai in Hawaii. The movie *South Pacific* enshrined in the collective consciousness of a generation of Americans the romantic image of World War II on exotic Pacific islands. It continues theatrically as a staple high school, college, and dinner theater production. In the spring of 2001 the old musical was remade as a prime-time network TV production starring Glenn Close and Harry Connick, Jr. The updated version still portrayed the South Pacific in a soft romantic glow, though a few graphic jungle combat scenes were added to bring some of the reality of the Pacific war to the modern TV audience.

James Jones witnessed the Japanese attack on Pearl Harbor, served in the Twenty-seventh U.S. Infantry Regiment, was wounded in combat on Guadalcanal, and survived to become a prominent author. Many of his works were based on his wartime experiences in the Pacific. He revisited the horror of what he lived through on Guadalcanal in his 1962 book *The Thin Red Line*. With the renewed cinematographic interest in World War II in the late 1990s,

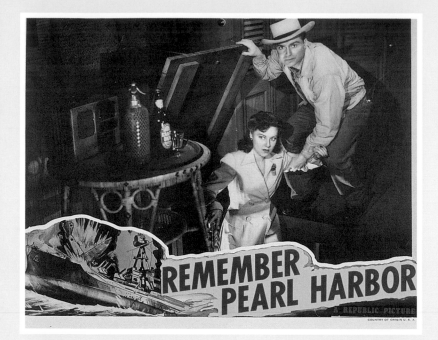

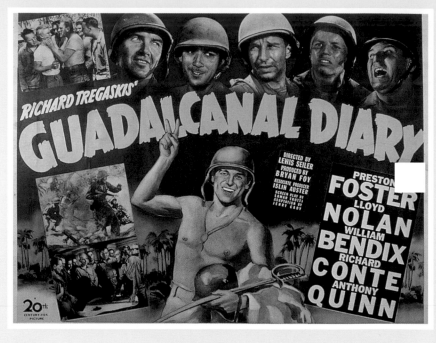

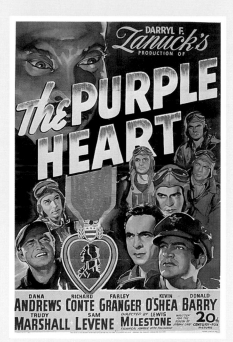

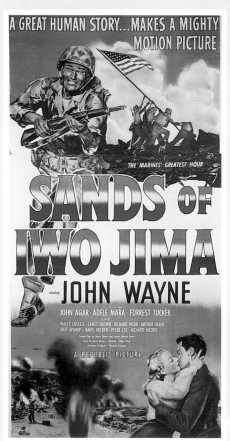

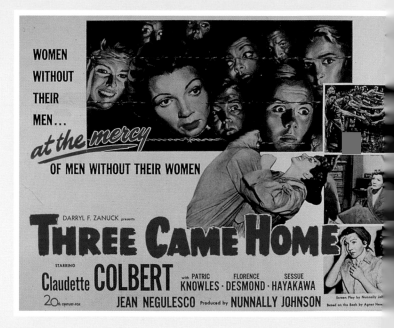

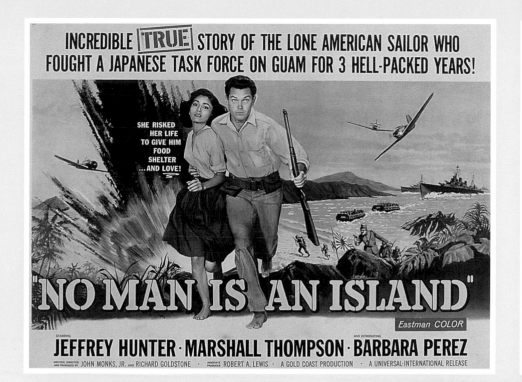

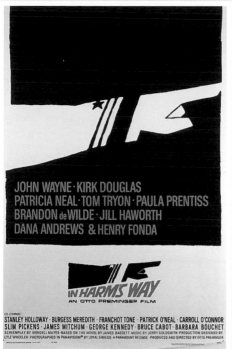

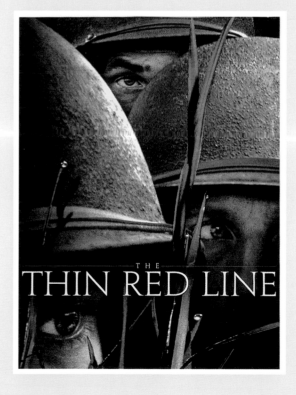

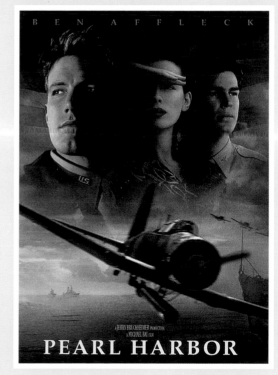

Remember Pearl Harbor, 1942

Guadalcanal Diary, 1943

The Purple Heart, 1944

Sands of Iwo Jima, 1949

Three Came Home, 1950

No Man Is an Island, 1962

In Harm's Way, 1965

The Thin Red Line, 1999

Pearl Harbor, 2000

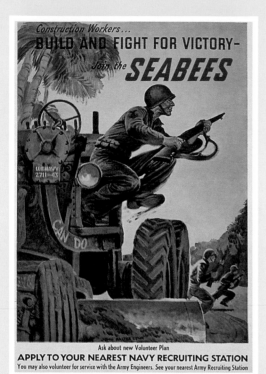

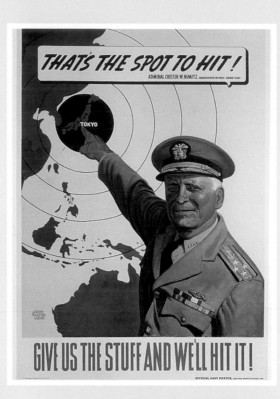

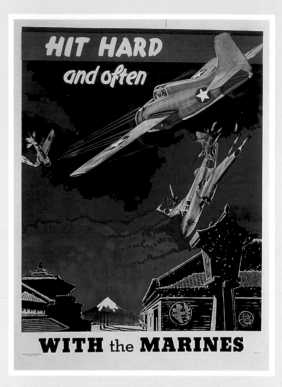

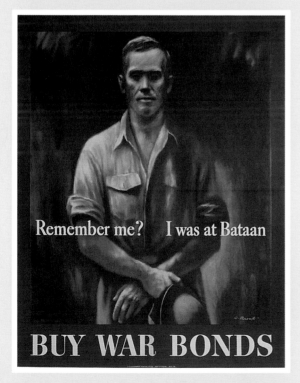

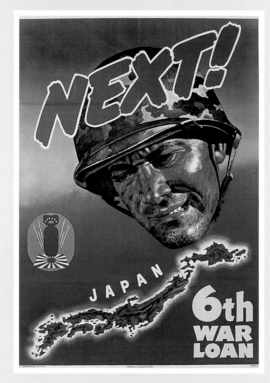

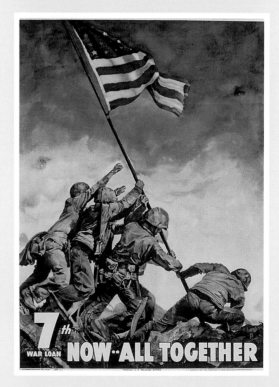

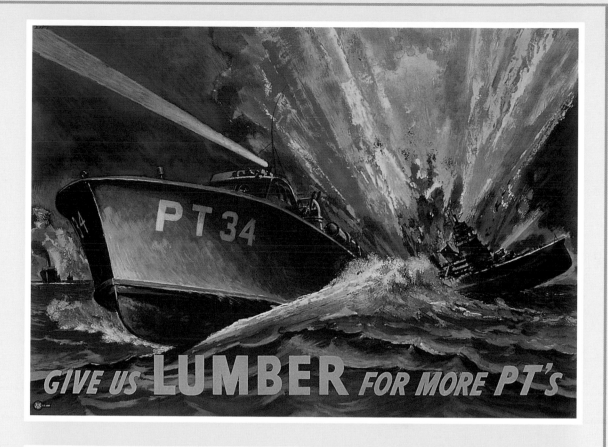

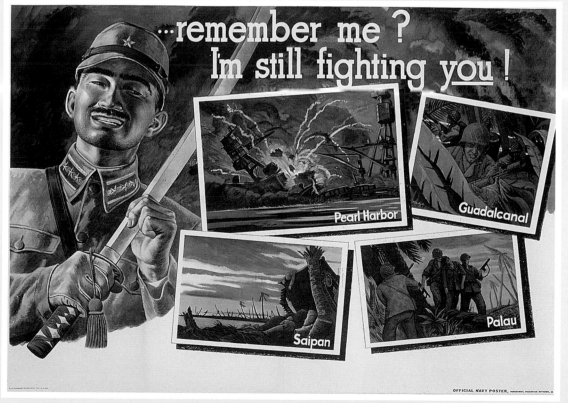

his book was made into a 1998 movie, filmed partially on Guadalcanal just before the political situation there deteriorated. Directed by Terence Malick, *The Thin Red Line* was nominated for seven Academy Awards including best picture and best director.

Another big-budget Hollywood retelling of World War II in the Pacific was the 2001 Disney production *Pearl Harbor*. No expense was spared to recreate some of the most dramatic moments of the Pacific war. The December 7 attack, actually filmed on location at Pearl Harbor, used vintage World War II aircraft, including the first genuine Japanese Zeroes to strafe Hawaiian naval facilities since 1941 (the other Hollywood studio recreation of the Pearl Harbor attack, the 1970 film *Tora Tora Tora* that won the Academy Award for best visual effects, used replica Zeroes). The vintage World War II Essex-class aircraft carrier *Lexington*, now a museum ship in Corpus Christi, Texas, doubled as the USS *Hornet* to recreate the Doolittle raid. B-25s lifted onto its deck were able to take off into a stiff sea breeze even though the *Lexington* was stationary. Then Japanese planes were put on the deck, and the *Lexington* was disguised as the carrier *Akagi* to film the takeoff scenes for the start of the Pearl Harbor attack.

Like the Civil War, fascination with World War II has carried on to subsequent generations even as the original participants pass from the scene. When the last eyewitnesses are gone, though, the texture and sense of the Pacific war will change forever. The only legacy then will be the physical remains on scattered islands, recorded accounts from those who were there, descendants' memories, and the socioeconomic imprint on the constantly evolving political landscape of Pacific island countries and other nations altered by events of the early 1940s. But no more will the veterans who actually saw Japanese dive-bombers coming at them on December 7, 1941, bring to life the feelings of that day for visitors to the *Arizona* Memorial in Hawaii. Pacific islanders who were terrorized by the Japanese and then had to move out of the way as Americans turned their tropical real estate into sprawling bases will no longer be around to tell what it was like to have their lives and islands so suddenly transformed forever. Their descendants will point to old runways, concrete foundations, and rusting junk they think used to be jeeps and landing craft, and try to recall what auntie or grandpa used to say it all meant.

James Michener, in *Tales of the South Pacific*, anticipated this transition, along with the legacy left by his generation and those who fought the battles in the Pacific. "They, like their victories, will be remembered as long as our generation lives. After that, like the men of the Confederacy, they will become strangers. Longer and longer shadows will obscure them, until their Guadalcanal sounds distant on the ear like Shiloh and Valley Forge."

SELECTED BIBLIOGRAPHY

Alexander, John W. *Flight Quarters: U.S.S. Belleau Wood.* Privately published unit history, 1946.

Alexander, Joseph H. *Utmost Savagery.* Annapolis: Naval Institute Press, 1995.

Alvarez, Louis W. *Alvarez: Adventures of a Physicist.* New York: Basic Books, 1987.

Barber, Joseph, Jr. *Hawaii: Restless Rampart.* New York: Bobbs-Merrill, 1941.

Belote, James H., and William M. Belote. *Corregidor: The Saga of a Fortress.* New York: Harper and Row, 1967.

Birdsall, Steve. *Saga of the Superfortress.* New York: Doubleday, 1980.

Bulkley, Robert. *At Close Quarters: PT Boats in the United States Navy.* Washington: Naval Historical Division, 1962.

Clapper, Raymond. *Watching the World.* New York: McGraw-Hill, 1946.

Coleman, John S., Jr. *Bataan and Beyond.* College Station: Texas A and M Press, 1978.

Commonwealth of the Philippines. *Facts and Figures about the Philippines.* Manila: Bureau of Printing, 1939.

Conner, Howard M. *The Spearhead: Unit History.* Washington: Infantry Journal Press, 1950.

Cook, Haruko T., and Theodore F. Cook. *Japan at War: An Oral History.* New York: New Press, 1992.

Cooney, David M. *Chronology of the U.S. Navy 1775–1965.* New York: Franklin Watts, 1965.

Coox, Alvin. *Japan: The Final Agony.* New York: Ballantine, 1970.

Cressman, Robert J. *A Magnificent Fight: The Battle for Wake Island.* Annapolis: Naval Institute Press, 1995.

Crew members of LST 831. *U.S.S. LST 831.* Privately published unit history, n.d.

Donovan, Robert J. *PT 109.* New York: McGraw-Hill, 1961.

Evans, Clay Bonnyman. *Bones of My Grandfather: Reclaiming a Lost Hero of World War II.* New York: Skyhorse, 2018.

Foss, Joe, with Donna Wild Foss. *A Proud American: The Autobiography of Joe Foss.* New York: Pocket Books, 1992.

Gibney, Frank. *Five Gentlemen of Japan.* New York: Farrar, Straus and Young, 1953.

Hallas, James H. *Killing Ground on Okinawa.* Westport, Conn.: Praeger Publishers, 1996.

Hammel, Eric M., and John E. Lane. *76 Hours: The Invasion of Tarawa.* New York: Tower Publications, 1980.

Hoffman, Carl. W. *Saipan: The Beginning of the End.* Washington: U.S. Marine Corps, 1950.

_____. *The Seizure of Tinian.* Washington: U.S. Marine Corps, 1951.

Hough, Frank O. *The Assault on Peleliu.* Washington: U.S. Marine Corps, 1950.

Hoyt, Edwin P. *Japan's War: The Great Pacific Conflict.* New York: McGraw-Hill, 1986.

Ienaga, Saburo. *The Pacific War 1931–1945.* New York: Random House, 1979.

Jablonski, Edward. *Air War.* Vol. 2. New York: Doubleday, 1971.

Jacobson, Richard B., ed. *Moresby to Manila: The Story of the 54th Troop Carrier Wing.* Privately published unit history, 1945.

Kerr, E. Bartlett. *Flames over Tokyo.* New York: Donald I. Fine, 1991.

Leckie, Robert. *Helmet for My Pillow.* New York: Random House, 1957.

Lodge, O. R. *The Recapture of Guam.* Washington: U.S. Marine Corps, 1954.

Lord, Walter. *Day of Infamy.* New York: Henry Holt and Co., 1957.

MacArthur, Douglas. *Reminiscences.* New York: McGraw-Hill, 1964.

Mahood, Robert. "Guadalcanal: A Veteran's Remembrance." Personal account, 1990.

Manchester, William. *American Caesar.* New York: Little, Brown and Company, 1978.

_____. *The Glory and the Dream*. Toronto: Bantam, 1974.

_____. *Goodbye Darkness*. New York: Little, Brown and Company, 1979.

Mercey, Arch A. *Sea, Surf and Hell*. Englewood Cliffs, N.J.: Prentice Hall, 1945.

Michener, James A. *Tales of the South Pacific*. New York: Macmillan, 1947.

_____. *The World Is My Home*. New York: Random House, 1992.

Morris, Eric. *Corregidor*. New York: Stein and Day, 1981.

Moses, Maj. Frank B., and Maj. Paul A. Conlin. "I Have Returned." *Coast Artillery Journal* 88 (1945).

Onoda, Hiroo. *No Surrender: My Thirty-Year War*. Tokyo: Kodansha International, 1974.

Piccigallo, Phillip R. *The Japanese on Trial: Allied War Crimes Operations in the East, 1945–1951*. Austin: University of Texas Press, 1979.

Raymer, Edward C. *Descent into Darkness*. Novato, Calif.: Presidio Press, 1996.

Rentz, John N. *Marines in the Central Solomons*. Washington: U.S. Marine Corps, 1952.

Ross, Bill D. *Iwo Jima: Legacy of Valor*. New York: Vanguard Press, 1985.

_____. *Peleliu: Tragic Triumph*. New York: Random House, 1991.

Russ, Harlow W. *Project Alberta: The Preparation of Atomic Bombs for Use in World War II*. Los Alamos, N.M.: Exceptional Books, 1984.

Schultz, Duane. *The Doolittle Raid*. New York: St. Martin's Press, 1988.

Sherrod, Robert. *Tarawa: The Story of a Battle*. New York: Duell, Sloan and Pearce, 1944.

Sledge, Eugene B. *With the Old Breed at Peleliu and Okinawa*. Novato, Calif.: Presidio Press, 1981.

Smith, Rex Alan, and Gerald A. Meehl. *Pacific War Stories: In the Words of Those Who Survived*. New York: Abbeville Press, 2004.

Smith, S. E. *The United States Navy in World War II*. New York: William Morrow, 1966.

_____., ed. *The United States Marine Corps in World War II*. New York: Random House, 1969.

Spencer, Louise Reid. *Guerilla Wife*. New York: Crowell, 1945.

Steinberg, Rafael S. *Return to the Philippines*. Alexandria, Va.: Time-Life Books, 1979.

Stockman, James R. *The Battle for Tarawa*. Washington: U.S. Marine Corps, 1947.

Thomas, Gordon, and Max M. Witts. *Enola Gay*. New York: Stein and Day, 1977.

Toland, John. *The Rising Sun*. New York: Random House, 1970.

Tregaskis, Richard. *Guadalcanal Diary*. New York: Random House, 1943.

Tyson, Carolyn A. *A Chronology of the United States Marine Corps*. Vol. 2. Washington: U.S. Government Printing Office, 1965.

U.S. Bureau of Yards and Docks. *Building the Navy's Bases in World War II*. Vol. 2. Washington: U.S. Government Printing Office, 1947.

U.S. Navy. *United States Naval Aviation*. Washington: U.S. Government Printing Office, 1970.

Wallin, Homer N. *Pearl Harbor: Why, How, Fleet Salvage, and Final Appraisal*. Washington: U.S. Navy Naval History Division, 1968.

Walton, Frank E. *Once They Were Eagles*. Lexington: University Press of Kentucky, 1986.

Wheeler, Keith. *The Road to Tokyo*. Alexandria, Va.: Time-Life Books, 1979.

Wheeler, Richard. *Iwo*. New York: Harper and Row, 1980.

Wilson, Earl J. *Betio Beachhead*. New York: G. P. Putnam, 1945.

Wolfert, Ira. *American Guerilla in the Philippines*. New York: Simon and Schuster, 1945.

ACKNOWLEDGMENTS

WE ACKNOWLEDGE, WITH SPECIAL RECOGNITION, the veterans who so unselfishly provided us with a wealth of written and tape-recorded personal experiences, but who will not find them in this book. We wish we could have included every one. Unfortunately, however, we were forced by the barrier of practical book-length to make a great many difficult and even heart-rending decisions about which accounts to include and which to leave out. Your contributions, however, have been neither wasted nor lost. They will be placed in research archives for the use of other historians and will become, thereby, permanent additions to the history of the Pacific War. To all the veterans who contributed material or interviews, we sincerely appreciate your help, because without you this book would not have been possible:

CARL ALBRITTON, DELMAR ALDRICH, GEORGE BEHRENS, RUEBEN BEST, BILL BOWER, GREGORY BOYINGTON, BOB CARON, ROBERT CLACK, CLARENCE COOK, HOMER CROSS, MILO CUMPSTON, WYLIE DAVIS, FRANK DIDIER, JOHN ENDRES, FRED EVERETT, GEN. HARVEY AND JEAN FRASER, FRED FREEMAN, RUSSELL FRINK, HARRY FUKUHARA, HOWARD FURAMOTO, GUY GABALDON, VERNON GARRETT, MANNY GOLDBERG, KEN GUENTHER, DAVE GUTTERMAN, AL HAHN, CARL HAMILTON, ALAN HANCOCK, MINORU HARA, BILL HASTINGS, HOADLEY DEAN, COL. EUGENE HOLMES, WAYNE ("JIM") JOHNSON, PERRY ("MAX") JOHNSTON, E. FAY JONES, DALE KILLIAN, A. C. KLEYPAS, PAUL KURODA, KARL LEFFLER, CHARLES LEONARD, OSCAR T. ("OZ") LEVERENZ, DAVID LEVY, CHUCK LINDBERG, FRANK LIPERE, DOUG MCEVOY, CHARLES MCNEAL, PAUL MEEHL, LOUIS MEEHL, MIKE MICHEL, JIM MILLIFF, JOHN WILLIAM MURPHY, STEPHEN NISBET, ROBERT NOBLE, ALBERT OHLMACHER, ROBERT PHELAN, DALE PLUMMER, BILL POND, JACK RASMUSSEN, BILL REYNOLDS, ROBERT SHEEKS, CECIL SPECK, JOHN SPORDONE, JIM SPRIGGS, CLARENCE ("DUDE") STORLA, IRVING STROBING, DON VANINWEGAN, JOHN VAYHINGER, DR. JOHN VINZANT, WALTER WAGNER, HARLAN WALL, MIKE WEST, JIM WESTBROOK, BOB WHITTEMORE, FRED WOLKEN, AND JOE WOODS.

WE ALSO THANK the Pacific islanders who spoke with us about their experiences during World War II, in particular those who contributed stories or interviews:

KIMIUO AISEK, FALAVI, TANGIE HESUS, ANDREW KUGFAS, ALONSO LADORE, TUK NAUAU, POKA, AND MILTON SIOSI.

ADDITIONALLY, we are grateful for contributions to the text or other assistance provided during the preparation of this book from:

JAMES AND EDITH BELOTE, WILLIAM BOLHOFER, JOHN BROWN, JOE CONNOLLY, ROBERT DONOVAN, MIKE AND MICHELE ELY, DOROTHY AND ROSS GREENING, AKIRA KASAHARA, LAMONT LINDSTROM, DANIEL MARTINEZ, MARLA MEEHL, EILEEN MEEHL, MARK MEEHL, JANET MEEHL, VIKKI AND MIKE MUSTO, SCOTT RUSSELL, PAUL SHANKMAN, DON WALL, AND LONI DING, PRODUCER OF "THE COLOR OF HONOR" (SHE CAN BE CONTACTED AT THE CENTER FOR EDUCATIONAL TELECOMMUNICATIONS, INC., 1940 HEARST AVE., BERKELEY, CA 94709).

PICTURE CREDITS

Front and Back Matter

Front cover: GM. **Back cover** TL: GM; TC: U.S. Army Museum of Hawaii 2307; TR: NA 80G-413988; BL: David Levy; BC: NA 80G-700777; BR: GM. **Half title**: NA Marine Corps 50898. **Title spread**: NA 80G-414423. **Contents**: NA 111-SC-334277. **4**: NA 208-N-41607. **9**: Gerald A. Meehl.

Chapter 1: THIS IS NO DRILL!

23: U.S. Army Museum of Hawaii 2307. **25**: GM. **26** T : NA 80G-451114; B: GM. **27** T: U.S. Army Museum of Hawaii 2310; B: NA 80G-30554. **28** TL: NA 80G-30550; TR: U.S. Navy; CR: NA 80G-32923; BL: U.S. Army Museum of Hawaii 3041; BR: GM. **28–29**: NA 80G-32424. **30** T: NA 80G-19941; B: NA 80G-1021538. **31** T: GM; BL: National Park Service drawing by Jerry Livingston; BR: GM. **32** T: NA 80G-204505; BL: U.S. Navy; BR: GM. **33** TL: U.S. Army; TR: GM; BL: GM; BR: GM. **35**: GM. **36–37**: U.S. Naval Institute. **37** T: GM; C: NA 80G-315177; B: NA 127G-315173. **38** TL: GM; CL: NA 80G-346846; CR: GM; BL: NA 80G-346810; BR: GM. **39**: All GM. **40**: NA 80G-41190. **41**: Bill Bower. **42** TL: NA 51233 A.C.; TR: NA 80G-41196; B: NA 80G-324199. **44** T: Bill Bower; C: NA 92731 A.C.; B: Bill Bower. **45**: Bill Bower. **46** TL: NA 25757 A.C.; TR: Bill Bower; BL: Bill Bower; BC: Bill Bower; BR: Ross Greening.

Chapter 2: THE TIME-BUYERS

58 T: NA 127-GR-111-114538; B: NA 127-GR-111. **59** TL: NA 127-GR-111-114542; TR: NA 127-GR-111-114540; BR: U.S. Defense Department. **58–59**: U.S. Defense Department. **60**: GM. **61** T: NA 111-SC-595885; BL: GM; BR: GM. **62** TL: NA U.S. Army; TR: GM; BL: NA 111-SC-595870; BR: GM. **63** T: James Belote; B: NA 111-SC-265357. **64** T: Japanese Army; BL: William Bolhofer; BR: William Bolhofer. **65**: Japanese Four-teenth Army, reproduced with permission of James Belote. **66** TL: James Belote; TR: GM; B: James Belote. **67** T: Japanese Fourteenth Army, reproduced with permission of James Belote; CL: GM; CC: NA 111-SC-595863; CR: GM; BL: James Belote; BR: GM. **68** T: U.S. Army photo courtesy of Col. Reilley E. McGarraugh, reproduced with permission of James Belote; BL: GM; BR: GM. **69** T: Japanese Fourteenth Army, reproduced with permission of James Belote; BL: GM; BR: NA U.S. Army.

Chapter 3: THE LONG ROAD BACK

86: NA 80G-10567A. **87**: GM. **88** TL: NA 80G-30073; BL: GM; TR: NA 80G-16322; CR: GM; BR: GM. **89** TL: NA 26204 A.C.; TR: GM; B: NA 80G-34887. **90** TL: NA Marine Corps 50898; TR: GM; B: NA 80G-30517. **91** TL: NA 80G-41286; TR: GM; BL: NA Marine Corps 53510; BR: GM. **92–93**: All GM. **94** T: NA Marine Corps 53489; B: GM. **95** TL: NA Marine Corps 79341; TR: GM; BL: GM; BR: Rex Alan Smith. **96** T: NA Marine Corps 66040; B: NA Marine Corps 56392-A. **97** T: Al Hahn; B: NA 80G-412406. **96–97**: NA Marine Corps 52171-A. **99**: David Levy. **100** T: David Levy; BL: NA 80G-250935; CR: GM; BR: David Levy. **101**: All David Levy. **102** TL: Al Hahn; TR: John F. Kennedy Library; BL: GM; BR: NA Marine Corps 104485. **103**: All GM. **105** T: NA 80G-65444; B: NA 80G-65450. **106** TL: U.S. Navy; CL: NA 80207A.C.; BL: NA B-80207A.C.; R: NA 70647A.C. **107** TL: NA Marine Corps 60459; TR: GM; CL: NA B-80560A.C.; CR: GM; B: NA SC-326397. **108** TL: NA 80G-56465; CL: NA 80G-54305; BL: NA SC-194828; R: GM. **109** TL: NA Marine Corps 60469; TC: GM; TR: GM; CL: GM; CR: GM; B: NA SC-242700. **111** T: GM; B: NA 80G-12717. **112** TL: GM; TR: U.S. Army; BL: NA 80G-12718; BC: NA 80G-5644; BR: NA 80G-3764#10. **113** TL: GM; TR: GM; B: NA 80G-5678. **114** TL: NA 80G-4720; TR: NA 75092; B: GM.

Chapter 4: A THOUSAND HONORED DEAD

129: NA B-65141A.C. **130**: GM. **131** TL: NA Marine Corps 64099; TR: GM; BL: NA Marine Corps 63754; BR: NA Marine Corps 64321. **132** T: NA Marine Corps 63575; BL: NA Marine Corps 63473; BC: NA Marine Corps 63474; BR: NA Marine Corps 63470. **133** T: NA Marine Corps 63458; BL: GM; BC: NA 80G-213472; BR: NA Marine Corps 63787. **134** TL: NA 80G-57405; TC: GM; TR: GM; B: NA Marine Corps 63578. **135** TL: GM; TR: GM; BL: NA Marine Corps 63632; BR: GM. **136** T: U.S. Marine Corps; BL: NA 80G-57406; BC: NA Marine Corps 64168; BR: GM. **137** T: NA Marine Corps 64071; B: GM. **138** TL: NA Marine Corps 77968; TR: GM; BL: NA Marine Corps 63656; BR: GM. **139** TL: NA Marine Corps 71729; TR: GM; BL: NA Marine Corps 77950; BR: GM. **140** T: NA A-63199A.C.; B: GM. **141**: All GM. **142**: All Rex Alan Smith. **143** T: NA 80G-335710; B: Rex Alan Smith. **145** L: GM; R: NA 80G-287264. **146** L: NA 59044A.C.; R: GM. **147** TL: NA Marine Corps 89471; TC: GM; TR: NA 80G-237566; B: GM. **148** T: Robert Sheeks; BL: Robert Sheeks; BR: GM. **149** TL: NA Marine Corps 125098; TR: GM; CL: NA 80G-238395; CR: GM; BR: Scott Russell. **150** L: GM; R: GM. **151** T: NA 63716A.C.; CL: GM; CR: NA 63732A.C.; B: GM. **152** T: GM; BL: NA Marine Corps 125648; BR:

GM. **153** T: NA Marine Corps 91044; BL: GM; BR: GM. **154** T: NA Marine Corps 152072; BL: NA64485A.C.; BR: NA 91634A.C. **155** TL: GM; TR: NA 80G-46572; BL: NA 75046 A.C.; BR: GM. **156–57**: All GM. **158** T: NA 88167; B: GM. **159** T: NA Marine Corps 87390; B: GM. **160** TL: U.S. Naval Institute; TR: GM; BL: GM; BR: GM. **161** T: GM; B: NA 80G-238983. **162** T: NA A-59002 A.C.; BL: GM; BR: NA Marine Corps 110186. **163** L: NA 59056A.C.; R: GM. **164** T: NA 55163 A.C.; BL: NA 60985 A.C.; BR: GM. **165** T: NA 59027 A.C.; B: NA A-59780 A.C. **166** T: NA 111-SC-268230; B: GM. **167** T: NA 3424; B: GM. **168** TL: NA Marine Corps 59392; TR: NA 80G-357315; C: GM; BL: Clarence Cook; BR: GM. **169** T: NA 7611 A.C.; BL: GM; BR: GM. **170**: GM. **170–71**: NA 23592 A.C. **171** T: NA 65226 A.C.; B: GM. **172**: NA 60161 A.C. **173**: All GM. **174**: NA 50803A.C. **175**: GM. **176**: GM. **178** T: NA Marine Corps 95256; B: GM. **179** T: Marla Meehl; BL: NA 80G-257339; BR: GM. **180** TL: NA Marine Corps 107912; TR: NA 127-GW-736I; BL: GM; BR: Marla Meehl. **181** TL: NA 127-GW-736-107717; B: GM. **182** T: GM; BL: NA 127-GW-739; BR: NA B-54871 A.C. **183** T: U.S. Naval Institute 95947; B: GM. **184** TL: NA 127-GW-698-100375; TR: Marla Meehl; B: NA 127-GW-697-98401. **185**: All GM. **186** TL: GM; TR: NA 127-GW-741-96475; BL: GM; BR: GM. **187** T: NA 127-GW-734-96102; B: NA 127-GW-734-98569. **188** TL: GM; TR: U.S. Naval Institute 95947; BL: U.S. Naval Institute 95947; BR: GM. **189** TL: NA 127-GW-712-102087; TR: GM; BL: U.S. Naval Institute 95947; BR: NA 80G-48358. **190** TL: U.S. Naval Institute 95947; TR: GM; BL: NA A68293 A.C. **190–91** BC: GM. **191** T: NA 111-SC-212870; BR: GM. **192**: NA 70780 A.C. **193**: All GM. **194** T: NA 127-GW-716-97921; B: GM. **195** T: NA 80G-45323; B: GM. **196**: All U.S. Naval Institute. **197**: GM. **198** T: U.S. Naval Institute; BL: NA Marine Corps 73090; BR: NA Marine Corps 105559. **199** TL: NA Marine Corps 78454; TR: NA Marine Corps 77329A; BL: NA Marine Corps 74083-A; BR: NA Marine Corps 70958. **200** T: Rex Alan Smith; B: NA Marine Corps 80892. **201** T: NA Marine Corps 78500; BL: NA Marine Corps 55779; BR: NA Marine Corps 50939. **202** TL: Rex Alan Smith; TR: NA Marine Corps 52948; B: NA Marine Corps 58274. **203** TL: NA Marine Corps 81359; TR: Rex Alan Smith; BL: Rex Alan Smith; BR: U.S. Naval Institute. **204** T: NA Coast Guard 26-G-2291; B: NA 80G-284947. **205** TL: NA 111-SC-341675; TR: NA 80G-258485; BL: GM; BR: GM. **206** T: NA 111-SC-349595-2857; B: GM. **207**: All GM. **208** T: NA 80G-288310; BL: NA 80G-47901; BR: NA 111-SC-262447. **209** T: NA 80G-273409; BL: GM; BR: GM. **210** TL: Fort Santiago; TR: NA 80G-273361; BL: GM; BR: GM. **211** TL: GM; TR: GM; CL: Rex Alan Smith; CR: NA 80G 273357; BL: GM; BR: GM. **212** T: Rex Alan Smith; B: GM. **213** T: NA 80G-3196921; TR: GM; BL: GM. **214** TL: NA 111-SC-202592; TR: GM; CR: GM; BL: NA 111-SC-271142; BR: NA 111-SC-203061. **215** TL: NA 111-SC-271117; TR: NA 80G-32818; B: GM. **216** T: NA 111-SC-203063; B: GM.

Chapter 5: UNCOMMON VALOR A COMMON VIRTUE

230: NA 80G-415308. **231** T: NA 70510 A.C.; C: GM; B: GM. **232** T: NA 80-G 48557; BL: GM; BC: NA Box 14, 127-GR-90-111,688; BR: GM. **233** T: NA 80-G-304865; BL: NA Box 14, 127-GR-90-110,111; BR: GM. CR: GM. **234** TL: NA Marine Corps 116325; TR: NA 80G-413988; BL: NA Box 69, 26-G-4140; BC: GM; BR: GM. **235** T: NA Box 14, 127-GR-93-109,604; BL: NA Box 14 127-GR-93-110603; BR: GM. **236** T: NA +57013 A.C.; C: NA 70337 A.C.; B: GM. **237** TL: NA B-70578 A.C.; CL: NA 62464 A.C.; BL: NA 64823 A.C.; R: NA B-67934 A.C. **238** T: NA +57431 A.C.; B: GM. **239**: All GM. **240**: Robert Sheeks. **242** T: NA 80G-498153; B: Robert Sheeks. **244–45**: All Robert Sheeks. **246–47**: NA Marine Corps 54377. **247**: NA 80G-17080. **248** TL: Col. S. D. Slaughter (ret), photo reproduced courtesy of Lamont Lindstrom; TR: Col. S. D. Slaughter (ret), photo reproduced courtesy of Lamont Lindstrom; B: U.S. Army. **249**: All GM. **250L**: NA 80G-281800; R: NA 80G-417628. **251**: NA 80G-44553. **250–51**: NA 80G-294131. **252**: NA 127-GW-670-124927. **252–53**: NA 127-N-120053. **254** T: NA 127-GW-618-120099; B: NA 127-GW-580-130792. **255** TL: NA 127-GW-580-122273; TR: GM; CL: GM; CR: GM; B: GM. **256** T: NA 127-GW-618-12333; B: GM. **257** T: U.S. Marine Corps; B: GM. **258** T: NA 127-GW-580-124737; B: GM. **259** TL: NA 127-GW-684-123919; TR: GM; B: GM. **260** TL: U.S. Army; TR: GM; C: GM; B: GM. **261** TL: GM; TR: GM; B: NA 80G-330153. **262** T: U.S. Navy; B: Marla Meehl.

Chapter 6: ENDING THE PACIFIC WAR

278: GM. **279** TL, TR, BL: NA 77-BT-122, 77-BT-115, 77-BT-116; BR: GM. **280** TL: NA 59475A.C.; BL: NA WWII #162; TR: NA; BR: GM. **281**: NA 80G-373264. **282** TL: Hiroshima Library; TR: NA U.S. Army; B: GM. **283**: All GM. **284** TL: NA 77-BT-177; TR, CL, CR: NA 77-BT-176, 77-BT-175, 77-BT-174; BL, BR: NA U.S. Army movie footage. **285** TL: GM; TR, Nagasaki Atomic Bomb Photograph Investigation Association, Nagasaki Atomic Bomb Museum; B: Atsushi Hirota, reproduced with permission of *After the Battle Magazine*. **286**: All GM. **287** TL: Atsushi Hirota, reproduced with permission of *After the Battle Magazine*; TR: NA 80B-264897; B: GM. **288** T: Rex Alan Smith; B: NA 80G-700777. **289** T: Michele Ely; BL: GM; BR: GM. **290** T: NA 80G-495894; BL: Guy Gabaldon; BR: GM.

EPILOGUE: PACIFIC LEGACY

302–3: Photofest. **304–5**: Meehan Military Posters.

INDEX

Page numbers in italic refer to illustrations

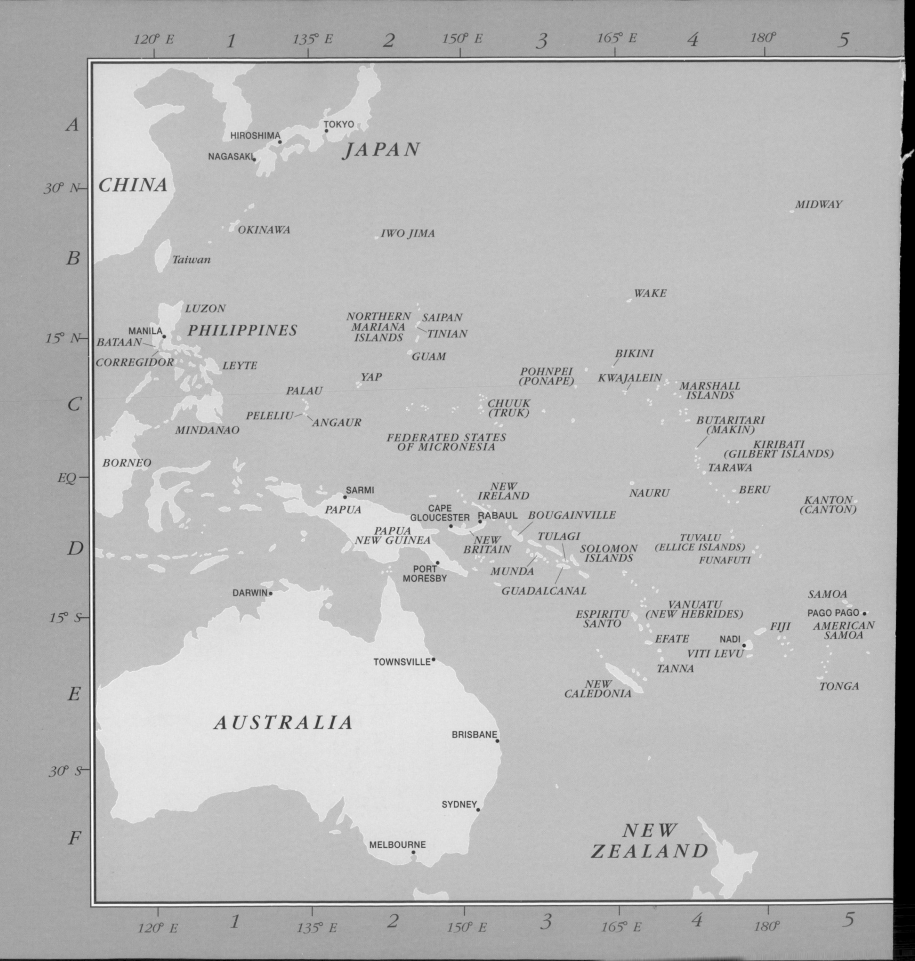